# Don't Call Us MOLLS

## Women of the John Dillinger Gang

ELLEN POULSEN

Clinton Cook Publishing Corp., Little Neck, New York

The genealogical information contained herein has been fact-checked to the best of the author's ability. The author is not responsible for lapses in accuracy in the entry of data into documents on public record.

William Helmer, a former senior editor at *Playboy,* is the author of *The Gun That Made the Twenties Roar,* and the coauthor of *Dillinger: The Untold Story, The Quotable Al Capone,* and *Baby Face Nelson: Portrait of a Public Enemy.*

Book design & typesetting by Liz Tufte, Folio Bookworks
Cover design by Dunn+Associates Design
Copy editing by Elise M. Oranges
Back cover writing by Susan Kendrick Writing
Cover photo courtesy of AP/Wide World

Printed and bound in the United States

Publisher's Cataloging in Publication
(Prepared by Quality Books)

Poulsen, Ellen, 1953–
Don't call us molls : women of the John Dillinger Gang / Ellen. – 1st ed.
p.cm.
Includes bibliographical references and index.
LCCN: 2002100692
ISBN: 0-9717200-0-2

1. Women outlaws—United States—Biography.
2. Mistresses—United States—Biography.
3. Dillinger, John, 1903–1934—Friends and associates. I. Title.

HV6785.P68 2002 364.1'092'273
QBI33-351

*In Memory Of My*
*Father,*

*Leo A. Poulsen*

SVB:HMD

November 11, 1935

Superintendent
U.S.Detention Farm
Milan, Michigan

Dear Mr. Ryan:

I have had a letter from Warden Johnston and he calls my attention to the fact that there are four women in your institution whose husbands are at Alcatraz, Kelly, Waley, Cherrington, and Spark, and that the three last-named write and receive letters every month, whereas, Kelly has received only one letter since he arrived at Alcatraz.

I think there is no getting away from the necessity for treating all these cases alike and hereafter all of these cases will have to be subject to the same ruling, namely, the wife may write to her husband one letter every two months, and receive an answer thereto, provided of course they have not forfeited their privileges. This should be on the future understanding that the correspondence deal with matters of a legal or business nature and not be indulged in for the purpose of institution gossip or comparison. You are authorized to withhold any letter which is of a frivolous or improper character.

Very truly yours,

Director

# Contents

# Foreword

Most "true-crime" writers are historians, scholars, criminologists, cops, or crime buffs who happen to be male and who assume the same is true of their readers. So unless they're researching Bonnie and Clyde, they rarely give more than passing notice to the women who prolonged the criminal careers of their boyfriends or husbands by renting apartments, buying cars, treating wounds, acting as couriers, and serving as camouflage. At long last comes Ellen Poulsen to remedy this. *Don't Call Us Molls* is a carefully researched examination of the often frantic lives of the girlfriends and wives of John Dillinger and fellow gang members who terrorized the Midwest during 1933 and 1934, when the failure of local law enforcement to capture interstate criminals led Congress to expand the authority of an obscure Justice Department agency soon to be known as the FBI. It already was a federal offence to drive a stolen car across state lines, and this technicality would prove valuable against a number of interstate fugitives; but that law had been passed nearly a decade earlier, mainly to expedite recovering the vehicle. When the Repeal of Prohibition coincided with the Depression and banks became national villains, the revival of armed robbery (or at least a renewed interest in it) gave the newly elected Roosevelt administration the opportunity it needed to wage the country's first "war on crime," declaring "motorized bandits" to be a national problem requiring a federal solution. Even Americans who on principle had opposed any law-enforcement agency that might turn into a federal secret police soon found themselves caught in an exhilarating game of cops 'n' robbers as the country's new breed of glamorous "G-men," trained in the forensic sciences, first publicized and then pursued "public enemies" with colorful names like "Pretty Boy" Floyd, "Machine Gun" Kelly, and "Baby Face" Nelson.

Since the women themselves rarely stormed banks or robbed payroll messengers, local authorities previously had shrugged them off as thrill-seekers or witless bimbos attracted by easy money; and reporters could disparage them as "molls," a term vague enough to avoid lawsuits even if mistakenly applied. However, no such qualms restrained J. Edgar Hoover, who often exaggerated their complicity and vilified them as disease-ridden harlots who could be prosecuted for harboring fugitives unless they turned on their men. (When the FBI's focus eventually shifted from old-time crime to war-time sabotage and then cold-war Communism, the "gun moll" lost her news value and became, more simply, the kind of girl our mothers warned us about.)

As a New York policeman's daughter in the increasingly feminist society of her college years, Ellen Poulsen developed an interest in the outlaw gangs of the 1930s; and she combined this with a special talent for both research and writing to finally give "molls" their own lives, longings, dilemmas, disappointments, and personalities. Easy money and loose morals might go with the territory, but their tolerance for or attraction to outlaws often mirrored their self-image as social outcasts, products of childhood abuse or neglect, with emotional needs ranging from rebellion to dependency to loyalty construed as love. Presented here is a thoughtful and long-overdue study of the complex relationships between gunmen and their "gun molls" that belongs on every true-crime bookshelf for its originality, but which would be equally valuable in a social history course or a women's studies program.

— *William J. Helmer*

# Introduction

*By Ellen Poulsen*

The story of John Dillinger took place during the Great Depression. The events surrounding him were a reflection of his time. His female confederates came under a social microscope. They were the first generation of women allowed to vote and wear makeup, to seek office work, and use birth control. They balanced wildly, tottering between lost Calvinism and the new world.

John Dillinger's parole in 1933 coincided with the social activism of Franklin D. Roosevelt's New Deal. Uncle Sam, himself, had promised to place that famous chicken into every pot. Never again would an American citizen be solely responsible for himself.

The New Deal was offering programs previously unheard of. It looked like the dole to some, that dreaded home relief associated with the poorest people in the land: Social Security, an eight-hour work day, jobs funded by the federal government. Reluctantly, the populace relinquished the concept of "pulling yourself up by your bootstraps."

At the same time, intellectuals were questioning the subordination of prisoners, women, and African-Americans. The National Association for the Advancement of Colored People (NAACP) and the Communist Party called attention to the plight of the Scottsboro Boys in Alabama. In spite of the domination of the Hearst press, the Left was being heard. Their message trickled into the parlors of the old conservatives. Subliminally, the seeds of social revolution were planted.

Dillinger and his gang, who sprang to the headlines late in 1933, were home-grown terrorists. Dillinger's record was splashed everywhere. He'd served nine years for an armed robbery committed while a teenager. After five years he'd been denied a parole and was sent to a maximum security prison.

He seemed familiar in a vague way. The novelist Theodore Dreiser had recently published *An American Tragedy*, which blamed the criminal mind on fate and circumstance.

As Dillinger began to dominate the headlines, a conduit of editorials questioned the punitive philosophy of the Indiana prison system. Dillinger's long sentence, imposed upon him while still a juvenile, came under attack.

The social ambivalence surrounding the outlaw would taint the months of his notoriety. The desperado was photogenic. He manipulated public opinion with a piercing stare. In the arrogance of his Dayton mug shot, taken at the height of his confidence, people saw something that they themselves had lost. It was the old college try, the optimism that America had tried to fulfill before the stock market crash of 1929.

Dillinger reflected the national disillusionment with American life. Out of the poverty of the Depression had arisen a new rebellion on the part of the common man. The crash of 1929 had ushered in the Age of Hypocrisy. It was hard to find a mainstream newspaper with the editorial courage to damn the Depression. Throughout the worst economic plunge in history, readers had to burrow through society luncheons to find the broken lives of businessmen and sharecroppers. Beyond the feature stories of debutantes and Cotillion Balls lurked the awful stories. As broken bankers jumped into the canyons of Wall Street, backwoods farmers killed their children to ward off death by starvation. Others, less deranged by circumstances, killed only themselves in shame and despair. While society crumbled, prisoners like Dillinger's henchman, Harry Pierpont, remained oblivious to the debacles outside their walls.

Pierpont and the principals of the Michigan City prison break of 1933 could not predict the far-reaching effect of their plans, which sent them hurling through the barriers. They crashed into the lap of a public hungry for vengeance and thirsty for violence. Through horror expressed with perfunctory outrage, the readers were fascinated.

Pierpont would become known as many kinds of men before the electric chair placed him into the final category. He was "Pete," the trigger man of the Dillinger Gang, the man police derisively referred to as "Handsome Harry." Likewise, his girlfriend could not escape the attention. Mary Kinder, dubbed the "Queen of Gangland," ascended higher than other women in her stratum. She asserted her voice, which found its genre in a new wave of print journalism. From the rustic quotes attributed to her in the first days of notoriety to the polished appearances later hosted by the *Chicago Herald and Examiner*, she asserted a radical social viewpoint. The New Woman was a "moll."

The word itself had become generic. Originally coined to denote a female pickpocket, it evolved to "gun moll" during Prohibition. The year 1934 brought the hunt for the "public enemies" into the forefront. In the early stage of Dillinger's criminal career, the women were a shadow of the men. Unknown save for the occasional description furnished by an informant, there were no pictures, no concrete images. People assumed she was a sexual creature. This libertine enjoyed freedom. She ran with gangsters, basking in a sordid yet beckoning glamour.

As the hunt for John Dillinger escalated, the arrests of their women dominated the front pages. They were easier to capture than their agile boyfriends, and they often were abandoned—Baby Face Nelson's last mention of his wife at the Battle of Barrington was, "we can't take her now." Once in custody they were photographed, often during or immediately after attempts to apprehend their male companions, while emotions ran high.

The death of Bonnie Parker in May 1934 coincided with the first public appearance of Helen Gillis, Jean Delaney Crompton, and Marie Comforti. When news photographers were able to shoot high-speed photographs of women going into custody, their subjects hid their faces. Designed to discourage later identification, these gestures were exploited by the press as physical acts of contrition—the aftermath of fear, shame, and modesty. This was comic-book titillation at its best.

The incident at Little Bohemia Lodge shoved the Dillinger gang women into the headlines. The thrill was cheap, costing three cents, the price of a newspaper. The attraction was the sleazy glamour of the fallen women. With sex an unapproachable subject in 1934 America, this served up a juicy substitute.

These were not the usual humdrum stories about the proper women of Midwestern society. Yet the reporters took their cue from the style employed in reporting on ladies' auxiliaries and church socials. These women, always referred to as "girls," were described in terms of their tears, laughter, and confidential revelations.

"I've been sick, and have to build up my strength," Helen Gillis was said to have confided into the ear of a journalist. This same writer, who claimed to have garnered a confidence that hordes of Justice Department agents could not elicit through days of grilling, also credits Jean Delaney Crompton with a special request.

"Please, don't call us molls," she allegedly begged.

The lounging pajamas that Jean Delaney Crompton and Helen Gillis wore at the time of their capture launched a new mystique. Clad in her Butcher Boy silhouette pajamas, she was a nostalgic throwback to the flapper of the Roaring Twenties. While the early feminists had worn bloomers under short skirts to protest the constrictions of women's dress, the Butcher Boy had a free-swinging back and loose-cut top. With the Depression influencing style, and the hemlines dropping to exactly twelve inches from the floor, pants were a radical concept in women's dress.

During the height of the Depression, the culture remained in the grasp of nostalgia for the flapper who'd gone to her symbolic death in the crash of 1929. Her degenerate opulence was obsolete. Through gang "girls," the lost freedom of bobbed hair and flattened breasts could still thrive. The moll was not stopped by the repentant culture of the Depression.

Bonnie Parker had one good outfit and the timing to be immortalized wearing it. Claudette Colbert copied the look as she hitchhiked with Clark Gable in *It Happened One Night*. Dillinger's girlfriend, Evelyn Frechette, wore stripes when arrested in Tucson. These were the stripes of women in rebellion. Bonnie Parker, through her Joplin photo shoot, leant style and performance to the role of the woman desperado. Yet her very creativity isolated her. Through her epic poems about life with Clyde Barrow, Bonnie took on a solitary form. None of the women of the true underworld cared to emulate her.

Yet women who laughed at conformity enjoyed popularity—Marlene Dietrich and Jean Harlow triumphed at the box office. Out of this genre a darker film character was born. She was sinister through Ann Dvorak's interpretation. Sylvia Sidney made her plain and untainted. When John Dillinger dragged his friends to the movies, the women were buoyed by the celluloid gun molls. Faith and passion in the face of arrest, trial, and death leant credence to their existence. Suddenly they had a prototype by which to judge their own experience.

Before 1934, the moll was portrayed through the pathos of W. Somerset Maugham's ill-fated prostitutes, unredeemed and discarded in the gutters of the Lost Generation of the First World War. The stark realism was short-lived. On March 21, 1934, a change in attitude catapulted

Bonnie Parker, in her famous striped dress.
(Author's Collection)

Hollywood into a new era of censorship.

The Hays Office of the Motion Picture Producers and Distributors of America placed a ban on any movies about Dillinger.

"Such a picture would be detrimental to the best public interest," said a Hollywood representative. It was the same censorship office that had recently relieved Betty Boop of the frolic in her short dress, placing her modestly into a calf-length shirtwaist. Ever on the lookout for new challenges, the commission described its Dillinger censorship as "the most definite action ever taken against pictures delineating criminal exploits."

Out of news blackouts and Hollywood censorship arose the print alternative. The decision of the Hays Commission coincided with the conclusion of the Lima, Ohio, trial of Harry Pierpont, Russell Clark, and Charles Makley, the three principals of the "Trigger Gang." At the same time, Mary Kinder was sighted everywhere. Like an apparition she was stalked and charted, viewed and quoted. She was reportedly spotted in Lima, Chicago, and Tucson at the same time.

Pat Cherrington was photographed while answering charges of harboring Dillinger. Her tight-fitting suit leant her the aura of a bull dog in a spiked collar. Accompanying Cherrington was her sister, Opal Long, on her way from Chicago to St. Paul to answer similar federal charges. Opal Long appeared broken. This was a less aggrandized image of life on the run. If movie images of gun molls fell short of reality, nowhere was the true life of crime more closely depicted than in Opal Long, who signed her prison letters "jailbird." The irony is that Opal Long, in her domestic fierceness, embodied the woman the gang members wanted. These former farm boys wanted women with rough hands, the kind that did the housework of crime.

Once inured with a wanted fugitive, these women stayed in to cook, or sneaked covertly out for take-out meals under the cover of darkness. John Paul Chase's girlfriend, Sally Bachman, testified that she helped the wife of Baby Face Nelson with the job of bringing wrapped restaurant food out to the gang, who never entered the public arena of a restaurant.

Other job descriptions included buying and renting cars, procuring apartments, and opening safe deposit boxes under assumed names. Evelyn Frechette confided her thriftiness to Beth Green in a conversation where she outlined her strategy for saving rent money. You never put too much down on a hideout, she felt, because a "bump out" by police meant a lost deposit. This and other strategies comprised the variations of domesticity under which they lived. Ironically, they'd been raised to perform household chores and very little else by school systems unwilling to train girls into full employment possibilities. Even more tragically, their prison terms put them face to face with useless "homemaking" classes. The otherwise progressive Alderson Industrial Facility, the destination for three-quarters of the women of the 1930s Midwestern Crime Wave, tracked the women into decorating, sewing, and housecleaning instruction.

The doting consorts, as well as wives, risked abandonment due to the transient nature of their activities. Separation anxiety permeated the minds of women who had come to depend completely upon the dubious security provided by these gunmen.

Throughout their troubles and travails, the women of the Dillinger gang were profiled through their gender. Female stereotyping was a given in 1934. Predating feminism by thirty-five years, the paperwork maintained by various policemen in the hunt for Evelyn Frechette and her confederates is replete with racist, derogatory statements. Within intelligence furnished by Indiana State Police Captain Matthew Leach, who was instrumental in the Dillinger hunt, Evelyn is described as having a "heavy type face, almost Jewish in appearance."

These policemen were provincial, with a limited scope of culture outside their own. Not confined to the pen of Captain Leach, common prejudices echoed throughout much of the official memoranda being written on the Dillinger gang. It was a time when the First Lady of the land, Eleanor Roosevelt, asked the public to accept a new kind of racial and religious unity in the nation. It was to go side by side with the New Deal. Yet in the populist Midwest, change would be slow in coming.

The contempt and disregard for their prisoners was fueled in part by the assumption of police officers. They felt the women were whores. It was not sexual prejudice—police often lived double lives themselves. In spite of the written code of the time, the unwritten one predominated throughout society. Sex without cover of marriage must benefit a woman materially. In those days of back-alley abortions, sex offered the damnation of unwed motherhood on the one hand and possible death on the other. It was too risky to be entered into casually by a woman. As a result, smart arrangements always contained basic compensation. A man was expected to provide a new suit of clothes or money for a dentist. The pitfalls of sex would find their balance in material gain.

In the case of Mary Kinder, materialism was one motivation that stood out of the complex set of circumstances that drove her to Harry Pierpont. She had a photographic memory for the amounts spent on everything she acquired. She would recount, years later, these amounts to the penny—numbers confirmed, amazingly, in FBI memoranda.

Other factors engendered the hatred of policemen, who were outraged that a moll could have sex with cop-killers. One Justice Department agent wrote pointedly in a memo that "Mary Kinder cohabited with Harry Pierpont on the night that he shot and killed Sheriff Sarber in Lima." Through the transfer of semen, Mary Kinder became the accessory after the fact. Often judges and prosecutors shared this view. Certainly the Justice Department, under the straight-laced vision of J. Edgar Hoover, believed this.

When Dillinger entered the realm of federal jurisdiction as he violated the Dyer Act in his escape from the Crown Point County Jail, he brought his girlfriends along with him. The Justice Department was now free to pursue Federal Harboring Indictments because Dillinger had broken the provisions of the National Motor Vehicle Theft Act, 18 U.S.C. S408. The Justice Department's Division of Investigation—it had not yet christened itself the FBI—employed this law in breaking down the fabric of the gangs.

By 1935, the backlash in gun moll culture had begun to circulate in the form of morality shows, pamphlets, and newspaper articles. Evelyn Frechette authored such a brochure upon her release from the Milan Federal Facility in Michigan in 1936. Entitled, "The March of Crime," Evelyn revealed that, upon her mother's death, shortly before Dillinger was killed at the Biograph Theater, the prison administration refused to allow her to attend the funeral.

The supreme commander over all investigations, Director J. Edgar Hoover, fought the morality trend in a heated campaign. He drew on the statement he first issued after Dillinger's escape from the Justice Department at Little Bohemia:

"She is more dangerous to society than the desperado himself. It is she and her kind who make him seek a life of crime," he vehemently declared.

This bride of Frankenstein was Hoover's first public commentary

After her release from prison, Evelyn Frechette went on tour.

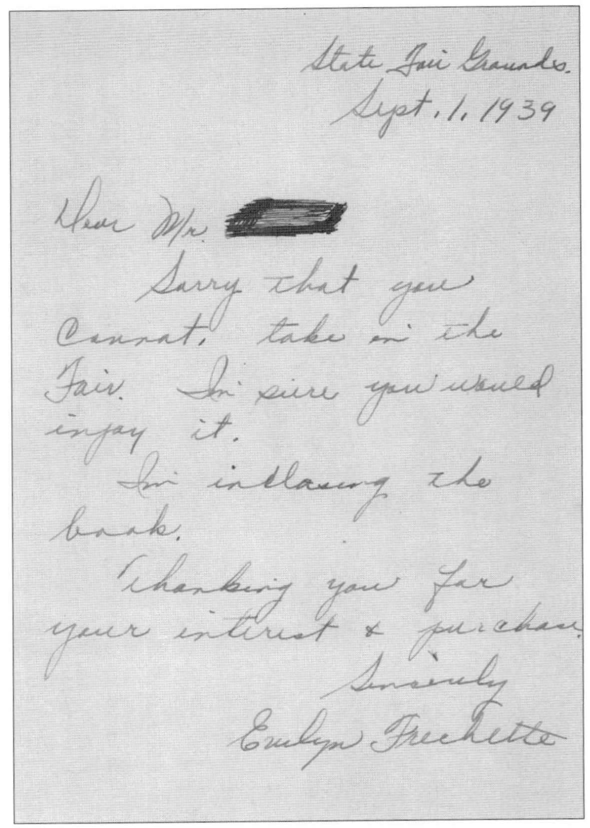

State Fair Grounds.
Sept. 1, 1939

Dear Mr. [redacted]

Sorry that you cannot take in the Fair. I'm sure you would enjoy it.

I'm enclosing the book.

Thanking you for your interest & purchase.

Sincerely
Evelyn Frechette

(Author's Collection)

about the women who traveled with the major public enemies. It would not be his last.

Years later he attacked the women, long after they had served out their sentences, by waging vaginal wars with myth grounded in ancient stereotypes. In his published essays, he accused them of carrying syphilis and gonorrhea. This was largely erroneous; the Federal Bureau of Prison records on incoming prisoners indicate that most were not infected with sexually transmitted diseases.

The underworld had its cures for sexually transmitted conditions, including pregnancy. With severe abdominal problems plaguing Pat Cherrington, Marie Comforti, and Helen Gillis, the cures rested often in gangland hospitals and underworld physicians. One notorious spot was the Vallejo General Hospital in California, the resting place for Helen Gillis and hideout for Baby Face Nelson, "Johnnie" Chase, and "Fatso" Negri. The underworld doctors in St. Paul treated the women's ailments, as in Dr. Mortensen's treatment of Pat Cherrington while the gang resided at the Little Bohemia Lodge. Mortensen took credit for the discovery that Pat's gall bladder was missing, a fact he claimed Pat was unaware of.

By 1934, one Midwestern abortionist, Joseph "Doc" Moran, had been released from Joliet State Prison after serving time for killing a girl during a botched abortion. Like Dr. May, the co-defendant to Evelyn Frechette who was tried with his nurse, Augusta Salt, for harboring Dillinger, he had a history as an abortionist. The abortionists were licensed physicians in good standing. Many practitioners would maintain one office for legitimate patient care and another office for the treatment of venereal diseases and abortions. Criminals needing plastic surgery, fingerprint removal, and treatment for gunshots filled out their schedule. It was not unusual for an abortionist to leave a bank robber's festering wound to treat a "girl in trouble," the euphemism of the day. The fee was usually $50.00. Occasionally a patient died, as in the case of Doc Moran.

These doctors were protected by corrupt local governments. Local organized crime paid municipal graft, which allowed the abortionists to thrive. The rhetorical "back alley" was usually a flat in an apartment house, where landlords and janitors were paid to look the other way. These outfits were supervised by women with ties to organized crime. Often they had gleaned some practical nursing experience before entering the lucrative work of illegal abortion. Often they served as mistresses to attorneys who kept them out of jail.

After the end of the era, Hoover's wrath was levied at challenging the morality pamphlets and appearances at "Crime Does Not Pay" spectacles. He published essays drawing on archetypes to embellish his imagery. The moll, especially through the persona of Kate "Ma" Barker, took the form of a decadent shrew. She was unstoppable as she supervised the moral collapse of the males around her.

Hoover elaborated on his theme. The first female mastermind he created was Kathryn Kelly, convicted in 1933 and sentenced to life imprisonment for her part in the kidnapping of oil millionaire Charles F. Urschel. With Kathryn Kelly, the idea of a woman with superior criminal intelligence came into being. Her husband, George "Machine Gun" Kelly, went down in history as that pathetic creature, a hen-pecked man.

The vilification of the gun moll reached a deep level of misogyny by the late 1930s. As the morality pamphlets were discarded, the "Crime Does Not Pay" spectacles fell dead as vaudeville. The last remaining women behind bars were paroled. Yet Hoover's tone remained misogynistic, as he alluded to the "straggly breasts" upon which criminals fed.

The Director's outrage was understandable as seen through one important perspective. He wanted to lift the sexual amnesty that he believed protected women from equal treatment and prosecution. He was frustrated with short sentences, ranging from one year and one day to the exceptional five-year sentence meted out to Dolores Delaney.

It can be argued that through the genre of the morality pamphlets and lecture series, Evelyn Frechette and Mary Kinder did revert to nineteenth-century values, which asked that society forgive them their shameful antics.

Mary Kinder managed to leave her imprint in a sad postscript: "I figured I should tell a lot of other young people of all the trouble you can get into when you get smart and think you can break the rules. You pay in the end and keep on paying. I ought to know."

# Part I

# Bad Reputation

## August 1932 – March 1934

During her trial in St. Paul, Evelyn Frechette confers with Louis Piquett and A. Jerome Hoffman, her counsel. (AP/Wide World Photos)

---

"Miss Frechette knew at all times the identity of John Dillinger. She was aware that he was an escaped convict, that he had stolen an automobile. Whether she was aware there had been a federal warrant is a matter for you to determine. Consider her relations with Dillinger prior to his escape from the Crown Point, Indiana, jail. Consider the admission she is alleged to have made to federal officers regarding Dillinger's theft of an automobile."

*Judge Gunnar H. Nordbye, Charge to the Jury*
*U.S. v. Evelyn Frechette, et al.*
*U.S. District of Minnesota , May, 1934*

*"It was just one of those things. I just wanted more money than I had and that looked like the way to get it."*

*—Welton Spark*

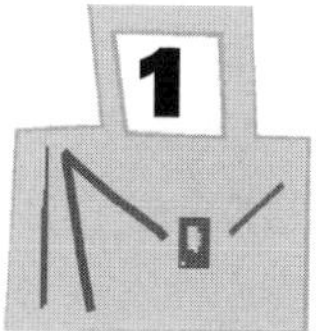

# Throw No Rice

Traces of home life crawled over the Cook County Jail's visiting area. While reeking of a bleach-stained washtub, it sounded like a maternity ward. On the hot morning of August 2, 1932, County Chaplain E.N. Ware checked off his roster of duties. Periodically, he consulted his clipboard. Throughout the day, he'd given counsel and absolution while ignoring the din of screaming babies and frazzled people. Beyond the cage that separated them, he avoided the stares of the visitors. They sat huddled or sprawled, depending on their attitude.

Calling loudly, Reverend Ware summoned Patricia Young and Evelyn Frechette, mispronouncing the latter's name as "Frisbetty." The woman named Frechette rose. She pulled her friend Patricia out of the seat beside her. The two faced the minister as Patricia flicked a cigarette, her thumb and index finger forming a rigid catapult. She crushed the butt beneath the toe of her sling-backed, high-heeled shoe, her hips jingling in unison. Miss Frechette, however, appeared calm. The lone indication of turmoil, her eyes, radiated a fierce, black hue. In contrast to Pat's snug hat that rested in a point over her eyes, Billie's hair bobbed loosely around her sharp features.

They'd come to marry two men bound for the U.S. Federal Penitentiary at Leavenworth, Kansas. Dressed as they were in their dark, crepe dresses, the fashionable twelve inches from the floor, they didn't look like brides. Nevertheless, they answered the questions posed to them by Chaplain Ware. Knowing that paperwork defined one's life behind bars, they duly produced the *ex parte* marriage licenses they'd obtained without their intended spouses.[1]

They'd learned about bureaucracy like traditional apprentices, trained at an early, impressionable age. Recently, they'd also become hardened to jail. The two had been arrested along with their boyfriends on June 13, 1932, in Michigan City, Indiana. The state of Indiana released the women and dismissed their cases. The men, Welton Spark and Art Cherrington, parolees from the Illinois State Prison at Joliet, returned to Chicago as parole violators.

Evelyn's man, Welton Spark, was charged, along with his accomplice, Roy Little, for post office embezzlement and stealing mail. On May 31, 1932, they had robbed a clerk of personal property in Postal Station No. 231 in Chicago.

These were unsophisticated thieves. For the crime of stealing $100.87 and $47.32 from the U.S. Mail, they'd be going to Leavenworth. Along with a third man, Patricia Young's boyfriend Art Cherrington, they heard their fate in a federal district court. The parolees were sentenced by Judge Barnes in the U.S. District Court of Northern Illinois to three concurrent terms of ten and five years. They would spend at least eleven years behind bars.

"It was just one of those things," Spark remarked at the sentencing. "I just wanted more money than I had and that looked like the way to get it."

With unfocused eyes and spiky, thick hair, Spark was unstable. He'd been diagnosed as having a "constitutional psychopathic state." At Joliet he was profiled as a dangerous, hardened, and habitual offender.

"I've only been free a few months in twelve years," he liked to say. It was an odd means of self-introduction.

To Evelyn Frechette, Spark was an exciting renegade. His height was perfect for her, at five feet and ten inches, with a stocky build of 186 pounds. He had a deep scar running between his eyebrows, and his face wore a loaded expression. There was a sadness, a fundamental gap within this man that Evelyn could understand. Both Spark and Frechette were native to Wisconsin. They'd each lost their fathers in childhood. Both had run away from home, never to return with any commitment. She'd lost a baby, while Spark had played the role of lost child all his life.

Evelyn met Welton Spark shortly after his parole from Joliet on February 15, 1932. For a short time, they lived with Evelyn's sister, Frances "Patsy" Schultz, at 3512 North Pinegrove in Chicago. Spark supported Evelyn with a series of petty stick-ups. This culminated in the Chicago post office robbery of May 31, 1932. Shortly afterward, when Spark and Evelyn Frechette were staying in Michigan City, Indiana, as "Mr. and Mrs. James E. Malone," they were arrested on June 13, 1932. Arrested with Spark and Frechette were Roy Little, Arthur Cherrington, and Patricia Young, who were traveling under the aliases of Mr. and Mrs. Jack Riley.

On June 14, the day following the arrests, Arthur Cherrington and Welton Spark were extradited to Illinois, for violation of their parole. The women's cases were dismissed.

Once installed in the Cook County Jail, Spark joined the ranks of inmates looking for an angle. His priority was to make the time go easier. He knew he could get more commissary money by marrying Evelyn Frechette. As a ward of the Menominee Reservation, she received a small federal allotment every month. As her spouse, the allotment could be assigned to him. The benefits of marriage would help Evelyn and Patricia as well. They'd each be entitled to home relief, in the form of a cash stipend, as the indigent spouses of federal prisoners. It was an early form of welfare.[2]

On the stifling afternoon of August 3, 1932, County Chaplain Ware met Evelyn Frechette and Patricia Cherrington, the brides-to-be, with a perfunctory smile. For a short moment, the four enjoyed the glow of positive attention. It felt vaguely hopeful, akin to the revival meetings of Patricia's Southern Baptist childhood.

Chaplain Ware knew otherwise; the act of saying "I do" netted benefits for an incarcerated man. With irreverent thoughts distracting him, he sanctioned the union of the two couples before him. Welton Spark

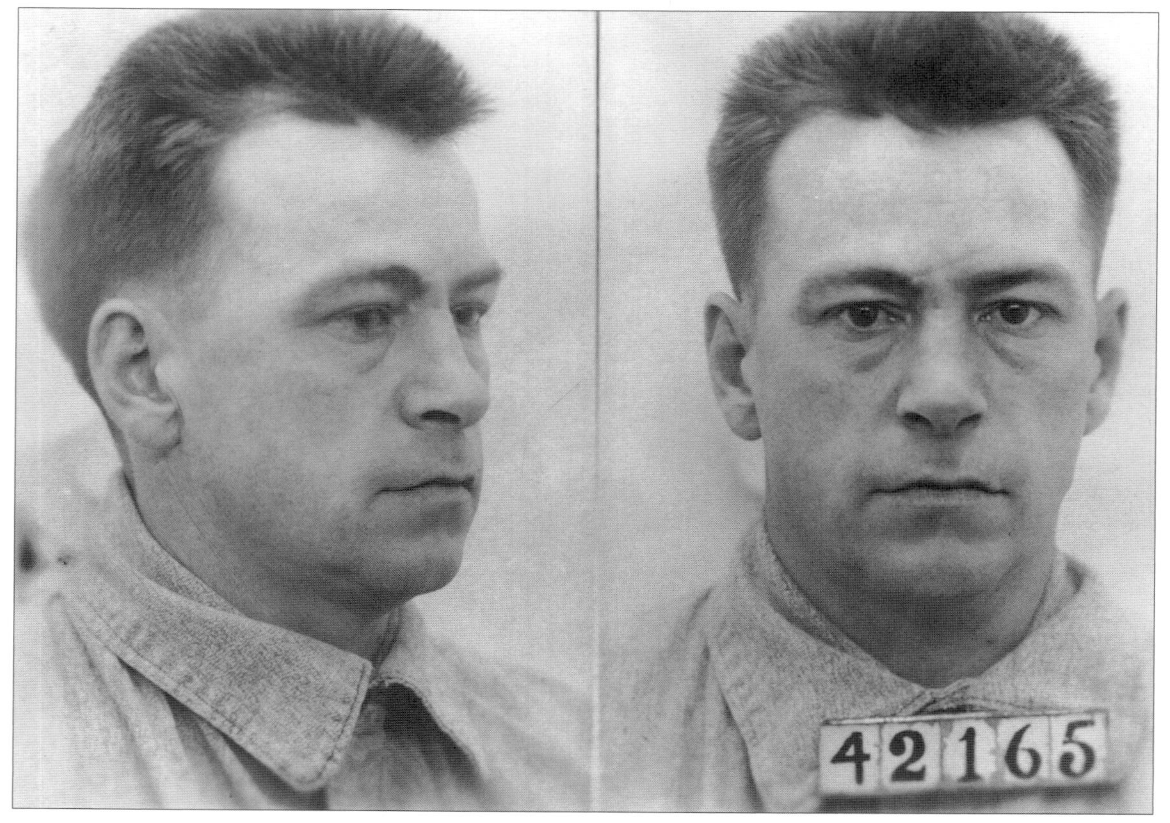


Welton Spark (above) and Arthur Cherrington (below) married Evelyn Frechette and Patricia Young on August 3, 1932, en route to Leavenworth. (National Archives)

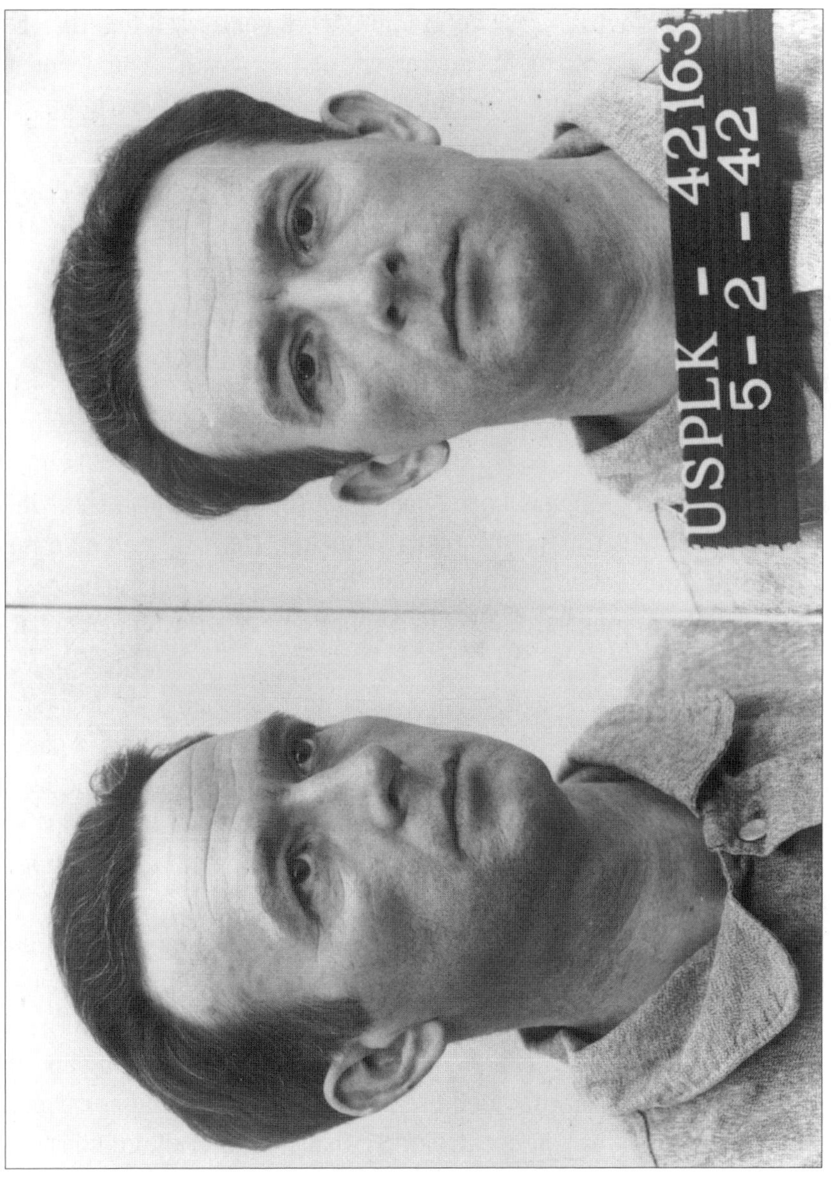
USPLK - 42163
5 - 2 - 42

scratched his name Walter Spark. As Art Cherrington exchanged vows with Patricia Young, Evelyn Frechette kissed Welton Spark. Nobody threw rice.

Just days before the wedding, on July 20, 1932, Spark, at age thirty-three, and Cherrington, age twenty-nine, were sentenced together to a term of fifteen years, to be served at Leavenworth. The mandate, delivered by an unsmiling judge in the Federal District Court, was the closest the couple would get to the traditional champagne toast.

Within the next few days, Welton Spark exchanged his name for Number 42165. Evelyn wrote to him, signing her correspondence "Mrs. Welton Spark." Frechette allotted her "Indian Headright" to Spark.

In the days that followed the sentencing, Welton Spark and Art Cherrington went through a battery of intelligence and psychological tests as part of a progressive intake procedure. It appeared that Spark and Cherrington had formed a symbiotic twin relationship—two felons, mysteriously welded to each other. Prison social workers learned that Arthur S. Cherrington was born November 13, 1903, in Jackson, Ohio, to William Cherrington and Marcella Whitaker. He had been a promising student, but the lure of petty theft had destroyed his artistry. He was paroled from Joliet in 1932 with a rudimentary knowledge of charts and band performance.[3]

Art migrated to Chicago, finding work in the small jazz orchestras performing in the speakeasies. There he met Patricia Young, a dancer who showed a sorry sense of judgment when moving among the hucksters of the nightclubs. She later claimed to have read "books and poetry" with Art. The couple did share a raw, instinctual appreciation of jazz. Like Art Cherrington, Patricia was talented.

Patricia "Pat" Young was born Patricia Long on September 26, 1903, in McClure County, Arkansas. The family had migrated to Texas, where her younger sister, Opal "Bernice," was born. A boy was later born into the family, but he died in childhood. Her parents, William Long and the former Goldie Jacquas, provided for the family by working as farmers. Patricia once told a prison social worker that her paternal grandparents had owned a plantation.

The family, living within Baptist traditions, broke apart in 1909 with the death of Pat's father from cardiac arrest at the age of thirty. Patricia's mother moved the family to Dallas, Texas, to live with her own mother, the girls' maternal grandmother. Patricia's maternal grandfather was a traveling railroad inspector whom the girls seldom saw.

Nervous and unruly, Patricia showed signs of creative intelligence. She found no outlets for her creativity as the family moved from Dallas to Chickasha, Oklahoma. Pat completed the eighth grade early, at the age of eleven. After two years of high school, she left home. At thirteen she was claiming to be a student at the University of Oklahoma. In this ruse she expressed a wish that her social position couldn't support. Her tragedy was that she never comprehended the advantage of her intelligence.

"I have a pretty good record as a student," was all she'd say.

In May 1920, at the age of fifteen, she married her boyfriend, in Tulsa, Oklahoma. For three months in 1920 she worked as a telephone operator, earning $7.50 per week. In this early period of independence, Patricia resembled an ill-fated heroine of Theodore Dreiser's novels. She personified the plight of the young, career-oriented woman with no training to back up her ambition. Her daughter's birth stopped her from working temporarily. J Young (a pseudonym) was born on June 8, 1921. The birth, called instrumental in its day because of the use of forceps, left Patricia disabled for one year after the baby's birth. A growing dissatisfaction with her husband, whom she claimed neglected her, forced her out of the quicksand of physical discomfort. It was the dawn of women's rights, and Patricia fell into step with the times. She wore the short skirts forbidden to her mother's generation, and started smoking. In 1922, Patricia took her baby and ran away from her husband.

She moved through Detroit and Chicago. There she was forced to board her daughter and find employment in another locale. She found a Chicago care-giver named Betty Naetz Minor, a married woman with a small son. Mrs. Minor boarded the baby in her apartment, 2-E, on 524 Beldon Avenue. Patricia told Mrs. Naetz Minor that she was going to New York to work as a waitress. After a while living "back East," as she called it, Patricia returned to Chicago, where she worked in odd jobs. She obtained a formal divorce in October 1925, during which proceeding she fought Young, her ex-husband, for custody of her daughter, and won. Even after freeing herself from the old, teenage marital fling, she reasoned that she was no better off. Her frustration flew like a poisoned arrow. For the first time, she chose a profession, one befitting her nervous creativity. Perhaps as a way of fighting her constant abdominal pains, she struggled to learn the art of chorus line dancing. To perfect her skills, she hung around the nude dancers in the bars of Prohibition.

In that spirit, she embellished herself as a woman of culture and sophistication. Using an early alias, Pat Riley, she found work as a dancer, earning as much as $75 per week, a fortune for a single woman in the 1920s. She built upon the bogus credentials she'd established years earlier, by augmenting her academic background, which now included both the Universities of Oklahoma and Pennsylvania.

She danced in choruses and specialty numbers in Chicago's Keith Circuit and the Orpheum. When she performed in teasing routines and chorus-line numbers, Patricia smiled with lips closed and secrets intact. A master of illusion, she hid her missing teeth behind a posed, pouting grin. On stage, she kicked her fashionably chubby thighs in unison with other dancers as desperate as she. Her smiles masked her labors under constant abdominal pain. The malice of a faulty gallbladder, and the need for surgery she couldn't afford, added to her problems.

In 1929, Patricia's mother died of heart disease in New Orleans. Patricia visited her daughter as often as she could, and sent the babysitting fee of $6 per week to Betty Neatz Minor. Occasionally, the care of the child was assumed by Patricia's sister, Opal Long, who'd been working in Chicago as a waitress since 1926. Known to the little girl as "Auntie," Opal Long was the child's second mother.[4]

After her mother's death, Patricia made the acquaintance of Evelyn Frechette in Chicago. The two women would develop a trusting, female friendship. With Evelyn "Billie" Frechette, Pat Cherrington shared an unearned legacy of mediocrity. Both had born children while still children themselves. Each had been deprived of the experience of raising her child. Their parallel lives were marked by the early loss of their fathers. They'd each been cast out as young teenagers to fend for themselves, their only tool their wits.

"Billie" took her nickname from the father she'd lost.[5]

The community that had ushered Evelyn Frechette into the world on September 15, 1907, in Millford, Wisconsin, had struggled to bequeath its heritage upon her under the microscope of the local Agency of the Department of the Interior's Bureau of Indian Affairs (BIA). As a resident of the Menominee Reservation, she grew in the knowledge that, before anything else, she was a ward of the United States government.[6]

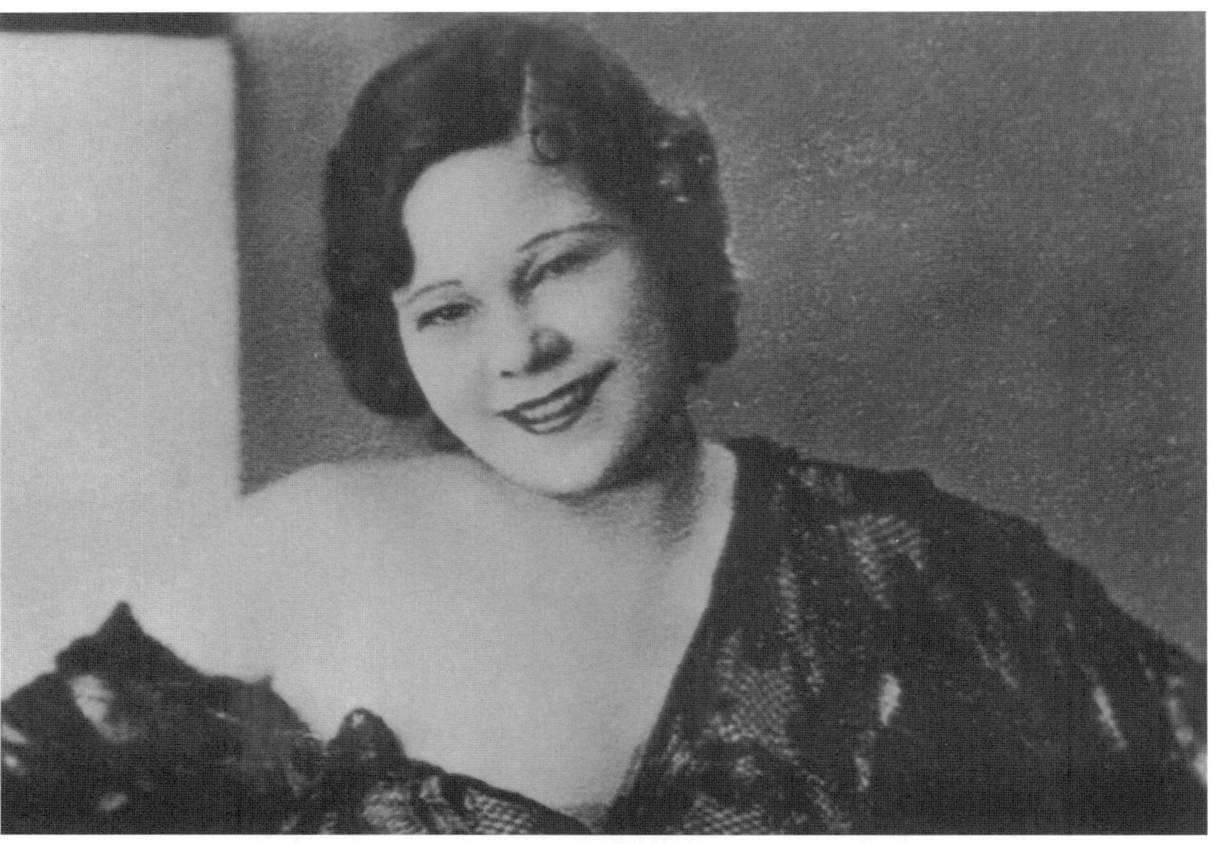

Pat Cherrington's pose hints that her career as a Chicago lounge dancer, may have included stripping. (FBI)

She pronounced her name without the 'e', like "Freshet," as her father had done. William Frechette had lent his Menominee, and French Canadian blood to his daughter, while his wife and Evelyn's mother, Mary LaBelle Shopwosekaw, born in 1880, brought her own French Canadian, Menominee blood to the marriage. This blended heritage had begun in 1634, when French explorer Jean Nicholet, visited the Menominee Indians in Wisconsin. This resulted in the French fur trade imbedding itself in the region. The French infiltration climaxed in 1671, when all of the Indian tribes of the area were declared French subjects.[7]

Because the French loved to mingle with the aboriginals, the Menominee were a people of blended lineage. In the 1930s, the deferential would make little difference in a nation torn by racial ambivalence. With her black hair and round face presenting a mask, she was taken for a "foreigner," that is, Mexican, Italian, or Greek. This misidentification grew as an offshoot of the isolationism gripping the United States in the years between World War I and World War II.[8]

Evelyn was also subject to racial slurs levied against Native Americans. Yet she lumbered under the weight of her heritage, with 7⁄16 Menominee blood. Defined first and foremost as an "Indian," she was controlled by the white hierarchy. It would distort her heritage while permanently branding her with it.

The first step to assimilation was St. Anthony's Catholic mission school in Neopit, which opened its doors to 70 elementary school children in September, 1913, when Evelyn was six years old. Run by the Franciscan Sisters of Christian Charity, the school would educate the children of workers drawn to the Shawano Lumber Mill, which had opened in 1909. At St. Anthony's Catholic Church, the priests kept active in affairs of the governance of the small town. These priests were social workers in clerical garb, overseeing classes for children, while hosting fish fries and mixers—otherwise known as "boring Neopit dances"—for the young people home from the boarding schools.

Under the protective tent of the Catholic Church, Evelyn's identity developed with familiar customs. The Menominee people had lived in the land of Wisconsin through the tribal development of five clans: the ancestral Bear, Eagle, Wolf, Moose, and Crane. Indigenous to the state of Wisconsin, the homeland of the Menominee Reservation was situated on their ancestral territory. Thus, their language, practices, and traditions were passed through the generations. Evelyn learned the native dances of the tribe, performing them with her brothers, Sylvester Thomas, born October 4, 1914 and Elmer Charles, born February 6, 1911, and sisters Anna and Frances, at community gatherings and church socials. They called themselves "The Indian Players," dancing to skits called "Little Fire Face" and "The Elm Tree" while dressed in feathers, beads, and painted faces. She learned to cook parched corn, wild rice, and other Native American dishes, and to prepare wild game, such as squirrels, and freshwater fish with Anna, one year older, and Frances, four years older. "She could cook anything," her husband, Art Tic, later said of her. "She could hunt and fish, and she could cook deer and partridge," he boasted in an interview.

Evelyn's father, William, died in Neopit on April 4, 1916, when she was nine years old. Her mother took a job as a janitress in the BIA.

Her childhood was pastoral yet marked by poverty. Evelyn's family moved around, a condition which subjected her to several different schools. In a combination of financial need and pressure from authorities at the BIA, Indian families sent their children to the St. Joseph Boarding School in Keshena. Evelyn later reported having attended "St. Joe's," as did her brother, Elmer Charles, in March, 1928. The BIA supported the Catholic boarding school, with its sanctioned administration by the Pulaski Franciscans.

"The conditions were terrible," recalled a Tribe Elder in an interview. "They hit small children with rulers and belts. They wouldn't let them speak their language. The children would often go home to parents who couldn't understand a word they said."

A representative of the Catholic Church denies that St. Joseph ever participated in the kidnappings, performed by child "bounty hunters" employed by the BIA to populate the secular boarding schools erected for the tribal children of the Great Lakes. Evelyn Frechette was subjected to a variety of these boarding schools. Wards of the Menominee tribe attended the Tomah Indian Industrial School in western Wisconsin. Tomah enrolled pupils in the elementary grades from various tribes. While taking nine children from the Menominee Reservation, it served as a melting pot of children taken from the Chippewa, Sioux, Quapaw, and Winnebago (now called Ho-Chunk) Reservations, along with others of the Great Lakes' region.[9]

When Evelyn went to Tomah, she had her immersion into the baptism of the government's agenda to whitewash the Native American. The administration at the Tomah School was ignorant of the nuances of each tribe. One government inspector who visited Tomah in 1916 registered surprise in viewing the student population. "While composed of ten tribes," the inspector jotted down in his report to Washington, "these students do not strike one as being heterogeneous."

The main component to assimilation was to teach the "tots," as they were called, the English language. "The teachers . . . are earning the love and gratitude of their pupils and the respect of all who see their devotion to duty," said the report of an inspector in a memo to the Department of the Interior. "It is a beautiful thing to see the primary grade. The teacher put words of three and four syllables on the board with proper sound accents and the tots pronounced them perfectly although they had not seen them before."[10]

Poetry of this sort captioned the cozy world pictured in this correspondence, which neglected to mention that these children were interned here, taken from their parents for a minimum of three years. The component of racial hatred supported the concept of the Indian schools. It cloaked itself in a cover of advocacy.

For Evelyn, boarding school got her away from the poverty of the reservation. In the classrooms she developed a graceful, fluent handwriting, through which she conducted her gentle manner of self-expression. She left Tomah in 1920 as a candidate for the Riggs School at Flandreau, South Dakota. A high school, Flandreau drew its population from the Great Lakes' tribes. Evelyn was eligible to attend for the minimum three-year tenure that was required. She arrived in the midst of several epidemics. The administration strove for sanitation—towels were used only once, for example, and toothbrushes were collected every day. Yet measles, pneumonia, and trachoma, as well as the less severe ailments of grippe and bad colds, had invaded the buildings.

In her separate girls' quarters, Evelyn had the benefit of her own room, filled with her meager possessions. The clean sheets and relative privacy compensated for the steel ceilings and walls painted white over dark green. Covert dime novels circulated throughout the school. The matrons, in charge of stifling the budding sexual awakenings in these girls, ascended the soapbox of morality, decrying this "scandalous mix of true stories . . . and romances."

These pamphlets dismayed the BIA inspectors, who demanded the school elevate the level of fiction. The suggestions were futile, as Flandreau was an agricultural school that gave literature a low priority. The curriculum emphasized farming skills for boys. For ten weeks per year, girls learned "home training, cooking, poultry raising, sewing, laundering and nursing." In the hands of unaccredited, aging teachers, these subjects set a tone of servitude, both in the home and in the workplace.[11] On May 26, 1924, Evelyn graduated.

Native Americans graduating from these schools were unprepared for the sophisticated workplace developing in the cities. For any unmarried woman seeking employment in the 1920s, the classified ads presented only two choices, domestic work or clerical jobs in business firms. The lack of such abilities tracked Evelyn's classmates into a career of low-paying, domestic labor. The school operated on the premise that the girls would return home to get married. Evelyn became involved with a young man living on the Menominee Reservation named Melvin Fairbanks. His early romantic designs carried with them the weight of common sense; they were both part-blood Menominee living in a world of prejudice. Yet Fairbanks became disillusioned with Evelyn, as she failed to conform to his plans. He would, in the days of her notoriety, profess his disapproval of her "loose conduct" loudly among their family and friends.[12]

Had Evelyn followed the established pattern for teenaged girls, she would have married Fairbanks, or another young man, by the age of sixteen. Young married men hoped to gain employment in the Menominee Lumber Mill at Shawano. The mill gave the men of the Menominee Reservation their livelihood. It cast over Neopit the ambiance of a factory town, by placing the workers under the umbrella of the BIA. Employing the talents of the Indian loggers, it manufactured the local white pines, hardwoods, and northern hemlock.

Charles "Charley" Frechette, born in 1876 to Mose Frechette, was her father's brother. He was a jobber who acted as chairman of the advisory board and liaison between the Menominee mill and the BIA. A union representative, he stood up for the rights of the workers. For Evelyn, he embodied the power that was out of reach. He "went to Washington to do things for the Indians," she later wrote. He walked within a mystique that connected the indigenous community to the governing hierarchy. In reality, Charles Frechette worked as a liaison between the mill, the BIA, and the workers from the Tribe. His vocal pleas to the BIA were meant to stand up for the rights of the Menominee workers.

His philosophy embodied the spirituality and wisdom of the Menominee. When a training program was instituted at the mill by the BIA's Indian Affairs Office, Charley Frechette responded passionately. "I do not want to create the impression that I have any quarrel with the idea of a training program . . . all men are not born leaders, and no amount of study will create a successful leader. The Menominees have demonstrated, in their desire for greater learning, an interest in the training program. Well and good, give us the full prescription so that in the end we will not be found wanting."

From the text of his letter, it is evident that Charles Frechette feared that the training would result in a loss of traditional skills among the workers. He seems to have walked a tightrope in his liaison capacity between the Tribe and the U.S. Department of the Interior.[13]

A block of tents erected near the old Stockbridge Reservation, south of the Menominee, formed the local red-light district. As a result of visiting the brothel site, married men were becoming infected with venereal disease. By 1929, the epidemic was rampant. The BIA installed a medical clinic to treat the infected for syphilis.

Dr. L. Culp, in one month alone during 1929, treated seventy-seven residents of the Reservation. Unknown to the trusting sufferers who lined up for the first of several intravenous treatments for the disease, he spent his evenings begging the Washington office to relieve him of this station. "Cured cases, if any be made, will go right out and become reinfected . . . by lack of common judgment on the part of many parents young girls from their early teens are practically directed in the paths of prostitution. They hang along the walks and in vile places like the red light districts of the cities, beckoning and baiting the male contingent which needs no urging."

Yet the problem of prostitution came closer than "red-light districts of the cities." The Menominee mill housed many transient men.[14]

The mill offered the surety of employment for the men. By comparison, there was no such opportunity for the women. Evelyn followed the only prescription offered to women, a job as a domestic. She called herself a "nurse girl," finding work out of slender offerings. Finally, she acknowledged that she could no longer stand the boredom of Neopit. The Catholic Mission dances, with their stupefying lineup of local boys, became intolerable. She thought about Chicago, the promised land for Midwestern girls born in the Progressive Era. Her generation had grown to adulthood in time to be dazzled by the optimism of the 1920s.

On April 23, 1923, Evelyn's mother, Mary, remarried Henry Sprague, of the Stockbridge Reservation.

In 1924, Evelyn went to Milwaukee. In the gush of sexual freedom that followed, she became intermittently involved with four men in Gresham. Soon she was pregnant. It was a time when unsmiling society branded an unwed mother a "wayward girl." Government programs and social welfare were still controversial theories.

In July 1927, she arrived in Chicago. Doctors at the Bryant Hospital at 351 Grant Place confirmed that she was two months with child. She listed herself as nineteen years old and single, Catholic, with no occupation. From there she went to the Salvation Army Hospital in Chicago, at 2040 North Crawford Avenue, where a social worker named Miss Thomas referred her to the Beulah Home for Unwed Mothers.[15]

The Beulah Home housed itself at 2144 North Clark, on the same block that staged the St. Valentine's Day Massacre, at 2122 North Clark. The Beulah Home, in an inconspicuous way, dealt a benign form of violence on its inhabitants that rivaled the famous gangland execution.

When Evelyn arrived with her dresses straining at the seams, her spirit almost broken from the long and lonely pregnancy, the Beulah Home was raging with an epidemic of head lice. The inmates, as they were called, brought their own soap and towels, yet were systematically denied bathing water. The squalid conditions proved to be too much for some, who simply left for the relative safety of the streets. One young mother later told authorities that she'd run away because she "couldn't stand the dirt."

Reverend and Mrs. Edward L. Brooks, the operators of the institution, sent the "girls" out to collect castoff food at the Sprague-Warner wholesale grocers. The head of the canning division of this company, Charles Riemenschneider, complained about their condition to Reverend Brooks, saying that they were inadequately dressed and too far along in their pregnancies to be out begging for food in the streets.

In a bartering arrangement that tendered work for room and board, the pregnant women did the physical upkeep of the almshouse, which included scrubbing the floors. Childbirth didn't exempt them from employment. In one instance, a sixteen-year-old girl was sent to her outside job on the day following the birth of her baby. In another situation, a married woman forced into the home by the abandonment of her husband gave birth to a baby girl with the intentions of keeping the child. The proprietors promised the child in adoption to an affluent woman willing to pay for a baby, while telling the birth mother that the child was too sick to leave the home with her.

While a virtual captive of this Victorian workhouse, Evelyn relied on her inner strength. For these strangers, her smile would hide her agony. She made the best of the situation up to and including the birth of the baby. On a freezing day in February 1928, she went into labor, to the smell of chloroform and ether, which permeated the dust-covered operating room of the home. This torture chamber contained three pieces of furniture: a flat operating table on large, old-fashioned wheels; a table for instruments; and a cabinet containing surgical dressings, medical books, bottles labeled and unlabeled, iodine bottles, and alcohol.

Beyond sat a dank kitchen piled with blankets and baby clothes. The recovery room contained a hospital bed, baby crib, a sign on the wall that stated self-righteously:

*"This is a house of peace; rest ye here in safety."*

She named the baby William Frechette, after her father, and lent to him her own adopted nickname, Billie. In her pauper status, she had no alternative but to leave Baby Billie in the dubious care of the Beulah Home as she went home to Neopit to stay with Vivian Tourtillott Warrington. In her application, she had listed both her parents, William Frechette as well as Mary Frechette Sprague, as dead. In the months after the birth, she stayed with Vivian, and fought the ravages of bereavement and depression. Late in 1928, she left Neopit for Milwaukee. She chose to live for a short time with the man whom she believed to be the baby's father. Upon her eventual return to Chicago, her efforts to retrieve the baby were met by a stone wall set up by the sixty-five-year-old proprietor of the Beulah Home. She wrote anxiously for word of the baby's welfare. What Evelyn didn't know when she penned her letter was that Billie had died between the ages of three and five months of age.

> *Neopit, Wisconsin, Nov. 15, 1928:*
> *Dear Mrs. Brooks,*
> *I have been thinking so much lately that I just had to write and find out how Billie is. Is he still with you there, or has he gone to a different place? Please Mrs. Brooks tell me all about him. I'm so anxious to know and I wish I had a picture of him. I would be satisfied. I just imagine how big he would be now.*
> *I'm stranded here. I haven't any money to get out of here, but I'm going to wait until after Xmas before I go back to work, and when I do I'll be right over to see you. And I hope Billie, too. -I will now close. I remain as ever,*
> *Evelyn F."*

Reverend Brooks employed the practice of obtaining money from the bereaved mothers for burial of the babies who died and then buried them himself, at no expense. He most likely used this ploy on the hapless Evelyn, or he side-tracked her claim for custody on the grounds that the baby was too sickly to leave his care. A grand jury investigation later disclosed that babies under the care of Edward L. Brooks met their death by either poison or violence, although the advanced state of decomposition made it impossible to prove the assertions. A body wrapped in a newspaper was found in 1935 in a frozen Michigan cemetery. A death certificate identified the child as William Frechette, date of death, July 24, 1928.[16]

*"We thought he got a raw deal."*

*—Delbert Hobson*

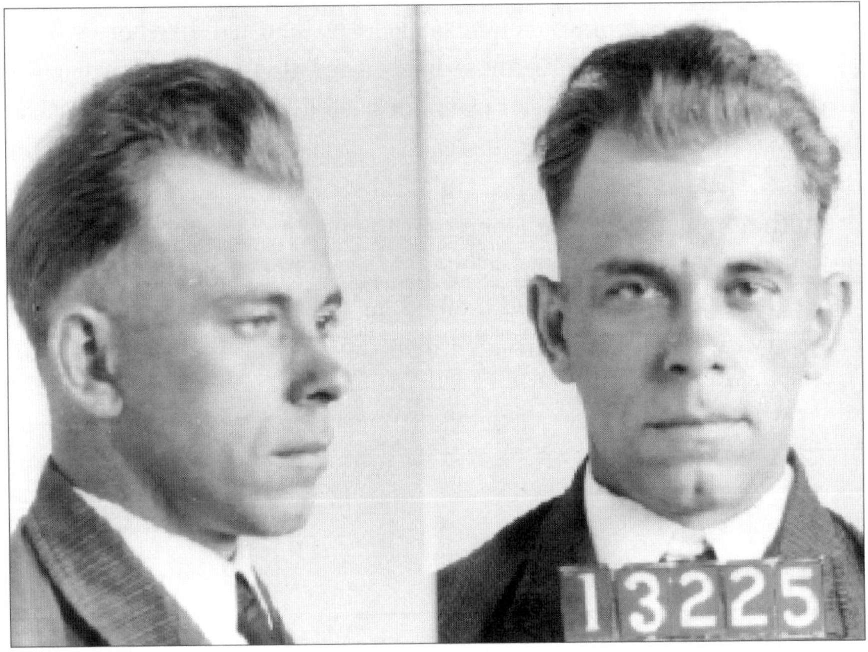


John Dillinger (Indiana State Prison)

# Running the Lines

In 1929, a prisoner of the state of Indiana was transferred from the reformatory to a state prison. During this routine procedure, he was asked to reiterate his original offense, in writing. The poor diction and wobbly grammar, not characteristic, betray his emotional strain:

> Saturday night of September 7, 1924, while under the influence of alcohol, me and my companion Edward Singleton attacked Mr. Morgan, a grocer in Mooresville, Ind. I had a gun a thirty two revolver when I struck him and hit him on the head with a bat and then ran we didn't get the money he had on him which was three hundred and twenty five dollars. I was arrested the next day and taken to Martinsville but I denied the charge. On September 14 my Father and Sister came to see me and told me that they had arrested Singleton two days before and he was a state witness against me having told all he

> knew of the crime. The prosecutor said that if I would plead guilty they would be linient [*sic*] with me. My Father and Sister asked me to plead guilty they were sure the county would be linient with me so I plead guilty next day Monday 15 Edgar Singleton when [*sic*] before Judge Williams and he asked me if I plead guilty and I said yes and he sentenced me to the Indiana Reformatory 10 to 20 years for assault and battery with intent to rob and 2 to 14 for conspiracy, sentenced to run concurrently. Then Singleton plead not guilty . . . and he had two jury trials and eventually received 2 to 14 years at the Indiana State Prison. I was told that I and the three others who come with me were transferred to play ball although it wasn't told to me by the Superintendent.—John Dillinger #3225.

Dillinger's attempt to rob Mr. Frank Morgan, the grocer, with Edgar Singleton surprised everyone, in spite of Dillinger's prior brushes with the law. On September 15, he had gone before Judge Joseph Williams of Martinsville. He was sentenced to two concurrent sentences of two to fourteen years and ten to twenty years on charges of conspiracy to commit a felony and assault with intent to rob.[1]

Delbert Hobson, his boyhood friend, was aghast at the sentence. "We thought he got a raw deal," said Delbert Hobson in an interview. He was referring to Singleton's sentence, in comparison to his young accomplice. Mr. Hobson saw this as the turning point.

"Dillinger had lots of good in him, but Edgar Singleton was never any good," said Mr. Hobson, as part of his lifelong attempt to vindicate his childhood friend. He insisted that Dillinger was led into the attack on Mr. Morgan. "Dillinger wouldn't have gone into it by himself."[2]

One thing is certain. John wrestled with his victim while his accomplice, Edgar Singleton, hid in the darkness. John broke free in confusion, didn't see the vanished Singleton, and, unbelievably, stumbled up the hill to his father's farm. He didn't have time to get comfortable.

Circumstantial evidence coupled with his reputation as a troublemaker placed him at the scene of the crime. He confessed to the police in nearby Martinsville. His family had no idea, they later said, how to help him. With Singleton arrested and turning evidence against Dillinger, the prosecutor conferred with the elder Mr. Dillinger and Audrey Hancock, John's sister. A guilty plea would bring the young man a light sentence, he assured them. They believed him, and counseled John to trust the court and plead guilty.

"It broke my mother's heart to see the way he went," said Audrey Hancock's daughter, Mary, in an interview. "He was brilliant; he could have gone another way."

The sentence levied upon Dillinger by Judge Williams, without benefit of counsel, was excessive even for that conservative community. "We all knew that the judge wanted to make an example of him. That was why he was given such a long sentence," said Mary.[3]

In spite of his friendship with Delbert Hobson, Dillinger had never liked the pastoral life of Mooresville. "He liked to read books about Jesse James," said Mr. Hobson in an interview. "It was all he'd read. We used to go 'uptown' together, and John would wear his cap on the side of his head," related Mr. Hobson. "All the rest of us, we wore our caps on the top of our heads. But John wanted to look different."[4]

The community of Mooresville, Christian and conservative, had lacked the exotic component that Dillinger had demanded from life. While still a teenager, he'd displayed his religious ambivalence through the theft of a car from the local Christian Church parking lot while the owners attended religious services inside. The act was a metaphor. Dillinger's primal loss, which began at the age of three with the death of his birth mother, cast the seed for his moral dilemma.

Mollie Dillinger had given birth to John Herbert on the night of June 22, 1903. Mollie's time with her son was short; three years later she became sick and, before her child's fourth birthday, she died. The Dillinger family buried the young mother in their newly purchased plot in Crown Hill Cemetery in Indianapolis, while they grieved in disbelief.

Back at home, John's sixteen-year-old sister took over. Audrey Hancock was already married. This fact was recalled years later by Mary, Mrs. Hancock's daughter. "My mother had to go back home to take over the care of John, as his mother died when he was only three years old. She raised him as her own."[5]

Mr. Dillinger eventually married the woman who was to become John's stepmother, Elizabeth Fields. He then sold his Indianapolis retail establishments and bought a farm in nearby Mooresville. The farmhouse sheltered the growing family, as three children, Doris, Frances, and Hubert, were born.

His imprisonment removed him, at the age of nineteen, from society for nine years. When he entered the Pendleton Reformatory, that world still included his wife.

Berlie Dillinger, in faith and love, passed the time by writing pretty letters. Their marriage lasted as long as she was willing to pen these florid notes, while cherishing the ones she'd received from him. On monotonous prison stationery, he would write in his rather delicate, slanted handwriting the desperate words of hope and humor.

At the age of nineteen, John had married Beryl Hovious. Known as "Berlie," she was born on August 6, 1906. When she was seventeen, John released her, literally, from her pinned shirtwaist and high, upswept hair. She was four months short of her eighteenth birthday when she married John. They wed on April 12, 1924, in a wild step out of their rural backgrounds, where she'd learned embroidery, cooking, and prayers in preparation for life as a Christian housewife. A native of neighboring Martinsville, she reflected the domestic ideal of femininity—a Gibson Girl.[6]

As she entered this marriage of thwarted hopes, she soon learned that it was to be a life of waiting. Their small room in the farmhouse had doors that opened both to the kitchen and the parlor.[7] With little privacy she'd watch for him from the highway window. Later she would wait in the same patient way for visiting day at Pendleton Reformatory.

By the time he'd married Beryl Hovious, crime was a way of life. The car he'd stolen in front of the Friends' Church had taken him for a ride which had led to the Navy to avoid prosecution, then AWOL from the U.S.S. Utah in 1923 to escape the Navy. Wedding bells didn't stop the treadmill; marriage was quarrelsome and directionless as they attempted to live in the farmhouse with the elder Dillinger, later moving into an apartment in nearby Martinsville. But the young couple fought constantly.

In the waning sunlight of the autumn of 1924, the pain of the incarceration took hold of them both. That summer of anger, the heat of the nights that had climaxed in the violent robbery of an old man, receded as though in a dream.

As inmate number 14395 of the Pendleton Reformatory, symbols of his inability to tolerate authority surrounded him. These were the days

Beryl Hovious (Courtesy of Tony Stewart)

predating the modern concept of prison as a social program. The administration hired guards who had no formal training, and no trouble understanding what they were there to do. They faced their job unhampered by notions of sensitivity. In doing so, they made a fair match for the class of men that they were paid to control.

The U.S. Federal Bureau of Prisons had begun to implement progressive changes in penology. Social workers, trained in psychological and intelligence evaluations, had instituted programs in some of the newer federal prisons. However, these changes were slow in coming to state and local facilities. At Pendleton, these ruined farm boys were assigned to the Singer industrial sewing machine. Dillinger couldn't easily adjust to prison life and went on a long course of petty infractions and impulsive escape attempts.[8]

His wife, at home, continued to wait. She visited Dillinger in the Pendleton Reformatory. Yet the small sacrifices dutifully performed were less and less appreciated by him. They would peer at each other through the small dirty window. She began to dread the visits to her husband in his shrunken world.

Their marriage lasted, miraculously, for five years, until she filed for divorce. Judge Chester Vernon granted a divorce to Beryl in Morgan County on June 20, 1929.

This transition left John Dillinger without an important outlet for his romantic sentiments. He now faced his time without the emotional buffer of a woman waiting at home. For the next four years of his incarceration, with a subsequent transfer from the Pendleton Reformatory to the state penitentiary at Michigan City, women as romantic or sexual beings existed for him only in an abstract way.

The other inmates, some of whom he befriended, enlivened the seemingly dead time. Homer Van Meter would prove to be a loyal confederate. "Van" would eventually outlive Dillinger by only one month. He was two years younger than Dillinger, and skinny at 5 feet 11 inches and 133 pounds. He'd occasionally worked as a waiter, and at one point had the word "Hope" tattooed on his right forearm. He bore a 1-inch scar in the middle of his forehead. Van Meter took his inspiration from Eddie Cantor, the singing and dancing comedian who conquered with joking one-upmanship. Van had been imprisoned at Pendleton since March 25, 1925, when he'd been sentenced to ten to twenty-one years on two robbery counts. He'd been transferred to Michigan City on July 28, 1926. Van

Anchors away – Dillinger before he went AWOL (FBI)

Meter's innate sense of survival was threatened by his fatal flaw; he watched everything. He refused to "lay low," trusting no one and nothing.[9]

The natural leader of this prison gang was Harry "Pete" Pierpont. Pierpont, at twenty-seven years of age, exerted an innate sense of hierarchy because of his strikingly handsome appearance. He was tall and fair-haired, with an omnipotent personality. His enigmatic mood swings, coupled with his dazzling physical attributes, set him apart. In a departure from the usual flat prisoner classifications, the record department listed his hair as "light chestnut," his eyes as "grey azure."

Pierpont, sentenced to ten to twenty years for a well-publicized bank robbery, had little hope of release. He was not eligible for parole for ten years, at which time he would be threatened with eleven years of a former sentence dating from 1922, mostly unserved for assault and battery with intent to commit murder, which had netted him two to fourteen years when he was only nineteen years old. The handsome "Pete" Pierpont was a role model for Dillinger, a Jesse James he could smell.[10]

Both Van Meter and Pierpont had entered Pendleton as jaded seedlings. When they were transferred from Pendleton to the higher-security Indiana State Penitentiary at Michigan City, in 1928, they joined a tougher crowd. On July 16 of the following year, Dillinger followed. He was officially transferred because the Michigan City baseball team needed a good shortstop. Dillinger had played ball both in Martinsville and later at Pendleton.

In his new location, he became friendly with an assortment of felons, all serving long sentences. Russell "Boobie" Clark, was 6 feet, 1 inch and weighed 167 pounds, which was large for the time. His size had brought fame when he attempted to enlist in the Marine Corps during the First World War. The Terre Haute recruiting station reported the largest man ever to enlist, Russell Lee Clark. His good intentions had not resulted in a life well lived, however. He was dishonorably discharged from the armed services a scant four months after enlisting. On December 12, 1927, he was convicted in New Castle, Indiana, and sentenced to a twenty-year term for bank robbery. At Michigan City he left a trail of infractions. The most important were three escape attempts and a work strike that he organized in 1929.

Charles "Mac" Makley, a rotund bank robber doing a ten- to twenty-year sentence for robbery, was older than the others, at age forty-four.

On June 23, 1928, he was sentenced to 10 to 20 years for bank robbery. He was of a medium to heavy build at 180 pounds and 5 feet, 7 inches. He had gray eyes and dark chestnut hair, his skin was swarthy, and he walked with a slight limp due to a shortened right leg. His wife, Edith, had not joined in the pilgrimage made by his family to visit him, although she did attempt to write to him. Makley could have followed in the footsteps of his respectable Ohio family had he not expressed his contempt for the working man so often, and so well.

Edward Shouse had been sentenced to twenty-five years on June 4, 1930, for auto theft. He was only twenty-seven years old, weighing 150 pounds at 5 feet 7 inches tall."[11]

John "Red" Hamilton, a freckled, Irish redhead, was a Canada-based Chicago bootlegger. He was sentenced on March 16, 1927, to twenty-five years for auto banditry in South Bend, Indiana. At the time of the offense, he'd been living with his wife, Mary, and two young boys. His wife had run away from him, taking some of his money. After she had left him, she died of cancer in 1930. The woman's mother took in the boys, and the fragmented family was living on home-relief in Toledo. Although he'd not seen them, Hamilton was rumored to have set up a trust fund for his sons.[12]

These men gazed through one mirror of bitterness. Their jagged looking glass reflected grudges and lack of personal culpability. They lived on cell block "A" like neighbors forced by varying circumstances into the low-rent district. This housing unit stood closely behind the Administration Building and the Chapel. The three buildings formed a cornerstone of the prison community that moved coal, or "ran the lines," along the railroad tracks that mazed through the grounds. The industrial landscape of Michigan City formed a road map for the extensive escape route in the planning stage.[13]

As the years progressed, both Pierpont and Dillinger began shedding the soft edges to their faces. Their hairlines began to recede. Pierpont's frame thinned out, lending him the appearance of an austere, determined intellectual. Dillinger also lost weight, but it had the effect of casting over him a hawklike, haunted look. The friendship of Dillinger and Pierpont was an association that would, over time, see the two men leave the impulsiveness of their twenties as they crossed the threshold to manhood and their destinations.

*"He told his father that he was treated like an animal in prison, and that they had taken nine years of his life and they owed him."*

*—Jeff Scalf,*
*great-nephew of John Dillinger*

# The Highwayman

Hubert Dillinger, John's half-brother, brought him home to Mooresville, Indiana in May 1933. While riding through the main section of town, Dillinger stared longingly at the women strolling past the shops. Their skirts were longer than he remembered, almost touching the sidewalk. A sobriety of dress, the severity of face and hair, cloaked the figures of the housewives as they pushed their perambulators down the center of town. He heard crystal sets playing jazz from the opened doors of storefronts.

Peering out the window of the passenger seat in the car driven by his brother Hubert, John Dillinger gazed blankly at the symbols of the New Deal. The curious drawing of the National Recovery Act (NRA) eagle with its legend, *NRA—We Do Our Part,* posed on the cover of the newspapers and storefront windows of Mooresville. The controversial NRA had swept the country as a symbol of hope, offering solace and a broad way out of the poverty that had replaced the prosperity of prior years. The Great Depression had meant little to the convict, who had been cut off from the economic changes that had transformed the country.

Green farmland and the warm brick of the Quaker Church beckoned as they made their turn to begin the last leg of their journey. The road curved past the high school that Dillinger had never wanted to attend. They turned onto the uphill driveway. The car always rolled backwards during the shift—they knew that the only way you got up that hill was to gun the gas pedal. Otherwise, you just slipped down, precariously backwards. With a jump-start they bolted home.[1]

Quaker Church, Mooresville (Author's collection)

The Mooresville School. The arch says, "Enter to grow in wisdom." (Author's collection)

John Dillinger's elation at his release from prison darkened as he arrived. His stepmother, Lizzie, had suffered a stroke on or about May 18.[2]

As though in a trance, John watched family members walk out of the kitchen onto the porch that faced the open farmland. His sister, Audrey, cried as his father, face set in a grimace, greeted him on the wooden porch. His young half-sisters, in their oxfords and horn-rimmed glasses, waited for the chance to kiss their half-brother. A shocking aura of death wafted out of the kitchen door on to this group of country people. Elizabeth Fields Dillinger, John's stepmother, had died an hour before. The group tracked back into the large kitchen, overcome by the loss of one and the return of another. Dillinger's gaze wandered past the kitchen, into his old bedroom.

In the turbulent period after his parole, he became grounded in the belief that he owed nothing to the state of Indiana except revenge. He felt the prison system had stolen his human dignity. John's great-nephew, Jeff Scalf, related a conversation between the outlaw and his father, John Wilson Dillinger. "He told his father that he was treated like an animal in prison, and that they had taken nine years of his life and they owed him," recalled Jeff Scalf.

Dillinger managed to soothe his own scars, raw as meat, with a neutral plaster of objectivity. Within days he was on the road, tracking down a list of fixers. He'd been prepared to meet Dewey and Pearl Elliott by Harry Pierpont while the two had been in prison. Pierpont had talked about New Harmony repeatedly. In the annals of prison bravado, New Harmony was Pierpont's big score. Pearl and her husband, Dewey Elliott, had been Pierpont's associates and suspects in the 1925 New Harmony bank job. The police had failed to connect their activities and, after questioning them for hours, were forced to dismiss their culpability for lack of evidence. Pierpont and his co-defendants had been living at Pearl's rooming house when they robbed the New Harmony Bank on March 11, 1925. Bringing the money back to Dewey and Pearl at 714¼ North Washington, the robbers had counted out $11,128. The take had amounted to $4,828 in cash, $4,300 in liberty bonds, and $2,000 in unnegotiable securities.

To celebrate the success of the bank robbery, the Deweys threw parties for Pierpont and his partners, Thaddeus Skeer and Louise Brunner, Skeer's girlfriend. While both Skeer and Brunner would later testify against Pierpont, they agreed to keep mute about the Elliotts.

The abundance of liquor and women was noticed by the local townspeople. Pierpont and his friends staged these orgies of lust for sheer pleasure, both material and sensory. At one such party, a proprietor feared that he wouldn't get paid. To assuage his concerns, one of the revelers spilled gold coins into his hands.

It was to be a short month for the young bandits, however. Pierpont's winning streak ended when he was arrested on April 2, a mere three weeks after the robbery. In the flurry of arrests, Pearl and Dewey Elliott managed to avoid prosecution, although they were picked up for questioning.

Harry Pierpont adamantly denied their involvement all throughout the trial and subsequent imprisonment.[3]

In the early summer of 1933, Dillinger traveled to Kokomo as Jack Donovan, to visit Pearl and Dewey Elliott. His orders were to spot a roadhouse located seven miles north of Kokomo, on a main highway. Near a bridged creek, he was to find a small cottage, a few hundred feet from the roadhouse on a knoll. He was to enter from the main road and drive to the rear of the roadhouse. When Dillinger approached the house, he watched for a flickering signal flashing from a lamp in the window facing the road. It was safe to advance if the light was on; the absence of a light meant danger.[4]

The Elliotts would work primarily as messengers, running from place to place delivering messages for the mob. Over the course of their association, Dillinger would give the Deweys amounts adding to $15,000.[5]

Pearl Elliott was a broadly masculine woman living in the subculture of prostitution with her husband, Dewey Elliott, whom she less than affectionately called "Mr." She was 5 feet, 10 inches, and weighed 150 to 160 pounds, with a large bust and slender hips. Her voice was deeply masculine. A prostitute in the pioneer tradition of the nineteenth century, she surrounded herself with women. The one holding the most prominent position among Pearl's associates was Ruby Kosmal, also called Ruby Ickes.

Pearl Elliott was born on October 21, 1887, in Hillesburg, Indiana, and was raised by her parents, a Scotsman named John Newton McDonald and his wife, Mary Bell Booher, whom he married on July 17, 1886. Pearl, the first child of this marriage, grew to womanhood with a massive back and shoulders. Her voice developed into a bass. She preferred the rough and tumble horseplay of her brothers, Roscoe and Verne, to the rag dolls of the girls around her neighborhood. She would remain close to Roscoe throughout her life.

Pearl McDonald tried to resist the pressure to leave the household as a properly wedded wife. At the advanced age of twenty, she married Earl Crawford on December 17, 1907. Pearl's mother brought some cheer but little hope for this marriage. She knew that Pearl would not fit the mold of a submissive wife. Her strong-willed daughter fought with her husband, Earl Crawford, soon leaving him altogether. The marriage ended in divorce, freeing Pearl to gamble with marriage a second time. She wed Charles McGrath on November 10, 1910. Pearl could not reconcile her no-nonsense personality with domestic frills. The requirements of a housewife—the details of lace and muslin curtains, keeping cookbooks and the family Bible—were lost on her. She thought like a man, having no feel for the sentiments that went with homemaking. While married to McGrath she met a local hoodlum from Kokomo by the name of Dewey Elliott. She divorced Charles McGrath, which allowed her the freedom to go the criminal route with Elliott.

Dewey Elliott was a gambler who towered at six feet tall and weighed close to 250 pounds. Born in 1900, he was 33 years old at the time he became involved with Dillinger. His father, William, hailed from Lebanan, Kentucky, where he'd been born on April 17, 1861. William settled in Indianapolis with his wife, Anna. He made a living as a station fireman. Anna had kept house for the family of six children. While living with his parents as a young man, at 1136 South Delphos Street in Indianapolis, Dewey worked as a machine operator. He was twelve years Pearl's junior and, rather than try to dominate her, he joined her as an equal partner.

Kokomo was called "The Junction" because of the railroad tracks running through it since the 1860s. It was a wide open town where it was rumored that any ex-convict could run for political office—and win. Pearl and Dewey thrived in an unconventional marriage, living at 606 N. Market Street. She worked as a prostitute and madam, under the name "Pearl Mullendore."

Pearl was arrested several times on public morals' charges. She called off the dogs with the help of her cousin, "Uncle" George Bonham, the mayor of Elwood, Indiana. This association sheltered Pearl's prostitution racket, which she ran with the help of her cousin, Ruby Kosmal, alias Ruby Ickes and Ruby Church. Ruby also affectionately addressed Mayor Bonham as "Uncle" and lived in his house at 2029 South Elwood Street in Elwood, Indiana.

Dillinger visited Pearl Elliott's "joint," in the summer of 1933. Within the twenty-one room rooming house at 714¼ North Washington, a customer could enjoy dining, entertainment, and, if desired, the company of a prostitute. One such lady was the 250-pound Tiney Cypher, who had graduated to the position of Pearl's assistant in the administration of the establishment.

Dillinger gave Pearl and Dewey Elliott the first of several deposits toward the purchase of groceries, an apartment, and a car. The Deweys accepted the money with the promise of supplying a new Dodge. Dillinger was to learn that they would pocket the money and then deliver less than the original bargain. In this instance, the car they eventually delivered was not the new Dodge they'd promised; it was a stolen Chrysler. Dillinger later noticed other small transgressions. Pearl Elliott never got any change at the grocery store. Dillinger found that no matter what he gave her for a purchase as low as $4—from a $50 bill to a $100 bill—Pearl never gave him the change. Dewey Elliott was important as a connection in Chicago and, for that reason, Dillinger tolerated the petty theft that he constantly endured at the hands of Pearl Elliott. Dewey assured Dillinger that his syndicate connections could guarantee the gang a safe place in Chicago. Dewey was known to Capone's people and could supply them with guns and ammunition.[6]

Dewey, who worked mainly with Michigan City parolee Harry Copeland, made the important arrangements to advance the design of the Michigan City breakout. He connected Copeland with his friend Homer Brown, who had written letters to Pierpont under an assumed name, while the latter was incarcerated at Michigan City. Brown lived a double life as both a theater owner and mobster. As part of a deal made with Copeland, he purchased a large carton of thread from the American Thread Company in Chicago, and then consigned it to the East Coast Shirt Company, which operated within the Michigan City Penitentiary. They planned to use the cartons of thread to hide three .38-caliber automatics, which would be delivered to the shirt factory where Russell

Clark was assigned on a work detail.[7]

In the company of Harry Copeland, Dillinger visited brothels in Muncie. His immersion into the reality of prostitution, garnered with two women named Sarah Goodnight and Mickey Shea, had taught him that sex was not going to come giftwrapped. Trying to pursue a relationship, Dillinger called on twenty-three-year-old Mary Longnaker. She was the sister of his friend, James Jenkins, who remained in Michigan City. Although he was disliked by Pierpont, Jenkins had hoped for inclusion in the impending jail break.[8]

Mary Longnaker. (Lori Hyde)

Mary Longnaker tried to look attractive, wearing stylish spectator pumps, flowing crepe dresses, and brown bobbed hair. Thin at 5 feet, 6 inches and weighing 125 pounds, she carried herself with an air of limp resignation. Before meeting Dillinger, she'd spent the days aimlessly in her rented room at 324 West First Avenue in Dayton, Ohio.

Mary was born Mary Ruth Jenkins on August 14, 1910, in Bedford, Indiana, to the former Veena Burke and George Jenkins. She had a sister named Veena, and a brother, James "Jimmy," who was Dillinger's close friend in Michigan City. After her mother died, her father moved with his girlfriend, Jessie, to Kansas City, Missouri. With James in prison and her father relocated to another state, Mary married Howard Longnaker at the age of nineteen. Longnaker, a farmer from Pleasant Hill, Ohio, was two years older than Mary, yet less mature, and with a stubborn streak that would only grow worse with marriage. When they'd stood before a magistrate at Newport, Kentucky, on February 28, 1929, and declared their devotion to each other, they began a relationship that would result in two baby daughters.

Her legal battle to end her marriage began on April 21, 1932, when she left Howard in Ohio, charging him with cruelty and neglect. She started going out during the summer of 1932 to dance halls in Dayton. Mary spent a great deal of time going to parties. Howard Longnaker felt justified in taking Mary's two children out of her custody. He steadfastly refused to return them. To hurt Mary further, he refused to allow her to visit the girls. This trapped Mary into a hopeless and vicious circle; he wouldn't reveal their whereabouts to the Domestic Relations Part of the Ohio court system. To make matters worse, the judge showed no interest in locating or retrieving the children for Mary.

She first heard from Dillinger while in the midst of her custody battle. Dillinger spent large sums of money on Mary, yet he could not lift her from depression. Her despair over the loss of her little girls, who were three and four years old, gave Mary such stress that Dillinger intervened. He confronted Howard Longnaker. The two got into a fistfight, with Longnaker refusing to budge on the issue of child custody. On July 15, Dillinger visited the law firm of Pickrel, Schaeffer and Young in their offices at the Union Trust Building. After being admitted to the office of an attorney named Johnson, he offered to pay for Mary's divorce. "Take care of it, now," he ordered Johnson. "This is a favor for a friend." The attorney threatened to throw him out the front door.

This useless encounter forced Mary to accept the loss of her children. She half-heartedly embraced her new role in life. She would act as hostess to Dillinger during his inconsistent visits to her Dayton boarding house.

Mary Longnaker was expected to provide help with the escape plan. As the sister of an inmate, she could enter Michigan City without arousing suspicion. They planned the visit while eating at "Pete's," a Greek restaurant at Third and Wilkinson Streets, an underworld hangout. Since the divorce attorney wouldn't accept money, Dillinger gave it to Mary. It did help to keep things rolling in the Domestic Relations Court. The cash was flowing in from his jobs, a series of armed robberies.

He and Mary Longnaker made an opulent couple, enjoying the profits from these robberies in this dreary year of the Depression. He invited Mary and her girlfriend, Mary Ann Buchholtz, to Chicago. Mary Ann, a German girl from Dayton, believed the "businessman from Indianapolis" line, at least until they got to Chicago. It appeared legitimate enough; the three stopped at John's father's farm in Mooresville. It was a stay lasting about ten minutes. Then they drove to a filling station where Dillinger left $10 with an attendant for his brother Hubert.

In Chicago, they stayed for almost two weeks at the Crillon Hotel, located near the grounds of the 1933 World's Fair. The three tourists, who registered under their true names, appeared to be the picture of respectability; Dillinger had his own room on the second floor, next to the one occupied by the two women.

With seemingly unlimited cash, they went to the Chicago Century of Progress of 1933. In the World's Fair on July 20, they saw every exhibit and went on all the rides. John was pleasant. He never showed suspicion of anyone, not even policemen. Their inflated holiday ended on the first of August. As the detours began, Dillinger's mood darkened. They drove through the Indiana Dunes, which bordered Michigan City. Hailed as the scene of "beautiful beaches where tired city dwellers can go out to the pure air and see the sun rise and set over the lake," the Dunes flanked the Indiana State Penitentiary. Mary was going to visit her brother, James Jenkins. Prior to the stop, they bought a basket of fruit. The couple stripped the skins from a dozen bananas. They stuffed money into the soft meat of the fruit and then restored the skins to replicate fresh bananas.

Mary went in with her friend, Mary Ann Buchholtz. Dillinger, barred from the institution as an ex-inmate, waited outside in his maroon coupe. During the prison visit, Mary stood on line with wives, mothers, and sweethearts, all holding trays of food slowly gathering bacteria in the stifling visiting area. Mary submitted the bananas. As she did so, she handed a guard $50, on the pretense of petty cash for Jenkins' commissary. The visit took half an hour, at which time the two women walked across the wide road separating the Administration Building from the parking field.

The next stop lent an ominous climax to the grand vacation. When they stopped in Fort Wayne, Indiana, Dillinger made the two women wait in the car while he entered a run-down, gray frame house. The girlfriends sat passively in the Chevrolet, left to stare at the sinister shack at 604 Third Street. This shanty, the flip side of the glamour of the World's Fair, was a hangout visited by many underworld characters. Dillinger, who stood on the front porch, began a conversation with a woman who came to the door. Miss Buchholtz could hear bits of their discussion. The person Dillinger had stopped to visit was gone—he'd been arrested.

Upon arriving home to Dayton, Dillinger spent the night in Mary Longnaker's rooms at 324 West First Street. He left the following day for Indianapolis.[8]

At around the same time that Dillinger began seeing Mary Longnaker, he moved away from the humiliating string of grocery store and soda fountain robberies to bank jobs. Like an obsessive breadwinner, he was fueled to the task of providing the means for the Michigan City escape. With his important connection to the Elliotts established, Dillinger next contacted Fred Berman and Clifford Mohlar, two Fort Wayne bank robbers. For this meeting, Dillinger drove through the tree-less expanse of Indiana's flat roadways. He rode through twisting, rural back roads that ushered in the scenery of East Chicago, Indiana. In 1933, the town was controlled by the graft of the local police.

On May 25, 1933, he met his old friend, Homer Van Meter, who had been paroled on May 19, 1933, just before Dillinger. On the advice of Harry Copeland, Dillinger regrouped with Michigan City ex-con Sam Goldstine. They roomed in the Beverly Apartment Hotel at Madison and 8th in Gary, Indiana, and split the $75 per week rent.

Dillinger, during this gestation period, traveled to St. Paul in a fruitful reunion with Van, who was elated at his recent release. With Van and Harry Copeland, he stayed sporadically during July and August of 1933 at English Lake, Bass Lake, and St. Pierre, Indiana. He then helped to plan a job in Ohio, at the New Carlisle National Bank. This first attempt at bank robbery found Dillinger in his perpetual supporting role. Together with Harry Copeland and Homer Van Meter, he joined Sam Goldstine on June 10. They left the bank and went directly to East Chicago, Indiana. They collected $10,600, an inspiring sum of money with which to grace the growing web of payoffs, protection, and supplies. The gang-of-four comprised of Van Meter, Dillinger, Copeland and Goldstine also robbed a bank in Grand Haven, Ohio.

Dillinger and Copeland formed a hybrid gang out of an original team who had joined Dillinger doing petty stickups. They were known as the "White Cap Gang," because they wore straw hats during their holdups, out of some vain desire to make a physical impression. The next robbery would be staged in Indiana, at the Bank of Daleville on July 17. The plans were interrupted with the arrest of William Shaw and "Lefty" Parker, who had comprised the members of the "White Cap Gang." Dillinger hit Daleville with Harry Copeland. Although they collected a mere $3,500, Dillinger discovered in Copeland a professional partner and mentor. The two staged a robbery at the First National Bank of Montpelier on August

4 with a third man, netting $10,110; on August 14, they hit the Citizens National Bank of Bluffton, Ohio. Dillinger narrowly escaped arrest with the Indiana State Police staked out at the apartment that he shared with Sam Goldstine. Goldstine was arrested, along with Fred Berman and Clifford Mohlar, as they left the apartment.

Dillinger, who would always prove to be a better soldier than strategist, realized how desperately he needed Harry Copeland. It was humiliating for him to accept that he couldn't operate on his own finite ability. Yet in accepting his meager status in all its limitations, he was renewing the supporting role he'd always played.

On September 6, he joined with Hilton O. Crouch, who was having an affair with a fifteen-year-old girl. With a third man, they held up the Massachusetts Avenue State Bank in Indianapolis. During the holdup, Dillinger climbed to the top of a partition.

"This is a stickup," he shouted to assistant bank manager and acting teller, Lloyd Rinehart. His threats became louder as Dillinger theatrically slid to the floor. Rinehart connected Dillinger's straw hat to the many newspaper articles written about him. He allowed Dillinger and the two other robbers to scoop between $21,000 and $24,000 from the tellers' stations. They took Rinehart as a shield, letting him out en route to Ohio. Hilton Crouch, a car thief operating in Indianapolis before he'd been convicted on February 2, 1928 and sentenced to five to twenty-one years, had never seen so much money.

Unknown to Dillinger, two boarders took a room on the first floor of Mary's rooming house at 324 West First Avenue in Dayton, Ohio. Two detectives, Russell K. Pfauhl and Charles E. Gross, had gotten Mary Longnaker's name from the visiting records at Michigan City, when she had visited her brother, James Jenkins. Jenkins was known as Dillinger's associate, and his suspected homosexual "punk." With Mary's address in hand, Pfauhl and Gross set up a surveillance of Dillinger's comings and goings from the boarding house. They broke into Mary's room and hit the jackpot with the discovery of Dillinger's love letters.

Dillinger had a date with Mary on September 21. Neither of the detectives was in the boarding house at the time of his arrival, which was late at night. Mrs. Stricker, the landlady, called the desk sergeant, W.J. Aldridge.

"He's here," she cried excitedly into her wall phone.

"Who's here, and where?" Aldridge asked with bored impatience.

"John Dillinger," she cried. It woke the desk sergeant out of his lethargy. At 1:30 a.m., Sergeant Aldrich and Detectives Pfauhl and Gross went to the boarding house at 324 West First Street.

With the house surrounded by plainclothesmen, Mrs. Stricker knocked on the door. After the landlady identified herself, the police barged in. Dillinger was standing in the middle of the room under a drop light, looking at their vacation photos from the Chicago Century of Progress.

Detective Gross shoved a machine gun against Dillinger's chest. "Hold them high, John," Gross said. "We're police officers and you're under arrest." Mary pretended to faint. They told her to crawl across the room. As she slithered on all fours, they never took their eyes, or their guns, away from Dillinger. His automatic lay helplessly under a pillow on the bed. Mary Longnaker became hysterical as they searched her room, finding a sack filled with cash. Much of the currency was packaged in Indianapolis bank wrappers.

In the station house, located over the old city market on Main between Third and Fourth Streets, Dillinger faced down Sy Yendes, Chief of the Detective Bureau. Yendes had a reputation of breaking an arm or a leg if a prisoner talked back. Dillinger became cocky.

"I want to call my lawyer."

Yendes retorted that he had "lots of time," and began grilling him. Dillinger insisted that the bag of cash was his life savings, and denied knowing anything about bank robbery. At the end of the long night, Dillinger laid his rings and watch on top of his pocket money and went into a solitary cell on the third floor of the jail.

Dayton criminal lawyer Jack Egan, who maintained a practice in both Chicago and Dayton, appeared for him. He specialized in *habeas corpus* proceedings, which got his client out quickly. In spite of Dillinger's criminal trail in Indiana, Indiana State Police Captain Matthew Leach had been unable to make any charges stick. Dillinger was only wanted in Ohio—in Allen County, for the robbery of the Bluffton bank. Egan insisted that the Allen County warrant was valid, knowing that his client would never be released on bail. Judge Patterson was faced with the realization that Montgomery County could not hold Dillinger without evidence.

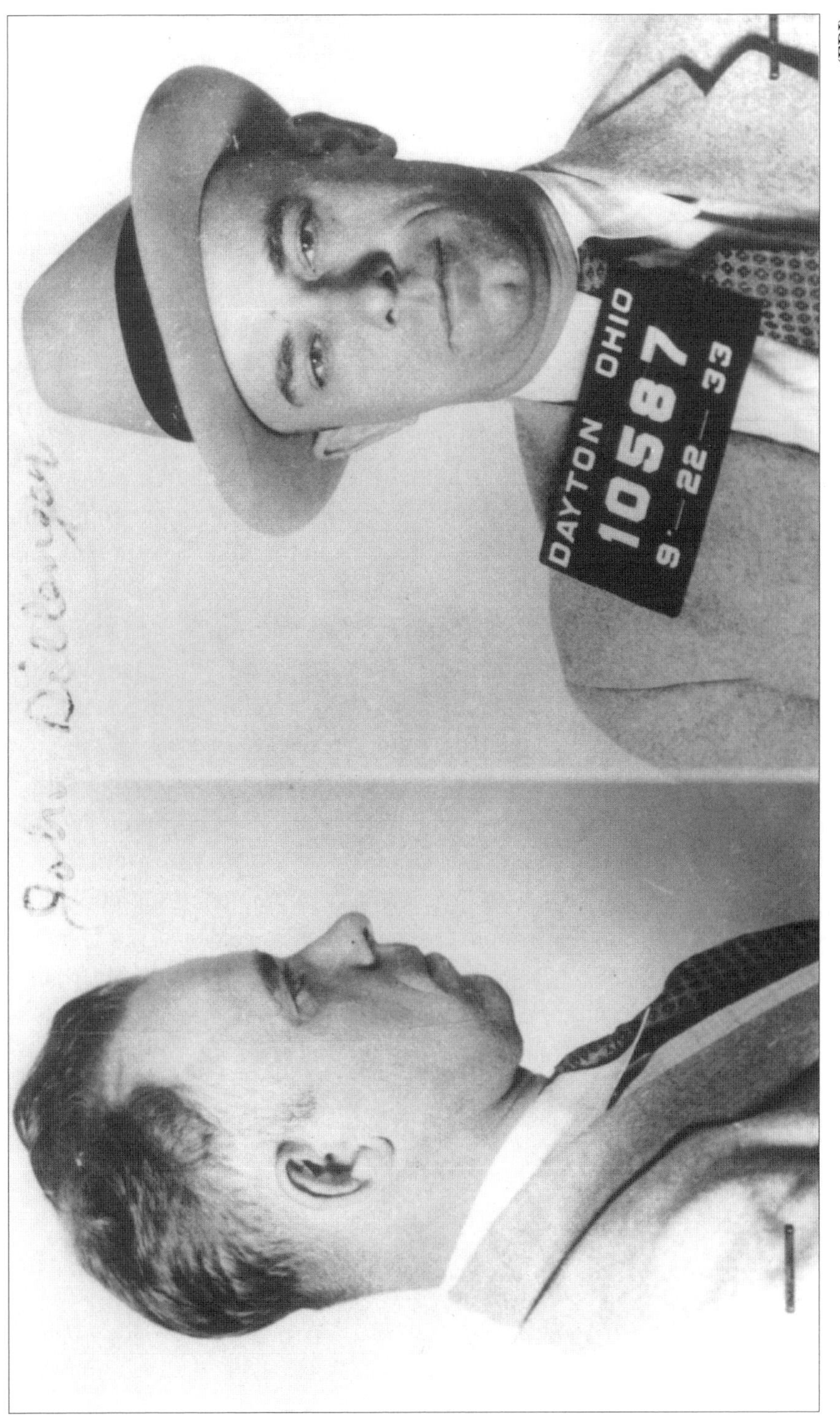


(FBI)

Jack Egan, his attorney, then made a bold move. He made a request to take his legal fees in payment from the Indianapolis bank bonds, found in the bag in Mary Longnaker's room. The only objection came from a few reporters. Egan responded in a high-pitched, loud voice.

"We will insist that it was his life savings," he answered. Judge Patterson made no attempt to intervene, claiming that the money was a "matter between the attorney and his client." The Dayton police released Dillinger's recently purchased Essex Terraplane to Jack Egan. The attorney kept it in the family by seeing that it went to Hubert, Dillinger's half-brother. Hubert, in turn, parked the sleek automobile outside his house at 409 LaSalle Street in Indianapolis.[10]

The arresting officers had all but ignored Mary Longnaker. Sy Yendes confirmed her fears that John believed she had turned him in.

Mary Longnaker waited for Dillinger, with little hope of seeing him again. She had one consolation. She paid for her final divorce decree and picked up where she'd left off, devoid of her children. After Dillinger's arrest, she moved to 214 Clay Street and lived in Apt. #1 with another girlfriend, Ruth Kennedy, and a new boyfriend, Sherman Claude Constable.[11] She missed Dillinger and hoped to see him again, wanting to assure the desperado that she hadn't given the Dayton police the tip that had resulted in his arrest. While Dillinger sat behind bars, convinced that Mary had tipped off the Dayton police, she readily forgot him in favor of the gainfully employed, honest Claude Constable. He represented stability to Mary: Claude was employed, a huge selling point for an eligible bachelor during the Depression. He worked as a welder at the General Motors' Delco Plant in Dayton. His father, Thurman Constable, was a deputy sheriff at Richmond, Indiana, who was running in the next election for the sheriff's position. In spite of his fears of Dillinger, Mary Longnaker's man vowed to get "some big reward money" if Dillinger ever came back.

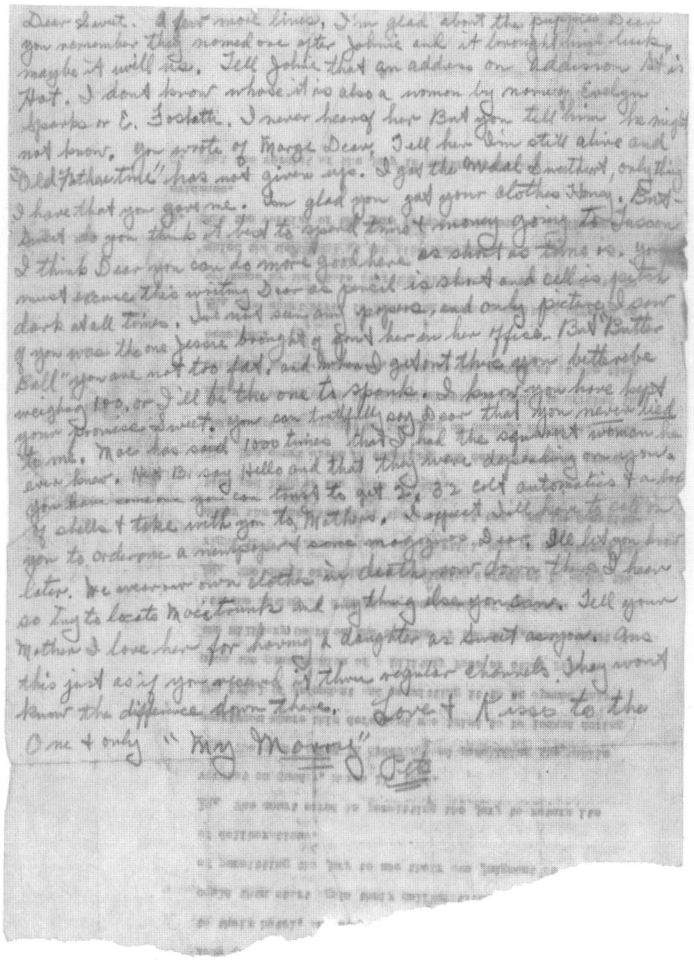

Dear Sweet. A few more lines, I'm glad about the puppies Dear you remember they named one after Johnnie and it brought them luck, maybe it will us. Tell Johnnie that an address on Addison St. is Hot. I don't know whose it is also a woman by name of Evelyn Sparks or E. [illegible]. I never heard of her But you tell him he might not know. You wrote of Marge Dear, Tell her I'm still alive and "Old Father time" has not given up. I got the medal Sweetheart, only thing I have that you gave me. I'm glad you got your clothes Honey. But Sweet do you think it best to spend time & money going to [illegible] as short as time is. I think Dear you can do more good here. You must excuse this writing Dear as pencil is short and cell is pitch dark at all times. [illegible] papers, and only picture I saw of you was the one Jessie brought of [illegible] her in her office. But "Butter Ball" you are not too fat, and when I get out there you better be weighing 100, or I'll be the one to spank. I know you have kept your promise Sweet. you can truthfully say Dear that you never lied to me. Mac has said 1000 times that I had the squarest woman he ever knew. Mac & B. say Hello and that they were depending on you. If you have some one you can trust to get 2, 32 colt automatics & a box of shells & take with you to Mothers. I expect I'll have to call on you to order me a newspaper & some magazines Dear. I'll let you know later. We wear our own clothes in death row down there I hear so try to locate Mac's trunks and anything else you can. Tell your Mother I love her for having a daughter as sweet as you. [illegible] this just as if you passed it thru regular channels. They won't know the difference down there. Love & Kisses to the One & only "My Mary"

Pete

Harry Pierpont wrote to Mary Kinder from death row, then kited the letter through his attorney. (Author's Collection)

*"It was love at first sight, but I never saw Harry outside the courtroom."*

*—Mary Kinder*

# Earl "The Kid"

Sheriff Jesse Sarber was assigned to hold Dillinger temporarily in his Allen County jail in Lima, Ohio. When he arrived to take custody of Dillinger, one reporter remarked that Sarber looked more like a bank president than a lawman.[1]

On Friday, September 22, 1933, Dillinger entered his cell in Lima, Ohio. At the same time, Walter Detrich, a bank robber, opened a carton of thread that was smuggled into the shirt factory of Michigan City. Marked "East Coast Shirt Company," it contained the guns that would empower the jail break.

Harry Pierpont never revealed that Copeland and Dillinger planned the thread delivery during the September 1933 visits to Pearl and Dewey Elliott. At their behest, Homer Brown had packed three .38 automatics with extra clips and shipped them to the shirt factory.[2]

This was the second try at getting the guns inside. Dillinger had tried throwing three .38 automatics over the wall on September 3. He knew

"The Wall"—it had been built by men such as himself, convicts, in 1859. The height and depth of the twenty-five-foot barricade, with its eight-foot-wide base and three-foot-wide top, had its foundation drilled deep into the ground. Dillinger's Herculean effort landed the package in the yard, a maze of streets comprising the prison city.[3]

The three guns were picked up by an inmate clerk. This trustee turned the guns into the warden, who earmarked the weighty contraband to one of Pierpont's friends, Daniel McGeoghagen. This convict, a South Side beer gangster serving twenty-five years, was thrown into the newly built Solitary and Seclusion section with two associates, Jack Gray and Edward Murphy. McGeoghagen, alias Danny Davis, lost his chance to get out with the others. John "Red" Hamilton decided that, if the crash out went as planned, he'd go straight to McGeoghagen's wife, Marie, in Chicago. He wanted to give her the news that her husband wouldn't be around for a while. Marie McGeoghagen was first on his visiting list; Hamilton also planned to see his two sons. All the escapees wanted reconciliation with their family members.

Charles Makley had lost touch with his wife, Edith. Having made a brief effort at corresponding with him in prison, she'd declined to visit him. While his family bolstered his morale with formal, well-composed letters of support, Edith gradually withdrew from him. He'd allowed his home ties to fray. A native son of St. Mary, Ohio, Charley Makley seemed like an orphan. Unlike the others, whose home towns offered hideouts and relatives willing to tend them, Makley's family members had not been involved in his criminal activities. They were solid, working people, had supported him in criminal court and would stand ready to do so again.

Russell Clark would be meeting Opal "Bernice" Long, the ungainly sister of Patricia Cherrington. Opal Long informed her boyfriend, Larry Streng, that they could continue to meet on occasion in Chicago, as long as their relationship stayed platonic.[4]

Others would go their separate ways. Walter Detrich and Joseph Fox, bank robbers, would be recaptured. James Clark, who was no relation to Russell Clark, turned himself in days after the escape, sick with ulcers. James Jenkins would be shot to death by a sheriff's posse after being ejected from Pierpont's car. Edward Shouse would remain with the Pierpont gang until being thrown out over a money dispute. Joseph Burns would remain free, although his name would come up as a suspect in several bank jobs associated with Dillinger.

Deputy Warden H.D. Claudy, who Pierpont had eagerly hoped to kill during the break, lost his credibility upon admitting to prior knowledge of the smuggled guns.

Corruption charges hung in blurry shadows, neither proven nor disbursed. Tangible security lapses created the climate that nurtured the escape: New officers brought in with Indiana Governor Paul V. McNutt's administration had been trained by inmate clerks, or trustees; guards carried no weapons, but chose to store them in the tower and guardhouse. Most damning was the fact that there was no check on inventory delivered into the prison.

Harry Pierpont viewed the impending escape as the natural offshoot of his failure to obtain a parole hearing. In the past several months, he'd written to the foreman of the jury at New Harmony, John Linnville, asking him for a parole recommendation. He managed to obtain the names and addresses of several of the jurors. He wrote to them with the same request for a parole hearing, to no avail.

Another conspirator, Pierpont's co-defendant, Earl "The Kid" Northern, did not get out with the others. Northern's tuberculosis had forced him into the infirmary. The young man was not destined to live much longer; he would die of the dreaded lung disease in three years, on June 29, 1936, while still an inmate.[6]

Earl Northern's sister, Mary Kinder, was waiting for them both. She dreamed of rescuing Earl from the dampness of the nearby "Indiana Dunes." She spoke constantly of spiriting him away to Arizona where his lungs could start their healing process. Mary was a good sister to Earl Northern. As a surrogate mother to his co-defendant, Harry "Pete" Pierpont, she faced tough competition. Pierpont had a domineering mother.

Harry Pierpont displayed an odd quirk to his hardened persona. He was a mama's boy who'd held his mother's hand during sentencing. Lena Pierpont blindly disputed Harry's culpability. An odd triangle formed between Mary, Lena, and the young man they both loved. Pierpont's affections toward Mary Kinder filled Lena with jealousy. Mary lent her ministrations toward Pierpont, overshadowing his mother with the added allure of sexual overtones. Pierpont responded like a hungry infant to the young, vivacious woman. She reigned in fantasy, the convict's dream girl. Yet Mary Kinder would not content herself with merely dreaming. Her interest in Pierpont was vested with complex motives. She was a worker who never tired of playing roles for him.

She was, by the summer of 1933, deeply involved in the lives of four men incarcerated at Michigan City. The connection to two held fast through family. Besides Earl Northern, her brother-in-law, William Behrens, stood convicted of bank robbery. His wife and Mary's sister, Margaret Behrens, was a local character nicknamed by the Indianapolis police as "Silent Margaret." Pierpont would fondly call her Margie.

The third inmate was Mary's legal husband. On a whim she'd married Dale Kinder, the son of a sergeant on the Indianapolis police force, Claude Kinder. Dale had dishonored his father by descending in rank to that of convict; he was now doing time for the robbery of a store.

Mary discarded Dale Kinder in favor of the fourth prisoner, to whom she leaned the closest. The twenty-two-year-old woman craned her neck to view Harry Pierpont's face. He stood six feet to her petite, five-foot frame. She loved his placid countenance, which masked a wiry cruelty.

She was no stranger to crime herself.

Mary Ellen Northern was the eighth in line of thirteen children, born on August 29, 1908 in Martinsville, Indiana, to Lewis Northern and the former Viola Tansy. The family lumbered under the weight of the constant births coupled with the deaths of five of her brothers and sisters. Lewis Northern later moved his family from the farm to Indianapolis, finding work on the Pennsylvania Railroad Indianapolis Limited. He died when Mary was sixteen years of age, forcing Viola out of the house and into a factory in an attempt to support her many children. This put a burden on Mary to take care of her siblings at home. She had to leave the Emmerich Manual Training High School after completing only two years. Enforced domesticity at an early age programmed her into the nurturing tendencies that would always rule her. No matter where she found herself, she would start cleaning and begin cooking. This was a unique work ethic among her siblings.

Some of the older members of the family were starting to live on the fringes of the law. Mary, though, combined food service and counter jobs with factory work. She grew up believing that life had shortchanged her.

"I never had a chance," she said in looking back. "I suppose it was a strange kind of love affair, but that's all I could expect in my kind of life."

The life that Mary referred to was an existence that was ruled by the ever-present specter of poverty in the large, fatherless household.

The clannishness peculiar to families who operate on the fringes of the law wasn't lost on the Northerns. They hovered over the youthful offenders, offering their familial love and protection.[7] Earl "The Kid" was convicted on bank robbery charges. Mary's brother, Charles, was brought up on charges of weaponry in a gun fight that had erupted with bootleggers over twenty-four gallons of whiskey. He'd also done time at Michigan City. Silent Margaret Behrens had been christened by the Indianapolis Police Department for her refusal to give information during a trial of her husband, William Behrens, for bank robbery.

The family's problems brought Mary to a premature adulthood. Through her growing-up process, she'd learned how to combine an easy-going, sadly comical innocence with a comfortable knowledge of the fringe element. She was in her sixteenth year when the two decisive, traumatic events occurred. Her father died. Then her brother went on trial for bank robbery as a three-time loser, with two prior convictions for car theft. He went on trial with Harry "Pete" Pierpont, an irresistibly handsome associate who'd been around the Indianapolis neighborhood since Mary was a nine-year-old Catholic school student.

Harry Pierpont was put on trial amid the huge headlines of a small town. The offense was the robbery of the New Harmony Bank in 1925, which had netted a fantastic amount for that time.

It would also force Pierpont into the fleeting limelight that accompanies sensational trials. While at the court, he became attracted to Mary. Standing by her brother, she impressed upon his mind the same benevolent air of his own ever-present mother. It was the beginning of a mutual obsession that would drive them wild with frustration in the face of barriers to a physical relationship.

Mary never had the opportunity to touch the object of her deepening affection. As she later put it, "It was love at first sight, but I never saw Harry outside the courtroom."

Nearing the conclusion of the 1925 trial, Pierpont changed his plea to

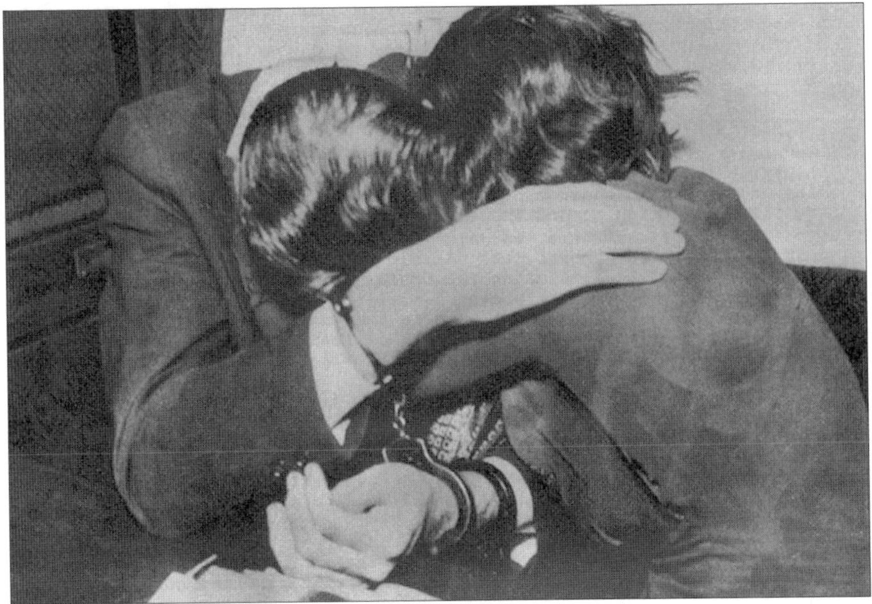

Mary Kinder bids goodbye to Harry Pierpont as they board the train that will separate them forever. (Lori Hyde)

guilty. The eyewitness evidence had piled up against him and climaxed as his accomplice, Thaddeus Skeer, implicated him on the witness stand. To protect three accomplices, Pierpont narrated his own version of the story at the close of the trial. He took his personal code of silence seriously, denying he'd ever known Earl Northern, in spite of the fact that the two men had done time together at Jeffersonville prison.

Pierpont was convicted of the bank robbery in a swift decision of the jury. The prosecuting attorneys, Homer R. Miller and Earl B. Barnes, had declared in their closing arguments that the question was not of guilt or innocence, but of how much time the defendant should serve.

"A sentence of two to fourteen years will give the defendant a chance," said Barnes, perhaps sardonically. "He might reform."

The jury apparently agreed. Fifteen minutes after they received the case, the jury returned with their verdict and delivered it upon the smiling, boyish Pierpont, who kept his arm around his mother during the sentencing.

Pierpont returned to the court to take the witness stand after his conviction, to further vindicate Mary's brother from any implication in the bank robbery. As Mary sat hysterically with her mother and their

Mary Kinder begged to keep her St. Joseph Medal in Tucson. It was to be an "aid to her prayers." (Library of Congress)

attorney, Jessie Levy, who everyone called "Miss Jessie Levy," they realized that Earl's redemption was threatened by the habitual criminal act, which took offenders known as three-time losers and put them away for life. In the language of the law, it weighed heavily on the two pathetic women, Mary and her mother, Viola, as they sat in the courtroom: "If a defendant is convicted twice of felony and upon conviction a third time, he may be charged with being a habitual criminal, and if found guilty, shall be sentenced for life."

As Pierpont testified a second time, attired in a new suit yet lacking his prior arrogance while still a defendant, he withstood the scrutiny of the prosecuting attorney. He continued his attempt to exonerate Earl Northern. The effect of his oration was not lost on Mary, who cried openly with her mother, Viola, during Pierpont's testimony. She felt, at that moment, an overwhelming sense of gratitude toward Pierpont. She watched his handsome figure, elegantly clad in his three-piece suit. He was desirable and, yet, unattainable.

In spite of Pierpont's mendacious oration, the court convicted Earl Northern of bank robbery. To the intense relief of his family, however, he was mercifully acquitted of a life sentence on the habitual criminal charge.

Pierpont entered the Pendleton Reformatory and began his letter-writing campaign to the jurors. He begged them for recommendations of exoneration.[8]

Five years after the trial, Mary met a soldier who had been stationed at Fort Ethan Allen in Vermont before coming home to his native Greenfield, Indiana. Dale Kinder was the son of an officer in the Indianapolis Police Department. It was a whirlwind courtship for Mary. She married her man-in-uniform on March 3, 1931. By 1932, Dale was wanted for robbery in Herricks County, Indiana. The police arrested Mary, holding her pending Dale's arrest. After putting him behind bars, they released Mary. Dale Kinder left Mary with his name, and little else. The desperation of her life deepened with the arrival of a baby. Mary always said her child had died. In recounting her life, she spoke of a child as having been born into the marriage of Kinder and herself. She later described these years as being "tough at home all the time."[9]

For all her troubles, she continued to serve as dutiful daughter to the overwhelmed Viola, helping with the many chores in the house. She

Russell Clark (Lori Hyde)

developed the habit of slaving in the dreary kitchen. With her mind somewhere else, she hashed up frogs' legs and cheap, days-old chicken for the voracious consumption of a large family. To color her disappointing life, she created a scenario in her mind. If she had to toil like a slave, she would be Pierpont's slave, pleasing him, feeding him. Through her visits with Earl, Pierpont would whisper his strict instructions to his doting pseudo-wife. Mary Kinder embraced Dillinger and joined the conspiracy that now stretched from Kokomo to Hamilton, Ohio.

Knowing that there was no check on inventory delivered into the prison, Walter Detrich, with Russell Clark, set the escape in motion at 2:00 on the afternoon of September 26. They worked in the shirt factory as receiving clerks, through a self-sustaining system that allowed private industry to enter and hire the convicts at cheap wages. On this muggy afternoon, they sauntered over to their superintendent, G.H. Stevens. Stevens braced himself for the common request for water. They looked thirsty and stiff.

"There's a couple of men downstairs to buy shirts," they said chokingly.

Thinking this a routine matter, the superintendent accompanied the men to the basement to meet the fabled buyers. Through the barred window, Stevens noticed that the hovering clouds were low and dark.

In the basement, Stevens realized that he'd been tricked. John "Red" Hamilton, flanked by another inmate, stuck a gun in his ribs and pushed him into a tunnel that connected the shirt factory to the power house. There three convicts greeted him. The members of this welcome-wagon dragged him out to stand behind the shirt racks.

Albert Evans, the Assistant Deputy Superintendent, walked into the trap and was made to join Stevens behind the shirt racks. They tied up the shop foreman, Dudley Triplett. Five innocent convicts, ignorant of the escape plan, came in. The marauders pushed them into the conduit tunnel.

On an ordinary day, the convicts' routine was a march in two-quarter time from work stations to the cell house for lockup and count. It was the practice of "running the lines." On this day that was not ordinary, they faced the maze of streets called the yard. In order to get safely through, a routine appearance had to shroud their actions. The men formed a slow and winding parade, with Evans in the rear and Stevens leading.

It was a curious color guard. Bearing not flags but piles of wagging shirt-sleeves, they passed in covert review over 600 feet of yard between the shirt factory and the guard room. Hundreds of unsuspecting convicts, guards, and administrators missed the cues that something was amiss.

They inched through the crowded streets, over a railroad track that wound its way through the maze. These tracks supported the rail cars that were used for the delivery of coal.

The band of escapees got to Main Street, the natural barrier between the bustling prison city and their heralded destination, the Administration Building. This was the first of three checkpoints separating them from freedom.

Charles Swanson and Guy Burklow were standing at the gate to the guard room. They waved to Stevens, now walking straight toward them. Swanson floundered as Stevens began clawing at him.

"They've got guns! Open the gate or they'll kill us," he pleaded. Swanson and Burklow complied, opening the first steel gate to the outside. Swanson numbly opened the gate and joined the desperate march. At the second gate, Burklow opened it, allowing access to the last gate. By the time the group reached this third gate, which served as the outer exit leading to the lobby, chaos took over. One of the group slugged the guard, Turnkey Fred Wellnitz, with a pistol butt and knocked him unconscious.

Assistant Deputy Superintendent Evans, who had been forced to walk behind the procession, reacted to this attack on Wellnitz. He pushed and yelled in frenzied outrage. Pierpont turned on him and unleashed his peculiar, awful temper. He knocked Evans down. Then, in a wild, spontaneous move typical of Pierpont, he demanded that Evans locate and produce Chief Deputy Warden D.H. Claudy. Pierpont wanted Claudy to release Daniel McGeorhagen, the inmate who was thrown into solitary when the first cache of guns was found.

The convicts found the keys on the unconscious form of Fred Wellnitz. They unlocked the third gate, allowing the long-awaited entrance to the Administration Building. They passed the gracefully wide staircase that led up to the offices on the second floor, adorned by the festooned lamps that stood as a remnant of the long-past gaslight era. They formed a majestic welcome for ten convicts dressed in drab prison blues with wooden-soled shoes.

The layout of the Administration Building opened to the warden's office on one side and the general office on the other. They swarmed here for three minutes, locking eight civilian employees into a vault. As one elderly clerk, Finley Carson, moved slowly into the vault, the delay enraged one of the convicts, who shot the seventy-year-old man in the abdomen and thigh. As Carson lay bleeding from the two wounds, people began screaming.

With hysteria taking over, Pierpont yelled obsessively for Deputy Warden Claudy, to no avail. Warden Louis Kunkel, a warden despised by the inmates, stood unrecognized with the civilians. As he was forced into the vault with the others, no one thought to identify him, thereby saving his life.

In the lobby the gang, by now delirious with power and fear, recognized the Superintendent of prison industries, Lawrence Mutch. In their last act of intimidation, they demanded that he open the arsenal. He refused, and was beaten to the ground for his bravery.

The ten left the Administration Building, pouring into the parking lot across the road.[10]

---

*"Mary Kinder was a gang member. Unlike the other women, who were just girlfriends, Mary participated fully in the gang."*

*—Joe Pinkston, curator,*
*John Dillinger Historical Museum,*
*Nashville, Indiana*

---

# A Young Army

The escaped men, in the public eye, assumed the size of gladiators. The press, bent on sensationalism, dubbed them the Terror Gang. Fueled by Matt Leach, the *Chicago Tribune* opined that the "extraordinary procession" that had marched through the prison yard under the threatening sky was about to begin an unprecedented crime wave. In the suspense and delirium, Matt Leach, captain of the Indiana State police, made a prediction.

"The persons responsible for the covert delivery of the guns," Leach announced, "will continue to help them."

The escaping group had split into factions after their liberation through the doors of the Administration building. The group comprised of Joe Burns, Walter Detrich, Joseph Fox, and James Clark forced themselves into a car driven by Sheriff Charles Neal, a weathered lawman who had run into the prisoners on their way out. The other group, Harry Pierpont, Russell Clark, Charles Makley, John Hamilton, James Jenkins, and Ed Shouse, went to Indianapolis. On September 27, Pierpont's party

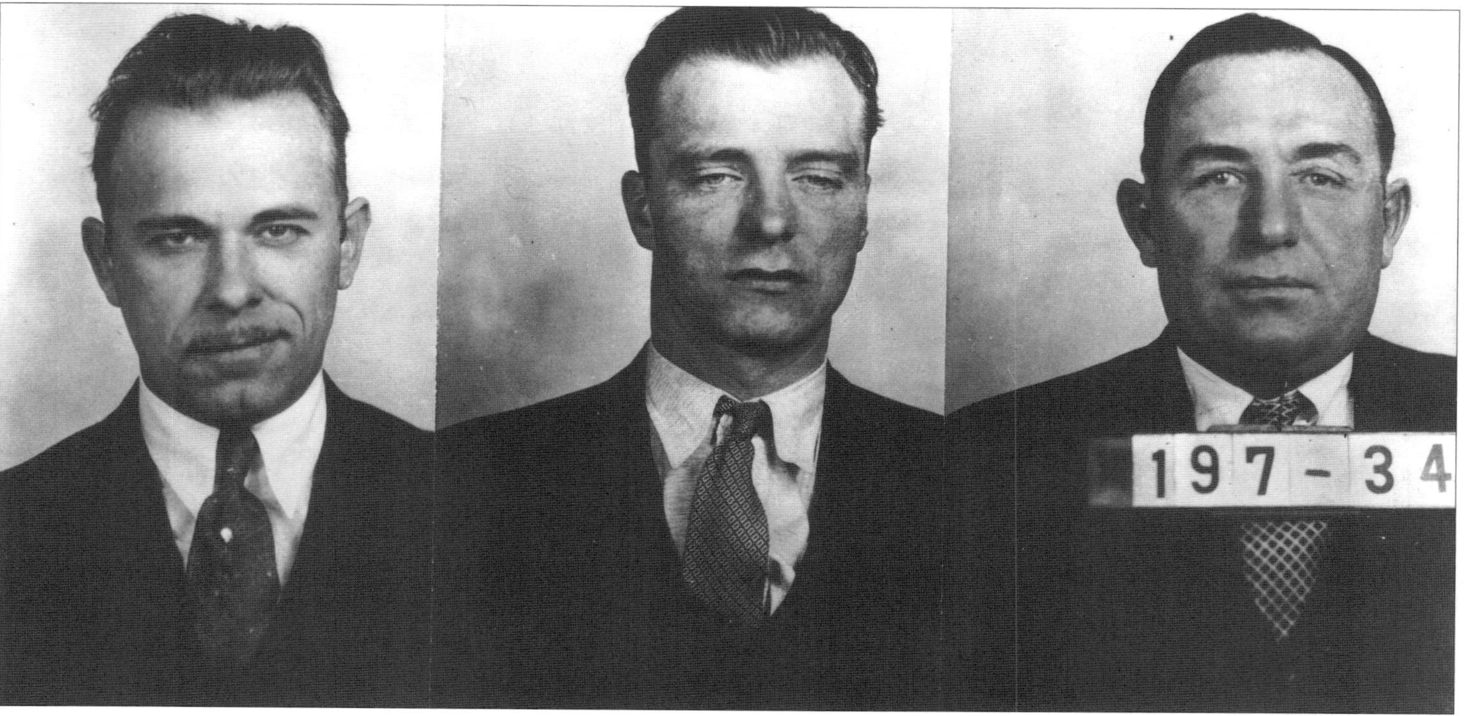


L to R: Dillinger reflects sarcasm; Pierpont arrogance and Makley shock upon their arrest in Tucson. (Arizona Historical Society/Tucson)

arrived at 316 North Luett Street, Indianapolis, the home Mary Kinder shared with her mother, remarried as Viola Paterson, and sister, Margaret Behrens. The men were disoriented and, without admitting it, frightened. Viola Paterson imploded with sorrow at the sight of them. Earl, her son, was in the relative safety of the prison infirmary, not part of this caste of untouchables. Viola would go through months of terror. Once Mary left with Pierpont, Viola was afraid to pick up a newspaper. She couldn't listen to a radio, for fear she would hear that the police had shot her daughter.

Pierpont's charm with women, fresh and strong after eight years behind bars, brought out the latent instincts in the tiny, ninety-five-pound Mary. The waiting game was over. She fell into step, prepared to do the housework of crime. She purchased clothes for the tired men, by now scratching and smelly in their prison blues. While out, she made a series of phone calls from a public telephone. She led the gang to the home of Ralph Saffel, a casual friend, at 343 McCleed Avenue. While the men held Ralph Saffel hostage, Mary located Pearl Elliott, who rushed to Indianapolis for a covert reunion with Pierpont. They left Indianapolis, and on September 30, they ejected Jenkins like a litter would kill the runt. They threw him from the car with the police in pursuit. A posse shot and killed Jenkins on a two-block stretch that comprised the main drag of Beanblossom, a hamlet five miles from Nashville. Now Mary Longnaker shared a sad covenant with Mary Kinder; neither woman would see her brother to freedom.

The group stayed with Russell Clark's associates at 1052 South 2nd Street on October 2, in a cottage on a river bank behind the house. There they met with labor racketeer Bill Davis. Davis, who usually hung around Chicago, had developed a relationship with Dillinger before the arrest. Hubert Dillinger, John's half-brother, joined them, driving his brother's Essex Terraplane that Jack Egan had retrieved from the Dayton police pound. Hubert transferred the title by registering it in the name of "Mrs. John Dillinger," actually Mary Kinder, at the 1052 South 2nd Street address. In Hamilton, Charles Makley talked of his dream of robbing the First National Bank in St. Mary, his old hometown. The gang carried out the plan on October 3. Mary Kinder went along, positioned at the wheel of a second getaway car, which they left in a nearby cornfield. In spite of her submission to Pierpont, she held an important position.

"Mary Kinder was a gang member," recalled Joe Pinkston, curator of the John Dillinger Historical Museum and personal friend to Mary Kinder. "Unlike the other women, who were just girlfriends, Mary participated fully in the gang."

The men returned to the car, carrying their heist of $11,000. Shortly after they left Hamilton, police raided the hideout on October 9. At the time of the raid, the gang had moved to a camp on the Miami River, ten miles southwest of Hamilton. From there they went to the Pierpont family farm in Leipsic, Ohio, arriving on October 11. Fred Pierpont, Harry's brother, drove the Oldsmobile used for the robbery of the First National Bank in St. Mary. He brought it out of the rough, hilly terrain of Hamilton and hid it within his barn.[1]

Basking in the sordid country comfort, Mary Kinder planned a celebration for Pierpont on Friday night, October 13. Superstitious connotations aside, the party was destined to be canceled by the long-awaited release of Dillinger from the Allen County Jail. In the short time that they stayed in Leipsic, Mary Kinder and Pierpont made a love nest in the barn. She later recounted: "It was our honeymoon, if you want to call it that. But we couldn't have very much fun. We had to watch out for coppers all the time. There were plenty of them."

The Leipsic farm housed the fragments of a bereaved family. The Pierponts' lives were driven by the grief that both shattered and bound them together. In addition to the loss of their son, Harry, to a childhood insanity inquest and prison, they had also lost their teenaged daughter, Fern, to the ravages of disease. The remaining members of the family were Lena; her husband, Joseph G.; and their son, Fred. He'd been arrested and charged with smuggling a hacksaw into Harry's cell in 1925, but was acquitted. In a new decade, he'd maintained the family value of unquestioning loyalty to Harry. Lena Pierpont was the standard-bearer of the family code of silence. Her brushes with the law dated back to the period immediately after the New Harmony Bank robbery, when she'd been arrested with her husband once Harry was established as the suspect.

Lena Pierpont, the former Lena Croutt, with her husband, Joseph G. Pierpont, had buried their only daughter. Nineteen-year-old Fern was buried on August 7, 1919, after a wake in the family home at 54th and Keystone Avenue in Indianapolis. She succumbed to tuberculosis in an

John "Red" Hamilton during his bootlegging activities, c. 1920. The truck was filled with beer and whiskey.
(Author's Collection)

epidemic that ravaged Marion County during the 1920s. This epidemic also infected Earl Northern.[2]

With no direct communication from Dillinger, the gang members planned to crash Dillinger out of the jail at Lima, Ohio. "I don't think they would admit it," Opal Long later said in a newspaper interview, "but they were all afraid of the job they had ahead of them."[3]

It was inappropriate language, more finely tuned for a New Deal work contract than a violent jailbreak. They embarked from the Pierpont's family farm on October 12, to prey upon the quiet administration of Sheriff Jesse Sarber, the Allen County Sheriff. While Dillinger awaited a hearing on the Bluffton bank robbery charges, he played cards with other convicts. He also talked glibly. Mentioning Harry Pierpont's name, he bragged about the success of the escape from Michigan City.

At around 6:00 p.m., three men entered the office of Jesse Sarber. Ed Shouse remained at the door. Sheriff Sarber was a pleasant man. Pierpont and Makley told Sarber that they were "from the Indiana State Prison and had come to get John Dillinger, a parolee from that institution." Sarber took a long look at Pierpont. He challenged him to show his credentials. Pierpont pulled a gun and shot the lawman.

"This is my authority," the witnesses thought they heard him say.

Sarber then made a move to reach his own gun, which was on the desk, and as he did so Pierpont fired a bullet through the sheriff's abdomen. Makley dealt the fatal blow, by jumping on Sarber and beating his uncovered head with the butt of a pistol. Sarber's wife, who was there to fix dinner, became hysterical. Another attacker turned to the Deputy Sheriff Wilbur L. Sharp, in attendance also, and demanded the keys to the cells. Mrs. Sarber rushed to the spot where the keys were kept and handed them over. The raiders opened the door of the jail and ordered Sharp and Mrs. Sarber to enter. The two remained locked in the cell.

Not offering to free Mrs. Sarber, so that she might assist her dying husband, they yelled for Dillinger. After firing another shot wildly, to discourage the other inmates from joining them, the group escorted Dillinger out. They escaped with two .38 colts belonging to Sheriff Sarber and Deputy Sheriff Sharp.

The bandits left Sharp and Mrs. Sarber locked in the jail for twenty-five minutes. It took that long for rescuers to torch and knock off the cell door. This prevented Mrs. Sarber from touching her husband in his final

moments of life. He went without medical aid during the first crucial fifteen minutes after his injuries were inflicted, and died two hours later in the hospital. The blows to his head, rather than the bullets, caused death.

Police Chief J.W. Cooke led a posse to the farm in Leipsic, thirty-five miles from Lima. They arrived at 10:00 p.m. and confiscated a photo of Harry Pierpont. Dillinger, whose talk to a cellmate had provided the lead to Leipsic, went possibly to Rankin, Illinois, to the home of a contact named August Carleson, where he reputedly stayed for a week. Carleson had gone to the World's Fair with Dillinger the summer before.

Mrs. Sarber and Deputy Sheriff Sharp partially confirmed Pierpont's identification. Police linked another member of the Terror Gang almost immediately through a bizarre piece of evidence. The gang had left their Oldsmobile, linked to the St. Mary robbery, in the garage. The Lima

Police immediately dispatched a wire to the Automobile Protective and Information in Chicago and were told that this Oldsmobile had been sold by the Sheair Motor Sales Company of Chicago to Arthur S. Cherrington, who had lived at 2318 Sunnyside Avenue, Chicago. Fred Pierpont, who could not reasonably explain the presence of the car, fingered Harry Copeland as being the owner. Copeland had indeed stolen Art Cherrington's identity, with permission from the grieving jail widow, Patricia Cherrington. The alias would have provided a strong cover had not Fred Pierpont talked during an intensive grilling that lasted for days.

The local police had arrested Fred, while holding his mother for questioning. Fred finally relented, throwing a bone in the form of Mary Kinder's name and address. The Ohio police wired Matt Leach in Indianapolis, who raided Viola Paterson's house. Surprisingly, the stoic Lena Pierpont broke under the interrogation. She admitted that Harry, Russell Clark, Charles Makley, Edward Shouse, and Harry Copeland had visited the farm. Copeland, wanted for the Daleville robbery committed with Dillinger back in July, was now linked to the escapees from Michigan City. His fate was sealed when Deputy Sheriff Sharp identified a photograph of Copeland as the man who had held the gun on him.[4]

Forced by now to leave Ohio, the gang launched two strategic moves in one week, the robbery of two separate police stations for ammunition. They hit two police station houses in rapid succession. After raiding Auburn, Indiana, on October 14, they hit Peru, Indiana, on October 20. They procured two machine guns; one tear gas gun; five rifles; two sawed-off shotguns; a repeating shotgun; twelve bulletproof vests; one .32 and a .45 caliber automatic; three .38 specials, and five police badges.[5]

Not yet a pariah to the syndicate, the Dillinger gang entered Chicago triumphantly in mid-October 1933. The underworld in Chicago, controlled since the imprisonment of Al Capone by Frank "the Enforcer" Nitti, was open to the Dillinger gang. Frank Nitti supervised the delivery of whiskey in Chicago. At this point, with the police chasing Dillinger down blind alleys, the gang enjoyed the obscurity that opened doors to Chicago's organized crime.

Dewey Elliott was connected to the gambling rackets in Chicago. In late October 1933, Dillinger, Hamilton, Makley, and Shouse went on Dewey's tip to the hangout of two remaining members of Capone's gang. Frankie Pope ran Chicago gambling under Frank Nitti. With his brother,

"Big" Pope, he ran the Idle Club at 602 Forquer Street, and the Steuben Club, on the 700 block northwest of Congress and Tilden Streets. Padlocked since 1932, the Steuben Club had emerged just after the Michigan City escape. In its new and improved presentation, it stood four stories high, with its third and fourth stories consisting of private rooms used for hideouts. When the escapees arrived at the club, they were permitted to enter through their alliance with Dewey Elliott. They were nevertheless barred from entering the special club room, reserved exclusively for members of the Pope and Capone gangs.

The place made Dillinger nervous. Dewey Elliott tried to reassure him that it was the spot for "really hot" criminals.

"Gangsters who are wanted badly in Chicago hang out there," said Dewey Elliott.

When the Dillinger gang arrived, they had to enter through an office with a sentry. They checked their guns, blackjacks, and any other weapons. They were greeted by Frank Nitti and "Big" Pope. He brought them to a horseshoe-shaped bar containing a bottle case filled with liquor and cigarettes. Pope pushed a button, swung the bottle case, and eased it as it opened into a sixteen-foot square room, called "The Arsenal."

"Take what you want," said Pope as the men tried to hide their amazement. "There's enough there for a young army."

They picked and chose from the thirty rifles and sawed-off shotguns; eighteen machine guns; and scores of revolvers, ammunition, and "pineapple" bombs. Like kids in a demented toy store, they helped themselves to three machine guns, placing them in a large traveling case. They loaded themselves up with pistols, ammunition, and several bulletproof vests. After stuffing everything into traveling bags, they hoisted them over their shoulders. They were directed to leave the premises through an underground passage. They had to maneuver their guns through an opening and then slide down a brass rail like the ones found in firehouses. This took them to the basement of the building, and a secret getaway leading to the garage. Dillinger felt that the Steuben Club, called a safe place by the underworld, was a dangerous trap.[6]

*"I got a little headache this A.M.*

*but that don't amount to much."*

*—Pearl Elliott*

Pearl Elliot vowed to "personally beat up Matt Leach and several other members of the Indianapolis Police Department," for splashing her photo throughout Indiana.

(Author's Collection)

# "Two Sisters . . . Names Unknown"

In Chicago, another police veteran joined the chase for Dillinger, quietly and without fanfare. Captain John Stege and Sergeant Frank Reynolds took over a special division within the Chicago Police Department in late October. Called the "Dillinger Squad," it kicked off with forty city policemen.

John Stege had been around when Dion O'Banion was murdered by the Torrio and Capone gangs in 1924. Stege's vocal epithet, that "O'Banion was a thief and a murderer, but look at him now, buried 80 feet from a bishop," had lingered, settling in as part of Chicago's lore as the city of sin and virtue. He'd recently made the papers again, by extracting a confession from Dr. Alice Wynekoop, a prominent physician whose daughter-in-law, Rheta, had been chloroformed and murdered on a basement gurney. The case, delivering *noir*, true crime to Chicago's newsstands, was a tabloid sensation. Through Captain Stege's role in the confession, he'd maintained his self-containment. Neither the press nor other police bureaus had found him to be gregarious. In his reticent personality, he contrasted the style embodied by Matt Leach, who wore his badge like a billboard.[1]

After leaving the hospitality of the Steuben Club, the men returned to Harry Copeland's place, where he lived with Patricia Cherrington at 115 North Parkside Avenue. A woman they called "a dark-skinned Indian" had begun to travel with Dillinger. She was Evelyn Frechette. According to Patricia Cherrington: "I did not ask questions regarding the activities of 'the crowd.'" She later admitted in prison, "[We] had a good time and . . . past activities or present enterprises were not discussed." During the prison interview, Patricia said they "seemed to thrive on excitement." She had known Evelyn Frechette for "quite some time before meeting her with the Dillinger crowd."

Pat Cherrington and Evelyn Frechette had supported themselves in Chicago since the mutual incarceration of their husbands. They'd both waived the home relief that was available to them as wives of federal convicts. Patricia's reason was cut and dried: She needed to avoid the system. Because she was a mother, the arrest with Cherrington of June 13, 1932 had thrown her into a panic. She feared that her daughter, whom Arthur Cherrington had never met, would be claimed by her ex-husband in a move to get custody. She didn't want nosy social service clerks questioning her child's welfare in the babysitter's home. She made a decision to support herself. Her autonomy would keep the social workers away from her daughter.

On September 6, 1932, Pat had moved into the Hotel Wil-Mar at 11 West Division Street, and reported her address to the prison authorities. She worked several engagements per week as a dancer. It was the height of the Depression and the money wasn't coming in like it used to. The salary she'd gotten in the 1920s for dancing, $75 per week, was harder to come by now.[2]

Her sister, Opal Long, joined "the crowd" and chose to live with Russell Clark. In her way, she was the perfect gang woman. Opal Long wanted to be ignored by society. In this respect, she differed from her outgoing sister, Patricia. To Opal's endless chagrin, she remained visible through an overweight, ungainly physique. Her bespectacled eyes, accustomed to a bleak landscape, could squint in raw suspicion. Her smile, stingy and rare, sulked within a kinky frame of natural, bright-red ringlets. At 5 feet, 8 inches and weighing 164 pounds, she suffered from the critical nearsightedness that had plagued her childhood. Her green/gray eyes squinted behind thick, rimless eyeglasses. Her red hair fell in childish banana curls around her weathered face, casting a sense of sulking expectancy about her. Opal Long had no pretensions of glamour inherently out of her reach. At age twenty-seven, her nomadic life showed itself on her person; she dressed with little care. One police description listed her as "dissipated in appearance."

She was born in Texas, to William Long and his wife, Goldie Jacquas, on March 20, 1906. Her sister, Patricia, was older, having been born before the family moved from McClure, Arkansas. The sisters differed in personality and had little in common physically. Yet Opal Long, fiercely loyal to those she loved, remained close to Patricia and her child. She'd lived in Chicago since 1926, working in The Triangle Restaurant on Oak Street. She'd resided, since 1930, in a cheap residency hotel called the Marshall Hotel, at 1232 North LaSalle.

When Patricia stopped dancing due to gall bladder pain that required surgery, in February 1933, she had no money coming in. She lived with Art Cherrington's brother, Ira, and his wife, Vera, at 1832 Belmont Avenue. In the spring of 1933, Patricia left the Belmont Avenue apartment and moved in with her sister at the Marshall Hotel. It was a well-known underworld hangout. As she moved into the Marshall, Patricia carefully avoided the desk register, dragging her leather valise through the darkened lobby filled with potted plants. Her luggage bumped in a succession of resting points on the stairs, as Opal looked around carefully. They lumbered past a sign prohibiting profanity while on the premises. In their rented room, Patricia went for the telephone, clicking her heels as she did so. With an aura of crisp efficiency, she placed thirty-nine local phone calls to members of the underworld. One of these calls was to Harry Copeland. As he picked up the receiver, he heard Patricia's voice. Her vivacious vocal chords, interrupted with the rapid sucking of a cigarette, excited him.

To Copeland, Patricia meant the resurrection of sex, the smells of perfume, flesh and fluids, drying in the aftermath of a furnished room. He had these and other plans for their union.

Copeland had been sentenced, in 1927, to two to fourteen years on second-degree burglary. He'd stayed as trim as possible, weighing in at 147 pounds, and 5 feet, 10 inches. His face sported a thick, sensuous mustache. He felt young, at age thirty-seven or thirty-eight, and ready for action. He boasted the highlights of his life upon his sleeve. His left hand bore a heart; his right arm wore a circus girl and a sailor's head over his initials, HEC. This faded ink resisted change even as he shed his convict's skin.[3]

Opal Long soon moved in with Russell Clark. Before being incarcerated for bank robbery, he had run liquor across the Detroit River from Canada in the 1920s. For Opal Long, whose nearsightedness had restricted her movement, the dashing pirate lent her a sense of freedom. The two matched up physically. He, handsome and just over six feet tall, loved the large-woman appeal of the fleshy Opal Long. Through her black sense of humor—she could make a joke out of a funeral pyre—she wooed him with her aggressive, unsentimental loyalty. They kindled their lovemaking like married people, holding hands while listening to hillbilly music on the crystal set. She assumed responsibility for the housekeeping, along with Mary Kinder. Opal Long was described as "industrious, and willing to fuss around the kitchen" by government agents who talked to informants.

The "dark-skinned" Billie Spark, as Evelyn was known at that time, joined "the crowd" as Dillinger's woman. At first, the other gang members balked at hanging out with an "Indian." Mary Kinder, in particular, was afraid to drink with Evelyn.

Dillinger looked a bit like Welton Spark to Evelyn Frechette. Both men were stocky and under six feet tall. Both men had square-jawed, hatchet-shaped heads. Dillinger's hair, growing like a weed patch, was slightly thinner than Spark's. They shared a tendency toward making eye contact through a hard, piercing stare. While Spark's face was set in a grimace, Dillinger had a hard, determined laugh.

In contrast, Evelyn seldom laughed. She had a way of smiling inwardly, as though relishing a private thought. And her thoughts, by this time, were seldom happy. After her hasty marriage to Welton Spark, she took a North Side job as a hat check. Given the economic climate of this, the darkest year of the Depression, it was a good job. She'd worked with layers of Max Factor pancake powder coating her tired face. Her long hem alluded to the plight of the nation's economy. Yet the stock market crash hadn't changed her fortunes. To one congenitally poor, the economy didn't matter. Her one great hope resurrected itself daily, found in the collective pockets of the men she dated. Even the one-nighters could be counted on for some help—a bit of cash, a ride in a Hudson or Ford. She'd started going with a man named Miles Burphy. The two often traveled to Detroit, and occasionally returned to the Reservation in Neopit. Sometime in the summer of 1933, she broke off with him.

She lived with inner trepidation that was masked by recklessness. No longer the teenager who had stuffed her dreams into a suitcase, she had little to lose. From her experience, Chicago had never listened when she'd cried.

In the summer of 1933, Evelyn met the people who filled her longing for prosperity. In the darkness of the lounges, the shoddy and the cheap could shroud itself in mystery. In this atmosphere, where any stripper could call herself a foreign dancer, Evelyn immersed herself in the ambiance. During Prohibition, racial prejudice against Native Americans had kept her out of the speakeasies. As a club employee, she could drink without arguments and side glances. Once part of "the crowd," she came under added scrutiny; Pierpont didn't like drinking. Mary Kinder, who struggled with the early stages of alcohol addiction, drank with Billie. In doing so, she overcame her initial fear of "drinking with an Indian," her reference to indulging with Evelyn.

In contrast to Mary's initial aversion to Evelyn Frechette, Dillinger was fascinated by his new girlfriend's religious and cultural background. At once Native American and Roman Catholic, she appeared primitive and mystical. She hooked him with her black, glistening eyes and haunted beauty. He'd been raised within Protestant traditions in the largely rural Midwest and knew nothing of the nuances of religion. Evelyn's Roman Catholicism, which she'd learned from the priests of St. Anthony's Catholic Church in Neopit, was an enigma. To Dillinger, filled with guilt and religious ambivalence, Evelyn's complex persona offered a route to his self-understanding.

When Evelyn Frechette looked at Dillinger, she was reminded of that fundamental gap, the void within the eyes of Welton Spark. She was attracted to wild men, those motivated by forces darker than they readily understood. Dillinger, schooled to the ninth grade, stood unequipped to see himself through a world's eye view. He missed his own reflection in the anti-heroes of literature, driven by fate to crime and punishment.

Told in the way that legitimate men boast about their college days,

Dillinger filled their nights with his stories. They unburdened his soul: endless instances of gang rape, sadistic guards, and unrelenting con games.

In her growing trust, she wanted to bring him home to Neopit. He'd never know her, she believed, until he could see where she'd been.

Together they drove out of Chicago, the roads winding through primal farmland. North near Neopit, the big Wisconsin sky narrowed as the Shawano forests shivered around the tin building of the BIA Office of Indian Affairs. Then the forests once again parted, widening like an umbrella over the old Indian cemetery. Homemade wooden crosses presided over graves marked *Crow* or *Bear,* according to the clan of the deceased. Ancient, dried bouquets waved from these crosses, the flags of barren lands.

They arrived thirsty, going straight to the general store on the stubby road of town. They bought some unfiltered Camels and a few bottles of pop. The shoppers watched her keenly, peering through the aisles of the airless hut. The store, central to the neighborhood, offered among its wares some dusty foodstuffs, politics, and gossip. She'd known such attention, and had come to expect the side comments, uttered out of lips that neither smiled nor moved. As she stepped out onto the wooden porch of the general store, the sun pierced the hot fibers of her black crepe dress. The veiled, black hat that shadowed her dark, wavy bob was alien to this dusty outback as she, once more the conquering heroine, stepped from another white man's car. And what she engendered, to the community that had watched her grow up, was a mixture of envy, awe, and disdain.

Talk of her behavior had traveled to the Office of Indian Affairs in nearby Keshena. While the Menominee were a people disinclined to be brief, Evelyn Frechette had gotten herself paraphrased. She "bore a bad reputation."[4]

While in Chicago, the gang members disbursed into separate apartments. Russell Clark and Opal Long boarded with Charles Makley and Ed Shouse. Opal sensed some tension between Shouse and the others, yet she doted on Makley, with Russell Clark's sanction. The brotherhood between Clark and Makley was a strong one, able to sustain some friendly flirtation from the women. They depended upon Opal Long. They shunned restaurants, out of fear of recognition. She cooked huge meals for the men, spending her nights cleaning up the kitchen. She went on errands as well as her visual handicap permitted.

Harry Copeland, in another part of town, wasn't looking for a maid. His legal wife, Myrtle Dirk, had deserted him in Muncie, and was living in Muncie near his mother. With no illusions of love, he asked Pat Cherrington for a favor.

When Harry Copeland first met Patricia Cherrington, she appeared small, at 5 feet, 4 inches, with big hips. Her brown hair smoldered under her hat. A black veil shaded her slanted eyes, rife with intention. She sized him up with the instincts of a predator. That easy-going smile of his, broad and expansive, could mean he was generous and would be good to her. Pat fell into line easily, clinging to his arm and remaining by his side. His jokes and amiable grin helped her to forget the unemployment that had resulted from her chronic illnesses; she'd stopped menstruating, although she wasn't pregnant. Yet she brought a dowry, something of value to the relationship. Besides offering her dubious loyalty to Harry Copeland, she gave away Art Cherrington's identity. Copeland adopted it as an alias. In September 1933, he purchased an Oldsmobile under the name of Arthur S. Cherrington. While living at 1941 Warren Boulevard, he registered the car to a Chicago address at 2518 Sunnyside Avenue. Copeland, in his gratitude, lifted Patricia from her shared room in the Marshall Hotel.[5]

With Opal Long committed to Russell Clark, a decision had to be made on the care of Patricia's daughter. She'd been in the itinerant care of both Betty Neatz Minor and Opal Long since 1932. They had recently left the child in the home of Mae Clark, Russell's mother, in Detroit, Michigan. One afternoon in late October, the two couples set out to bring Pat's daughter back to her prior babysitter. Betty Neatz Minor had noticed that Patricia "got money without working." Regardless of what people said about her, Pat loved her child and wanted to keep her.

"The best people wanted her but I'd never adopt her out," she would later tell a parole board. Betty had kept her daughter from 1930 until August of 1932, when the girl had gone to live intermittently with Opal Long. After the events at Michigan City, neither Pat Cherrington nor Opal Long, whom the child called Auntie, could take care of her.

In the interim, Betty Neatz Minor had returned to her estranged husband, Verne. The woman was still available, and agreed to take the child for $26 per month. She was attempting to reconcile her stormy marriage, with their own twelve-year-old son in residence. Now their family unit would include their sporadic foster child.

For the occasion of parting with her child, Pat donned a white wig that covered her naturally dark hair and, so disguised, delivered the twelve-year-old to the destination where she would spend the next four months.

The girl was small, eighty-five pounds with the same dark brown hair, eyes, and complexion as her mother. As she rode up to Michigan sandwiched between her bewigged mother and Auntie, she listened to them banter with two men they called Lee and Harry. Copeland, of course, marked the time in speedometers. The girl already knew the value of confidentiality. Her features were heavy and prominent. Impassive, she'd learned early to withhold her emotions.

The sight of Betty was familiar, as the child had been with her when she was only eight years old. Now Betty introduced the child to her husband, Verne, who took a dim view of this new addition to his already strained household. As she watched her mother's party drive away in a new Plymouth, the shiny Illinois license plates held her gaze until the car was well out of sight. It was en route to a cheap hotel called the Seaver in downtown Ithaca. Pat acted out of the desire to shield the girl from her criminal associations.[6]

While Harry Copeland moved around freely, Dillinger and Pierpont rented an apartment at 4310 Clarendon Avenue, taking Evelyn and Mary with them. As woman-of-the-house, Mary put down $90 for the first month in the apartment, which had one bedroom for each couple, a living room, dining room, kitchen and sun porch. This came out of her $1,000 household allowance. She deposited the cash in a bank under the name of Mrs. Fred Ross. Mary handled money in varying amounts for the gang, often taking packages to safety deposit boxes without even asking the amount involved. Her position of monetary responsibility lent to her an aura that the other women didn't share.

Denied the dental care they needed due to prison and poverty, all of the escapees, and their girlfriends, went to the dentist. Pat Cherrington was missing five teeth when she finally got the money for dentistry.

Mary and Evelyn went on shopping sprees. Dillinger wanted the women to dress in the somber hues that he preferred. He believed that conservative dress would ensure that they would not stand out in any crowd. Evelyn, for one, disregarded the arbitrary dress code. She liked wearing pink and black.

Chicago's bitter cold rolled upon the city, ascending toward a spiteful climax. By September, the winds off Lake Michigan drilled painfully through the ears of the women. They bought new coats and hats, which adorned their bobbed, marcel waves. The men armored themselves in herringbone. All purchased expensive, leather valises and trunks. They would be living out of these trunks, ready at a moment's notice to abandon their dashing clothes, should escape become a necessity.

For now, the domestic arrangements were casual and happy. If Mary ever had a honeymoon, as she called it, this was it. She employed her housekeeping talents and did the cooking, and she tried to fix the foods that the men liked the best. John helped wash the dishes. Dillinger enjoyed the movies and went to see everything in town.

The gang pursued their craven pleasures. This revolved around gambling, which Mary Kinder enjoyed. Patricia Cherrington liked cards, a vice that she shared with Dillinger. The women would drink while the men favored sobriety. They played the crystal set, moving around their apartments to the sounds of pre-swing, big band instrumentals from the orchestras of Fletcher Henderson and Fred Rich. They'd seek outside entertainment in after-hours places like the Terrace Garden and the College Inn.

They basked in this culture of the Depression, a mixture of pathos and jaded sophistication. A decade before, these men had been yanked out of the decadent pleasures of the jazz age. Now they sought to replace what they had lost.

One night before police raids forced them to leave Chicago, Mary Kinder broke the gang's taboo against drinking. She went on a binge. In drunken confusion, she got lost going from one tavern to another. Separation was a cause of sheer panic. As she put it, she "was trying to forget all the trouble she was in." Mary was slipping into the early stages of a life-long struggle with alcoholism.

"I started to drink one night," she later told newspaper reporters.

"That was against the rules. Dillinger had forbidden liquor. A little beer maybe, but nothing else. Of course he was right, because otherwise you can't keep your head the way we all had to."

As Mary tells it, she got herself into trouble, asking the bartenders for "free champagne for everyone." With her tips coming to $10 a drink per waiter, they were happy to oblige. Her behavior sent someone to a phone to notify the police, who came into the Nut House at 1022 North Clark. Mary had just left when the place was raided. Stewed and sodden, she somehow found one of their hangouts, a hotel where she remembered that the "gang had stayed once or twice." She found herself marooned, waiting for what seemed like an eternity for the men to realize that she might be there.

"I couldn't stand it there all alone. I began to hear policemen tramping up the hall to my door. I wanted to scream. I had to get out. Maybe Harry was killed. So I got in a cab and told the driver to go up Humboldt Park and just keep driving till I told him to stop."

Eventually Mary found her way back to her gang, but not before her cab passed the Humboldt Park address, and Mary looked through the opened shades to see "hundreds of cops" inside.[7]

On October 23, Pierpont, Dillinger, and Makley walked into the Central National Bank of Greencastle, Indiana, making off with $18,000 in cash and over $56,000 in stocks and bonds. Ed Shouse drove the getaway car.

Shouse and Makley tried to fence the stolen bonds from the Greencastle Bank robbery around Chicago, negotiating with Arthur "Fish" Johnson and Jack Perkins. "Fish" Johnson lived with his girlfriend, Jean Burke, at 1742 Humboldt Boulevard in Chicago.

The Greencastle job caused some in-fighting when Ed Shouse fought both Dillinger and Pierpont to get more of the take. It was the first dissension in this tight group who went by two creeds, one of which was to avoid involvement with other factions, like the Touhy gang. Dillinger would gradually drop this insular philosophy as the pressures for protection increased. The other tenet was to distribute the profits of all the jobs equally, whether or not any one of the gang did not take part in the robbery.

Shouse claimed they'd broken their promise. His earnings reflected a shortfall of $8,000. He pulled a gun on Pierpont, who returned the favor by drawing his own pistol. Shouse backed down, escaping in Russell Clark's car. His exit prevented a double homicide from ending the Terror Gang. He vowed to get even, and he eventually did—from the back room of an Indiana police station to a witness stand in Lima, Ohio.[8]

Captain Stege and his Dillinger Squad raided 4310 Clarendon Avenue on November 17. Chicago Deputy Chief of Detectives William V. Blaul, with four detective squads, tore through the hideout so lovingly tended by Mary Kinder. Their search turned up nothing; the residents were settling themselves in other parts of town.

Dillinger, Pierpont, Mary, and Evelyn were forced to abandon Clarendon and the apartments at 150–154 Parkside Avenue. With the exception of John Hamilton, who kept his place at 5510 Winthrop Avenue, apartment 207, they went one step ahead of the police. The permanence so cherished by Mary Kinder was an illusion. When Mary later reminisced about her homemaking arrangements, she referred to something that only lasted for about two or three days at a time, before being hastily disbanded.

Two days before the raid on Clarendon, on November 15, Dillinger and Evelyn had narrowly escaped a trap set for the bandit by Captain Matt Leach. He had learned from an informant of the couple's whereabouts. A figure who would act as Dillinger's petty tyrant, informant Arthur "Marty" McGinnis, was handing out information to the police of Indianapolis and Chicago. Police, and later federal agents of the Justice Department, went after the marginal associates of criminals. Police were known to threaten the hangers-on with threats of investigation into their affairs, which could result in arrest. These were the people who, generally, turned informant while still in the mob. Some, like Art "Fish" Johnson, would promise to inform, be released, then disappear back into the streets. McGinnis, though, was trusted by both the police and by his underworld friends. Paroled from Michigan City, he had performed some errands for Dillinger. He became a valuable aide to Matt Leach.

Dillinger had gotten ringworm around his hair follicles. McGinnis told Leach of the outlaw's plans to visit a physician. The trap was set at the office of Dr. Charles H. Eye at 4175 Irving Park Boulevard, a three-way intersection.

A dozen men, led by Lieutenants John Jenkins and Chester Butler, and Detectives Arthur Keller and Eugene Ryan, waited outside the building for Dillinger. Evelyn Frechette had been left in the car, probably as a lookout. When her man, upon leaving the doctor's office, noticed several officers walking toward him, he dashed for the driver's seat.

The squads of police had assumed that Dillinger, because of the direction of the parked car, would drive in a southward direction. He surprised them by backing his car around the corner into Irving Park Boulevard, facing east, and gunning the accelerator. When the firing started, Dillinger drove with one hand and shot back over his shoulder.

Once the windshields on the Indiana police cars were shattered, they dropped behind Dillinger's car. He then swung to the southeast into Elston Avenue, rounded a side street, and was lost around Grace Street and Western Avenue. In the confusion, Evelyn, wearing a blond wig, would later be credited with firing the bullets that sprayed the windshields of the Indiana and Chicago police cars. The newspapers reported that a porthole had been opened, through which a mysterious gunner fired on the pursuing vehicles. Through a fusillade of facts and fabrications, the two got away. Once out of danger, the couple got to the apartment kept by Russell Clark and Opal Long. They walked in from the cold, clear twilight, out-of-breath and totally unnerved.

On this night, the northwest winds blew gently through Chicago's streets, in a soothing change in the weather. Yet the couple, whose urban honeymoon had been broken by the knowledge that they had been stalked, hardly noticed the romantic, starlit night.[9]

Evelyn Frechette, as the woman with Dillinger, was identified as Mary Jenkins by the press. Police circles identified her as Pearl Elliott. McGinnis gave Matt Leach the name of the woman, as she was known on the street. This didn't offer a clue as to her true identity, however. Leach circulated her description:

"Billie Spark has raven black hair cut in long bob. Heavy-type face, almost Jewish [*sic*] in appearance. Wears small, close fitting hat and coat of Persian lamb which is black in color. Also carries a small Persian lamb muff. Fair complexion, skin coarse tending to pimples. With John Dillinger almost constantly." Leach coined a similarly racist descriptive into the widely circulated Identification Order of Clark:

"Russell Clark always wears gray clothes, and presents a striking figure. Considered well-dressed, wearing a 'nigger-head' [*sic*] blue-black overcoat, topped with light, soft hat."[10]

The incident on Irving Park Boulevard put Dillinger in the forefront of the search for the Terror Gang. For the first time, the *Indianapolis Star* featured Dillinger's face on the front page. "Indiana's most noted criminal," he was captioned as the leader of the gang, and mistakenly tagged under a $10,000 reward. While as yet unfounded, the reward helped to fan the fire of hysteria surrounding his name. The next day, Dillinger's car was found in front of 7600 Greenview Avenue, with its body and bulletproof glass windshield dented by twenty-two bullets. There were no blood stains inside the sedan, which had been registered to Dillinger's alias, Joseph Harris of 2847 Washington Boulevard. Both he and Evelyn had miraculously escaped injury, and on November 20 Dillinger participated in another bank robbery. The new mark was the American Bank and Trust Company in downtown Racine, Wisconsin. The gang had planned the job in the Triangle Bar in Milwaukee, under the protection of Casey Jones, an ex-con from Leavenworth. There they hung out with a Pearl Elliott connection named Heck Trimby.

At Racine, the gang timed the job with a psychological component. Their time of arrival, 2:30 p.m. was a half-hour to closing. When Pierpont, Dillinger, Leslie Homer, Makley, and Clark hit the curb, they hoped to find sleepy, inattentive tellers.

Four of the men, with weapons under their overcoats, walked into the bank screaming hysterically. They threatened death. This escalated when one of the robbers released a spray of machine-gun bullets to the floor. With the gong tolling in front of the building, it rang like a call to arms. A crowd pulled together and rushed toward the building, punctuated by a police car screeching from the station house two blocks away.

The robbers scooped up the sacks and made haste to escape with the $50,000 they'd been able to get. To escape, they shot into the crowd. None of the bandits were themselves hit. Still, they took no chances.

Helen Cespken was a bookkeeper who worked in a cage at the rear of the bank lobby. She and her co-worker, Jeanette Williams, were to accompany them out of the bank. The young women were sucked into the crowd, unnoticed by their captors.

"I got my worst moment when they started to leave and took Jeanette and me with them. The fellow guarding us stopped to load his machine gun and that's when I was sick with fright."

She felt that her life would continue at the robbers' discretion.

"The click of those bullets going into the gun was horrible," Helen Cespken told reporters. By the time the thieves got to the door with their hostages, a crowd of between 50 to 100 people had gathered. Some locals thought a mad dog had been shot by a policeman. Kenneth Lee, of

Racine, recounted that the citizens who surrounded the bank were paralyzed with fear. Yet, in a morbidly curious fashion, most stood fixated on the action.

"The crowd seemed to want to get as close as possible," said Lee, in relating what he had witnessed.

The gang sped off to Highway 41, taking several hostages. One by one they released them into the cold afternoon as they sped for the Illinois state line.

Grover Weyland, the bank president who was also taken hostage, recounted to police that the robbers had treated their passengers in a manner that was "courteous, without insults or rough language."[11]

Leslie Homer was arrested shortly after participating in the holdup. He was arraigned right in the town of Racine. During his arraignment, he talked at length to police. Between his revelations and those of McGinnis, Captain Matt Leach discovered the existence of Pat Cherrington and Opal Long. He attributed to them their sisterhood, at least, without knowing their surnames. They were two sisters whose names [are] unknown:

> *Pat*—33 or 34 years, 5'5", 140 lbs., chunky build, hair was red and now dyed black, formerly a cabaret entertainer; *Opal*—35 years, 5'5", 140 lbs., ruddy complexion, straight red hair, wears glasses, is not a neat dresser and is rather homely. Makley, Clark and Shouse had an apartment together. Opal was keeping house for them.

In early November, Pat Cherrington, who never kept house for anyone, stepped into her spectator pumps and hopped a train to Kansas City, where she was said to have relatives.

On a Chicago street corner, while embroiled in an argument with a prostitute, Harry Copeland lost his cool and his cover. On the same afternoon that his friends were robbing the bank at Racine, he got into a fight with a prostitute in the front seat of his car. As their argument escalated, he pulled the car over. Whipping a gun out of his pocket, he held it on the woman, while accusing her of stealing his wallet while he'd slept off their sex-for-pay in a hotel just a few hours before. In his livid state, he waved a gun on a street corner. A passerby, noticing the gun, called the police. Patrolman Edward McBride and his partner, John Ryan, were just finishing up their tour. They answered the routine call of a nuisance at the corner of North and Harlem. They arrested Copeland and the woman.

At the station house, Captain Thomas Duffy, on a hunch, felt that there was more to the story. He shared his feelings with Captain Dan Gilbert. They decided to order Copeland, who called himself John Santon, brought to the Justice Department to be fingerprinted. This method of identification, still in its infancy, had amazingly not yet become a routine part of arrest procedure.

Within hours, his prints identified him as a member of the Dillinger gang. Captain Duffy, in a quick series of moves, rushed Copeland's picture to Lima, for the perusal of Sheriff Jesse Sarber's wife and the Deputy Sheriff who remained at her side on the fateful night of October 12. They identified him simultaneously as one of the party of men who had raided the jail. Within hours, the Allen County prosecutor, Ernest Botkin, immediately charged him with culpability in the murder of Sheriff Sarber.

In this fashion, Copeland went from a successful bank robber to Ohio's premier candidate for the electric chair. In his news photograph, taken with the arresting officers with broad smiles all around, he appeared confused. The very next morning the lights went out for him, literally, as he was returned to the Indiana penitentiary for violation of parole.

The gang didn't hear of the arrest right away. The capture was kept secret by Lieutenant Richard Barry, who held Copeland for the evening at the station house at 11th and State. He posted squads of men holding machine guns and shotguns at the doors. "There won't be any jail delivery here," he cryptically announced when news of the arrest leaked out.

It is doubtful that Pat Cherrington ever returned to the love nests she kept with Copeland at 820 Montrose and 1941 Warren. Captain Stege put these locations under surveillance.[2]

Based on crossed wires, Pearl Elliott was identified as living with Dillinger and Pierpont at 150-154 Parkside. Dillinger's true association with the Elliotts took place within the confines of their bootleg, gambling, and prostitution joint in Kokomo. Initially he'd gone there with Copeland, staying for entertainment and meals. After a while, they brought Evelyn, whom Pearl later referred to as the "dark-skinned girl." Pearl called Patricia Cherrington the "red-haired girl." The habit of the group was to stay until 2:00 or 3:00 in the morning. Leach, who gleaned through McGinnis the connection between the Elliotts and Harry Copeland, got a police photo of Pearl and designed an Identification Order placing her with Mary Kinder. He believed that the girls, as he called them, were the gang's eyes and ears.

Pearl Elliott lost her cover as a result of John Dillinger. The police had placed her at the Parkside and Clarendon addresses, based on a tip from McGinnis. This exposure represented a change in her fortunes. She adamantly denied having had anything to do with Mary Kinder or the Michigan City escape, maintaining that she knew Dillinger only through his visits to her joint. In spite of her denials, Matt Leach nailed her picture to every wall in her home state of Indiana. Suddenly, the Elliotts realized that they'd brought the heat on themselves; too many people knew that Dillinger frequented her joint. She was forced to abandon her lucrative fun house in November, 1933, leaving the business at 714¼ North Washington to the management of her friend, Tiney Cypher. Tiney, who weighed 250 pounds, had at least three illegitimate children, one just an infant at the time Pearl left the house under her supervision. Tiney was Pearl's stand-in on those occasions when Pearl wanted to travel to Frankfurt to visit her mother's house at 501 North Main Street.

On the assumption that she'd left her house with a trusted partner, Pearl accompanied Dewey to Madison, Wisconsin; to Milwaukee; and finally to Houston, Texas; where Dewey worked in the gambling rackets. They parted temporarily when Dewey went to Oklahoma.

When Pearl returned to Kokomo in early 1934, she walked into an empty house. In her absence, Tiney had mismanaged the bawdy house, causing it to fall into the red. As a way out, she emptied the twenty-two-room house of its furniture. Pearl found out that Tiney had gone to live with her father in Windfall, Indiana, where she planned to open up her own house.

Pearl, protected by her political connections, put Tiney on her private "hit" list. Prominent on this mythical wish list were a few police officers and others that Pearl planned to "beat up" if she ever got into physical shape. Pearl expressed her thoughts on Tiney's betrayal in a letter to her mother:

> *"My darling Mother and All:*
> *I got two letters from you and I sent you two from here. How is everybody, fine I hope. I am O.K. I got a little headache this A.M. but that don't amount to much. Don't write to Tiney or tell her nothing, she sold part of my things. I am going to Ruby's, leaving here Sunday A.M. and be there Monday night, on business. . . . Write me a big letter at Ruby's right away. Love to one and all. I am as ever yours."*

Pearl Elliott's cousin, Olin Holt, was a former convict who was the Mayor-Elect of Elwood. Under his jurisdiction, Kokomo was to be an open town, starting with his administration commencing on January 1, 1935. Holt promised Pearl that if she were arrested for her connection to Dillinger, he would "put her on the bricks." On this promise, Pearl remained close to Elwood and Kokomo. Her business had gone to ruin through the combined efforts of Matt Leach on one side of the law, and Tiney Cypher on the other. Dewey had remained in Oklahoma, with no immediate plans to return to her. Most disturbing to Pearl, though, were the unbearable pains in her stomach. She made plans to return to her mother, Mary McDonald, in Frankfurt.

Pearl reluctantly went to doctors. They operated and found numerous cancer cells, which had spread throughout her abdomen. They sewed her back up and placed her on morphine. She returned to her mother's home with a ten-month prognosis.

In the knowledge that she was dying, Pearl developed an addiction to the morphine, which relieved her physical agony. Like a dowager of the old Orient, she became addicted, reclining her masculine frame on a pillowed divan rank with body odor. Her narcotic-induced conversations often went to rambling. As she moved slowly toward death, one thought comforted her. She vowed to rise from her bed to "personally beat up Matt Leach and several members of the Kokomo police for the publicity they had given her."[13]

*"These people were not rowdy and no complaint was made by anyone in the neighborhood."*

*—caretaker,*
*201 South Atlantic Avenue,*
*Daytona, Florida*

# "Good Piece of Company"

Mrs. Margaret Shanley washed the floor quickly. She checked off the date, December 14, on her kitchen calendar. It was eleven days to Christmas. Not expecting company, she started nervously when the bell rang. At the door stood Frank Hopkins, from her husband's squad. In halting tones, he told her that there had been an accident. Her body flashed hot and cold. Without a coat, she ran up her block, ringing doorbells. She quickly found neighbors to come in and sit with her six-year-old son and wait for the other three children, who were due in shortly. Patrolman Hopkins took her to Edgewater Hospital, where she was led to her husband. In the confusion, she didn't understand that Bill was dead.

"His eyes are moving," she insisted, as she held his hand in those last fatal moments of hope that he was still alive.

When Margaret Shanley returned home in a radio car, she noticed the mop, still in the pail where she'd left it hours before. She fell into bed, leaving the arrangements to her sister. The couple's four children, ages twelve; eleven; nine and six, were sent out to play with the neighbor's children. It was easier than explaining. Their mother could not stop crying.

Their home on 1415 Thome Avenue became a madhouse, as the people running in and out prepared for a visit by Mayor Kelly, who would arrive with Police Commissioner Allman. Margaret would be unable to compose herself through visits from dignitaries such as these, and also from the parish priests at St. Gertrude's, where Shanley had served as a church usher.

The slain policeman would be coming home, and would lie in state in the parlor where he had played with his children.

William Shanley had won the *Chicago Tribune's* Monthly Hero award for entering an unlighted crime scene alone, to capture two armed men, back on January 2, 1922. The family and friends of the slain man had considered him to be invincible. Slowly, with hushed tones, the rumors began circulating. William Shanley had been shot by a member of the kill-crazy Dillinger gang.

John Hamilton was seeing a waitress named Elaine DeKant Sullivan Dent. He was her sugar daddy. When he handed her an $80 deposit on a shiny green roadster, she took it eagerly.

She'd just gotten fired from the dining room of the Stevens Hotel for drinking with a customer. She believed Hamilton, a patron, when he told her that he was a businessman. After she was fired, he shuttled her between two apartments, one at 5510 Winthrope Avenue and another at 1342 Argyle.

Thinking that she'd found an end to her money problems, she clutched the title to the car, which had been registered in her name. On the afternoon of Thursday, December 14, she and Hamilton arranged to have its fender straightened. They left it with a mechanic at 5320 Broadway. The two then went to the movies. Nearby, Chief of Detectives Schoemaker, of the "Dillinger Squad," had traced the car to the garage. He sent an urgent radio call to Sergeant William Shanley and his partners, Patrolmen Martin Mullen and Frank Hopkins. They were ordered to locate the car "somewhere on Broadway."

Sergeant Shanley's eight-to-four tour was ending. Schoemaker had warned him that this might be a member of the Dillinger gang. But

Shanley, possibly distracted, maybe tired, viewed it as a routine detail. After coasting along Broadway, they found the car in the garage. He also found Hamilton, returning from the movie with Elaine Dent on his arm.

Shanley was a hero accustomed to dealing with thugs by himself. He'd been cited for just that type of bravery.

"Is this your car?" asked Shanley.

"No," said Hamilton, turning to Elaine. "It belongs to my wife."

At her cue, Elaine produced the receipt. Shanley, who should have had Hamilton seized by his partners, single-handedly ran his hands over the desperado's hip pockets for a weapon. Hamilton, quick to the draw, pulled the sought-after .45 out of a shoulder holster and shot Shanley twice. As the policeman fell amid a pool of blood, the couple flew like bats out of the garage, separating on the sidewalk. Elaine was caught.

Mrs. Dent decried her ties to the Dillinger gang and explained her genealogy—maiden name De Kant; married first to Sullivan and later, Dent. Of Hamilton, she said she'd known him as John Smith. Captain Stege shrugged her off as insignificant. When she walked into the oblivion of the streets, she signed a bland postscript on John Hamilton.

"He was good to me . . . bought me this coat and the car."

Before the bier that held the body of Bill Shanley, Margaret's sister, Edna Bender, expressed the outrage felt by those who had loved the home-loving man who lay in a coffin in the parlor.

"Something like this had to happen," she said bitterly. "This family was too happy."[1]

After that, fifty men were assigned to Captain Stege in ten squads. They formed the new and improved "Dillinger Squad." These latest recruits were detectives, who replaced the forty city policemen who had been searching for Dillinger. Their first official arrest would be to nab Art "Fish" Johnson, a familiar face in the neighborhood of Sheridan Road and Irving Park Boulevard. A bookie manned the phones at the infamous Lakeview 1–0159, located in a pool hall owned by Otis Murphy at 3939 Sheridan Road. The arrest of Art "Fish" left the gang scattered without a means of making contact.

"Fish" Johnson had been fencing $56,000 in stocks and bonds from the robbery of the Central National Bank of Greencastle, the job that had caused Ed Shouse to defect. "Fish" belonged to a clique that included Bill Davis, the go-between in disposing of the bonds; Jack Perkins; and

Jimmie Murray, who ran a roadhouse on North Avenue.

Captain Stege's new squad arrested "Fish" Johnson on December 17 in his apartment at 1742 Humboldt Boulevard, with his twenty-four-year-old girlfriend, Jean. She was young, pretty, and had been seeing "Fish" since the days when she'd hung out on Clark and Diversey. Had Stege looked into Burke's apartment at 1840 Humboldt, he might have found some of her girlfriends: Mary Kinder, who'd been calling herself "W. Ryebolt" hung out there, as did Evelyn and Pat Cherrington, as "Irene Hunter."

Finding four shortwave radios capable of getting police calls, Stege conducted the raid with tear gas bombs and bulletproof shields. Their weapons were no match for Jean Burke's mouth. She lashed into Stege, keeping up a running tirade for hours. Stege finally threw her out of the station house. "Fish" Johnson, who hinted he might inform on messages coming through his telephone station, followed her out the door.

On December 20, a tip came in to the Chicago office of Captain Stege that a woman companion of the Dillinger gang was headed for 1428 Farwell Avenue. Stege, with his partner, Sergeant Frank Reynolds, charged over with his "Dillinger Squad." In their zeal, they entered the apartment and fired forty-four shots into three men in the hopes that they were Hamilton, Pierpont, and Dillinger. This resulted in the instant death of three gangsters named Louis Katezewitz, Charles Tattlebaum, and Sam Ginsburg. No woman was found at the bloody carnage, but there were some articles of female clothing.

Mayor Edward J. Kelly lauded Stege for "showing what the Chicago police can do." This official acceptance of the "shoot-to-kill" crusade meant that the gang women could also meet instant death. The thought so upset Mary Kinder's mother, Viola, that the woman stopped reading newspapers and listening to radio broadcasts.[2]

After the gang kicked him out of Chicago on November 21, Shouse drifted with Ruth Spencer and Frances Colin of Fort Wayne. On December 20, Matt Leach learned that Shouse was planning a bank robbery in Paris, Illinois. Buoyed by official and public acceptance of Captain Stege's actions in Chicago in the mistaken-identity killing, Leach issued his orders: "Shoot and kill and take no chances."

Lieutenant Chester Butler fired a shot intended for Shouse, as the gunman pulled up in front of a hotel accompanied by the two women.

Eugene Teague, a handsome bachelor who had recently joined the state police, was hit instead. The sight of this enraged Police Officer Albert Stepp. He shoved the muzzle of a revolver against Shouse, who surrendered. In Paris, Lieutenant Butler collapsed upon learning that his bullet had killed Eugene Teague. As the prostrate Lieutenant was injected with tranquilizers, Matt Leach refused to comfort him. He focused his attentions on quickly hustling Shouse out to Michigan City. Shouse frustrated Leach by refusing to talk to him. The removal of Shouse left the reporters, who had gathered at the scene, to question Ruth Spencer.

"I'll pose for you in a bathing suit, if you'll find the suit," she offered.

With Shouse and Harry Copeland facing twenty-five years in prison, Hilton Crouch was arrested by Captain Stege on December 24. Crouch had broken from the gang and bought an interest in a tavern at 4433 Broadway after the Massachusetts Avenue Bank robbery in Indianapolis. He was caught quietly, with his sixteen-year-old companion, Violet Barretti. She tearfully claimed to have married Crouch two months before. She had thought he was a businessman named Bob Price, the name he'd used when they were married. Crouch agreed that he had fallen madly in love with his little teenager some five months before, upon meeting her at Drumm's tavern. Police found a Christmas card in his pocket, addressed "To My Dadee, [*sic*] From your Babee."[2]

The arrests of Crouch and "Fish" Johnson worked like cleanser to a claw-foot tub. It cleaned out Chicago. Before splitting up, the gang agreed to meet in Chattanooga.

"They didn't like to miss a date because it would be too easy to lose track of one another," Opal Long later wrote. She left Chicago with Russell Clark in a Ford V-8 on December 14. Dressed in a tweed suit and holding a pipe, Clark resembled a college professor. With the alias "Jess Wilson," a name he borrowed from a family friend in Detroit, he'd purchased the sedan by giving the nonexistent address of 428 South Oak Park Avenue in Chicago.

While riding through Indiana, Clark hit a truck broadside. Opal, who was struck unconscious, awoke to find uniformed paramedics placing her in an ambulance. With a gaping wound on her face, she began fighting.

"There we were with a wrecked car and a suitcase full of machine guns and pistols in the back seat. I told Russell I wasn't going to the hospital," she wrote.

Clark tried to calm his woman, afraid that she was attracting too much attention. He amiably agreed to file a police report while his "wife" went to the hospital. Opal, in a bilious fit, gave her name as "Mrs. Bernice Wilson."

"There I was with $4,500 in my shoe and I knew they'd try to take my clothes away from me at the hospital. I was afraid I'd talk under ether and get us all in trouble, so I had to hang on for dear life and grit my teeth while they sewed up the cuts on my face," she recalled later.

She was one tough and difficult customer to the unsuspecting hospital aides.

"The nurse tried to take my shoes away. That $4,500 packed under the sole of one shoe was all the money we were carrying. I fought like a cat until I got the shoes back and put them under my pillow."

Russell Clark, handsome in his pipe and tweed, checked "Mrs. Wilson" out of the hospital. With no car, they rode via taxi to an airport, where they took a chartered plane to Chattanooga. At the rendezvous point, they met Dillinger and Evelyn Frechette. She made Dillinger stop at a mailbox to send money to her sister, Anna, for Christmas presents. She may have been suffering from holiday melancholia. Her drinking escalated in the company of Mary Kinder. Prohibition had just ended. The latest fad was the cocktail, which was more potent than watered-down beer.

In Nashville, Mary Kinder got an $800 engagement ring with an $85 wedding ring to grace her symbolic union to Harry Pierpont. The net amounts mattered to Mary. She had a photographic memory for the money spent on everything she acquired while with the gang, and years later she would recount, to the penny, their expenses.

Dillinger arrived in Florida with Evelyn on December 19. From a rental office at 195 Ocean Avenue in Daytona, they rented the house at 901 South Atlantic Avenue. The couple paid with $100 up front. On the following day, three other couples joined them at the two-story frame building that faced the ocean. The caretaker pegged the group, who said they were from Chicago, as "gangster types." He left them alone.

Pierpont and Mary traveled to Daytona as "Mr. and Mrs. Evans." With Mary's sister, Margaret, they greeted Pierpont's parents. Lena would anger Mary Kinder by interfering in their conversations. She had a habit of misquoting Mary's words to Pierpont, in an effort to cause the two to quarrel. Mary found the woman's animosity to be a puzzling annoyance, at best.

Russell Clark and Opal Long showed up, exhausted from their automobile accident. Charles Makley, as usual, arrived alone.

In Daytona Beach, the gang did "a lot of drinking at night," in the words of the caretaker. "These people were not rowdy and no complaint was made by anyone in the neighborhood," he later told investigators. "They kept to themselves and had no outside contacts . . . no one was seen to visit them."

The underworld clique stayed here without a telephone in the seventeen-room house. Here the men enjoyed the fruition of dreams born of imprisonment and deprivation. They sat in the large, round living room, around one of the four open fireplaces. They rode horseback in bathing suits on the beach. Patricia Cherrington was impressed with Dillinger. She thought he treated every girl as a lady.

"He provided the best," she later told prison officials in an interview at Alderson, West Virginia. "He was modest in his tastes, never drank to excess and was a good piece of company."

Opal Long noticed the way the men pampered the women—all but her, it seemed. She'd planted herself in the kitchen, where she'd been fixing Charles Makley's "3–5 minute" eggs. While banging pots and pans, she noticed none of the others lifting their manicured fingers. With her red banana curls framing her face like Medusa, she fixed her gaze on the men and demanded attention.

"I, too, am on vacation," she hissed, casting a pointed frown at Mac. For the rest of the week, the gang ordered takeout plates from the local eateries.

The caretaker reported that the occupants of the house left after Christmas. Curiously, one gang member returned on January 13 in a new Studebaker sedan, Makley's car, to pick up bundles of mail. More mail arrived after he left, much of it postmarked from Georgia. The caretaker sent the bundles to the local dead-letter office.

Evelyn Frechette left without picking up a dental bridge she'd requested. It was typical of these indigent women to get their teeth fixed when they got some money. She'd gone to Dr. Sid Ney, who had an office at 256½ South Beach Street. He extracted a tooth and ordered a bridge. Evelyn was acquiring the accouterments of the middle class, to which she'd never before belonged. She wore a diamond ring and a platinum wristwatch studded with diamonds. In addition to her elaborate, if unfinished, dental work, she came into possession of an automobile. As "Frank Kirtley," John visited Notary Public D. R. Beach on December 26.

"I want to transfer a car to my sister," he explained. "I don't need it."

Mr. Beach dutifully notarized the transfer of title of his Essex Terraplane to Evelyn Frechette from Frank Kirtley. Mary Kinder also built up her assets. She'd won $200 playing dice on Christmas day. This unholy celebration continued into December 26. A decision was made to allow Evelyn to return to the Reservation for the remnants of the Holiday season. Amid rumors that there had been a fight between them, she left in the Essex Terraplane. Yet Evelyn's family members, to whom she returned after Florida, denied that John had been abusive.

"He never hit her; he wasn't mean like that," insisted a relative of Evelyn Frechette in an interview.

She left Florida after Christmas, en route to Chicago. When she got to Chicago she wired her girlhood friend, Vivian Warrington, that she'd "see her in Shawano."

Evelyn bounced into the Menominee Indian Reservation like a renegade Spaldeen ball. After spending New Year's with Vivian Warrington and her husband, George, she talked Vivian into accompanying her to Milwaukee. Once again, Evelyn wasted no time getting out of the Wisconsin woods.

Driving without a license, Evelyn discovered that she loved the speed of the Essex Terraplane. The exhilarating rush of freedom she felt beneath the wide Wisconsin sky ended in a minor traffic accident. Having no boyfriend to supply her with another means of transportation, she drove the damaged car to Milwaukee. Evelyn's mission in Milwaukee was to trade in her damaged Terraplane. With the survival instincts of a weathered fugitive, she employed the skills needed for a good automobile trade. Telephoning auto salesman N.B. Goulard, she made a deal. Upon a credit of $175, she would relinquish her car with its wrecked front end. She paid a balance of $220 in cash for a used car.[3]

Her purchase, a 1932 Terraplane coupe, would take the country's premier public enemy over the next thousand miles.

State of Florida.
County of Volusia.

I, Frank Kirkly, do hereby sell, transfer, and assign to Miss. Evelyn Frechette, of Neopit, Wisconsin., One Terraplane Essex Eight, Coupe, Car No. 70921, Motor No. 21192, key No. 404., free of all incumberances.

Mr Frank Kirtley .(SEAL)

State of Florida.
County of Volusia.

Personally appeared before a Notary Public in and for the State of Florida at large, Mr. Frank Kirkly, who signed the above Bill of Sale,
Witness my hand and seal at Daytona Beach, Volusia Co., Florida this 20th Day of December, 1933.

[illegible]

Notary Public, State of Florida at Large
My Commission Expires Mar. 21, 1936

Evelyn Frechette left Daytona in her own Essex Terraplane 8. It was a moment of independence for her. The name "Frank Kirtley" was signed by Dillinger before a Notary Public. (FBI)

*"A lady has to have considerable baggage when traveling."*

*—Evelyn Frechette*

# Every Means of Persuasion

The wreck of the Essex Terraplane rang as an omen. Through the noisemakers and revelry, Evelyn must have known that 1934 would be a terrible year. By pre-arrangement, having written to Vivian the month before, Evelyn spent New Year's Day with her friend, at the home she shared with her husband in Shawano. One week after arriving on January 7, Evelyn and Vivian left for Milwaukee.

In Milwaukee, Mrs. Bewersdorf, the innkeeper of the Jackson Hotel, on North Jackson Street, thought Evelyn Frechette's black eyes appeared glassy. She later told investigators that one of the two women in room 201 "appeared to have indulged in intoxicants." The two women hurriedly checked out on January 10, leaving for Neopit the next morning. Vivian returned to her husband, George Warrington.

Evelyn was beginning to miss her own man.[1]

The separation carried its own hardships. Now Evelyn would have to do some footwork to find Dillinger. From Chicago she wired Russell

Clark's mother, Mae Clark, in the hope of reaching Opal Long or Pat Cherrington. The messages transmitted through the Shawano telegraph office on January 16 show that she was laying the foundation for her return to Chicago. Pat Cherrington, disguised as Ann Jackson, answered her call. She knew how to reach Dillinger.

"Wire where I can call you at 6:00 p.m.," she relayed. "Important."

Evelyn had trouble understanding the answer that was expected of her. "Ann Jackson" wired a second time. She specified that Evelyn meet her, at once, at 75 East Windemer Street, Highland Park, Michigan, the Clark family home in Detroit.

Upon getting this later telegram, Evelyn hastily packed her bags and sent a wire of her own. She preferred to meet in a new apartment that Pat had rented in Chicago.

"Received your wire but cannot understand. Will meet you at 901 Addison Street."[2]

It was risky to roam Chicago; the windy city still burned from the January 7 arrest of Jack Perkins. One of the "Fish" Johnson crowd, Perkins had been arrested on the corner of California and North Avenues.

"Perkins absolutely refused to furnish any information regarding members of the Dillinger gang, although he was questioned vigorously and thoroughly, and every means of persuasion was employed to force him to talk," Captain John Stege wrote to Agent Sam Cowley of the Justice Department. Then, on January 6, Walter Detrich, remembered for his role in opening the box of thread in Michigan City, was captured in a hideout in Bellwood, Illinois. He'd been hiding out with Theodore "Handsome Jack" Klutas, who was killed in the ambush.[3]

When Evelyn drove her 1932 Terraplane into Chicago, she took a chance of being identified. She went to her new apartment at 901 Addison Street, two blocks from Wrigley Field. She was dressed to impress. On her finger perched a diamond engagement ring, given to her by Dillinger on Christmas Eve. She paired it with a wedding ring. Her platinum wristwatch, studded with diamonds, complimented her stylish leather jacket, sleek dresses, and berets. Rebellious styles mixed with bold, expensive jewelry ran counter to the somber mood of the Depression. Thus adorned, she visited her sister, Frances "Patsy" Frechette, at 3512 North Halsted Street on January 16. She came in at around 9:00 p.m., staying long enough to display her regalia. The next day, she kept a date with Dillinger, who preferred unobtrusive, conservative clothes for them both. To face the freezing winds of January, Evelyn donned an overcoat, shrouding herself in wool that dropped to her ankles. The icy temperatures mixed with John's ugly mood. Since January 15, he hadn't eaten, nor had he slept.

John Hamilton, with two other unidentified members of the gang, had been taken by surprise during a robbery of The First National Bank in East Chicago, Indiana. It was the desolate and decadent town he'd used as a hideout and base of operations. The town was wide open. The gang thought that their connections rendered them unbeatable there. One theory is that John Hamilton planned the robbery with the help of a Fort Wayne associate, Victor Fasano. Situated visibly in the center of Main Street, The First National Bank was an imposing building facing a two-way street.

As they walked in with their proverbial greeting, "This is a stickup," Vice President Walter Spencer picked up the phone.

"I'm being robbed," he cried.

A robber identified as Dillinger grabbed Spencer, taking him as a hostage. The message had alerted Police Officer Hobart Wilgus, who was the first to arrive.

"I went into the bank while the other three waited outside. I could not see inside because there weren't any windows to the bank, and I had to go through three doors before I got inside.

"When I stepped inside the first person I saw was Dillinger. He had me covered with a machine gun."

The man identified as Dillinger forced him to drop his .38 and line up with the rest of the hostages. He placed Wilgus in the position of being first in line for a bullet.

"Hamilton was looting the money drawers," continued Wilgus. "When he got through, Dillinger and Hamilton marched Vice President Spencer of the bank and myself out the door as shields. There were about thirty of us lined up before Dillinger's machine gun."

Officer O'Malley felt that he had a good shot and wanted Wilgus out of range.

"Wilgus," O'Malley screamed. Both Wilgus and Spencer jumped back, allowing O'Malley to fire four times. He couldn't foresee the devil's armor around the gunman's torso. Every bullet rolled off the robber's bulletproof vest.

"That machine gunner, who the police say is Dillinger, is a terrible man," said one eyewitness, no doubt prompted by police or reporters to emphasize Dillinger's name.

When Jeff Scalf, the great-nephew of John Dillinger, was asked whether his uncle was at the East Chicago bank robbery, he, like Dillinger himself, emphatically denied that John was ever there. Scalf had asked Mary Kinder, in an interview, if John had been involved in the East Chicago robbery and the shooting of Police Officer Patrick O'Malley. Mary maintained that John had stayed in Florida after she had left with Pierpont.

"I knew the good about Johnnie and I knew the bad about Johnnie. He knew the good about me and he knew the bad about me," said Mary Kinder. "He had no reason to lie to me because it wouldn't make no difference to me and he told me he was not there."

William O'Malley was a policeman, like Sergeant William Shanley, who had come into law enforcement by virtue of his family heritage. It was a time when the ranks of the department were dominated by second-generation Irish. They were large men, strong and tough. Yet their fathers had never contended with the high-powered munitions and bulletproof vests worn by these new criminals. Officer O'Malley wore no protective gear in this most deadly encounter. The gunman identified as Dillinger fired at least eight times in quick succession.

"He and Dillinger shot about the same time," Wilgus remembered.

"When they picked up O'Malley afterward, he had eight bullet holes in him. The bullets went right on through . . . not a bullet in his body," said Wilgus.[4]

While Dillinger escaped unhurt, Hamilton took a bullet in the lower back. The take, $20,376 in cash, would now be split and a good proportion would go to a local abortionist, Dr. Joseph P. Moran, for Hamilton's care. They brought Hamilton to the home of "Fish" Johnson's aunt, at 5740 South Homan Street, Chicago. When Jean Burke, Johnson's girlfriend, informed Pat Cherrington that they were there, she rushed over. Patricia nursed Hamilton through his gunshot wound at the Homan Street address. Hamilton fell in love with his sexy and vivacious nurse. In this way she rose from the banishment of Harry Copeland's arrest to become Hamilton's companion. Entrenched in a second affair with a Dillinger gang member, she was no longer a disposable item.

Pat Cherrington was motivated by her faulty gallbladder, which was crucifying her. Her abdominal pains were severe and affecting other areas of her health. She needed another operation, yet had no money to pay for it.[5]

While Pat Cherrington played nurse, Dillinger left for Tucson with Evelyn in her 1932 Terraplane. They adopted the aliases of Mr. and Mrs. Frank Sullivan, of Green Bay, Wisconsin.

When they pulled into St. Louis on the morning of January 19, Dillinger was gaunt from hunger and lack of sleep. In contrast, Evelyn had ascended to the ladylike stance that John had demanded as a disguise. She carried a small bull pup like an Edwardian dowager.

Mr. and Mrs. Sullivan stopped Louis Aikman, a mechanic at the Milton Oil Service Station at 22nd and Olive Streets. They needed to trade in their car. The mechanic sent them to the sales rooms of the Hudson-Frampton Company.

J.C. Jones, a car salesman, took them to the automobile show then being conducted in the Mart Building. Evelyn lingered behind, respecting the "No Dogs" rule that barred all canines except seeing-eye breeds from entering. Mr. Jones found Dillinger to be a certain type of customer, the kind with his mind made up. A seasoned salesman, Jones didn't try to talk him out of it.

"Give me a black Hudson with a long wheel base," John said. Mr. Jones persuaded him to accept the bison brown car then on the floor of the show. Dillinger wanted to get "his wife's approval." In 1934, a car purchase belonged to the domain of the man's world, and the salesman thought it was "sissy" to include the wife.

"Do you trust her to drive it?" he joked, jabbing Dillinger's rib with his elbow. At that point he felt the shoulder holster.

Dillinger laughed, and held the bull pup like a baby while Evelyn approved the car. The puppy, as slippery as its master, got loose. Security guards stationed in the convention hall joined Dillinger in the chase to catch the dog.

The couple decided to buy the 1934 Hudson Club Sedan, for a price of $1,229. They traded in the 1932 Terraplane for $275, which brought the price of the new car down to $954. Dillinger paid in cash, with a stack of old $20 bills bound with a bank stack wrapper.

As he returned the stack wrapper to his overcoat pocket, he bristled upon hearing that the car wasn't available immediately. He'd planned to be in Phoenix by January 25. On the recommendation of Mr. Jones, they agreed to stay in town to wait for the car.

"I need a place near the tourist attractions," Dillinger said eagerly.

Mr. Jones, who noticed that Mr. Sullivan's exhausted demeanor clashed with his desire to sight-see, offered to drive them to the Roosevelt Hotel in one of the company's demonstrator cars. After they closed the deal, Jones placed their luggage into the back seat. He was then forced to wedge himself into the front alongside Dillinger, Evelyn, and the dog. Stale sweat wafted from Mr. Sullivan, who admitted that he'd driven continually through the previous night. His body odor mixed with Evelyn's face powder and perfume, and the musky scent of the bull pup resting in her arms. At the Roosevelt Hotel, Jones lifted the suitcases out of the back seat. A large zipper-bag felt like it contained an anvil.

"A lady has to have considerable baggage when traveling," said Evelyn with great dignity.

Back at the dealership, the manager, Mr. Davis, had become suspicious. Thoughts of the Lindbergh case scouted through his mind. He didn't want to take kidnap ransom money, no matter how bad the times were. "That guy was carrying a gun in a shoulder holster," he thought. When Dillinger occupied the driver's seat, the pistol had protruded from under his coat.

Mr. Jones wanted to give his buyer the benefit of the doubt. He had, after all, waited patiently for the car. While the couple had declined to view the attractions that St. Louis offered, they did enjoy dancing on the roof garden of the Roosevelt Hotel.

The car arrived on the morning of January 21. Mr. and Mrs. Sullivan, in a cloud of smoke and dust, skipped town in one deft turn of the wheel. Employees at the Roosevelt Hotel later learned that the quiet man who'd worn smoked glasses, was clean shaven, and spoke very little was John Dillinger.

Evelyn Frechette, nestled in her feigned, material security, nodded vaguely toward a new destination. She'd previously visited Phoenix to meet the Hamilton, Ohio, associates of Russell Clark.[6]

Unlike Evelyn, Mary Kinder had no free hands with which to stroke and coddle a dog. In the midst of her inventory and packing, Tucson loomed in her mind with foreboding.

"Don't go to Tucson," a voice inside her head said with chilling finality. Frustration enveloped her, causing her to reevaluate her true importance within the gang. Her power had actually been in the social realm. In the decision and policy-making framework, she counted for nothing.

The Florida vacation had presented a bulwark in the figure of Lena Pierpont. She'd suspected that Mrs. Pierpont secretly engaged in a campaign of lying and sabotage. While glad to get away from Harry's mother, she did not want to go west.

"There's no use arguing with the boys," she shrugged in rationalization. She later wrote,

"You can't ever get settled. That's the way it goes. You're afraid to stay put, and you're afraid to go to another place where it's strange."

Mary, who had just won $4,000 at the racetrack, reluctantly packed the loot and ammunition. Through the torrid zones of hot weather they'd become accustomed to since Daytona, the gang filtered into Tucson by January 23. They came in three separate factions. Makley, accompanied by Russell Clark and Opal Long, had arrived earlier than the others. Dillinger and Evelyn showed up after Pierpont and Mary.

Opal Long shared Mary Kinder's fatigue and depression. Her face was still battered from the automobile accident she'd suffered with Russell Clark at the wheel.

In Daytona, the gang's quest for luxury had reached its climax. This period marked the peak in their friendship. The outlaw group had formed strong bonds in the four months that they'd spent underground. All used special, pet names for each other—"Johnnie and Billie," Opal Long as "Bernice," and Clark as "Boobie." Pierpont had always been "Pete," dating back from the Michigan City days. Mary went as "Shorty" to all but Pierpont—to him she was "My Mary." Once in Tucson, Charles Makley, who always went as "Mac," left the protective circle of the gang, and went out to womanize. He picked up torch singer Marge Metzger.

By January 25, two events occurred simultaneously. Russell Clark lost control of his drinking in the lounge of the Congress Hotel. This was exactly the kind of thing that the gang members had always sought to avoid; he had called attention to himself.

Then, a fire started in the hotel. Opal Long lent an official account.

"It put us in a terrible jam," she wrote. "If the fire ever got to the trunk, and set off the bullets in the machine gun clips, it would be a dead giveaway. The fire cut us off when we tried to run down the hall. We had to take to ladders and leave the trunkload of guns in the room."

The trio, staying on the third floor of the Congress Hotel, was actually lifted from rooms 329 and 330 by aerial ladders that firemen swung up to the window ledges. Makley, thinking of the guns, paid two firemen, William Benedict and Kenneth Pender, to save the luggage. These firefighters, accustomed to being observant, were astounded by the weight of the bags. The $12 tip given to the firemen by Clark and Makley did not detract from their suspicions.

Later on, one of the firemen picked up a copy of *True Detective* from a pile of magazines stacked in the living quarters of the firehouse. In an article about the Michigan City jailbreak, a series of photos lined the top of the page. One mug shot stood out in the grouping of escaped prisoners. He looked familiar. In the way that reality slowly wakes one from slumber, some of the others, relaxed from dinner and coffee, congregated around the magazine. Amid the advertisements for white teeth and weight loss stared the square jaw of Russell Clark.

"Isn't that the guy who gave you the twelve bucks at the Congress Hotel?"

The firemen called the sheriff's office, where they were referred to Maurice Guiney, a criminal identification expert. Guiney opened his photo files.

Together with Chief C.A. Wollard, the two men identified the mug shots in the files. With the collaboration of officers Harry Leslie, Jay Smith, Al Wein, Frank Eyman, Dallas Ford, Chet Sherman, and Mark Robbins, they matched the names on the hotel register to the pictures.

It has always been thought that an informant dropped the tip to Captain Stege in Chicago, or Matt Leach in Indianapolis, that the gang address was 927 East Second Street. This forwarding address was found on baggage claim checks at the Congress Hotel. For all the top brass working on this case, it was ironic that the job of catching the Dillinger gang would fall to Tucson's patrol and traffic officers.

Officers Frank Eyman, of the traffic squad with 3½ years' service; Kenneth Mullaney, a small, wiry traffic officer; and Chet Sherman, in plain clothes, paid a visit to 927 East Second Street. It stood in a moderately well-to-do neighborhood, with a university fraternity and church nearby. The neighbors had noticed the opulent luggage of the new residents.

It was 2:00 in the afternoon of January 25, several hours after the meeting in which Mary Kinder begged the gang to leave town. The police detail staked the house, then impatiently rushed to ring the bell. Chet Sherman spoke to Opal Long, who opened the door carefully. He tried a ruse, by waving a letter "addressed to Art Long." Opal Long's shrewd instincts told her not to believe his story. She tried to prevent their entry, finally slamming the door, and in the process breaking the finger of Dallas Ford. But three men had already entered the apartment to overpower Russell Clark.

Sherman aimed his gun at Clark. Clark, in response, grabbed the gun, and a tug of war ensued around the room. In his disorientation, Clark had forgotten where Opal had put his .38 automatic. Just then, Dallas Ford struck his gun against Clark's head. It was the decisive move in the battle.

Both Clark and Opal Long, large and bold, went down. Opal fought the policemen, punching and clawing at them. She got knocked in the face as they held her down while subduing Russell Clark. Clark's blood splattered the front porch as he and Opal Long were flung into the radio car. The scuffle had put more bruises on Opal's already battered face. She now had a black eye to add to her purple chin, a remnant from the car accident in Tennessee.

Clark's head injury had left him stunned and helpless. He was carrying $1,288.70.

The police quickly went back to the house on 927 East Second Street and waited until a 1934 Studebaker sedan pulled up. Makley had already come and gone, accompanied by his torch singer, and drove downtown. They traced him to the Russell Electric Company, where he'd gone to purchase a radio.

"You're under arrest as a fugitive from justice," said Mark Robbins, an identification officer with ten years on the force. For emphasis, he dug his .44 into Makley's ribs.

As Marge Metzger cried, Makley refused to be fingerprinted.

"Makley, we are going to fingerprint you whether you like it or not," said arresting Officer Mark Robbins. The system, still a fledgling science, was considered "deadly sure" as performed by Officer Robbins.

They then relieved Makley of his money belt. They knew that his girlfriend, who had the foresight to list herself as "Mary Miller," was a local entertainer with no connection to the underworld. They released her almost immediately. Marge knew she had a good job in Tucson, singing torch songs in a Mexican cabaret to a transient, male clientele. She didn't need this publicity. She looked on in shock as the police emptied Makley's wallet of $770. She would long remember the sight of her rich playboy exchanging his white flannel trousers and sport coat for handcuffs and leg irons.

By now, the neighbors at East Second Street had called the police. A Buick with Florida license plates had reached the front of the house and had quickly turned around to drive away.

Just then, a traffic officer, "Mickey" Earl Nolan, was starting this animated tour of duty. Recalling that he'd been stopped some days before by an attractive couple with expensive luggage and Florida license plates, he voiced his recollections. Nolan gave a good description of the motorist. He identified a police photo of Pierpont.

Jay Smith, in charge of the traffic squad; Frank Eyman, who would figure in three of the four arrests; and Mickey Nolan went out to find Pierpont.

Frank Eyman cornered Pierpont at 6th Avenue and 19th Street. Jay Smith had Eyman covered with a gun, raised at the ready but hidden beneath the car door. Nolan sat in the car, looking around innocently. They talked Pierpont into driving to the police station.

Eyman took the back seat, sitting on a suitcase that held the guns. Smith and Nolan, following them, continued their game of poker, showing no sign of the incredible tension they were all under in this move to bring Pierpont into the station house. They got him through the door in this amiable way.

Pierpont, hoping to talk his way out, made a surprise reach for his clip shoulder holster. He aimed at Wollard before being disarmed by Frank Eyman and Earl Nolan in a well-choreographed series of moves that included clubbing Pierpont to the floor.

Officers James Herron, Milo Walker, and Kenneth Mullaney went back out on the job, returning to the flush house of cards at 927 East

Second Street. Dillinger and Evelyn Frechette were just pulling up to the curb in front of the house. Seeing that all was dark inside, Dillinger stepped out, leaving Evelyn in the car and starting up the walk. Officer Herron, who had studied the photo of John Dillinger, knew the man was the last remaining fugitive of the gang. The woman, left in the car, said not a word as Herron followed Dillinger up the walk. But Dillinger, who observed Clark's blood on the steps, turned around to leave. Herron stopped him.

"Put up your hands," he ordered.

Dillinger hesitated, until he heard the words, "Put up those hands, or I'll bore you!"

Evelyn sat in the car, frozen with shock, as Milo Walker, a traffic officer, kept her covered. Quickly they got Dillinger's hands into cuffs, as his move for his gun was stopped by the officer's riot gun in his back.

"I'm Frank Sullivan, of Green Bay, Wisconsin," he protested meekly, as he was pushed into the police car and taken to the station. Beneath his brown business suit, the officers found rolls of bills suspected of originating in East Chicago. Mark Robbins took his fingerprints.

"Sign this, John Dillinger," Robbins said triumphantly. Leaning the fingerprint card against a file cabinet, the prisoner did as he was told.

Evelyn joined Opal Long and Mary Kinder in the women's ward. Evelyn's dog had been forgotten in the commotion. He was found later, hiding under the rear seat of the car that also contained their arsenal.

Mary Kinder was carrying some of Pierpont's money. When police confiscated $3,116.20, she claimed she'd won it at the pony and dog races. She considered this a personal violation, a moral injustice. She wanted to produce receipts to prove that the money was rightfully hers. She repeatedly asked the matrons to tell her what had happened to Harry. She'd heard they'd clubbed him senseless.

While Opal Long sat subdued by the black eye spreading over her pudgy face, Evelyn relied on her stoicism. She appeared to worry not at all about her boyfriend, the most wanted man in America. Her concern was mainly for her Boston terrier that had been left hiding underneath the back seat of the car. The matrons reassured her; the dog had been placed in the temporary custody of Mike McGuire, a retired officer.

Outside, crowds gathered in the hopes of getting a tour through this impromptu murderers' row. Back on East Second Street, hoards of fraternity kids drove past the gangsters' house. They hooted, laughed, and blew their horns, while a group of local businessmen gathered to exchange their own fragments of history.

One claimed to have taken in the laundry of the gang. The gun moll had said her husband was "very fussy about his clothes."

"He didn't want his shirts mixed up," said the proprietor. He was left with a tab for a pile of laundry, and a receipt with a fictitious name. Not even the police knew the true name of his petulant customer. A full twenty-four hours would elapse before anyone tried to identify the women. There was no fingerprint record from which to form a profile. All three gave assumed names, which added to the total confusion.[7]

Dillinger and Pierpont in Tucson. Behind Pierpont sits Marie Grott, Mary Kinder's matron. (Author's Collection)

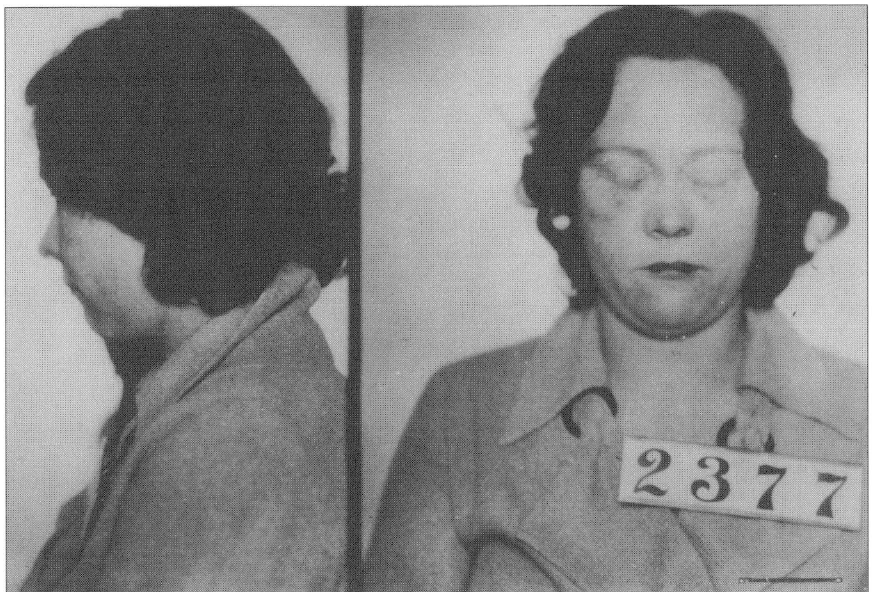


Opal Long's bruised face in Tucson, the result of resisting arrest. (FBI)

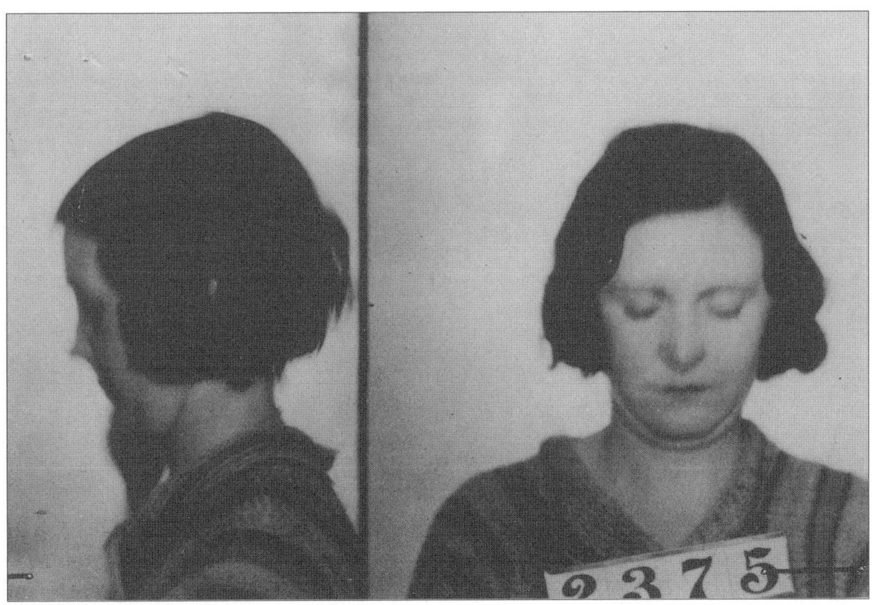

Mary Kinder tried to slip through Tucson as "Mrs. Harry Pierpont." (FBI)

*"John told me to 'take care of Billie.' He said, 'I'm not going to stay in this paper jail very long.'"*

*—Mary Kinder*

# "None of Your Business"

By nightfall on January 26, the police assessed that one of the women was most likely Mary Kinder. In the excitement, Mary's crimes were exaggerated: mastermind of the Michigan City Escape, she was the advance fixer, the "brains" of the gang, wanted in Illinois on charges of robbery and murder.

Mary Kinder called herself "Mrs. Harry Pierpont" when she was booked as a material witness. This charge was based upon her presence during Pierpont's apprehension, when he'd produced his concealed weapon and aimed it at Chief Wollard.

She was fingerprinted, photographed, and relieved of her jewelry. As she went before the intake photographer, she clamped her eyes closed to hinder future identification. Her hair style, cropped in the short, popular bob of the day, was sadly flattened. In her diminutive, innocent appearance, it was hard to believe that she was the common law wife of Harry Pierpont, the obscene, relentless gunman. He'd already been dubbed the true tough guy of the gang by identification expert Mark Robbins. Yet here was his woman—petite and pleasant.

Mary remained anonymous until Matt Leach arrived from Indianapolis with great fanfare. Leach recognized Mary from the grainy lady of the Indiana "Wanted" poster that had so enraged Pearl Elliott. Interestingly, as "Mrs. Pierpont," she was worth $5,000 in posted bail. As "Mary Kinder" she'd command a higher price; her bond increased to $100,000, matching that of the men. Mary, who had been wearing three rings, a watch, wristlet, and string of crystals, was allowed to keep only a chain bearing a small gold cross and a miniature of St. Joseph. It was weighted with sentimental value. She and Pierpont had purchased identical medals, each wearing one as a token of their union.

She begged to hold on to it.

"It's an aid for my prayers," she told the court. She wore the little cross as a symbol of devotion to Pierpont.

The second woman, "Bernice Thompson," conceded that her name was Opal Long. Matt Leach distinguished the big woman from her nearsightedness and naturally red hair.

Her battered face was unrecognizable. For the first time in her life, she took a mug shot, blinking in an attempt to distort her debut.

During the preliminary hearing that morning, she'd listened to the charges with head lowered and her coat pulled around her defensively. While in court, Russell Clark wouldn't look at her. Doubled over on a bench against the wall, his thick, sensuous hair a bloody muck, his head injuries were neither cleaned nor bandaged.

Evelyn, alone, bluffed her alias. The last of the women to have bail set, she signed her fingerprint card "Ann Martin" in stilted, stick-like letters.

"Evelyn made it through Tucson as Ann Martin," said Joe Pinkston, curator of the John Dillinger Historical Museum, in an interview. "This made it crucial for the rest of the gang to keep her real name a secret," he said.

The court set bail for her at $500 as a material witness, with an additional bond of $5,000 for resisting officers and obstructing arrest. Because Evelyn had not actually resisted arrest, it is probable that they pressed this charge to keep her from legally walking out.

Like Mary, Evelyn relinquished her hunks of jewels, including her platinum watch set with diamonds. Altogether, the jewelry taken from the gang was valued at $42,500. It was destined to be sold at a public auction.

Evelyn's purse netted a bonus: a slip of paper with the address of the house she and Dillinger had just rented at 1304 East 5th Street. This information led police there to find more money, ammunition, and luggage.

The morning after the arrests, on January 26, 1934, everyone was hauled into the Pima County Court to be arraigned before Justice of the Peace C.V. Budlong. They were charged as "fugitives from justice." All were held for a preliminary hearing set for Tuesday, January 30, 1934, at 10:00 a.m. The court set bail at $100,000 for each of the men.

They walked through a crush of between 1,500 and 2,000 people, all trying to get a look at them. The women, who weren't handcuffed, turned their faces from the cameramen, hiding themselves with their hands and the lapels of their coats.

In court, Evelyn sat next to John. She burrowed toward him, concealing her face in a gesture that said she wanted protection from the photographers and onlookers. She seemed to need his assurance. It was a fleeting moment when her impassive reserve broke down.

Dillinger acted like Samson after the haircut. He sat as Evelyn clung to his shackled hands. They listened helplessly to claims that $2,000 was found in his money belt, rolled between National Bank Notes on The First National Bank of East Chicago, Indiana, Serial Numbers A000919 to A001107.

Dillinger's great-nephew, Jeff Scalf, later pressed Mary Kinder in an interview, if the Tucson police authorities had found money and bonds from the East Chicago bank robbery in the gang's luggage after their capture in Arizona.

"Everyone was crooked," Mary said, "and they wanted to pin murder raps on all the guys to get rid of them." She stated that [the bank notes] had been planted on all of them.

"If it had been legitimate," she insisted, "they wouldn't have let [me] and the girls go because they planted some in their luggage as well as the guys."

During the proceeding, Harry Pierpont expressed a strange resentment that, out of the entire group, Evelyn alone was not identified. He yelled wildly as the gavel fell and proceedings on Ann Martin began. Pierpont, barely subdued, whispered something to their newly retained lawyer, John L. Van Buskirk. Pierpont wanted a marriage license drafted so he could marry Mary Kinder. It was the shotgun request of a doomed man. Upon receiving the vital statistics of the two, Mrs. Lenna Burges, Clerk of the Superior Court, typed away like a crackerjack. At ninety words per minute, Pierpont might have beat the clock to the altar. But fate stepped in. Someone said he'd heard a rumor that Mary was the daughter-in-law of an Indianapolis police officer named Claude Kinder.

Van Buskirk abandoned the marriage effort for another maneuver—to release the seven people from custody on application for a writ of habeas corpus.

Next, two Winchester 351-caliber rifles, mounted as machine guns, and three Thompson submachine guns were introduced as evidence, together with five bulletproof vests taken from the baggage of the gang. The total sum of money found in their possession, $25,000, was introduced as evidence in order to prevent a reoccurrence of what had happened in Dayton, when Dillinger's attorney took his payment from money found on the bank robber.

Clarence Houston, Pima County D.A., levied preliminary felonious charges:

- assault with a deadly weapon against Pierpont;
- resisting an officer against Clark and Opal Long;
- material witness against Mary Kinder;
- resisting officers and obstructing arrest against Ann Martin.

Until now, Tucson brass had held the credits in the arrests. Everything changed with a chilling message from Washington, DC.

The Federal Department of Justice, Division of Investigation, as the FBI was known in 1934, had arrived. The might and power of the Federal government showed up in the lone figure of the Special Agent in Charge of Tucson, SAC Carlton Endres. Mr. Endres announced that Director J. Edgar Hoover was "keeping in constant touch with all developments in the case." It was still a paper effort. They had no jurisdiction in this, a manhunt that had involved the four Midwestern states of Indiana, Illinois, Wisconsin, and Ohio. Lack of jurisdiction, however, didn't stop Hoover from sending Agent Endres into the Pima County jail to question the prisoners. They refused to answer the questions that the federal man posed to them.[1]

On the day that Matt Leach arrived from Indiana, he claimed jurisdiction over the prisoners, by virtue of their initial offense—the escape from the State Penitentiary at Michigan City, Indiana.

A support team was arriving on an airmail plane, to add weight to Leach's campaign to bring Dillinger back to Indiana. This group represented Lake County, the venue for East Chicago in the murder charge pending against Dillinger. The top official was Robert G. Estill, County Attorney. Carroll Holley, Deputy Sheriff of Lake County, accompanied the prosecutor. They'd brought witnesses: Nicholas Makan, Chief of Police at East Chicago, came with Officer Hobart Wilgus.

Wilgus was remembered as Officer William O'Malley's friend, who'd had a clear view of the shooting. When brought in to see Dillinger, he testified to all who would listen.

"I know he's the man that killed him and there'll be twenty-five more witnesses back in East Chicago to agree with me."

But Indiana would not get its native son without a battle. A delegation from Wisconsin came to Tucson, and wanted the men brought there to answer for the Racine holdup the previous November. The Wisconsin charges, "robbery with firearms," carried life imprisonment but no death penalty.

The officials from Racine had done their homework, wiring a $2,000 reward. The money had its weight. The Tucson police officers feared they'd lose their bounty to the other states without getting paid. The Racine district attorneys, Grover C. Lutter and John Brown, with Detective George Lyle, had prepared the proper extradition documents. They one-upped the East Chicago contingent, who had not completed the paperwork.

At the superior court hearing, Van Buskirk presented the waivers of extradition and asked that the fugitives be placed in the custody of Wisconsin officers. The fugitives had signed documents that declared they had officially waived extradition to Wisconsin.

The officers from Racine had prepared the statement, which the men had read in confusion. They initially refused to sign, because Racine would not be taking the women. It was an irrelevant dilemma, as charges against Ann Martin and Opal Long were not that serious.

Nevertheless, the prisoners demurred on this point. When told it would be a way to "beat the chair," they signed the statement stating that they "freely, voluntarily . . . agree to return to Racine, Wisconsin, to face felony charges . . . . "

In this game of war, Ohio joined forces with Indiana. In a triumphant announcement, Matt Leach declared that Ohio stood united with Indiana. They wanted Pierpont, Makley, and Clark brought to Lima in chains. They would answer for the murder of Sheriff Jesse Sarber.

Two days before, Allen County Prosecutor E.M. Botkin had arrived from Lima to claim Harry Pierpont. He'd already obtained a promise from Indiana for Harry Copeland and Ed Shouse to stand trial for the murder. Accompanying Botkin was Sheriff Don Sarber, the son of the murdered Sheriff Jessie Sarber, who declared that "we'll make every attempt to get them back here to stand trial."

Don Sarber from Lima and Hobart Wilgus from East Chicago listened to the politics of reward money without comment. One was bereft of a father, another a life-long friend.

Governor B.B. Moeur of Arizona made the final decision. Of course, the state with the most serious charges would get the men.

Neither Indiana nor Ohio wanted Opal Long and Ann Martin. The two women would be released from all charges on motion of the county attorney. On January 27, it became official: Opal Long and Ann Martin would be held another three days, before an unconditional release.

Indiana and Ohio overruled Wisconsin on January 29. In a sweeping move, the Arizona governor signed the Indiana requisition. Indiana won Dillinger. Ohio, by virtue of its alignment with Indiana, would get Pierpont, Makley, and Clark.

The D.A. in Lima promised that that prizes of $1,000 for Makley, Pierpont, and Clark would go to the Tucson arresting officers.

Lake County Prosecutor Estill decided to spirit Dillinger out of Arizona in a secret maneuver. They executed their coup covertly. Virtually no one knew it was happening until the plane left the Tucson airport shortly before 5:00 p.m. on January 28.

Most of the groundwork was laid for this plan during the period of harassment by the Racine officials. Once the requisition was signed by the governor, Dillinger was approached in his cell by A.O. Dunaway, the jailer, accompanied by Sheriffs Belton and Farrar. Upon hearing the words "East Chicago," Dillinger became hysterical as Farrar struggled to get handcuffs around him.

Pierpont, the proverbial anarchist, banged on the bars of his adjoining cell. He would then say his last words to the man who had been his closest friend for the past nine years. It was his swan song.

Dillinger was finally pushed against the walls of his cell and manacled. After being taken by a secret route through the streets of Tucson, he was put aboard a charter plane and taken to an American Airways plane, which left Arizona at 11:14 p.m.

The requisition party landed in the Chicago Municipal Airport at 6:12

As Dillinger posed in his Tucson, Arizona jail cell, crowds caused a commotion outside. (Author's Collection)

p.m. in the following evening after several stopovers to change planes. In Chicago, two lines of Indiana state police and 100 Chicago officers formed a gauntlet of machine guns, revolvers, and tear gas bombs.

Captain Stege, of the "Dillinger Squad," took custody of the trophy gangster in Chicago and remanded him to his next-in-command, Sergeant Frank Reynolds, who accompanied him by police car to the Lake County Jail at Crown Point, Indiana. Sergeant Reynolds' heroic record of numerous citations, including the *Chicago Tribune's* Hero award, formed a silent reinforcement. Credited with killing up to fourteen criminals, he now sat quietly next to Dillinger on the road to Crown Point.

The events that propelled the remaining four to Indiana had all happened very quickly.

Promptly at 10:00 on the morning of January 29, Judge Fickett ordered the writ of habeas corpus smashed. With a show of gavel and guts, he remanded the three men and Mary Kinder to the custody of the sheriff. He literally ran them out on a rail.

Mary Kinder was on her way back to Indiana, to face a grand jury investigation into charges that she aided the September 26 prison break. The charge carried a term of two to fourteen years. Her bail, originally $5,000, had been increased to $100,000. She was now worth as much as Pierpont, Clark, and Makley.

"I saw John and the others in the three days we stayed in prison," remembered Mary Kinder in a newspaper article.

"But it was all over," Mary said. "John told me to 'take care of Billie.' He said, 'I'm not going to stay in this paper jail very long.'"

At 11:00 on the morning of January 30, Pierpont, Makley, Clark, and Kinder went to the Southern Pacific station where a special chartered Pullman car had been attached to the back of the Golden State Limited. There, accompanied by Leach, they boarded. Six of his officers flanked the prisoners.

Mary Kinder, the only prisoner not handcuffed, carried some snatched clothing in a dirty pillowcase. She'd lost the bulk of her wardrobe and $2,000 worth of jewelry. When told she would be denied physical contact with Pierpont, she started shrieking. Animal cries emitted from the tiny woman. Police officers dragged her into a separate rail car.

"Why can't I ride with him?" she screamed. She cried from primal,

Crowds gather to watch the Terror Gang leave Tucson, Arizona. (AP/Wide World Photos)

ruptured dreams and rage. Matt Leach, who had made the promise to allow them to sit together, ducked into another rail car. The lawman was known to avoid emotional confrontation, and this was no exception.

At Kansas City, Mary was moved, with her pillowcase stuffed with shreds of clothing, to a train bound for Indianapolis. Pierpont, Makley, and Clark went on to Michigan City. Pierpont, watching Mary's departure, groaned loudly.

"I'd give $2,000 for a machine gun."

Left behind in Tucson, Ann Martin and Opal Long tried to retrieve their belongings. Their clothes and suitcases had been tied up with everything else confiscated by the police. After the dismissal of the charges against them, they begged Van Buskirk to get their things back. The lawyer had petitioned on January 28 for the return of their personal property and money.

The two freed women were prevented from taking anything by an injunction brought by the firm of Connor and Jones on behalf of the National Surety Company. It released their personal property, barring jewelry and money. This left them with only the clothes on their backs.

This essentially meant that they would leave Tucson penniless. The $67.90 taken from Ann Martin and the $181 taken from Opal Long when they were arrested was held pending further legal action in this and other suits. Their attorney argued this injunction, estimating that six months would be required to settle all of the cases.

Evelyn, at least, retrieved her Boston terrier puppy. She claimed him as her property and Mike McGuire, the ex-officer who had helped around at the county jail, was compelled to return the dog to her.

Without even a dollar, they were 2,000 miles from home. When the doors of the Pima County jail parted for them on January 30, they had only the clothes they'd been wearing for the past five days.

Now, these were resourceful women. Down-and-out was not a new experience for either Opal Long or Evelyn Frechette.

In the spirit of the true hustler, they arrived at a plan. Their "husbands" had put a deposit down for utilities, as was required when renting rooms. The two women ran over to the local utility company. With $20 deposited on power fixtures installed in the house they had rented, they might be able to retrieve it.

They didn't get too far with the tidy, coifed secretaries and receptionists. Lady luck was no lady in this case—she came in the person of a man.

Paul Hardwicke, the manager in charge of the billing department, listened to their story, fascinated by this new kind of creature, the gangster's moll. Evelyn, in spite of her recent travails, had a winning smile, while Opal Long twirled her pretty, red banana curls hopefully.

"Certainly we will refund your money," he said. "May I have your receipt?"

They looked at each other in dismay. He wanted a receipt? Was he kidding?

"The men have gone," they exclaimed. "We will probably never see them again," they cried, putting their hands up to their faces.

"Please, can't you make an exception in this case? We haven't a cent and we are hungry and haven't even a bed to sleep in."

Paul Hardwicke was a kind man. He asked for their signatures and advanced them $16.

"They were extremely courteous," Mr. Hardwicke said, "and a person couldn't help but feel sorry for them. After all," he said pensively, "they might not be as bad as people suppose."

The two then went to the telegraph office, to wire Detroit. Then they went to the Southern Pacific station, where they were cornered by onlookers. When questioned by reporters as to their destination, their "extremely courteous" deportment had lapsed.

"It's none of your business where we're going," they snipped. They bought two tickets to Detroit. They got off at Kansas City, Missouri, where Opal Long and Pat Cherrington had relatives.[2]

Evelyn was thinking of her sister, Patsy Frechette, in Chicago. In Chicago she'd have more access to information about Dillinger. Menonimee, her usual retreat, was out of the question. She wouldn't go back there penniless. The Reservation, for now, was not her destination.

*"[Zarkovich] practically wore a path between the grand jury room and Estill's office."*

*—Judge William J. Murray,*
*Lake County Circuit Court*

# "Take It on the Chin"

The sheriff's quarters at Crown Point resembled a stately Victorian home. Fronted by curtained windows and a wooden porch, the soft facade was deceptive. Behind it, the worst offenders of Lake County were housed pending their commitment to state facilities. The jail's proximity to the commercial streets placed it squarely within the mainstream. It was a time before television, when even a movie was a rare treat. Kids found ways to amuse themselves nevertheless, often through stolen looks into adulthood. The sight of the cells through the grilled windows, and the occasional glimpse of a prisoner, shadowed the children's games with grainy realism.

John Dillinger was delivered to Crown Point in a caravan of thirteen official cars on the evening of January 30, 1934. Upon his heralded arrival, the welcome he received broke the tension of the situation—a charge of murder of an East Chicago, Indiana, policeman during the course of a bank robbery, with a politically ambitious prosecutor who promised the death penalty.

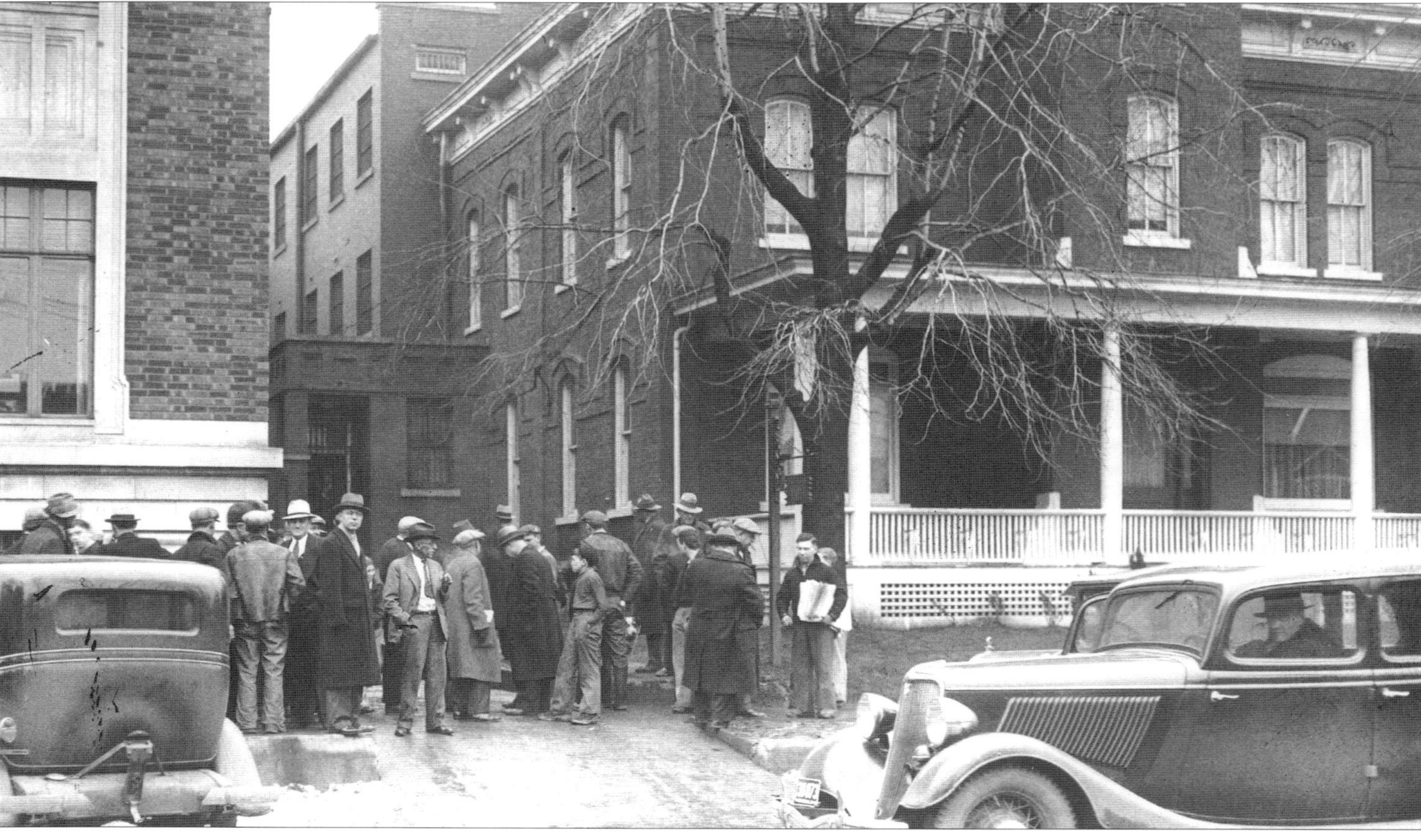

The Crown Point County Jail, with its attractive, Victorian façade.

(AP/Wide World Photos)

As he was led from the car and ushered into the building, still wearing the businessman's vest and white shirt of his Frank Sullivan persona, he was pushed before an assemblage of newsreel crews, photographers, and reporters for a group photo session.

This was to be a far cry from his first mug shot, taken at the age of nineteen. That long-ago photo had caught him candidly, revealing an uncomprehending felon.

On this night at Crown Point, the wanted man found himself touted like a prized trophy posed with the eager hunters. They earnestly pledged his continued incarceration, pending death by electrocution. No one really knows why the dreaded prosecutor hugged him, amid a deputy sheriff who flanked him with a grin, beside a female sheriff who suppressed a smile. In all the excitement of the frenzied news crews, calling the attention of the nation to this small town in Indiana, it is easy to understand the misguided show of determination. If all said "cheese" for the photographers, in a concerted attempt to look good, the effort failed. In the immediate aftermath, State Prosecutor Robert G. Estill, Sheriff Lillian Holley, and Deputy Sheriff Carroll Holley would blink away the glare of the cameras before their eyes.

Flash powder was a temporary annoyance, the price of dubious fame. More tenacious would be a naked gaze in the weeks to follow that would spotlight the loss of their credibility, political standing, and collective reputations.

If this photo session was to cause the collapse of the reining Democratic Party platform of Crown Point, it would mark a metamorphosis for John Dillinger as well. The snapshot caught a new look, evolved from the vapid stare of that first mug shot back at the Pendelton Reformatory.

For his illustrious moment, he gazed past the camera, in the direction of Sheriff Lillian Holley. In the picture broadcast throughout the United States and Europe, the bounty stands among the hunters. Yet he resembles less a broken jailbird than a pensive hawk.

The wanted man had never seen a female sheriff before. For Lillian Holley, freeze-framed as a uniformed Mona Lisa, her face reveals a cautious trepidation. She wore the badge out of the rural tradition bequeathing to widows the guns of husbands killed in the line of duty. A forty-two-year-old wife and mother, Mrs. Holley had taken the sheriff's

(AP/Wide World Photos)

post on January 23, 1933, after her husband, Roy Holley, was killed by Michael Lantars. A deranged farmer, Lantars had gone on a rampage, wounding several police and deputies before killing himself.

Roy Holley's widow, when faced with the question of how she was going to support herself and her children, had accepted the county commissioners' offer to finish her husband's aborted tenure. Needing the salary, she'd agreed to accept for one term. This decision kept the post in the family; it would further the career of her nephew, Deputy Sheriff Carroll Holley, who was eligible to run for the sheriff's post in the up-coming election.

With her title in place as firmly as the gun strapped around her hips, she choked back the grief, rage, and depression at the loss of the father of her twin daughters. As sheriff she would avenge the death of Roy Holley through small acts and daily deeds.

Prior to Dillinger's arrival, Sheriff Holley had carried out her responsibilities with no problems. She successfully guarded James "Fur" Sammons, one of the Chicago Crime Commission's official public enemies in the fall of 1933. Dillinger would, by his very presence, erase the good name she'd established in her own right. The prelude arrived in the publication on February 2 of a news photo of Captain Stege of the Chicago "Dillinger Squad" giving her a bear hug. He towered over her like a mountain, and the caption's "atta girl," didn't increase her stature to any definable degree. During Dillinger's time at Crown Point, hugs went all around, a preamble to the back stabbing that would follow his escape.[1]

As Mrs. Holley had followed the echo of her slain husband through a map of duty and reparation, another, very different woman moved in a parallel course. Evelyn Frechette, bereaved in her own fashion, stubbornly trailed the gait of her own man. The two women spun from their different worlds toward a crash course of their oddly placed, colliding tracks.

"I left Tucson without a dime," said Evelyn Frechette to anyone who would listen.

Dillinger's girlfriend had drifted to Chicago's North Side. Wearing the suede jacket and striped dress she'd been arrested in, Evelyn arrived by train after parting company with Opal Long. With her jewelry confiscated by the police, she had nothing to pawn. In her familiar limbo, Evelyn experienced her last days of rootless anonymity.

Sheriff Lillian Holley had successfully guarded James "Fur" Sammons without incident before Dillinger's arrival. (Author's Collection)

With Dillinger restrained at Crown Point, she stayed with her sister, twenty-nine-year-old Frances "Patsy" Frechette. Patsy was her anchor in those tumultuous days after Tucson. Less nomadic and more self-sufficient than her sister, Patsy was in the process of moving from 516 Cornelia Street to the second floor of 3512 Halsted Street with her roommate, Marge Edwards. Patsy had been employed as a domestic day worker for the past several years and had a good reference from her employer. Mrs. McGee, a Chicago homemaker, had been fond of Patsy.

Evelyn had lived in Chicago with her sister before. The sisters had shared a fashionable address on Pinegrove with Welton Spark back in 1932. Patsy had migrated to Chicago ten years ago from the Reservation, marrying Gerhardt Shultz in 1927. She'd borne him two children, a boy and a girl, before getting divorced shortly afterwards. The children had gone to both her ex-husband and her mother in Neopit, while she struggled to make a living in Chicago.

Evelyn and Patsy had gone home together that previous September for a short visit to Neopit. While Evelyn was on the road with Dillinger, she never forgot Patsy or her family at the Reservation, sending postcards from places as diverse as Mexico, Florida, Arizona, and Kansas.[2]

While Patsy and her roommate Marge worked as domestics, Evelyn lived on the money she could get from Dillinger's attorney, Louis Piquett.

A street-educated barrister, Louis Piquett hung on the fringes of politics and organized crime in post-Prohibition Chicago. His earliest recorded meeting with Dillinger occurred on February 1, when he received a call from Warden Louis Baker. Dillinger wanted to see him. The seemingly innocent telephone call was the initial move in an escape conspiracy between Piquett, the East Chicago police, and their entrenched associates of Lake County.

Piquett visited the Crown Point County Jail to discuss the issue of Dillinger's defense. The prisoner and the barrister argued over fees. Piquett left only to be met with more phone calls from the prison officials in Lake County. Dillinger wanted Piquett to sit in on his impending arraignment.

Piquett started a public relations campaign for Dillinger, using pat-on-the-back histrionics. At the same time, he operated a lonely hearts club for Evelyn Frechette and Opal Long. Mary Kinder, still incarcerated in Indianapolis, kited messages to Piquett through her lawyer, Jessie Levy.

As they called his office day and night—to stay informed of the progress of the court cases, to pass and receive money as it surfaced—it became clear that the recent dissolution of the gang, had left their widows bereft of support. Through the dreary days of February 1934, Evelyn haunted Piquett's office, sandwiched in a building overlooking the Chicago River. She leaned heavily on Piquett and his assistant, Arthur O'Leary. Working under the official title of investigator, O'Leary was a forerunner of the modern paralegal.[3]

Piquett sent Evelyn to Indianapolis to confer with Attorney Joseph Ryan, the first lawyer retained for Dillinger at Crown Point. With a pint of liquor in her purse, Evelyn made a definite impression on dispatcher Jim Maloney, who sold her a ticket for a $75 chartered flight.

He flew her out of the Chicago Municipal Airport early on the morning of February 8. Calling herself "Sadie," she seemed intoxicated to pilot Oscar Hanole, who flinched at the woman's conversation, which was spiced with profanities.

"If the Chicago cops know I'm up in the air, they'll come right up after me," she laughed, "because I was with Dillinger when he was arrested in Tucson." She then passed out. It took fifteen minutes to wake her up and get her off of the plane. Mr. Hanole felt sorry for "Sadie." No one was there to meet the woman at the airport, and she wobbled away from him, stooped and unkempt.

During her Indianapolis conference with Joe Ryan, Evelyn asked him to end her defunct marriage to Welton Spark. While doing his time, the convict had tried to maintain his marital relationship with Evelyn. He mailed his sentiments to the Menominee Reservation while Evelyn had lounged in the Florida mansion with Dillinger. Spark then obtained another address, possibly from Pat Cherrington. He sent a second letter to Evelyn in care of 901 Addison Street in Chicago on December 23. His frustration mounted as Patricia, the wife of his co-defendant Art Cherrington, was banned from his correspondence list.

On February 16, a notice was served on Spark that his marriage was over by virtue of a Divorce Judgment dated February 19, 1934. He stood to lose his beneficiary status to Evelyn's headright from the federal government, the stipend granted to Native Americans living on reservations. It had been earmarked to him. While it offered him little consolation, the impending divorce would relieve Spark of unfair complicity in the Dillinger case. Fingered as the husband of the mysterious Billie, Spark found himself irrationally connected as a gang member.

In contrast to the exiled Welton Spark, Dillinger sported a peacock tail at Crown Point. He received visitors frequently. Arthur O'Leary went in to see him on the day preceding Evelyn's much publicized meeting with the public enemy. Dillinger also saw Hubert Dillinger, his brother, who visited in the company of Attorney Joseph Ryan. With the trial on the calendar for March 12, Dillinger fired Ryan on February 19.[4]

Arthur O'Leary, Piquett's investigator, got his first glimpse of Dillinger during a visit to Crown Point with Louis Piquett. They were putting together an alibi and, to that end, brought an old associate from Michigan City, Meyer Bogue, along for a consultation. A dubious ally in Dillinger's cache of connections, he was known to hang around Happy Miles, an informant to Captain Stege in Chicago. An ex-con from Michigan City, Bogue was fencing stolen bonds from his room at the Southland Hotel in Chicago. He was prepared to testify to having seen Dillinger in Florida on January 15. His credibility was shorter than his rap sheet. Meyer Bogue had clocked twenty years in prison. Wanted in Detroit for a $9,000 robbery, he was the object of a Chicago police warrant. In spite of this, Piquett felt they had the "the best alibi case I've ever worked on."

Through the torrent of followers and fixers, Dillinger longed for his woman. When Evelyn Frechette rode into Crown Point from Chicago with Piquett on February 16, she dressed in the best clothes she could get. Upon her arrival, Sheriff Holley conducted the body cavity search, viewing the visitor through the bifocal lens of a cop and a woman. As she catalogued the woman's clothing, she noted the visitor's imitation fur collar on her black broadcloth coat. A cheap turban and crepe dress in matching black stamped the visitor as a person of little means to the solidly middle-class sheriff.

Evelyn Frechette appeared to be drunk to Sheriff Holley during the strip search. She called herself "Mrs. Dillinger," refusing to give a first name. The sheriff, who had her paperwork to consider, listed the woman's physical traits in lieu of legitimate identification papers. She attributed to "Mrs. Dillinger" a weight of 115 to 120 pounds, a conservative estimation. Evelyn balanced around 140 pounds, comfortable and round in the lean days of the Depression. The "swarthy" woman, twenty-five years of age, between five foot five or six inches in height, matched "very dark" eyes set in a "full round face" with a brown, long bob of hair. Her nationality, listed as either "part Indian, Mexican, or Italian," was a mystery to Sheriff Holley. She was a product of her time and place. With no experience in dealing with minorities, Holley had no way of knowing the difference between an "Indian," Mexican, or Italian.

These preliminaries completed, Evelyn sailed into the prison as easily as Dillinger later left it. The reunion in the dreary room brought them together for the first time since Tucson.

"Stand back," the officer in charge commanded them. Their passions like a pressure cooker, they talked in a controlled, businesslike manner. Evelyn spoke in words interlaced with the numbers 7, 11, 3507, or 50. They discussed the planned escape.

"Stop that kind of talk," the guards ordered, "or we'll terminate the interview."

Evelyn rode away from Crown Point in a pensive state. Alternating between memories of this depressing jailhouse tryst, she worried for the blank future that loomed as cold and gray as Chicago's winter.

She had left in her wake confusion over the identity of Mrs. Dillinger. Two theories reigned—the visitor was either Elaine Dent or Mary Kinder. The Chief of Investigation for the Cook County State Attorney's office announced the woman's identity decisively. Captain Daniel Gilbert went public with the announcement:

"We know that Mary Kinder visited him in jail, and it is possible that she acted as a go-between." The truth was, Mary was imprisoned in Indianapolis during February and would have needed a hacksaw to go anywhere.

On Saturday night, February 26, Evelyn went to a party with Marge Edwards at 638 Newport Avenue, the home of two sisters, named Faustina and Florence Tochida.[5] Evelyn wore one of the few dresses that she owned at this time, a black crepe with a shining ornament pinned to the shoulders. While there, Evelyn danced with three men named Bill, Gus, and Brisky.

For all she cared, they could have been Tom, Dick, and Harry. With no real interest in these men, she encouraged their advances out of frustration. Dillinger had filled a void within this sensual, complicated woman. The longing created by his absence, and her empty flirtations with other men, were short-lived. Satisfaction would come in one week's time.

Early the following Saturday, on March 3, Deputy Sheriff Samuel Cahoon entered Dillinger's cellblock at 9:15 a.m. A former inmate of the jail, he'd worked as a trustee for the past two years. This morning he'd taken too much out of the supply closet and had trouble juggling the soaps and towels of prison hygiene clumsily in his arms. The trustee was known to perform his weekly chores with the intent and purpose of the reformed. Today he looked sleepy and uncoordinated, dropping everything on the floor. He took a chance just this once; he walked in unescorted with the prisoners out of lock-up. For Dillinger, exercising in the corridor with fourteen other men, it was his cue.

"Do as I say, or I'll blow you apart," he ordered, pointing his mysterious gun at the trustee for emphasis. A myth would develop that the gun was wooden, whittled by Dillinger out of a washboard and darkened with shoe polish. The truth was later established that Piquett had arranged to have both a real gun and a wooden prototype smuggled into the prison.

Cahoon, dropping the last of his supplies on the floor, stood there acting numb and confused. Dillinger pushed him into a cell, taking the trustee's key ring. His next hostage, Deputy Sheriff Ernest Blunk, would cooperate fully with Dillinger. When asked to call Warden Baker, Blunk complied, walking to the rear of the facility, positioning himself in the middle of this corridor, and calling Baker's name. His voice echoed through the narrow, eighty-foot hallway. Warden Baker answered the call.

During the collusion of the two officials in the hallway, Dillinger appeared from the left tier of the cells. Pointing the gun to the warden's back, he walked him to the cell where he had already locked up six trustees who had been on the first floor. Blunk, still free to roam around with Dillinger, disappeared with the escaping prisoner. They returned with another inmate, an African-American named Herbert Youngblood. Dillinger and Youngblood had the foresight to steal a Thompson submachine gun from the jail office.

Blunk, who later insisted, "When I looked down the barrel, I was looking at a real gun," walked at Dillinger's side. They passed through the kitchen on the way out, and met three deputies and two women. They promptly locked the deputies into cells and the women in the basement laundry room. With all of the jail employees imprisoned, Dillinger and Youngblood, accompanied by Blunk, passed out the kitchen door, which they locked, and went around the rear of the jail. In their wake, they'd left thirty-three guards, inmates, and civilians locked behind bars.

Stopping in the jail garage, they couldn't start the cars, including two Nash automobiles, both the property of Lillian Holley. Dillinger broke the wire connections on both, preventing pursuit, and turned first into South East Street and then to another alley fifty yards further along the sidewalk. Their new destination was the public garage on Main Street. They were able to navigate Main Street without attracting any suspicion.

In the garage they met Edwin Saager. The mechanic had extended his night shift into morning, The excuse he gave for his presence was an urgent need to finish repairs on a Chevrolet. Dillinger, Youngblood, and Ernest Blunk entered. Dillinger walked up to Saager.

"Which is the fastest car in the garage?"

The mechanic pointed to a Ford sedan.

"There's your V-8 over there," Saager replied.

Youngblood moved through the front end of the garage, covering five garage employees and one mail carrier with the submachine gun. Dillinger forced Saager into the rear seat and told Youngblood to sit next to him. Dillinger, garbed in a cap and raincoat stolen from a trustee, told Blunk to drive. After a short distance Dillinger again played with the wooden gun.

"Do you think it was this that did it?" Dillinger pointedly asked.

"If I knew then what I know now, you wouldn't be getting away with it," Blunk replied. More double-edged banter went on between the two, as reported by Saager.

As they drove along Route 41, Dillinger pulled open a small drawer, a forerunner of the glove compartment, and noticed some buckshot shells and handcuffs. After passing the Indiana town of St. Johns, Blunk pulled to the side of the road and went to work removing the red searchlight that stuck out like a bloody nose.

On the road, Dillinger sang his own rendition of "The Last Roundup" and tenderly recited the prophetic lines, "Git along little doggy, git along." He told his hostages that this was his "last jail." A back-seat driver, he nagged Blunk about his driving.

"Don't go over forty miles," he ordered. The advice came a bit too late; they rolled into a ditch.

While Saager and Youngblood struggled with the car, Blunk and

Dillinger again put their heads together, talking quietly. At a place called Lilly's Corner, Illinois, they stopped.

"I think I'll get rid of you fellows here," said Dillinger. He checked to ensure that there were no telephones nearby. He offered Blunk and Saager money, with Blunk refusing and Saager accepting $4. Dillinger produced the $15 he'd collected from his prisoners at Crown Point. He gave the four bills to Saager. His car departed with a jolt, the wind bearing his parting admonishment.

"Be sure to keep your noses clean." With Youngblood seated in the passenger seat, the car sped south. Blunk would return to accusations that he'd taken part in the conspiracy to aid Dillinger's escape.

Back at Crown Point, the trustees, guards, and civilians locked into cells were yelling out windows to pedestrians on the street. The shock waves struck Mrs. Holley when a trustee ran into her bedroom with a shotgun in his hand.

"Dillinger's out," cried the trustee. Holley tossed him her pistol in a reflex reaction.

"Kill him."

The most crucial and immediate fact to establish was that the fugitive was driving a Ford V-8, Indiana license no. 674549. It would appear that the wrong number was released intentionally. Baker, a conspiracy suspect, released a totally different number, that of 679929. This critical error insured that Dillinger had plenty of time to get away. An official explanation was released to the newspapers, attributing the mistake to an *unknown person* who was sent to the car garage. This unidentified messenger performed the equation correctly, according to the report. The mistake occurred because it was picked up from the wrong auburn car, which accounted for the incorrect number being broadcast.[6]

Herbert Youngblood co-piloted the return to Chicago. As a "Negro" in 1934, he was acutely aware of the social conditions governing justice toward African-Americans. The Scottsboro Boys, wrongfully accused of rape for riding in a rail car with two white women, languished in an Alabama jail. Youngblood rightfully feared a lynching should he be caught with Dillinger. When the interracial escapees entered Chicago at around 4:00 p.m. that day, Youngblood remained crouched in the back seat. After being greeted by Piquett and O'Leary, who brought Evelyn to meet the car on Belmont Avenue, Youngblood ran off. He was killed by police bullets on March 16, after being trapped in a store in Port Huron, Michigan.

Winds blew in at a mild forty degrees but Evelyn was in a wild heat of excitement. She'd welded herself to her lover as Piquett asked his secretary to hide the couple. With the door slammed in his face, the decision was made to hide Dillinger for the night in Patsy's new Halsted Street apartment. With Evelyn beside him, Dillinger walked up the steps to the second-floor apartment.

They turned off the lights. In another part of the country, Washington, DC to be exact, the midnight oil burned throughout the night. The mechanics of the government's entry into the Dillinger hunt were simple and efficient. With a snap of a bureaucrat's clipboard, the entire face of this crime spree was about to change. Dillinger had made himself a federal fugitive when the car, found abandoned on Ardmore Avenue in Chicago, was labeled a stolen automobile driven over a state line. This constituted a violation of the Dyer Act, inviting the Justice Department to claim jurisdiction over a federal crime and formally enter the case.

The theft and interstate transportation of Sheriff Holley's car were presented to Assistant U.S. Attorney Edward A. Fisher in Chicago, who authorized the issuance of a complaint and warrant for Dillinger and Herbert Youngblood. On March 7, 1934, Special Agent T.F. Mullen signed a complaint before U.S. Commissioner Edwin K. Walker, charging Dillinger and Youngblood with theft and interstate transportation of an automobile, from Crown Point, Indiana, to Chicago, Illinois. A warrant was issued on the same day, and went to the hands of the U.S. Marshal in Chicago, Illinois. From that moment on, Dillinger became the primary concern of the nation.

His unknown female companion, likewise, came under scrutiny. The newspapers published half-baked accounts of the jailhouse conversation in numbers, provoking new leads in the search for the elusive "Mrs. Dillinger." Her obscure, numerical tongue fed the mystique developing around her. Out of the squad of amateur detectives came George Howard of Indianapolis, a "reporter and finger printer." He mailed his theories to the Justice Department. Requesting that his name be "kept dark," he wrote:

> Think just what this baby is—had this in the World War and this is my tip to you. 'The car was found' I think is

> around 50 or 5000. 'I love' [*sic*] is 3507. If the guards would tell more of her talk, you can get your men hot on the job.

While providing comic relief, Mr. Howard symbolized a vision of Mr. Citizen that was starting to emerge. As a one-man crime-stopper, he echoed the thoughts of many:

". . . and the jail picture, disgrace. The friendly photo of Dillinger and Estill . . . this is the SOS call. One finger down . . . and three fingers folded up. Look at it."

Letters such as these deluged newspapers and law-enforcement offices, written by self-styled detectives, preachers, and moralists.

Back at Crown Point, Sheriff Holley began her slow descent into the act of taking the fall. Her behavior was charted, dissected, and maligned at every opportunity. Her subsequent statements were misinterpreted. She lacked the public relations skills so aptly employed by Matt Leach and Louis Piquett, who were seasoned at handling reporters. In answering the press' queries with self-examination and honesty, she appeared inexperienced. Sheriff Holley became an instant and convenient scapegoat. She debated with Judge William J. Murray, of the Lake County Circuit Court. The published piece reflected well on Judge Murray. While it lent him much-needed credibility, it denied vindication to Mrs. Holley. *Chicago Tribune* Reporter Virginia Gardner wrote it up like a fashion page.

"Mrs. Holley," she purred, "had large hollows under her eyes." The article made note of her "blanched face devoid of softening makeup." Even the sheriff's shoulders became an issue, defined as "slight and satin clad, yet erect."

In spite of the desecration, Holley, the "wiry little woman sheriff," continued to perform with objectivity.

"I'm not a sissy. I can take it on the chin. But I feel that I'm getting the blame for this just because I'm a woman. I can't see where I was at fault."

During the course of the interview she bantered back and forth with Judge Murray, who glossed over his multitude of bad decisions in the case. Murray was bending under the criticism of his previous denial of a petition that would have removed Dillinger from the Crown Point jail for the surer security of Michigan City. Robert Estill had petitioned Murray for permission to remove Dillinger during his trial. The judge had denied Estill's petition saying, "the Lake County jail is strong enough to hold him." In his own defense, he invoked an old ordinance that withheld his power to order a removal unless the prisoner was threatened by mob violence.

Holley: "I think there was yellowness. I can't say what I would have done under the circumstance, but you'd think that one of the men Dillinger locked up, before he came downstairs, and got the machine guns, would have known the cells were searched the day before, that he couldn't have had a gun, and would have taken a chance. I think I would have."

Murray: "No one could blame those boys or call them yellow, as nearly everyone would have done likewise in their places."

Holley: "Dillinger took one chance in a million."

She explained that she took the job to avenge the death of her husband. Roy Holley had been a dentist, practicing in Hammond and Gary, who was commissioned to act as sheriff, when he was killed in the line of duty. Apparently, the custom of putting civilians into law-enforcement jobs at Crown Point had been in place before Lillian Holley stepped into her official capacity.

The reporter, herself a woman struggling in a male-dominated profession, responded by asking a preposterous question.

"Have you now realized the job is too big for a woman?"

"Oh, hell's fire! Of course not," Mrs. Holley retorted. "Everything went smoothly when we had 'Fur' Sammons here, and other prisoners who were tough," she remonstrated.

"How this could have happened, I don't yet see."

The Democratic Board of County Commissioners of Lake County met for the reported purpose of demanding the resignation of Sheriff Holley, for what they called neglect of duty. They launched an investigation, conducted by Robert Estill and Edward Barce, Assistant Attorney General of Indiana.

"Plain laxity was responsible for Dillinger's escape," said Board President Charles Baran. Curiously, nobody pushed for the resignation of Warden Baker. The warden, once he was released from the cell that

Sheriff Lillian Holley took responsibility for the "Wooden Gun" escape, unwittingly shielding the men behind the conspiracy. (William J. Helmer)

he'd been locked into by Dillinger, had given out the wrong license plate number, thereby assuring Dillinger's triumphant return to Chicago. But the board focused on the manner in which the jail had been run under Sheriff Holley, claiming that the ease with which Dillinger intimidated the guards was held to be *prima facie* evidence of laxity in the jail. The structure had been manned largely by trustees, marginal people placed prematurely into positions of trust.

Mrs. Holley commented on Ernest Blunk. He was "a weakling." The caustic remark was her only lapse from objectivity. Yet her insider's perspective continued to backfire, fueling the contagious feeding frenzy. Most reports erroneously had her in a constant state of morbid collapse.

The Democratic stronghold at Crown Point was precarious. Only four years prior, the Democrats had grabbed control from the Republicans. The two key issues under the Holleys had been the conviction and imprisonment of gangster James "Fur" Sammons in the fall of 1933. The next triumph, that of the success of county officials in getting custody of Dillinger, had confirmed a victory in the upcoming election. Now a split in the doomed Democratic ticket had developed. It would have included Judge Murray, Robert Estill, and Carroll Holley, the nephew of Roy Holley and incumbent Chief Deputy. The winning ticket was ripped in half by the escape.

Judge Murray soon fired his hand-picked grand jury, with the purpose of impaneling a new one. He also fired his former associate Robert Estill and appointed former Circuit Judge Martin J. Smith as special assistant prosecutor in charge of the new grand jury's investigation.

Rumors began to circulate. Editors at the *Chicago Tribune* circulated an interoffice memo stating that Dillinger had "greased" his way out of Crown Point with $3,500 in bribes. With no solid evidence, they withheld publication of the allegation. Louis Piquett, the suspected go-between, stepped in to cast light away from the idea of a bribe.

"Dillinger said he could win his way free with a toy pistol," he stated.

Captain Timothy O'Neill, of the East Chicago Police Department, was next granted permission by Governor McNutt to make an independent investigation of the jailbreak. O'Neill, who would go on to join the posse who would ultimately bring Dillinger to his death, was joined on March 18 by Sergeant Martin Zarkovich. They formed a questionable alliance in the climate of the escape. It is to be remembered that Dillinger had gone directly to East Chicago, Indiana, after his release from Michigan City, to benefit from the wide-open protection of an underground economy. The graft that proliferated in East Chicago was directly accountable, and protected, by the corrupt police department operating under Sonny Sheetz. So chilling was the presence of O'Neill and Zarkovich in Crown Point that former associates backed off. Judge Murray, who emphatically denied any favors or clemency on the part of Lake County toward the organized crime syndicate of East Chicago, denounced Zarkovich's presence at Crown Point as puzzling.

"[Zarkovich] practically wore a path between the grand jury room and Estill's office," Murray observed. Robert Estill, not wishing further affront to his dead career, stepped up to explain why he needed the East Chicago police: Zarkovich was an "ace detective." He continued to clarify that Zarkovich was not his chief investigator. That job was filled by James Regan, former chief of the East Chicago police. The police secret was that "certain" East Chicago policemen had made a deal with Louis Piquett and Arthur O'Leary to get the guns into the prison, for a price of $3,500. The meeting place had been either a saloon on Main Street, two blocks from the jail, or a bar in East Chicago.

Indiana Attorney General Philip Lutz Jr. stepped in to say that he hoped government investigators would take charge of the probe into the escape. He was afraid that the prosecution would be handled by Robert Estill, or some other person appointed by Judge Murray.

Then the federal government took the reigns in the hope of stopping the infighting. They entered on orders of U.S. District Attorney James R. Fleming at Fort Wayne, assigning an inspector to investigate Blunk's connection with the escape. Fleming pointed out that the Dyer Act, the theft of a car over state lines, would be brought in to prosecute Blunk, if it could be proved that he helped in the theft of the car.

Lutz then turned up information that Blunk, now suspended and out on a $2,000 bond, had locked a special guard in a cell right before Dillinger appeared in the corridor carrying a machine gun. Matt Brown, eighty-four years old, one of the special guards placed around the jail, had testified that Blunk led him down a jail corridor and locked a cell door on him "before I realized I had been decoyed into the cell."

Judge Murray, in spite of his patronizing attitude toward Lillian Holley, remained one of her few remaining defenders.

"She employed Lew [*sic*] Baker, a responsible and reliable person, as Warden," he commended. "She did her duty."

Sheriff Holley would repeat that she had personally searched Evelyn Frechette, to the point of removing the woman's clothing. Holly had strongly opposed the February 19 visit by Meyer Bogue, whom Piquett called "the alibi witness" in Dillinger's defense. When Holley and Estill refused to allow Bogue entry, Piquett appealed to Judge Murray. Murray had signed an order for Bogue and explained thus:

"I thought there was no harm in that so long as Bogue was searched and somebody was watching and there was a screen between him and Dillinger," he later told the Grand Jury.

It would be intimated that Piquett had paid a bribe. During his trial for harboring Dillinger and Homer Van Meter, which would take place two years later, four witnesses from Lake County would be called to testify: Holley, Saager, Baker, and Blunk would be subpoened based on Piquett's visits to Crown Point with Meyer Bogue. Judge Murray, of the Circuit Court at Crown Point, who refused to transfer Dillinger from the jail to prison, was never again questioned.

The bitterness of Mrs. Holley was understandable and apparent.

"If I ever see John Dillinger again, I'll shoot him dead with my own pistol. I have finally turned fatalist . . . I tried so hard to make good, but I just couldn't make it. And I wanted to be the ideal woman sheriff, too." Her self-effacement was complete.

"Don't blame anyone else for this escape," she said. "Blame me. I have no political career ahead of me and I don't care."[6]

The "lovely woman" had just taken the fall for the suspected collusion of Murray, Estill, and Baker at the top. She offered a buffer for Cahoon, Blunk, and Saager on the lower end of the conspiracy. In the Crown Point escape, she was victimized by three factors:

- her self-effacing series of quotes, which were embellished by the press;
- her forced deference to male colleagues;
- public sentiment, which denied the effectiveness of women in law enforcement.

Sheriff Lillian Holley would resign on New Year's Day, 1935, to give the sheriff's job to her nephew, Carroll Holley. He would go on to hold the post for the next four years.

The odd parallel that had brought Lillian Holley into play with Evelyn Frechette would continue to effect their mutual transformation. If Evelyn Frechette had been reduced to a substandard consort to a fugitive, Lillian Holley was diminished to a mincing, ineffectual girl tripping through the boys' game of cops and robbers.

*"Where is that gun? They play with it—now I want to play with it."*

*—Jessie Levy,*
*Trial of Charles Makley,*
*Lima, Ohio,*
*March 12–17, 1934*

# Squarest Woman He Ever Knew

Mary Kinder arrived in Indianapolis under the guard of fingerprint expert Marie Grott. Representatives of the press tried to interview Mary, hoping to set up a tabloid prototype of "Gangland's Queen." She still held the remnants of her wardrobe in the dirty pillowcase from the prison laundry.

The state had hoped for a grand jury indictment implicating her in the Michigan City escape. This, too, fizzled like a damp firecracker. On February 9, her attorney made a motion to quash the indictment, saying that the charges did not constitute a public offense. With no evidence with which to place her among the Michigan City conspirators, the Indianapolis Grand Jury dismissed the charges of aiding the escape on February 15. In the vain hope that some evidence would turn up, possibly through an informer, the state of Indiana held her until the end of the month.

On the last day of February, the Indiana Grand Jury, facing the limitations of state jurisdiction, released her for lack of evidence.

"If you're dumb you'll go back to the gang and end up in jail a long time," Judge Frank P. Baker cautioned her.

"I spent twenty-eight days in jail," Mary later told the press. "When I got out on February 28 I was lost. All my friends were locked up. My sweetheart was going to trial for murder. I didn't have a job . . . I had to go back . . . to my mother in Indianapolis."

Mary brought the plagues and locusts to Viola Paterson's house. Both the local police and federal agents knocked at any hour of the day or night for months afterwards. The backlash affected her estranged husband, who was serving time at Michigan City. Dale Kinder was transferred out just as Pierpont, Makley, and Clark went into solitary there. Kinder, with whom Mary had dropped all contact, would finish out his twelve-year sentence for bank robbery at the state farm at Putnamville.

"Three days after I went home," Mary later wrote, "Dillinger broke out of the Crown Point jail, and the cops headed straight for my place." Unknown to Mary, she'd been implicated further by former gang member Ed Shouse.

"If Dillinger were to go to Indianapolis," he told Michigan City officials, "[Dillinger] would immediately contact Mary Kinder . . . [she] would be the first person Dillinger would go to if he were not in Chicago," he confirmed in an interview with the warden.

Upon her release from jail, Mary went straight to the office of Bessie Robbins and Jessie Levy, at 928 Circle Tower Building. Jessie Levy, the old family retainer who'd handled Pierpont's 1925 defense in New Harmony, was a pioneer in her own right. Born in 1898, she studied law, and obtained her degree, in an era offering few opportunities for female lawyers. Now she would defend first-degree murder charges in Lima. The defendants' families had no money with which to launch a strong defense, and Jessie Levy was ill-equipped to help her clients "beat the chair." She would defend the three with a combination of courtroom histrionics and an alibi with as much substance as a baloney sandwich.

Agents from the Justice Department placed a wire tap on Levy's telephone, which allowed them to listen to the calls coming in hourly from both Mary Kinder and Opal Long, as well as Lena Pierpont. The three women were near hysteria. A conviction of first-degree murder made the death sentence mandatory. The only exception would be a jury's recommendation of mercy.[1]

Mary Kinder, the "Queen of Gangland." (Paul Gallo)

In Lima, the quality of mercy was quite strange. An Oxbow sense of frontier justice permeated the streets teaming with National Guardsmen. On March 6, Pierpont went on trial before Judge R.E. Everett. Lena held Pierpont's manacled hand throughout the trial. Less sympathetic was Mark Robbins, one of the Tucson policemen who captured Pierpont in Tucson.

"Dillinger is personally a coward," he said. "But not Pierpont. He is the real tough fellow of the gang."

Harry Pierpont would indeed appear in multiple guises during the next three weeks. He was tough but loved his mother. He was the Trigger Man, the leader of the Terror Gang. In his svelte, handsome appearance and decisive testimony, he dazzled the crowd that had come to see him condemned to die.

The prosecuting attorney, Ernest Botkin, would hasten in several key pieces of evidence that resulted in a guilty plea without the redemptive recommendation for mercy.

His opening statement, that Pierpont had been carrying Sheriff Sarber's small-barreled revolver, led the way for the damning testimony from the Tucson arresting officers that they had relieved Pierpont of his victim's service revolver.

"You carried that gun as a memento of the dastardly murder you committed, didn't you?" suggested Botkin.

"A man who carried that gun would have a lot of brains, wouldn't he?" Pierpont retorted.

"Now in Tucson," Botkin continued, "you had some guns on you when you were arrested?"

"Yes, two."

"And you would have used them?"

"I never have yet. I might have tried to bluff my way out. I probably should have had a wooden pistol."

"How did you manipulate the Michigan City prison escape?" Botkin asked in a wild-card attempt to implicate Mary Kinder.

"Well, I'll tell you," said Pierpont, fully aware of the intention behind the question.

"Through sources that I do not care to state, I received three pistols on September 26," he teased. "I asked several men if they would like to leave. They said yes.

"About 1:00 I went around to them in the shop and said to them, 'All right, if you want to go now and take a chance, we'll go.'

"There were ten of us. We ran into an assistant deputy warden. I lined him up with some of the other officials there. I was the third man in this line. I think John Hamilton was first. We each had a bundle of shirts in our arms.

"We walked forward to the large lobby and the first gate was opened. This was a violation of the rules. The gates are not supposed to be opened when a convict is in sight.

"Those gates were opened either by order or by mistake. There were a number of officers and policemen between this gate and the next one. Some of them cried and bawled and dropped on the floor.

"A sheriff was driving up with some prisoners at the time, and four of the boys took the car and the sheriff. The other six ran across the highway. I stopped a car and told the passengers to get out. I waited for the others and then drove away.

"I used money to get those pistols in the prison—also cooperation," he inferred in conclusion.

"Did the officials of the prison get that money?" asked the prosecutor.

"I don't care to state that."

None of the dramatic content of the testimony, however, could match the outrage generated when the Don Sarber, the twenty-four-year-old son of the slain sheriff, told the courtroom that he'd come home from a vacation to find is father bleeding on the floor and his mother locked in a cell.

Jessie Levy then tried to distance Pierpont by implicating Harry Copeland, who was facing charges in Indiana on the Greencastle holdup of the previous October. She asked Sarber's son if the man described as Harry Copeland had been the "trigger man." The cause of death had been established that Sarber died from the blow to his head delivered by Makley, yet Levy continued on the track of trying to divert the blame for the abdominal bullet wound.

Other testimony was given by the two witnesses to the murder. Deputy Sheriff Sharp and Lucy Sarber pieced together the identification of Pierpont as the killer. Sharp had been the attendant on duty that night who had tried to release Mrs. Sarber from her prison cell.

The icing on Pierpont's poison cake walked in with his head shaved and finger pointing. Ed Shouse testified that Pierpont had told him he'd killed the sheriff. Brought in for the occasion in a bulletproof automobile, Shouse endured Pierpont's curled lip and arrogant stare.

Ed Shouse returned to the Solitary and Seclusion hole in Michigan City. Harry Copeland occupied a similar cell. Attorney Bess Robbins, who worked with Jessie Levy, had dug up a forgotten Indiana law forbidding the extradition of any prisoner against whom charges were pending in another state. Since he was wanted in Indiana on bank robbery charges for the Greencastle job, the law was used to block his extradition to Ohio. This law kept both Copeland and Shouse in Indiana.

The defense staff issued their alibi that Pierpont was in his mother's house in Liepsic at the time of the jail delivery. It was useless. After fifty-five minutes of deliberation on the morning of March 11, the jury found Pierpont guilty of first-degree murder and did not recommend mercy. In the ensuing excitement, rumors that Mary Kinder was rushing to the scene from Indianapolis began to circulate.

Charles Makley went on trial after Pierpont. His sisters sat in on the proceedings, which commenced on March 12. In their solid familial presence, Florence and Mildred, who'd traveled from Kansas, hoped to lend credence to the dinner-time defense.

Other inferences rounded out the defense. Levy made it a point to say that Botkin was more interested in his reelection than at establishing the truth. She picked up Sheriff Sarber's service revolver.

"Where is that gun? They play with it—now I want to play with it," Levy cried dramatically.

Makley's trial was conducted in a similar manner to Pierpont's. The same witnesses came up to testify, with the exception of Shouse, who refused to return to Lima. The court established that Makley had taken Sarber's gun and struck him on the head in one or two blows, and then forced Mrs. Sarber to get the keys to the jail. Like Pierpont, he was found guilty on March 17 of murder without a recommendation of mercy. His sisters sobbed loudly in the courtroom.

He faced the wailing wall.

"Don't worry," he told his sisters, "everything will be all right."

Russell Clark, third on the match, was ironically spared. He was extricated, in part, by the image of his seventy-year-old mother, Mae Clark, who left her house in Detroit with her daughter, Beulah, and son-in-law, Andy. Both testified that Clark had been having dinner with her at the time of the murder. If the jury had been somewhat numbed by the repetition of the dinner-time defense, it may have felt waves of sympathy for Mrs. Clark, who was powerless to stop the criminal behavior of her handsome, ruined son.

On March 24, after Levy unsuccessfully petitioned for a retrial based on the fact that the jury believed in capital punishment and Clark did not, he was granted the coveted recommendation for mercy with the pronouncement of guilty. This obligated the court to pronounce a sentence of life imprisonment.

The verdict was delivered in a climatic atmosphere. Just the day before, Matt Leach had come from Port Huron, Michigan. There he had helped to identify Herbert Youngblood, Dillinger's African-American partner in the Crown Point escape. Youngblood had been loitering in a general store, bragging about his part in the Crown Point escape. Understandably, his moments with Dillinger had been too good to keep to himself. Word filtered to Sheriff Van Antwerp, Undersheriff Charles Cavanaugh, and Deputy Howard Lohr. When they arrived and shot at Youngblood, he returned fire. Van Antwerp and Lohr fell, seriously wounded. Charles Cavanaugh was mortally wounded and died shortly afterward.

Youngblood was taken to the hospital. As the orderlies washed his face, they discovered that it was deeply scared; burnt cork had covered the disfiguration. This gave rise to the rumor that Dillinger was traveling unnoticed around the country, his features disguised in the burnt cork and "black face" of minstrel shows.

Leach got his due respect in Lima. Louis Piquett, who arrived with Esther Anderson, his secretary, was given the state equivalent of the bum's rush. Amid rumors that the married Piquett was engaging in lewd behavior with Esther Anderson in a hotel room, the Ohio National Guard threw the couple into jail before escorting them out of town. Piquett did manage to confer with Levy and attorney Clarence Miller. Goaded by the pleas of Opal Long, Mary Kinder, and Lena Pierpont, he left money. Mrs. Pierpont slipped him a letter earmarked for Dillinger.

*". . . In the face of what is happening over there at Lima, it is making it harder and harder for Harry here, and we*

*should act quickly. I think if you will talk this over with the fellows, they will realize that Harry has been fair all the way through and wants to continue to be and that they will be willing to help you to help him . . . See what you can do because things are getting hotter for Harry every minute. Sincerely"*

The letter was unsigned.

With the jury still out on Clark, Pierpont was brought, clanking and cuffed, into court to hear the death sentence pronounced. Judge Everett overruled motions for new trials and set the date for July 13. Back in the pen, Makley and Pierpont spun the yarns of their common fate philosophically.

"Unlucky 13 again," said Pierpont.

"Well," added Makley, "you can only die once."

Simultaneously, Clark's verdict came in. White-faced, he leaned heavily on Jessie Levy as the foreman spared his life.

Through the hysteria of the trial, Mary Kinder was said to be lurking in every corner. While the sightings were reported in Ohio, Mary was in Chicago, where she met with Evelyn Frechette and Opal Long. From there she traveled to Indianapolis, to see Hubert Dillinger and Audrey Hancock. She deliberately avoided the laser beam of Lima. It was now crucial to lay low as a mole.[2]

Dillinger had just pulled off two bank robberies, performed in rapid succession at Mason City, Iowa, and Sioux Falls, South Dakota. As with his earlier bank jobs before Tucson, the women lined up for their pin money. With Pierpont, Makley, and Clark disenfranchised, the need for cash took on crisis proportions. The legal bills mounted for both the trials and forthcoming appeals. After sentencing, Opal Long prayed for the type of fix she believed had sprung Dillinger from Crown Point.

A change had come. Before Tucson, a cult of self-adornment had engulfed Opal Long and Mary Kinder. Now the two women adopted a new philosophy of utilitarianism. No more would they covet jeweled watches and furs, pockets stuffed with thousands of dollars. The conviction forced Mary to reevaluate her direction. On a personal level, Mary vowed to fight her growing reliance upon alcohol. She tried to stop drinking. The adrenaline rush she'd known in the days of the jack-hammer escape was gone. Replacing it was the low-grade fever, the grinding pace of the law.

The three prisoners were taken during the last week of March, under heavily armed motorcade, to Death Row in the State Penitentiary at Columbus, Ohio. They were accompanied by Chet Sherman, the Tucson policeman who had helped to bring them in.

"Once inside the prison they were meek as lambs," said Sherman. "I was surprised that such a change could come over men. Pierpont almost collapsed. He was crying. Clark, as usual, had nothing to say. Makley's demeanor appeared unchanged, but he was quiet."[3]

Right after the transfer to Columbus, Pierpont pencilled a letter to Mary. He scrawled it on a carbon copy of the appeal. Mrs. Levy tucked the smudged love letter among her folders and clipboards, and delivered it to Mary Kinder.[4]

> *"Dear Sweet,*
>
> *A few more lines. I'm glad about the puppies, Dear. You remember they named one after Johnie and it brought him luck. Maybe it will us. Tell John that an address on Addison Street is Hot. I don't know whose it is. Also a woman by name of Evelyn Spark or E. Foshetti. I never heard of her but you tell him he might not know. You wrote of Marge, Dear. Tell her I'm still alive and "Old Father Time" has not given up. I got the medal, Sweetheart, only thing I have that you gave me. I'm glad you got your clothes, Honey, but Sweet, do you think best to spend time & money going to Tucson? I think, Dear, you can do more good here as short as time is. You must excuse this writing, Dear, as pencil is short and cell is pitch dark at all times. I've not seen any papers and only picture I saw of you was the one Jessie brought of you and her in her office. But 'Butter Ball' you are not too fat and when I get out there you better be weighing 100, or I'll be the one to spank. I know you have kept your promise, Sweet. You can truthfully say Dear that you never lied to me. Mac has said 1000 times that I had the squarest woman he ever knew. He and B. say hello and that they were depending on you. You have someone you can*

*trust to get 2 .32 Colt automatics & a box of shells and take them with you to Mother's. I expect I'll have to call on you to order me a newspaper & some magazines, Dear. I'll let you know later. We wear our own clothes in death row down there I hear so try to locate Mac's trunk and anything else you can. Tell your Mother I love her for having a daughter as sweet as you. Ans. this just as if you received it through regular channels. They won't know the difference down there. Love and Kisses to the One & Only 'My Marry'.*

*Pete"*

# Part II

# Flash Powder

## March 1934 – May 1934

L to R: Opal Long, Patricia Cherrington, and Jean Burke. June, 1934. (Author's Collection)

---

"Perhaps the best diagnosis of a gun Moll is that she is a woman who wants what she has done nothing to deserve."

*J. Edgar Hoover*
*Director, FBI*

*"Evelyn Frechette and Opal Long are very chummy and closed to outsiders."*

*—Mr. and Mrs. Wilson,*
*Mae Clark's boarders,*
*Detroit, March 1934*

# Paramour

While Mary Kinder dodged the spotlight, Evelyn Frechette remained anonymous for one short week after Dillinger's Crown Point escape.

Encouraged by the progress made with informant Ed Shouse, Federal Agent T.F. Mullen entered Michigan City on March 9. Mullen traveled to Michigan City under orders of Melvin Purvis, Special Agent in Charge of the Chicago Field Office.

Shouse cracked the identity of "Mrs. Dillinger" in a terse interview laced with questions that ranged from the irrelevant to the integral.

Mullen: "Where do you think Dillinger would have been likely to go after his escape from Crown Point?"

Shouse: "Bill Davis, or his wife, on the West side." It was a reference to a connection who was to go on trial for a speakeasy murder. "He'd no doubt get in touch with Dewey and Pearl Elliott. Both of these people are very friendly with the Dillinger gang, and they both reside in Chicago. . . Dillinger might also contact Ann Martin, his girl, but Ann Martin is not her correct name."

Mullen held his breath. She was so close, he could taste her. Shouse continued:

"She is known to the gang as Billie. She is said to come from Wisconsin, and is the wife of a man by the name of Fancette, [*sic*] or some similar name, who is at present serving a sentence in the Leavenworth Penitentiary in connection with theft of some money being forwarded through the mails . . . A man by the name of Cherington or a similar name, is also serving a sentence in the Leavenworth Penitentiary, and Cherington is a pal of Fancette . . . Cherrington's wife had a sister named Opal Long, who was the girlfriend of Russell Clark."

Opal Long had already been identified at Tucson. In that moment, it all clicked. Opal Long and Pat Cherrington were sisters. Pat Cherrington was an associate of the "wife of Fancette."

The agents immediately contacted Leavenworth and in short order linked the two inmates, Art Cherrington and Welton Spark, as having been co-defendants in the action that had sentenced them to prison. They named Evelyn under this misspelled composition:

". . . one EVELYN FASCHETTI alias Spark alias MRS. WILLIAM Spark, the alleged wife of Wilton Spark, Leavenworth Penitentiary number 42165."

The composite was put together by Special Agent Jay C. Newman of the Chicago Division office and Sergeant Harry Newman of Captain John Stege's squad. Evelyn was found on Spark's mailing list at Leavenworth to be residing at Neopit, Wisconsin; and at 901 Addison Street and 911 Brompton Place, Chicago.

A request was then issued to Special Agent Endres in Tucson to retrieve the fingerprints and photo card of Ann Martin. He sent them via special delivery airmail from Tucson to Washington, DC and Chicago, where they were classified under the name "Evelyn Frechette alias Ann Martin."

The agents, exalted with the finished product, presented their Bride of Frankenstein to Lillian Holley and Robert Estill at Crown Point for positive identification as "Mrs. Dillinger." Shouse was also shown the picture.

An Identification and Apprehension Order was issued. Two thousand copies would be sent out within the next two weeks. In was drafted to contain her fingerprints, description, budding criminal record, and known relatives in Neopit and Chicago.

Unaware, the elusive Billie was enjoying a deceptive period of security with her man. There was a frightening quality to her coupling with Dillinger. To her, it felt more treacherous than it had before Tucson. In the past, he had shown exuberance in the controlled crime spree of 1933. The experiences of the recent months had seemed reckless in comparison. She needed the allusion of a sober man, someone who could chase away the tremors of uncertainty. Her drinking problem was escalating as a result of the constant stress.

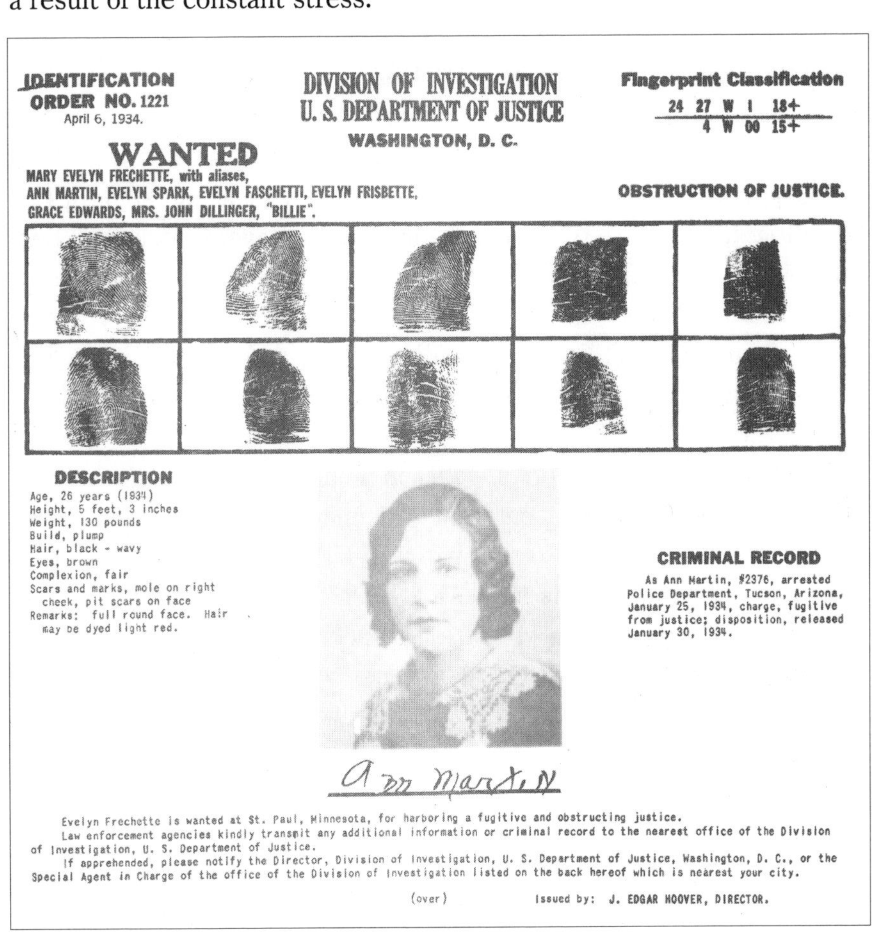

IDENTIFICATION ORDER NO. 1221
April 6, 1934.

DIVISION OF INVESTIGATION
U. S. DEPARTMENT OF JUSTICE
WASHINGTON, D. C.

Fingerprint Classification
24 27 W I 18+
4 W 00 15+

WANTED

MARY EVELYN FRECHETTE, with aliases,
ANN MARTIN, EVELYN SPARK, EVELYN FASCHETTI, EVELYN FRISBETTE,
GRACE EDWARDS, MRS. JOHN DILLINGER, "BILLIE".

OBSTRUCTION OF JUSTICE.

DESCRIPTION

Age, 26 years (1934)
Height, 5 feet, 3 inches
Weight, 130 pounds
Build, plump
Hair, black - wavy
Eyes, brown
Complexion, fair
Scars and marks, mole on right cheek, pit scars on face
Remarks: full round face. Hair may be dyed light red.

CRIMINAL RECORD

As Ann Martin, #2376, arrested Police Department, Tucson, Arizona, January 25, 1934, charge, fugitive from justice; disposition, released January 30, 1934.

Ann Martin

Evelyn Frechette is wanted at St. Paul, Minnesota, for harboring a fugitive and obstructing justice.

Law enforcement agencies kindly transmit any additional information or criminal record to the nearest office of the Division of Investigation, U. S. Department of Justice.

If apprehended, please notify the Director, Division of Investigation, U. S. Department of Justice, Washington, D. C., or the Special Agent in Charge of the office of the Division of Investigation listed on the back hereof which is nearest your city.

(over) Issued by: J. EDGAR HOOVER, DIRECTOR.

Justice Dept. Agents released Frechette's Identification Order shortly after Dillinger's escape from Crown Point County Jail. It would mark her public debut. (Author's Collection)

She now had to stay away from her family and her home. Both she and Patsy were forced to miss a family funeral. A distant relative posed a real threat, in the person of a detective who had married her aunt. Frank Bauler of the 1st District Station at South Market Street, Chicago, had made it clear that he would collar Dillinger if he "as much as showed up at the Reservation." During the funeral, the common talk revolved around Evelyn, the definitive black sheep of the family. In careful whispers, they passed the news: Their native daughter ran around with the notorious John Dillinger. Evelyn had been a favorite subject of gossip for years.

With the Reservation no longer a potential hideout, Evelyn joined Opal Long in early March at the Detroit home of Russell Clark's mother, Mae Clark.[1]

With Evelyn relatively safe in Detroit, Dillinger raced into St. Paul. His priority, to find the underworld person he could trust the most, brought him to his old friends, Homer Van Meter and John Hamilton. He was happy to see Van, and he dropped to his knees at the sight of Red Hamilton. It was more than their common prison history that lent them relief at the reunion. Van Meter would re-introduce Dillinger to the connections that Piquett had made for him while he remained in Crown Point: Tommy Carroll, Eugene "Eddie" Green, and Lester "Baby Face Nelson" Gillis. They operated in St. Paul under the protection of Harry "Dutch" Sawyer.

Dillinger's new gang were shoots and branches of the St. Paul underworld who had, in the recent past, frequented a saloon operated by Daniel "Dapper Danny" Hogan, who was killed five years earlier by a bomb placed in his car. His successor, Harry Sawyer, operated St. Paul as a safe haven by paying protection to people on all levels, from the highest government down to local law enforcement. He was the contact man for all elements of the criminal underworld operating in the Twin Cities. Sawyer was a crime boss of epic reputation in St. Paul. Van Meter's acquaintance with Sawyer was the decisive event of his criminal career.

The man he introduced to Dillinger, Eddie Green, was a local with a long record and a devoted mother who lived in St. Paul. He lived in a monogamous relationship with a woman who smelled the danger in people like Van Meter. Van Meter, with his girlfriend Marie "Mickey"

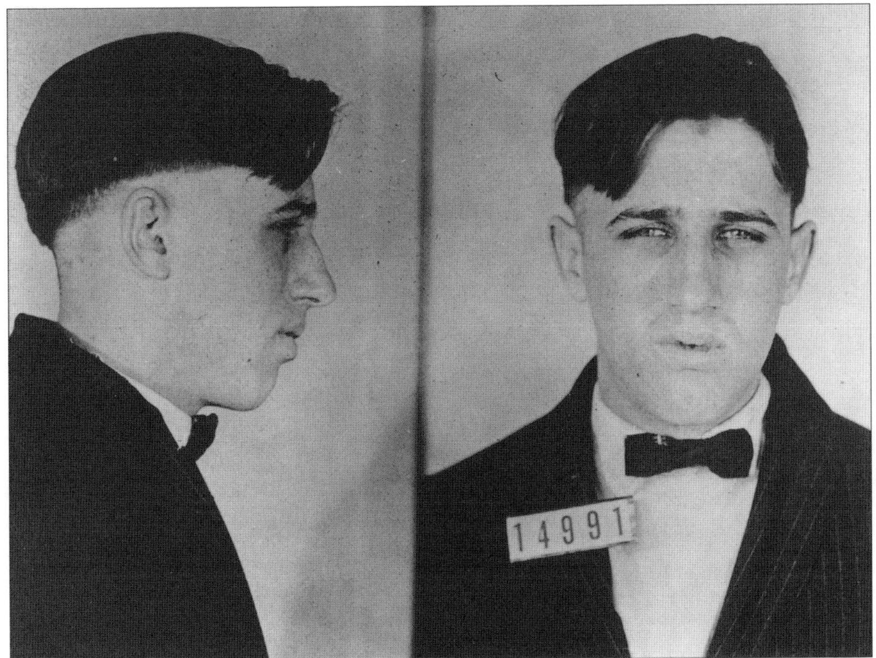


Homer Van Meter stayed close to Marie Comforti during her hospitalization in St. Paul. (National Archives)

Comforti, had been hanging out with the Greens and another couple, with whom they'd spent the previous summer.

Lester "Baby Face Nelson" Gillis had spent sporadic summer nights in a rented summer cottage at Long Beach, Indiana, during June 1933. The house had been hidden in between Stops 17 and 18 in the vacation spot known as the "Indiana Dunes." Lester and Mrs. Gillis, as "Mr. And Mrs. Jimmy Williams," had rented the cottage with the help of a priest.

Father P.W. Coughlan lived in Wilmette, north of Chicago, when he wasn't making deals while garbed in the Roman collar. He presented the impeccable image needed by sleazy underworld characters. In doing so, he dazzled Mrs. Gillis. A Polish Catholic, she trusted and depended on him. Gillis came to Father Coughlin by way of a previous introduction. He'd met the priest at the Oak Park Hospital through Tommy Touhy, who was being touted in the newspapers as "Terrible Tommy Touhy." When Tommy Touhy went into the Oak Park Hospital in June, 1933, Roger Touhy visited his brother there. Father Coughlan, who visited Touhy in the hospital, introduced Touhy, a Capone rival, to Baby Face

Nelson. Later, when Roger Touhy went on trial in the bogus kidnapping of Jake "The Barber" Factor, he denied ever meeting Baby Face Nelson. Upon leaning that Baby Face had wanted to rent a cottage, Father Coughlan agreed to accompany him to the Long Beach Realty Company. The broker, happy to do business with a man-of-the-cloth, accepted a down payment of $400 rent. Almost immediately, the house had filled up with Chuck Fisher, Earl and Hazel Doyle, Eddie Bentz, Tommy Gannon, Van Meter, Marie Comforti, Tommy Carroll and Jean Delaney Crompton. They were not divinity students, in spite of the good impression made by Father Coughlan; they came to plan a bank job.

The odd triad of Dillinger, Van Meter, and Gillis had formed back in May and June of 1933, between East Chicago, Indiana, where Dillinger met Gillis on May 25, and St. Paul, where Van Meter was introduced at the Commodore Hotel between June 9 and 22, 1933.

Dillinger had been put off by Gillis' volatile nature in the easy-living days after his parole. He was not so independent since he'd lost his gang in Tucson. Having no other choice, he was forced to work with Gillis. He owed Baby Face "some kind of debt," he said, and hoped to distance himself from Gillis after paying it off. Gillis had gifted Piquett with funding to pay the bribe that released Dillinger from Crown Point. Dillinger had inadvertently sold his soul to a petty tyrant: He never broke free of Gillis' grip.

Violent and intolerant, Gillis had hung out in San Francisco and Sausalito with John Paul Chase, and had been running liquor in northern California with Joseph Raymond "Fatso" Negri prior to the repeal of Prohibition Laws. Gillis had been staying in San Francisco with John Paul "Johnny" Chase in January 1934, calling himself James Rogers. Chase and Gillis were oddly inseparable. When Nelson came to St. Paul, Chase came up from Sausalito and San Francisco. There he stayed in Gillis' shadow.

The other member of the fledgling gang was Tommy Carroll. In contrast to Eugene "Eddie" Green, who was devoted to his common-law wife, Bessie, Carroll had wandered and womanized. The thirty-eight-year-old St. Paul bank robber was recklessly handsome at 5 feet 10 inches, with light blue eyes and dark chestnut hair. He was wanted in the murder of a San Antonio policeman that had occurred in November 1933.[2]

On March 6, 1934, Dillinger joined forces with Lester Gillis, John

Hamilton, Homer Van Meter, Eddie Green, and Tommy Carroll. They robbed the Securities National Bank at Sioux Falls, South Dakota. Gillis, always quick to use his firearms, shot policeman Hale Keith when he saw him running toward the bank. The patrons and tellers, detained in this impromptu house-of-horrors, related the incident.

The predators fled by lining the running boards of their car with innocent bystanders to protect them from gunfire. It was a remake of the Racine, Wisconsin, robbery of the previous November. The freezing, terrified hostages were hoisted upon the running boards of the cars like the dead sentries of *Beau Geste*. Nails were scattered on the roads to discourage pursuit. The take, $49,500, wetted the vampiric gang's appetite. They repeated the scenario one week later.

On March 13, the same group raided the First National Bank at Mason City, Iowa, and escaped with cash estimated at $52,000. This was a gang tough enough to endure the tear gas released by bank security guard Tom Walters, who had the advantage of a bulletproof cage. Yet the boastful experience and expertise of this group could not make up for what it lacked. There was no cohesion. With the exception of Dillinger, Hamilton and Van Meter, who had bonded through their prison experiences like college frat boys, there was no loyalty. The gentlemen's agreements of the previous gang were missing.

They had preyed upon the employees and patrons in these two institutions like terrorists. In a time when isolationist theories abounded in America, with foreigners looming as suspicious entities, the true enemy had struck from within. It seemed like danger was everywhere, from the wanton needs created by the Depression to the fear that the "public enemy" lurked around every corner.

Both Dillinger and Hamilton were shot in Sioux Falls. They got help from William Albert "Pat" Riley, who was known as Harry Sawyer's "Guy Friday." The right-hand man to the boss, Reilly brought the wounded duo to Doctor Nels G. Mortensen, the St. Paul City Health Officer. The respected physician treated them for shoulder wounds between March 13 and 15. As he cleaned them off, he suggested they "come back tomorrow." Predictably, they didn't return, and, more predictably, Dr. Mortensen failed to report the incident until authorities showed him pictures of Dillinger and Hamilton. Now he couldn't deny it. In his own defense at his suspension hearing, Mortensen claimed that he had planned to call the police upon the gangsters' expected return to his office. The underground patients skipped their follow-up visit and returned to Chicago accompanied by Van Meter and Gillis.

Enroute back to Minnesota, they stopped at "Louie's Place" for drinks and steak dinners. The proprietor, Louis Cernocky, a 300-pound Bohemian, was well regarded. He ran a contact place and hideout that drew anyone desiring to get in touch with the mob in Chicago.

The gangsters laughed when Cernocky's wife, who was as huge as he, screamed at him from the kitchen while she chopped frantically. While he lounged with the gangsters of post-Prohibition Chicago and St. Paul, Mrs. Cernocky worked a sixteen-hour day running the restaurant. The laughing stopped when Cernocky gave them the bill. He'd charged them a whopping tab of $20 a plate. They humbly paid the bill. Dillinger was anxious to return to the Twin Cities, where Evelyn waited for his return.[3]

He'd faced danger with other males in tribal circumstances. Now the primitive instinct was guiding him.

Evelyn was simply glad to get out of Detroit, where she'd been living with Opal Long. She didn't feel comfortable in the chaotic home of Mae Clark, who maintained a revolving-door policy. There were seventeen family members, with babies and toddlers in tow, joining the odd groups of people who straggled in and out at all hours.

The large, open household had also welcomed Opal Long in the aftermath of the Tucson arrests. She'd been there before, having visited in December before going to Florida. The house was a pressure cooker, with crying children, cigarettes overflowing in ashtrays, and a loud crystal set playing as whiskey glasses piled up around the sink. Opal tried to earn her keep by cleaning up the kitchen, but found that the grease had penetrated the wooden cupboards and tiles in an indelible coating. Added to the tensions inherent in an overcrowded house was the knowledge that the people residing within were being watched. The federal agents also had levied their attention on 75 Windemere, which belonged to Clark's sister, Beulah, and her husband, Andy.

Pat Cherrington, whom the agents knew as "Ann Jackson," soon joined them. It wasn't a mere social call. Sick with stomach ailments, she'd been interned in the Women's Hospital with a problem she'd explained as appendicitis. Opal had faithfully visited her sister in the hospital and was prepared to help the wandering Pat in the care of her daughter. Opal now juggled the girl's care with the responsibility of raising money for Clark's appeal.

Once inside the house, Evelyn remained very close to Opal Long, talking mainly to her and out of earshot of everyone else. The only time they left the rambling hideout was to go to the local drug store for phone calls. The house was under surveillance and they knew it. What they didn't know was that the agents had talked a married couple who lived there as lodgers, a Mr. and Mrs. Wilson, into working as informants. "Evelyn Frechette and Opal Long are very chummy and closed to outsiders," they reported.

The agents, who had rented a room across the street, watched the "gun molls" with interest. They were glimpsing a new type of female. These were women who flaunted convention and lived with men they hadn't married in an age when such an arrangement was considered immoral. With the responsibility to pen lengthy memos to the branch offices, a question arose as to the most appropriate euphemism. Someone coined the word "paramour." It stuck like the dye that plastered the heads of these women; they were at once exotic and foreign to the baffled agents.

When Evelyn and Pat left Detroit, Opal Long took over the care of Pat's daughter. She also agreed to tend Evelyn's bull pup. Opal Long said an uneasy "goodbye" to Patricia and Evelyn. She wondered if she would ever see them again.

The Boston bull pup, remembered for his mad dash around a St. Louis car showroom with John in hot pursuit, escaped from the overburdened Opal Long and ran out the door.

"I'll have to do much explaining to Evelyn when I see her," Opal ruefully told the observant Wilsons. The informants rushed to the local drug store to use the telephone.

On her rare trips outside, Opal Long bought a variety of newspapers. The *New York Journal American,* the *Chicago Tribune,* and the *Toledo Blade* were her favorites. She made her long-distance calls from the same drug store telephone that the Wilsons used in their calls to the Justice Department. Nearsighted, Opal brought a chaperon with her for better visibility.

After Evelyn left to go on to St. Paul, the Clark family vacated the house at 75 Windemere and moved in with Mae Clark at her residence at 531 Chandler Street on March 20. They hoped to lessen the police surveillance. At seventy years of age and weakened by the strain of the Lima testimony, the matriarch expressed strong disapproval of her daughters' drinking.

In spite of the chaotic atmosphere, Pat's daughter showed a remarkable resiliency. She attended the Highland Park School every day. The Justice Department sent its field agents to the school, They convinced the authorities to administer a "psychological evaluation." A Psychological Department was hastily assembled in the Highland Park Public School District for the purpose of aiding in the investigation. In this way the innocent girl was victimized twice, first by her mother's criminal associations and again by these intrusive "psychological" tests.[4]

In spite of her tender age, Pat's daughter could dodge the trick questions. In a letter to a friend, who attended the North Star School with her, she wrote,

"My mother has been in the hospital, but keep this confidential."

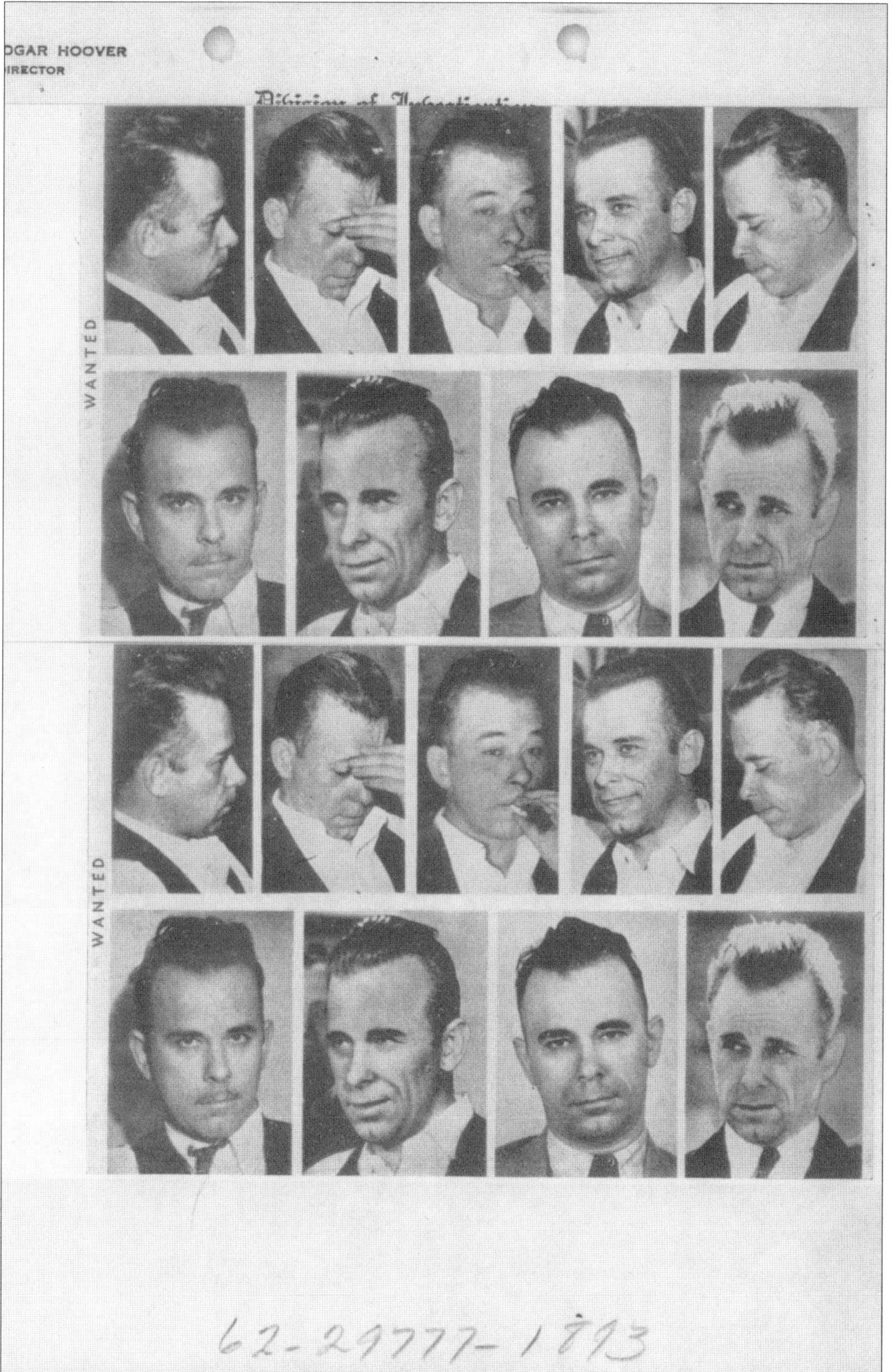

DGAR HOOVER
DIRECTOR
WANTED
WANTED
62-29777-1893

*"Bess could adjust her behavior to the situation."*

*—Myrna Otte,*
*great-niece of Bess Green*

# "On a Long, Hard Trip"

By the time she joined Dillinger in St. Paul, Evelyn Frechette was exhausted. They moved into no. 106 of the Santa Monica Apartments, 3252 Girard Avenue South, in Minneapolis, under the name "Mr. and Mrs. Irwin Olson." The apartment was situated around the corner from the home of Eddie Green and his common-law wife, Bess, at 3300 Fremont Avenue South. Dillinger's new money did nothing to help his status in the criminal community. The Greens, living under the blanket of "Mr. and Mrs. Stevens," disliked the close proximity to their new and unwelcome neighbors. They had a steady tenure in the underworld of St. Paul; by its standards, they were old family.

Eddie Green had a criminal record stretching back to his first arrest in Milwaukee in 1916 for grand larceny, which got him six months in the House of Correction. After that he served jail time intermittently from 1921 through 1923, when his fortunes brought him to an indeterminate term for robbery in the first degree. He had lived with Bess since 1932, first in St. Paul, then Chicago, then back to Minneapolis. Bess was eleven years older than Green, who was twenty-five. At thirty-six years of age, Bess had extensive underworld connections. Her living arrangement was unique in that she managed to keep her gang-related life separate from her young son, Skippy. According to Bess' great-niece, Myrna Otte, "Bess could adjust her behavior to the situation." Her versatility had shielded her son from the life she led.

She was born Bessie Hinds in North Dakota, on June 28, 1898. Myrna Otte's family history reveals that Aunt Bess "was the only daughter of a strong-willed mother." Bessie was one of six children, she being the only girl. The brother born before her died in infancy. According to her great-niece, "She was twelve years old when her family moved to Canada from Burnstad, North Dakota. At this point, her formal schooling ended. As part of a homesteading family in Canada, Bessie had to assume a lot of responsibility for household chores and care of the younger children while her mother helped her father with ground breaking and farm chores."

According to Mrs. Otte, Bessie's mother preferred outdoor labor to housework. Her daughter seemed to inherit the nontraditional approach to feminine roles.

"Bessie met Nelson Skinner as a teenager and eloped with him to California, where her son 'Skippy' was born," continued Mrs. Otte. "After her divorce from Skinner in St. Paul, she supported her son by working in or managing restaurants, night clubs or gambling casinos. She became the hostess of the Hollywood Inn."

Bess apparently decided that legal marriage was a flytrap. While working in the Hollywood Inn and living with Bob Walsh in 1928, she waited tables for Danny Hogan. After the lugubrious death of Danny Hogan by a car bomb, Bessie went to Harry Sawyer, Hogan's successor as the powerhouse of St. Paul crime. She managed his Green Lantern Cafe at 545 Wabasha, a combined cafe and cabaret run by Sawyer before it closed in 1931. Bessie took responsibility for the nuts-and-bolts administration of the place. When it closed, she bought the Alamo Night Club with her lover, Ray Moore. The Alamo was a roadhouse on Route No. 1, White Bear Road, in the White Bear Lake vicinity. She'd met Eddie Green during those years, when he once expressed a desire to purchase the place.

The Alamo, as its name suggested, played host to some dramatic collaborations. Volney Davis, Fred and Doc Barker, and Alvin Karpis behaved themselves there, in the company of the fifty-five-year-old woman they called "mother."

Bess and Eddie Green, who had been in their Minneapolis apartment for a long time by criminal standards, felt a strong dilemma after Dillinger moved into the neighborhood. They didn't want to leave, but they believed that there was great danger in living near him. Green had kept a respectable profile by going out of the house every morning, just like the other working men in the building. Bessie shopped for groceries with the other housewives, and was known and recognized by the butcher. She always counted out the same small change in front of the merchants, never flashing large bills or making an ostentatious purchase that might attract attention.

This couple, living quietly on the spoils of bank robbery and bootlegging, relented under the pressure to include Dillinger in their circle of friends. In the wave of enthusiasm for the aggressive new fugitives who were flooding the area, they accepted the situation.

From the first, the new alliance between the Dillingers and the Greens was one of fake laughter and real resentment. Green called Evelyn "Pearl," out of some confusion or because he had heard of Pearl Elliott, Dillinger's cancer-stricken friend from Kokomo. Green disliked and tried to avoid Evelyn, disapproving of her drinking. She was, in his words, "too foul-mouthed." Yet Evelyn felt a semblance of trust for Bess, who'd matured into her thirties, like her old friends Opal Long and Pat Cherrington. Bessie, a dyed redhead, was physically as well as psychologically imposing, at 5 feet 8½ inches with a dark complexion, blue eyes, and a wide mouth.

During Evelyn's visits to the Greens' apartment on Fremont Avenue, Evelyn would assail Bess' ears with stories of their adventures, embellishing in a way that made her sound wealthy and worldly.

Yet Bess, who "had a good, but somewhat risque or salty sense of humor," according to Mryna Otte, had lived too many lives and could sniff out a phony. With Evelyn, she sat poker-faced while extracting the truth from between the lines. She didn't bother to conceal her contempt for Dillinger, who disliked her as much as she reviled him. She gave lip service to Evelyn but drew the line at entertaining Dillinger; she retreated into the kitchen whenever he visited their apartment.

**IDENTIFICATION ORDER NO. 1230**
July 30, 1934.

**DIVISION OF INVESTIGATION**
**U. S. DEPARTMENT OF JUSTICE**
**WASHINGTON, D. C.**

**Fingerprint Classification**

$$\frac{20\ \ 5\ \ U\ \ 00\ \ 18}{1\ \ U\ \ 01}$$

# WANTED

**MRS. HELEN GILLIS, with aliases, MRS. JOSEPH J. MARR, MARIAN VIRGINIA MARR, MARION VIRGINIA MARR, MRS. JIMMIE WILLIAMS, MRS. LESTER M. GILLIS, MRS. "BABY FACE" NELSON, MRS. LESTER GATES.**

**HARBORING FUGITIVE**

## DESCRIPTION

Age, 21 years (1934); Height, 5 feet, 2 inches; Weight, 94 pounds; Build, small; Hair, brown, bobbed; Eyes, blue; Complexion, fair.
Scars and Marks - small brown mole 2 inches above left inner wrist; forehead has four horizontal lines from wrinkles.

Photograph taken April 25, 1934

## CRIMINAL RECORD

As Mrs. Marion Virginia Marr, arrested Sheriff's Office, Madison, Wisconsin, April 23, 1934; charge, harboring U. S. fugitive; released to U. S. Marshal.
As Marian Marr, #2984, arrested U. S. Marshal, Madison, Wisconsin, April 25, 1934; charge, harboring U. S. fugitive; sentence, 18 months; sentence suspended, placed on probation; probation revoked June 12, 1934.

*Marion Marr.*

Mrs. Helen Gillis is wanted by the United States Marshal, Madison, Wisconsin on charges of harboring John Herbert Dillinger and Thomas Leonard Carroll (both deceased), Fugitives from Justice, and for violating her probationary sentence.

Law enforcement agencies kindly transmit any additional information or criminal record to the nearest office of the Division of Investigation, U. S. Department of Justice.

If apprehended, please notify the Director, Division of Investigation, U. S. Department of Justice, Washington, D. C., or the Special Agent in Charge of the office of the Division of Investigation listed on the back hereof which is nearest your city

(over)

Issued by: J. EDGAR HOOVER, DIRECTOR.

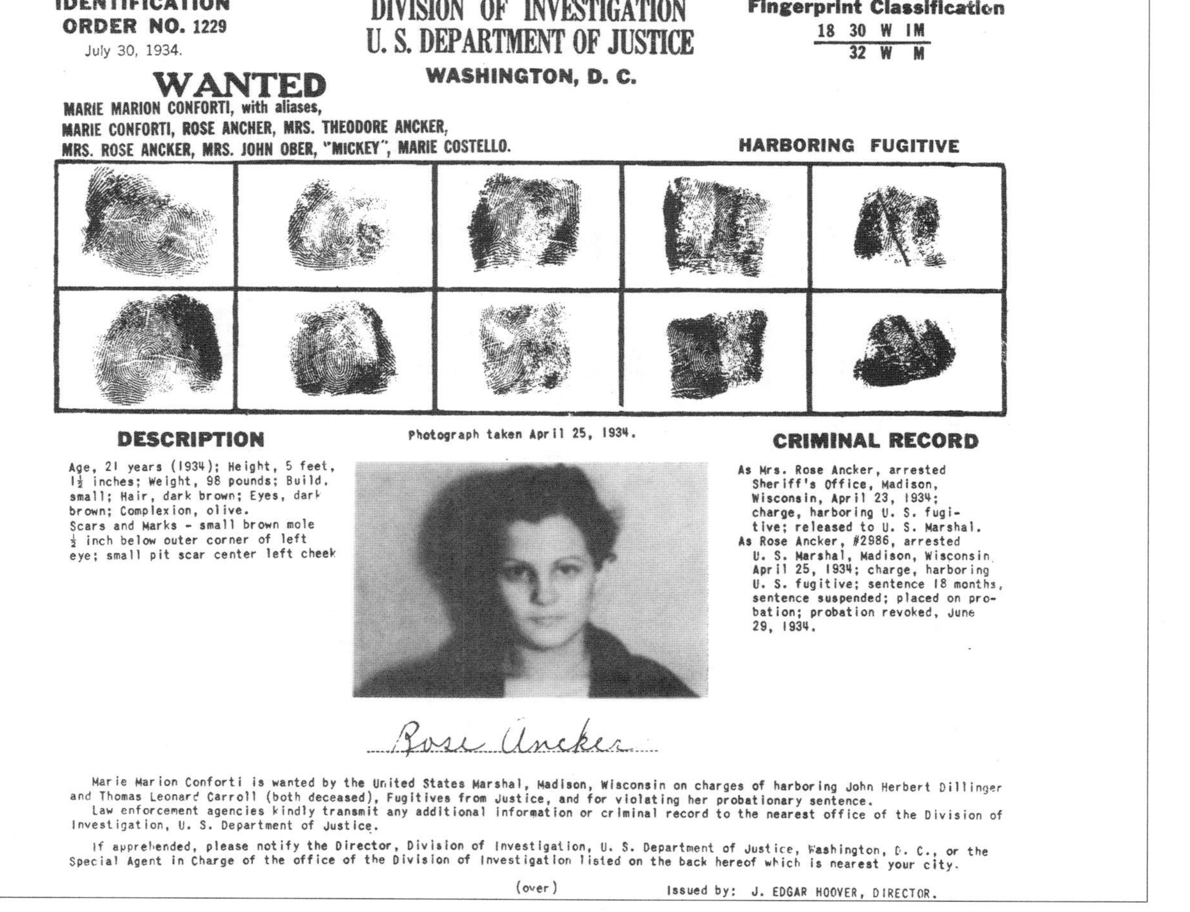

**IDENTIFICATION ORDER NO. 1229**

July 30, 1934.

**DIVISION OF INVESTIGATION**
**U. S. DEPARTMENT OF JUSTICE**
**WASHINGTON, D. C.**

**Fingerprint Classification**

$\frac{18\ \ 30\ \ W\ \ IM}{32\ \ W\ \ M}$

# WANTED

MARIE MARION CONFORTI, with aliases,
MARIE CONFORTI, ROSE ANCHER, MRS. THEODORE ANCKER,
MRS. ROSE ANCKER, MRS. JOHN OBER, "MICKEY", MARIE COSTELLO.

**HARBORING FUGITIVE**

**DESCRIPTION**

Age, 21 years (1934); Height, 5 feet, 1½ inches; Weight, 98 pounds; Build, small; Hair, dark brown; Eyes, dark brown; Complexion, olive.
Scars and Marks - small brown mole ½ inch below outer corner of left eye; small pit scar center left cheek

Photograph taken April 25, 1934.

Rose Ancker

**CRIMINAL RECORD**

As Mrs. Rose Ancker, arrested Sheriff's Office, Madison, Wisconsin, April 23, 1934; charge, harboring U. S. fugitive; released to U. S. Marshal.
As Rose Ancker, #2986, arrested U. S. Marshal, Madison, Wisconsin April 25, 1934; charge, harboring U. S. fugitive; sentence 18 months, sentence suspended; placed on probation; probation revoked, June 29, 1934.

Marie Marion Conforti is wanted by the United States Marshal, Madison, Wisconsin on charges of harboring John Herbert Dillinger and Thomas Leonard Carroll (both deceased), Fugitives from Justice, and for violating her probationary sentence.

Law enforcement agencies kindly transmit any additional information or criminal record to the nearest office of the Division of Investigation, U. S. Department of Justice.

If apprehended, please notify the Director, Division of Investigation, U. S. Department of Justice, Washington, D. C., or the Special Agent in Charge of the office of the Division of Investigation listed on the back hereof which is nearest your city.

(over)

Issued by: J. EDGAR HOOVER, DIRECTOR.

Marie Comforti. (FBI)

The four, so at odds from the first, had to learn to confine their small talk to benign subjects. Some of the lighter moments between the two couples involved the movies. Dillinger had gone to see "Joe Palooka" with Billie and joked about it to the Greens. He didn't mention that, while at the movies with Evelyn, they were surprised by an editorial newsreel that had shoved his father into the national limelight.

"John isn't a bad boy, they ought to give him a chance," he pleaded. "He only robbed some banks," the elder Mr. Dillinger said in clarification. This fiercely honest farmer spoke more from script than from heart. He'd read these simplistic lines as he stood poised against his tidy farmhouse. John Dillinger sat under the cover of darkness, choking back emotion barely audible to Evelyn in the seat next to his. According to Evelyn, John's only reaction was to be "glad" to see his dad.

With the dubious exception of Bess, Evelyn had no girlfriends in St. Paul. In their world, females had to bond when their husbands and boyfriends collaborated. These conditions of companionship forged few friendships. Rivalries also sprung up between women, with strong reasons to detest each other. The wives and girlfriends of these fugitives defined their friendships by the alliances of the men.

The women attached to Dillinger's new gang were younger than Evelyn; they were either teenagers or the other extreme. Both Kate "Ma" Barker, known in the underworld only as the reticent mother of Doc and Fred Barker; and Mary Gillis, the mother of Baby Face Nelson, were highly visible. Mrs. Gillis took care of Nelson's son, four-year-old Ronald, usurping this role from Helen.

Helen Gillis' relationship to her spouse was disturbing, even for this circle. She'd clung to her husband in the vise of a death wish; she wanted to "die with Les." Evelyn Frechette did not relate to the purity of this philosophy. Nor did she have luck befriending Marie Comforti or Jean Delaney Crompton; they were all twenty-one years old. With the exception of the sickly Helen Gillis, the women of the new Dillinger gang seemed silly and immature.

Evelyn soon got a respite from her friendless existence in St. Paul, when Dillinger charged her with the job of finding Pat Cherrington. John Hamilton wanted to find his nurse-substitute, who had helped him to recuperate after his wounding in East Chicago.

Using "Grace Edwards," her sister's roommate's name, as an alias,

Evelyn sent a telegram to Patricia in the Clark home at 75 East Windemere. Knowing that Pat was penniless, she wired $100. As "Ann Jackson," Pat was living in Russell Clark's mother's home at 75 East Windemere in Detroit: "If able travel and want to meet me check in at Greenview Hotel, 6234 So. Green Street, Chicago. Make reservation on 4:30 plane. Stop. Leaving here for north will be there few hours today. Answer immediately by Western Union to 3512 North Halsted Street, apartment 2. — Grace Edwards."

After getting the crucial $100 bill, Pat left Detroit on March 20, placing her daughter in the care of Russell Clark's mother. It was a stable arrangement, by Pat's standards. Pat Cherrington's fatal flaw, a taste for tough men, made it hard for her to stay with her daughter. She was a mother by accident, a gangster's moll by choice.[1]

The proverbial prison visit was the anti-climax of this choice. Pat performed this duty with rambunctious style. She'd just returned from a visit to Harry Copeland, who was incarcerated at Michigan City. Through the looking glass of the visit, Pat had worn a wig. The ex-dancer put her knowledge of physical illusion to good use, and she knew that Copeland enjoyed her in elaborate and glamorous disguises. A more practical consideration for wearing wigs was the mess she'd made of her own hair. From constant bleaching and dyeing, her hair was a haystack of streaks and artificial colors. Pat's rambunctious beauty was further challenged by the gall bladder removal of the previous February, which had left her sallow and emaciated.

In spite of her health problems, Pat's list of boyfriends read like a line-up. Within the time frame that she visited Copeland in Michigan City, she was writing to her husband, Art Cherrington in Leavenworth. A double-duty pen pal, she had just been kicked off Welton Spark's mailing list when it was discovered that the convict had been writing to the wife of his co-defendant. While juggling these prison relationships, Pat made haste to get to St. Paul to join John Hamilton as his common-law wife. It was an arranged marriage of sorts, and one that fitted their mutual profiles. She was in dire need of money—the $100 wired from Evelyn was all she had in the world.

Hamilton sought Pat because he disliked the women who gravitated toward the Barker-Karpis gangsters. They were a rowdy lot, strongly addicted to liquor and nightlife. Pat Cherrington seemed tame in comparison. His mail-order bride sojourned into St. Paul by packing her $100 bill and her sister, Opal Long. They met in Indianapolis where Evelyn was scheduled to meet Dillinger's siblings, Hubert and Audrey. Mary Kinder joined them, and hoped to get funds for Pierpont's appeal.

Audrey Hancock, John's sister, brought personal items that she wanted John to have. It was a small collection of his baby pictures, all captioned on the back with the wish that they be returned to his sister, Audrey Hancock.

Evelyn was entrusted like a loving wife with these family mementos. The Dillinger family had no fear of losing these precious photos if given to Evelyn. According to Mary, Audrey Hancock's daughter, "We all loved Evelyn. She was a lovely, wonderful woman. I'm sure they would have gotten married if things had turned out differently."

Evelyn returned to Minneapolis on a Northwest Airlines flight the next afternoon, March 20, accompanied by Pat Cherrington and Opal Long. Amazingly, the pilot's surname was Van Meter. The fellow, who would later be interrogated by the Justice Department, would have a rough time convincing the agents that there was no relation to Homer Van Meter.

Chartered plane travel was popular in 1934. Not surprisingly, the end of Prohibition had produced a drunk culture, people too intoxicated to be seen in the polite company of a railway car or bus. Mike Caffarello, in charge of the office at the Minneapolis Municipal Airport, was starting to notice that a large number of his hired flights transported persons who were inebriated at the time of the trip. He had arranged for Evelyn Frechette's wild flight to Indianapolis the month before and had treated the matter as routine, with a large number of legitimate businessman appearing for their chartered flights in the same intoxicated condition.[2]

It was old home week in St. Paul, with Opal Long camped out on the couch in the Dillingers' apartment, Pat Cherrington staying with John Hamilton, and Van Meter living nearby. The nervous, skinny gangster jumped around like a flea and made Bess Green especially nervous.

His girlfriend, Marie Comforti, with whom he was living as "John and Mickey Ober," had developed abdominal cramps and bleeding. She went to the Samaritan Hospital, where she was admitted. Van Meter had paid $200 for the procedure, a scraping of her uterus. The procedure was generally required after a miscarriage. Van Meter, in an unusual show of affection for Marie, went to Bess Green on March 19. He needed a hideout located near the hospital. The Greens felt that sinking sensation they'd experienced over Dillinger: Van Meter was dangerous. In their words, he "didn't know how to lay low." When they gave him the keys to apartment no. 106 at 2214 Marshall Avenue, they hoped it would keep him inside and out of public view.

With the gang becoming firmly planted in St. Paul, an apartment was rented for Dillinger's use at 93-95 South Lexington Avenue, Apartment 303. The woman of the house, Evelyn Frechette, did not secure the apartment. It was rented for her by Bess while she was in Indianapolis.

Louis and Margaret Meidlinger lived in the basement of 93 Lexington Avenue, as janitor and general caretaker for the buildings. On March 19, Bess appeared at the door and inquired about a furnished apartment.

Mrs. Meidlinger hesitated; she was not in charge of rentals. But the manager of the Lincoln Court Apartments, Mrs. Daisy Coffey, was out, so Mrs. Meidlinger took the woman to apartment 303. She noticed that the visitor, whose short, auburn hair was clean, made a nice appearance in a black fur coat and hat.

Bess inspected the apartment, not giving her name, and made one inquiry about linen and silverware, saying she would prefer an apartment on a lower floor. She walked through the rooms for a few minutes, shaking her head doubtfully. Thinking the matter routine—perhaps the girl had second thoughts; she didn't know or really care—Mrs. Meidlinger took her to the end of the hallway and bid goodbye as they parted company. The custodian's wife went down the back stairway, which was restricted to employees. Thinking the visitor had gone out the front stairs, Mrs. Meidlinger momentarily forgot about her.

A few minutes later, the caretaker went down to the cellar on a routine chore, only to encounter the red-headed woman. Composed, Bess walked past the janitor's wife, fur coat swaying around her silk-stockinged legs. Without saying a word of explanation, she left with a courteous smile.

Bess returned a few days later and talked to Mr. Meidlinger. As she stood in the doorway to the Meidlingers' flat, to ask for a key to apartment 303, Mrs. Meidlinger opened the door and glowered with suspicion; she still remembered the odd occurrence in the basement. The woman's appearance had altered and was markedly different from her first visit. Then she had appeared fresh and crisp, like a young office worker; now she looked tired, her makeup smeared and careless, with dark circles under her eyes. In Mrs. Meidlinger's words, the woman looked as though she had been "on a long, hard trip." She agreed to apartment 303, in spite of her preference for the first floor. When the manager, Mrs. Coffey, finalized the arrangements, they did not include the furnishing of references or the number of people who would occupy the apartment.[3]

The auburn-haired woman disappeared like an apparition. Then three men and two women appeared on the scene. It was difficult to determine which of these people were the actual tenants, listed on the rental agreement as Mr. and Mrs. Hellman.

When Mr. Meidlinger tried to install a toilet paper holder and roaster for the kitchen, one of these unsanctioned occupants opened the door a few inches. With difficulty he tried to see flashes of the woman's face but could only make out that her hair was black. Evelyn Frechette never removed the chain from the door. Her husband was taking a bath, she hissed, and he would install the rack himself. Meidlinger stood in the hallway holding the items in pregnant anticipation. This was not the woman who had rented the apartment; who was she? Opening the door only wide enough to take the items from his hands, the gracious Mrs. Hellman then slammed it shut.

A few days later, Mr. Meidlinger passed a blonde woman in the front of the house. Throwing her an idle glance, he was astounded to see Evelyn Frechette again, now sporting a big, platinum hairdo. She'd changed her appearance like a girl in a magic show.

Behind tightly closed doors, Mr. and Mrs. Hellman had scattered their personal effects all over the apartment. Evelyn by then had amassed a dazzling trousseau. The garish wardrobe bore a striking contrast to her former austerity, when she'd left Tucson wearing the same striped shirtwaist and leather jacket she'd been arrested in.

In St. Paul she'd bought nightgowns, slips, shoes, and undergarments in her favorite color, pink. She had scores of kimonos, silk pajamas, and nightgowns, mostly in black or pink. Her wardrobe included at least thirty dresses. These ranged from black velvet and silk evening gowns to plain grey wool and black shirtwaists. In the 1930s, women did not wear slacks on the street. Casual lounging pajamas served the purpose of comfort and flexibility, but only within the confines of one's home. Evelyn had everything from bathing suits and beach pants to mufflers. Her outerwear included five pairs of gloves, several coats, jackets, and hats. And she had her costumes, a nurse's uniform and the bushy blonde wig.

Also included was an assortment of house dresses. These came in a domestic array of flower patterns, red and white stripes, checks and gingham. These sweet, floral shirtwaists served as props. The Hellmans never asked for the vacuum cleaner, as tenants usually did. And, unlike the other women in the building, she never went to the basement to wash the clothes.

Dillinger's wardrobe was no less opulent. Contrary to his reputation for grey pinstripes, he'd stuffed his closet with a chinchilla man's overcoat.

On the day that Evelyn returned from Indianapolis, she decorated the apartment with the collection of photographs given to her by John's family. She put her personal touches into the effort by adding a toy pistol that they'd picked up, which was no bigger than a woman's little finger. Carved into the little pistol and colored with chalk was the legend "Souvenir of 1934." On the back of one photo, Audrey Hancock, Dillinger's beloved sister, had written, "John Dillinger in cherry tree 10 or 11 years old," while another said, "John, after the death of his mother, 3½ years."

In these photos, and in the domestic scattering of Evelyn's gingham housedresses, this pair of fugitives expressed the yearnings that all young couples experience. If the white picket fence wasn't what they'd opted for, they would at least have glimpses of the life they might have had. Dillinger and his Billie had gone through several aliases in the past several months. In choosing the name "Hellman," they were listing a deeply subjective metaphor for their existence—the "man of hell" and his misses.

Yet, as "Mr. and Mrs. Hellman," they consumated the highest potential of their relationship. Evelyn would dress in her black velvet and lace nightgown, a hardened night person. They would make love in the early hours of a shade-darkened morning, while the legitimate world existed outside their windows in some far-away dream. They must have sensed the nagging diminishment of time. Unknown to them, one of their closest friends had a posse of agents watching her every move.

Opal Long was again being followed. The conglomeration of agents from the Cincinnati office had been spying on the woman when she'd lived at Russell Clark's family home in Detroit. The surveillance, which had started as a furtive, peeping-Tom activity, had intensified, with the Clark family members moving from one house to another. It also had become mired in the familiar jealousy between law enforcers. Matt Leach, who also had men watching Opal Long, wouldn't cooperate with either the local police or federal agents. Tenacity paid off, as they developed a clear concept of the woman's habits and personality traits, as far as they could perceive from a distance. When she left Detroit for St. Paul, her shadow team followed her.

Enroute she'd stopped in Chicago to have a drink in the U Tavern on State Street with Larry Streng, her old friend. He'd been confiding information to an informant. With his easy affability, he allowed a great deal of information to leak into the wrong hands.

Through the Streng intelligence, the Justice Department learned that the recent wounds suffered by Dillinger and Hamilton had not been serious, and that the gang had plenty of money after the Mason City and Sioux Falls bank jobs. Some of the mob had been "shot up a little in these jobs," Streng had said, "but not serious enough for medical attention." As careful as Opal had always been, she was now unwittingly helping the agents by confiding in Larry Streng. In Chicago, Opal was trailed to the Commonwealth Hotel by agents who intercepted her telegrams to Mae Clark in Detroit. On March 19, they broke into her room. Besides installing a wiretap on her phone, they plundered her meager possessions. They broke into embarrassed laughter at the discovery of her vibrator, before listing it on their inventory sheets like wizened accountants. Through a March 29 wiretap, they learned she was checking out. On the train to St. Paul, this fox had attracted a horde of hounds.

In spite of her poor eyesight, Opal's reflexes had sharpened as a result of being constantly tailed. The usually cagey woman made a critical mistake in thinking she'd eluded her pursuers. They trailed Opal Long into St. Paul. They knew that she would meet Dillinger, to beg money for Russell Clark's defense.[4]

It was somewhat prophetic that on this same day, a Thursday, the Dillingers and Greens relaxed the tension inherent in their relationship.

Indeed, the recalcitrant Bess had agreed to visit the apartment on Lexington Avenue with Green. As usual, they entered through the back entrance of the building. Dillinger had softened his opinion of her.

Bess was a woman to be reckoned with. She had been put in charge of Green's take from Sioux Falls and Mason City, opening up a safe deposit box on March 16 at the Midway National Bank as Elizabeth Kline. She'd opened another at the Liberty National Bank under her maiden name of Hester Hinds, in which she had stashed money received for a cache of liquor sold by Eddie Green. She had also been instrumental in the purchase of Dillinger's new Hudson sedan.

Thursday, March 29, was a day that saw the two couples back and forth to the other's apartment. Evelyn paid two extended visits to the Greens. There she talked at length of her experiences with Dillinger.

"We lived in Chicago," Evelyn said, "in a lavish apartment, six rooms, completely furnished with a large amount of cut glass, all sorts of linens, beautiful dishes. Our silver service would have been sufficient to use at any sort of formal dinner." It was either a wish fulfillment or a means to impress the highly connected Bess with her refinement. The world-weary Bess merely listened, having little to add.

The older woman had the angle on most of the young girls running with the St. Paul gangsters. While not sharing her thoughts with Evelyn, she was critical of other women.

She disliked Helen Gillis, for one, and felt that the wife of Baby Face Nelson was a funny looking girl who acted very "queer."

She wasn't charitable to Dillinger's girlfriend, either, tolerating her merely as "that dark-skinned girl known as Billie."

The following day, March 30, was a Friday. Dillinger took Billie to see *Fashions of 1933*. After the movie, they visited the Green's apartment.

"Don't take Bess to see that one," laughed Dillinger to Green. "It'll put the wrong ideas into her head."

On Friday night, Evelyn continued her talkative and friendly demeanor. She shared her strategies about money management with Bess. Perhaps she sensed that this topic would be of interest to the former manager of the Alamo and Green Lantern Cafe. It was the old girl talk, a backbone of the conversations of female friendships.

"I can always spot a bargain," said Evelyn. Budgeting the receipts for a fugitive's life was tricky when you ran the risk of being chased out of a paid-up apartment. The best housing arrangements came with a tip-off, preferably from the local police station.

"If we know a raid is coming, we can get out quick," she advised, "without paying any advance rent for a place we won't use."

That day, Mrs. Coffey, the landlady, went to the post office. There she nervously confided in a postal inspector, the closest thing to a federal man she could find. Suspicious persons were occupying one of her apartments, she whispered, three men and two women who seldom left and permitted none to enter. One of the men drove a Hudson sedan, she said. The information went through channels, with the Justice Department quickly tracing the car as purchased on March 29 under the name Carl T. Hellman.

At the same time that Evelyn and Bess were having their nice conversation inside the apartment, two federal agents, Rufus C. Coulter and Rosser Nalls, arrived at the site. Opal Long had been followed there, and that, combined with Mrs. Coffey's admissions, convinced the agents that they had Dillinger. While standing outside, they saw nothing suspicious—unknown to them, everyone was coming and going through the back door.

Next morning, March 31, was a Saturday. The snow on the ground had hardened into a dirty mess on the sidewalk. The two agents, Coulter and Nalls, reported to Agent William "Bill" Rorer of Lynchburg, West Virginia, who had been in charge of the Bremer kidnapping investigation prior to the Dillinger case. Rorer advised them to see Chief Dahill, of the St. Paul Police, to secure assistance "in the immediate questioning of the occupants." Rosser Nalls stood alone in the hallway and awaited the hoped-for police backup. Chief Dahill, of the local police, granted one of his men to Rufus Coulter. City Detective Henry Cummings was grabbed by Chief Dahill, and together they went to the apartment.

Inside, a dwindling party fell flat as last night's cocktail. Hamilton left, bedecked by two adoring friends. Pat Cherrington, her hair a bleached kaleidoscope, and Opal Long, her mane a red mass of banana curls, flanked him on each side. They'd left Dillinger and Billie in their double bed, groaning in the unwelcome sight of morning.

A knock on the door roused Evelyn. She thought it was Hamilton, returning for some reason or the other. Opening the door to face Agent Coulter, she heard a request for a "Mr. Hellman." The stage name confused her. "My husband is not here," she said, trying to sound reasonable and unafraid. She told them she was undressed; she would open it after she had thrown on some clothes. Evelyn then closed the door with a terse click, attaching the chain latch. The sound of the lock sliding across the door contradicted her amiable response, and Coulter prepared for the worst.

Dillinger was already stepping into trousers and picking up as much as he possibly could to take with them. The quick strategy was to get his machine gun, collect his ammunition, and stall for time. He thought Hamilton would return and provide the backup to get him out of the apartment. He believed, in that frenzied moment of life or death, freedom or imprisonment, that deliverance was forthcoming in the figure of John Hamilton.

Rufus Coulter, meanwhile, telephoned headquarters from Mrs. Coffey's first-floor apartment and reached his friend Bill Rorer.

"I've got only one police officer, for pity's sake—and Dillinger trapped in the apartment," he cried. In response, Agent Rorer telephoned the St. Paul Chief of Police. Could they have some officers? This request for local reinforcements would have its own repercussions, as it would enrage the elitist J. Edgar Hoover.

Coulter returned to the suspects' apartment after the telephone call. He stationed himself outside the door, with City Detective Henry Cummings placed around a corner in the hall. Suddenly, a stranger appeared on the third-floor landing from the back steps. Unknown to Coulter and Cummings, it was Homer Van Meter. He went past Cummings, identifying himself as a soap salesman looking for a "Mr. Johnson."

"Where are your samples?" Coulter asked, his instincts telling him this was no salesman.

"In my automobile," Van Meter replied. He turned and cooly walked down the stairs, with Coulter following. Within the advantage of his five-second lead, Van Meter drew his gun on the first floor. Coulter also drew. Van Meter shot at Coulter. As Coulter returned the fire, Van Meter fled back into the building.

About half an hour had elapsed since the first knock on Dillinger's door. The pair had managed to pack one suitcase. Immediately after the exchange of the shots between Coulter and Van Meter, Dillinger fired his machine gun through the apartment door on the third floor. He'd been tricked by the sound of Van Meter's gun; he thought the awaited backup had come from John Hamilton. Coulter, following the close call, met Agent Nalls outside, who pointed out the Ford coupe that Coulter's assailant had arrived in. Coulter shot the tires, to ward off any possibility of an escape. Officer Cummings took cover in the hallway twenty feet from the door and returned fire.

With Dillinger showering machine gun bursts through the hall, Evelyn hopped down the back stairway, dragging a massive bag of ammunition. The adrenalin rush of fear enabled her to carry it. Evelyn then pulled the Hudson sedan from the private garage near the apartment house. She'd always claimed she was quick with an automobile, and now she put her money where her mouth had always been. She roared out of the garage and pushed the heavy door open for Dillinger to crawl into, slipping and bleeding in the dirty snow. The shooting had lasted one minute.

Coulter, from the first, knew he'd hit someone, as traces of blood dotted the rear of the apartment building. Van Meter had made his getaway, unseen and on foot. Evelyn drove Dillinger, bleeding from a bullet wound, to the Greens' apartment at 3300 Fremont Avenue.

The agents stormed into the apartment as soon as they'd deemed it safe to enter. They recovered a Thompson submachine gun, two automatic rifles, one .38 super colt automatic with twenty-shot magazine clips, and two bulletproof vests. The bygone sentiments of baby pictures sat amid a scattering of bullets, a getaway road chart from the Newton National Bank at Newton, Iowa to St. Paul, and Evelyn's receipt from her airline flight of March 19.

There was also a letter carelessly tossed on a table, but not before the signature had been ripped off. It was Lena Pierpont's terse epistle from Lima, delivered by Louis Piquett, which had demanded help for Harry Pierpont.

The agents immediately catalogued the belongings of the couple. Every item was treated as an important discovery, from the getaway road map to Evelyn's personal items. In an age when birth control was a hit and miss affair, they found Evelyn's personal contraceptive, her douche bag. It was duly inventoried, along with her "Jolly Girl" and "Gordon Uplift" brassieres, size 36, and one elastic girdle.

Yet the most important discovery was something that could be found anywhere, in anybody's cache of personal belongings. An innocent bottle of Listerine held a fingerprint of John Dillinger. Charles Tierney, Inspector of Detectives at the St. Paul Police Department, entered the apartment immediately after the shooting and obtained the Listerine bottle upon which the print was found. It was identified through records of the St. Paul Police Justice Department of Criminal Identification as being Dillinger's fingerprint.

One of the bulletproof vests had belonged to John Hamilton.[5] Dillinger's no-show backup, Hamilton, had also left his ammunition there. With Opal Long and Pat Cherrington, he had watched a curious crowd gather during the first exchange of gunfire, as Van Meter's arrival had coincided with his own departure. Rather than charge in, as Dillinger had so vainly hoped, Hamilton had cleared out.

*"You're a nut—you have to be everywhere."*

*—Bess Green, in a conversation with*
*Homer Van Meter,*
*April, 1934*

# "Bumped Out"

Through the stumps of tarnished snow, Evelyn brought the Hudson sedan just short of the Greens' house at 3300 Fremont Avenue. Leaving Dillinger bleeding in the car, she stumbled the few remaining blocks to their apartment. Responding to a knock, Bessie opened the door, to be confronted by Evelyn. She stood in high heels with no stockings, her hair a splintered frame around her face. Holding the cumbersome bag of ammunition, Evelyn fell through the door.

"We've been bumped out of our apartment," she cried, as the Greens sat motionless. "John's been shot but not serious, I don't know how badly hurt he is, there's a lot of blood and I don't know if he can walk," she said in a monolithic outcry. Their response was to listen silently.

"Please get us to a doctor," she begged Green, getting right to the point.

He agreed, and Bessie watched nervously as they left together. She waited for the next several hours, sure he'd gone off in search of Pat Reilly.

In the way that Harry Sawyer had ordained Pat Reilly to have Dillinger's bullet wounds taken care of after Sioux Falls, he arranged the medical treatment now. Reilly sent Green to the Masonic Temple Building in Minneapolis, which housed the office of Dr. Clayton E. May. He arrived there at 11:00 that morning. May, known to police as an underworld abortionist who later denied that he treated Dillinger willingly, clung to his story that Green had lured him to the gangster by saying his "friend" had been hurt in a bootlegging still explosion.

Green took Dr. May to Thirty-Third Street and Dupont Avenue South, where a disheveled Evelyn Frechette sat in the driver's seat. Dillinger slouched in the back of their car. A familiar smell of blood greeted the physician. They drove John to the home of Dr. May's nurse, Mrs. Augusta Salt, at 1835 Park Avenue, where they treated the fleshy part of his leg on two separate occasions that day. Green returned to Bess a few hours later, after leaving Dillinger and Evelyn at Nurse Salt's Minneapolis apartment, their car hidden in a garage behind the apartment. They would stay there for the next three days, leaving on April 3.

Almost simultaneously, Homer Van Meter showed up at the Greens' apartment. He had gotten away from the Lexington Avenue apartment house by stopping a large truck in front the house, threatening the driver with a gun and hitching a ride.

Bess grimaced at the sight of him. Her annoyance turned to blatant anger when she recalled that he used to park his car near the entrance to an alley close to their building. She yelled at Van Meter. He had even lied to her, in the past, about his parking place.

"You're hot," she lashed out. It was to be a long tirade.

"You're a nut," she reiterated. "You have to be everywhere." All the resentment against these people, who couldn't keep their faces low to the ground, was brimming over for the woman. "Don't ever come to this house again," she ordered Van Meter, as she stomped into her bedroom. Van Meter couldn't be trusted, not even to park his car in a discreet place.[1]

Since the shootout, the Justice Department had stepped up its activities. With as many as ten hideouts under surveillance in Chicago, Director J. Edgar Hoover sarcastically paraphrased Agent Rorer's desperate call to the St. Paul police in the minutes before the shootout.

"In order to have some courage, if [you] need a man in a blue uniform, then go ahead and take one," he would scathingly write.

On Monday night, April 2, Van Meter returned to the Greens' apartment with the welcome news: His gang was leaving town. Could he clean out the apartment on Marshall Avenue?

"There's nothing there that can get anyone in trouble," Van Meter lied. Somehow, the guns had to be delivered to Dillinger.

In response, the Greens contacted two women, Lucy and Leona Goodman, to ask them to clean out the apartment. Bessie's two associates had worked as maids, laundresses, and go-betweens for all the principals of the St. Paul crime wave, keeping quiet about it for years. Leona and Lucy had worked for the members of the Barker-Karpis conglomerate: Myrtle Eaton at 565 Portland Avenue, and Harry and Mrs. Gladys Sawyer at 1878 Jefferson Avenue. Now the two women would act out a new role, unwillingly forced to participate in the bureau's attempts to catch Eddie Green.

Employment for African-American women was limited to that of cooks and maids in the 1920s and 1930s. Nowhere was the inequality between the races more evident than in the evolution of the relationship between Bessie Green and Opal Whyte, sister-in-law of Lucy and Leona. Once the women had been friends, working together in kitchens that serviced the pleasuring instincts of the underworld. But while Bess had risen in the ranks to the highest levels of trust in Sawyer's operations, Opal Whyte had remained a kitchen worker.

Opal Whyte, who now followed the trail of openings and closings of restaurant-style cabarets, had had a long career as a cook. One of eleven children, she'd left Moberly, Missouri, in 1909 at the age of sixteen, to go to Kansas City and St. Paul. She married and divorced twice, and had a son.

Her first lucrative breakthrough came with St. Paul Chief of Police John O'Connor in 1912, when she worked as a cook for the corrupt policeman. Between 1912 and 1927, she worked continuously as a kitchen aid in a school, as a nanny and nursemaid, as a cook, and as a housekeeper. She had worked as a cook while Bessie waitressed in the Hollyhocks Club Casino, during Danny Hogan's reign of 1927. She followed Bess Green to the Green Lantern Inn. When she worked as a cook there, Alvin Karpis, who she knew only as "Slim," would ask her to fix a glass of milk for him, as he suffered from stomach problems. She also worked as a cook when Bess Green owned the Alamo, and was such a fixture that the prospective new owner, Eddie Green, wanted her to stay there if he took it over.

As Bess Green progressed up the rank and file of the St. Paul underworld, Opal Whyte became her housekeeper. The two women had been peers and equals when both worked in 1928 at the Hollyhocks Club Casino. Now Whyte didn't see Bess as a friend, but rather as an employer. She, Lucy, and Leona called Bess "Old Nuts" behind her back.

Opal Whyte knew Bess intimately, knew her history—that her maiden name was Hines, that she'd had a baby nineteen years earlier and had named him Leonard. She knew that the boy, "Skippy," occasionally went to live with his father in California. She was there for some of the crossroads of Bess' life. She'd seen Bess sitting on Green's lap, knew that they acted like sweethearts rather than like husband and wife. When Bess had run away from the violent Ray Moore, she'd gone to Opal Whyte for a favor. She'd asked Opal to hide some of his possessions at 27 Summitt Avenue. During this time, Whyte was employed in the cleaning of Myrtle Eaton's apartment, at 565 Portland. Myrtle was a shoplifter connected to the members of the Barker-Karpis gang, the perpetrators of the Bremer and Hamm kidnappings. Opal had also worked as a maid and laundress at 1095 Osceola Avenue for Charlie and Paula Harmon, who lived upstairs, and for Vi Matthis, who lived downstairs. Opal Whyte described Vi Matthis as a blonde, thin woman who called her lover, Verne Miller, "Sugar."

With other African-American women up from Missouri and Mississippi, she worked for the St. Paul underworld, believing them to be bootleggers, but certainly not gangsters. Yet Opal Whyte knew how to keep a distance from these people.

"The only white person I know is Agnes Mass," she often said, referring to her social ties to an entertainer at the Oakwood Club, a good friend of "Radio Sally," Bennett, Tommy Carroll's old girlfriend. Whyte's African-American heritage worked to her advantage in reducing her culpability to the white criminals she intimately knew. In the Jim Crow days of the 1930s, the crossover was a rare and difficult move to make.

On April 2, Bess Green telephoned Leona and Lucy. They were busy managing their restaurant on Rondo Avenue, in the heart of St. Paul's African-American community. Nevertheless, they responded to her request. Would they go to an apartment at 2214 Marshall Avenue to pick up a bag, a coat, and some laundry for her. At 11:00 a.m., that same morning, they stopped at Bess' home to get the key to Van Meter's apartment on Marshall Avenue. Bess told them to take $10 in silver dollars from the apartment, to keep as payment.

Unknown to all, the agents of the St. Paul Division of the Justice Department were right behind them. On that same day, a wiretap was connected to the telephone at the U Tavern in Chicago. The conversations of Opal Long's friend Larry Streng were yielding pertinent information about the Lexington Avenue shootout: Dillinger was shot in the leg. His companion was Evelyn Frechette. She drove the car. The woman with John Hamilton was Pat Cherrington. The gunman/soap salesman was Homer Van Meter. He'd occupied apartment no. 106 at 2214 Marshall Avenue and had disappeared on March 31.

On the morning of April 3, Agent Rorer, Chief of Police Dahill, Inspector of Detectives Charles Tierney, and Agent Werner Hanni gained entry to Van Meter's apartment on Marshall Avenue. The empty rooms exuded all the warmth of a vacant lot.

The janitor, Mr. Walter L. Pommerening, told agents that on March 15, 1934, a woman named Mrs. D. Stevens rented apartment 106 in this building, but nobody ever used it.

The policemen searched and found Van Meter's clothing, mostly functional items like underwear, socks, and towels, and a forgotten purse of Marie Comforti, which contained $16. And then the bullets, license plates, and getaway maps were found, along with a small bag containing first aid equipment—bandages, adhesive tape, morphine, and cat guts.

At 11:30 that same morning, Leona and Lucy entered the Marshall Avenue apartment, with the key they'd obtained from Bess. Met by a welcome wagon of agents, they identified themselves as maids who were hired to clean the apartment. When that excuse failed to convince the agents, they admitted that Green, known to them as Mr. Stevens, had asked them to get a bag, a coat, and some laundry from the place. After allowing them to take the bag, the agents accompanied the women to Leona's home at 778 Rondo Street, to wait for "Miss Bessie." Leona and Lucy were frightened and intimidated by the agents.

Then the endless wait for Eddie Green began. Leona's home at 778 Rondo was under siege, watched by the armed Justice Department agents, who staked themselves out in various places during the night of April 2. All waited for the Hudson sedan that would park in front of the house.

As twilight descended, at 5:30 p.m., Bess and Eddie Green parked their new 1934 Hudson sedan across the street from Leona's home at 778 Rondo Street.

The police had already decided to shoot on sight if Leona identified Eddie Green. According to the account given by the agents, Special Agents Gross, E.N. Notesteen, and Wood arrived at 778 Rondo Street. While they held Leona and Lucy hostage inside, Green came to the front door. He now had the precious cargo in his hands, and he was about to give his life for these items: a Thompson submachine gun stock, holster, field glasses, license plates, caliber automatic clips, shells for .380; .45; and .38 calibers, shot gun shells, .32 caliber bullets, money wrappers, getaway maps, and sales slips.

Leona, frozen with fear, had thrown the bag at Green and slammed the door in his face. She turned to the dining room on her right, to behold one of the government men, as she called them. Flanking her on the left was a bedroom and a living room, with two government men on that side of the kitchen. She couldn't see anything and mercifully missed what happened next.

As Green passed the window in front of which Agent Gross was sitting, he held the bag out, away from his body, and looked around. Agent Gross made a split-second decision: Green was holding his arms in a "menacing and threatening" manner. Agent Notesteen, coincidentally, also noticed a "menacing, threatening" gesture on the part of Green when he turned around.

"Let him have it," he called to his partner. Gross aimed the machine gun through the window, and fired.

Struck in the head and right shoulder, Green tumbled down to the grass between the sidewalk and the curb. Agent Wood turned to Green's auto and shot at the rear tires. Jumping from the Terraplane, Bessie ran toward Green.

In a collective, organized gesture, the agents wrapped newspapers around the license plates and placed a tarpaulin over the Terraplane, leaving Special Agent V.W. Peterson to keep a watch over the car. Green was taken to the Ancker Hospital.

Bessie was dragged into custody and found to be carrying $1,155. The money was immediately checked against the Bremer and Hamm ransom money with negative results. Her pocketbook disclosed that she had lived with Green under the name of Mr. and Mrs. T.J. Randall in apartment 207 at 3300 Fremont Avenue in Minneapolis.

Momentarily forgotten, the hysterical Lucy and Leona ran to their brother, Mose. He telegramed Opal Whyte and hinted that the two women were in trouble. Their sister-in-law was surprised, as she had never seen the two women in any trouble, nor had any of their group ever been in jail.

In her shock, grief, and horror, Bessie was herded to an unofficial location, her whereabouts a mystery for the next seven days. This intake procedure was tagged "incommunicado." The agents grilled her on Green, Dillinger, Hamilton, and all the St. Paul gangsters and racketeers.

"You shot him down without giving him a chance," she screamed, and then turned her head away in sick disbelief.

The agents claimed that with many cars passing the house and circulating in the vicinity, they took Green's hand movements as a signal for backup by gangster friends. J. Edgar Hoover immediately addressed the possibility of this accusation, by issuing a statement that the United States was declaring "endless war" against the Dillinger gang.

"This man [Green] has admitted that he participated in the gun battle with our men in St. Paul Saturday. That's going too far."

In this declaration, Hoover paraphrased the deathbed statements of Green. Mortally wounded, Green was delivering his soliloquy to an enthralled audience in the Anker Hospital. Surrounded by Justice Department agents, nurses, and family members, including his mother, he mumbled that he "walked away from 93 Lexington Avenue Saturday," adding with surprising practicality that they "must have lost a couple of bulletproof vests" on Saturday, also.

After the shooting, Bessie's home on Fremont was ransacked by the bureau. They found scores of maps and one eight-page getaway plan. Boxes of .22- and .32-caliber shells, clips loaded with .45-caliber automatic and .351 Winchester automatic rifle shells, bulletproof vests, Thompson submachine gun, with drum and shells, a 16-gauge single-barrel shotgun, and a first aid kit were found.

With Eddie Green hanging on to life, Bessie understood that she would be "sent up." It was probably the first time in her life that the specter of imprisonment as a gangster's woman would dawn on her. She knew she was considered "hot," knowing too much, and believed that the gang would raise a $100,000 bond for her. At the same time that she began to understand her predicament, the Justice Department realized just who this lady was. In the words of H.H. Clegg, an assistant to Hoover who had arrived in a flood of federal agents to the area, Bessie was "a smart woman, not at all dumb; having owned a night club there and run it herself." He made a brash determination regarding his prisoner.

"If she gets outside to see her lawyers, she won't testify, or give any information at all if she thinks she has a chance herself," he decided.

Within her increasingly confused state, she maintained a strong stance on one ringing issue. Her mothers' instincts toward her son overrode any concern she might have had for herself. She wanted her true identity to remain a secret from the public. Her innocent boy should never suffer from this notoriety. The Justice Department agents recognized her nineteen-year-old son, Leonard, as her Achilles heel and used the threat of exposure as a leverage from which to extract information from her.

Public curiosity ran high over the identity of the "red-headed woman," forcing the hand of the Justice Department in giving out some details. The first statements tossed out referred to Bessie by the euphemism "Beth Green." It was a symbolic as well as a practical baptism. She would never be Bessie Skinner, in the true sense of the word, again.

By April 10, family members had retained the services of counsel for the disappeared Bessie Skinner. The attorneys, John Edmund Burke, Edward K. Delaney, and Joseph P. Tracy, went in to the federal court with a writ of habeas corpus and charged before Judge M.M. Joyce that Justice Department agents had held her incommunicado for the entire week, and had refused to allow her to see an attorney.

"We have not even been permitted to interview Mrs. Green in the presence of Department of Justice officials," said Mr. Burke to reporters. "The only satisfaction we received was to be told that she did not want counsel. We do not know whether this is true or not, and we at least want to find out."

Agent Werner Hanni appeared at the bench with Assistant District Attorney George A. Helsey. In arguing against her release, Mr. Helsey used a paper debate—that the counsel team was not valid because it had been retained by unnamed "relatives." The writ would have to be signed by the person for whom the release was intended, he maintained.

Judge Joyce ordered Agent Hanni to bring "Mrs. Green" into the courtroom. Wearing the same tan suit, hat, and eyeglasses that she wore on the day of the shooting, Bessie was pushed in. She'd had no time to grieve, and no decent food, sanitary, or sleeping arrangements for over a week. Her face paled at dead-white, her expression was disoriented and frightened. She was ordered to look at the three hired attorneys. She did so, with an uncomprehending gaze.

"Do you accept these men as your counsel?" asked Judge Joyce.

"No," she whispered, and was ushered from the courtroom. In the same motion, the judge vacated the writ. Agent Hanni was now free to conduct the excavation into her activities.

It was encouraging to see the woman smashed like a discarded bottle. Bess gave a written order to the Midway National Bank and the Liberty State Bank for agents to make an examination of the contents of her safe deposit boxes, one at the Midway National Bank under the name of Elizabeth Kline; and one at the Liberty National Bank under the name of Hester Hinds, with the two boxes totaling $9,000 inside. About $4,000 of it was the result of a sale of a truckload of alcohol by Eddie Green. The bills were not ransom notes but had figured in an illegitimate alcohol transaction. The other box contained $4,700, the proceeds from Sioux Falls.

Then she talked about Tom Filbin. This admission was seen as a clean indication that Bess had broken. She'd conducted an automobile trade of two cars with the automobile financier to the St. Paul underworld, in order to provide Dillinger with his Hudson sedan. Filbin, evading capture through his lawyer, would admit to the transaction but, like everyone else, denied he knew of any connection with Dillinger. This information was confirmed by none other than Eddie Green, raving in his hospital bed. He spoke openly about Bess getting the cars from Tom Filbin. Green was flanked in the hospital by his mother and brother, Frank. An interview was conducted over a period of six hours, between 7:00 p.m. on the night of April 3 and 1:00 a.m. on the morning of April 4.

The dying mobster, raving and incoherent, was deemed rational by the agents of the St. Paul division of the Bureau. Agent R.T. Noonan questioned him. He admitted his presence at the Security National Bank in Sioux Falls, South Dakota, and he implicated Van Meter and Tommy Carroll.

He then said to Agent Hardy, "Tell Tommy I will be over when I feel better."

"Tommy who?" Agent Hardy inquired.

"Tommy Carroll."

"Well, where can we find Tommy Carroll?"

"Carroll at 16th and Chicago in Minneapolis."

He identified Dillinger's girl as "Pearl," his mistaken idea of Evelyn's name, and said that she was drunk the day before yesterday at his place.

"Who shot the copper at 93 Lexington Avenue?"

"Jack shot."

"What did Dillinger do?"

"He opened up with the Tommy and then went out the back way."

He was given a hypo at 1:10 a.m. by Nurse Marie Tinklenberg, who was sure he was dying. He kept yelling that he had Dillinger's keys. "I got the keys—he wants them."

Green then asked for Harry Sawyer, when he called for "Harry,"giving no last name. He said he knew Alvin Karpis, admitting that he'd seen him recently "downtown."

Agent Noonan casually mentioned Bess.

"I see that your wife was with you at the time you got hurt."

"Did Bess see the paper on me, did she call up the hospital about me?" he cried.

"Where did Bess get the $1,500 she had on her?" the agent asked.

"I want to call up my home and see if Bess is there, and have her come over."

He thought the nurse was Bess and he told her, "get the belongings out of the apartment on Marshall Avenue, they belong to John."

As an afterthought, he decided against that.

"Don't take them to John," he ordered. "Dillinger doesn't like Bessie."

"The only time Bessie should go to see Dillinger is when I am along, and I don't feel well enough to go."

He called to Nurse Tinklenberg.

"Give my suitcase to my partner, Red." This was a reference to John

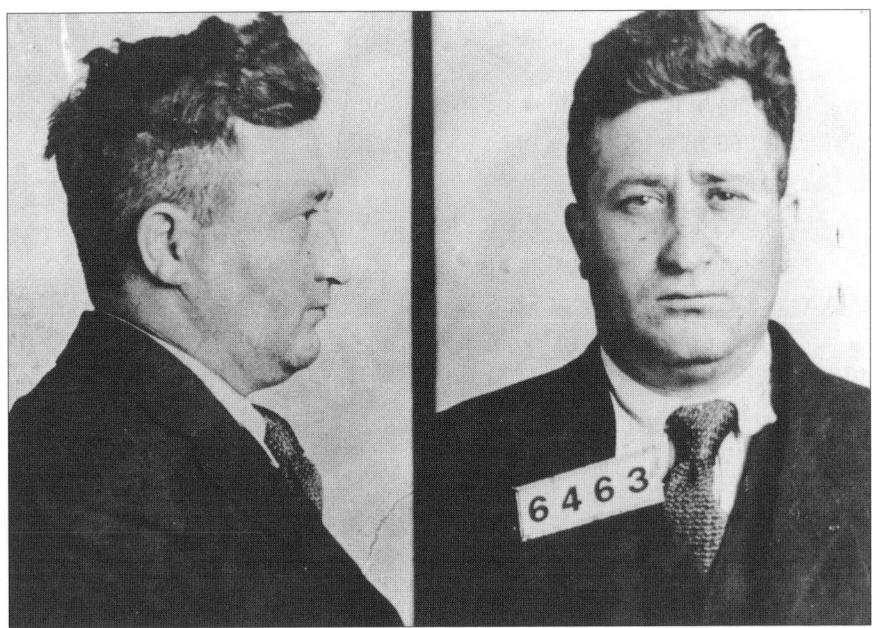


Harry Sawyer had argued with Beth Green. Their old friendship was over by 1934. (National Archives)

Hamilton, who, on Green's lips, sounded to the nurse like "Pencilman."

The name Homer Van Meter invoked the familiar paranoia. When asked if he knew Homer, Green became agitated.

"What are you trying to do, get me in the penitentiary? I don't know those fellows."

Right before Green died, the agents brought Bessie in to see him. It was a flat disappointment for the woman, an anti-climatic viewing on a past life. Her Eddie was in a coma and didn't know she was there.

Right after that, a complaint was filed against her. The pleadings listed her legal name as Beth Green. Under this pseudonym, she would tell "everything." She insisted on one catch: She wouldn't talk until Eddie was dead in the ground.

Bess' metamorphosis was the result of several factors. She knew she couldn't help Eddie Green get a lighter sentence—he was null and void; his death was imminent. By the time the attorneys had been hired, it was already too late for her to go back to the street. She'd inadvertently thrown out information while delirious and sleep-deprived.

Had Harry Sawyer arranged the fix to get her out of jail, things could have been different. Sawyer ignored Bess; they'd been "on the outs" for the past several months.

Bess was livid at the thought that Dillinger and Van Meter were free, and flattened in the truth that Sawyer withheld the fix. The federal government was above and beyond the bribery that enveloped St. Paul. This remained beyond her objective understanding. Deprived of her lover, her freedom, and even her real name, she had nothing more to lose.

On April 10, right before the three hired attorneys had tried to have her released on the writ of habeas corpus, she had been arraigned before W.T. Goddard, U.S. Commissioner, on charges of conspiracy to harbor and conceal a fugitive from justice, John Dillinger. The charges were based on the escape from the Lexington Avenue Apartment building of March 31. Her bond was set at $25,000. The commissioner read the complaint to her and she interposed a statement, at first denying she had visited with Dillinger in his apartment on Lexington Avenue. Two days later, she changed this story, by saying that she had seen Dillinger wearing shirt sleeves in his apartment, on Thursday or Friday before the shooting.

Through her statements, the Justice Department began to understand the depth of this woman's involvement in St. Paul:

- She was employed with Danny Hogan at the Hollyhocks Inn, from which she opened her roadhouse, which became the rendezvous for the likes of Frank Nash, Thomas Holden, and Francis Keating, all of whom were escaped from the Leavenworth Penitentiary;
- Eddie Green knew Harry Sawyer, Volney Davis, Alvin Karpis, Fred and Doc Barker, William Weaver, and Myrtle Eaton through Bess' intervention. Green had first met Bess when he'd walked into The Alamo in 1932 with his offer to buy it.
- Eddie Green worked with the Barker-Karpis gang in the Fairbury National Bank robbery on April 4, 1933, along with Volney Davis, Karpis, the Barkers, Frank Nash, the deceased Earl Christman, and Jess Doyle. He was an accomplished bank robber in his own right.
- During the spring of 1933, Bess and Green had lived in

Chicago, on Kedzie Avenue, in the same building that had housed the Barkers. In Chicago, the Greens had spent a great amount of time with Alvin Karpis and his sixteen-year-old mistress, Dolores Delaney.

- In fall of 1933, the Greens had been in contact with Jess Doyle and his girlfriend, Doris O'Connor, who was the sister of the notorious Edna "Rabbits" Murray, a three-time prison escapee known to the police as "The Kissing Bandit." The two couples spent several weeks on Sawyer's farm and at a Minnesota summer resort.
- Lester Gillis had visited the Greens' apartment with Helen, his wife, their son, and Gillis' mother. Tommy Carroll also visited the 3300 Fremont Avenue place with his girlfriend, Jean Delaney Crompton, the sister of Dolores Delaney.
- Homer Van Meter had visited the Greens, with Marie Comforti, during January 1934, when they'd lived next door as Mr. and Mrs. John Ober, in apartment 201 at 3310 Fremont Avenue.

Eddie Green died at 12:55 p.m. on April 11. That same night, Bess was removed from the secret holding cell and placed in the county jail. Right after he died, the Ancker Hospital invoiced the St. Paul Justice Department headquarters for his treatment. Agent Clegg, stuck with the bill, reasoned with Hoover to pay it.[3]

"The opinion prevails that because of the fact that the hospital officials, the nurses, and the doctors cooperated fully with the Division in efforts to procure information from Green . . . it would be the proper thing for the Division to see that these claims are properly settled."

The outstanding balance of $327 was paid to the Ancker Hospital by the Justice Department.

*"They called me 'Dirty Indian.' They kicked my stomach, pulled my hair, slapped my face, to get me to tell them where he was . . ."*

*—Evelyn Frechette*

# "Miss Cuttin' Up with You"

The crackdown in St. Paul had left Opal Long an outcast. While Van Meter was blamed—he caused the heat in St. Paul with his "ducking in and out of every place," in Bess' words—Opal Long suffered a worse stigma. She carried the weight, by all accounts, for bringing the agents down on the gang.

When visiting Dillinger on Lexington Avenue, Opal had worn an oversized housedress. Thus adorned, she'd left the apartment with Hamilton and Pat Cherrington on her proverbial mission of stocking the food pantry. After the shootout, she pushed through the melee with a grocery bag in her arms. Assuming the pose of a concerned neighbor, she innocently asked about the commotion. Upon hearing of the shootout, they rode around in confusion. Eventually, Pat Reilly came to mind. Hamilton drove to McCormack's Restaurant, a local hangout, to wait for Sawyer's "Guy Friday." When Reilly arrived, he ushered the trio into a Ford sedan and tried to decide what to do with them. He'd wanted to take them out to Sawyer's place in the country, but the plan was rescinded when a tip came in by Officer McMullen of the St. Paul Police Department that a raid on Sawyer's place was imminent.

Harry Sawyer was under subpoena to testify at a grand jury investigation and had taken a hiatus in the countryside with his wife, Gladys, and their child. The old Green Lantern Cafe at 545 N. Wabasha Street, which had been closed for two months, had just been raided and an arsenal of two shotguns, a rifle, and a suitcase full of dynamite was taken by St. Paul city detectives. The St. Paul gangs had begun to play hot potato, with the object being to keep away from the Dillinger gang. It was a policy that would eventually cost Hamilton his life.

In this spirit of insulation, Reilly firmly ejected the trio from his Ford sedan. Opal left her two companions and went into temporary exile. She awoke in the funnel of a cheap hotel with the stale bag of groceries her only companion.

"Next day was Easter Sunday and I stayed in this place all day, afraid to go out because I didn't have anything on but an apron," she later wrote. "I didn't even have a hat. I sat there all day and ate the bread and sausages."

It was a sad irony for Opal Long. Past sacrifices meant nothing. Word quickly spread around the Twin Cities that she'd been trailed to St. Paul from Chicago. She'd managed to visit Bess in the hours after the shootout.

"The agents followed me from Detroit," she'd said in that meeting. "But I gave them the shake in Chicago," she'd lied. Opal's attempt to vindicate herself was to no avail. Her problems with the law had escalated also. After she'd gone into hiding, the Justice Department established that she had visited the Lexington Avenue apartment, leaving before the shooting occurred. Her old boyfriend and confidant, Larry Streng, let this drop in one of his conversations with a Justice Department informant. She was now a shoe-in for a prison sentence as a harborer of a federal fugitive. Whether or not Opal knew how deep her complicity ran, she got herself out of St. Paul, where the danger came from the underworld as well as the police. She returned to Detroit and went to 531 Chandler Street, to stay in the overcrowded Clark house with Pat's daughter.

In one sense, she remained undaunted, obsessed with the $50,000

Informants close to Opal Long gave this snapshot to Federal agents. (FBI)

she believed Dillinger had in his possession. Opal felt sure she could do some "fixing," as she'd told Bess.[1]

The last desperate plan to spring Pierpont, Makley, and Clark from the Ohio State Penitentiary was a concoction of foolish ideas. Under the false assumption that there was only one guard in the death house at night, with none at the walls, they felt they could "buy off" the few guards and stage a raid. With no committed accomplices, Dillinger hoped to launch the escape from a farm twenty-five miles away from Columbus.

In Lima, Jessie Levy had been expecting Opal. She contacted the Clarks on April 4:

"Is Bernice with you. Answer immediately to Millers Office Lima. Important.—Nell." Sensing Opal's complicity, the defense team refused to use real names. They located Opal, who went to the state prison in Columbus, Ohio, to visit Russell Clark. It is at this point that Opal Long changed her name to "Bernice Clark." Without the married providence, she would not have gotten in to visit him. Whether married or not, she was valued as a person that agents could shadow on the street. For that reason, she wasn't arrested. Accompanied by the Clark family, she met Mary Kinder, Lena Pierpont, and Jessie Levy on April 11.

During the prison visit, Opal longed for a private moment with Russell Clark. She was tired of being one of many and wanted some individual attention from the man she claimed she'd married. She was lucky in one respect. Unlike much of the prison correspondence, this letter was delivered, and Clark actually got to read it:

*Mrs. Bernice Clark*
*531 Chandler Street*
*Detroit, Michigan*
*April 12, 1934*

*"Dearest Russell,*

*"I don't hardly know what to write about after just being down there yesterday but thought a few lines might help to break the monotony. Honey, you sure looked mighty good to me after not being able to see you for so long. I like you much better without your mustache. Was terribly disappointed that I didnt [sic] even get to kiss you, but was more than glad just to see you and talk to you. We stopped in Lima on the way back and I talked to Jessie and Mary for a little while. The lawyers are very busy working on the appeal cases."*

(After some chatty news about the Clark family, Opal Long continued.)

*"Mac and Harry seemed in very good spirits yesterday.*

*I'm glad they are taking it like that. Tell them both hello for me . . . I bet Mac misses his 3–5 minute eggs. But I guess he dont* [sic] *need them now. They make him too frisky. Its going to seem like a long month before time to visit you again, but I guess I'll just have to get used to it. But there are a lot of things I'll have to get used to. I miss cuttin-up with you, plenty.* [sic] *Life seems very dull now, but this is a dull day maybe thats it."*

(She talked some more about his family and then concluded)

*"I think if you'll behave yourself down there that you'll get a fair break. Everybody says that they treat prisoners nice there. I hope that you'll be out of that death row soon, as it gives me the shivers to think about it. I'm afraid they might make a mistake and put you in the chair (Ha ha). Well I said I didn't know much to write but looks like I've done pretty good. Guess I better ring off before I get writers cramps. When you can, try to write just to me instead of the whole family and tell me a lot of nice lies. You know I'm just foolish enough to like to listen to them. Can't begin to tell you how much I love you so will close now.*

*Your loving wife,*
*Bernice."*

Easter Sunday also lent Mary Kinder time for reflection. On Friday, March 30, she'd written to Harry Pierpont. He never got the letter. Through its contents, prison authorities ascertained that Mary was rebelling against Pierpont. He still played the role of boss; Jessie Levy was his messenger. He expected Mary to travel endlessly, finding items long lost and impounded by the Tucson police. She still transported guns, money, and clothing but reaped nothing tangible. To a woman as concerned with material gain as Mary, this unrequited loyalty began to wear thin.

On April 11, Pierpont was visited by Mary and his mother, Lena Pierpont. He issued his directives, ordering Mary to go the next day to St. Louis.

"Find a guy named John O'Connell," he said. "Get a key to his apartment, pick up the machine guns, then get rid of them—You know how to do that."

It was an order she'd ultimately refuse to follow. Her veneer was scratched away by gut instincts: Pierpont went to his mother for the love that Mary felt belonged to her.

*Mrs. Harry Pierpont*
*930 Daly Street*
*Indianapolis, IN*

*"Dear Darling Husband,*

*Gee honey I sure was glad to get your letter today and hear that you are O. K. and still in love with me...just tell me how much you love me and that is all that is necessary for a while. How could I get tired of hearing that when I love the man that writes that. I am going to do what you said in your letters for awhile I mean with your mother . . . Darling when I make a promise I keep it and honey that is one I am going to keep until we see how things come out.*

*"I went out to the dance about three times but I have never did anything I would be ashamed of or wouldn't want you to know. I have not been drinking hardly at all. Marg and I have been going to the shows lately and you should see how they watch me honey afraid I will meet some one."*

(Mary's hostile relationship with Pierpont's mother surfaced.)

*"She acts sometimes like she doesn't trust me and God knows I never did anything to her and I am trying to do all I can for you kids. I get pretty peeved at her sometimes, I don't know half the time what she is doing . . . I went to town today and got me a permanent wave and it looks real nice and talk about Red, you remember my red suit, well I got red shoes, red hat and purse to match, all dressed in red and it makes a nice looking outfit. I wish my honey was here to take me somewhere in it. Would you darling? Honey I lost your picture that you gave me, the only ones I have are the newspapers. See if you can have pictures and I will have one taken and send you so you can kiss me goodnight. Did*

*you get that medal and get to keep it? I still have mine."*

The next paragraph contained a hint of battle fatigue:

*"What about clothes honey write and let me know about them and what you need, I will send you and Mac the money tomorrow morning when the post office is opened and will send you some magazines. Anything you want write sweet and I will send (if possible). If you dont [sic] ask for impossible things. Sunday is Easter and I am going to church for a change and see if that wont help.*

*Love and Kisses and ?*
*To my darling husband*
*From your wifie."*

Pierpont never read these wishful tidings of frustration. The letters mailed to him were dissected and copied before being withheld. Mary's visitor status was under attack. The warden had gotten her to admit that she was not Pierpont's legal wife.

She was in the process of relocating from the Daly Street apartment to 516 Luett Street in Indianapolis on April 7. With her mother, sister, and brother, she admitted the police to the new dwelling. They helped the family unpack their possessions by staging an impromptu raid. Mary was taken to Indiana Police Headquarters and held overnight for questioning. Matt Leach's men found nothing that could be used against Mary or point them to Dillinger.[2]

While Mary Kinder's family was targeted by the local police, Evelyn Frechette's kin was tracked by the Justice Department. Most prominent in the investigation centering in Chicago was Melvin Purvis. An aristocrat from South Carolina, Purvis had come to the Justice Department holding a degree to practice law. Intelligent and determined, his personal quest for Dillinger was fueled by his protectiveness toward his fellow agents. He combined bravery with analytical thinking and masked an extremely sensitive nature with a hard facade. This thespian talent helped him in the hours he would spend interrogating the people who knew Dillinger.

He'd assumed command of the Chicago field office in November 1932. He'd monitored the Dillinger case unofficially until his violation of the Dyer Act brought the Justice Department into the case. When

Evelyn Frechette's identification order was released, it contained the names of her sisters. One of them was Frances. Purvis found Patsy and Marge Edwards at 3512 N. Halsted Street. Frances told Agent Metcalfe that she had quarreled with Evelyn in February and had not been on speaking terms with her since. She brushed Dillinger off as a nonentity.

"I've never met or seen any of that crowd," she said with pretentious disdain. Then she confided in him softly.

"It's a lie that Evelyn has pockmarks," she whispered. "I'm the one in the family with the pockmarks." Noting Patsy's face, smooth save for a small mole on each cheek, Purvis conceded.

Other agents, stationed in Wisconsin, made the trip to Neopit. Many were surprised to see the poverty of a reservation; perhaps some came to understand the conditions that brought a woman to the likes of John Dillinger.

They drove past St. Anthony's Cemetery, noting the humble graves beneath wooden crosses, many of which told of the infant, child, or teenager buried there.

After their arrival to the corrugated tin village, the agents infiltrated the homes of Evelyn's family and friends. In spite of the extreme poverty of the town, inside the houses were cheerful and inviting, decorated with paintings and vintage photographs of American Indians, with decorative bows and arrows on the walls. They visited Evelyn's girlhood friend, Vivian Warrington. With her husband, George, at her side, she spoke of Evelyn as a good and loyal friend who had kept her company during her long illnesses of the previous year. She wisely neglected to mention that Evelyn had visited their home accompanied by Dillinger.

The agents found Evelyn's mother and stepfather, Edwin Sprague. The Neopit chief-of-police accompanied them to the house. He apologized in their Menominee language as the agents ripped apart their things. The searchers found an old letter from Evelyn, mailed in Tennessee during the Christmas season of the previous December. This prompted Mary Sprague to emphasize her daughter's generosity; not only did Evelyn enclose money during Christmas, but she graced many of her relatives on the Reservation with financial help. Thoughts of her daughter caused the woman to become hysterical. Through heaving, guttural sobs she revealed her constant fear: Evelyn would be sentenced to the electric chair, or shot.

"I'd do anything to find her," she cried. The usually skeptical agents believed her.

Far from her childhood home, Evelyn cleaved to John Dillinger. In the hope of getting married in Mexico, she had gone to Chicago attorney Michael H. Bodkin to have her divorce finalized. In the same useless vein, Dillinger was stashing money. It would be their nest egg: Evelyn would leave the country with him, and they would get married under assumed names.

In the midst of their planning, Evelyn's fingerprint card lay in stacks around the nation. In her poised, prim headshot wearing a lace collar, she could have been any young woman planning to marry her high-school sweetheart. Now that "Mrs. Dillinger" had a face, it was seen everywhere. Nowhere was this more evident than in the case of mistaken identity involving the wife of Chico Marx.

The member of the famous Marx Brothers comedy team was married to a woman who remotely resembled Evelyn Frechette. The thirty-seven-year-old Betty Marx, at 5 feet 2 inches and weighing 125 pounds, had jet-black hair and an olive complexion. The brown-eyed beauty did bare a slight resemblance to Frechette, with one exception: Evelyn's French-Indian eyes shimmered to black hues.

Mrs. Marx was on the way to meet Chico in Manhattan's Park Central Hotel on April 4. On the plane she chatted with attorney Allen Schwartz. Their animated conversation came to the attention of two detectives on the plane. In Chicago, Mrs. Marx stopped over and then boarded a United Airlines plane bound for Newark, New Jersey, at 11:30 p.m. The detectives telephoned the Justice Department and subsequently seven agents from New York greeted her in Newark, on the pretense that she resembled the wife of an embezzler from a Los Angeles national bank. She insisted that she was Mrs. Chico Marx, of 1152 Sunsetdale Avenue, Hollywood.

When it became apparent that this was a case of mistaken identity, the agents graciously insisted upon driving Mrs. Marx to her hotel in Manhattan. After seeing that she was checked in, they offered yet another friendly gesture: They drove her to Reubin's Restaurant on Madison Avenue near 58th Street, home of the New York grilled Reubin sandwich.

This scenario could have played itself out in one of the Marx

Brother's movies. The irony of being mistaken for Dillinger's girlfriend was not lost on Betty Marx. A naturally vivacious woman, she playfully introduced one of the agents by the pseudonym of "Mr. Smith" to proprietor Reubin.

"Miss Betty," answered the unsuspecting restauranteur, "I haven't seen Chico tonight."

Evelyn Frechette had never seen New York City. Just as the slapstick between Mrs. Marx and the Justice Department played in Manhattan, Evelyn was helping Dillinger out of the apartment kept by Nurse Salt in Minneapolis.

On the night of April 5, they went home to Dillinger's father in Mooresville. Somehow, the airplanes, police cars, and telescopes stationed across the farmland failed to detect their presence.

For his father, life had become a fireball of pressure.

"We were all in bed . . . I myself was worrying about what might have happened to him . . . he knocked on the door. I let him in, and almost at once was clasped in his strong, young arms. Great criminal, maybe, but my son," he would tell the newspapers in hindsight.

Evelyn was no stranger to John's family. They loved her and wished that the two could have been married, like Hubert and his bride, Connie.

Dillinger spent much of the day with Hubert in the barn, working on a car that Hubert had just bought for his brother's use. Then the brothers went to Indianapolis. They drove past two Justice Department agents and two local police officers, who didn't recognize them. In Indianapolis they stored the car downtown and kept a rendezvous, arranged by Mary Kinder, with the parents of Harry Pierpont.

On the way back, while traveling seventy miles an hour on U.S. Highway 31 at Noblesville, Hubert fell asleep behind the wheel. The two got away from the wreck and limped home. The Dillingers and Hancocks attended Sunday services at the First Christian Church at Mars Hill while hiding John in the farmhouse. He sat with Evelyn in the parlor, which afforded him a view of the highway from atop the hill. Through the door rolled two bedrooms to the left, one in which he'd lived conjugally with Berlie so many years before. On the right was the farmhouse kitchen, where Audrey, Connie, Mary, Doris, and Frances prepared the dinner, to which the elder Dillinger contributed two freshly killed chickens. Dillinger presided at the head of the table, his hair dyed a red never before seen in rural Indiana. Some of the conversation touched upon the famous wooden gun. The family had it in its possession since Evelyn had delivered it during her Indianapolis visit of March 19. While they ate, "shaking off that feeling of dread and proceeding to make the dinner a joyous family event," according to his father, fourteen carloads of Indiana State troopers, Indianapolis policemen, and federal agents and inspectors raided three Dillinger/Hancock family residences: that of Hubert and his bride, Connie; Connie's parents; and the Hancock home in Maywood.

Jeff Scalf, Dillinger's great nephew, related that John's father had pressed his son on the issue of the East Chicago shooting. According to Scalf, "John Sr. stated that he needed to know whether John had killed anyone so he could pray, if need be, for his son's forgiveness. A very solemn Dillinger told his father and his half-sister, Doris, that he was in Florida at the time of the robbery. He went on to say, 'Dad, I haven't killed anyone and I don't intend to.' John continued by saying that if it comes down to him going back to prison or shooting it out with someone, he said, 'I ain't [*sic*] going back to prison, but I don't want to hurt anyone.'"

Before leaving, the family took photographs outside the house. John posed first with his guns and then with his girl. Preening with Evelyn like a benevolent husband—his smile streaked with pride; she secure in his shadow. Neither of them could know that this was to be their curtain call.

When they prepared to leave the farmhouse on Sunday afternoon, at 4:00 in the afternoon, all had tears streaming down their faces.

"For my part," recalled John's father, "I had been living the life of a parent who had been informed, in effect, that his child had an incurable cancer. I knew that there could be only one finish to the 'illness' of my boy. That finish would be death."[3]

They drove all night, arriving in Chicago by morning. They had heard from Opal Long, who assured them that Larry Streng could put them into a hideout. Streng, forty-four, was trusted; he'd dated Opal Long for three years and was friendly with Evelyn Frechette. Yet three days before, Streng had unwittingly told an informant of his planned meeting with Dillinger. On the night of April 8, Evelyn went alone to his room, at which time she made an appointment to see him the next day at the Austin-State Tavern, sometimes called the "U" Tavern.

416 State Street was a tiny storefront wedged beneath an ominous water tower. Fire escapes loomed above, making canyons of the street below. It was sunny noon of a bustling, average weekday. While Dillinger remained in the car, Evelyn entered the tavern alone. In a naive lapse of judgement, Dillinger thought she'd be safe even if arrested, because she was unarmed. This was his reasoning. Neither could know that Larry Streng had been arrested minutes before her arrival. As soon as she walked in she was surrounded by men holding machine guns. Melvin Purvis took charge of her. A sea of somber, suited men hoisted her through the congestion of State Street to a waiting automobile. Careful to shield him, she did not look in Dillinger's direction. In a cloud of cigarette smoke, Dillinger blinked through the windshield and took one last look at his Billie.[4]

Left within the tomb of his silent car, Dillinger drove shakily away, bound for the comfort of his attorney, Louis Piquett. Piquett was in Washington, DC, and Dillinger drove frantically in search of a private telephone. On the empty seat, her scent lingered, mocking and taunting him in his grief. The dream of marriage under assumed names and the flight to Mexico or South America had given him the hope that he could go on to live a normal life. Her absence would leave him in the abyss of despair.

Like Bess Green, Evelyn was held "incommunicado" and kept secretly without formal charges. Purvis placed her under the supervision of Agent Murray C. Faulkner and Harold Nathan, who was first assistant to J. Edgar Hoover and a recent arrival to Chicago. During a three-day interrogation, she presented a bulwark of resistence.

"I want to see my lawyer," she answered doggedly.

"If you don't talk, you're not going to need a lawyer, you're going to need a doctor or an undertaker," someone allegedly joked.

Evelyn revealed a weathered shell. She had suffered many indignities in her lifetime. She surprised her interrogators, who had been buoyed by the cracking of Bessie two weeks before.

Evelyn threw them bones of scant, cursory information, such as the year she'd met Dillinger, and that she'd been married to Welton Spark. The questioning continued for the next two days, until Louis Piquett, Dillinger's flamboyant attorney, leaked the news of her arrest. This forced the Justice Department to make its first written clarification of the woman's arrest, which was issued on Wednesday, April 11, in a crisp memorandum for Sam Cowley from J. Edgar Hoover:

> Mr. Purvis telephoned this afternoon to advise that the Chicago American had printed a story to the effect that Evelyn Frechetti [sic] was in custody, and that Mr. Purvis had denied this fact. Mr. Purvis was inclined to feel that it would be better to tell them the complete story to avoid the sarcastic comment that would inevitably follow. I told Mr. Purvis, however, that I felt it would probably be wiser for him to continue to refuse to make any comment.
>
> I telephoned Mr. Nathan, and he agreed with this decision. Mr. Purvis advised that they are renting an apartment and that the Frechetti woman will be kept there tonight.
>
> Very truly yours,
> Director

Melvin Purvis, buckling under the pressure of the newspaper reporters, called Sam Cowley in Washington on April 11. The *Chicago American* had published the information that Evelyn Frechette had been taken into custody. Should he continue to deny the arrest?

Purvis, under orders from Sam Cowley, issued a statement:

> Mary Evelyn Frechette, a paramour of John Dillinger, was taken into custody Monday night; in Chicago, Illinois . . . she is being questioned at the present time . . . she denies having seen Dillinger since his escape from the County jail at Crown Point, Indiana . . . she [will] be prosecuted on charges of harboring a fugitive from justice.

Upon hearing this, Hoover brought thumbs down in a furious cry of veto. He commanded Purvis to make no further statements to the press regarding Evelyn Frechette.[5]

On April 12, a warrant was issued by Edwin C. Walker, U.S. Commissioner in Chicago, to remove her from Chicago to St. Paul to face charges of harboring Dillinger in the Lexington Avenue apartment. By Friday night, April 13, bail was set at $60,000, on charges of aiding

John Dillinger to escape from the Lexington Avenue apartment. She was arraigned late Friday before Commissioner Walker on a removal warrant.

The $60,000 bail was an amount that Piquett tried to get reduced to $500, while threatening to fight her removal to St. Paul. Always the orator, he privately composed a series of statements that he would drop upon the fascinated public readership. His talent was to take the jargon of the legal system and translate it into the easy copy of layman's language.

"All the Federal Government has on Dillinger is a Dyer Act Case," Piquett would go on to tell the press.

"The Dyer Act prohibits the interstate transportation of stolen automobiles. Well, Dillinger stole Sheriff Lillian Holley's automobile when he escaped from Crown Point, Indiana, jail into Illinois . . . anyone will agree that $2,500 bail is a reasonable figure in a Dyer act case. Yet here is Billie Frechette, charged with harboring a $2,500 defendant, and her bond stands at $60,000. It should be $500."

The tie to St. Paul was Dillinger's fingerprint on the Listerine bottle. It had been taken from the Lexington Avenue apartment and had been left in the St. Paul Police Department of Identification, where Inspector Tierney guarded this crucial evidence. Agent Coulter claimed he'd also lifted Evelyn's print from the apartment, along with that of John Hamilton, and that her print had been identified in the division laboratory.

Further evidence linked Evelyn to a conviction in St. Paul. Agent Werner Hanni, in the hours following the shootout, had taken Evelyn's tan coat from the apartment and had it identified as belonging to her from tags sewn inside the seams. Special Agent T.G. Melvin took it over to the Young-Quinlan Company at 9th and Nicollet Avenue, Minneapolis, and exhibited it to saleswoman Vee Clancy. She recalled selling the coat on March 27 and, when shown Evelyn's photograph, identified her as Mrs. J. Hughes, the buyer of the coat.

After Louis Piquett had pushed his way in to see the prisoner, Evelyn rendered her tale of beatings and insults. Piquett and her other defense attorney, Jerome Hoffman, shared her indignation.

"They called me 'Dirty Indian,'" she maintained. "They kicked my stomach, pulled my hair, slapped my face, to get me to tell them where he was . . . ."[6]

Evelyn Frechette entering courtroom, St. Paul (Tom Smusyn)

*"Van Meter doesn't even like Marie. He's with her because she's the most convenient thing available."*

*—Jean Delaney Crompton*

# "She Was Just Like Him"

As Beth Green, as she was now called, was indicted and committed to the Ramsey County jail, the U.S. Commissioner for the District of Minnesota, W.T. Goddard, swore out a Complaint that substantiated her confession.

This document was to usher in a new strategy of law enforcement. In the fight against the crime wave sweeping the Midwest, it promised to erode the fabric of the gangs. In its words, numbers, and symbols, the Federal Harboring Law would fall upon the gangs like divine restitution. Section 141 of the United States Criminal Code, 18 U.S.C. 246, said basically that "technically, the Government can prosecute for the act of harboring in any one of the federal districts in which the harboring occurred."

The Complaint, dated April 9, was a pioneer of its kind. It said that the Greens conspired "together unlawfully to harbor and conceal in the City of St. Paul aforesaid, in the County, State and District aforesaid, one John Dillinger, a fugitive from justice. . . ." The small detail that had brought Beth Green into such culpability was the Dyer Act, which was cited in the text of the Complaint as the source of the federal jurisdiction of these charges. Dillinger had violated the National Motor Vehicle Theft Act, and the Greens were charged with preventing "Dillinger's discovery and arrest." A hearing was scheduled to take place on April 23. Crouching under an imminent prison sentence, Bess continued to cooperate. Like a modern-day Scheherazade, forced to weave a story to save her own life, she told a plausible tale.[1]

Bess described the wife of Baby Face Nelson as "weird" and "funny looking" in an unflattering portrait. Yet the life of Helen Gillis could not be pigeon-holed into the biography that Bess provided.

Helen Gillis was a blue-eyed, small woman, at 5 feet 2 inches and weighing 94 pounds. She took her place at the side of Baby Face Nelson with an abiding sense of wifely duty. She said she wanted to die with him. Yet with two small children, she lacked the freedom to assume so esoteric a stance. The babies, Ronald and Darlene, were farmed out to Gillis' relatives and brought to see their mother when the hideout and time permitted. Helen Gillis was sick, recently hospitalized, and obsessed with imminent death. Her forehead was engraved with deep wrinkles, and, at twenty-one years of age, she looked far older. In her insular detachment from the real world, she garnered very little sympathy and much contempt. Called pretty by some, ugly by others, at once pathetic and calculating, there was no easy explanation for her.

She was born Helen Warwrzyniek in Chicago on March 23, 1913. The family had emigrated to Illinois from Germany. In spite of political upheavals, the family identity had been staunchly Polish Catholic.

Her mother, the former Kasmiria Popeleski, bore four girls, Helen, Sophie, Wanda, and Marie, who died, and three brothers named Steven, Frank, and Leonard. Kasmiria died in childbirth in 1924. Her death tore apart the fabric of the family. Helen's father, Vincent Warwrzyniek, supported his brood by working at the Fullerton Packing Company as a meat packer. Money was scarce and Helen went to work in the toy department of Goldblatts on Western Avenue. Helen soon strayed from the strained, bereaved household. She fell in love with a former inmate of the Illinois State School for Boys, Lester Gillis.

Lester J. Gillis had been born to a Belguim immigrant, the former Mary Dogueg, and Joseph Gillis in 1908. In 1922, Gillis was arrested in

Helen Gillis, wife of Baby Face Nelson. (Author's Collection)

Chicago for car theft. After two years of reform school, he was paroled in April 1924. On Christmas Eve, 1924, Lester's father died at the age of fifty-five. Lester was returned to the state school shortly after being paroled and received a second parole in July 1925. Once again he violated, returning to the state school in October 1925. He received his third parole on July 11, 1926. He became active in Chicago's tire theft and bootlegging rackets, meeting people in the caliber of Tommy and Roger Touhy, Ed and Ted Bentz, and other notorious figures. He also met Helen.

Her tenure would begin with a leap of faith and the hem of her skirts; at three months' pregnant, she eloped with Gillis on October 30, 1928, to Valparaiso, Indiana. Both lied about their birth dates on the application. Thus, Helen began her new life, living with Lester's family in their brick, middle-class home on the South side. On April 27, 1929, Ronald Vincent Gillis was born to the couple.

The following year, on May 11, 1930, Helen returned to the Garfield Park Hospital and gave birth to a girl, Darlene Helen. Helen Gillis cared for her children with the assistance of Lester's mother and married sisters, Leona and Juliette. Another sister, Eugenie, had died at the age of twenty-five.

Helen's problems accelerated when Lester was arrested by the Chicago Police in Chicago on January 15, 1931, and charged with bank robbery. On July 9, 1931, he was sentenced to one year to life in the Illinois State Penitentiary at Joliet, and on July 17 he was received at Joliet to begin his sentence. Helen remained with his mother, Mary Gillis, in a flat on 2000 South Ogden Avenue in Chicago.

Lester would escape from jail on February 17, 1932. During the process of being removed from prison to stand trial at Wheaton, Illinois, on a charge of robbing the Itasca State Bank of $4,000, he was found guilty and received another term of one year to life. It was a short-lived sentence; while being taken from the Du Page County Circuit Court, he escaped from his guard.

From there he slithered through a type of underground railroad system, reaching Reno, Nevada, and a connection named Joe Pirrenti, a bootlegger. Helen lived with "Les" in Reno through December 1932 as Mr. And Mrs. James Burnell. A man of many names, including the most theatrical tag ever vested on a contemporary criminal, he used Jimmy Burnell most of the time.

Pirrenti introduced Gillis to William Graham, who, together with James McKay, headed the underworld in that region. Graham provided refuge for Gillis and sent him to James Griffin at the Andromeda Cafe, at 155 Columbus Avenue, San Francisco.

The Andromeda, a short distance from Chinatown, stood sandwiched

Dillinger was indentured to Baby Face Nelson for "a favor." Dillinger hoped to pay him off. (FBI)

on a crowded street. The gangsters always sat upstairs, in a balcony fashioned with windows that allowed them to view the saloon, embellished with ceiling fans and a mirrored bar. There was a secret exit through a door at the bottom of the stairs, which contained a passage connecting to pirates' catacombs. Dating back to the days of the Barbery Coast, it emptied to a maze that stretched seven miles to San Francisco Bay. Barring an attack of claustrophobia, a fugitive could snake beneath the streets of Chinatown to freedom.

It was in this exotic setting that Baby Face connected with the most important people he would know. They were Anthony "Soap" Marino, Louis "Doc Bones" Tambini, and Joseph Raymond "Fatso" Negri. Gillis met John Paul Chase when the latter worked for Hans Strittmatter in Sausalito. Strittmatter introduced the two men. Gillis, as Jimmy Burnell, and John Paul Chase became instant friends, blending like a two-toned shoe.

Chase would thereafter introduce Gillis as his half-brother. Lester sent for Helen in April 1932. She left the children and met a contact who drove her to a highway south of Chicago. There, Nelson waited under the cover of darkness for his wife.

The brotherhood established between Gillis and Chase was somewhat cooled with the arrival of Helen, who settled with him in the Mohn Apartments in Sausalito. In June 1932, the two, as Mr. and Mrs. James Burnell, moved to 126 Caliente Street, in Reno. She was joined from time to time by his mother, Mary Gillis, who brought little Ronald along. Lester couldn't live without seeing his son, but Darlene's needs could not be met. She was cared for by Lester's two sisters, tentatively settling in Bremerton, Washington, with Leona, who was married to William McMahon, at 2119 6th Street, and occasionally returning to Juliette Fitzsimmons at 5516 South Marshfield Avenue.

Helen had surgery under the name Helen Burnell on September 12, 1932, at the Vallejo General Hospital in Vallejo, California. The institution operated a strange sideline: It was a meeting place for the local underworld, run by mobster Thomas "Tobe" Williams. In the spirit of this camaraderie, Helen provided the name of her closest relative, the head of the syndicate in that region, William Graham, and his address at 548 California Avenue, in Reno, Nevada. She stayed until September 17, 1932. Gillis, who was living at the Casa de Vallejo Hotel in Vellejo, visited her every day, often accompanied by John Paul Chase and Fatso Negri.

By December 1932, Lester and Helen Gillis, as Mr. and Mrs. Burnell, lived in Reno, Nevada at 126 Caliente Street. They stayed through the end of January 1933, during which time John Paul Chase expanded his bootlegging activities in Sausalito. While Chase would remain there, Nelson took Helen to East Chicago, Indiana, in May 1933, living there as Jimmy Williams.

It was here that the associations were formed which would connect Gillis to the Dillinger gang. Nelson's introduction to Homer Van Meter was consummated through the intercession of a bizarre character. Father P.W. Coughlan was a Roman Catholic priest. He was disconnected from parish life and had left the rectory for the home of his sister in the northern Chicago suburbs.

Unknown to all, he would eventually kneel to the Justice Department, serving as chief confessor of the sins of Lester Gillis. To Helen, he was the embodiment of her Catholic childhood, a scrabble of ethics and religious confusion. In the spring of 1933, Father Coughlan lived in Wilmette, Illinois, at 1155 Mohawk Road with his sister, Mrs. T.J.

Carney. Working for Gillis, he found a summer home in Long Beach, Indiana, for them to share with Homer Van Meter and Tommy Carroll.[2]

Van Meter had met a young woman from Chicago, Marie Santorini Comforti. She was nicknamed "Mickie," and was rather disliked by the other gang women. Before joining Van Meter as his common law wife, she was involved with Chicago's notorious "42 Gang." The syndicate operated bootlegging operations and a dime-a-dance hall under Anthony "Tough Tony" Capezio. He'd been given a joint called the Silver Slipper, in Stickney, Illinois, which had operated under the remnants of the Capone gang. Many of the area residents had worked in the syndicate's bootlegging operations in the neighborhood that housed the Silver Slipper. Inside, the dancers tried to coax their partners into a house next door, set up for a prostitution racket.

Marie had recently run away from her own family, comprised of an adoptive mother and a half-brother. She hung out with her friend, Angeline "Bobbie" Harland. The two girls had one thing in common. Both had come from respectable families before straying to the young toughs of the neighborhood. Bobbie, a Sicilian girl, limited herself to Italian boyfriends. When she met "Wayne Heuttner," his Anglo-American face did not pass her criteria. She passed him on to Marie, who ran away from the "42 Gang" to join Van Meter.

Her adoptive father had recently died. Marie's family, bereaved and disrupted by the death of William Costello, distrusted her new boyfriend. She rebelled, jumping into his Graham Paige sedan and thinking she'd made the big time. To a young girl, Van Meter was a catch.

Yet her family was not as gullible. They had been insulted by Wayne's lack of good manners. He never entered the house and avoided the usual pleasantries. Sarah Costello, Marie's adoptive mother, had met him only occasionally when she learned that her troubled daughter was leaving her protective nest in order to "get married," a polite euphemism in those days. The two cohabited both in the Diversey Arms and later the Lincoln Park Arms Hotel in Chicago before leaving for Texas in November 1933.[3]

They'd been invited for Thanksgiving Dinner in San Antonio, to the home of H.S. Lebman, a Texas gun dealer. Lebman had been engaged by the gang to convert automatic pistols into machine guns and to supply the gang with firearms. To the bounty came Nelson with Helen; Charles

Fisher; and Tommy Carroll with his girl, Jean Delaney Crompton. Carroll, who would work with Dillinger both in the Mason City and Sioux Falls Bank holdups, was there to make a buy.

Tommy Carroll was accompanied by Jean Delaney Crompton, the sister of Pat Reilly's wife, Babe, and Alvin Karpis' sixteen-year-old girlfriend, Dolores Delaney. Young, pretty, and outrageously bold, the Delaney girls wielded strength reminiscent of ancient matriarchies. In their numbers, in their powerful marriages, pregnancies, and affiliations, they influenced the toughest men of the Barker-Karpis and Dillinger gangs.

In spite of the unsavory tastes in men that she shared with her sisters, Jean Delaney Crompton had an introspective, studious side to her personality. While living as Carroll's mistress in Minneapolis, she had been a frequent visitor to the Uptown Library. She paid her initial deposit, borrowing and duly returning the novels under the name "Jean Lane."

These women of the new Dillinger gang were yearlings as compared to Opal Long and Pat Cherrington. All were twenty-one years old, 5 feet 2 inches or shorter, and all weighed less than 110 pounds. Even when compared to Mary Kinder, who was also in her early twenties, they seemed young, inexperienced, and childish. Jean Delaney Crompton started flexing her rank over Marie Comforti and openly expressed her disdain for her. Jean perceived herself as a member of Harry Sawyer's St. Paul empire, while Marie was a dark horse. Van Meter never gave Marie much money; her purse was never found to contain more than $50.

"Van Meter doesn't even like Marie," Jean snarled. "He's with her because she's the most convenient thing available."

In her relationship with Tommy Carroll, Jean Delaney Crompton lived under his domination. Carroll had tired of his recently estranged girlfriend, "Radio Sally" Bennett. His wife, to whom he'd been married years before, Viola, had been a heroin addict who'd tried to kill him with a fireplace stoker. His brush with female rage had left Tommy Carroll with a taste for a submissive woman. When he met Jean Delaney Crompton through her brother-in-law, Pat Reilly, she was exhausted from her dissolved marriage to a musician, during which she'd had a miscarriage. Attracted to the handsome Carroll, she soon learned what the terms of her new love would be. She tried to discuss Dillinger, and Carroll's answer was to beat her up. She later expressed her fear of the gunman. In her words, if she asked a question, he would "slap her down."

Having little to say about the way her life had gone thus far, Jean accepted her fate and offered her acquiescence. Carroll controlled her with a rigid code of behavior, forbidding her to smoke, drink, or mingle with the other members of the gang. She had a higher code of ethics than the other women in this circle and thrived under Carroll's domination. She perceived herself as living within a moral structure, even if it was imposed by a bank robber.

The three women had paid high interest on their moments of excitement and thrills. The terms, quite individual, imposed a usury way out of bounds. Marie Comforti gave herself in vain; Jean Delaney Crompton tithed her free will; and Helen Gillis sacrificed her health.

Interrupting her vacation in the Indiana Dunes in May 1933, Helen Gillis accompanied Lester to St. Paul with Father Coughlan. Driving in an Essex Terraplane, they registered at the Commodore Hotel in St. Paul and stayed from June 9 to 22, 1933. Gillis, with the priest, met Tommy Carroll. All went to Louis' Place in Fox River Grove. Lester and Helen spent the summer at the Indiana Dunes, returning there and staying until September 1933. On Thanksgiving, 1933, Gillis, Helen, Marie Comforti with Homer Van Meter, and Chuck Fisher had dinner at the home of H.S. Lebman at 111 South Flores Street, San Antonio. Sometime in early December 1933, Helen became sick. Lester went through Reno, on December 18 and 19, arriving at Spider Kelly's cabaret on the Barbary Coast in San Francisco. He went directly to Spider Kelly's cabaret to see Fatso Negri. Gillis handed Negri seven $100 bills. He wanted to put Helen back into the hospital. On January 7, 1934, he brought her to the Vallejo General Hospital. She remained there until January 20, 1934. Her name had been changed again, and she now lay under the hospital chart as Helen Williams. Dr. Edward Peterson of the Vallego General Hospital said that Gillis visited her almost daily, except for three or four days during which he had gone to Portland, Oregon. She remained in the hospital until January 20, 1934.

She was still sick on February 3, 1934, when John Paul Chase drove to Chicago and contacted Mary Gillis, Lester's mother. Upon hearing of Helen's situation, she flew out to California with Ronald, the couple's son. On February 21, all three crossed the California border.

Mary Gillis accompanied young Ronald in Chase's Plymouth. Helen and her husband rode into Reno, Nevada, alone. On February 23 they left Reno, arriving in St. Paul three days later. They got rooms at the Commodore Hotel. On March 1, they rented apartment number 106 at 1325 W. 27 Street in Minneapolis. On March 5 they left the premises early in the morning. On March 8 they arrived in Bremerton, Washington, where Mary Gillis remained with Ronald. She would stay there until July 1934.

On April 13, Van Meter and Dillinger, carrying machine guns, raided the Warsaw City police station and obtained two revolvers and four bulletproof vests. The men fled in a black sedan. Jud Pittinger, the night policeman on duty who was slugged over the head by one of the gunmen, said he was quite positive one was Dillinger. Van Meter was tentatively fingered as the other assailant. The two fled to the Evening Star Camp five miles east of Cedar Rapids, Michigan.

Van Meter had sent Marie Comforti to live with "Babe" Reilly, Jean Delaney Crompton's sister and Pat Reilly's estranged wife. Marie was recovering from her own operation and was recently released from the Samaritan Hospital. Marie Comforti stayed with Helen "Babe" Reilly until April 17, when she took the night train for Chicago, meeting Van Meter at the Northwestern Depot. The two went to the Wil-Mar Hotel, where he registered them into a second-floor room as Mr. and Mrs. J.O. Williams.

He made up for the weeks he'd disappeared. With the promise of a vacation, he gave her money to buy clothes.

"We're going up north," he told her, leaving out the other geographical details. She went out to buy her own version of the popular "outing" ensemble of the day, seen in the society pages of the Sunday paper. She came back to the Wil-Mar Hotel with a green riding habit, complete with high boots and knickers. A girl born of the teeming streets of Chicago, she could not be blamed for this fashion mistake.

The trip north was actually a desperate plan to unite the errant members of the gang, who needed to regroup. The Lexington Avenue shootout and the death of Eddie Green had scattered the remaining people like ants. Arranging a meeting was to be a complicated matter. In order to make contact, Gillis and John Chase sent an intermediary known as Bruce to go to Father Coughlan's home in Wilmette. On April

10, the spoiled priest followed orders to go to the familiar hangout, Louis Cernocky's place, at Fox River Grove, Illinois. He was to meet Gillis, Van Meter, Carroll, and Chase.

Louis Cernocky greeted the gangsters, who had dined with him after the Sioux Falls holdup. A rotund, friendly restauranteur, he extended his hospitality over the period of April 16 to April 19. In attendance were the dubious cleric, Mr. and Mrs. Gillis, Tommy Carroll with Jean Delaney Crompton, and Homer Van Meter and Marie Comforti.[4]

Carroll and Crompton had come from Nashville, Tennessee, and Louisville, Kentucky, where they'd met with John Hamilton and Pat Cherrington. The original plan had been for all to meet at Louie's Place by April 20. But Hamilton took a detour and brought Pat to Chicago, where they picked up John Dillinger. They formed a trio, and went on the road to Sault Ste. Marie, Michigan, to visit John Hamilton's sister. Dillinger felt like a sorry, third wheel. Obsessed with Evelyn, he was grieving her loss. His monologues centered on attorney Louis Piquett's work on her upcoming defense.

Pat Cherrington, while concerned with Evelyn's plight, had pressing concerns of her own. She was, like Helen Gillis and Marie Comforti, chronically ill. Her stomach hurt her constantly. The sutures of her February operation were not setting properly. She had other problems, adding to her stress and pain. Right after Evelyn's arraignment, using a key found in the Lexington Avenue apartment, Justice Department agents opened Cherrington's safe deposit box in the Lincoln Safe Deposit Company on the North side of Chicago. They were looking for bank robbery money but took her jewelry, a watch, and several rings valued at only a few hundred dollars. To this indigent woman, it was a violation that left her bereft of any financial security. The loss of the property was minuscule, though, as compared with the larger picture: Her name was printed in the papers for the first time. She was now publicly associated with Dillinger.

Pat had been living with John Hamilton as his wife, but the road allowed for little accumulation of wealth. She knew that, without Hamilton, she'd be penniless. She accompanied him with Dillinger up to Algonquin, a Sault Ste. Marie suburb of Michigan. They visited the home of Hamilton's married sister, "Fat Anna" Steve, at 1201 Fourteenth Street, on Tuesday, April 17. They left one of their cars, to avoid the suspicious appearance of two autos trailing each other.

The visit lasted for about two hours. Pat and her sweetheart posed for a picture. Hamilton tried to contact an old friend while there, Paul Paukette. They squeezed the last remnants of family gossip into the short time that they had. Hamilton left a car with his sister, a Ford V-8 sedan that he'd recently bought in Nashville. Anna Steve would be arrested in short order, arraigned and indicted under the tentacles of the federal harboring law. As she watched her brother drive away, she wondered if she would ever see him again.

Two days after her brother left with Pat Cherrington and Dillinger, federal men burst into her home and searched it. They said she'd allowed them entry. She disagreed—the search, without a warrant, was conducted against her wishes. Nevertheless, they confiscated the keys to the car, with the invoice, delivering it to the U.S. Attorney in Grand Rapids, who claimed it as an abandoned automobile. The outraged woman filed a petition to get the car returned to her. Her petition was dismissed, on the grounds that she failed to prove it was rightfully hers.

Dillinger, Hamilton, and Pat Cherrington met the group in Fox River. They were making plans to leave Louie's Place. Cernocky was sending them to his friend, Emil Wanatka, who operated a large restaurant and lounge in the north woods of Manitowish Waters.

Emil Wanatka and Cernocky went back to the days of jumping ship in New York Harbor. Cernocky's European trade, horse harnesses, rendered him obsolete as a feudal serf. He'd become friendly with Wanatka in New York, migrating into Chicago later on. Their stories were similar. As a young man in Europe, Emil's family had wanted him to be a priest. His answer was to stow away on a vessel bound for North America. He jumped ship at the West side pier and melted into New York. He was caught stealing food from a restaurant, and, to avoid arrest, he agreed to stay and work.

He followed the Manifest Destiny and went out to Chicago. He opened the Little Bohemia Restaurant in Chicago. There he met Louis Cernocky. In Kenosha, Cernocky would open a place he'd lovingly call Louie's Crystal Palace. During these years, Emil met a nice young woman, Nan Voss. She hailed from a remote section of northern Wisconsin, where her family had founded Voss Birchwood Lodge in 1909. This resort, nestled on Spider Lake, Wisconsin, catered to upper-class businessmen seeking rest and refreshment. They married, and Wanatka opened up his own place about a mile from the Voss Birchwood Lodge.

Cernocky gave Lester Gillis a letter of introduction for Emil Wanatka, who did not expect them. The epistle instructed Emil to "treat well the individuals whom he is sending to his place."

On the morning of April 20, Lester Gillis, Helen, Tommy Carroll, Jean Delaney Crompton, Homer Van Meter, Marie Comforti, and Pat Reilly left Louis's Place. Enroute, near Portage, Wisconsin, Gillis' car was wrecked and they had to place it in the Slinger Garage, in Portage. Chase, who didn't go with the others to the Little Bohemia Lodge, went to Chicago to visit the home of Juliette Fitzsimmons, Gillis' sister.

Frank Traube, a waiter at Little Bohemia, already knew Lester Gillis, having met him in the Channel Lake region near Fox Lake, Illinois, and also at Louie's Crystal Lake Dance pavilion. His father, Frank Traube Sr., had been one of Emil's associates in the Chicago bootlegging operations. With astonishment, Traube recognized Marie Comforti when she arrived. He could swear he'd danced with her when she'd worked as a dime-a-dance girl in a barroom at Cicero and Harlem in Chicago during 1931 and 1932. Remembering the dancer, he kept it to himself and thus prolonged his life.

Marie arrived in distress and discomfort. In her riding outfit with the stiff boots, she must have felt her anticipation of a great adventure wavering as time passed in the endless droning of the car. Gradually the farms diminished, until not even a cow could be seen from the highway. By the time they passed through Wawsaw, the area was completely desolate. The billboards faded first; then even the horses disappeared. An occasional silo broke into the dark landscape like an introduction to the narrowing road, the country becoming etherial and wild. They found Route 51N, a two-lane highway past farms and rolling hills with an occasional farmhouse. Trees formed a distant horizon.

The dusk shrouded their destination, the Little Bohemia Lodge. The first night offered strange blackness. Not even starlight got through, with the tree branches stretching 100 feet into the sky. Dillinger arrived on Friday afternoon with John Hamilton, Pat Cherrington, and Pat Reilly, whom they'd picked up after leaving Hamilton's sister. It wasn't Dillinger's first choice for a hideout; he'd wanted to get in touch with Victor Fasano, who had harbored Dillinger and John Hamilton around the time of the East Chicago bank robbery in January.

Nevertheless they toted their baggage, expensive leather suitcases stuffed with clothes. Dillinger carried silk boxers with buttons and lots of ugly socks. They filled closets full of dark, conservative suits and heavy, woolen overcoats. All the women brought satin pumps, except Helen Gillis. The life had taken her bloom of youth away; she never wore high heels, nor any sought of personal adornment. They carried pocketbooks of leather patchwork with wooden handles framed in leather.

Helen Gillis unpacked in the cottage some feet away, hanging up her blue and white gingham dress in seersucker. A surprisingly domestic dress, it had an empire waist with a white eyelet ruffle in the seam and puffed sleeves. A veteran of the warmer climate of the West coast, her lightweight dresses couldn't serve her in these aboriginal woods.

Tommy Carroll and Jean Delaney Crompton arrived in a Buick driven by Tommy Carroll. Jean's secret pregnancy, coupled with Carroll's restrictions, meant she would spend her time alone in their room. She'd brought along her newest novel, *Twenty-Four Hours*, by Louis Bronfield. She planned to read quietly, unlike the others, who played cards.

In the small town of Manitowish Waters, where many people were connected through extended family, word spread that a group with fancy sports cars had arrived. It was unusual for that time of year, with the roads caked with ice, to get visitors such as this.[5]

At the Voss Birchwood Lodge, Nan Wanatka's niece drove over to Little Bohemia to see what was going on. A young, attractive art student, Audrey Voss was home from her university for spring recess. The success of the lodge, opened by her mother and father in 1909, had ensured that she would grow to be educated and cultivated.

Sophisticated, a modern career woman, Audrey Voss was unimpressed with the new arrivals.

"John Dillinger didn't seem like any extraordinary person. He was in the corner playing cards with Emil. When he looked up at me, he looked right through me. His bleached red hair looked orange. It was not attractive. In those days it was very unusual for a man to dye his hair. I could tell that it was dyed from his dark eyebrows. He had a mole and very piercing eyes."

Without knowing their identities, Audrey sensed their unsavory nature.

"They were not the types who usually came in here. No one had expected them. They were sent here by a man who had known Emil at the Little Bohemia in Chicago."

The women seemed especially out of touch with the surroundings. Crompton was simply not visible, staying up in her room in blind obedience to Carroll's orders. Comforti looked ludicrous in her riding outfit. Helen Gillis made a poor impression on the young Miss Voss.

"She was small, didn't wear makeup. Her hair was short and plain-cut. She had a dog in her arms."

These were not the usual businessmen's wives nor the occasional mistress brought up for a stolen weekend of good wine and native Bavarian cuisine.

"Anyone who was hanging out with them was a gun-moll, not a lady," Audrey Voss opined.

The first night passed in agony for Pat Cherrington. By Saturday morning, she was doubled over with abdominal cramps. Pat Reilly offered to take her to Dr. Nels Mortensen in St. Paul. They left right away, and would not return until the following night.

The light of the morning brought Helen Gillis into the forefront of Audrey Voss' attention.

"Helen Gillis was hanging around the kitchen to keep an eye on things. It's a lot of bunk that they were helping out with the cooking," she said, responding to rumors later fostered by newspaper articles.

"They were keeping an eye out. Every time the phone rang they looked to see who it was."

Audrey Voss would not forget the acridity of Helen Gillis for many years.

"She was a hard-boiled gun moll. She looked like she ran the show, that she would tell the other women what to do. She was just like him and he was tough. You could tell he meant business and her too."

George Bazso was the bartender at the Little Bohemia Lodge. Twenty-six years old, he'd tended the establishment since its opening. Accustomed to watching the behavior of the various patrons who'd flocked into the saloon, he noticed that this group didn't linger in the public areas. After dinner, they always went right upstairs to the bedrooms.

"Van Meter was quiet; Hamilton very tall; John Dillinger a typical

Indiana farm boy," said Bazso in an interview. He remained surprised that Dillinger, an "unassuming guy," had gotten all of the publicity.

"The others seemed like they were in charge." Bazso only remembered that the women were untouchable.

"I didn't talk much to the girls because of who their men were. Suicide!"

It was easy to avoid the women, who purposefully kept their profiles in the background.

"They were not at all obnoxious," Miss Voss was quick to notice. "They didn't want people to take a big note of who they were. They were quiet, well-behaved."

On Friday night, Baby Face Nelson impressed Bazso as the youngest and most talkative.

"Jimmie gave me a $5 tip, a fortune in those days."

Early Saturday morning, Bazso received special orders from Wanatka.

"I got an emergency order to go to Ironwood for food. They would follow me, but I wasn't supposed to know. They were driving a Ford sedan; they came in behind me, and I saw that they had a rifle. They had followed me to Ironwood and back. If I would have stopped to talk to a cop, they may have gotten me.

"When I was unloading the truck, I heard shots and I asked Emil what that was. He said, 'The customers are taking target practice.'

"I didn't go down to look. I didn't want to get involved with them in the daytime."

Pat Cherrington shared her opinions later with prison officials. She respected Van Meter; the brains of the outfit, he was, in her estimation, "a good man for bank jobs." Patricia perceived Lester Gillis as a "very hardened criminal." He was a "blood-thirsty individual," in her own words. As Dillinger's confidant, Patricia knew that his tactics were not approved of by the other members of the gang. Dillinger was totally disgusted with Nelson. He'd told Hamilton that he owed Nelson a favor, or else he would have severed his connections with him.

Local customers, some from the Civilian Conservation Corps, came to drink beer, listen to piano music, and bask in the warm, darkened feeling of the paneled decor of the lodge. To the displaced men of the CCC camp, it had the heart of home, enhanced with aromas wafting from the kitchen. Nan Wanatka was supervising the cooking, resentful of the gaze of Helen Gillis. As Nan worked at the huge, blackened stove, her eyes kept darting to the wall clock. Emil knew they were the Dillinger bunch, and he had not kept this a secret from his wife. Nan was a responsible proprietress and, more importantly, a mother who was frightened for the safety of her son, Emil Junior. She left the stove sporadically to check the cellar door, just outside the kitchen. It would make a safe haven should the unspeakable occur.

Nan was afraid to use the telephone while the gangsters were there. She felt sure the phones were bugged because of the way that everyone was behaving. A chance to leave the lodge presented itself, when she accompanied Emil Junior to the home of her nephew, Calvin La Porte. It was his birthday party.

"In those days, it was just coffee and cake," Calvin La Porte recalled in an interview.

"If you were lucky, you got ice cream. It was the Depression, you know."

With a child's sense of things, he wondered why he and his playmates were not allowed to play outside the house that day.

"I kept wondering why they were all in the back room talking, if it was my birthday," he recalled. His cousin, Emil Junior, didn't return to his own house at the Little Bohemia Lodge that night. He would sleep over. Calvin La Porte learned years later why his cousin stayed the night.[6]

"That was the pretense to get him out."

*"It wasn't Purvis' fault. He didn't know the layout of the land. When he heard Dillinger was planning to leave early, it upset the entire plan. He had to rush on in."*

*—Audrey Voss*

# The Raid Proper

George La Porte, Calvin's father, presided over the birthday party conference that troubled Saturday afternoon. With Nan Wanatka and Audrey Voss, they planned a hurried strategy.

Audrey Voss would drive the family car to Rhinelander, to place a telephone call out of hearing range. And drive she did—all that night at top speed, with her father, Henry Voss, at her side. Audrey's grandmother sat in the back, thinking it a routine trip; her presence would remove suspicion should they happen to meet any of the gang.

When they got to Rhinelander, Henry Voss telephoned the Milwaukee police, but Milwaukee's chief, Jacob G. Laubenheimer, was not to be found. Henry Voss next called Frank Prohasen, Captain of Detectives.

The Captain ill-advised them to contact the Vilas County Sheriff. This would have put them back where they started, and would have been too dangerous. Dillinger was a national threat, not a local nuisance. Henry insisted the Milwaukee police contact the Chicago office of the Justice Department. The call was returned by Melvin H. Purvis, instructing them not to telephone any other local police department.

The calvary would march from two office headquarters, Chicago and St. Paul. Purvis left in a twin-engine airplane, while the St. Paul office sent two flights leaving Minneapolis. The Voss family remained at Rhinelander, with instructions to meet the raiders at the airport. Henry was to wear a white handkerchief tied around his neck for purposes of identification.

The initial meeting with the Chicago chief established that this was no social call. The special agent was tense and unapproachable. Yet Purvis' lofty attitude was due in part to his own awareness that he would answer for anything that was about to happen.

"Anyone who was in a position of responsibility felt that they were going to be criticized," Audrey Voss recalled.

"It wasn't Purvis' fault. He didn't know the layout of the land. When he heard Dillinger was planning to leave early, it upset the entire plan. He had to rush on in."

The main problem facing Purvis was timing; there was no time to plan a strategy. A local police battalion would have helped to familiarize the government men, but a collaboration with city or state officers was out of the question. The sting of Hoover's scathing remarks to the Lexington Avenue combatants, which had suggested they'd needed a "man in a blue uniform to give you courage," still reverberated in everyone's mind.

This paranoia was exacerbated with the arrival of Special Agent William Rorer. The direct recipient of Hoover's stinging criticism, he arrived with three other agents from St. Paul in two separate planes. Accompanying this group was Hugh H. Clegg, a master interrogator but unproven combatant.

Clegg had been called away from the Beth Green case, where he was garnering her trust in the process of bringing her confessions into the record. Curiously, as Clegg had captured the mind of Beth Green in St. Paul, Melvin Purvis had dominated the arrest of Evelyn Frechette in Chicago. The custody of both had initiated the two special agents into a close awareness of the women of the gang. Yet neither of these officers had engaged in combat with their armed, male opponents.[1]

They carved out a hasty strategy. "Their purpose was to surround, and if possible, to apprehend Dillinger," Clegg later testified in the jargon of hindsight. By Sunday's late afternoon conference, they had decided to wait until dawn, planning to go in between 4:00 or 5:00 in the morning.

While they were still unloading the planes of their machine guns, rifles, shotguns, tear gas equipment, and short arms, Mr. Voss came rushing back onto the landing field. The gang was planning to leave right after dinner. The agents appropriated four cars. Two were wrecks that soon broke down. Twelve of the agents piled into the two remaining vehicles and rode through the freezing night by whatever means possible; hanging onto the running board was the method chosen by default. Other manpower had been held back at Rhinelander.

Eight men stood on the running boards, holding ammunition while trying to keep from losing their balance on the speeding vehicles.

According to Agent Clegg, Little Bohemia was approached at first from the front. Then, at the point between the detour from Highway 51 and the lodge, the soldiers broke into two groups in order to surround the house.

"One group of men stood to the right of the house," he later testified, "another on the left, and there was a group connecting these two lines in front. No agents were stationed behind the lodge."

This strategy was based on their ignorance of the terrain: Little Star Lake, lapping quietly behind the inn, was flanked by a ten-foot embankment upon which a person could stand, walk, or run. This ridge also provided a perfect cover for a person wishing to flee unseen. The men, blinking in the darkness, saw no boats moored on shore. As a potential escape hatch, it was written off. The agents left it unguarded.

They focused instead on the garage, which they thought held the cars of the mob. Fatefully, three customers took that moment to leave. Stationed in Ironwood was a branch of one of President Franklin D. Roosevelt's alphabet agencies arising out of the New Deal. The Civilian Conservation Corps, a rural attempt to provide employment to lumberman and carpenters, operated a camp that provided a livelihood to previously unemployed men.

Eugene Boisoneau, a twenty-one-year-old employee of the Civilian

Conservation Corps, had been inside drinking in the ambiance and fellowship. He left in the company of two of his older co-workers, John Hoffman and John Morris, and climbed into Morris' car. Through the silence of the countryside, somebody yelled the order to "Stick 'em up." The three were listening to big band radio and didn't hear a thing.

The three workers, enjoying the last strains of band music on this Sunday night, started away from the resort. As the car gained speed, one agent ordered the others to "fire at the tires." An instant firing squad hit the men inside the car. John Hoffman and John Morris were wounded, and Eugene Boisoneau was killed.

Emil Wanatka, standing on the porch, also heard the order to "Stick 'em up." This movie dialogue was later changed by Clegg to "Stop, Federal Agents," in the inquest, with "Federal Officers and Federal law," added in the hearings conducted afterwards. The phrasing was immaterial because the three never heard the federal agents. Hugh Clegg testified that the car came between a direct line of fire between the cottage and the federal officers in front of the main lodge.

"They fired to the right side of the car," he explained.

"As the car gained speed it backed around in a more or less sidewise position."

The car rolled toward the detour road leading to the highway; then it stopped.

Bartender Traube clarified the version told by Wanatka, because he also heard the strange command issued from the darkness near Highway 51.

"As they walked to the car, someone said 'Stick them up' and I complied to [*sic*] the orders." Traube testified that immediately after that, the shooting started, issuing from a different direction from the voices that had ordered the men to stop—"From the cottage," he later said, "around the house."[2]

He, Bazso, and Wanatka ran down to the basement when the firing started. George Bazso, who has been credited with saying, "Don't fire," never said it. He also maintains that the popular story of the barking dogs having alerted the gang to trouble was untrue; the dogs, Collies, were very friendly, and their barking wouldn't have elicited any alarm. According to this eyewitness, the gang did not stop to return the fire.

"They were gone before the shooting even started," he later insisted.

Outside, with Boisoneau shot, Morris stumbled out of the car and fell down beside it, wounded. The agents stood poised with their guns pointed at him. Still unaware that they had a civilian, they yelled "hands up." Oblivious, he ignored them.

Pat Cherrington picked this moment to enter the scene. She was back from her visit to Dr. Mortensen, medicated and drowsy. Pat Reilly drove the car, on a mission to bring additional funds from St. Paul.

"When we got to the lane the thing started," she later testified.

"We drove right into the midst of it; we drove up the lane and got out and then they started shooting at me."

A bullet grazed her eye, leaving it black and blue. The fragments fractured her arm. Reilly drove the Packard sedan wildly out of the driveway.[3]

The sound of the gunfire directed at the CCC workers had alerted the gang to the trouble. The men jumped out of the upstairs windows, hit the banks, and ran under cover of the black night. There were no agents back there to check them. The fleeing men slid down the ten-foot embankment to the deep mud on the shore of the lake.

Although the fugitives had checked the area by daylight, the night-time conditions were black as pitch. They couldn't detect trees two steps ahead of them as they ran. The lake cast no reflection. Occasionally the branches of a small pine loomed in front like a spiderweb.

As the gang sloshed through the mud with the speed of gliders, Wanatka, Bazso, and Traube hit the stairs.

"I ran immediately down the cellar," George Bazso recalled. Thinking himself fast, he was surprised to greet the three girls nestled among the coals.

"In the coalbin, they were very calm," he related. "We were more upset then they were."

Van Meter, in his room with Marie Comforti, had heard the dogs barking at 9:30. But the shooting, not the dogs, sent him sliding down the roof. He somehow joined Dillinger and Hamilton. They ran north, to a neighbor's place called Mitchell's Lodge.

At the moment the gangsters landed on the embankment, the agents blew a second round of fire at the quiet building. This maneuver was officially known as the "raid proper."

In the melee, the agents went on their instincts. Return fire seemed to be coming from two points, the cottage and the roof. Bullet holes left imbedded in the bricks pointed to the cottage occupied by Nelson. The only shot returned by the gang originated there. No ballistic evidence was left to support the claim that any bullets were fired from the roof.

"I had information that shots were fired from the roof of the main lodge," Hugh Clegg testified.

The ballistic evidence later pointed to the government's assault as originating from the north, with the bullet-ridden panes telling the story from the northeast window. There was only one single bullet hole from the west, which would indicate that Nelson fired a shot from his cottage before abandoning it. There were no bullet scars on the west, east, or south walls, while the stove chimney was left with numerous scars. In the small house where Gillis was, a chair was left with a single bullet hole.

Dillinger, Hamilton, and Van Meter, who had run to Mitchell's Resort, north of Little Bohemia and just south of George La Porte's house, were prepared to take a hostage. They awoke Mr. and Mrs. Mitchell. Dillinger pointed an automatic at them, while Hamilton stood outside with a sawed-off shotgun.

The group of hostages and criminals left on foot because the Mitchells didn't own a car. They walked to the house of the caretaker and yelled up to a bedroom window and awoke Robert Johnson, a carpenter who lived upstairs.

"Mrs. Mitchell is sick and needs a doctor right away," they lied. Falling for the ruse, Johnson quickly donned work clothes and bedroom slippers and went out to face the men, holding revolvers and a sawed-off shotgun. At gunpoint they crowded into Johnson's small 1930 coupe, with a third person packed into that peculiar symbol of the era, the rumble seat.

One other member of the gang, Tommy Carroll, had gone his own way. He'd escaped from the vicinity after creeping over a bridge into a field of pines and brush. He found the Northern Lights resort, where he stole a car.

Back at the Little Bohemia, the Justice Department halted its onslaught. In the freezing darkness, they came to a realization: Their prey had gotten out on foot.

"No escape by automobile was possible after the raid proper," Werner Hanni later testified.

Agent Hanni, who arrived from St. Paul only after the entire thing was over, was one of the lucky ones. He hadn't been killed, and he would not be asked to take responsibility for the deaths that did occur. This blame went solely to Melvin Purvis, who would shoulder it for antiquity.

When the shooting began, Lester Gillis left his cabin. Helen Gillis, still in the lodge, joined the group in the coalbin, but her enraged husband acted alone. Instead of running, he backed away, shooting at the agents from the cottage. Then, rather than make his escape like the other gang members, he chose to stay in the area. He seemed to want involvement in the bloodbath. In addition to the desire for revenge, particularly against Wanatka, he had purely practical reasons for staying in the vicinity. According to George Bazso, "Jimmy went to Koerner's because the calls came in there. He wanted to know what was coming in."

At around 10:30 p.m., Gillis first knocked on the door of Paul W. Lang and his wife, who lived in a small house on the shore one mile south of the Little Bohemia. Gillis must have had trouble getting there in the pitch blackness, as the terrain sloped dangerously downward directly into the bank of the lake. When he arrived, he petted their dog while he aimed his gun at the couple.

"I won't harm you if you do as I say," he suggested, his baby voice tender as a hatchet. The three got into the family car and drove with the lights off along Highway 51.

Baby Face obviously did know that Koerner's Lodge, two miles away in Spider Lake, had a telephone station that handled all of the area's phone calls. In his increasingly primitive state of panic, Nelson asked about the gas—was there enough in the car? Paul Lang had to assure him that there was. When they got to Koerner's, he pushed Lang to the door.

"Go to the window and show your face so they will know who you are," he commanded.

Alvin Koerner, with his wife, two boys, and small daughter, with an employee named Flora Ella Robins, opened the door. Gillis shoved him inside and pointed his large, automatic rifle at everyone there. He instructed both Mr. and Mrs. Koerner to get their car. He wanted them to drive him to Woodruff.

"I can't leave my children alone," wailed Mrs. Koerner.

Gillis, hair combed back and dressed in a brown suit, next turned to Koerner.

"Then you come," he negotiated. This elicited another cry from Mrs. Koerner.

"I can't stay here alone with the kids," she insisted.

This standoff ended with the sounds of people yelling outside. Emil Wanatka, George Bazso, and Frank Traube had arrived from the Little Bohemia. Traube later testified that they had left the three women in the coalbin and went upstairs after the second storm had stopped. They surrendered to the agents with their hands up. With permission, Traube had telephoned Alvin Koerner.

"Get over here as soon as you can," Koerner had cried into the phone. With the excuse that they had gone to Koerner's to get warmer clothing for themselves, they took Nan and Audrey's cousin, George La Porte, who had left his home for the Little Bohemia after hearing the initial gunfire in his living room. Accompanying them was civilian Carl J. Christensen, whom La Porte had bumped into while seeking medical aid at the CCC camp for the injured workers. The two had parked La Porte's 1930 Ford sedan at the entrance of Koerner's house and went right in.

George Bazso recognized Baby Face Nelson. He was "Jimmy," of the bar and grill.

"I thought he was my friend because he'd given me a $5 tip for a piece of pie," recalled Bazso in an interview. The bartender quite forgot himself, greeting Baby Face with an amiable, "How are you doing?"

The gangster responded to Bazso's greeting.

"He answered me by saying, 'Shut your god dammed mouth and get against the wall,'" recalled Bazso with an ironic smile.

Nelson surveyed his captives. He walked toward Wanatka and Koerner, grabbed each of them by the arm, and ordered them into the car that had been driven by La Porte.

"Don't give me no monkey business," he threatened. "Because I'm gonna kill somebody if we don't get going."

The three walked out of the house. From Mr. Koerner's recollections, the gun was not in view at that point. At the gate, Wanatka got into the driver's seat, and Nelson pushed Koerner into the back. He then took his place on the passenger side of Emil Wanatka. Just as Emil was trying to get the car started, a Ford V-8 driven by Special Agent J.C. Newman, with W. Carter Baum and Constable Carl C. Christensen, drove into the entrance to Koerner's. Agent Newman lowered the window on his side and announced that he was an officer looking for Mr. Koerner. Gillis jumped out of La Porte's car with his automatic in hand and proceeded to Newman's driver's side.

At this distraction, the two hostages, La Porte and Wanatka, jumped out, running like wild dogs from Gillis. He hardly noticed them. His attention was on the policemen; knowing them to be armed, his bloodthirsty instincts erupted. Gillis pulled out his weapon and gunned down the three lawmen.

Alvin Koerner and Emil Wanatka started back to Koerner's house. Civilian Christiansen remained in the back seat.

"I was running and I heard some shots . . . quite a few," Koerner was to testify. "I heard someone say 'somebody is hurt,' and 'let them in,' but I refused to let anyone in," he said honestly.

Audrey Voss had hid in the woods with her grandmother when they heard the shots fired by Gillis. They'd fled their attic hiding place for safety in the forest, where they'd burrowed under a tent base, afraid to venture out. Their last gesture, before going into hiding, had been to serve dinner to the two agents.

Audrey Voss recalled the meal. The agents had appreciated the sophisticated quality of the hospitality.

"Carter Baum was a nice, friendly, young, family man," recalled Audrey Voss, with a sad shake of her head. "He was at our place when the call came to send reinforcements to Koerner's Lodge." He was the father of two infant daughters close in age, who lived in Washington, DC, with their mother.

The agents had come to Koerner's Lodge at that moment in response to a charge of a stolen car. Special Agent J.C. Newman, who had been assigned the job of tailing Opal Long in Chicago, with W. Carter Baum, were sent to investigate the news that a Packard sedan had just been stolen from the garage of a neighbor, Henry Kuhnert. In this first crucial interaction with local police, the government agents followed orders to consult Constable Carl C. Christiansen, forty-two years old, of Spider Lake, who had information concerning the theft. The two agents had gone to his home at 10:30 p.m. Upon meeting Constable Christiansen, they invited him to get into their Ford Coupe. Baum was in the middle, with Newman driving.

They returned to the Voss Lodge, where they were told that a car was parked without lights on Highway 51, a short distance from Koerner's residence. They located the car and noted that it was empty. They then went to Koerner's.

They were met in the darkness by Gillis, who darted to the left side of Newman's car and covered the agents. He held his gun even with the door, within four or five inches of the nearest occupant.

"I know you have bulletproof vests on . . . I'll shoot you in the head. Get out of that car," he screamed prophetically.

While Newman tried to get at his own .38-caliber automatic from his top coat pocket, Gillis told Newman to keep his hands away from his pockets. He tried to get out of the car, and, as he was about to step off the running board, Gillis shot the agent, striking him in the forehead and rendering him semi-conscious. As Newman fell and crawled in front of his Ford Coupe, he heard several additional shots. Gillis shot Constable Christiansen as he opened the car door on his side of the Ford Coupe. He fell into a ditch with nine gunshot wounds. Amazingly, he would live. Carter Baum, hit in the thorax, would die, shot as he followed Christiansen out of the car. He fell sideways over a fence parallel to the road, his machine gun falling on Christiansen. Gillis, still firing, took possession of the Ford Coupe and backed away. From the ground, Newman opened fire on the fleeing Coupe but failed to halt it as the killer left the scene.

Agent Newman went back to Voss Birchwood Lodge, where he met the newly arrived reinforcements from St. Paul: Agents Werner Hanni, G.F. Hurley, T.J. Dodd, and C.G. Hall. The four agents took Newman back and found Constable Christiansen slouched in a half-sitting position, leaning against a fence. Newman took the light belonging to Christiansen and jumped over the fence to find Agent Baum, who was lying face down in a small pool of blood. There was no pulse.

They placed the wounded Christiansen in Werner Hanni's car. The body of Agent Baum was first brought to Voss Birchwood Lodge before being placed in a truck belonging to Emil for removal to the CCC camp before reaching its destination at Caffney's Mortuary in Eagle River.

Before dawn, George La Porte drove back to the CCC camp and asked for Major S.M. Roberts, the camp doctor. Doctor Roberts, who was asleep, was awakened with the news that one of the boys was seriously injured at the Little Bohemia. La Porte waited while the doctor anxiously dressed; then he drove him to the scene of the seize. The doctor shone his flashlight on the body of Eugene Philip Boisoneau, still in the car at its odd resting place near the detour road. He then looked at the car, noting that all twenty-two bullet holes came from the right side, the side from which the agents had fired. He presided as Morris and Hoffman were taken to Grand View Hospital in Ironwood. The body of Eugene Boisoneau remained in the car, heaving on flaccid tires before the disgraced militia.

As dawn approached, the barrage that would be called the "third raid" by the bureau commenced. The agents threw tear gas into the building. Marie Comforti, Jean Delaney Crompton, and Helen Gillis, who had spent the night in the coalbin, came out coughing with eyes streaming.[4]

Three days later, Calvin La Porte returned to the Little Bohemia Lodge with his cousin, Emil Junior. The extended sleepover, which had kept young Emil at Calvin's house in the days after raid, had gotten boring. The boys wanted to get some toys out of Emil's room. Calvin recalled the pungency of the gases.

"We went up the stairs toward Emil's toy room. The tear gas burned our eyes. This was three days later." The aftermath left bartender George Bazso with an enduring sense of chaos.

"It was a real mess," he stated simply.

"I still can't figure it out today."

L to R: Jean Delaney Crompton, Helen Gillis and Marie Comforti took cover in the coal bin during the raid on Little Bohemia Lodge. (AP/Wide World Photos)

# THE CAPITAL TIMES

*Only Madison Paper With Associated Press Service*

MADISON, WIS., WEDNESDAY, APRIL 25, 1934 SIXTEEN PAGES PRICE THREE CENTS

# 'Molls' Under $150,000 Bail

## Dillinger Girls Camera Shy --- Hide Pretty Faces From Photographers

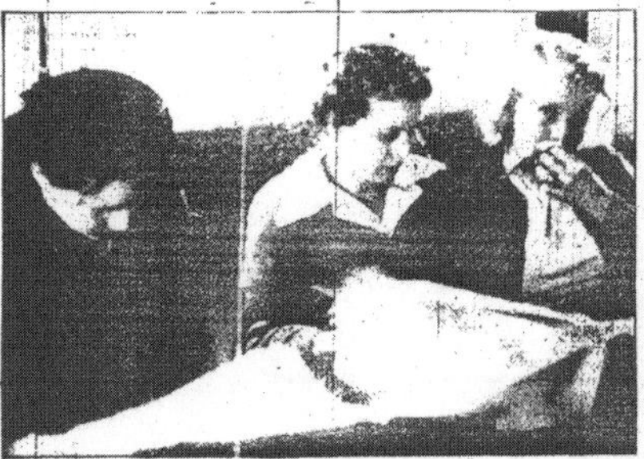

Here are the three Dillinger molls now held in the county jail here under $50,000 bond each. They are shown seated on a davenport in the Vilas county sheriff's living quarters reading accounts of the Dillinger man hunt. Left to right: Rose Anker, 19, petite miss with auburn hair; Marian Marr, 21, brunet bride of two weeks of one of the gangsters; Ann Southern, 18-year-old blonde with a diminutive Mae West figure. All said they came from Chicago.—Associated Press Photo.

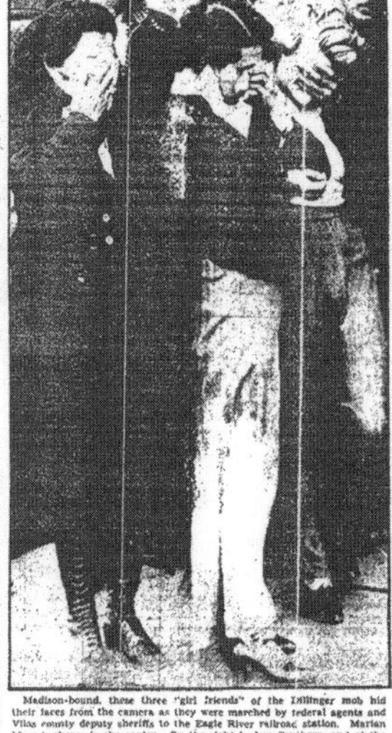

Madison-bound, these three "girl friends" of the Dillinger mob hid their faces from the camera as they were marched by federal agents and Vilas county deputy sheriffs to the Eagle River railroad station. Marian Marr is shown in the center. On the right is Ann Southern, and at the left is Rose Anker. Federal agents have refused to let newspaper cameramen take pictures of the girls since they were brought here.—Associated Press Photo.

## Deep Secrecy Shrouds 'Jail Cell' Hearing

### Girls Show Fatigue After Severe Grilling as They Plead Not Guilty to Charges; Believe Fictitious Names Given

SHROUDED in complete secrecy, the three girl companions of John Dillinger and his mobsters today were arraigned before U. S. Court Commissioner J. J. McManamy in the county jail at 12:30 p. m. Bail was set at $50,000 each, and they were bound over to the federal grand jury which convenes in Madison May 7.

Refusing to give addresses or ages, the trio gave their names as Ann Southern, Rose Anker, and Marian Marr.

They pleaded not guilty to charges contained in warrants accusing them of concealing persons for whom federal warrants have been issued.

Though arraignments before a federal commissioner are supposed to be public—this was admitted by Asst. U. S. Dist. Atty. Harold E. Hanson — newspapermen were barred from the hearing, which apparently was directed by Federal Agent Hardy, who loomed mysteriously in the background of the proceedings.

**Girls Appear Weary**

Seen through the windows as they were brought to the jail office, the girls appeared quite weary and fatigued.

Marian Marr, a comely brunet in lounging pajamas, is about 5 feet 8 inches tall. She is said to be the wife of one of the escaped gangsters.

Ann Southern, a blond of the Mae West type, appeared to be about 5 feet 4 inches tall, weighing about 130 pounds.

Following these two was Rose Anker, a petite auburn-haired girl, 5 feet 3 inches tall, about 110 pounds. She appeared to be the best looking of the trio.

According to the sheriff, the girls are being kept incommunicado in separate cells. The separation has been effected for purposes of questioning, it is said.

**Chicago Agents in Control**

They will probably be turned over to U. S. Marshall John M. Comeford within a week. Until that time they will be in custody of federal agents. Indications are that the department of justice agents will leave here in a week.

The hearing was held in the office of the Dane county jail. Doors to offices were locked and window shades pulled down during the proceedings. By the time reporters were admitted, the girls had been led back to their secret cells by another exit.

**Guard Is Heavy**

During the hearing, vigilance of the heavily-armed guards increased, if that was possible. Nearly a dozen crowded into the small jail office, and a score of others patrolled surrounding corridors.

Before the hearing proceeded, Commissioner McManamy assured a Capital Times reporter that he would be admitted to the hearing.

"These hearings are always public," he said.

But at 12:15, when it appeared that the proceedings had got under way, Sheriff Fred T. Finn, guarding the jail door, refused admittance to anybody. He said:

"It can't be done. The federal government is running this hearing, and I have been given orders to admit nobody."

**Officials All Silent**

Commissioner McManamy, reminded of his promise to make the hearing public, said:

"I'm taking orders from the department of justice."

U. S. Dist. Atty. Harold E. Hanson came out of the jail office with Marshal Comeford, who refused to comment on "anything connected with the case." Hardy then peeped shyly around the corner, but ducked back when a cameraman aimed his camera at him.

"Let's have no more of this," he warned.

The girls were brought to Madison for keeping in Dane county jail by federal agents after their capture Sunday night in a resort known as Little Bohemia near Eagle River, Wis., in Vilas county.

**Tighten Defense Lines**

As one of the most extensive manhunts in the history of Wisconsin proceeded throughout the state, defense lines around Madison were tightened to thwart a possible raid by Dillinger or his associates.

One of the most [illegible] threats of [illegible] was seen in the report [illegible]

## Loot Ohio Bank; Suspect Dillinger

[By The Associated Press]

AKRON, O. — The Mogadore Savings bank in suburban Mogadore was held up and robbed of $4,000 by two bandits shortly after noon today. The robbers kidnaped two clerks and two customers, releasing their captives about 1½ miles north of the city near the Cleveland-Akron road.

The captives gave Akron police Illinois license No. 181-193 as the one attached to the robber's car. The police began an immediate check to determine whether this was one of the "Dillinger gang" cars which fled a trap in northern Wisconsin 48 hours ago.

The captives said it was a Ford V-8 1932 model. A similar car carrying one of the license numbers broadcast by federal operatives as those of a "Dillinger car" was seen at Muncie, Ind., Tuesday headed toward Ohio.

**6 Raid Farm Home**

ST. PAUL—(AP)—Four armed men and two women raided a farm home near Elk river today, took a small amount of cash and then fled, causing a general alarm to Twin City police who at first were told that the gunmen had commandeered an automobile.

First reports led the authorities to believe that the raiders might have been members of the John Dillinger gang who have been sought in this area since they shot their way through a large force of federal men who surrounded a Mercer, Wis., hideout Sunday night.

**5,000 Join In Search**

[By The Associated Press]

MERCER, Wis.—America's million dollar murder, with a puny $25 price tag on his head—and the blood of 13 men across his bullet-blazed trail—mocked today an army of more 5,000 officers who hunted him. But—

"We'll have John Dillinger before long," said the department of justice through its division of investigation at Chicago.

The earnestness of the government's determination was witnessed by both the great number and high calibre of agents they threw into the hunt.

**Has Cost $2,000,000**

There was no word of the desperado despite the intensity of the hunt. Rumors flew, but all simmered down to the fact that John Dillinger vanished Sunday night from the Little Bohemia resort near here and has been unreported since.

In a criminal career dating only from last June—not yet a year—this 31-year-old, small-town man from Indiana has cost an estimated $1,500,000 in law enforcement funds and another $500,000 in loot from banks

(Continued on page 4)

## Reporter Attacked By Fed; Tells of Assault

Federal Agent Hardy, in charge here of the Dillinger investigation, this morning assaulted a Capital Times reporter, R. D. Linton, assigned to "cover" the arraignment of three girls accused of being members of Dillinger's gang. The attack occurred when Linton refused to answer Hardy's questions to his satisfaction and would not turn over to the agent an exposed plate which the agent thought contained his picture. Hardy destroyed all of Linton's plateholders, in addition to the one the agent had demanded. Following is Linton's own account of the incident:

By R. D. LINTON
(Of The Capital Times Staff)

NOW I know how it feels to be "questioned" by a federal agent.

Now I know how a federal agent behaves when a person doesn't answer questions to the satisfaction of said agent.

This morning I was assigned to "cover" the expected arraignment of the three Dillinger "mollettes" before U. S. Court Commissioner J. J. McManamy.

**Waited for Photographs**

I waited in the seventh floor corridor of the Bank of Wisconsin building ready to interview and photograph anyone connected with the case as they left the commissioner's office.

When Federal Agent Hardy, in charge of the case here, left the office I took a "speed flash" photograph of him. We rode down in an elevator together.

"Did you get my picture?" Hardy asked me.

"I don't know," I answered.

We discussed the case and the strange mantle of secrecy with which it has been shrouded by the federal agents ever since it became known agents' bullets probably killed an innocent bystander during Sunday night's battle.

As we walked over to the county jail Hardy frequently [illegible] his question:

"Did you get my picture?"

I repeated my answer.

**Appeared Friendly**

He appeared fairly friendly, although reluctant to talk. He said that if he were in charge of this case he would be willing to grant permission to photograph the girls, especially since pictures of them had been published elsewhere.

But he would not make a definite statement as to whom application for permission to take such a picture had to be made.

In the county jail courtyard, I left Hardy and started talking to two other newspaper cameramen.

Hardy suddenly rushed over from the jail doorway and demanded:

"I want that picture."

I answered:

"I don't know that I have your picture and I can't give it to you. You'll have to put me under arrest to get it."

"Oh, no, I won't," Hardy said, "I'll take it away from you."

He tried to grab hold of two plateholders I held. I tried to run away.

(Continued on Page 4)

## Bandit Robs Oil Co. Station Second Time And Gets $25

### Luther Rondell Is Victim Again at Johnson St. Place

A bandit returned to the Standard Oil Co. filling station, at Johnson and Livingston sts., Tuesday night for the second time this month, escaped after robbing Luther Rondell, attendant. The bandit secured about $25 Tuesday night.

Rondell told police the robber is the same man who robbed him of $60 on Apr. 7.

The bandit is about 28 years of age, five feet and nine inches in height, weighs about 160 pounds, wears a brown, imitation leather raincoat and dirty, gray cap, has a red face and sandy mustache, Rondell declared.

**Calls at 8 P. M.**

The bandit entered the station shortly after 8 Tuesday night, the same time as his previous robbery.

As on the previous visit, the robber entered the station while the attendant was alone.

The bandit, on neither occasion, displayed a gun. But his right hand was in his coat pocket. Rondell believes the man had a gun in his pocket.

Upon entering the station, the bandit commanded:

"Get over there in the corner and give me your money."

Rondell reported to Detective Romain York Sr. that he was forced to unlock the safe. There was but $10 in the safe and he handed it to the robber, Rondell said. Then the robber forced him to hand over approximately $15 he had in his pockets, the attendant reported. The bandit did not take the attendant's change belt.

**Locked in Room**

Before running from the station, the bandit forced Rondell to enter the wash room.

Police began to scour the vicinity a few minutes after the robber fled but their search was unsuccessful.

## County Relief Costs Nearing Peak Levels

### March Total $16,825 Over February, Hein Reports

Dane county relief costs are climbing toward the pre-CWA era again, according to E. C. Hein, county relief director.

Costs for March totalled $83,388.45, an increase of $16,825.75 over the $66,562.70 cost for February, Hein's figures revealed.

The number of persons seeking relief is growing daily, the relief director said. He added that many persons never before on relief are applying for aid now in the hope of getting FERA jobs.

"We had about 2,400 able-bodied men on the relief rolls on Apr. 1," Hein said. "But our total work program will take care of only 1,200 to

(Continued from Page 4)

## Regents Favor Gregory Ouster In Secret Meet

### U. W. Board Silent on Charges Worker Made Against Officials

Working under a shroud of secrecy, the university board of regents today confirmed dismissal of Otto Gregory as an elevator operator for the university department of dormitories and commons.

This action was taken by the board in executive session, while reporters "cooled their heels" for two hours in the corridor outside Pres. Glenn Frank's office.

In taking this secret action, the board failed to clear up publicly certain charges which had been made against the university and the department of dormitories and commons in connection with the Gregory case. One of these charges concerned alleged irregularities on the part of the university and the department's business management in their relations with certain Madison business firms, from whom the university purchases supplies.

Questioned by reporters after the executive session, Pres. Frank and Regent Harold M. Wilkie disclosed that three members of the board had voted against the dismissal of Gregory.

Regents who opposed the dismissal

(Continued from Page 4)

## Governor Sees Hopkins; Relief Talk Is Delayed

WASHINGTON.—(AP)—The conference Gov. Schmedeman of Wisconsin had hoped would result in allocation of more federal relief funds was interrupted this morning and was to be resumed later today.

Harry L. Hopkins, federal relief administrator, received the governor and a group of his advisers, but could give them only a few moments because of an appointment.

The governor is asking federal assistance to avoid, if possible, the necessity of calling the legislature in session to provide relief funds.

James Borden, state budget director, who accompanied the governor here, said about $760,000 of state relief money had not been collected partly because it was tied up in closed banks. This money was raised by a surtax on incomes.

The governor said he had time this morning only to outline the situation as a whole and had not reached a discussion of figures.

He said no specific amount was being asked.

## Ask School Board Explain Insurance Vote

### E. Side Socialists Adopt Resolution Condemning Action

The city board of education has been requested to explain its action in placing school insurance with the old line companies instead of the state insurance fund at a public hearing in a resolution approved by the East Side Branch of the Madison Socialist party.

The resolution approved by the Socialist organization is as follows:

"Whereas, the school board has seen fit to reverse itself on the question of insurance of school buildings and has voted to continue to insure with old line companies and,

"Whereas, the citizens of Madison have lost more than $75,000 dollars by such action in the past 10 years,

"Be it resolved that we citizens of Madison organized as the East Side Branch of the Socialist Party of Madison condemn this action of the school board and especially the action of Miss Regina Groves in reversing her vote on this matter, after the election and

"Be it further resolved that we call on all patriotic taxpayers, unions and civic organizations to unite in condemning this action of the school board, and

"Be it further resolved, that the school board be requested to attend a public hearing and explain its action to the voters."

## Ask Penalty for Death at Mendota

### Kin of Juda, Wis., Victim Want Dane County to Prosecute

MONROE, Wis.—(AP)—Relatives of Clark Lyman, Juda, Wis., whose death at Mendota hospital in 1931 recently was investigated by the legislative committee have written to Thomas H. Caffrey, chairman of the committee, demanding punishment for those responsible for the death.

They asked Caffrey to help launch a speedy prosecution and said that they were consulting the Dane county district attorney, who, they said, explained that the records of the investigation were held by the board of control.

The relatives ask that the board of control turn the records over to the prosecutor.

## Two Nabbed Here On Speed Counts

### Joe Taylor is Fined $5; Hans Schlucher Fails to Appear

Two persons were arrested on speeding charges here Tuesday.

In superior court today, Joe Taylor, route 3, was fined $5. Hans Schlucher, 139 Gilman st., failed to appear to answer to a similar charge.

**WIBA TALK TONIGHT**

Gerald Brown, representative of the [illegible]

## Herbert E. Lawsons' Divorce Is Set Aside

Mr. and Mrs. Herbert E. Lawson, divorced last Oct. 28, have reached a reconciliation, it was revealed in a petition filed by them in circuit court Tuesday asking that their divorce be set aside. Judge A. G. Zimmerman granted the request, enabling the couple to resume their marital life.

## Ex-Wausau Woman Shoots Self in Hotel

MILWAUKEE, Wis.—(AP)—A woman identified as Miss Margaret Al-[illegible]

## Girl, 3, Is Killed by Truck at Wiota, Wis.

DARLINGTON, Wis.—Mavis Thoreson, 3-year-old daughter of Mr. and Mrs. Silas Thoreson, was struck by a truck and killed instantly while she played in a small wagon at Wiota, a [illegible]

## County Jail Is 'Honeymoon Hotel' to Gangster Girl

### Marian Marr Held in Cell Here as Groom Dodges Bullets in Man Hunt

A PRETTY brunet girl, who claimed to be 21 years old, but looks 18, is resting between the grillings of federal agents who are seeking a clue to the phantom-like disappearance of John Dillinger and his notorious henchmen.

She told police her name is Marian Marr.

This is the sequel to a honeymoon as adventurous as any girl ever had . . . spent with one of the five gangsters who, leaving a trail of 13 ruthless murders in a wild flight through the Middle West, blasted their way out of a trap set by federal agents near Eagle River, Wis., last Sunday night, eluding a determined army of 5,000 men assigned to the capture of him and his chieftain, after deserting his bride of two weeks.

The only part of the trousseau she has is her lounging pajamas, now a little soiled from the wear and tear of four days spent in two jails . . . her "Honeymoon Hotels."

With her in the Dane county jail are two other girls giving their names as Ann Southern and Rose Anker.

**Lonely for Pet Pup**

Marian, it is said, has expressed a loneliness for a little Boston bull dog, "Rex," who was left behind when she walked out of the tear-gassed, bullet-riddled resort in Vilas county.

**WEATHER**

*"They ran away from the lodge, leaving me, Mrs. Crompton and Marion Marr, deserting us."*

*—Marie Comforti*

# Their Honeymoon Hotel

After the women surrendered, the government cloistered them with an edict: no photographs, no interviews. Once the Justice Department brought down the curtain, the frustrated reporters had no choice but to embellish the news blackout with sensationalism.

For two days the women dabbed at their eyes, which were still wet from the tear gas. These gestures, caught in an explosive photo, were fabricated as proof of shame and modesty. On the morning of April 23, the three sleep-deprived women entered the Vilas County Jail.

The Bureau's domain over the prisoners angered one news reporter. Disgruntled by official refusal to allow his cameraman to photograph Dillinger's baggage and munitions, he drafted a petition demanding the suspension of Agent Purvis. This action slowly added fuel to the sentiments in Mercer. The town's animosity was heightened by speculation as to why Purvis did not contact the Mercer police before the raid. They were personally insulted, taking the Bureau's exclusion as an insinuation that the area might be controlled by a corrupt police department. Hoover's standard position on the exclusion of local police was that, typically, criminals were notified of an impending raid by the very police who were supposed to be executing it.

The Justice Department answered the call-to-arms that would have had Purvis publicly disgraced. While Hoover had no compunction about privately stripping an agent's power, he was not going to allow a public execution. He made a report to the attorney general, the only area of government to which he was judicially accountable. He declared that Purvis had never been in charge of the investigation—Inspector Clegg, rather, had led the raid. Hoover knew, with his customary insight, that Purvis would remain the scapegoat of the Little Bohemia, and that Clegg's role would go unnoticed. In one stroke, he lessened the national dissatisfaction with the affair and took the first step in the calculated diminishment of Melvin Purvis, that would result in his eventual dismissal from the FBI.[1]

On April 24, at 9:30 a.m., the three women were transferred from the relative comfort of the sheriff's home in Vilas to the Dane County jail in

Embankment behind the Little Bohemia Lodge. The FBI didn't know of the grading which aided the escaping gang. (Author's collection)

Madison. They were separated, with their hearings held behind closed doors.

"The Federal Government is running this hearing," said Sheriff Fred Finn. "I have been given orders to admit nobody," he announced. The Justice Department had pulled rank on his station.

Officially, they had to be placed under arrest, and this was quickly accomplished by Harold E. Hanson, as Assistant U.S. Attorney for Wisconsin's Western District. This assured that there would be no state interference to hamper the government's case against them. With the local jurisdiction quashed, Hoover then asserted his dominance over the Western District Federal Court, which was next on the pecking order. Dane County was chosen because Madison cushioned the federal offices. To be argumentative, Hoover touted his Chicago field office as headquarters. It was a slap in the face of the U.S. District Attorney at the Madison Federal Courthouse.

At the core of the controversy was the fact that the women didn't cooperate either, giving assumed names and refusing to talk. Unknown to them, they had been crowned by the press. As stars in the thrilling chronicle of girls-gone-wrong, they were demoted from their early twenties, becoming "three girls, all in their teens." More significantly, these abandoned, physically ailing women had become overnight sexual bombshells.

Marie Comforti, alias Rose Anker, was typecast into the bland category of "petite miss with auburn hair." At the moment of capture, she more closely resembled Bela Legosi's movie *Dracula*, with her dyed widow's peak prominent upon her forehead and her riding coat draping morbidly around her green vest. In spite of this, she was dubbed "the best looking of the three."

Jean Delaney Crompton gave the name of Ann Sothern. This inspired a Hollywood ambiance and her description as an "eighteen-year-old blonde with a diminutive Mae West figure." She'd been arrested while wearing the latest style, Butcher Boy silhouette pajamas. They were a darkened throwback to the carefree flapper of the roaring twenties, a rare reminder in the greying days of the Depression.

Similarly attired, Helen Gillis, alias Marion Marr, was the "comely brunette bride of two weeks" whose trousseau, her lounging pajamas, were now a "little soiled from four days spent in two jails . . . her 'Honeymoon Hotels.'" It was the year of Busby Berkley's fantasy musicals, with their synchronized songs of unbridled sex. In the days of censorship, these veiled allusions to libertine pleasures were enjoyed in the dark seclusion of movie theaters. The comparison of the three young women of Little Bohemia to these licentious themes, added to their aura as objects of freedom, of pleasure outside of society's rules. The three were hardly aware of the hype, however. As women in custody, they were coming to the attention of J. Edgar Hoover. He released an unsubstantiated statement.

"Some unscrupulous woman helped Dillinger to escape," he declared. "Catch the woman who has cheered Dillinger in a career of murder," Hoover continued, "and you will catch Dillinger. She is more dangerous to society than the desperado himself. It is she and her kind who made him seek a life of crime."

Knowing they were charging the women under aliases, by April 25, Tuesday morning, the Western District of Wisconsin issued a Temporary Mittimus charging Rose Anker, Ann Sothern, and Marian Marr with harboring Dillinger under Section 246, Title 18 U.S. Code. According to the new language, which had also helped to implicate Bess Green and Evelyn Frechette, they had concealed John Dillinger on the 21st and 22nd of April at the Little Bohemia Lodge. To obtain information, the agents employed the methods already used on Frechette and Green. They soon gleaned Jean Delaney Crompton's true identity. Sleep deprivation, in particular, would break Marie Comforti. By Friday, she would be ready to dictate a confession.

"They ran away from the lodge, leaving me, Mrs. Crompton and Marion Marr, deserting us," she cried. Her interrogators were elated at this show of anger directed at Van Meter and, curiously, Pat Reilly. Unlike the other two women, she was a novice and the only one to give a truthful confession.

"My name is Marie Marion Comforti. I have also used the aliases Mrs. Rose Anker and Mrs. Ted Anker and Mrs. Theodore Anker and Mrs. John Ober and Mickey and Marie Costello.

"I met Mrs. Helen Reilly, wife of Pat Reilly, at a beer tavern in Chicago during the summer of 1933, and was with her for three evenings, got to know her quite well, and when she returned to her home in St. Paul, Minn., she gave me her address and she invited me to visit her. I worked until Christmas, 1933, in Chicago, Illinois, and then met Van Meter, just picked him up, and about Jan. 1, 1934, I started living with him as his wife, although we were never married . . . "

In this, her five-page confession, Marie Comforti essentially named Pat Reilly and his ex-wife, the sister of Jean Delaney Crompton, in complicity with the Dillinger gang. Her actual connections were doubtful, as flippant as she was about a close relationship to Helen "Babe" Reilly. An orphaned girl, she was not visited during her tenure at the jail in Wisconsin, which stretched to five weeks until their probation on May 25. While Helen Gillis was visited by her sister-in-law, Juliette Fitzsimmons, and Jean by her own sister, Helen "Babe" Reilly, Marie went without a visit while the Justice Department researched her family.

As a girl, she had been raised in a foster home by the woman she was to call "Mom," Sarah Costello. She was born in Chicago on April 14, 1913, to seventeen-year-old Elinor Krause and Rocco Comforti, an Italian immigrant. Marie Santorini Comforti, her legal name, was orphaned at the age of 2 years when Rocco died. Her mother, though still alive, entered a sanitarium as a paralytic. Eleanor Krause had no choice but to relinquish her little girl. Her friend, Sarah Costello, took the child in an unofficial adoption, with her husband, William, and son, Charles. As the little toddler entered into her new family, her birth mother's condition worsened and, by September, 1922, she was formally installed in the facility where she would live out her life: the Infirmary of the Oak Forest Sanitarium at 1444 Farrabe Street, Oak Forest, Illinois. To clarify the natural mistake of spelling the name "Conforti," Eleanor Krause insisted that the father of the child had spelled his name, "Comforti." Yet the correct spelling didn't stick any more than family ties for the orphaned child.

Little Marie had a dark widow's peak and huge, brown eyes that stared blankly out of her face. Sarah raised Marie with the help of her husband, William, sending her to the Locke Elementary School. The girl grew into a petite, 98 pound teenager of 5 feet 1½ inches, with a seductive mole beneath her left eye that lent a winking attitude to her pert face. She never attended high school, however, and began to rebel after leaving eighth grade. It was a time when teenage girls grew to maturity very quickly, often leaving school to marry or hold a menial job. The idea of a rebellious teenager was vaguely understood in boys; in a girl it smothered as a shameful secret kept by a panicked family. She went to work as a clerk at Scott's 5 & 10 Cents Store, located on North Avenue between Crawford and California Streets in Chicago. Her fate seemed sealed with the death of William Costello, her stepfather, on February 15, 1933. She hung out with a West Side crowd with roots in the Capone era: the 42 Gang that ran a dime-a-dance hall called the Silver Slipper, operating under the fist of Anthony "Tough Tony" Capezio. When she met Van Meter, she'd already begun to feel comfortable with people from organized crime. Had she started work in the Silver Slipper, she'd have nowhere to go but down: The rooming house next door provided a bed for customers who preferred paid sex to dancing.

According to Sarah Costello, her foster mother, Marie lived a "very independent life" after her father's death. She made strange, new friends and stayed away from home for a month at a time. By nineteen years of age she left the Costello home at 2631 N. Montclare Avenue to reside in a rooming house at 1740 Adams Street in Chicago. In September 1933 Marie had wired home to say that she'd been married in St. Paul to Wayne Huettner. Mrs. Costello had met the man only once, on the day before the alleged wedding. She would identify an old mug shot of Van Meter, the bogus groom.[2]

At the time that Marie Comforti was implicating her, Babe Reilly, the ex-wife of Pat Reilly, was enroute to the Dane County Jail. She would ignore the plight of the unrepresented Marie Comforti. Bad blood had developed since the prior March, when Marie had recuperated in Helen's home after the scraping of her uterus in Samaritan Hospital in St. Paul. At that point, Marie was still trying to keep peace with her adoptive mother, sending her $25 for her birthday, postmarked from Babe Reilly's house at 288 Thomas Street.

Now, Babe would pay only the bail of her imprisoned sister, Jean Delaney. The woman received $100 from Tommy Carroll through the intercession of a third party. By the time the money went through all the channels, it had dwindled down to $30. Crompton, who was in the early stages of an ill-fated pregnancy, was receiving softer treatment than the others, out of concern for her condition. On May 10, accompanied by St. Paul lawyer Thomas J. Newman, Mrs. Reilly endured a long session with U.S. District Attorney Hansen. Babe lived up to her reputation among police circles as a tough-talking, flippant woman who kept herself entirely in control.

The reporters waited for Babe at the door of the probation hearing of her sister. They were brave to approach the woman, in light of their tabloid pieces showing her as an "older married sister who could not be separated by 500 miles, jail walls or disgrace."

When cornered outside, Babe told off the reporters in expletives most likely censured in translation.

"If you put in any more sob stuff about me, I'll tear your old paper in two," she allegedly retorted.

Of more concern to Helen Reilly was the allegation that the bail money for Jean, brought by her from St. Paul, originated from Bremer kidnapping funds. It was a hysterical and far-fetched conclusion. It arose out of the fact that the third sister was Dolores Delaney, the mistress of Alvin Karpis, the main suspect in the kidnapping of St. Paul businessman Edward Bremer. Jean Delaney Crompton denied all knowledge of the Barker-Karpis gang, limiting her confession to her relationship with Tommy Carroll, whom she would call "Jack Sothern." Jean and Helen Reilly kept quiet about Dolores to investigators; the Bremer kidnapping connection was enough of a mine field without adding their sister, Dolores, to the fray.[3]

The fabled Alvin Karpis' gang, from its humble tradition of southwestern banditry, had branched into an interconnected syndicate. The people involved floated through two main groups. Called the Barker-Karpis and Nash-Miller gangs, they operated within the Midwest and Southwest from 1931 to 1934.

Karpis' associates, Fred and Arthur "Doc" Barker, were born to a woman of the Cookson Hills of Oklahoma. Kate "Arizona" Clark, called Arrie by her friends, would marry a man named George Barker on September 14, 1892. The four sons of the marriage, Lloyd, Herman, Arthur, and Fred, arrived as the family migrated through Missouri and Oklahoma. The Barker boys became associated in childhood with Volney Davis and Harry Campbell in a hangout known as Central Park in Tulsa. Fred Barker befriended Alvin Karpis while the two served time in the Kansas State Penitentiary. The gang bonded in youth, which is the origin of Ma Barker's reputation as a criminal mastermind in apron strings. In reality, Kate lacked the brains or the status to plan anything more complicated than a grocery list. Logic should have placed her in the ranks of those prosecuted under the Federal Harboring Law, with two to

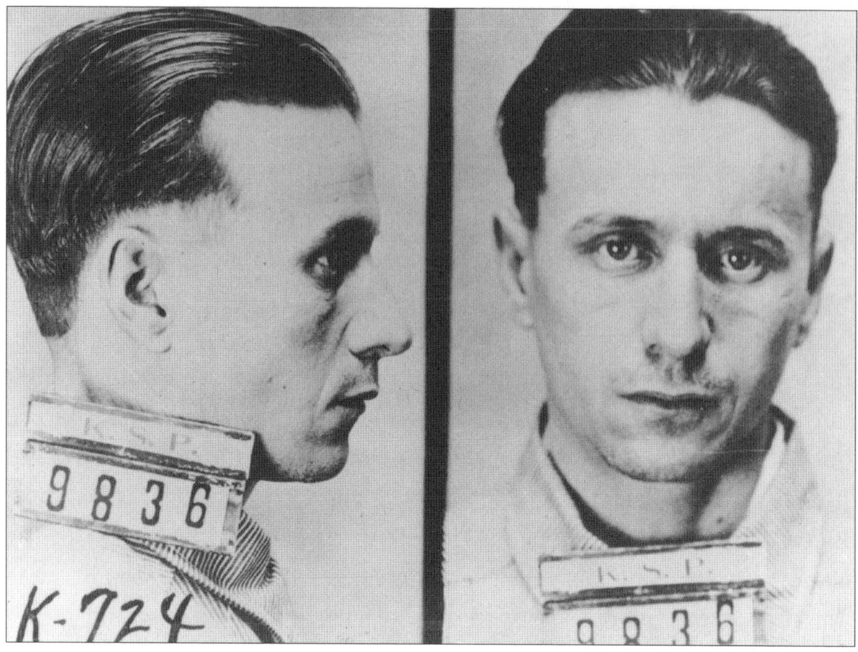


Fred Barker (National Archives)

five years served in a federal facility. Ma Barker was not destined for the court system and had never even been arrested. In the annals of public enemies, she would receive a posthumous pedestal in the criminal hall of fame.

As a mother figure who accepted the wanton ways of her sons and their friends, she was a magnet for the problem kids kicked out of more righteous homes. In this way, Alvin "Old Creepy" Karpis became her surrogate son. As his nickname suggests, he was colorful in a moribund way. Born Raymond Albin Karpavicz to law-abiding parents on August 10, 1907, he was moved through Topeka and Montreal, finally settling in Chicago. After a string of small-time robberies and convictions, he found himself in the Lansing State Prison on May 19, 1930, where he became inseparable with Fred Barker. The two were released in 1931. Kate's other son, Herman Barker, had killed himself on August 29, 1927, while cornered after killing a police officer in Wichita. Lloyd, the fourth son, was in Leavenworth for mail robbery, serving a twenty-five-year sentence.

In 1931, Fred Barker and Alvin Karpis were mutually acquitted and

"Mother," who gained posthumous fame as a criminal mastermind. (National Archives)

released. The two ex-cons lived in a hideout near Thayer, Missouri. A store robbery was committed in West Plains, Missouri, where a De Soto car had been used. On December 19, 1931, Sheriff C.R. Kelly walked over to the De Soto that was used in the robbery the day before. They shot Sheriff Kelly, killing him. It was part of the Barker's pattern of wanton depravity and disregard for human life.

Fred and Alvin Karpis lived with Kate and her companion, Arthur "Old Man" Dunlap in South St. Paul, hiding on South Robert Street. They hung out with Fred "Shotgun George Zeigler" Goetz, bankrobber Charles Harmon, Frank "Jelly" Nash, Verne Miller, and Harvey Bailey, who was later convicted of the Charles Urschel kidnapping along with Machine Gun Kelly and his wife, Kathryn.

Harry Sawyer's protection had been purchased through a contact named Herbert Farmer, who sent Karpis to St. Paul. A landlady's tip was intercepted by a police clerk on Harry Sawyer's payroll, and it took hours for the police to arrive at the hideout, which had been quickly abandoned. Fred and Karpis blamed the unfortunate Dunlap, who was an unwelcome addition to the clan. He was knocked off like a roach on a dinner plate, shot to death. With Dunlap's body a myth was created. That archetypal prop, a woman's blood-stained glove, was said to be found next to Dunlap's nude body, pocked by three bullets. This glove was most likely placed after the fact, a figment of someone's Freudian imagination.[4]

On June 17, 1933, other associates of the Barker-Karpis gang would participate in the Kansas City Massacre, the botched escape attempt of Frank "Jelly" Nash that occurred in Union Station. Verne Miller, Charles Pretty Boy Floyd, and Adam Richetti would be held accountable for the incident, which resulted in the death of Nash, several agents of the Justice Department, and Kansas City police officers. It was called, at the time, the nation's most vicious crime. Richetti would die in the gas chamber at Missouri State Prison, Miller would be murdered by the underworld, and Floyd would be gunned down in a cornfield by a squad of Justice Department agents headed by Melvin Purvis.[5]

June 15, 1933, Doc and Fred Barker, with Alvin Karpis, under the guidance of mastermind Fred Goetz alias Shotgun George Zeigler, and with the help of Charles Fitzgerald and William Bryan Bolton, kidnapped William A. Hamm, Jr., of the Theodore Hamm Brewing Company of St. Paul. The family paid $100,000 ransom. After Hamm's release on June 19, 1933, the gang moved to Chicago. They instigated a payroll robbery, during which time one police officer was murdered and another was paralyzed. Harry Campbell joined the group in September 1933. All went to Reno, meeting Baby Face Nelson, then back to St. Paul, to meet with Fred and Paula Harmon, Volney Davis and Edna Murray, and Harry Campbell and Wynona Burdette. They met Eddie Green; he would prove a dependable bank robber.

Green frequented Harry Sawyer's saloon at 545 Wabasha Street and also the Hollyhocks, places where Bessie Green managed the restaurants. Bess would witness many nights of drinking, heroin, and marijuana use. Nude dancers provided entertainment.

The women attracted to the Barker-Karpis people were a tougher, more deeply entrenched breed than the women of John Dillinger's gang. They were of a practiced criminal element. Edna Murray, the girlfriend

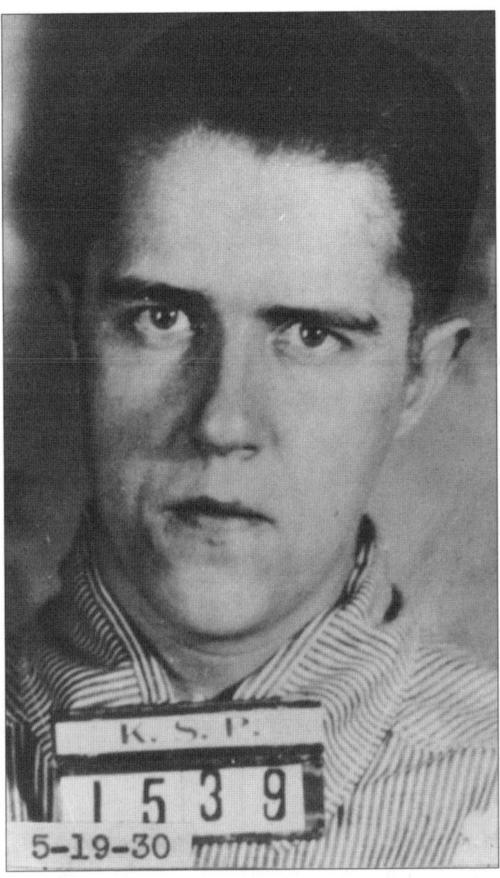


"I got plenty of dough and want the best for the little girl." So said Alvin Karpis to a Miami physician. His teenaged girlfriend, Dolores Delaney, was expecting a baby. (National Archives)

of Volney Davis, was a known escape artist. She'd earned her two most prominent nicknames, the Kissing Bandit and the more gritty "Rabbits," after having first escaped from jail in 1922 and then later in 1931 and 1932 from the Missouri State Prison. Her friend, Myrtle Eaton, was a shoplifter with a long criminal record. Eaton was at first the girlfriend, and later the stalking victim, of Bill Weaver. Jaded, sophisticated women of crime, they relished the nights of drinking and depravity. Bess Green later told the Justice Department that the women "liked the wild excitement of night life." Yet one thing they didn't like was Ma Barker. Most of the girlfriends of the Barkers and their associates stayed well away from her. They trusted her like a poisoned snake. The one exception was supposed to have been Dolores Delaney. Karpis insisted that Ma was fond of her, perhaps because she was young and easily manipulated. Sometime in December 1933, Dolores was moved to Chicago. Despite the proximity to Doc Moran, Chicago's notorious abortionist, Dolores would choose the harder road for women like her. She would bear Karpis a son.

Abortionist Joseph P. "Doc" Moran had started out like many of that lost generation of 1917. He served as a second lieutenant in the aviation section of the Reserve Signal Corps with service in France during the

Dolores Delaney, Sister of Jean Delaney Crompton and Helen "Babe" Reilly.
(National Archives)

First World War. He'd been an honor student at the Tufts Medical School in Boston, but by 1928 he had a drinking problem. It was a time before the effects of war-related stress had a name or a face, and help was non-existent. Either you "took it like a man" or you fell into alcoholism. In the case of a physician, the easy availability of drugs made one a prime candidate for drug addiction.

In 1928 he'd performed an abortion in which the woman died. He was sent to Joliet Penitentiary on a plea of guilty and was put to work treating convicts, and obtained drugs for them in a lucrative sideline. While there, he saved the life of a diamond theft racketeer named Ollie Berg, who, when released simultaneously with Moran, brought the doctor to Chicago to meet with higher-ups in the politically connected syndicate. Moran followed the standard abortionist's script in the years prior to *Roe v. Wade,* which legalized abortion in the United States. He practiced straight medicine on one hand, while performing abortions and treating wounded bank robbers on the other. Before long, he would be asked to save the life of John Hamilton.

In St. Paul, the Barker-Karpis gang's coupe-de-grace took place with the kidnaping of Edward G. Bremer, a businessman, on January 17, 1934, for $200,000 ransom. Adolph Bremer, the victim's father and a personal friend of President Roosevelt, demanded proof that his son was still alive before agreeing to pay the ransom. Bremer was released alive. By April 30, $197,000 of the ransom money was still missing. The most powerful piece of evidence linking Karpis to the crime was a set of fingerprints on a gasoline can found in the Bremer hideout, which brought the Justice Department officially into the chase.

What connected the Barker-Karpis gang to Dillinger was Jean Delaney Crompton's admission that a man named Slim had met her with Carroll and the Nelsons in Chicago on April 18, the day before they set out for the Little Bohemia. Slim Gray was also mentioned by the other women within the course of their sleep-deprived, rambling confessions. The connection was made to a Slim connected with the Bremer case, Roy "Slim" Gray, who was implicated in exchanging the ransom money. Through Helen Riley's attempt to set bail for Jean Delaney Crompton, the connection between the Dillinger and Barker-Karpis gangs was suddenly illuminated.

A more concrete connection had been established through Eddie

Green, when Dillinger had entered St. Paul after Crown Point. The terms of the Twin Cities' umbrella policy would involve payoffs by Dillinger that were applied to Tom Brown's campaign for sheriff. Dillinger's contribution, along with six other men, amounted to $1,500.

Bess Green, that St. Paul maven of the underworld, would be visited after Little Bohemia by agents asking her to identify a mug shot. She was shown the image of the woman calling herself Marion Virginia Marr, or Mrs. Joseph J. Marr, wife of a bootlegger. Bess identified Helen Gillis and mentioned the Gillis' children, thereby giving law enforcement a ram to crack the facade of the wife of Baby Face. They were in for a surprise.

In a memo rife with frustration, St. Paul Agent D.L. Nicholson reported that,

> "Every method of attack has been used by agents in an effort to get this woman to talk, but without avail. It was thought that possibly her weak point would be her children, which this agent brought into the picture at length. She finally would no longer deny that she had children but would not admit them. On two occasions, when discussing her children she broke down and wept at length, but would not give in. She refused agent's offer to call relatives or friends but stated repeatedly that she was expecting a lawyer. On several occasions she was frank enough to admit that she would not talk and later regret it."

After Attorney Carl N. Hill of Madison, sent in by the Gillis family, arrived, Federal Judge Patrick T. Stone gave permission for him to go in on May 4. Her attorney strengthened her resolve. In their refusal to let her eat or sleep, the agents brought on an attack of dehydration in Helen, who was weakened from previous health problems. When Helen became ill during the interrogations, the wife of Sheriff Finn had called in a doctor out of fear that Helen would die. In spite of breaking down physically, her mental resistance remained firm. She never said another word, except to deny complicity in the Bremer kidnapping case, and to deny ever seeing Dillinger or Evelyn Frechette. She also denied being married to Baby Face Nelson.

With her memory rifled yet intact, Helen's husband and the cause of all her troubles had stayed in Wisconsin.

"Talked more like baby than like man," said Ollie Catfish, who was forced to sit with his family and watch Baby Face Nelson devour his food supply. He was referring, in his native vernacular, to Nelson's high-pitched voice. Catfish guarded his family from the killer, who forced them to sit passively on the Lac du Flambeau Indian Reservation for three days with him.

"Little fellow came my house Monday noon. He didn't sleep. Watched me and woman and kids all time. Didn't play with kids. He didn't shave. Cleaned his fingernails."

Nelson, armed with three guns, in Ollie's words, generally did not shoot civilians. He left by forcing Ollie to walk seven miles with him, stealing a Plymouth sedan, releasing the "Indian" on Highway 70, and headed in the direction of St. Paul. His ultimate destination would be the restaurant owned by Jimmy Murray, on Harlem and North Avenues in Chicago.[6]

Dillinger, Hamilton, and Van Meter, tandem fugitives, had traveled back to the area around the Little Bohemia to pick up some hidden ammunition before evicting Robert Johnson, their hostage, from Mitchell's lodge. On April 23, they were sighted by Deputy Sheriff Al Johnson of Douglas County, who signaled them to stop. They turned and fired on him. An expert marksman, Johnson returned fire, hitting Hamilton in the back and wounding his liver. Dakota County Deputies Larry Dunn and Norman Dieter, with Hastings Deputy Sheriff Joseph Heinen, pursued them.

With Hamilton bleeding profusely, Dillinger and Van Meter eluded the police, eventually catching up with a young family. They forced Ray Frances, driving with his wife and baby, onto the road four miles south of St. Paul. Frances would tell police that they had carried a man into the backseat before driving away.

Shortly after, at 1:30 p.m., the car in which Hamilton had been hit was discovered. The bullet holes were positioned in a way that confirmed that someone had been shot, and the deep stains soaking the upholstery of the back seat with blood clots confirmed this.

Dillinger was dragging his ailing friend through the channels that promised medical aid. The bullet had mushroomed, and in the 1¼" diameter bullet wound on the left center of his spine, gangrene was setting in. Lead fragments had lodged in Hamilton's lower spinal column, causing intense pain. With death rattles issuing from the man's throat, no underworld doctor would help and the ambulatory group was turned down wherever they went. After they'd brought Hamilton to a restaurant in Chicago, where he was placed in the back of a saloon, a minor member of the Barker-Karpis gang, Russell Gibson, agreed to contact Doc Moran. The alcoholic underworld physician and abortionist had treated Hamilton once before, after the latter was shot in East Chicago. The worst smack in the jaw for the gang was the refusal by Doc Moran to have anything to do with them. He had gotten into a fight with Hamilton after treating him after East Chicago. Moran was angry at the entire Dillinger gang at the time that Hamilton was dying. Also, he doubted that his fee, averaging $5,000 for the care of a wounded gangster, would be paid. Without a doctor to administer quinine or another pain killer, Hamilton is assumed to have died.

The remaining members of the Capone gang passed the word to Dillinger to stay well away from Chicago. Frankie Pope, their former connection, had recently taken the last ride. Murdered on March 7, 1934, Pope had been the lone survivor of the Frank Nitti clique that had harbored the Dillinger gang after Michigan City. They now brought too much heat and would not be welcomed in underworld hangouts. This was a fall from grace for the desperadoes, who just months before had enjoyed the sanctuary of the Steuben Club, a refuge for the Pope and remaining Capone gangs. Dillinger, who had been welcomed in the place where "really hot" gangsters could hang out in peace, was told to get out of town.

The grapevine passed the word that Hamilton's wound was the size of a silver dollar. Jack Perkins heard it from Baby Face Nelson and passed the word around through Art "Fish" Johnson and other hangers-on in Chicago. Jean Delaney Crompton would also confirm to the Bureau that Hamilton had died. Notwithstanding this intelligence, he continued to be a suspect and would actually be identified as a bandit at the June 1 robbery in South Bend, Indiana, for one year after his death.

A grave would be exhumed on August 28, 1935, just outside Oswego, Illinois, in the vicinity of Aurora. The corpse had an injury to the left center of the spine, a ruptured spinal column, but not penetrated. Lead fragments had lodged in the fifth lower vertebrae. Apparently the dental records at Michigan City Penitentiary would match up with the corpse, although there have always been doubts. John Hamilton's fingers had decomposed, and the missing fingers that could have identified him were nonexistent.

Not knowing that her brother was dying, Hamilton's sister, Anna M. Steve, was arrested on April 24. She'd turned 40 on Feb. 6. On April 19, federal agents had gained entrance to her home without a search warrant. They alleged the search was conducted with her consent; she said it was forged against her will. They seized the Ford F-8 that Hamilton had left in her possession and brought her in to be arraigned before U.S. Commissioner John A. Colwell. A law-abiding citizen, she would spend the next six weeks in a jail cell.

To Anna Hamilton, it was one more nightmare to survive. With her brothers John and Foye doing prison time, she'd weathered the process of broken trust, false hope, and despair. After marrying Isaac Steve, she'd made a home in Sault Ste. Marie, Michigan. While she'd vowed to keep her brother inside her heart, he was firmly out of her life. She might have found her peace had Hamilton not escaped from his jail sentence in the notorious flight from the Michigan City Penitentiary. The agents delivered the car keys, with the Nashville bill of sale, to the U.S. Attorney in Grand Rapids, who claimed it as an abandoned automobile. Mrs. Steve filed a petition to get the car returned to her. She claimed that she had a right to it and cited violation of due process in the entry of her home by federal agents. This only increased her culpability. In the eyes of a harsh district court, she'd lost her credibility as the self-appointed heir to Dillinger's automobile. Her petition was dismissed, on the grounds that she failed to prove that the car was rightfully hers.

In an order denying her petition, the court said that "no person has yet established to the Court that they are the true and lawful owner of the car." A preliminary examination was set for May 16 on federal harboring charges, and she was held on $1,000 bail.[7]

By the end of April, both Helen Gillis and Jean Delaney Crompton had attorneys, and questions arose about who was going to represent Marie Comforti. Neither attorney for the other two women had any information about her. She seemed more of an orphan than ever, with Helen Gillis visited on May 14 by Juliette Fitzsimmons, the sister of Baby Face

Nelson. Like Babe Reilly, she went before U.S. District Attorney Harold Hanson, U.S. Marshall John M. Comeford, and Special Agent Robert Gillespie. The mother of six, Mrs. Fitzsimmons had driven over with her husband Robert. They brought three of the children with them.

Waiting to mob Mrs. Fitzsimmons, the reporters asked about Helen's own family. Juliette would prove to be the talkative, public-relations member of the Gillis clan. They asked how Helen had managed to keep her own family out of the limelight.

"Helen's relatives haven't any money and so can't help her any, and figure there's no use coming here to be badgered by the federal officers," she explained, not revealing that Helen's maiden name was Wawrzyniac. "They don't even know she's in trouble or they would have tried to get in touch with her by now."

Jean Delaney Crompton's name was publicized on April 29 and identified as the former sister-in-law of Pat Reilly. Tommy Carroll, the only member of the gang whose whereabouts had not been traced immediately after the raid, was still listed as "missing." Helen was listed only as the wife of "Baby Face Nelson," and Marie Comforti was still unidentified in the press. Her biggest regret was the loss of her puppy. The pedigreed Boston bull pup that Evelyn had brought to Tucson was also carried by Helen Gillis. Dolores Delaney had four of them. Marie would never get hers back.

"I'm particularly bitter against the Sheriff of the Eagle River Jail in Wisconsin, who kept my last gift from Van Meter, a pedigreed Boston bull," she would later say.

They would be released on May 25, after pleading guilty, on eighteen months' probation under suspended sentences of a year and a day each after testifying before Judge Patrick T. Stone. Their departure from Madison was coated with the insipid reportage that had marked their capture and detention.

They left amid a fabricated story about a shopping spree enjoyed by the three women, complete with a fancy ladies' lunch with a reporter.

"I must keep up my strength," Helen Gillis was said to remark over a "hearty luncheon," that quaint custom of the 1930s. Then the "girls" supposedly went shopping.

"A car horn tooted as they left the restaurant," reported one newspaper. "Mrs. Fred Finn, the sheriff's wife, waved to the girls, as she drove past with a car full of children."[8]

The three were not the only women of the Dillinger gang to undergo redemption, and weight loss, in the eyes of newspaper reporters. In St. Paul, Evelyn Frechette was hauled out of segregation and pushed into the limelight in the Ramsey County Jail. Under the gaze of Dillinger's attorney, Louis Piquett, she lent her commentary on the Little Bohemia.

She was said to be "reclining comfortably" in jail, which was a stretch unless you could see solitary confinement as being comfortable.

Like the women of the Little Bohemia, Frechette suddenly became "attractive and pert." She was asked if she'd harbored Dillinger.

"I didn't harbor him. I just went up to visit him like any sweetheart would."

With "a cigarette sending smoke curling away from her 110-pound frame," she'd somehow managed to lose 20 pounds. Evelyn had never been a small woman; her frame had always carried around 130 pounds, and she was round and womanly. Yet this new prototype of the "gang girl," a throwback to the lean flapper, had been established days before in Wisconsin.

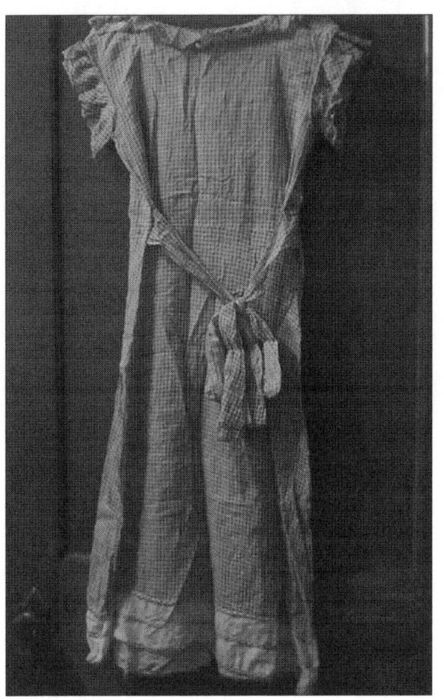

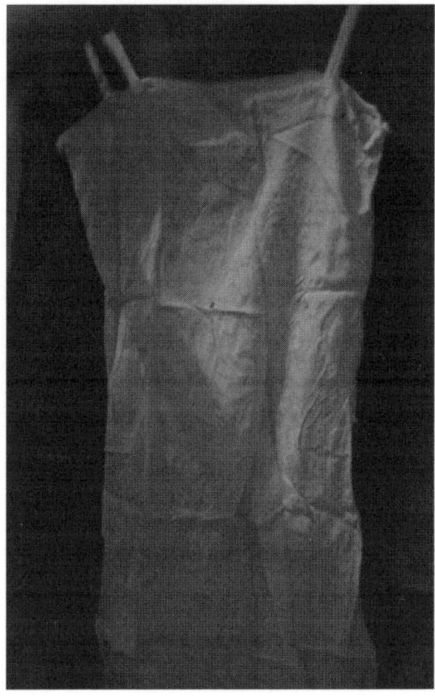

A dress, with slip, left by one of the three women of Little Bohemia. The shirtwaist frock was a wardrobe staple in 1934. (Author's Collection)

*"It may be of value to note that, on occasions, Frechette is very moody in temperament and she assumes a hostile attitude and . . . when she becomes sullen and snarling, a two- or three-day treatment of solitary confinement has a very tame effect upon her disposition."*

—*St. Paul FBI Agent Hugh Clegg*

# "I Saw Miss Frechette Ironing"

Placed on a podium to withstand the trial scheduled for early May 1934, Dillinger's sweetheart bore her scarlet letter with vapid arrogance. In the Ramsey County Jail, Evelyn Frechette lent her commentary on the Little Bohemia.

"I do not believe John is in this part of the country," she said. "And even if he is, the Federal government will never get him, dead or alive—he is too good a man."

Dillinger's attorney, Louis Piquett, had allowed reporters access to Frechette in the daily articles that described the prisoner as resting comfortably in jail. Agent Hugh Clegg would later phrase her "experience in St. Paul" in a more accurate light:

"It may be of value to note that, on occasions, Frechette is very moody in temperament and she assumes a hostile attitude and . . . when she becomes sullen and snarling, a two- or three-day treatment of solitary confinement has a very tame effect upon her disposition."

Louis Piquett, her buffer to the hostile world, was an obtrusive counsel. At age fifty-one, with bulging eyes protruding over a sullen mouth, his pugilistic face lacked redeemed shades of pathos. His affiliation with Dillinger had thrust him into the bogus position of a criminal law specialist. With little formal education, he'd pursued a quiz course in law during 1918 and 1919, passing the bar on his third attempt in 1920. Piquett was never admitted to the Chicago Bar Association because of rumors that he had been central to police graft, vice, election fraud, and police fixing in the old 21st Ward under Mayor William Hale Thompson. In 1922 and 1923, Piquett's name appeared on grand jury indictments as a defendant in a scheme to "rake off" fifty cents a ton on coal sold to the board of education. When Thompson left office, Piquett lost his stature and set up shop at 228 North LaSalle Street, overlooking the Chicago River. Here the most wanted criminals in America would waft through his office, elusive as the radio's Mrs. Calabash.[1]

As Evelyn's mouthpiece, Piquett's tongue slipped around like a loose wire. In this, he performed a disservice to his client. When public opinion demanded contrition from its fallen "moll," her lawyer would deliver no such thing. He preferred to represent Evelyn with blubbery speeches that discredited her.

"If Dillinger walked in here now and I introduced you to him, you'd fall in love with him in half an hour," he stated modestly. "He's just a nice boy—not one of those ego guys. How did I meet him? Well I've known him for some time. He sent for me. Of course, we weren't school mates."

Ironically, Dillinger had reaped more formal education than his lawyer. The gangster went to high school; Piquett quit school in the eighth grade to run away from his father, who was employed as a blacksmith. In his rejection of the pastoral life, Piquett bore a resemblance to his fugitive client. Dillinger had also rejected his father's livelihood, refusing to take it as his own.

The familiarity that Piquett had shown Dillinger wasn't lost on the journalists of the Twin Cities. They responded to the "school mate" analogy and issued a challenge of their own.

"If the government would guarantee to prosecute Dillinger only on the Dyer act charge," they fired, "could you surrender him?"

"That's stretching a point," Piquett answered. "I don't know if he could be surrendered."

"Who employed you to defend Dillinger, and who paid the fee?"

"His father, an Indiana farmer."

"Who employed you to defend the Frechette woman, and who is paying the fee in this instance?"

"Her sister," he lied, knowing that Dillinger had paid $500 to his investigator, Arthur O'Leary, as a retainer.

Louis Piquett, described by Leavenworth officials as "self-confident, brazen, contemptuous, evasive, antagonistic and bitter." (Author's Collection)

Piquett had been in the Willard Hotel in Washington, DC, on the day of Evelyn's arrest. Dillinger had telephoned him and spilled out the details in a high-pitched, distressed voice.

"Billie's been arrested . . . we were in the car . . . in Chicago . . . I sent her out with a message when the government men grabbed her . . . I left in the car."

At that point, Piquett had called Chicago attorney Paul Pomeroy to serve a writ of habeas corpus. Piquett then leaked the story of Evelyn's arrest, which had, until then, been kept a secret by Melvin Purvis.

She'd been held incommunicado in a Chicago apartment when the extradition proceedings came through on April 13, four days after her arrest. She couldn't pay her bond of $60,000 and, with no other choice, accepted St. Paul as her trial venue.

When Edwin K. Walker, U.S. Commissioner, served Melvin Purvis with a warrant, Piquett delayed her removal. He needed time to pull together $2,000, the cost of disbursements in St. Paul. His announcement that Frechette needed to purchase a "new spring outfit" precluded the logistics of a shopping spree while locked up. He kept her in Chicago until April 24, when she was taken to St. Paul.

Prior to that, on April 18, agents in St. Paul arrested Dr. Clayton E. May and Augusta Salt, his nurse. The two were held in the Ramsey County Jail on $100,000 bond, which was soon reduced to $20,000.

They were indicted on April 27 and added to the list of conspirators with Beth Green, John Hamilton, Evelyn Frechette, and Edward Green.

All were accused of violating Section 88, Title 18 of the U.S. Code 246. A misdemeanor with a maximum term of six months and a $1,000 fine, the deceptively benign penalties could be imposed in consecutive layers.

In district court the prosecutor declared that Evelyn Frechette would be tried with Dr. May and Nurse Salt. Upon hearing this, Frechette's co-attorney, A. Jerome Hoffman, jumped up.

"We will move for severance on the grounds that the testimony of the other co-defendants may be prejudiced to our case," cried Hoffman. Less colorful than Piquett but certainly more rational, he chose to argue over banal technicalities.

"Miss Frechette does not know Dr. May or Nurse Salt and we feel that, under such circumstances, she is entitled to be tried separately."

Upon hearing this, Prosecutor Sullivan interjected a retort, swearing that the three would stand trial together.

A grand jury investigation had already taken place in the District Court of Minnesota, and by the time the findings were completed, the names of Pat Riley and Homer Van Meter were added to the list of St. Paul conspirators. Evelyn's specific culpability would be more directly targeted within this document. She was charged with an "overt act" that linked her with the co-defendants. In legal rhetoric, Evelyn "did accompany the fugitive aforesaid from the City of Saint Paul [to] 1835 Park Avenue, City of Minneapolis . . . for the purpose of obtaining for said fugitive professional medical and surgical attention and treatment required by him."

This language was very deliberate. It essentially bound up Dr. May and Nurse Salt to Evelyn Frechette by implicating all three in the treatment of Dillinger's gunshot wound. The prosecutor's oath had been prophetic. Evelyn Frechette would stand trial with Clayton May and Augusta Salt.

On May 3, Evelyn was taken under heavy guard to the Federal Building, holding a handkerchief to her face to shield herself from photographers. Like her co-defendants, she entered a plea of "not guilty."

The dark-horse defendant, Beth Green, pleaded "guilty" on May 5 to "conspiracy to harbor and conceal." She had been held in the county jail in St. Paul in lieu of $25,000 bail and was the last of the four defendants to appear for arraignment.

The specter of Beth Green had hovered like a ghost until this moment. Nobody had seen her; rumors abounded. Unnoticed, her attorney had cemented the deal made when she traded her real name for the anonymity of her young son. Her true surname would remain secret. She would identify photographs of Fred Barker and Alvin Karpis, wanted in connection with the Hamm and Bremer kidnaping, and connect them to a 1932 bank robbery. She revealed that Dillinger had contributed to Mayor Tom Brown's political campaign in St. Paul.

In the bargain, Beth Green revealed that Dr. May had known Eddie Green since 1922, treating Green for ailments ranging from a sore throat to a gunshot wound after a payroll robbery. In court she stood silently as attorney John Burns entered her guilty plea. At the request of Prosecutor Sullivan, Judge Joyce deferred sentence pending the disposition of the cases of the other co-defendants.

She bore herself with the same stylish air that had once impressed the caretaker when she'd rented the apartment at Lexington Avenue for Dillinger. Dressed in the brown coat she'd worn on the day of her arrest, she appeared docile. She didn't act like a gangster's moll, people noted with surprise.

The woman had undergone a form of brainwashing in those first days after her arrest. She had suffered shock when she witnessed the execution of Eddie Green, and this, combined with sleep-deprivation and harassment, had pushed her over the edge to the shadow world of a government informant. She leaned upon Agents Clegg and Hanni, depending on them for support as she entered her guilty plea. She would say nothing to reporters or the curious spectators lining the route to the courtroom.

The case for Evelyn Frechette was assembled in Louis Piquett's office, where he'd previously set up a scam of charging fees from fired city employees with the promise to have their jobs reinstated. One of his victims, a discharged policeman who paid Piquett $500, had gone before the bar to complain. In Piquett's presence he declared that he "wouldn't shake hands with you or any other lawyer who would go around defending people like Dillinger's sweetheart and other dogs and just take honest people's money."

At 228 N. La Salle, above the murky waters of the Chicago River, a secretary pounded out Evelyn's pleadings on a manual typewriter. Dust gathered on the rotund books of law that were arranged just for show. No legal research had gone into defending Evelyn Frechette. No one had searched for precedent cases, forming arguments around prior decisions. The shallow defense used in Evelyn's case would set an unfortunate precedent of its own. At the heart of its basic tenet was one elusive declaration: A person in love with a federal fugitive should be exempt from harboring charges.

The trial commenced on May 15, 1934, in the U.S. District Court of the District of Minnesota, Third Division in St. Paul, with Judge Gunnar H. Nordbye presiding. For the occasion Evelyn donned the "new spring outfit" alluded to by Louis Piquett in stalling extradition. Deliberately conservative, it featured a clean, white collar, blue gloves, and a small blue hat. It was, coincidentally, the kind of low-profile garb that Dillinger would have preferred Billie to wear while she was out with him. A matron lent her lipstick, and Evelyn eagerly applied the bow shape worn by Jean Harlow. The result backfired, with the crimson hue accentuating the creeping prison pallor of her skin. Yet Evelyn welcomed the makeup. Her appearance had changed for the worse after her forced withdrawal from alcohol. Now she was facing the cameras in ill-fitting, ugly clothing that she had not chosen for herself.

When she stepped out of her Ramsey County cell, she joined her jailer, Bernard Anderson, and five St. Paul detectives. This happy group walked the two blocks to the courthouse, where she was met by Louis Piquett. Her chagrin deepened when he held her hand like a suitor and leaked the latest news he'd heard "through the grapevine."

"Dillinger has fled to Mexico or South America," he declared. "Miss Frechette planned to marry Dillinger although she still is the wife of George Spark, an inmate of the Leavenworth Penitentiary, but she is seeking a divorce," revealed the gossipy Piquett.

"Will that be her defense?" the excited reporters shouted.

"She is innocent, and that will be our defense," interjected A. Jerome Hoffman. The more sensible member of the legal team, he was quick to jump in, hoping to dispel the quips and banter. Spectators, many of whom had waited on line all night, were disappointed to hear that the courtroom would be filled to capacity with government witnesses.

Once inside, Hoffman made a motion to admit Louis Piquett as the attorney for Frechette; George F. Sullivan and Lewis N. Evans were named for the United States of America; and Thomas W. McMeekin and

Peter Scott appeared for Dr. May and Nurse Salt. When the courtroom broke for lunch at 12:30 p.m., Evelyn surged out in the crowd of fifty-odd people chosen for the jury panel. The overflow spilled out the door onto the street. Like a swimmer caught in a riptide, Evelyn moved toward the exit.

Edward Pincha, a bailiff for Judge M.M. Joyce in the adjourning courtroom, noticed her move for the door.

"I was walking along the hall," said Mr. Pincha, "just coming up to the door of Court Room No. 2, which is nearest to the judge's bench. She came right out in front of me and she was all alone. I asked her where she was going." Instinct told him to grab her arm.

"She didn't say anything, but gave me a kind of a cute look and a little giggle," Pincha recalled. "I turned her around and walked her back into the courtroom and Marshall Ruderson was there and I turned her over to him." Pincha noticed that two newspapermen had witnessed the whole thing.

"They didn't make any attempt to stop her," he noted.

Louis Piquett clowned about the incident.

"I suppose she was just trying to find the way back to jail to get her luncheon," he joked.

There was no laughing in Washington. The hogwash was cleaned by Agent Hugh Clegg, who wired Hoover to explain that ". . . newspaper accounts are untrue and grossly exaggerated and U.S. Marshall Ruderson personally was looking at Frechette when Picha took her arm . . . and states she was coming to him at his instructions."[2]

The afternoon agenda held the selection of jurors. The lone woman called was chosen as foreman. Mrs. O.F. DeGroat, a housewife from Owatonna, would preside upon the jury with great dignity, refusing to speak to the press even after the verdicts. The remainder turned out to be local, working-class white men.[4]

Prosecutor Sullivan then stated the case to the court and jury on behalf of the plaintiff.

The next morning found Evelyn facing a specific charge, that of conspiring with John Hamilton and the Greens to "unlawfully harbor and conceal" Dillinger on March 29.

She hid a slight smile of remembrance as Louis Piquett handed her a copy of the pleadings. The title put her many incarnations into a capsule:

"U.S. v. Evelyn Frechette, alias Billie Spark, alias Ann Martin, alias Mary Evelyn Frechette alias Evelyn Spark, alias Evelyn Faschetti, alias Evelyn Frisbette, alias Grace Edwards, alias Mrs. John Dillinger, alias 'Billie.'"

The parade of witnesses for the prosecution would tell the story of Evelyn's unbridled life after the escape from Crown Point. It seemed as though Dillinger himself was standing trial by proxy. All the frustrated effort that had gone toward catching the fugitive now went toward prosecuting his woman. That effort was reflected in the witnesses: Agent Thomas Mullen, who had investigated the Crown Point theft of Sheriff's Holley's car; Edwin Saager, the mechanic who had driven Dillinger out of Crown Point; Mark Robbins, a Tucson arresting officer; photographers John Juricek and Harry Hall who traced Dillinger's path after Crown Point; and Dillinger's arresting officers in Dayton.

Next came Evelyn's neighbors in St. Paul. While Evelyn didn't know them, they had watched her come and go while pretending not to notice the strange Mr. and Mrs. Hellman. One was Daisy Coffey, the landlady of the house on Lexington Avenue.

"Do you see anyone in this room who was in that apartment last March?" Sullivan prompted.

"Yes," replied the landlady. "That woman there." As she pointed, Piquett nudged Evelyn to stand up. Mrs. Coffey had delivered extra bedclothes to the apartment upon the request of the mysterious occupants and had seen Evelyn Frechette enter through the back door of the apartment house on March 26 carrying several bundles.

"And isn't it possible," cross-examined Hoffman, "that you could not have seen the defendant entering by the rear door, because Miss Frechette might have come in the front door and walked up the rear stairway?"

This useless question confirmed Mrs. Coffey's resolve. She shook her head emphatically.

"I saw Miss Frechette ironing one night from across the apartment house court and there was a strong light on her and the window shades were up. Another time, I saw Miss Frechette wiping dishes."

The image of a gun moll toiling in the hideout, spotlights showcasing her domestic tendencies, carried an evocative appeal. Yet these hindsight observations were doubtful. None of the staff at Lexington Avenue had gleaned a clear idea of anyone's identity while the gang was hiding there. Evelyn had been a shadow, viewed elusively behind cracks in the doors with chain locks bursting at their hinges. But the defense let this strong identification remain unchallenged.

Mrs. Coffey's portrait of Evelyn as the prudent woman-of-the-house had little bearing in fact. The janitor had noticed that the Hellmans never asked for the vacuum cleaner, nor had they tried to use the laundry facilities.

The next witnesses were Louis and Margaret Meidlinger, the caretakers. They identified a photograph of Beth Green, which was admitted as an exhibit, along with two photographs of the Lexington Avenue apartment. The Meidlingers recalled the day the snappy young redhead had paid $60 in advance for the apartment, renting it under the name of Carl Hellman. Yet the Meidlingers failed to place Evelyn in the apartment, as their only real interaction had been with Beth Green. Mr. Meidlinger denied knowing Frechette. On the day he had tried to bring in the toilet articles to the apartment, she'd remained an unseen recipient who'd slammed the door in his face.

After the noon recess, more witnesses lined up like dominoes. The previously anonymous agents who'd spent the past three months tracking Dillinger through St. Paul assumed a clarity on the witness stand. Detective Henry Cummings and Agents Rosser Nalls and William Rorer, veterans of the Lexington Avenue shootout, were joined by St. Paul Police Officers, Tom Jansen, Tom Grace, Fred O'Rourke, Ed Fitzgerald, and John Tierney.

It was a long day and the most explosive witness would be saved for last. Harold Reinecke, the Department of Justice Agent accused of mistreating Evelyn, was briefly introduced to the court. The next two days would be the worst moments of the trial for Evelyn. By now, the "new spring outfit" felt smelly and wrinkled as it hung on her frame. She was tense and guarded as Reinecke was recalled by the prosecution and then cross-examined by Hoffman. Throughout, the agent denied Hoffman's allegations that he had beaten Evelyn while she was held incommunicado before she was formally arrested.

"Isn't it a fact," said Hoffman, "that Miss Frechette asked you to call W.W. O'Brien when you talked with her last April 10th, and didn't you tell her that if she didn't talk, she would not need a lawyer, she would need a doctor or an undertaker?"

"No such thing," replied Reinecke.

"Didn't you tell her she would stay there weeks or months if she didn't talk?" Hoffman pressed.

"No."

"Is it not true that Miss Frechette was not given a chance to rest from Tuesday morning, April 10th until 1 a.m. Thursday morning?"

"That is untrue."

"Did you slap her?"

"No."

"Did you threaten her with your fist?"

"No, I placed my fingers gently underneath her chin, and asked her to please make eye contact with me."

"And isn't it true that Miss Frechette sat at a desk facing a battery of high-powered lamps?" Hoffman continued.

"I do not recall seeing high-powered lamps in that room. The only light is a ceiling lamp," Reinecke coolly retorted.

Evelyn, usually impassive, became upset at this line of questioning. To her way of thinking, she had been treated like dirt. Murray Faulkner, the second agent that Evelyn had accused of mistreating her, sat among the witnesses.

"And isn't it true," questioned Hoffman on his return, "that Miss Frechette was taken by about fifteen federal agents armed with machine guns?"

"I don't know that," Reinecke countered with a smile. "For all I knew, she could have walked into my office."

Although it would have no bearing on the outcome, Reinecke admitted that Evelyn had been held incommunicado when she was questioned in Chicago.

Rufus Coulter, the St. Paul agent who had knocked on the door of the Lexington Avenue apartment on the morning of the shootout, next took the stand to place Evelyn in the apartment with Dillinger.

"There is no doubt in my mind," he said, "that Miss Frechette is the woman whose voice I heard in the Lexington Avenue apartment when myself and two other officers surprised Dillinger there last March 31. Miss Frechette," he concluded, "has an unusual voice."

Agents Werner Hanni and John Brennan stepped up to present three items. Like artifacts of a lost empire, Evelyn's powder box, the beer and Listening Bottles were hauled from the police lab where they'd been sequestered since the March 31 shootout.

Agent Thomas Dodd, who'd been instrumental in the arrest of Dr. May and Nurse Salt, testified that "Green was killed on the night he was supposed to have paid the medical fees."

Dr. May's police reputation as an abortionist was kept out of the transcripts and the newspapers. Although he'd been indicted by a Hennepin County grand jury in 1932 for performing the illegal procedure in apartment number 6 at 131 E. 14 Street in Minneapolis, the charges had been dropped when the complainant and all witnesses left the state or disappeared.

By Friday, May 18, a blanket of lazy dust hung over the room. The appearance of young Wallace Salt sprinkled cold water over the sleepy crowd. The adolescent son of Augusta Salt was compelled by law to testify against his mother. He spoke with childish earnestness while she pressed her face into a handkerchief. Mrs. Salt, who had gone to nursing school and had become a registered nurse seven years ago, was a widow with four children to support. Wallace, the only child in the house during Dillinger's tenure, had been grilled ten days before by the Department of Justice. The boy, sputtering and unsure of himself, had identified Dillinger from a photograph. He also recognized Frechette as one of the two women who came with the bullet-wounded Dillinger to his mother's home.

Now, on the witness stand, he repeated the story.

"Who were these people?"asked Sullivan.

"Evelyn Frechette was there," he said. "They came Saturday, the last part of March. I ran errands for Miss Frechette, like getting papers and magazines at the drug store and getting anything they wanted."

"Was there anyone else?"

"Yes, a man I know now as John Dillinger."

After running through the gauntlet of questions, during which he placed Dr. May twice inside the house, Wallace rejoined his mother. He handed Mrs. Salt the $10 he'd received as his payment for having testified as a government witness.

During the lunch break, speculation buzzed over the next scheduled witness. The appearance of the doctor's mistress promised to climax this day of fractured loyalties.

Twenty-two years old, Dolores Smart was May's companion on the night that Ed Green had contacted the physician at his office in the Masonic Temple Building. After dressing the wounds the doctor had returned to Beth Green's apartment with Miss Smart. Beth had watched in disgust as the two had guzzled gin while groping each other.

Not trusting a subpoena in the hunt for Dolores Smart, Prosecutor Sullivan had sworn out an order on May 14 that demanded that the woman offer $500 or else be detained. The prosecution staged a "hunt" for her, claiming she was missing. She gave herself up, declaring she had no money for recognizance.[5]

A new angle in the government's case was about to be introduced. It would be hotly disputed in the appeal and deemed a sneaky attempt to prejudice the jury. A Chicago *Herald* clerk, Albert Whitehall, stepped up and identified a March 8 newspaper stating Dillinger's status as a federal fugitive. The inference, that Dillinger was as familiar as the Dionne Quintuplets, was clearly drawn. Nobody could deny knowing who, and what, he was.

With a total of sixty-three exhibits and close to forty witnesses, the United States rested its case.

On May 19, Clayton May was to be the first of the three to testify in his own behalf.

"Dillinger threatened to blow out my brains," he told Thomas McMeekin, his attorney. He admitted that he drove his criminal patient to the home of Mrs. Salt at 1835 Park Avenue, where Dillinger's leg was dressed. Next he implicated Frechette. If there had been honor among these thieves, he might have remembered that Evelyn had denied meeting him during her tortuous nights of interrogation. Regardless of her silence, Dr. May now fingered Evelyn and placed her in the Park Avenue apartment with Dillinger.

Evelyn's own testimony was worthless. With the government's case a weighted stone in her rowboat, she took the stand in her own defense. Under cross-examination, she admitted coming to St. Paul and Minneapolis with Dillinger after the escape from Crown Point on March 3. She'd known that Dillinger was a bank robber.

"I loved him just the same," she said.

Augusta Salt next testified as a witness on her own behalf. Through guttural, heaving sobs, she admitted that she'd dressed Dilllinger's wounds. She had seen a gun, she said, and acted under the coercion of the weapon.

As it was Saturday, the courtroom doors closed with a bang of relief for some and a cry of anguish for others. Evelyn, who had not managed to engender the pity rendered on Mrs. Salt, went back to her cell in the Ramsey County Jail. She spent her weekend on the stingy cot with the nervous cockroaches for company. Confinement came as no surprise to this veteran of the Indian Boarding Schools. She was once again a ward of the U.S. Government.

On Monday morning, Dr. May was recalled and, during his cross-examination, Dolores Smart entered the room. Freed from jail, she wore silk and flowers with a wide-brimmed hat. The doctor stopped his testimony to smile and preen at her.

The next day, May 22, Louis Piquett delivered the bended-knee defense. He asked the court and jury to forgive Miss Frechette, that she loved John Dillinger. She should not be held accountable for harboring. Sullivan offered his summation, before bowing to Judge Nordbye for the charge to the jury. Nordbye's oration took ninety minutes.

"Miss Frechette knew at all times the identity of John Dillinger. She was aware that he was an escaped convict, that he had stolen an automobile. Whether she was aware there had been a federal warrant is a matter for you to determine. Consider her relations with Dillinger prior to his escape from the Crown Point, Indiana, jail. Consider the admission she is alleged to have made to federal officers regarding Dillinger's theft of an automobile."

He then said that Beth Green, whom the jury had never seen, had already pleaded guilty. He made clear that these defendants were charged with entering into a conspiracy.

"A conspiracy, in this case, is the unlawful act of harboring and concealing of Dillinger. When we think of conspirators, the mind is very apt to visualize a dark room where there is performed or arranged an unlawful act. It need not be a conspiracy in writing. It is not necessary that it be expressed in words. . . ."

After these opening statements, he took up the Frechette case.

"I do not believe you will have trouble in deciding whether any one made an arrangement with John Dillinger. It is admitted that Evelyn Frechette told government agents, when she was summoned to the door of an apartment at 95 South Lexington Avenue, that Hellman was not in."

The judge then went into the case of Dr. May, concluding with a statement that would set the precedent for many harboring defenses that would follow in the next few months:

"One cannot excuse a criminal act merely because he is threatened with harm. There must be more than mere threats. . . ."

"Keep a broad mind regarding the specific knowledge the defendants had of Dillinger's status as a fugitive. . . . "

The next day, Wednesday, May 23, was called a "Day of Retribution." Clyde Barrow and his girlfriend, Bonnie Parker, had been shot dead by officers in Gibsland, Louisiana. In St. Paul, the jury would return with a verdict in the trial of Dillinger's friends and allies. It seemed as though the battlefield was yielding to the rightful victors.

At 9:50 in the morning, the jury returned from the deliberation room, wading through the sea of used ballots that littered the floor. They were faced with Mrs. Salt's lamentations, which had by now reached a fever pitch. Her loud moaning did nothing to quiet the nerves of the other defendants who were destined to face the bench. Evelyn, sitting behind the panicked nurse, was stoic as usual. Her black eyes, known to shine and glisten, were described as "flashing" by reporters who watched for every nuance of emotion she might display.

Dr. May, no longer buoyed by the figure of his shapely girlfriend, clutched his hat and looked regrettably at Mrs. Salt. He stood before the bench and said he had no comment. Mrs. Salt's screams formed the backdrop to her acquittal, while Dr. May was found guilty and sentenced to two years and a $1,000 fine.

As he took his seat, Evelyn stood up and walked forward.

"Have you anything to say?" Judge Nordbye asked her.

"No," she said, then lowered her shoulders to absorb the verdict.

"We, the jury in the above-entitled action, do find the defendant Evelyn Frechette, alias Billie Spark, alias Ann Martin, alias Mary Evelyn Frechette, alias Evelyn Spark, alias Evelyn Faschetti, alias Evelyn Frisbette, alias Grace Edwards, alias Mrs. John Dillinger, alias 'Billie' guilty as charged in the indictment."

On May 24, Evelyn Frechette was brought before Judge Nordbye for commission to an "institution of the Industrial Reformatory type," for a period of two years. She was fined $1,000, a sum she never would pay.

Acting Attorney General William Stanley, center, congratulates Melvin Purvis, right, Special Agent in Charge of the Chicago Field Office, after Dillinger's death. J. Edgar Hoover, left, wanted to oust Purvis from the Division of Investigation. (AP/Wide World Photos)

Originally sentenced to the Alderson, West Virginia, Industrial Reformatory, she was recommitted to the Milan Federal Correctional Facility in a move designed to separate her from Beth Green. Attorney General Homer Cummings decided that "the government does not want the two women confined in the same prison."

Evelyn, as prisoner number F-11, became the first consort of a federal fugitive to experience the attorney general's new policy of "steel bars for female incorrigibles." Marshall Ruderson, the guard who had taken the blame for Evelyn's near escape on the first day of trial, moved her to the women's annex at Milan, Michigan, on June 3.

Beth Green would serve fifteen months as compared to Evelyn Frechette's nineteen months. Green was delivered to Alderson amid rumors of a Chicago talk with Melvin Purvis. But the woman failed to respond favorably to Purvis. She'd done most of her talking to another federal agent who held her firm allegiance. She trusted Hugh Clegg, her earliest and most attentive interrogator. After leaving Chicago, she wrote to him from Charleston.

"The country here is beautiful. Hope you arrived home O.K. We have about 150 miles to drive tomorrow. So by the time you see this, I'll be quite settled."

In his St. Paul field office, Hugh Clegg kept the little note on his desk. He read the letter, penned on hotel stationery with a matching envelope. For a pensive moment, he thought about this sharp-witted woman he'd come to respect. He would not keep the note, of course. The director would have to be advised. He banged out a memo, to Hoover from H.H. Clegg, with regard to this recent correspondence from Beth Green.

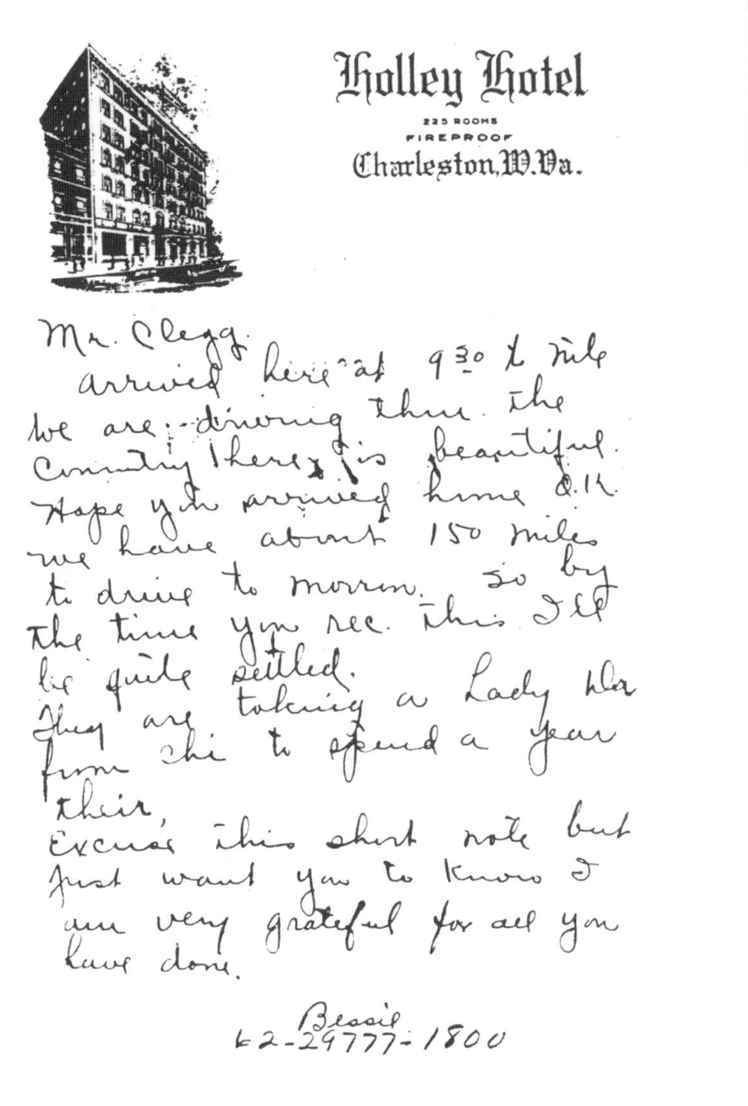

Holley Hotel
225 ROOMS
FIREPROOF
Charleston, W. Va.

Mr. Clegg.
arrived here at 9:30 & will
we are driving thru the
country there is beautiful.
Hope you arrived home O.K.
we have about 150 miles
to drive to morrow. so by
the time you rec. this I'll
be quite settled.
They are taking a Lady there
from Chi to spend a year
their,
Excuse this short note but
just want you to know I
am very grateful for all you
have done.

Bessie
62-29777-1800

(FBI)

IDENTIFICATION
ORDER NO. 1227
May 21, 1934.

DIVISION OF INVESTIGATION
U. S. DEPARTMENT OF JUSTICE
WASHINGTON, D. C.

NATIONAL MOTOR
VEHICLE THEFT ACT

WANTED

MRS. ROY THORNTON, aliases BONNIE BARROW, MRS. CLYDE BARROW, BONNIE PARKER.

DESCRIPTION

Age, 23 years (1933); Height, 5 feet, 5 inches; Weight, 100 pounds; Build, slender; Hair, auburn, bobbed; originally blonde; Eyes, blue; Complexion, fair; Scars and marks, bullet wound left foot next to little toe; bullet in left knee; burn scar on right leg from hip to knee; Peculiarities, walks with both knees slightly buckled.

RELATIVES:

Roy Thornton, husband, Texas State Penitentiary
Mrs. J. T. (Emma) Parker, mother, 1216 South Lamar St., Dallas, Texas
Mrs. Billie Parker Mace, sister, 1216 South Lamar St., Dallas, Texas
Hubert (Buster) Parker, brother, Gladewater, Texas
Nellie Gonzales, half-sister, Harwood, Gonzales County, Texas.

CRIMINAL RECORD

Arrested sheriff's office, Kaufman, Texas, June 16, 1932; charge, burglary; released.

WANTED

CLYDE CHAMPION BARROW, aliases CLYDE BARROW, ROY BAILEY, JACK HALE, ELDIN WILLIAMS, ELVIN WILLIAMS.

DESCRIPTION

Age, 23 years; Height, 5 feet, 7 inches, bare feet; Weight, 150 pounds; Build, medium; Hair, dark brown, wavy; reported dyed black; Eyes, hazel; Complexion, light, Scars and marks, shield and anchor with "U.S.N." on right forearm, outer; girl's bust, left inner forearm; bullet wound through both legs just above knees.

RELATIVES:

Henry Barrow, father, Rural Route 6, Dallas, Texas
Mrs. Cunie Barrow, mother, Rural Route 6, Dallas, Texas
L. C. Barrow, brother, County Jail, Dallas, Texas
Marie Barrow, sister, Rural Route 6, Dallas, Texas
Mrs. Artie Winkler, sister, Sanger Hotel Apartments, Dallas, Texas
Mrs. Nellie Cowan, sister, Sanger Hotel Apartments, Dallas, Texas
Mrs. Jim Muckelroy, aunt, Martinsville, Texas
Mrs. Belle Briggs, aunt, Dallas, Texas
Frank Barrow, uncle, Eureka, Navarro County, Texas
Jim Barrow, uncle, Streetman, Texas
D. Brown, cousin, Martinsville, Texas
Bertha Graham, cousin, Tyler, Texas
Claud Linthicum, cousin, San Angelo, Texas
Rommie Linthicum, cousin, San Angelo, Texas.

CRIMINAL RECORD

Criminal record and fingerprints can be obtained from Identification Order No. 1211, issued October 24, 1933.

Clyde Champion Barrow and Bonnie Parker constantly travel together and extreme caution must be exercised by arresting officers as they are wanted in connection with assault and murder of officers.

Complaint was filed at Dallas, Texas, on May 20, 1933, charging Clyde Champion Barrow and Bonnie Parker with transporting Ford Coupe, Motor No. A-1878100, property of Dr. E. L. Damron of Effingham, Illinois, from Dallas, Texas, to Pawhuska, Oklahoma, on or about September 16, 1932.

Law enforcement agencies kindly transmit any additional information or criminal record to the nearest office of the Division of Investigation, U. S. Department of Justice.

If apprehended, please notify the Director, Division of Investigation, U. S. Department of Justice, Washington, D. C., or the Special Agent in Charge of the office of the Division of Investigation listed on the back hereof which is nearest your city.

(over)

Issued by: J. EDGAR HOOVER, DIRECTOR.

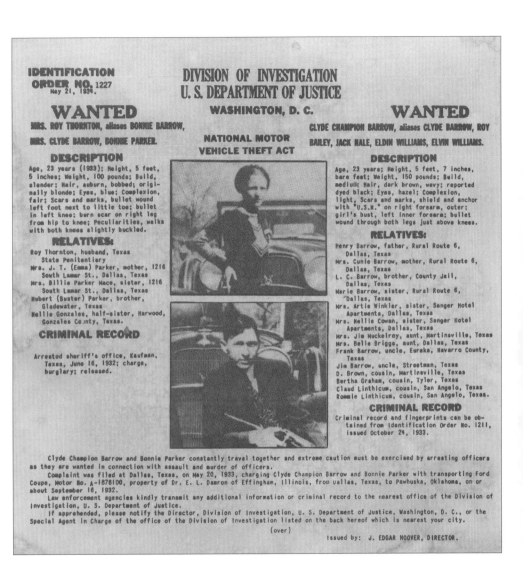

Evelyn Frechette was convicted on the day that Clyde Barrow and Bonnie Parker were killed in Louisiana. (Author's Collection)

**Part III**

# Lock-Down

## May 1934 – March 1935

Dolores Delaney.
(National Archives)

---

"Girls must understand that it is not heroic to aid crime."

*Judge Halsted L. Ritter*
*U.S. District Court,*
*Southern District of Florida;*
*U.S. v. Dolores Delaney, March, 1935*

*"No one will ever know what I went through those eight days he lived knowing I should be with him and then when I did go to the Hospital it was too late to talk to him."*

*—Beth Green*

# "Mrs. Nelson Has Gone to the Show"

Beth Green's prize in the game of cooperation was anonymity. During her move to the Chicago House of Corrections, she asked for one more favor. A better mattress and more blankets would ease the discomfort of the forty-eight-hour holdover, during which time she was scheduled to meet with Melvin Purvis. It seemed like a good idea to keep her in "as good spirits as possible." He made one phone call to the county jail with instructions to change her bedding. Unfortunately for Purvis, his dime dropped in more ways than one.

An insider leaked the news that Beth Green was "talking" to Chicago authorities. As the news hit the papers, Hoover demanded to know how an unsubstantiated rumor in St. Paul had found confirmation in Chicago. Purvis prepared his response. It was one more mishap to explain to the boss.

"Other girls leaving the county jail would see that Beth Green received better accommodations," he wrote.

Beth Green failed to respond favorably to Purvis. She'd done most of her talking to another federal agent, and he held her firm allegiance. She trusted Hugh Clegg, her earliest and most attentive interrogator.

When Beth arrived at the Federal Industrial Reformatory at Alderson, West Virginia, she entered a new era of social reform. She was headed for the minimum-security campus that some were calling a college for female cons.

Alderson was the product of the progressive mood taking hold. After women won the right to vote in 1920, the remaining activist factions undertook a new challenge: a model of humane treatment for the women convicted in a federal court.

On the night that Prohibition became effective in the United States, January 16, 1920, a new category of U.S. prisoner was born—female, active in bootlegging, often by association with husbands and brothers. Three years into the Volstead Act, nineteen state institutions notified the Department of Justice that they would no longer house federal prisoners. Women prisoners especially suffered, because they were being incarcerated in wings of men's prisons with no regard for their special needs. With Assistant Attorney General Mabel Walker Willebrandt leading the campaign, a three-point "pressing need" plan was presented to the Federal Department of Prisons in 1923.

The Enabling Act of 1924 sent the concept of Alderson Industrial Reformatory into motion. When Congress approved the architectural plans on March 4, 1925, they contained a radical proposal: to house inmates in communal cottages. These cottages, which could shelter up to thirty women, were christened with hopeful names like "Jane Addams Hull Cottage."

Dr. Mary B. Harris would preside over the custody of the women convicted during the height of the crime wave of 1933/1934. The warden who would officiate over Beth Green, and later Pat Cherrington and Jean Delaney Crompton, was born into resplendent academic and cultural advantages. Yet Dr. Harris, who could have devoted her life to educating the padded factions of Midwestern society, chose instead to work in penology, applying herself in Hull House and Blackwell Island in New York. She was appointed to the fledgling facility at Alderson under the mandate that its warden, and most of the staff, should be female.

Alderson would offer a progressive program, although some courses followed the usual maudlin categories. Domestic skills like house decoration seemed like a far-fetched goal for the transient women who

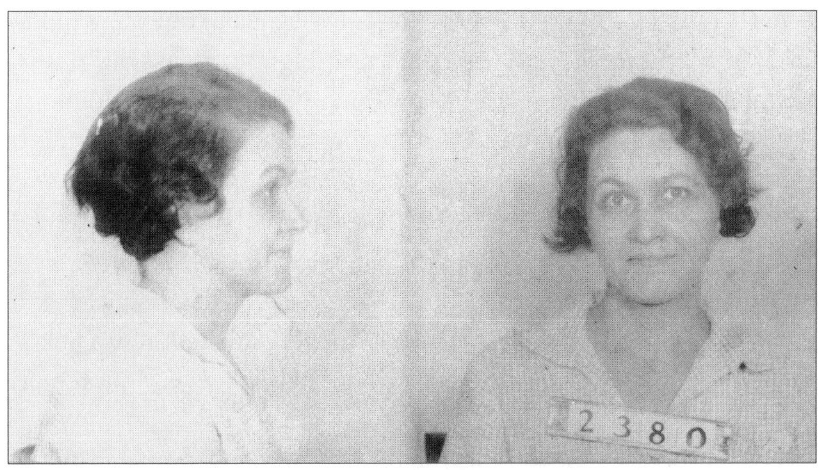


Bess Green, who brought the St. Paul underworld to its knees.
(Federal Bureau of Prisons)

had drifted into crime. Dr. Harris, herself liberated from homemaking chores by virtue of her upperclass background, was amazed at this track's popularity. Perhaps "phases of home-making" satisfied some wish for a settled life.

Beth Green arrived among the excitement of Eleanor Roosevelt's annual visit. The appearance of the First Lady occurred simultaneously with the intake procedures that turned the person of Beth Green inside out. She was given tests for venereal disease, which came back negative. There were also intelligence tests and personality evaluations.

"She is doing nice work, has splendid attitude. Is joining the cottage book club," her intake counselor would say of her. In spite of the business courses offered to Bessie, her real work would be the healing of her troubled and traumatized psyche.

Once away from scrutiny, her remembrance of the painful events of the past few weeks came flooding back. She was finally free to accept the reality of her bereavement. In a letter to the mother of Eddie Green, she released her grief.

"No one will ever know what I went through those eight days he lived knowing I should be with him and then when I did go to the Hospital it was too late to talk to him."[1]

After mortally wounding Eddie Green, the government planned to take the bigger catch alive. On the day that the prosecution rested in

Frechette's trial, May 19, the grand jury in Wisconsin, reporting to Judge Patrick T. Stone in Federal Court after an eight-day session, returned indictments against John Hamilton, Tommy Carroll, and Homer Van Meter. Dillinger and Tommy Carroll were indicted for harboring one another, with Lester Gillis charged with murder.

Pat Reilly, Marie Comforti, Jean Crompton, Helen Gillis, and Pat Cherrington as "Pat Young," were charged with conspiracy to harbor John Dillinger. The "harboring" terminology was taking its place among the tactics of law enforcement. J. Edgar Hoover had instituted a policy to "surround a hunted man so thoroughly that his every protector is frightened."

Giving weight to these indictments was a series of nine crime bills that had been placed before Congress by Attorney General Homer Cummings. Congress approved the ground-breaking legislation, and, in May 1934, President Roosevelt signed them into law.

This was a major breakthrough for the federal law enforcement officers who had previously had only the Dyer Act as the leverage point upon which to prosecute the Dillinger gang. With the crime bills, it had become a federal offense to assault or kill a federal officer, to rob a federal bank, to flee from one state to another to avoid prosecution or give testimony in certain cases, to carry stolen property worth $5,000 or more across a state line, and to use interstate communications such as telephone and telegraph in extortions. The federal Kidnaping law was amended. Now an interstate abduction was a federal violation, even if ransom or reward was not the motive. This hoped to discourage a receding fugitive from taking hostages over state lines. Also, the agents now had full power of arrest and full legal authority to be armed. Amazingly, prior to these crime bills, agents had to have special authorization to carry weapons.[2]

The three women of Little Bohemia were officially released on May 25, after pleading guilty, on eighteen months' probation under suspended sentences of a year and a day each by Judge Patrick T. Stone. They were held for a few days longer while an immense network of informants and shadow men was set up to trail them. The belief was unanimous that the women would go back to their men. In the Chicago office, they were brought before Melvin Purvis and another lawman, a looming, thirty-four-year-old former Mormon missionary named Samuel Cowley. No stranger to the Dillinger case, he had been Harold Nathan's assistant in Washington when, on June 1, he was called into Hoover's office for his transfer to Chicago's Special Squad.

"Go anywhere the trail takes you," Hoover had ordered, "taking everyone who ever was remotely connected with the gang."[3]

After the women paid their due respects to both Purvis and Cowley, they were escorted to the Chief Federal Probation Officer in Chicago, William McGrath. After warning them to report weekly, he released them. Agent Gillespie stayed with them awhile, riding the train until they got off. Impending freedom brought Helen Gillis out of her introversion. She became talkative.

"I expect to be followed the rest of my life," she said, with her usual fatalism. With Mrs. Gillis, one's life span was quite relative. She intended to follow Baby Face, her "Les," to the grave. Her feeling was that they were going to be killed in short order.

The shadow team, made up of six special agents, had a mission that would prove impossible: to cover the three women at all times. The lack of manpower handicapped them, as they shuttled between Chicago and Fort Wayne, Indiana, where Dillinger and Van Meter were reputedly hiding. They also watched a Nelson hideout at 152 South Crawford, but to no avail; Nelson was reputedly staying in a house of prostitution in East St. Louis, Illinois.[4]

On the other side of town, Marie Comforti was returned to her foster mother's home and told "not to associate with any criminals whatsoever." Also ordered to remain in Chicago, Jean Delaney Crompton moved into the Fitzsimmons home. The house at 5516 South Marshfield Avenue had become a fish bowl. Agent Hollis, with his shadowing team, focused on preventing their escape back to the men. The agents hung out in a nearby filling station for a few days and then rented an apartment directly across the street from the Fitzsimmons home at 5515. Not easily intimidated, Helen Gillis contacted her Madison attorney, Carl Hill, with a request. She wanted to reclaim Baby Face's car, which was being stored in Portage, Wisconsin. Carl Hill wrote to U.S. Attorney George Sullivan requesting the ticket for the Ford. The government shoved her request aside while looking for a loophole, which they found in her bill of sale. The car had been purchased with the help of Tom Filbin, the St. Paul underworld financier. Armed with this paperwork, Hugh Clegg advised Sullivan that the terms of her probation expressly stated that she was not to associate with criminals, a club of whom Filbin was, undoubtedly, a member. They got their loophole; she lost the car.

Hoover noted dryly that Helen Gillis showed no desire to see her babies, only to rejoin her "baby faced rat." Her hurried dash from the company of four-year-old Darlene tends to confirm this callous observation. In their need to escape back to the underworld, the women lacked the awareness of an imminent prison sentence or sudden death, unless you counted Helen Gillis' fantasy of dying with Baby Face. Restricted by their social class and lack of education, they yearned for excitement. Their dangerous men fed their cravings for thrills. There had never been a moment's doubt that this was what they wanted.

On May 31, Father Coughlan slipped a message to Helen Gillis at the Fitzsimmons home. She lifted herself from a bored, desperate catnap. Her petite frame left its impression on the chenille bedspread after she'd gotten up. She kissed her daughter Darlene, age four, and roused Jean Delaney Crompton. In a staged scene, she asked Jean to accompany her to a local movie house. They left with only a purse tucked under their arms. Outside the house, Helen greeted Father Coughlan, the intermediary sent by Gillis to bring her back. Helen trusted Coughlan, not knowing that he acted as a double-agent to the watchful shadow team. Not wishing to interfere with the "informant's contact," the agents remained in their apartment across the street. They neglected to follow them, sensing no danger of losing the women, who carried no luggage or other sign of transport. They neglected to take one fashion fact into consideration: A desperado's woman could, and did, abandon her wardrobe in a fast escape.

Fifteen minutes elapsed. When their informant did not return, they found him sitting in a car in front of the theater with another woman in the passenger seat. He looked up to see a group of incredulous men staring pointedly in his direction.

"Mrs. Gillis has gone to the show," he glibly volunteered.

When Sam Cowley heard that Helen was gone, he grew livid. Melvin Purvis agreed that the shadow shouldn't have interfered with the contact. They heard nothing more until June 8, when Father Coughlan telephoned Sam Cowley in the Chicago office to say that Baby Face had just left Chicago. It was typical of Father Coughlan to play both sides. He'd waited until Baby Face was far out of sight before reporting on his whereabouts. The only thing left for the Justice Department to do was revoke Helen Gillis' probation. On June 12, a warrant was issued for her arrest.

In a bizarre double-play, the women had slipped away without ever buying a movie ticket. They'd joined their men, who idled in a car that Tommy Carroll had stolen from a dealership.[5]

The shadowing techniques used to trail Helen Gillis and Jean Delaney Crompton had only recently been refined. The proving ground was the tailing of Opal Long in Chicago, when everything she'd owned, including her vibrator, had become fodder for the agents' imaginations. With police tactics on one side and poverty pressing on the other, Opal had recently become obsessed with retrieving the valuables she'd lost in Tucson. She went to John L. Van Buskirk, the attorney to whom the Dillinger gangsters and their molls had assigned $34,000 in currency, cars, and jewelry in Tucson after their arrest. He scored a legal point in Superior Court when Judge Fred W. Fickett denied a motion made by Gerald Jones, counsel for the National Surety Corp., a plaintiff in civil actions against the money and property. Van Buskirk won on the grounds that the cars had been assigned to him and that they belonged to him. Now Opal's things had legally gone to Van Buskirk, and she wondered if she was really better off. Of special value to the woman was her jeweled cosmetic case, lost in the debacle of the arrests. She treasured the memory of that long-ago treasure trove of lipstick, powder, and perfume. These lost symbols of her sexual life with Russell Clark would remain elusive. So, too, would credibility as his legal wife, a problem that was caused by Opal's mixing of her aliases with her legal names.

The government acknowledged her only as Opal Long, in spite of her endless battle to become known as Bernice Clark. She couldn't convince the warden at the Ohio State Penitentiary that she was actually married to Clark. When he suspected that the certificate that she provided to him was false, he wired the Justice Department to say that she had made changes on an old marriage license, passing it off as her conjugal imprimatur.

Early in the morning of May 10, Opal left Detroit with Pat Cherrington, who was up there to visit her daughter at Mae Clark's house. Enroute to Columbus, where Opal would attempt to see Russell Clark, they crashed their car. This forced Opal to hock her diamond ring to pay for the repairs. Momentarily defeated, the two returned to Detroit, forgetting a plan to bring money to Harry Copeland's mother in Muncie. Pat sent it instead through an intermediary.

In the middle of May, they looked up Larry Streng in Chicago. It is curious that Pat still trusted him, with his reputation for having set up the arrest of Evelyn Frechette. Pat, in the frantic days after Little Bohemia, had appealed to him on April 30. "Let's go drinking," she'd said, "let's go anywhere." Climbing into her Checker cab, he'd found the drive to be harrowing. They were being followed. Not heeding Dillinger's gut feeling, Pat stayed in close proximity to Larry Streng. In the same scenario played out so many times before, the two sisters checked into the Chateau Hotel, at 3838 Broadway. They'd dragged their meager belongings, heavy legs, and ailing spirits into the cheap walk-up. While there, they learned of John Hamilton's death. In a letter sent to Bernice Norton, Clark's sister, Opal Long would later write from prison:

"We got a note from Frank before we got pinched and he said that Red had passed on about a couple of months before that and we were supposed to see him but never got a chance to." The elusive "Frank" was an attempt to prevent authorities from knowing that she'd seen Dillinger. It is doubtful that this death bell tolled in Sault Ste. Marie, Michigan, where Hamilton's sister still waited to post bail. Arraigned before Federal Judge Fred M. Raymond on June 7, she pleaded "not guilty" while furnishing a bond of $1,000 for her appearance at the October term of the Federal Court at Marquette, Michigan.

At the same time, Pat Cherrington became the subject of a grand jury indictment and warrant for her arrest. On June 1, she was resting with Opal Long in the Chateau Hotel. Police Captain John Stege and his "Dillinger Squad" raided the room, herding the women down to the Marquette police station. At the same time, Larry Streng stopped at the pool hall where Art "Fish" Johnson and Jack Perkins hung out and mentioned that Cherrington might have been arrested. Johnson ordered his girlfriend, Jean Burke, to go to the station house to confirm the rumor. Burke walked past the twin green lights of police headquarters, only to find herself mugged with Cherrington and Opal Long. Larry Streng, never tagged as an informant, had now figured prominently in the arrests of Cherrington and Long, as well as Evelyn Frechette.

Stege's Dillinger Squad had walked into the Chateau with a mistake-

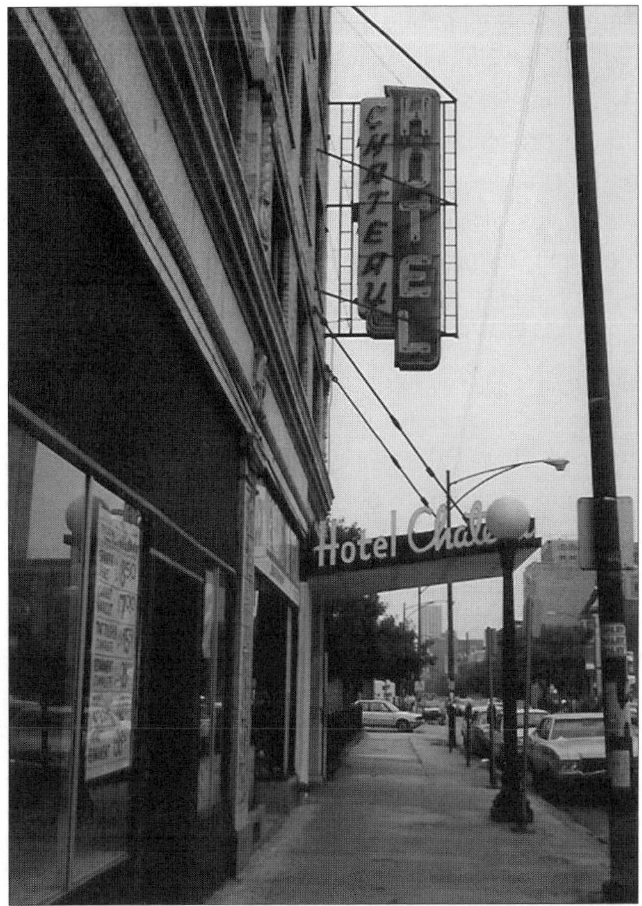


Transient women, Opal Long and Patricia Cherrington lived in Chicago residence hotels like the Marshall and Chateau.
(Author's Collection)

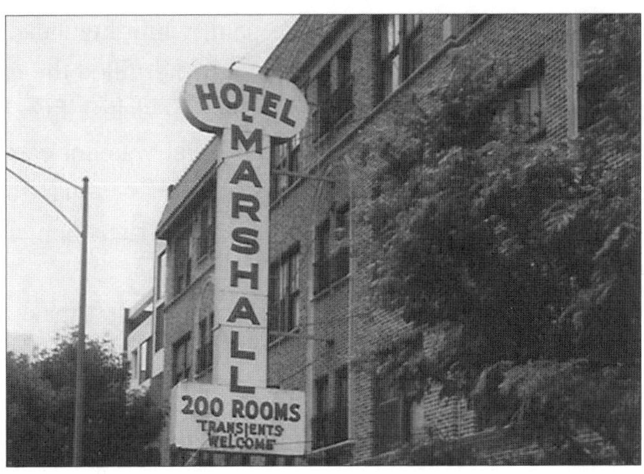

proof warrant and supporting indictments. Having intact paperwork would avoid the problems such as they'd had with Anna Steve in Michigan, who had claimed that the entry into her home was against her will and without proper justification.

In a rare effort at cooperation between city police and federal agents, Stege delivered his prisoners to Melvin Purvis later that night. Stege then revealed that his preferred plan had been to relinquish custody to Matt Leach in Indiana. As Hoover disliked and distrusted the Indiana police captain, that was not likely to occur.

On one thing they could agree: Pat Cherrington and Opal Long were leftover sediments of an earlier era. The police moved in only after being convinced that Dillinger wasn't expected to contact either woman. The gang was glad to be rid of them, with their endless grubbing. Van Meter, especially, cursed Pat Cherrington whenever her name came up in conversation.

Pat Reilly had instigated this feud when he'd driven Cherrington from Little Bohemia to St. Paul while the gang had stayed at the lodge. He'd picked up $4,000, an amount that was owed to Van Meter from Tommy Gannon. When their return to the lodge was aborted by gunfire, they fled, rolling into a ditch in the process. Reilly claimed that while he pushed the car out and onto the road, Pat rolled him, taking the money from his pouch. When Reilly delivered the money to Van Meter, the original $4,000 had dwindled down to $300, with Pat getting the blame.

In Bridewell Prison, Pat did three days in the hole. "Incommunicado" had become a systems-normal treatment for women of Dillinger's gang. In this spirit, Pat was kept in solitary confinement. Her postoperative ventral hernia had her doubled up with pain, while her head throbbed with the migraine that plagued her. The moldy diet filled the gaps in her teeth but not her hungry stomach. By now she'd lost five teeth, the cumulative result of poverty and neglect. Yet Pat was not easily cowed. The federal men, as she called them, questioned her intermittently during this confinement. She later bragged about her tight-lipped response to this treatment.

"When I made up my mind not to talk, they couldn't make me, and I didn't."

Exacerbating Pat's problem was Louis Piquett. He didn't appear for her, although he did report for Opal Long on June 18. She waived examination and was held to the U.S. District Court for the District of

Minnesota and ordered to post $10,000 bond for the crime of "unlawfully and feloniously concealing and harboring a fugitive, with knowledge that a warrant had been issued for said fugitive." Lacking the bail money, Piquett shrugged with apathetic relief as she left for the holding pen, bound for the Cook County House of Correction. Both women would remain in Chicago.

Long, picked up on charges of joining Dillinger on March 31 in the Lexington Avenue apartment, answered for the social call because Dillinger had broken the provisions of the Dyer Act a scant three weeks prior to Opal's visit. Prosecutor Lloyd C. Moody ordered a payroll made in the amount of $44.30 for the appearance of two witnesses. Daisy Coffey, the landlady who placed Evelyn Frechette at the ironing board, would return to identify Opal Long.

Opal Long continued to fret over Clark. Her worries revolved around his mother, who was now solely responsible for the care of Pat's daughter. Opal wrote to May Clark after her arrest.

> *"If you can come here, you can get the car. It hasn't been tied up that I know of. It is at the Marquette Police Station in care of Captain John Stege. You can see Piquett, but don't let him talk you out of any money. Tell Russell hello, and give him my love. Tell him I was just trying to help the kids. That's why I am jammed up and you can tell that to Mrs. P.P. [Pierpont] if you ever see her. Mom, get Mary's [Kinder] address from Levy and ask her if she'll send me some spending money when I go to St. Paul. They can appoint me a lawyer. . . . "*

Amazingly, Mrs. Clark did receive Opal Long's clothes, car, and rings. In another letter, written to Clark in cell E1, Columbus, Opal wrote:

> *"It isn't so bad here. They play the radio till 9 at nite.* [sic] *Last nite we heard mountain music and it sure did make me think of you and all the nites we used to sit home and listen to it. Tell young-old [sic] Mac I said 'hello' and best regards to Pete. Hope the lawyers are still working on that appeal. . . . "*

The two sisters were realistic about Louis Piquett. The lawyer did visit Pat in the Cook County Jail, merely to advise her on a guilty plea. It was advice based on financial incentives. She refused, holding out for "not guilty," even as she flew to Madison on June 20, leaving Opal Long to go to St. Paul.

In Madison, Patricia answered to federal harboring charges based on her stay at the Little Bohemia. She asked Judge Stone to appoint her counsel. When asked if Piquett was her attorney, she said,"I don't know if he's going to defend me or not." Then the court set her bond at $25,000. "Can you raise bond?" Judge Stone asked.

"I could raise $20,000 bond," she said, laughing "but I'd rather not. Every time I go anywhere they raid the place and I don't want to get any innocent people into trouble for nothing, so I prefer to stay away."

The reporters liked Pat instantly. The ex-dancer and entertainer was a feisty firecracker, a born star. They asked her why she didn't plead guilty.

"I haven't done anything to plead guilty to."

"Hey, maybe the sheriff's wife will give you a job peeling potatoes," they laughed.

"I didn't do any work before they got me and I don't expect to," she replied with a wink.

But Pat Cherrington would crash from her perch as queen of the tabloids. On July 6 she changed her plea to guilty. Her snappy attitude, though, remained. When she went before Judge Stone for her violations of S. 88 and 246, Title 18, U.S. Code, she bore herself without remorse. "Your Honor," she addressed Judge Stone, "I've worked in practically all the exclusive clubs in Chicago."

Requested to be more specific, Pat was quiet for a moment and then named the "Frolics" and "Minuet" as two places she'd plied her trade as a dancer in Chicago.

"When and where did you first meet Dillinger?"

"I first met him in Chicago about a year ago."

"How did you come to meet him?"

"I don't remember."

"Oh yes you do."

Pat would temporarily be assigned to Alderson, a candidate because of her medical condition. She was ignorant of the cause of her postoperative pain. When she'd seen Dr. Mortensen in St. Paul during the days the gang had stayed at the Little Bohemia, she told him she'd had a "gall bladder operation." He surprised her with the revelation that her gall bladder was gone. The bile was now passing through a new outlet, one that was too small to allow free flow to the digestive tract. She was expected to endure the pain for the next few months, during which time the new outlet was expected to expand.

Under sentence of two years, she went to Alderson on July 11, during a searing heat wave. As number 2417-W, Pat's tailored outfit was taken from her and replaced by the generic shirtwaist worn by the inmates as an official "alternative to gloom and drabness." She was photographed and fingerprinted, probed internally, and interrogated. A test for venereal disease was administered to Pat, as it had been previously to Beth Green. The cultures came back negative. Neither woman was found to be infected with sexually transmitted diseases, although Hoover was irrationally convinced that they were.

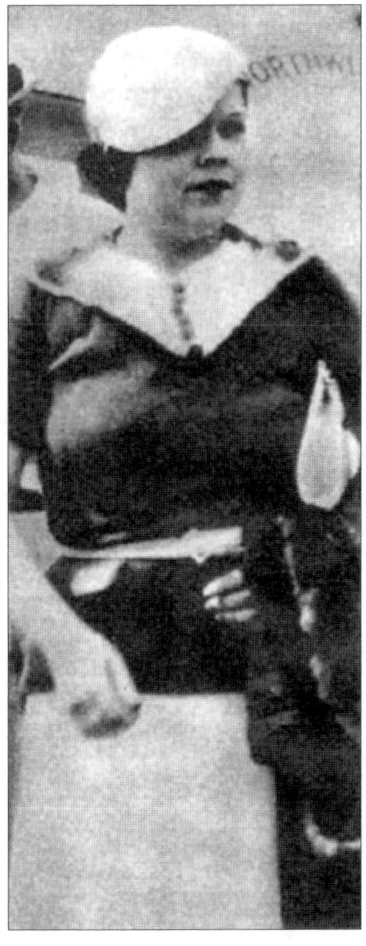

Pat Cherrington entered Alderson during a 110-degree heat wave. (Sandy Jones/John Dillinger Historical Society)

A crude psychological test and a Binet-Simon intelligence test were administered, on which Pat scored 105. In a move away from the antiquated practice of putting females to work on sewing machines, the Federal Bureau of Prisons offered Pat a chance to type and take stenography.

"She has a pleasant personality—is a vivacious type. She tries to analyze herself, is always studying the people with whom she comes in contact. She likes to read—is particularly fond of poetry." In this and subsequent interviews, Patricia resurrected Art Cherrington from Leavenworth. "We had books and poetry in common," she said. Her time with him was "the only happiness she had ever known."

Pat's tenure at Alderson would be

short, although they liked her and wanted to place her in the library. Her only blemish was a refusal to identify the people with whom she'd traveled on "certain occasions." She would stay at Alderson for two months until August 5, when she would be deemed inoperable—the lining of her stomach had worn too thin, with surgery too risky.[6]

Pat Cherrington would not benefit from the social reform of the past decade. Considered a real security risk, she was removed from her cottage, her poetic memories, and her sten pad, bound for the U.S. Detention Farm at Milan, Michigan. The Board of Prisons, no doubt goaded by Hoover, acted when the female consorts of the "high-profile" gangsters were aimed at their progressive institution. By the time Pat Cherrington entered the facility, a determination was quickly made.

"The Federal Industrial Institution for Women at Alderson was not designed and is not equipped to handle women who are desperate and incorrigible," said Sanford Bates, Director of the Prison Board. "We cannot risk the possibility of an attempt to rescue forcibly the wife or sweetheart of any organized gangster. Consequently, we have set aside a portion of the Federal Detention Farm at Milan, Michigan, for the housing of a small group of female prisoners. Here they can be adequately guarded by armed officers and housed in the more traditional type of steel cells."

Yet Milan was not a maximum facility either. In spite of its three armed watchtowers and barbed wire fences, it was considered less

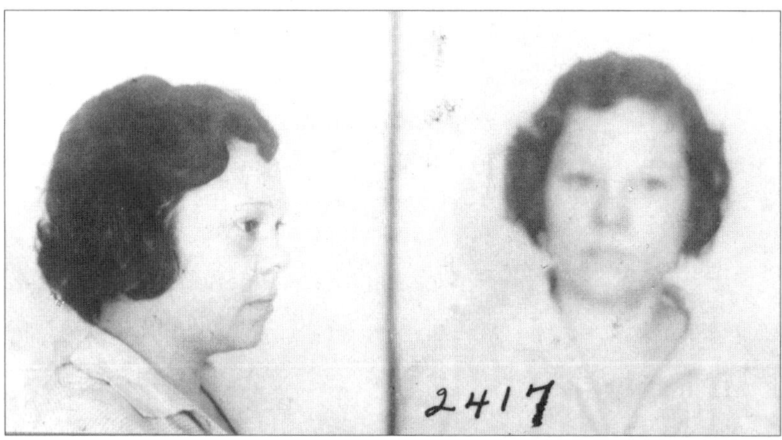


Patricia Cherrington was taken from Alderson's progressive cottages, and placed in Milan, where she found "steel bars for female incorrigibles."

(Federal Bureau of Prisons)

secure than Leavenworth and Atlanta. It was built for "improvable criminals." When it was completed and just opening its doors to prisoners on April 21, 1933, its original intent was to house 600 males on a short-term basis from the Detroit-Toledo area. Its only exercise area was an exposed area formed within a rectangle of buildings.

In all fairness to the personnel at Milan, the medical division went to special trouble for the ailing Pat Cherrington. She was entitled to a special support belt to relieve the pain of her hernia. The surgeon placed a frantic request to Alderson for the specific belt measurements.

Opal Long would also go to court, appearing in the St. Paul venue that had hosted the trial of Evelyn Frechette. Unlike Pat, Opal Long openly showed her remorse. Lacking the brass of her colorful sister, she went before Judge M.M. Joyce quietly. Her banana curls hung sadly around her freckled, tough face. In analyzing her situation, she'd exhibited more common sense than her showy sibling.

"I pleaded guilty to that charge because I knew I'd have to sit around in jail for six months anyway, waiting for a trial," she said, and pleaded guilty on June 28. During the proceeding, the district attorney reiterated her role.

"She was a visitor in the Lexington Avenue apartment on March 29, from which Dillinger shot his way out of a police trap on March 31," claimed Charles F. Sullivan.

Opal's attorney, A. Jerome Hoffman, interrupted him, making a fuss over the date in question. With the same attention to insignificant detail that had characterized his losses in representing Frechette, he contradicted the U.S. attorney.

"She did not visit the flat until the afternoon of March 30," he announced with vapid emphasis. "And she didn't go to the flat to see Dillinger, John Hamilton or Homer Van Meter," he continued, "but to see a sister who was there."

Sullivan responded by quoting from the affidavit made by Mrs. Daisy Coffey. Opal Long had been the "woman with a towel around her head on at least one occasion." She recalled Pat Cherrington as the "girl with the large hips."

"Would you please consider the 29 days which Mrs. Clark already has been in jail and that this period be credited against this term?" he requested.

Judge Joyce denied the plea, asserting that the penalty could have been much more severe. She was sentenced to six months. Opal Long lifted herself up to answer the judge.

"Well, this is the last time I will be in a court room for a long while—I hope."

If the fairy godmother of this broken Cinderella heard one wish, she granted it. Hoffman moved to change Opal Long's name to Bernice Clark. Her commitment papers bore the title, "U.S. v. Bernice Clark." Finally, she'd received validation as Clark's wife. As the newly crowned "Mrs. Clark," she went to the Ramsey County Jail in St. Paul. She was bound for the Minneapolis Workhouse.

Known as Camden Station, the Minneapolis Workhouse had been placed under the control of the Minneapolis Board of Public Welfare in 1920. The facility had housed only women since 1925, when a working farm to house the men went up at Parkers Lake. While the women's facility offered "free liquor cures given to all who desire," Opal Long was written up as "moderate in her habits" upon her entry on June 30, 1934. She claimed to be married, a Baptist, and was weighed in at 164 pounds that day. The only relative she listed was her niece, with no name given. The $5.01 she carried was taken from her. She was judged able to read and write. She listed her address as 3838 Broadway, the location of the Chateau Hotel. Once the intake procedure was completed, Opal was assigned to an ironing board. Somehow, she kited out a letter to Russell Clark's mother:[6]

> *"Dear kids and everybody:*
>
> *Will dash off a few lines while I can. Hope you will receive O.K. as I am going to try to send it out with a girl who is leaving tomorrow. My pencil is so short I can hardly write so don't blame me if you can't read this. Be sure and don't mention about this letter when you write as things are tough enough here as it is without any extra trouble. Try to save all the papers about Johnie as we don't get much news in these papers here. I have the job of ironing now and my feet sure do give me hell but am getting more used to it now . . . I've eaten so much darned candy today I feel sick. I have never been outside in the yard since I've been here but think*

*maybe I might get to now a little later on. We also get locked up at 5:30 and can read till the lights go out. Four girls just got put in the "hole" today and I guess I'm lucky I didn't get put in too. I sure was mad at some stool pigeon in here so if you don't get any letter from me for any length of time you will know they have taken my writing privilege away from me. However, I am trying to be good for it sure is hell not to get any mail so try to write as often as you can all of you. Be careful how you answer. Tell everybody hello and give June my love and tell her to be a good girl.*

*love to all,*
*jail bird*

*"She was well spoken, and sounded educated . . . you'd never know that she was a gangster's moll."*

*—Reporter Francis Veach,*
*recounting his impression of Jean Delaney Crompton*

# "The Old Innocent Act"

Jean Delaney Crompton spent her first hours reunited with Tommy Carroll in the New Lawrence Hotel. In the monolithic high-rise on Lawrence Avenue in Chicago, the old dynamic resumed. He was jealous, with particular hatred for college boys and their lustful wolf whistling. When a young man yelled, "hey blondie," Carroll ordered her to dye the yellow tresses that so attracted attention. The resultant mud-brown color cast a pallor on her skin, making her appear years older. The life she led wasn't helping to preserve her youth. The fugitive couple would have less than one week to consummate the unfinished business of their relationship.

She had called their reunion "a rescue." Her later statement to the agents, that she'd had "no alternative but to go with him," left a controversial issue open for conjecture. Sometime within the next week, Crompton's pregnancy, which she'd claimed was viable upon her arrest at the Little Bohemia, terminated. When Crompton was discovered to have lost the child, it topped off a debate, with some law enforcers calling it a back-room abortion. She maintained that she'd lost the baby through miscarriage. It was a hot subject, with Hugh Clegg opining that it had been a miscarriage and others saying that she was never pregnant in the first place.

While in Chicago, they met Dillinger, who surprised Jean by looking different, the result of recent plastic surgery. Shortly after their stop at the New Lawrence, they joined Lester and Helen Gillis and traveled to the Lake Como Hotel, at Lake Geneva, Wisconsin. It was a known hangout for mobsters. At Lake Como, Lester Gillis stayed with Helen in the main hotel. Carroll and his Jean stayed in The Doll House. Three days later John Paul Chase arrived.

Lawrence Hotel, 1020 Lawrence Avenue, in Chicago, where Tommy Carroll stayed with Jean Delaney Crompton enroute to Waterloo. (Author's Collection)

The Doll House was operated by Lucille Moran, the former wife of George "Bugs" Moran. The Dillinger gang had gone to The Doll House many times, seeking shelter in the post-Capone years from Scarface's former people. One of the "big four"—comprised of Capone, John Torrio, and the Aiellos—Bugs Moran had been connected with Dion O'Banion before the latter was murdered on November 10, 1924, by the Torrio-Capone mob. Moran later shot Johnny Torrio in retribution for O'Banion's death. Now descended from the old O'Banion gang, it had been a contender for Capone's cookeries, wine and beer distributors in the late 1920s, when five of Moran's people were killed in the St. Valentine's Day Massacre by Capone's mob. Tommy Carroll would hold on to a Lake Como matchbox. An underworld calling card, it was one connection that hadn't dried up. It had stung the gang to know that Moran's old adversary, Frank "the Enforcer" Nitti, and his people hadn't cared if John Hamilton lived or died.

As Jean Delaney Crompton burrowed into The Doll House with Tommy Carroll, her mother, Mrs. Helen Delaney, was making a decision to avoid going to Chicago, which she called "sin city." Mrs. Delaney had an aversion to the criminal element that her daughters didn't share. Mrs. Delaney had known sorrow in the path her daughters chose to follow; she hated the criminals in St. Paul, especially Pat Reilly.

The best of her girls, undoubtedly, had been Jean. Born into the harsh Cincinnati winter on February 1 or 2, 1912, she grew into a book-loving girl whom Mrs. Delaney said she'd "never had to punish." Modest and pretty, Jean lived quietly in her mother's home in St. Paul, at 365 Maria Street. It was an address from which the daughters left as soon as they could. The house on a quiet residential street paled in comparison to the excitement of Harry Sawyer's nightclubs, which had attracted both Babe and Dolores. Jean followed her two sisters out the door, although she bypassed the Barker-Karpis cliques. She found work as a cashier in a Chicago lounge, eventually marrying Eddie "Lonzo" Crompton, the master of ceremonies there. They were married on May 5, 1931, and were separated by June 1932. She later claimed he'd abandoned her, most likely to obtain an uncontested divorce. He would later talk to police, who found him at work in the By-Lin Tavern, at 3837 Lincoln Avenue.

"We were married in the Subway Café at 507 North Wabash Avenue on May 5, 1932," he said, although the divorce papers would later state the year as 1931. "I was a singing waiter and Jean was also employed there. We lived together until seven months ago, when she decided she wanted to go to St. Paul and live with her mother."

There she drifted into her sisters' clique and began dating Tommy Carroll. The bank robber was the veteran of tumultuous love affairs, including a near-fatal attraction.

His first wife had been a troubled heroin addict. Viola Carroll grew up in a reform school where she was nicknamed "The Rattlesnake." She graduated into prostitution and shoplifting before marrying Carroll. Carroll helped his junk-addicted wife with cash gained by his post office holdups. Adept with a machine gun, he drifted into bank robbery by "casing jugs," as Viola later explained it. Working with the Barker-Karpis group through three major robberies, he also became known as a machine gunner who could control a group of hostages, which he did during the robbery of the Security National Bank in Sioux Falls.

Viola's stronghold on Carroll was short-lived. He threw her over for a new woman, named "Radio Sally" Bennett. When Viola found out, she augmented the attempted stove-poker murder by taking poison. Sally Bennett, while connected to the underworld, had her head on a bit straighter than the maniacal Rattlesnake. A Chicago night club entertainer living in the Fossmore Apartments at 5125 Kenmore Avenue, she was reputedly hiding Joseph Burns, who had escaped with Dillinger from Michigan City. Her two brothers, Charles in St. Paul and Joseph in Minneapolis, worked in line with Tommy Carroll. Joseph helped Tommy to the extent that he would receive mail for him, and he once hosted a get-together with Gillis, Helen, and their son.

Viola, waiting slavishly for Carroll's return, found out about Jean Delaney Crompton after Little Bohemia. The feature photo of the three women sent Viola into a depression. She would write,

"Another girl's picture showed in the papers this time. A pretty girl named Jean Crompton, not more than twenty years old. A girl half my age. And a vivacious child, judging by appearance. I had once been as pretty as she. That was long ago."[1]

As Tommy Carroll drove into Waterloo, Iowa, on June 7, his thoughts were on Jean, not the "Rattlesnake." His love now huddled beside him in a car stolen from a Chicago showroom. He was desperate for money, with only $700 left from the $785 that he'd exchanged for a bond in a St. Paul bank. That morning, they were midway between a Cedar Rapids tourist camp and a visit to Jean's mother in Minneapolis. In the heat of the day, Jean felt dry as the upholstery in the tight, stuffy car. The commercial section of Waterloo looked benign. Carroll decided to stop there for gas. He made the mistake, like his predecessors in Tucson, of writing off the people there as hicks.

The nationwide search for the Dillinger gang had turned every citizen into a private eye. Carroll's out-of-state license plates, which were hidden beneath the battery, glistened like stolen jewels when the mechanic lifted the hood. He tried to keep an impassive expression as he worked on the car. Meanwhile, Carroll had escorted Jean to the restrooms. When she came out, she told him she was thirsty. She wanted a glass of 3.2 beer, the brew of 1934. They drove to a bar on Lafayette Street. While Jean perched precariously on a barstool, police were gathering outside on the mechanic's tip to check a Hudson sedan with Missouri plates. When the couple returned to their car, two plainclothes police officers jumped out of hiding. Detective Emil Steffen and fifty-seven year-old veteran Sheriff P.E. Walker leaped in front of Carroll.

"Walker and I covered the car and waited some time before this fellow and a girl showed up. We stepped up and identified ourselves" Emil Steffen later said.

Carroll reached for his gun, but Walker shot him a fist to the jaw, knocking Carroll's gun out of his hand. But Carroll got up and grabbed his gun, making a run for his car. Steffen held Jean down on the ground and managed to get three shots into Carroll. His white shirt, stained a gruesome, coagulated mess, glistened on the sidewalk as Jean went crazy—kicking, screaming, and crying as Walker struggled to hold her by the wrists. It was Eddie Green all over again. Like Bess, Jean watched her lover take five bullets—in the left armpit, the chest, and three in the spine. He was pocked with four bullet holes in his upper torso.

Emil Steffen rode to the St. Francis Hospital with Carroll. A reporter named Francis Veach followed the ambulance to the hospital. There he met Dr. Wade Preece.

"I'm hit, buddy," Carroll told Dr. Preece. As nurses cut Carroll's clothes away from his body, he turned his head toward a detective.

"Don't try to steal my watch," he threatened. Dr. Preece confirmed that Carroll died with last rights administered by a priest.

"Death was caused by hemorrhage of the lungs," Dr. Preece confirmed in a later interview. His only request was for Jean, whom he did not mention by name.

"Tell her I'm all right," Carroll mumbled.

Dr. Preece then went to the Blackwell Jail, where he told Jean that Carroll was paralyzed.

Francis Veach, the *Courier* staff writer, followed the group into the police station to meet Jean Delaney Crompton.

"There wasn't anything to those stories about all the things he had done," she told the reporter. She sensed that Veach was sympathetic and tried to tell him that her boyfriend had been "really a nice fellow." Francis Veach liked her. The woman moved him to pity.

"She was well spoken, and sounded educated . . . you'd never know that she was a gangster's moll," he recalled in a later interview. He shared his recollections with the author and recalled Jean's request to him as he left for the hospital.

"Tell him I still love him . . . tell him not to die."

When Veach got to the hospital, armed with his message, Carroll had already expired, at 6:55 p.m. The reporter learned that some detectives wanted to shock Jean with the sight of Carroll's body—on the pretense that she was going to be visiting him.

"[They] planned to bring her in to see him lying on the slab," he related. "The idea was that she would break down and tell him where Dillinger could be found. [They] supposed it would shake her."

Veach intercepted the plan. He told her of Carroll's death.

"I went back to the Blackwell County Jail," said Veach. "She sat with her cellmate, an old woman serving time for bootlegging. I made her feel better by saying I gave him the message that she'd loved him."

"When can I see him?" she asked simply.

"It's too late." Veach retreated in shock when Jean fainted, leaving the elderly bootlegger woman to revive her.

When Jean came back to consciousness, she became angry. She felt she'd been "double-crossed."

"They said if I answered their questions, they would take me to see him. They took me to see him in the morgue. It was the first time I had ever seen anyone dead."

The Waterloo Police Department hadn't informed the Justice Department of the shooting. Finally someone from the Associated Press thought to notify them. Special Agent in Charge Werner Hanni, to whom the call was forwarded, reacted with dismay—no field agents were remotely close to Waterloo, Iowa. He dispatched Rufis Coulter, a veteran of the Lexington Avenue shootout, and Agent G.J. Gross, also from St. Paul.

Sheriff Walker became the subject of a letter-writing campaign to obtain the cash reward. The petition was based on recent acts of Congress that appropriated maximum rewards to officers who killed the gangsters. The request went as far as the U.S. Senate before an unequivocal "no" came back from the office of the assistant attorney general. The appropriation, a clause of the Deficiency Bill, was still unsigned by President Roosevelt.

Carroll's death revealed that he was a wanted man in his own right, for crimes committed long before his involvement at Mason City and Sioux Falls. He was a prime suspect in the slaying of H.C. Perrow, a San Antonio, Texas, city detective who was shot to death on December 11, 1933. His presence there had been confirmed by an informant who

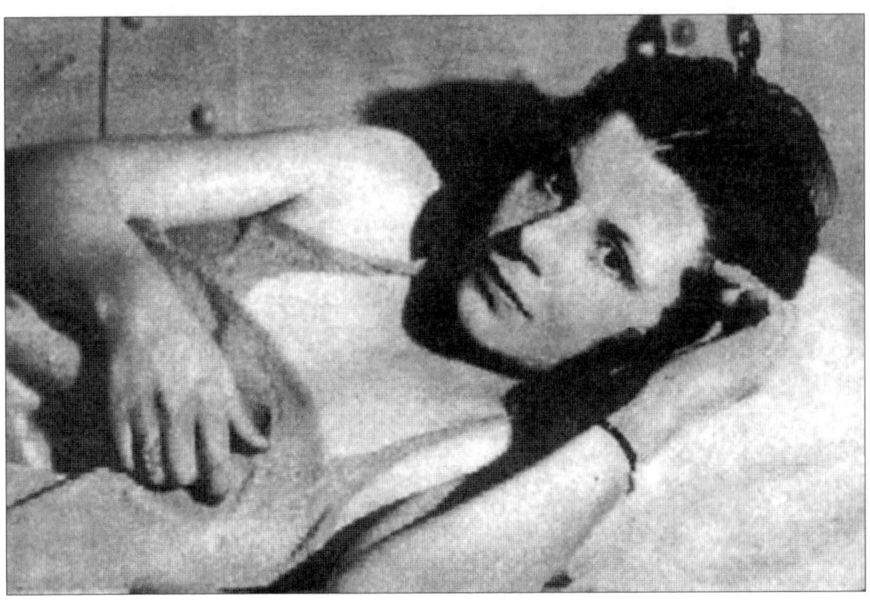

Jean Delaney Crompton, in shock after witnessing the shooting death of Tommy Carroll in Waterloo, Iowa. (Sandy Jones/John Dillinger Historical Society)

revealed Carroll was there to make a buy from gun dealer Hyman Lebman, attended by Carroll and, most notably, Homer Van Meter and Lester Gillis.

Carroll's body was displayed on a slab at O'Keefe and Towne Funeral Home. He was stripped to the waist, which displayed the bullet holes in an impromptu crime-does not-pay exhibit. Meanwhile, his death was driving Viola "Rattlesnake" Carroll to necrophilia. She stepped out of her room in a St. Paul hotel, where police believed her to be operating as a prostitute, and telephoned the newspapers. She was in charge of his burial, she said. Carroll's brother, well aware of the excesses to which Viola was prone, went alone to Waterloo to receive the remains. Viola settled for a photograph and bull session.

"It was I who had the right to be there, by his side. It was I who loved him, and to whom he had always turned when his luck had been the worst." In newspapers, her grainy photo straddled Jean's forlorn picture.[2]

Jean was returned to Madison, Wisconsin. The wife of Sheriff Fred Finn had been burdened with the women of the Little Bohemia for an entire month. She had seen to it that Jean Delaney Crompton had gotten preferential treatment, out of concern for her alleged pregnancy. When Crompton had said goodbye to the sheriff's wife, both thought it was a final farewell. Neither woman could guess that within two weeks the girl would return to her cell at Madison.

Crompton was brought into federal court at 7:00 a.m. on June 9 for revocation of her probation and arraignment. Judge Patrick T. Stone presided over the decision on her place of confinement for violating probation.

"Your order of probation has accomplished at least one thing," scolded the judge. "It has resulted in the removal from society of a desperado who has terrorized this country for a couple of years."

"He couldn't have been all those things they said about him," she cried. Hoover would call this the "the old innocent act." She brought up the lost pregnancy.

"He knew I was going to have a baby, and he wanted me to come with him."

"Are you in that condition now?" the judge asked.

"No," she replied without further explanation. She was sentenced to one year and a day in an "institution to be designated by the Attorney General." This was key language. The Justice Department answered only to the attorney general. This gave Hoover the power to dictate where Jean would serve her time, and, to her detriment, she had made him angry. He was "tired of all her talk about how 'brave' Carroll was." Again before Judge Stone on June 11, Jean appeared to be in denial, defending Carroll as though he were still alive.

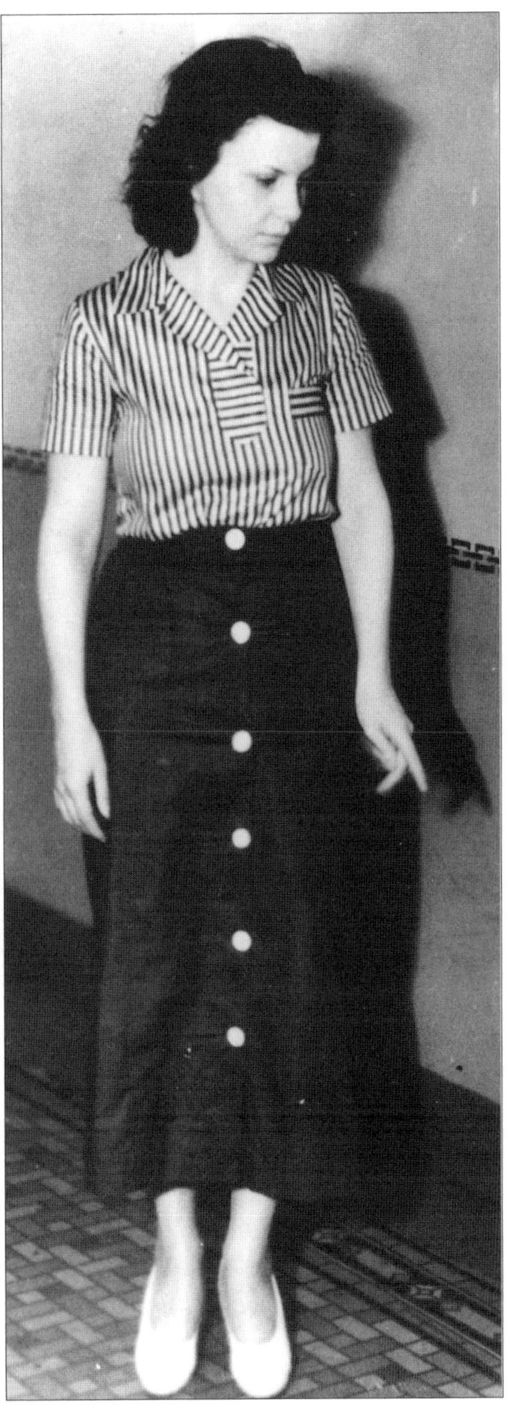

Jean Delaney Crompton, in custody after Tommy Carroll's death at Waterloo, Iowa. (Kathi Harrell)

Crompton was placed in a cottage with Beth Green, a decision that had come down from Washington. Assistant to the Director, E.A. Tamm, who had taken the seat vacated when Sam Cowley had formed the "Special Squad" in Chicago, wrote to the Bureau of Prisons requesting a two-day delay in placing Jean. Because she was fresh off the scene, unlike the women they'd had in custody for months, Crompton had more information than anyone else. Hugh Clegg suggested that Hoover place the girl in the same cottage as Green.

After Jean's revocation of probation, agents of the St. Paul office, under SAC Thomas Dodd, paid a visit to Babe Reilly and placed her under arrest for five days. She refused to talk, saying that although she was not especially interested in Reilly, she would do nothing to turn him in.

"I won't be a stool pigeon, not for a $10,000 reward each," she boasted. After releasing the lock-jawed Babe, they followed her to the home she kept with her son. Any preconceived notions about the spoils of crime were dashed when the agents found the woman living in comparative poverty with Reilly's five-year-old son. She didn't even have a home of her own, moving back and forth between her own mother, Helen Delaney Setzer, at 365 Maria Avenue, in St. Paul, and at other times with Pat Reilly's mother at 78 Sherbourne Avenue in St. Paul.

"She is quite a bluffer," they agreed. "With her sister likely to be sentenced to a term in the penitentiary, she may adopt a more serious attitude and be willing to cooperate," they hoped.

Of Jean's mother, the agents had observed that she was of a higher moral character than her daughters. "She seems to have some vestige of principle left in her makeup and will cry profusely if she is talked to about the status of her daughters," an agent wrote to Hoover from St. Paul. "She insists that they were not brought up to form associations with the type which they have developed. She utterly hates Pat Reilly. . . . "

Indeed, her letters to Jean reflect intelligence and introspection. She'd seen one daughter go to a federal prison; the other was pregnant with Alvin Karpis' child. After leaving Madison, the senior Delaney collapsed, remaining in bed for three days. Her biggest consolation would be to see Pat Reilly arrested on June 27 in his apartment in Minneapolis. She confided to Agent Hugh Clegg, who visited her at home, that she felt Reilly had been responsible for a great deal of her unhappiness. She had no objection to turning him in, she told them. They took the bait, offering her $500 for any one of the Dillinger or Barker-Karpis scalps. Money, however, could not replace the losses.

*"I have gotten so old looking the last few months that I can't get used to myself,"* she wrote to Jean, after her daughter had been committed to the Alderson Industrial Reformatory.

*"I worry a lot about going to Chicago to live. It is a wicked city and I wonder if I would be able to get along there. Pat Riley was found and he is*

*in jail here and I'm not sorry either. Perhaps I shouldn't tell you."*

Jean arrived at Alderson displaced, her moods swinging from the hormonal imbalances of the lost pregnancy. She found comfort in letters home, particularly to her mother.

*"There are some pretty decent girls here, and then there are the others of course."* Jean fit herself into this "decent" contingent of the prison population. It was an important step toward reclaiming her self-respect.

*"The majority are in for narcotics. There's a girl from St. Paul here Bess Green, I don't think you know her. She is very nice, we work together in the dining room."*

Beth, feeling pressured by the promises she'd made to Agent Clegg, reported Crompton's conversations to Assistant Superintendent Hironimas. She confirmed to her superior that when Jean saw Dillinger in Chicago, his face had been changed.

In her letters, Jean complained of the oppressive heat. In spite of the original intent of the Enabling Act, which suggested a geographic location in a moderate climate, the temperature was climbing to 115 degrees.

*"It has been so dreadfully hot here. It was 110 in the shade. The nights are fairly cool, though."*

Jean appeared to be finished with the life of crime's excesses. Unlike Opal Long and Pat Cherrington, whose correspondence was replete with the "boys" long after they were gone, Jean wanted a fresh start. She'd started typing classes, and was going to Catholic Mass. A local boy had started writing to her and expressed a desire to marry her.[3] To him, she wrote,

*"You should see me in my gingham dress and white stockings and black shoes, and my nose all shiny and I weigh 103 so you can see there isn't any danger of my getting fat."*

*"Something is coming off soon."*

*—Patricia Cherrington,*
*before the robbery of the*
*Merchants National Bank*
*at South Bend, Indiana, May, 1934*

# 22

# Coffee Klatsch Bravado

June 2, 1934, marked the day that Pat Cherrington and Opal Long lost their freedom. As they were herded into the Sheffield Avenue police station, Louis Piquett and Arthur O'Leary were making a deal on the other side of town. That night, a thirty-four-year-old Chicago woman got into a spat with her live-in lover over their domestic situation. James "Jimmy" Probasco, her boyfriend, was turning their place into a boarding house.

"There'll be a little bit of money in it," he explained.

On May 28, the woman had returned from work to a spectacle: one man lying shirtless on a bed and another standing over him. A panicked Probasco refrained himself from putting his hand over her mouth.

"I'll buy you a new outfit," he pleaded. "Just keep your mouth shut."

She'd just witnessed the home-grown plastic surgery performed on Dillinger's face by Wilhelm Loeser, a chemist whom everyone called "the old man." With his young, dissipated assistant, Harold Bernard "Cass" Cassidy, Loeser had smoothed over Dillinger's chin cleft, erased the seams in his cheeks, and removed a mole on his forehead. The operation was the fruition of plans first introduced by Piquett to Loeser on the first of May.

James "Jimmy" Probasco, age sixty-seven, a friend of the restaurant owner James Murray, was making good on his promise to harbor Dillinger for $40 per day. The friendship of Probasco and Louis Piquett had spanned thirty-five years, to the time when Probasco, an ex-pugilist and athlete trainer, had been arrested on bootlegging charges.

The next day in the kitchen, Dillinger complained constantly of the pain; he'd swallowed his tongue while under ether as his doctors frantically pulled it back with forceps. As his disgruntled hostess listened in the glare of the kitchen light, Dillinger spoke of Homer Van Meter.

"Now he'll have to go through what I've been through," he said protectively. Homer Van Meter was the next one to submit to the plastic surgery. He underwent two separate procedures. One removed the bump on his nose and changed the shape of his lips; the other attempted to eradicate his fingerprints. His postoperative behavior was hysterical.

"He just can't take it," Dillinger said to the others.

The atmosphere didn't lighten with the appearance of Gillis. He falsely claimed that he'd gone to "kill that filling station attendant who'd put Tommy Carroll on the spot." On the subject of Waterloo, everyone concurred that "Carroll should have hidden his license plates before pulling into an unknown service station."

Van Meter, Gillis, Dillinger, and Piquett sat around the kitchen table, the dirty dishes spilling out of the sink behind them. Their cigarettes left ashes dropping onto the oilcloth around the grimy cups and saucers, as a small kitchen radio blared news of the manhunt. The yellow lamp, hanging from a cord above the table, illuminated their thoughts on the amazing events of the past weeks. Little Bohemia had "cost them plenty." Baby Face bragged about the shots he managed to "get off," in his words. Dillinger said he wanted to "get" Emil Wanatka. He knew Wanatka was behind the actions of his wife, who had written the letter to the federal agents. He didn't blame Nan Wanatka, just Emil. As Louis Piquett listened to the gang converse, he decided he liked Van Meter the most. He was the "nicest" of the gang, in Piquett's estimation.

The next day Louis Piquett met O'Leary, Loeser, and Cassidy at 536 Wrightwood Avenue. He split the money between himself and his assistant, O'Leary, while a third portion was divided between Cassidy, Loeser, and Probasco. In one act the lawyer dug his own professional grave. A federal indictment, trial, conviction, and disbarment for harboring Homer Van Meter would soon follow.

While relishing the company in Probasco's kitchen, Gillis' presence in Chicago was business, not pleasure. Arriving in Chicago at the same time were John Paul Chase and Fatso Negri. The three began having meetings behind a schoolhouse in Chicago, and would be joined there by Van Meter and Dillinger.

Dillinger soon recuperated enough to leave Probasco's house at 2509 North Crawford. Ready, willing, and able to work, he resumed his chosen profession.[1]

On June 28, Van Meter took a ride to the Merchants National Bank to practice his vocation. As the advance man, he changed a $20 bill on the commercial strip at Michigan and Wayne, in the town of South Bend, Indiana. Gillis had gone to the neighboring drug store two days before that, to purchase gauze bandages. With their nerve enlarged like a prostrate gland, they planned their attack.

The Dillinger gang would begin their research two or three days before a bank robbery. They would ride the country highways and dirt roads, called the cat roads, and set their speedometer at zero. One man would drive the car and another would sit in the front seat and call off each tenth of a mile. All signs would be noted, as well as identification marks in the road. Every bump and all curves would be noted by a man sitting in the back seat of the car, who would jot down all pertinent information. This "log of a road" would be used as a getaway after the robbery.

The retreat was rehearsed, also. The men would plan to travel approximately 75 to 100 miles away from the scene of the proposed bank robbery, and after each robbery they would remain at the hide-out for two or three days. They then would take an 800 or 1,000 mile trip for the purpose of getting just as far away as they believed necessary from the scene of the robbery.

For South Bend, Dillinger collected himself and Van Meter, while Gillis brought in Jack Perkins, part of the clique around Art "Fish" Johnson. Larry Streng had told Pat Cherrington that Perkins was involved. Pat knew that "something is coming off soon." She was arrested with the knowledge, and kept it to herself.[2]

On the morning of June 30, Dillinger, with Homer Van Meter, Gillis, Jack Perkins, and an unidentified 200-pound man, walked into the Merchants National Bank at South Bend, Indiana, at 11:30. They'd dressed in populist garb, their denim overalls bulky over their bullet-proof vests. A straw hat topped Dillinger's obscenely bulging figure. He wore octagon-shaped sunglasses and carried a machine gun with drum. Gillis, also, wore darkened glasses. Van Meter chose to face the day without the benefit of this disguise. They carried rugs in an effort to resemble workers in dry goods. Simultaneously, the post office had just deposited $9,000 with a teller. Van Meter, whose real work had been to case the place for days before, now guarded the front with a .351 rifle. Gillis watched the car.

William Weaver was transacting business when Dillinger, standing in the center front of the bank lobby, pulled the rug away to reveal a machine gun.

"This is a stick-up," he screamed. Ordering everyone to hit the floor, he shot at the ceiling. The fat man and Jack Perkins flanked him, screaming in unison. Armed with a .15-caliber automatic revolver, the fat man went behind the second, third, and fourth tellers' cages and took the money. Bypassing the vault, they grabbed stupidly, perhaps hampered by the sunglasses, and took only what they could readily see. They managed to miss $35,000 that was in front of them. The robbery took five minutes.

Homer Van Meter stood in front of Kisley's Shoe Store with machine gun and black square magazine drum attached. He ordered a passer-by, Mr. Arthur Stilson, to stand next to him. Mr. Stilson had never seen a machine gun, and he obeyed, spellbound. Together they walked up and down the street. The three looters came out of the building with three of the employees and headed to their double-parked Hudson. They were fired upon by P.O. Hanson and Herb Zell, who was shot by Homer Van Meter. Delos Coen, a cashier, was one of the hostages.

"I asked the man in the lobby where I should go, and he answered that I should go with him," he later testified. "I walked out of the bank in front of the man who was standing in the lobby, when we turned south on Michigan Street with my hands in the air. Someone from the rear shot me through the leg; I proceeded by limping. When they got into their double-parked car at the northeast corner of Wayne and Michigan, I flopped to the ground." Three more people were shot at this point—two in the legs, another through the eye.

On the street the robbers met Van Meter. They fired from both the machine gun and a .351 rifle, raking the street with fifty shots. There were hundreds of people, who seemed to converge all at once on the corner of Wayne and Michigan. Detective Edward McCormick and Plain Clothes Detective Harry Henderson of the South Bend police fired shots into the getaway car. McCormick fired two shots at the head of the Hudson driver, Homer Van Meter, wounding him. He also hit Perry Stahly, director of the bank and one of the hostages. Many witnesses claimed it was "impossible to distinguish the bankers from the bandits."

A story of the battle was told by Mr. and Mrs. Kenneth F. Beers of Cassopolis, Michigan, who escaped without a scratch, although they came closer to death than any of the hundreds who saw the holdup when bullets smashed through the windshield of their car, missing their heads by inches and spraying them with flying glass. A killer with a submachine gun stood twenty-five feet away firing point blank at them. He had just shot down a policeman.

"We had just driven up to the intersection of Wayne and Michigan," Beers said. "We were on the right hand side of the street headed south and we had to wait for the traffic signal." When we heard the machine gun, "I knew what that sound was. It meant death for someone."

Gillis had just walked into Kisley's shoe store and ordered everyone to stand outside the store as shields. He was identified through his oddly high-pitched voice by two witnesses, Mrs. William Weaver and Mr. L.J. Smith.

"People were yelling and screaming all around us. Over on the southeast corner of the intersection stood a traffic policeman. He had his gun out and was shooting at the bandit. The killer with the machine gun turned his gun on the officer." Standing south of the bank, near the Brumode Hosiery shop, one of the robbers, either Van Meter or Gillis, fired at Police Officer Howard Wagner. The twenty-nine-year-old patrolman fell in front of the plate glass of the People's Store, mortally wounded. One bullet had hit his right chest, hitting the liver, and another passed through his right arm. He died in the hospital, a few minutes after being shot, at 11:30 that same morning, of a hemorrhage.

The killer displayed a maneuver popular with Gillis but never before demonstrated by Van Meter. Gillis followed his recurring pattern of murder by spraying the intersection with bullets. Mr. Beer would recount his own narrow escape.

"I think that bandit deliberately tried to kill us because we saw him shoot the policeman." Five eyewitnesses identified the killer as being Gillis, based on stature and the high-pitched quality of his voice. Admittedly, eyewitness identification in the South Bend affair is sketchy and unreliable. The identification of Wagner's killer remained inconclusive.

A gas fire had erupted at the northeast corner of the intersection. It seemed as though hell were advancing, with the inferno, the frantic crowd, and the dead man. Executed with the savage quality of a desperado's last stand, the reign of terror grossed only $28,323.29.

Among the witnesses would be Detective Harry Henderson of the South Bend Police Department and Lieutenant Hudson of the Indiana State Police, who identified Ted Bentz as being at the robbery. At 218 pounds, with a build described in his mug shots as "heavy," Bentz became a prime contender for the unidentified "fat man" position.[3]

The investigators trying to unravel the mysteries surrounding South Bend would depend upon women for their answers. They went first to Pat Cherrington. She placated them by explaining the nuances of the bank robbery plan—the preliminary visits to the neighborhood, the plotting of escape routes—but she remained silent on the connection to Jack Perkins.

Federal agents next visited another woman who was close to the Holden-Keating and Barker-Karpis-Nash groups that were falling like parachutes. Kathryn Kelly had lived at the Milan Penitentiary since her October 12, 1933, commitment for life in the Urshell kidnapping. At her trial she'd presented a theatrical pose beneath a smart hat and tidy bobbed hair. On November 14 she'd entered Milan under the same "incorrigible" clause that had destined Evelyn Frechette and Pat Cherrington to the steel-barred wing of the men's prison.

She'd resurfaced only once since 1933, spliced into a documentary film that was part of the morality genre coming into vogue. A voice-over had called her "the first woman to be sentenced to life imprisonment under the new Federal Kidnapping Law." She was briefly shown sitting

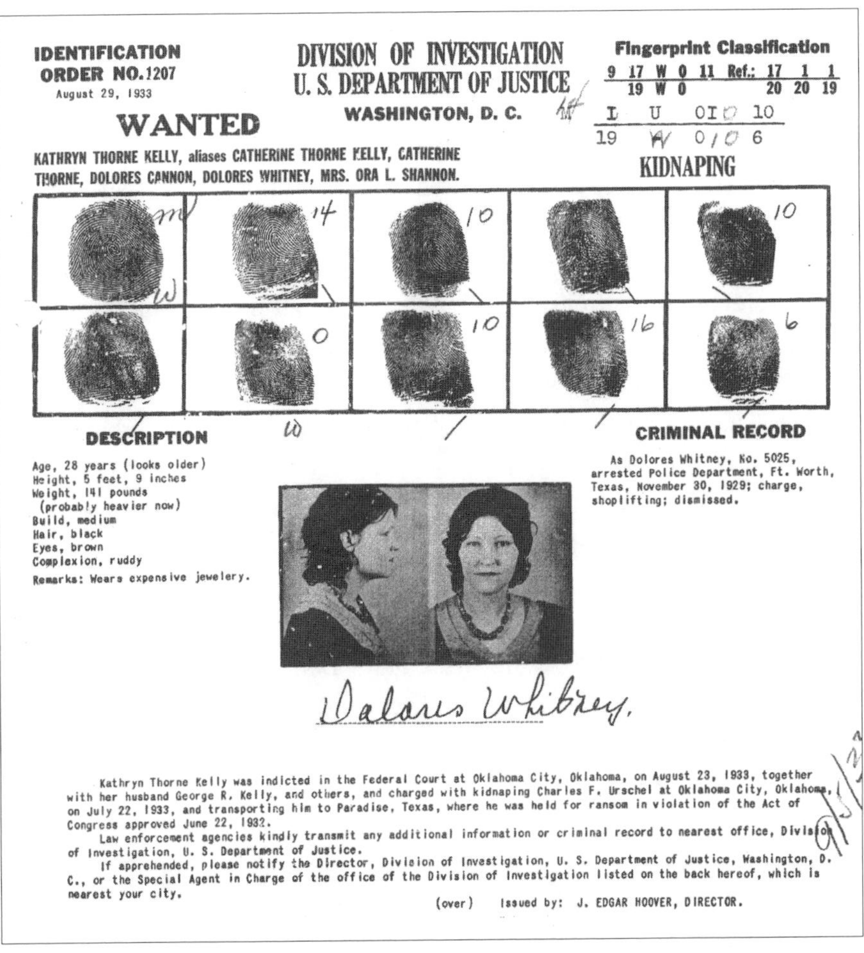

IDENTIFICATION ORDER NO. 1207
August 29, 1933

WANTED

DIVISION OF INVESTIGATION
U. S. DEPARTMENT OF JUSTICE
WASHINGTON, D. C.

Fingerprint Classification
9 17 W 0 11 Ref.: 17 1 1
19 W 0 20 20 19

KIDNAPING

KATHRYN THORNE KELLY, aliases CATHERINE THORNE KELLY, CATHERINE THORNE, DOLORES CANNON, DOLORES WHITNEY, MRS. ORA L. SHANNON.

DESCRIPTION

Age, 28 years (looks older)
Height, 5 feet, 9 inches
Weight, 141 pounds
(probably heavier now)
Build, medium
Hair, black
Eyes, brown
Complexion, ruddy
Remarks: Wears expensive jewelery.

CRIMINAL RECORD

As Dolores Whitney, No. 5025, arrested Police Department, Ft. Worth, Texas, November 30, 1929; charge, shoplifting; dismissed.

Dolores Whitney.

Kathryn Thorne Kelly was indicted in the Federal Court at Oklahoma City, Oklahoma, on August 23, 1933, together with her husband George R. Kelly, and others, and charged with kidnaping Charles F. Urschel at Oklahoma City, Oklahoma, on July 22, 1933, and transporting him to Paradise, Texas, where he was held for ransom in violation of the Act of Congress approved June 22, 1932.

Law enforcement agencies kindly transmit any additional information or criminal record to nearest office, Division of Investigation, U. S. Department of Justice.

If apprehended, please notify the Director, Division of Investigation, U. S. Department of Justice, Washington, D. C., or the Special Agent in Charge of the office of the Division of Investigation listed on the back hereof, which is nearest your city.

(over) Issued by: J. EDGAR HOOVER, DIRECTOR.

Agents visited Kathryn Kelly in her jail cell after South Bend, hoping she'd name the unidentified bank robber. (FBI)

forlornly at a sewing machine. Her name was not mentioned. While another lifer took a moment to express her remorse, Kathryn remained silent.

She'd had no visitors since her revised image graced the documentary, so it came as a surprise when she was greeted by government agents. They wanted her to rake her memory and tell them: Who was the anonymous fat man?

Like an aging Norma Desmond, with no connection to contemporary life, she implicated people from the old Holden Keating reign who were either dead, imprisoned, or about to be put away for life. She revealed only that Boss McLaughlin, implicated in Bremer, hung out at the Tivilei Grill. Her only clue as to the fat man was obscure: a bank man named "Big Homer." He had taken part in robberies with Machine Gun Kelly's crowd, Albert Bates and Harvey Bailey, always fighting to be the one to go behind the counter and take the money from the teller's cage. At the time of the interview, Leslie "Big Homer" was already imprisoned for his part in the Racine holdup with the Dillinger gang. Kathryn most likely referred to "Big Homer" Wilson, who robbed banks with the Holden-Keating/Barker-Karpis crowd. Wilson, according to researcher Rick Mattix, "was about six feet tall and weighed over 200 pounds. He died in Chicago, under the alias of John Wilson, of natural causes, on November 29, 1934."[4]

Helen Gillis would also be interrogated on the unanswered questions of South Bend. Upon her capture later that year in November, she would be asked to confirm the assertion that Pretty Boy Floyd and Adam Richetti, notorious for having participated in the Kansas City Massacre, had joined her husband at the Merchants Bank. This information was part of the intelligence garnered from the confessions of Raymond "Fatso" Negri. Gillis' old friend told the Justice Department late in 1934 that Pretty Boy and Richetti may have been involved with the Dillinger gang at the time of the robbery. In her conversations with federal agents after Gillis 's death, Helen Gillis repeatedly denied that her husband had ever known Pretty Boy Floyd. In spite of her rebuttal, the Pretty Boy Floyd connection became entrenched in lore.[5]

Homer Van Meter was tentatively identified. The getaway car bore the license plates that were used in a Fostorio, Ohio, bank robbery the prior May, when Chief of Police Frank Culp was killed. Van Meter, a suspect, was linked. Then, a physician named Edward Laird came forward and advised that a wounded man, with a bullet wound to his head, had demanded medical treatment—and cocaine—on July 1. He confirmed Van Meter's identity after seeing his old mug shot from Michigan City. Five witnesses eventually identified Gillis as the man who had shot Police Officer Howard Wagner from the street corner. Just as many identified Homer Van Meter as the killer.

A sprinkling of witnesses claimed that the deceased John Hamilton was there. Theodore "Ted" Bentz, who had been hanging around Dillinger right after John Hamilton's death, was also believed to be in on it. Bentz, who would always maintain that Hamilton's body had been thrown into a swamp outside of Minneapolis, incriminated himself by telling the story of Hamilton's death to police during one incarceration. Months later, he would be indicted for complicity in the South Bend affair, only to be cleared.

Other eyewitnesses, including bank director Perry Stahly, maintained that the machine gunner was Pretty Boy Floyd. Jack Perkins, a gambler who hung around the poolroom at 3939 Sheridan Road with Art "Fish" Johnson, would be implicated later by "Fatso" Negri. The last suspect to remain alive, Perkins would "take the rap" for the curbside death of Police Officer Wagner. He would stand trial for the murder one year later, and would be acquitted. Eventually, the government admitted defeat in its attempts to identify the other two bank robbers at South Bend. Prosecutors were reduced to charging, within their indictments, those old stand-ins, John Doe and Richard Roe.[6]

For weeks after South Bend, Van Meter wore adhesive tape on his head, with three shaved patches around his bullet wound. Looking like a raw, plucked chicken, Van Meter hounded Dillinger to leave "that woman he was seeing north by Diversey." In the role of soothsayer, he bode ominously.

"Be careful," he told his old friend. "You don't know anything about her."

*"The woman informant is not sure whether they are going to the Marbro or the Biograph Theater."*

*—FBI Agent Samual Cowley in a memo to J.Edgar Hoover, July 21, 1934*

# Silver Screen

On July 13, 1934, Eddie Green's mother visited the outlaw's grave in St. Peter's Cemetery. There she planted a rose bush. It had been Bess' gift to her, offered in love before Eddie's death had changed everything. Mrs. Green returned to her St. Paul home and sat down at a wobbly desk that she rarely used. The drawers resisted as she pulled them open, searching for paper. Her scented stationery, bought some years before, had yellowed around the edges. Mrs. Green penned her thoughts to the grieving Beth, addressing the envelope to the Women's Industrial Reformatory at Alderson, West Virginia.

> *". . . Oh Beth it is a cruel world and trubbel* [sic] *comes when we least expect it and we never know how mutch* [sic] *we can stand till we have to part with one we dearley* [sic] *love . . . truble does not kill us we just have to suffer in this world I hope for better in the next."*

Evelyn Frechette, incarcerated at Milan, received the parcels that slipped past the censorship committee. Mary Kinder, who'd promised Dillinger she'd check on his girlfriend's situation, traveled to Milan. There she attempted to cheer up her old friend and confederate. Evelyn had not heard from Louis Piquett on the forthcoming appeal. She knew he would stop the appellate process if Dillinger's payments became too erratic. Mary held back on talking about "Johnnie's new girlfriend." Dillinger became involved with Rita Hamilton Keele on the rebound. He was still obsessed with the idea of seeing Evelyn one last time. In the unemotional language of men, he conveyed his anguish to Louis Piquett. Evelyn had been a "good kid," he'd said. "He'd never be happy 'til he saw her again," he repeated endlessly. His attorney, a shrewd observer, had felt John's desolation beneath the brevity.[1]

Known to everyone as "Polly," Rita Hamilton Keele bore an amazing resemblance to Evelyn, with dark wavy hair and prominent cheekbones. Polly's family was English Canadian. After Polly, given name Edythe, was born in Canada in 1909, the family migrated to the U.S. Her natural father died, leaving her mother, Edith, to raise young Edythe, and her brothers, Ercyle and Robert, in Fargo, North Dakota. Polly's concerned expression could open into a bright smile. She had a steady job, working as a waitress at the S & S Café on Wilson Avenue. In her earliest days in Fargo, North Dakota, she'd worked as a dancer in a road show. She left her mother and brother in Fargo and moved to Gary, where she found temporary security in marriage. She had been married to a Gary, Indiana, policeman named Roy Keele on October 17, 1929. They separated on June 1, 1933. He filed for divorce on February 13, 1934, charging that she "failed to take care of her home as a person in her position would." They had no children during their marriage, and he got his divorce on April 30, provided he was willing to pay the costs.

She remained in Gary, choosing not to return to Fargo. She made her living after that helping to run the Kostur Hotel, a notorious establishment that operated in Gary. With ties to East Chicago, Indiana, she was not entirely unknown to Dillinger, as Van Meter had thought. Dillinger had gone to Gary since his parole, when he'd boarded with Sam Goldstine in an apartment in the Beverly Hotel.

On the Fourth of July, James Probasco, who had hosted Dillinger's plastic surgery and postoperative period, confronted Piquett while the

Polly Hamilton (Author's Collection)

two were dining at Jimmy Murray's place. He was not happy with the situation of Dillinger and Homer Van Meter coming and going "in the open." Could Piquett possibly talk them into leaving his house?

Dillinger was being pushed out of Probasco's lair and desperately needed a place to go.[2]

Anna Sage, paid by Piquett through the intersession of Sergeant Martin Zarkovich, had known Polly Hamilton in Gary. It is conceivable that Dillinger met Polly in Gary, when he'd visited the joints in and around Hammond in the days after his parole. Sage now had an apartment in the fashionable, exciting neighborhood in Chicago's near North section. The house was just down the block from the place kept by Evelyn's sister, Francis "Patsy" Frechette. Dillinger's entry into Sage's apartment at 2420 Halsted Street bore a strange parallel to another period of his life. The house where Evelyn Frechette stayed while he had been held in Crown Point County Jail was one block away from Mrs. Sage's apartment.

While settling into his new hideout, Dillinger pressed Polly's photo into his watch. There were differences, he decided, gazing at the miniature. Evelyn's face never opened, as Polly's did, into that wide, inviting smile. The cadence washed over him again—she'd been a good kid; he'd never be happy 'til he saw her again. Like a foster child, he placed his trust in the keeper of the keys to 2420 North Halsted.

Mrs. Sage had a history of arrests for both prostitution and that worn-out euphemism, "keeper of a disorderly house." She was a forty-three-year-old Romanian national with a rotund face and huge eyes that housed a quiet fury. In June of 1933, the Department of Immigration and Naturalization had made a decision to deport her back to her country. To make it stick they took her passport.

Born Ana Cumpanas on November 30, 1892, in a small Banat province, within the village of Costanza, Roumania, she joined the huddled masses in 1908, landing in Baltimore on the "Breslau." She returned to Europe, during which time she married Mike Chiolek on January 15, 1909 in Comlosul, Banatean, Romania. Back in the United States, she separated from him on December 10, 1918, when she charged him with beating her and failing to provide support to her and their baby, Steve. In the Gary courtroom where she filed an Affidavit of Non-Residence, never having adopted American citizenship, she signed her name with an "X."

While her divorce pleading said she'd "become ill and had been unable to work," she embarked upon a lengthy criminal career as a prostitute. At the same time, she developed a strong friendship with Sergeant Martin Zarkovich, of the East Chicago, Indiana, Police Department. Professionally, this relationship helped her to avoid prison in spite of constant arrests.

Sergeant Zarkovich first noticed Anna while she'd worked in a bar run by Big Bill Subotich, on Guthrie Street in East Chicago. After Subotich died, Mrs. Sage took over the operation of the bar, moving to Gary, where she worked in the Kostur Hotel on 1349 Washington Street. The police called the Kostur Hotel the "Bucket of Blood," due to the high incidence of gunfire and knife fights breaking out among the tough population of European immigrants.

On March 20, 1920, Zarkovich's wife, Elizabeth, the mother of his five-week-old daughter, filed a divorce petition against him, charging him with neglect, chronic physical and financial abuse, beatings, and unprovoked verbal assaults. At the time, he worked as a chauffeur on the patrol wagon at the Indiana Harbor Station, with a monthly salary of $150. Within this pleading she made an allegation that "on the 16th day of March, 1920, at Indiana Harbor, Indiana, the defendant and at various other times committed adultery with one whose name the plaintiff does not care to divulge at this time."

At the same time, Anna Sage had adopted the persona of "Katie Brown"—all-American, in spite of her heavy Eastern European accent and carriage of a nineteenth-century dowager, at 5 feet 7 inches and 165 pounds. In her choice of an alias, she alluded to another trans-Atlantic figure, Molly Brown, Titanic survivor and oil millionairess.

This unsinkable Katie Brown was arrested in Gary on Lincoln's Birthday in 1923. The charge: prostitution. While the case was dismissed, she was rearrested as Katie Brown on May 25, 1924, for keeping a "house of ill-fame." She was found not guilty. By now she had earned the notorious title of "Katie from the Kostur Hotel," the wide-open disorderly house located at 1349 Washington Street. She was again arrested, as Anna Sage, on February 8, 1930, for overseeing another house of prostitution. Found guilty this time, she was sentenced to ninety days in the Women's State Prison and fined $25 and costs. On March 19, 1930, she pleaded "nolo contendere" before a federal judge, T.W. Slick, at Hammond, Indiana, and was sentenced to pay a fine of $100. The prior prison sentence was suspended pending good behavior. Amazingly, she was immediately rearrested, on September 20, 1930, found guilty, and sentenced to sixty days in the state prison with a $60 fine. Appealed to Lake County Criminal Court, it was dismissed by the prosecuting attorney. She was arrested again on October 25, found guilty, and finally served time—thirty days in the Lake County Jail, which was, coincidentally, the scene of the "Wooden Gun" escape. There were more arrests, in November and then again in December. She was finally convicted in February 1931. On December 15, 1932, she was pardoned by then Governor Harry G. Leslie of the two prior convictions in Lake County, dating back to November and April 1931.

Mrs. Sage had friends in high and powerful places in the state of

Anna Sage was dubbed "the Girl In Red" as the FBI secretly removed her from Chicago. (FBI)

Indiana. While Lake County Prosecutor Robert Estill, who had lost his reelection after the Crown Point "Wooden Gun" escape fiasco, denied ever having interceded on Mrs. Sage's behalf, it was common knowledge that Martin Zarkovich was on close terms with the Crown Point prosecutor and also Judge Murray in the years that Anna Sage swung through the revolving door. Sergeant Zarkovich operated within a maze of graft, originating with East Chicago "Big House" proprietor Sonny Sheetz.

Policemen Martin O'Brien and Lloyd Mulvihill, an expert detective team of the East Chicago department, knew who collected graft, knew the gangs, and knew their relationships in and around East Chicago. They were slain on May 24 under circumstances never explained. They were murdered near midnight, in their police car on the old Gary Macadam Road in the southeast and swampy section of East Chicago. The report that the Dillinger gang was responsible would later be circulated by Matt Leach, among other officials. The detectives had left the police station only fifteen minutes prior to the mysterious killing. They were riddled with machine-gun bullets. Matt Leach charged that they knew too much.

Martin Zarkovich had acted rashly after Dillinger's Crown Point escape, first appearing on the scene on March 18. Rumors said he was involved in the plot to deliver Dillinger from jail, with a bribe paid by Louis Piquett in a Main Street saloon near the courthouse. Lloyd Mulvihill and Martin O'Brien, the doomed detective team, were said to have unwittingly interrupted a meeting of the conspirators. After the Crown Point escape, many of Zarkovich's former associates kept a healthy distance from the cop who looked dirty. In his personal life, Zarkovich was extravagant, living well beyond his means as a policeman. Nicknamed the "police sheik" because of his fancy clothes and jewelry, he nominally supported his daughter, who was now fourteen years old. She received $30 per month for her support while her mother, Elizabeth, worked as a domestic. His old flame, Katie Brown, had separated from Alex Sage, whom she'd married on May 16, 1928. She kept the surname of Sage, using an Americanized version of her provincial name of Ana. The newest variation of this chameleon, Anna Sage, was an evolved, sophisticated woman who was desperate to hold onto her police sheik. When the U.S. Immigration authorities issued a warrant for her deportation to Romania on June 12, 1933, she bought time in the United States with a writ of habeas corpus, which legal experts felt could never be sustained in her case.[3]

When Dillinger decided to trust her, it was with a deep level of fatalism. Most likely the largest component in his decision to accept her protection was desperation. Her fight with the immigration authorities was not a secret. It just never occurred to Dillinger that his scalp would become the main point of her negotiation.

On July 6, Polly told her brother, Robert, that she "had a new boyfriend who was taking her to night clubs and dances." Dillinger had left the cloistered world of Probasco's house, going around Chicago with the throngs of summer people.

He and his "Countess," as he called Polly, threw a birthday bash for themselves.

"The two-day party we had celebrating his birthday on the 22nd of June and mine on the 23rd, was just about the most important thing that ever happened to me," she said in an interview with the *Chicago Herald & Examiner*.

"He sent me two dozen roses, and bought me the amethyst ring, and we spent the evenings at the French Casino. He must have been in love with me. Lots of times he talked about a home, and kids of his own. He used to say he was going to retire from his Board of Trade job and buy a chicken farm, but I never took him very seriously on that . . . his favorite songs were "All I Do Is Dream of You" and "For All We Know."

Dillinger and Polly went out with Mrs. Sage's son, the twenty-three-year-old Steve Chiolak, who noticed the facial scarring but refrained from comment.

"You don't ask a man about his face," he later said in a newspaper interview.

This vapid, scarred man, an obvious fugitive living as "Jimmy Lawrence," took the friends out on his evenings off, ostensibly from a clerking job with the Chicago Board of Trade. As a group they had fun, often going to the movies. They went to see *Viva Villa* and W.C. Fields comedy shorts. The heat wave that summer drove people into the theaters, to sprawl near the huge blocks of ice stationed before whirring electric fans. Dillinger dressed in the sports style popular in the summer of 1934, preferring the "Air Cooled" Dobbs Straw that retailed for $4. In the world before air conditioning, men dressed in fabrics like seersucker and straw, materials that circulated air around the head and body. Dillinger sported hot-weather, linen suits that sold for $18. It was an era when no occasion, no matter how casual, justified sloppy attire. In this atmosphere, fun was a high priority and all enjoyed the climax of mirth-making. Steve Chiolak liked his mother's friend, because, in his words, "he always paid the bill."

"He didn't act tough and he didn't talk tough," Chiolak later told reporters.

Polly Hamilton's newspaper recollections hint that Dillinger was finding a domestic anchor that he'd never before known.

"All he asked was a home cooked dinner. Baking powder biscuits and chicken gravy, just like they have on the farm, were what he liked best. Tomatoes, green onions, and radishes, he had to have, too. When it was hot weather, he always brought ice cream, for he liked it so. Sometimes he'd bring half a dozen boxes of strawberries. He liked steak for meat, but when he was feeling particularly happy, nothing but frog legs from Ireland's would do."

Yet, Dillinger had ways of reverting back to his true character.

"We went to Riverview Park often. He couldn't get enough of the rides . . . Now that I know he was John Dillinger, I can understand why he always liked the shooting galleries so. He was a crack shot. The customers would always line up to watch him knock over the targets."

On July 21, Anna Sage reverted to her own true character. Leaving the frogs legs and strawberries to brew in her caldron, she accompanied Zarkovich on a date with Sam Cowley. The cop and the madam were an old item. Nobody questioned the alliance when, in the company of East Chicago Police Captain Timothy O'Neill, they met Cowley in a parked automobile. During the meeting, Zarkovich arranged Dillinger's execution. The bureau promised amnesty for East Chicago in exchange for Dillinger's betrayal. Zarkovich benefited from the deal, in that Dillinger would die silent. In death he couldn't reveal the instances of graft that had paved the way for him since his parole in May of 1933. Mrs. Sage left the meeting relieved, thinking she'd also receive amnesty in her deportation hearing. Everyone walked away from the deal feeling like they'd triumphed.

True to his professionalism, Cowley went back to the field office and typed out the first in a series of telegrams to the director in Washington.

"The woman informant," he wrote that Saturday afternoon, "is not sure whether they are going to the Marbro or the Biograph Theater."

The next day was Sunday. At 7:30 in the evening, Melvin Purvis and Agent Brown scrambled to the Biograph Theatre at 2433 Lincoln

Avenue, while Sergeant Zarkovich and Agent Winstead went to the Marbro. The rest of the twenty-five agents on standby remained in the Chicago office awaiting telephone advice concerning which theater Dillinger would actually attend. At 8:50 p.m. Dillinger and the two women were observed entering the Biograph, and this information was telephoned to the Chicago office. Two special agents, Clarence Hurt and Ed Hollis, were assigned to grab Dillinger as he left. They were soon joined by Agent Winstead.

Charles Winstead had taken the oath on July 27, 1926. A veteran of World War I, the experience would greatly color his politics and his outlook; he was a strong believer in democracy. He'd been assigned to an East Texas field office when the call came from Washington, DC, to join the Dillinger Squad.

Flanking him on Lincoln Avenue were East Chicago Police Officers Arthur Sopsic and Stretch Conroy. Others were placed on the north and south sides and across the street. Some sat in a car parked in front of the theater, while others crowded into the alley directly north. Purvis stood under the marquee. Cowley remained in a roving position. So many strange men crawled around the place that the manager thought they were going to be robbed.

John Dillinger, Polly Hamilton, and Anna Sage were late for the movie. The theater was filled, which forced Dillinger to place himself and Polly in the third row. These were not the most comfortable seats from which to watch *Manhattan Melodrama*. Anna Sage, dressed in an orange skirt, had to separate from the two and sat by herself in the back. A prophetic theme arose within the film: betrayal.

Gangster Blackie Gallagher, played by Clark Gable, confronts his best friend from boyhood, the district attorney, played by William Powell. The two bonded as orphans, having lost their parents in the General Slocum disaster in New York's East River. Now grown men, they compete for the love of Myrna Loy.

In these characters, Anna Sage had an opportunity to view a role she'd never played herself. Myrna Loy has left the racketeer for the goodly virtues of the district attorney. She's rejected crime and avarice for the simple pleasures of the policemen's ball. Blackie Gallagher also exudes a proletarian glamour. He's a bad guy with integrity. His character holds a mirror image to the persona that John Dillinger unwittingly

Polly Hamilton, who watched *Manhattan Melodrama* from the third row of the Biograph Theater with Dillinger. (Author's Collection)

created—a mystique held up for public consumption.

Clark Gable's Blackie Gallagher filled Dillinger's last hours.

The film comes to a spiritual and moral crescendo. A clock appears as a floating oracle.

"Young Man, Observe the Time and Turn from Evil," states the legend. Clark Gable walks to the electric chair with a stoic look of impatience. His Gablesque expression mirrors his resolve. Blackie Gallagher is doing the right thing.

At 10:20 p.m., Dillinger emerged from the Biograph, walking south on Lincoln Avenue. Special Agent in Charge Melvin Purvis, stationed beneath the marquee, struck a match and lifted it up to his cigar. Dillinger caught the gesture, became apprehensive, and started to run. Some say he grabbed for his gun. Agent Winstead fired one shot, then two more, while backed by the fire of Agent Clarence Hurt.

Dillinger fell into an alley with two wounds to his chest, one of which was just below his heart, and a third that entered the rear of the skull and emerged from the lower portion of the right eye above the cheek bone. Dillinger lay dying for twenty minutes. At 10:30 p.m., Agent Hurt, with Agents Hollis and Gillespie, watched as Zarkovich frisked the body. Those present issued a statement that no money was removed from his person. The story has since been reputed. He would have had several thousand dollars, yet, was said to have been carrying a mere $7. He'd been wearing a ruby ring when photographed in the morgue wagon; that also disappeared. One item that caught the attention of the agents was his watch. The agents scrambled for it. Its compartment with Polly's photo had to be hidden away from newspaper

The Biograph Theatre, shortly after Dillinger's death. (Author's Collection)

reporters, or the director was sure to reprimand them for the indiscretion. With fear of Hoover's ire motivating their actions, they felt it imperative to hide the timepiece from the newspaper reporters. The body was taken by patrol wagon to the Alexian Brothers Hospital. It was not removed from the vehicle, and was examined in the parking lot, where a staff physician declared Dillinger dead.

Two women had been hit during the taking of Dillinger. Theresa Paulus received a flesh wound in her hip, and Eta Natalsky was shot in the leg between her knee and thigh. J. Edgar Hoover later authorized the Division of Investigation to pay their medical bills. The women who'd accompanied Dillinger to the theater ran off in different directions. As Dillinger was cornered and shot, Polly Hamilton Keele was forgotten. She walked to the corner and turned, bound for the Fullerton Avenue train station. The block to the elevated train took on a dimension of terror. She walked quickly, afraid to attract attention. Jumping into the northbound train, she rode to Wilson Avenue and Broadway. She got off at the Wilson Avenue stop, the location of the shop where she worked as a waitress. The narrow steps made her dizzy. She stepped down slowly, gazing at the metal gratings with raw fear. They looked like prison bars spinning through a vortex.

Anna Sage, in contrast to her friend, had remained at the theater, welding herself to the instant crowd. She slithered to her apartment, which welcomed her like a bunker. In her small bedroom, she pulled off the orange skirt with haste and no vanity. In dark clothing, she returned to the Biograph, standing quietly with the sweaty throng of revelers. Later that night, she assembled Dillinger's cache of weapons. With a physically strong accomplice, she moved silently toward the public beaches of Lake Michigan, directly off the city streets. They dropped the bundle into a canal under the Diversey Bridge. Swimmers near the Lincoln Park Gun Club would discover a Thompson submachine gun, a .45-caliber automatic, one colt super .38 automatic with the identification numbers removed, five clips, one loaded machine gun drum, one canvas bag containing seventy-five rounds of .45 automatic shells, and one bulletproof vest.

Dillinger's body would be transferred to the McReady Funeral Home, as several South Bend witnesses arrived to perform post-mortem identifications.

Soon John Wilson and Hubert Dillinger arrived from Mooresville,

The bedroom of Anna Sage. (Author's Collection)

bringing with them a temporary coffin. The black wicker sepulcher would cart John home to Maywood for a funeral in the home of his sister, Audrey Hancock. The police officers who shielded them from the mobs treated them with respect and kindness.

Mr. Dillinger elicited pity from one police officer, who said, "We're not at all satisfied at the way things had been done."

With the memory of the death of Chicago City Police Sergeant Shanley on the minds of every patrolman, this ambiguous statement largely reflected the shame of the local police at their exclusion from the ambush. So infuriated was Captain Stege, still commander of the special "Dillinger Squad," that he hauled Jean Burke back into custody and picked up Frances "Patsy" Frechette. They were both released almost immediately. His luck changed with a tip from an unknown waitress named Maxine Dunn.

Twenty minutes after the shooting, Polly had entered the restaurant at 1209½ Wilson Avenue, where she'd worked as a waitress until her rich boyfriend had told her to quit. Two weeks before, she had given notice when Dillinger had demanded more attention from her. As she arrived, breathless, she forgot that her boyfriend's name was supposed to be Jimmy Lawrence. She confided that Dillinger was dead. Apparently, an alias becomes null and void with death.

Maxine Dunn had little patience when Polly called her after leaving the diner.

"Could you pick up my clothes at the Malden Plaza Hotel?"

"No," she replied curtly. Then she called Captain Duffy of the Sheffield Street Station.

Polly had left a trail of clues as to her destination. Her phone calls placed out of the restaurant at Wilson Avenue had given Chicago police a lead to Anna Sage's address—they traced the call made to "Lincoln 3436." Captain Duffy ran to the address at 4619 Malden Avenue, to be greeted by the hotel manager. All he cared to admit was that she'd left her apartment five weeks ago, coming back only to pay the rent on the empty place.

Stege's squad arrested Anna Sage and Steve Chiolak in front of their building on July 24. She was tagged as the "Girl in Red" the minute she entered the Sheffield police station. When she realized that her involvement with Zarkovich would be in the papers, she dissolved into anger. In her estimation, it was enough to "put her on the spot." When Sam Cowley arrived at the station house and demanded custody of his informer, Captain Stege initially refused.[4]

Hoover called from Washington and demanded that his newly promoted inspector smoke out the other woman and hold her incommunicado. Cowley pointed out that to do so would be violating the request of the informant and the "people at East Chicago." Not knowing what she really wanted, Anna Sage demanded to be allowed to leave town with Polly. Then she relented, realizing that her sudden disappearance would look suspicious. Money finally settled the matter. If they could be paid off, they'd be willing to leave town. Anna Sage had tried to protect Polly, although the sanctions couldn't be easily honored with the woman in hiding. She agreed to accompany Cowley and Zarkovich on a search.

While Cowley wrestled with the Chicago Police, Melvin Purvis wooed the East Chicago men. He took Captain Tim O'Neill, Sergeant Zarkovich, and the East Chicago Chief out to lunch on July 24. During entrees they agreed that too much news had leaked. Purvis made two promises simultaneously. He assured East Chicago that a blackout would be effected. After lunch, he returned to his office and answered a call to the director. Concerned because Purvis was going to be commended by the attorney general, Hoover issued Purvis a warning to be "brief and modest . . . and emphasize the cooperation of the East Chicago, Indiana Police," which would have a "good effect upon local law enforcement officers."

They decided to grant one half of the $10,000 reward to Anna Sage. Then an old boyfriend showed up with a claim that he'd been defrauded of $4,000 by Mrs. Sage, when she'd lived at 3504 Sheffield Avenue in April of 1933. Holger Burglum's accusations sent a red flag up for the government, afraid that the man would put a lien on the reward money. They considered making the check out to the woman under an assumed name.

A major distraction occurred when agents raided Probasco's Chicago hideout three days after Dillinger's death. During a break in the interrogations he fell from the rear window of the nineteenth floor of their office at 202 South Clark Street. Calling it a suicide, Deputy Coroner Schewel's inquest determined that Probasco's crushing injuries to his head and trunk "resulted when the deceased jumped out

# The Indiana

Generally fair tod

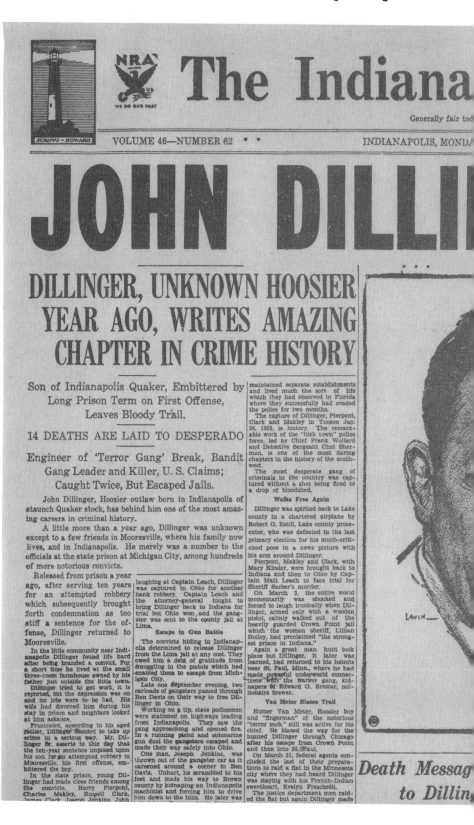

VOLUME 46—NUMBER 62 • • INDIANAPOLIS, MONDA

# JOHN DILLI

## DILLINGER, UNKNOWN HOOSIER YEAR AGO, WRITES AMAZING CHAPTER IN CRIME HISTORY

Son of Indianapolis Quaker, Embittered by Long Prison Term on First Offense, Leaves Bloody Trail.

### 14 DEATHS ARE LAID TO DESPERADO

Engineer of 'Terror Gang' Break, Bandit Gang Leader and Killer, U. S. Claims; Caught Twice, But Escaped Jails.

John Dillinger, Hoosier outlaw born in Indianapolis of staunch Quaker stock, has behind him one of the most amazing careers in criminal history.

A little more than a year ago, Dillinger was unknown except to a few friends in Mooresville, where his family now lives, and in Indianapolis. He merely was a number to the officials at the state prison at Michigan City, among hundreds of more notorious convicts.

Released from prison a year ago, after serving ten years for an attempted robbery which subsequently brought forth condemnation as too stiff a sentence for the offense, Dillinger returned to Mooresville.

In the little community near Indianapolis Dillinger found life hard after being branded a convict. For a short time he lived at the small three-room farmhouse owned by his father just outside the little town.

Dillinger tried to get work, it is reported, but the depression was on and no jobs were to be had. His wife had divorced him during his stay in prison and neighbors looked at him askance.

Frustrated, according to his aged father, Dillinger decided to take up crime in a serious way. Mr. Dillinger Sr. asserts to this day that the ten-year sentence imposed upon his son for an attempted robbery in Mooresville, his first offense, embittered the boy.

In the state prison, young Dillinger had made close friends among the convicts. Harry Pierpont, Charles Makley, Russell Clark, James Clark, Joseph Jenkins, John

laughing at Captain Leach, Dillinger was captured in Ohio for another bank robbery. Captain Leach and the attorney-general fought to bring Dillinger back to Indiana for trial but Ohio won, and the gangster was sent to the county jail at Lima.

**Escape in Gun Battle**

The convicts hiding in Indianapolis determined to release Dillinger from the Lima jail at any cost. They owed him a debt of gratitude from smuggling in the pistols which had enabled them to escape from Michigan City.

Late one September evening, two carloads of gangsters passed through Ben Davis on their way to free Dillinger in Ohio.

Working on a tip, state podicemen were stationed on highways leading from Indianapolis. They saw the gang approaching and opened fire. In a running pistol and submarine gun duel the gangsters escaped and made their way safely into Ohio.

One man, Joseph Jenkins, was thrown out of the gangster car as it careened around a corner in Ben Davis. Unhurt, he scrambled to his feet and made his way to Brown county by kidnaping an Indianapolis machinist and forcing him to drive him down to the hills. He later was

maintained separate establishments and lived much the sort of life which they had observed in Florida where they successfully had evaded the police for two months.

The capture of Dillinger, Pierpont, Clark and Makley in Tucson Jan. 26, 1933, is history. The remarkable work of the "hick town" police force, led by Chief Frank Wollard and Detective Sergeant Chet Sherman, is one of the most daring chapters in the history of the southwest.

The most desperate gang of criminals in the country was captured without a shot being fired or a drop of bloodshed.

**Walks Free Again**

Dillinger was spirited back to Lake county in a chartered airplane by Robert G. Estill, Lake county prosecutor, who was defeated in the last primary election for his much-criticised pose in a news picture with his arm around Dillinger.

Pierpont, Makley and Clark, with Mary Kinder, were brought back to Indiana and then to Ohio by Captain Matt Leach to face trial for Sheriff Sarber's murder.

On March 3, the entire world momentarily was shocked and forced to laugh ironically when Dillinger, armed only with a wooden pistol, calmly walked out of the heavily guarded Crown Point jail which the woman sheriff, Lillian Holley, had proclaimed "the strongest prison in Indiana."

Again a great man hunt took place but Dillinger, it later was learned, had returned to his haunts near St. Paul, Minn., where he had made powerful underworld connections with the Barker gang, kidnapers of Edward G. Bremer, millionaire brewer.

**Van Meter Blazes Trail**

Homer Van Meter, Hoosier boy and "fingerman" of the notorious "terror mob," still was active for his chief. He blazed the way for the hunted Dillinger through Chicago after his escape from Crown Point and then into St. Paul.

On March 31, federal agents concluded the last of their preparations to raid a flat in the Minnesota city where they had heard Dillinger was staying with his French-Indian sweetheart, Evelyn Freschetti.

The justice department men raided the flat but again Dillinger made

LAVIN

*Death Messag*

*to Dillin*

# polis Times EXTRA

PRICE TWO CENTS
Outside Marion County, 3 Cents

JULY 23, 1934

Entered as Second-Class Matter at Postoffice, Indianapolis, Ind.

# NGER SLAIN

John Dillinger

## EXTRA

## FEDERAL AGENTS KILL CRIMINAL IN CHICAGO THEATER

The body of John Dillinger was expected to be re-returned to Maywood late today. Funeral services will be held in Maywood, with burial in Crown Hill cemetary.

*By United Press*

CHICAGO, July 23.—John Dillinger, America's public enemy No. 1, was killed last night by a handful of the army of federal agents who had sought him for months.

The country's most notorious bank bandit, jail breaker and killer was shot as he came out of the Biograph theater with two women.

Dillinger was shot three times. One bullet penetrated his neck and came out above his eye; two others struck below his head. Traces of recent wounds in gun battles with police were found on the body.

Two women, innocent bystanders who sought to escape the heat by going to a moving picture, were wounded. Theresa Paulus was shot in the hip and Mrs. Etta Natelski was struck in the leg by a bullet.

Melvin Purvis, Chicago chieftain of the department of justice agents, headed the party that waited two hours for Dillinger to appear. He had a dozen men from his own department and five East Chicago policemen.

In the excitement, Dillinger's women companions escaped.

At the city morgue, where Dillinger's body was taken, it was found that he wore no bullet proof vest. In the pockets of the man who had led bank raids which had netted him thousands of dollars was $7.80.

**Carried Sweetheart's Photo**

A picture of Evelyn Freschetti, Indian-blooded sweetheart of the gangster, was found in the back of

Last night perhaps it was too hot for the vest.

Dillinger had none on. He was clad instead in a sporty summer outfit including gray pants, white shoes, a straw hat, a white shirt and no undershirt.

He wore no coat but he carried one pistol under his arm and another shoffed in his belt.

Officers from Sheffield Avenue police station were on the scene because of a call which they received from the manager of the theater.

The manager told them that there were some suspicious looking men lurking about the foyer. The men proved to be federal agents.

Purvis received a "tip" late last night that Dillinger was going to the Biograph theater last night to see the motion picture, "Manhattan Melodrama."

Working without the aid of Chicago police, Purvis rounded up his agents and called in the five East Chicago officers. The party loitered about the foyer of the theater. The men had been instructed that Purvis would give the signal when Dillinger came out.

After a wait of slightly more than two hours, Dillinger came into the foyer. He was accompanied by two women. Purvis recognized him instantly although Dillinger's hair had

## e Shock ... ger's Father

### MARY IS TEARFUL

Mary Kinder, companion of the Dillinger gangsters when they were captured by the Arizona "hick cops," and her sister and a companion were driving away from the Green Lantern last night to "go on of a window . . . with suicidal intent while in a despondent frame of mind." This prompted the wife of John "Boss" McLaughlin to send a telegram to Assistant Attorney General Joseph B. Keenan in Washington that her husband had been dangled from a window, in an attempt to make him confess to involvement in the Bremer kidnapping. E.A. Tamm sent an urgent note to Hoover and wired Cowley.

"Was there any indication we were using any wire rope on [Probasco] when he jumped out of the window?"

"There was not," Cowley replied. Amid this speculation and accusations of brutality, Samuel Cowley instituted the paperwork to pay Anna Sage $5,000 from the $10,000 in reward money. The other half would go to Sergeant Zarkovich and Captain O'Neill. They each received $2,500 as their share of the reward from William Stanley, U.S. Assistant Attorney General. At this point, Cowley authorized that the Justice Department pick up the hospital tab for the two women shot by flying bullets at the Biograph.

On July 30, Hoover asked the Immigration Service in Chicago to hold up deportation proceedings. The plan rested on Frances Perkins, the Secretary of Labor, to intervene because the jurisdiction belonged with that agency. The first woman to hold a U.S. cabinet post, Secy. Perkins nevertheless did not view her role as one of advocacy for women's rights. As an official, she'd been criticized by women's groups of the day for having no political empathy for women. Anna Sage would get no preferential treatment. Secy. Perkins agreed only to honor the acting attorney general's request that the deportation proceeding be delayed for three months.

Feeling assured that she would get the reward money, Anna Sage asked Cowley to move Polly and herself to Detroit for two weeks. But after only one week, the women decided they'd had enough of the company of the Justice Department, and demanded to go back to Chicago. They returned on July 31, 1934. Polly then disappeared back to her hometown of Fargo, North Dakota, where her family, in a reverse public relations campaign, had bought every newspaper to keep the towns from reading about Polly's involvement with Dillinger. She would return to Chicago by October 1934, when she agreed to join the growing ranks of Dillinger-gang women to tell her story to the *Chicago Herald & Examiner*.

Hoover, who had taken control over the custody of the women once they returned to Chicago at the end of July, made a strange decision. "If they don't care about their own safety, why should I?" he reasoned. The director's main thrust in keeping Mrs. Sage and Polly away from Chicago had been to to prevent Captain Stege from questioning them. Angry over Sage's rebellion, Hoover decided to make no special effort to "rush the payment of the reward money to her." Besides, he reasoned, how could he help in her deportation proceeding if she returned to Chicago?

His final statement set up the climate that resulted in her eventual deportation. This would occur against Purvis' promise that she'd remain in the United States.[5]

"The immigration authorities will probably deport her before we have all the kinks ironed out," said Hoover in prophetic postscript.

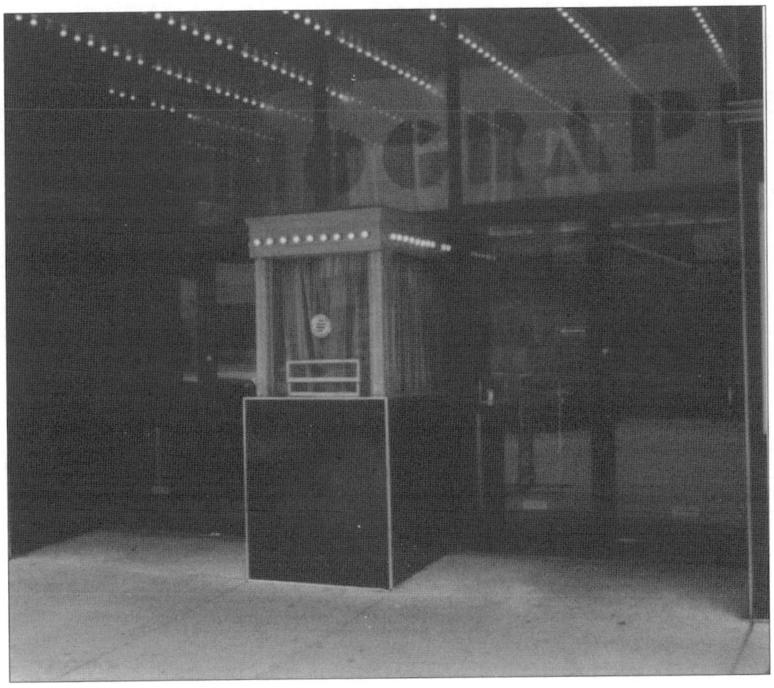

Biograph Theatre Box Office. (Author's Collection)

*"We're having nothing more to do with the St. Paul police."*

*—E.A. Tamm, Assistant to J. Edgar Hoover*

# Truck Stop Men

The shooting at the Biograph delivered Marie Comforti from the dreary Calumet City hideout she'd inhabited since June 13, when she'd violated her probation. Upon hearing of the death of Dillinger, she jumped into a pickup truck and headed for St. Paul. The comfort of Van Meter's large Buick sedans had disappeared from her life. She'd moved down in the world and looked it: Her new persona was that of a peroxide blonde named "Mrs. Hank Adams" who was dependent upon two strangers for safety.

William Finerty later confessed to making "arrangements to have him live at my home, and a day or two later Van Meter arrived with Marie Comforti, using the name 'Mickey.'" For the use of the place they'd paid $25 per week.

Once installed in the home of William and Ella Finerty at 492 Freeland Street in Calumet City, Illinois, Marie had found herself once again dumped. She passed the time in a local gambling house, seeing very little of her man. Over two days on June 28 and 29, Van Meter showed up, accompanied by John Dillinger. Here, Comforti had lived until the day that Dillinger died.

The renewal of her vows had disintegrated. The tired waiting game was still preferable to her post-probation life at home with the Costello family. The shadow team had kept a high profile outside the house and, in her words, "hounded her into going back with the gang while she was trying to go straight, working as a waitress." She put it this way:

"They took me on long rides, trying to make me break and trap the others. They took me to the home of Mrs. Gillis, and made me pretend I was trying to get clothes from her . . . they thought they would get something on Baby Face that way."

If her "clothes" problem had been a ploy to find something out, she repeated it as soon as she arrived in St. Paul after Dillinger's death. With Tommy Gannon, who drove them around in his own Ford truck, she visited Mrs. Helen Delaney while Gannon and Van Meter stayed in the truck. Marie asked the beleaguered woman for some clothes that she insisted Babe had been holding. "Mickey," looking tanned with her hair dyed a taffy blonde, wore a small-brimmed hat with a feather. She told a sad tale: She would not be able to purchase clothes for the coming winter. That night, Marie went to the Lyric Theatre while Van Meter went to the Spalding Hotel to rejoin Tommy Gannon.

An identification order was distributed on Marie that week. Showing her mug shot taken at Madison and her fingerprints, it was circulated from Washington, DC, across the nation.

On July 27, Harry Sawyer's farm was raided, as part of a crackdown on every beer joint and garage in St. Paul and Minneapolis. Angered by the reappearance of Homer Van Meter, whose reputation for "not laying low" had been established last April with the Lexington Avenue shootout, Sawyer sent a message to the desperado that warned: Keep under cover, or bring serious consequences to yourself and others.

The former Dillinger lieutenant was now relegated to the lowest strata of the underworld. Unlike Gillis, who maintained a large network on the West coast, Van Meter was a loner who now paid a price for his independence. On August 3, he made the last mistake of his life: He trusted Thomas Frank Kirwin.

Operating one step above skid row, Kirwin was a recent parolee from the North Dakota State Penitentiary. He was a heavy drinker who'd known incarceration since 1912. He'd gotten to know many people while in Leavenworth and Joliet during the 1920s, including the Touhy gang and Gillis. After his parole from the State Penitentiary at Bismark, North Dakota, in March 1934, he somehow got possession of a diamond ring and two cars. Then he went to Harry Sawyer, who fenced them for $260. The tiny nest egg went to St. Patrick's Day beer. It was a binge that would last until the middle of May, after which he became desperate for money. A hustler, he got more credit out of Sawyer and also Jack Pfeiffer, who lent him $500 for a car. The credit lasted only until August 17, when Pfeiffer's people came to repossess the car.

In desperation, Kirwin started double-dipping with a scam to invest in restaurants with proprietor John Colburg. He borrowed $200 from Colburg, while Tommy Gannon went after him for a bad loan made under the pretext of buying an ice box.

On August 5, Tommy Gannon's girlfriend, Marie McCarthy, helped Van Meter find a hideout. Her brother, Tom McMahon, operated a commission house on the corner of 11th and Jackson in St. Paul. Under Gannon's directions, she sent her friend, Meady LeClaire of Bears Island

Homer Van Meter (National Archives)

View, Leech Lake in Brevik, Minnesota, a card introducing a couple named Hank and Ruth Adams. "Treat these people nice," wrote McCarthy, "they are friends of mine."

From August 9 through 13, Van Meter and Marie stayed at LeClaire's resort, together with Tom Kirwin, William Gray, and Marie McCarthy. The accommodations were uncomfortable and crowded. Van Meter left Marie at Bears Island View, where she amused herself with food. "Mrs. Adams" had made a nice impression on LeClaire's granddaughter, who liked the nice Italian girl who asked for spaghetti with her meals.

By August 22 the couple returned to the Twin Cities. Van Meter had taken Kirwin on an errand to Gary to collect a debt. The sack had amounted to very little—$680 and "two grand short," according to an angry Van Meter. Van Meter went into Minneapolis the next day with the idea of dumping his car. He borrowed Frank Kirwin's black Chevrolet. Marie left her suitcases in this car and attended a movie as instructed to do so by Van Meter. He was meeting "someone." Her suitcases would be lost, with her cherished RCA Victor phonograph. The next afternoon, August 24, Frank Kirwin drove Van Meter to the corner of University and Marion Street in the Chevrolet sedan. According to Thomas A. Brown, former chief of police and acting head of the police identification bureau, Van Meter's death went this way:

> "For two weeks we've had a line on Van Meter and we've been right on his trail all the time. At 5:00 Chief Cullen, Jeff Dittrich, Thomas McMahon and I jumped into an automobile and drove to University Avenue. We had two machine guns and two shotguns with us. At University Avenue and Marion Street we saw Van Meter walking along the street. He had a moustache, which he ordinarily does not have, but we recognized him. We took up positions nearby out of his vision. Chief Cullen and I shouted a command for him to stop. He whipped out a pistol and fired twice. The bullets narrowly missed me. Then all four of us opened up. I guess we fired about 50 shots in all. Van Meter whirled around and started to run toward the street. At that moment a woman got in the line of fire between him and me. I, as well as the other

> three officers, had to stop shooting momentarily. When the woman got out of our way all of us opened up again. I saw blood streaming from his left hand. We chased him almost a block and finally landed him in an alley. There he dropped. When we got to him he was dead. He had a pistol in his hand."

Van Meter had thrown his hands in front of his face during the shooting and, as a result, his fingers were shredded. Comparisons of his altered fingertips were made with existing prison fingerprints to establish his certain identity. A white line running diagonally across the bridge of his nose confirmed that plastic surgery had been performed. He had $2,000 in a zipper bag when his possessions were inspected by Agents Coulter, Ladd, and Pranks. Curiously, on the day after Van Meter's death, Kirwin relinquished the Chevrolet to Jack Pfeiffer. Getting Van Meter had been relatively simple in the open city of St. Paul. The system that protected the criminals also made it easy to snuff out the undesirables.

On August 27, Pat Reilly confirmed the betrayal in the Ramsey County Jail after a visit from Babe. Van Meter's reputation for "not staying under cover," which had so angered Beth Green, had caused his death. When he'd returned to St. Paul after Dillinger's death, the warning that he ignored drove the underworld to make a deal with Tom Brown.

Pat Reilly had been turned in by a parole violator the previous June named Opal Milligan. Wild rumors flared up connecting Milligan to Van Meter—she was his new girlfriend—her family hated him and put him on the spot—soap opera speculation that resulted in Milligan's parole revocation. On August 28 she was returned to the Women's Reformatory at Sack Center, Minnesota.

Predictably, the St. Paul field office appeared at the first news of Van Meter's passing. The St. Paul police glibly said they'd gotten a tip that Van Meter was in town only ten minutes before the shooting. Obviously, Tom Brown wanted no federal interference in his police business. The Justice Department shared the icy sentiment, learning in hindsight that their informant had "sold his wares to somebody else . . . after we had sponsored him for a considerable time." The bitter rivalry that had started with the Lexington Avenue shootout had become a full-fledged war. E.A. Tamm in Washington sent a directive: "We're having nothing

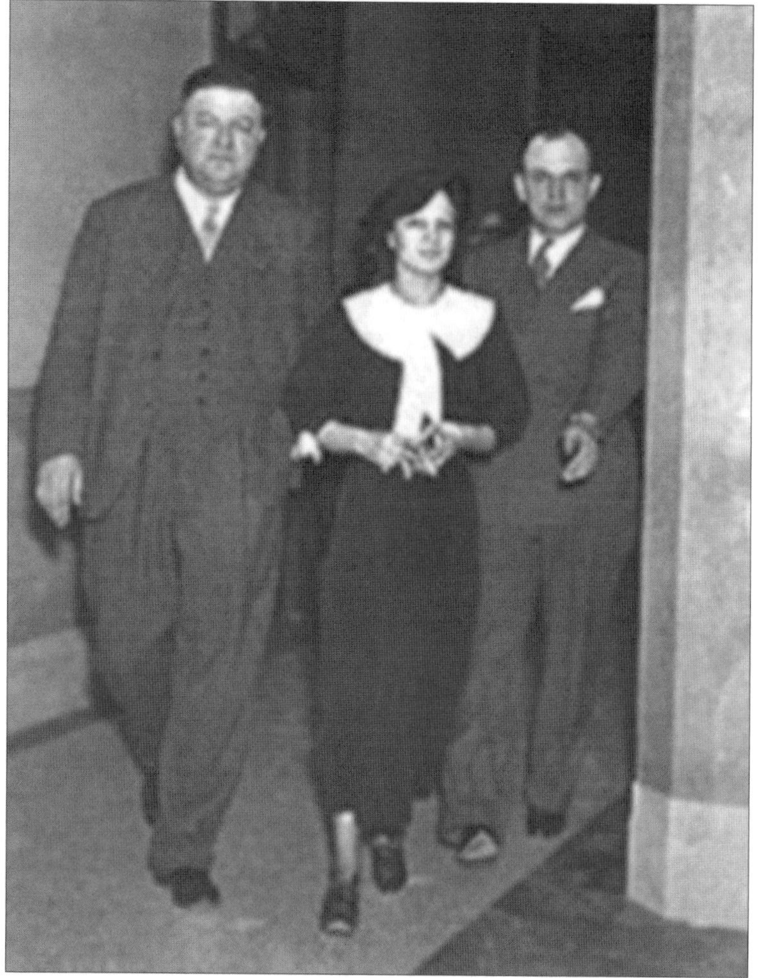

Marie Comforti surrendered after Homer Van Meter's death. (Lori Hyde)

more to do with the St. Paul police." Hoover had long been disgusted with St. Paul's reputation for openness and intimacy between local police and the gangland population. This contrasted sharply with his attitude toward East Chicago.

On August 26, a broken Marie Comforti returned to Chicago. She had no suitcase, having left it in the Chevrolet, nor did she carry a purse. All she had was one key and $41.44. At 9:00 that morning, she'd found a telephone on the corner of Van Buren and Laflin Streets and called her stepbrother, Charles Costello. Accompanied by a neighbor,

Anne Solesky, he went to the location and met Marie. At the same time, Marie's foster mother, Mrs. Costello, called Sam Cowley and asked him to meet the group on the street corner. The group of agents caused a stir in arresting the woman but kept the fact of her arrest secret for three days.[1]

That night, Sam Cowley picked up Arthur O'Leary in Chicago. Cowley confided to Agent Peterson that "they worked vigorously on O'Leary most of the night until about 4:30 or 5:00, and he admitted his part in the operations. . . . " Lacking an indictment, the agents released him. On September 7, the plastic surgery team was arrested: Louis Piquett, Harold Cassidy, Arthur O'Leary, and Wilhelm Loeser. The four would be tried together. On September 6, the grand jury for the U.S. District Court in Chicago issued an indictment charging the group with conspiracy to harbor, for purposes of performing plastic surgery, on Homer Van Meter at 2509 North Crawford Avenue on June 2, and taking money thereafter. The deceased client, John Dillinger, was not listed on the indictment. The language used by the grand jury was simple, stating that the "surgical operations upon the fingers and fingertips of the said Homer Van Meter, alias Henry Adams" would prevent the "detection and identification and arrest" of the gangster.

While Van Meter's death elicited little public response, sympathy for the deceased Dillinger still drowned out other sentiments. Mrs. Shanley stepped up to speak for the families of policemen who "will feel relieved of the anxiety they felt while Dillinger was still at large." The widow of Patrick O'Malley also lent her voice.

"I can't understand how anyone could entertain the slightest sympathy for so vicious a criminal as Dillinger. If everyone could appreciate the sorrow and suffering that he brought to our home, they would join with us in congratulating the authorities on their work."

Other widows also were interviewed for weeks after his death. Mrs. Carter Baum had gone directly to Hoover's office to congratulate him. She had moved in with her parents, the Rev. and Mrs. John Grose in Maryland. Rev. Grose made a statement:

"Naturally, we are glad that Dillinger is out of the way. We, of course, had nothing further to fear from him, but we are glad for others whom he might have endangered."[2]

Sadly, the relief was premature. Lester and Helen Gillis had also

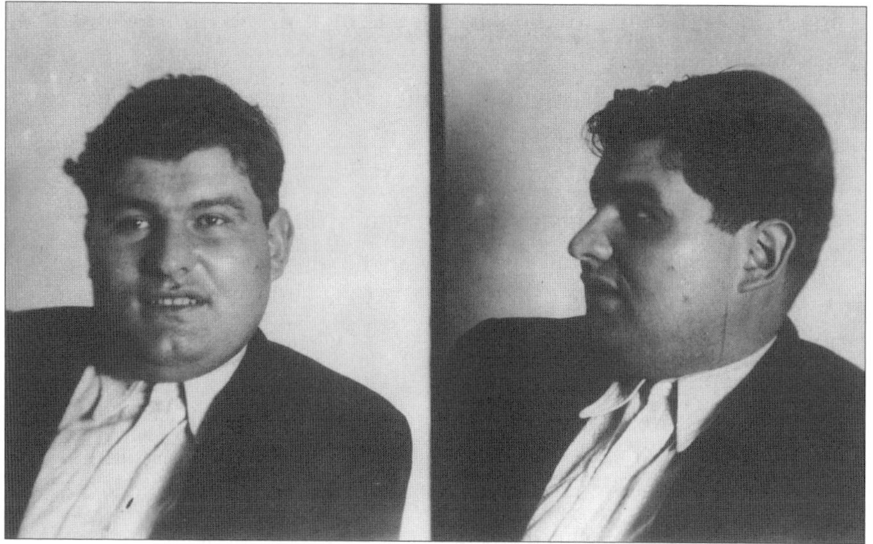

Lester Gillis and "Fatso" Negri visited Helen Gillis every day in the Vellejo Hospital. (FBI)

scampered out of Chicago after the shooting. During one of his last interactions with Dillinger, Gillis and John Paul Chase contacted Fatso Negri, who had checked into the Fullerton Hotel at 3919 Fullerton Avenue. He was hanging out at the roadhouse operated by James Murray, at North and Harlem Avenues. The three robbers met Fatso Negri in their schoolhouse meeting place. Both Van Meter and Gillis were lying on the ground. Crying that he "nearly got killed," Gillis gave Negri a satchel containing $1,500, the tithe from both Chase and himself. John Paul Chase would later give him a briefcase containing $12,000 or $13,000 in payoff money. Dillinger paid Negri $1,000. The denominations of $1000 bills soon appeared around the area.

They went out to California and, by July 31, were settled in El Verano. They traveled with Jack and Grace Perkins and the couple's 2½-year-old baby, a thin, sickly looking boy. He was so pale, he prompted a concerned passer-by to suggest that the child get some sun. Gillis' two children were being kept in Chicago with his family. Agents who knew this had trouble deciphering the identity of the child currently traveling with Gillis.

Reunited with Fatso Negri and John Paul Chase, Gillis remained in San Francisco. Chase's girlfriend, Sally Backman, had the perfect job for a resident of San Francisco: Golden Gate Ferry ticket seller at the foot of Hyde Street. Her first attempt to venture away with Chase had resulted in rejection; Gillis didn't like having an unknown woman about. Chase demanded that Sally be accepted, and he soon sent two "rough-looking men" to spirit her away from her job at the ticket booth. The rough-looking men referred to were Frank "Soap" Moreno and possibly Fatso Negri, who called for her on August 17, 1934. In this fashion she was taken away from her job, her livelihood, and any connection she'd had with the legitimate world. That world had included the lively women she saw every morning going to work—the laughing young secretaries waiting to line the wooden benches of the Sausalito ferry in knitting cliques. From this wholesome slice of Americana she slipped underground. In September the couple parted from Gillis, bound for the St. Andrews Hotel in New York City.

Helen Gillis was denied the basic luxury of a cheap hotel. The last months of her conjugal life with Les were pocked with low-life hideouts. They slept in hills and mountains, much like the glamorized gangsters in movies like *High Sierra* and *The Petrified Forest.* The real-life saga contained no elements of Hollywood. Gillis traveled from Las Vegas to Reno. They climbed the mountains of Nevada, living in an abandoned mountain cabin near Ely. On September 29 they went back to the Vallejo General Hospital. Gillis asked Thomas "Tobe" Williams, who'd been keeping money for him, if he could arrange a meeting between himself and Alvin Karpis.

"Come back in the spring of 1935," Tobe Williams told him. If it sounded like a brush-off, it was.

They were back in Chicago on November 1. While Chase would stay in hotels, Gillis and Helen slept in a pickup truck. Gillis loathed checking into lodges and gas stations for fear of recognition. As winter approached, they returned to Lake Como, hoping to secure an apartment for the duration of the coming season.

Based on the information received on Lake Como, Agents Winstead, Metcalfe, and McRae had stationed themselves there on November 27. Gillis and Chase had met the night before with Fatso Negri and Clarence Lieder to arrange an ammunition buy. With plans to regroup within twenty-four hours, they'd left Helen in the old neighborhood, during which time they stole a Ford V-8.

While they were thus engaged, she took a prophetic, yet nostalgic walk. From a hiding place on the street, she watched her father's house. She couldn't get near it; government agents lined the front porch. The house of Juliette Fitzsimmons was also guarded. She went to a movie, returning to a pre-fixed location to join up with Gillis and Chase. To follow their pattern, John Paul Chase went to a hotel, and Gillis drove his wife out into the country to sleep with her in the stolen Ford.

The next day, before their scheduled meeting with Fatso, Helen and John Paul Chase drove up to the house on Lake Como, looking for the owner, Hobart Hermanson. Gillis was met by Special Agent Metcalfe. He was hesitant to finger Gillis, remembering the civilian casualties of the Little Bohemia and the margin of error that had caused it. As the party left, Metcalfe made a positive identification of Helen Gillis, who sat in the front passenger seat. Gillis was disgusted at hearing that Hermanson was not there. He knew that they were agents.

Metcalfe ran inside and placed a call to Sam Cowley's office. Cowley dispatched Agents Thomas M. McDade and William C. Ryan, stationed on the north side of Chicago, to proceed to Lake Geneva. Inspector Cowley and Special Agent Herman Edward "Ed" Hollis jumped into their car to join the chase.

About five miles from Barrington, Bill Ryan and Tom McDade spotted a Ford sedan with 1934 Illinois license plates, the last three numbers of which were 578. They turned their car around on the road and saw that Gillis had also turned his car around on U.S. Highway 12. About one-half mile from Fox River Grove, Illinois, these agents, traveling in a southeasterly direction, observed a Ford sedan occupied by Gillis traveling in a northwesterly direction. They turned around to follow. The agents, who carried only side arms, were unnerved by the sight of Chase aiming a machine gun. Tom McDade sped away from the car to gain distance and fired shots into the gangster's car, disabling it by piercing the radiator. Bill Ryan and Tom McDade sped away from car, losing it.

Sam Cowley and Ed Hollis had proceeded from their office armed with a shotgun and submachine gun. They met Gillis on Highway 12, coming from the same northwesterly direction. Upon spotting Gillis' speeding car, they followed him for several miles. At the entrance to the North Side Park in Barrington, Illinois, Gillis suddenly turned off the Northwest Highway and stopped. Agents Cowley and Hollis were unable to stop until they had passed the Gillis car and proceeded on the Northwest Highway about 200 feet east. Before the agents were able to get out of the car, Gillis and Chase jumped out of the Ford V-8 and began firing on them. With seventeen slugs in his body, Gillis advanced, then crawled to his Ford V-8, took his guns out, and moved them to Cowley's division car. Chase jumped behind the wheel.

"Where's Helen?" Chase cried at his friend.

"We can't fool with her now," screamed Gillis. "We'll have to leave her." Helen resurrected herself from a ditch, where she'd taken cover. They drove away.

Sam Cowley died in the Sherman Hospital in Elgin, Illinois, as he clung to his wife's hand. Melvin Purvis stalked from the room with Cowley's empty revolver protruding from his coat pocket. The special agent had presided over Carter Baum's body at Koerner's Lodge. Now Gillis had taken two more of Purvis' men, one his closest associate. His anguish would last for years.

Ed Hollis, twenty-eight years old, who would have celebrated his seventh wedding anniversary on Thanksgiving Day, had died instantly. He'd been planning to go out to dinner with his wife that night, to celebrate. She was waiting in his office with her four-year-old son when she overheard strangers discussing his death. Her son began to cry.

"Will they kill us too, mama?"

Inspector Cowley's body was sent to Salt Lake City, Utah, accompanied by his dark-haired wife, Lavon Chipman Cowley, and her two children, John, seven months, and Samuel Jr., three years. Cowley was given a civic funeral in the assembly hall of the Morman temple the Sunday after Thanksgiving. His wife would receive $96.25 per month because she had two children. Agent's Hollis' widow, who accompanied her husband's body back to the Ambrose Cathedral at Des Moines, Iowa, would receive $75.75 because she had one child. These meager amounts upset Purvis, who felt they were entitled to more.

The guns of both slain agents were found empty. The car abandoned by Gillis was recovered. With thirty bullet holes in it, it's front right seat, which had been occupied by Gillis, was saturated with blood.

As these remnants of the bloodbath were recovered, Gillis, Chase, and Helen drove to Father Coughlan's sister's house at 1155 Mohawk Road, in Wilmette, north of Chicago, and requested shelter for the dying

Gillis. Not allowing them in, he instructed them to follow him. The still conscious Gillis told Chase to turn off and shake Coughlin; his instinct told him the priest was going to turn them in. They detoured to a nearby house located on Walnut Street. Helen was already acquainted with two men who met the car, one about sixty-five years old and the other a younger man. A woman named Mary, according to Helen's later testimony, mentioned that she had a young teenaged son and daughter. She gave them entry through a driveway and garage and then stayed out of sight.

At first they placed Gillis on a chair, but they then quickly realized that he'd have to go on a bed. Chase and the other man carried Gillis to a small bedroom in the back of the house. The solemnity was broken when the two men screamed at Chase to "get the car out of the garage."

"Don't leave me now," begged Gillis. The only medical attention the dying Gillis received was a few ripped sheets to stop the bleeding.

"Don't leave me," he chanted. Chase ignored the wishes of his pal and left in Cowley's car, bound for a rail to Chicago. Gathering no moss, he answered a quick ad for a convoy to drive to the West coast. Left behind, Helen cut the clothing from Gillis' body and stayed with him as he died.

She maintained a vigil until one of the two men approached the room.

"We'll have to take him out," he suggested.

"I would like to take him to the undertakers," she said.

They wrapped the body in the sheets and pillowcases from the bed, taking an extra blanket from the house. They drove with Gillis propped up in the seat like a Beau Geste legionnaire. Her driver had a "funny, queer look." It frightened her, she later reported to federal agents.

"Are you going to take him to the undertakers?"

"No, we're not going to take him to an undertaker."

She persisted to give him the name of Sadowski's Funeral Home on Hermitage Avenue and begged her ghoulish accomplice to call him up. She later placed the call herself. After they dropped the body at the edge of St. Paul's Cemetery in Niles Center, she drove with the men for a few miles and tossed the clothing from the car. She left the impromptu hearse and hailed a cab into Chicago. Once there she walked the streets.

The next day was Thanksgiving. She went without food or water.

Then she gave a young girl a dollar and asked her to bring a note to Juliette Fitzsimmons, asking her to meet her at the Lafayette School.

On November 28, Arnie Lindeman of Niles Center, telephoned the police captain to say that a bundle of bloody clothing was in a ditch at Railroad and South Howard Avenues. At 7:55 a.m. Helen reached undertaker Philip Sadowski, to advise that the naked body was located at Harmes Road and Lincoln Avenue, Niles Center. The body was discov-

II

Emil Wanatka sworn for pltf.
Govt X. D + E + F rec'd
Deft. X 1 rec'd.
Meady Le Claire sworn for pltf.
Delia Coleman " " "
Govt. X G. rec'd
" X H rec'd
" X I rec'd
Adjourn to 10 am Dec. 18, 1934
12-18-34
Marie Marion Conforti sworn for pltf.
R. C. Coulter recalled for pltf.
Govt X J. rec'd
Recess to 2 PM
R. C. Coulter recalled
Richard N. Pranke sworn for pltf.
Meady Le Claire recalled for pltf.
Delia Coleman recalled for pltf.
Harry L. Pratt sworn for pltf.
Govt X K marked
George Katz sworn for pltf.
Kenneth Fabynske sworn for pltf.

Marie Comforti testified against her former protectors. Court reporter's notes indicate that Rufus Coulter, FBI agent who fired at Van Meter in the Lexington Avenue shootout, followed her as a witness for the prosecution. (National Archives)

ered by Agent McKee at the intersection of Long and Niles Avenue. Crowds gathered at the county morgue in the hope that Mrs. Gillis would show up for a last look.

Death was fixed at 8:00 p.m. He'd been shot five times in the stomach, twice in the chest, and five times in each leg. Helen Gillis later claimed she did not know what happened to his money belt.

The newspapers declared Helen the new "Public Enemy No. 1," who was under a shoot to-kill-order. Melvin Purvis later denied that this directive had come from the bureau, calling it a newspaper trick. Helen's father, Vincent, mis-identified as "John Wawrzyniak" in many newspapers, said that Helen had "surrendered rather than face government bullets."

The next night, Helen Gillis turned herself in the way Marie Comforti had—on a Chicago street corner, in the company of her relatives. She was brought to the Cook County Jail, where she stayed for a short time before going to Milan. On a trip to the neighborhood where her husband had died, she pointed out a house at 1605 Walnut Street as possibly being the one she'd entered on that decisive night. The house she fingered was the home of Clinton B. Cochran, who had four children with his wife, Anna, a mine operator. A former village trustee, Cochran was a small-time politician.

She'd gotten the address wrong by a few houses; the address was later determined to have been 1627 Walnut Street.[4]

Undertaker Phillip Sadowski, a friend of the family who had supervised their other funerals, did eventually get Gillis' body. Gillis was buried in Chicago's St. Joseph's Cemetery by the undertaker chosen by Helen at the hour of his death. His mother, Mary, cried while Juliette Fitzsimmons and her husband, Robert, supported her. The 200-deep crowd was comprised of spectators and federal agents.

Helen was taken back to Madison, Wisconsin, wearing the dark coat and hat, black shoes and stockings of mourning. Her dress, dark blue, was the only color adorning her. Sick at ninety pounds with anemia, her eyes stared out of dark pockets of sadness. Juliette Fitzsimmons stayed with her, along with 150 spectators on December 7, when she faced Judge Patrick Stone. He'd been hoisted into a pulpit before by the return of the three women of the Little Bohemia to his courtroom. Helen Gillis had an understanding with the judge and had readily admitted having broken her probation. She waived the services of an attorney, who claimed to be there from Chicago, as she faced the reproaches of Judge Stone in the revocation of her parole.[5]

"What about your two children, you love them don't you?"

"Yes, very much."

"Your husband was an outlaw who was certain to be caught. If you loved your children how could you leave them behind with relatives and follow your husband around?"

"Well, I knew that Les didn't have very long to live and I wanted to be with him just as long as I could."

*"Now about the Fair. I am just to talk a few minutes and sell these articles I wrote. Honey I have an agreement with a man in Chicago who is to pay my expenses and buy me a few evening gowns and give me 25% of what we make."*

*—Mary Kinder in a letter to Harry Pierpont on death row, August, 1934*

# "The Government is Simply 'Piling it On'"

The death of the Dillinger gangsters left their widows with little incentive to uphold secrets. Marie Comforti had relinquished her Brownie points with charges aimed at defaming Sam Cowley's hero reputation. Her remarks were offensive, but the timing was worse. Just as Sam Cowley was being eulogized by his colleagues in both Washington and Chicago, these tasteless remarks found their way to Hoover's desk:

"I don't regret the death of Agent Samuel P. Cowley one bit . . . he used to get real tough with me . . . he chained me to a chair and every few minutes he would ask me, 'Where is Gillis?' Every time I said I didn't know, he slapped me and punched me. Once when I couldn't stand it, I yelled, 'You shot Dillinger in the back.'"

She became the target of the wrath of Hoover for her defamation of Sam Cowley. Thereafter, her work in bringing down the "Rogues Gallery" of those harboring Van Meter lost its validity.

Nevertheless, she became a witness for the prosecution after learning that Frank Kirwin fingered Van Meter. She identified William and Ella Finerty as they were brought in for questioning on August 27. Marie watched the couple who had harbored her through a two-way mirror. The new policing device, then called an "x-ray mirror," enabled her to observe the couple without being seen. William Finerty readily admitted to having hosted Van Meter on "two occasions" and identified Dr. Cassidy as the physician treating the gangster after South Bend.

On September 10, bench warrants were issued for William Finerty in the amount of $10,000; Ella Finerty for $2,000; and the already-imprisoned Marie Comforti for $5,000.

In September 1934, Marie Comforti was indicted in Duluth, Minnesota, with William and Ella Finerty for harboring Van Meter at 492 Freeland Street in Calumet City, from the period of June 13 to July 22, the day of Dillinger's death. On September 12, Ella Finerty was arrested in Chicago and held on $2,000 bail. The Finertys entered pleas of "not guilty" on September 12, 1934, while Comforti, a material witness, pleaded "guilty" before Judge John P. Barnes. There she received a parallel sentence to the one she'd garnered at Madison, one year and one day, which was to run concurrently with the sentence imposed at Madison, Wisconsin. The Finertys were released on bail posted by their family members and friends. The indictments reflected Van Meter's itinerary from the day of Dillinger's death to his own, which occurred one month later. Tom Gannon was the first to plead guilty, on October 9, 1934; the others elected to go to trial. On December 6, 1934, Marie Comforti became a material witness against Tom Kirwin, Frank Connolly, William Gray, William "Bill" Harris, and Marie McCarthy. Although slated to serve her original "one-year" sentence under Judge Stone in Madison, she feared more time should she refuse to cooperate. As the others pleaded "not guilty," she accepted her guilty plea and went on record for the plaintiff. This entitled her to minor protection, such as a special guard when she was moved around from Chicago, where she'd stood trial with the Finertys.

A jury trial commenced on December 17 in Duluth, with Comforti testifying for the U.S. Government. As she stepped down from the witness stand, Rufus Coulter, who had faced Van Meter in the hallway on Lexington Avenue, was next to testify. He recognized two mug shots taken of Van Meter, one from March 5, 1925, and the second, taken as he was paroled. These photographs, requisitioned from Pendleton, showed Van Meter's transformation from a young angry kid to a wizened, solitary man within the space of a few short years.

Emil Wanatka testified, as did Meady LeClaire, who had harbored Van Meter at Leech Lake. He blamed Marie McCarthy, saying that she'd sent Van Meter to their establishment on Bear Lake. He produced the guest book and register from the Bear Island View Resort. He accused Tom Kirwin of having gone to Gary, Indiana, with Van Meter to make the cash pickup.

The plaintiff was challenged to link the defendants and Van Meter, by proving that they had known his true identity. On top of that, the court had to link Van Meter to his own "Overt Acts," and so they resurrected the indictments dating back to the charges made in Madison after the events at the Little Bohemia. They also alluded to the original indictments against Eugene and Bessie Green. The guilty plea of Tom Gannon, together with the testimony of Marie Comforti, were two elements that went with the identification issue. The jury had to be convinced that the defendants had knowledge of the identity of Van Meter while the "alleged conspiracy" existed. The jury found all defendants guilty on December 20.

The Honorable Robert C. Bell, the presiding judge, doled out the sentences.

- Kirwin was sentenced to two years in Leavenworth and fined $10,000. Kirwin would leave prison on July 28, 1936, upon the Oath of Poor Convict and a waiver of $10,000 fine.
- Bill Gray was sentenced to one year and six months in Leavenworth and fined $5,000.
- Marie McCarthy, alias Marie McMahon, was sentenced to Alderson for one year and six months and ordered to pay a fine of $5,000. She stayed in the Ramsey County Jail until March 1935, when her transfer to Alderson became effective.
- Marie Comforti, Marie McCarthy's opponent in the courtroom, went to Madison on December 24, immediately following the trial. There Judge Stone revoked her probation and sentenced her to serve one year and one day, the sentence imposed upon her after Little Bohemia. The

> sentence of the District Court in Duluth, of one year and one day, would run concurrently, at Alderson.[1]

To Comforti, incarceration replaced one type of bordeom with another. Helen Gillis likewise found that imprisonment offered comforts relative to the hardships she'd endured. Her life with Gillis, which included sleeping in cars and trucks, had been physically hard and emotionally unbearable. She felt that she'd performed her duty as a wife and took comfort in the knowledge that he'd gotten a decent funeral.

Remembering how John Paul Chase had abandoned her Les on his deathbed, she readily placed him at Barrington after his arrest on December 27, in Mount Shasta, California. In February 1935, both Helen Gillis and John Paul Chase admitted in Purvis' office that they had accompanied Gillis to Barrington on November 27, 1934, and had engaged in the gun battle that had killed Agents Hollis and Cowley. She reiterated the humdrum testimony that, in light of Barrington, seemed weak and unnecessary.

"So then of course you knew and had known both from magazine articles and newspapers and what the authorities had told you when you were arrested that your husband was a very much wanted man by the Government, didn't you?"

"Well," she replied, "if I say no I am a liar."

Chase was charged with the murder of Ed Hollis on New Years' Eve, 1934. As the bells tolled and 1935 was heralded in, the U.S. Government looked forward to a new year of retribution. On January 28, 1935, Chase was also charged with the murder of Sam Cowley. Helen had agreed to testify before the grand jury as to his presence at the scene of the death of Cowley and Hollis, known only as "the crime." Of deeper relevance was her agreement to name Chase as the killer.

Upon her entry to Milan, on January 5, 1934, Helen Gillis also agreed to inform on Cherrington and Frechette in Milan. On March 22, it was decided that Helen Gillis, who was still in Milan, would be left there for the time being. U.S. District Attorney Dwight Green announced that, for the present time, he would not call Mrs. Gillis.

One of the Dillinger women who had remained free, Mary Kinder, knew that her freedom was the result of having been arrested before Dillinger came under the federal warrants. She maintained her relation-

Helen Gillis, angered at John Paul Chase's deathbed abandonment of Baby Face Nelson, later placed Chase at the Battle of Barrington. (National Archives)

ships with Pat Cherrington and Evelyn Frechette, who were also at Milan with Helen Gillis. Evelyn Frechette was one of fourteen women prisoners at the Women's Annex at Milan. She spent seven hours a day ironing in the prison laundry. It is tempting to think that perhaps Hoover had something to do with this. It could have been his idea of a sick joke to have "Miss Frechette, who was seen ironing," appointed to an ironing board. Her appeal, funded by Dillinger, had ended with Piquett's arrest. Like a benevolent husband, Dillinger had given $2,000, earmarked for the appeal, to Art O'Leary.

Warden J.J. Ryan would not permit Evelyn Frechette to be interviewed. On July 5, her mother was hit by a car, and died. The warden would not permit her to attend the funeral. She'd first been removed from her mother when only a child, as an Indian ward of the U.S. Government boarding schools. She felt this to be a worse persecution—an exercise of authority that denied her the proper avenue of grief.

Apparently, it was a comfort for Evelyn to share the prison experience with Pat Cherrington. Mary made note of this observation in a letter to Pierpont on death row:

"Jessie went and seen Billy and she said Pat was there with her and honey she lost her mother when Johnnie died. She sure is blue and discouraged. I sure feel sorry for her. I am going to write to Opal this eve. . . ."

Mary's every move had been watched by federal agents since Tucson. Harry Pierpont's parents had opened a barbecue stand and a sideline: they informed on Mary in the hopes of some leniency for their son. The couple was suffering from trauma. They'd buried their daughter at the age of nineteen and now were facing an execution date of their beloved son.

Based on the intelligence furnished by the Pierponts, a shadow team was formed to trail Mary. Agent Winstead, a veteran of the Biograph killing, moved into her newest domicile, the Linwood Hotel. With Jessie Levy's legal bills causing her anxiety, Mary met John Dillinger in Chicago on May 21, 1934. Low on funds, he refused her request for money.

The Pierponts notified the Justice Department on June 12 when Mary Kinder made a trip to South Bend, Indiana. Lena was especially quick to point out that Mary's new boyfriend, Carl J. Waltz, took her out to the local beer halls like the Green Lantern and the Alpine Club.

Mary didn't know that Waltz was chatting with federal agents about her activities and said that he couldn't question her for fear of causing suspicion. It is doubtful that Carl Waltz knew very much about his new sweetheart. She kept her relationship to Pierpont separate, making sure the doomed man never found out she was seeing another man.

Mrs. Pierpont also told John Dillinger to stay away from the Lima defendants, hoping for a motion for a new trial. As death row inmates, Pierpont and Makley were entitled to one visit per week. Pierpont was being drawn into the last days of a twenty-one-year condemned man in the adjoining cell. The young man would spend his time singing. The Irish folk ballad, "When Irish Eyes Are Shining," which the youth sang constantly, particularly upset Pierpont.

With his date of execution approaching, Pierpont had become belligerent to the people who were trying to help him. He found out that Mary had given the series of articles to the *Chicago Herald & Examiner* and wanted to know what she'd said. He resented the fact that his mother did not visit, nor write, as often as she was allowed by law. He questioned Mary's motives as he found out that she had begun selling her story. In a defensive answer to him, she explained:

". . . the only thing they wanted was my name to it and I seen a chance to help you kids out. I gave it to [Jessie Levy] as the understanding it was to go for you and Mack's trials. I gave her $300 . . . I asked her why she never told you all about it and she said you acted like you wasn't interested in it so she shut up about it. . . ."

Pierpont was further upset to hear that Mary had joined the Carnival shows that the Dillinger family had already taken on the road. From his perspective, it appeared that while he was about to die, Mary had continued to live. Her last letters were filled with explanations and apologies. Pierpont went to his death unaware of her new boyfriend's commitment to marrying her. She protected him from the truth through practice garnered by hours with the district attorney. Mary responded only to the questions Pierpont posed:

"Now about the Fair. I am just to talk a few minutes and sell these articles I wrote. Honey I have an agreement with a man in Chicago who is to pay my expenses and buy me a few evening gowns and give me 25% of what we make."

Mary rode on whatever publicity, and money, there was to help her get through the tragedy of Pierpont's death. She gave a radio interview, stressing that her life on the run had been one of extreme stress.

"[My mother] she worried herself sick all the time," she revealed. "Everytime she got a newspaper it gave her something new to worry about. The papers said we were here and there and everyplace and getting shot at. . . ."

Charles Makley and Harry Pierpont did try to cheat the dreaded chair. During an attempted escape from death row, using a gun carved out of soap, Makley was shot and killed. Pierpont, however, was placed in the infirmary with gun shot wounds. On October 17, 1934, Pierpont was executed at 12:09 a.m. and pronounced dead at 12:14.

Mary Kinder had never come under federal jurisdiction and, as such, was free to go her own way. Helen Gillis' freedom would be harder to obtain. Her testimony was pertinent to a grand jury inquiry in San Francisco. The proceedings were put on hold until February in order to ensure that Federal Prosecutor H.H. McPike would be able to interrogate her. As he predicted, her testimony began to unravel the mysteries

Mary Kinder at the bier of Harry Pierpont, who met his death in the electric chair for the murder of Sheriff Jesse Sarber. (Robert Bates)

buried in too many conflicting facts. Her sworn statements brought sixteen people into custody on February 4, 1935. The resulting trial would bring to light other startling facts: A nurse at the Vallejo Hospital, Myrtle Jordan, the victim of a "hit-and-run," was murdered because she knew too much; a missing Reno bank teller, Roy K. Frisch, was kidnaped and murdered to prevent his testimony against William Graham and James McKay, two Reno gamblers and politicians who were now being brought up on bank fraud charges.

Investigations into Vallejo Hospital revealed that Alvin Karpis had been to see Tobe Williams the previous October for a face-lift. Williams had thwarted Gillis' bid to be united with Karpis with his sarcastic advice to "Come back in the spring."

In spite of his Bremer money, which came on the heels of the kidnaping of William Hamm, Jr., the year before, Karpis had become less welcomed as the hunt for him intensified.

Karpis' trail had woven through several states after delivery of the Bremer ransom in Cleveland the year before. His speed was challenged at times by the slow gait of his pregnant girl. She was still a teenager.

Dolores Delaney was the little sister of Jean Delaney Crompton and Babe Reilly. Dolores had met Karpis in the same way that Jean had met Tommy Carroll, through Pat Riley and Harry Sawyer. Of the three sisters, all of whom were involved with underworld characters, Dolores was considered the true rebel. She'd fallen in love with "Raymond" while she was only sixteen.

She'd acted as an alibi witness for cop killer Clarence Devol, an early associate of Karpis' before he became involved with the Barker brothers. The commission of this perjury lent to her a tough and worldly self-image. She had affected a sidelong glance, as though viewing the world through her own peculiar lens. Beth Green, that student of human nature, had sized up Dolores as a "poor, dumb little thing."

She possessed none of Jean Delaney Crompton's gentility nor Babe Riley's sarcastic wit. Yet she was tougher than her sisters and strong enough to endure the lonely, empty hideouts that he'd set up for her. Her longest stay would be in Miami.

Karpis had installed her there in May 1934 with the help of Joseph H. "Joe" Adams, who rented a cottage in a suburb of Little River on 84th Street. In Miami, she became pregnant. Bypassing the back-alley route, she insisted on bringing the child to term.

Karpis had gone to Miami to see Joe Adams, a well-connected Florida businessman. A contact in Grosse Point who'd sent Karpis to Adams arranged to unload the Bremer ransom in Cuba, for a 15% charge. Karpis left his guns at the Biscayne Kennel Club, a dog track owned in part by Joe Adams. Under the protection of Adams, guarding his passage to the Keys, Karpis discovered the hot pleasures of Havana. His pregnant teenager followed, compliant as the bull dog pup that she carried everywhere.

They took a boat out of Key West for Havana and stayed in the Veradero, a summer result where the Cuban president spent his holidays with American millionaires. Their contact there was Nate Heller, who owned the Parkview Hotel in Havana. They sailed on the SS Cuba on September 21, 1934, staying until November.

After ransom money turned up in Cuba an Agent Kingman was sent down. But Karpis spotted the agent and took Dolores back to Miami. The two traveled as Mr. and Mrs. Wagner, on November 14. Four days later Dolores returned to Havana, traveling on Pan American Airways. She again flew, on November 18, back to Miami, returning to the house in the suburb of Little River, at 1121 Northeast 85th Street.

Here Dolores sat out her third trimester, while Karpis drove to Cleveland to meet Arthur "Doc" Barker, who'd come over from Chicago just before his arrest. While in Florida, Freddie apparently visited Karpis in Miami. Freddie and Karpis drove up to Cleveland and met Doc. From Cleveland they drove to Lake Weir, Florida, where Fred had gotten a house for his mother from Joe Adams.

The house where Kate Barker would live in tentative retirement had been in the family of Adams' connection, Carsen Bradford, for two generations. It had been loaned to Joe Adams the prior summer, as a honeymoon cottage for Adams and his bride.

Fred and his mother adopted the name of "Blackburn." The alias revealed elements of the Barker psyche, just as "Hellman" had revealed Dillinger's image of himself.

Kate "Mother" Barker settled into a slow life there. Not a woman's woman, she nonetheless offered her hand to Dolores. Vulnerable in her pregnancy, Dolores brought out the latent tenderness in the rawhide woman of the Ozarks. Yet the only thing the two women had in common, besides Karpis, was their real estate broker. Joe Adams had found the place for Dolores in Miami while arranging Karpis' trip to Cuba for the purpose of passing the ransom money. The Barkers had settled into the two-story cottage on Lake Weir after renting it from Bradford in Miami. Adams' official title was that of general manager of the Biscayne Kennel Club at Miami Beach, of which Bradford was president.

During the isolated confinement, Karpis hired a physician for Dolores. Dr. Carl Surran, a police surgeon, later recounted that Karpis had retained him.

"We've got plenty of dough and we want the best for the little girl," the mobster had instructed him.

In January 1935, Dolores was eight months' pregnant and cast with Wynona Burdette, the girlfriend of Harry Campbell. Winona had radio ambitions and an arrest record dating back to Tulsa in 1932. She was released by officers upon the unkept promise of a relative who promised to put Harry Campbell "on the spot." Harry and Winona Burdette, traveling as "Mr. and Mrs. Summers," drove down to Karpis' hideout in Little River, Miami. They picked up Karpis and the men drove to Ocala, to pay a visit to Fred and Ma. Dolores was sitting with Wynona when Joe Adams called the house with grim news: Fred and his mother were dead.

They had been located through a game of maneuvers that had incorporated elements of chess and charades. It had started with the arrest of Doc Barker in Chicago a few days before. Melvin Purvis had shadowed the Barker women, who led the special agents to the Pine Grove address where Doc Barker, Byron Bolton, and Slim Gray were hiding out. An agent stationed in the Chicago office, John Madala, raided a Chicago apartment fourteen blocks south and arrested Doc.

The January 9, 1935, arrest was done simultaneously with the arrest of associate Byron Bolton and the death of Russell Gibson, who, in the words of Agent Madala, "decided to fight it out." Under interrogation, Byron Bolton revealed that he had heard Doc talk of a lake in North Florida and an alligator named "Ol Joe." Five agents, under the command of Earl Connelley, stalked through Florida in search of the newest name on the Barker's hit list—a reptile. The agents zeroed in on Marion County in Central Florida and, using guile, asked a local huntsman about "Ol Joe." At eighteen feet long, living in a dredge hole and feeding on a constant diet of turtles, he sounded like an even match for the Barkers.

The Florida native replied, "Yes, I know two such alligators. One is in Lake Walberg near Gainesville, and the other is in Lake Weir." This correlated with a map leading to Lake Weir that was found in Doc's apartment. With only one telephone, the wooded county town of Oklawaha had pleasant houses nestled behind overgrown hedges and Spanish moss.

Warren E. McGahagin was ten years old when Fred and Ma Barker checked in. A long-time resident of Ocala, he confirmed the story of "Ol Joe" in an interview.

"According to the local talk, he was 18 feet long, and was living a couple of miles west on the north shore. There was a den and there was a dredge hole and he made his home in there. He swallowed a turtle whole and digested it, and regurgitated a skeleton."

Mr. McGahagin maintains that the Barkers were not reclusive.

"We thought they were rich people because they had New York license plates on their car. She looked like the wealthy people of the day who dressed more for show than for style. Her clothes, always dark in color, were expensive but not well-fitting. Ma looked more like a man than a woman. With the bright rouge on her cheeks, her clothes hanging like socks, she looked garish," he shuddered.

The Barkers went to school plays and mixed with the people. Freddie liked to flirt with the single women. Warren McGahagin recalls a game that Fred played with all the kids.

"They would offer three pennies in one hand or a nickel in another and you could take your choice. I took the three pennies, which made Fred laugh. They didn't seem to be evil. But Fred would defer to her. She had the voice of steel, and you could hear the authority."

The Blackburns came to ingratiate themselves with the people. Fred had his Buick coupe serviced at the Gillis & Gale Garage and made small talk with Raymond Gale, the mechanic. Kenneth Hart, who hung around the service station, liked Fred and shared the community's regard for his mother. "He was just a real friendly guy."

The man and his mother had settled in with a cook named Willie Woodberry who was called "Beigh" (pronounced "beej") by everyone, including his wife, who shared the housekeeping duties. Fred quickly acquired a reputation for deferential behavior around his mother. Beigh could see that Ma was the "boss."

"She was definitely the one who called the shots in that house," he said later in a newspaper interview.

The agents knew that Fred Barker traveled with his mother. The house that was to be her Florida retirement home held her in a place that was to be shaded, secluded, and quiet until the bullets of early morning broke through the film of dawn. The presence of a swampy alligator acted as the tip-off in a bizarre reversal of roles where the hunter becomes the hunted.

The morning of January 16 marked the one-year anniversary of the Bremer kidnaping. Fred Barker had arisen early and was neatly dressed, but the supper table was littered with dishes. Beer had been drunk. Fred was dressed in tan woolen trousers, tan shoes dyed black, brown socks, and a white shirt open at neck. Ma wore a red-checked housedress and no stockings. Earl Connelley, who had succeeded Sam Cowley, quietly formed a posse around the house. The agents had gathered from Texas, Oklahoma, Missouri, and Chicago. This was the fruition of the prior day's events, when an agent stood fishing off the Bradford dock. Fred had gone up to him and asked, "How's fishing?"

"Nothing doing," the agent replied, as he made his identification. "You must have caught all the fish in this vicinity."

The agents chose to converge on the house, rather than try to take Fred on the fishing docks where he would have been unaccompanied. The bloody end of Bonnie Parker, killed in the previous May, had desensitized peace officers to the prospect of shooting a woman who may or may not have been an active, gun-wielding accomplice.

The agents, after the Battle of Barrington, understandably wanted as much cover, and element of surprise, working in their favor as they could. With the memory of Sam Cowley and Ed Hollis alternately fueling and freezing him, Connelley walked to the door in that still, swampy morning.

Agents had surrounded the house, mounting machine guns on the bank of the lake and behind big oaks at the sides of the house in a grapefruit grove in the rear. Connelley, backed by Rufus Coulter, walked up to the front door and stepped back into the yard. Ma Barker came to the door.

"Is your son here?"

"Who wants him?"

The Barker Death House today, reclusive and unapproachable. (Author's Collection)

"A federal officer."

"If you will come out one by one," he suggested, "no one will be hurt."

"Well, go ahead," Kate invited. Fred simultaneously began to fire from an upper window.

The barefoot woman ran back into the house. Her son appeared downstairs in a moment. He had a Tommy gun and it sprayed lead into the dawn. Bullets spattered around the feet of the federal men, causing Connolley to jump behind an oak tree. Then, a burst of fire came from one of the federal posts at the side of the house. Tear gas was also fired.

As the fighting continued, the Barkers were driven by bullets to the upstairs front rooms.

Choking with gas, they were crowded to windows to make their last stand by returning fire. At intervals, agents ceased shooting to give the Barkers a chance to come out alive.

They ceased fire around 11:00 a.m. The road was blocked by agents to keep out the crowd of onlookers that had begun to assemble. They went to the adjoining house to retreive Beigh, the cook. He'd been lying on the floor for hours. They asked Beigh to go into the house. The thinking was that Barker wouldn't be inclined to kill the man who had shown him kindness. Beigh dashed up to the porch, but the door wouldn't open.

"That door's shut," he yelled with some relief.

"Well . . . go back and cut the screen and kick it down," the agents insisted.

When Fred Barker's fire stopped, the cook was sent into the house by the officers.

"They are all dead," he called from the house.

An agent called the Pyles Mortuary at 14 S.W. Fifth Street.

"Send the wagon down here. We've got two stiffs."

The crowd blocked the road while Sam Pyles tried to get his ambulance through. For the next eight and a half months, the bodies would remain at Pyles. Hundreds of locals and tourists would stream through the funeral parlor.

Harold Martin, the embalmer, had to keep oil on the bodies to preserve them.

"Her skin was just like a piece of leather," the mortician elaborated.

The process of removing mold from the bodies, periodically required

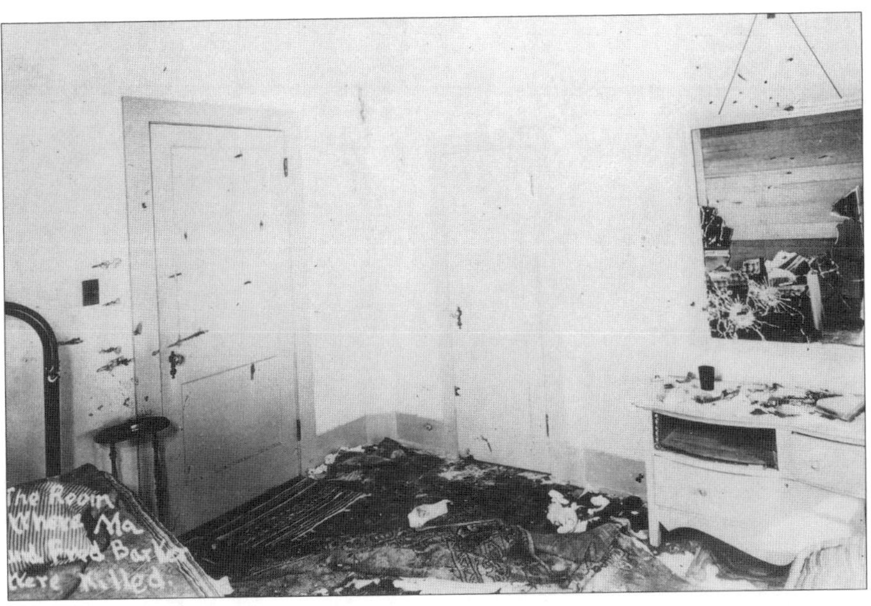

The room where Fred and Kate Barker held the agents at bay, destroyed in the aftermath. Bullets smashed the beveled glass mirror over the dressing table. (Author's Collection)

while they were held in Florida, ended with the appearance of Kate's estranged husband. He surfaced after eight months to remove the bodies to Oklahoma.

Through the morbidity that surrounded the death of Kate Barker, troubling questions arose regarding the life and death decision made by Fred Barker. Couldn't Fred, whose time was up, have surrendered in order to spare his mother her horrible death?

The earliest coverage of the shootout hosted Kate's promotion from a passive figure traveling with the Barkers to the "Brains" of the Barker gang. Previous references to the mother of the Barker boys were nondescript. She was called merely "mother," the woman "kept" by the Barkers.

She'd been the quiet figure known only to a few policemen and insiders to the Barker gang. Kate changed into "Ma" Barker overnight. The image, created in the newspapers, gathered speed. Like a sacrificial lamb she accepted the guilt for an era. Hoover's conclusion, written in the florid, antiquated language he preferred, was that Kate Barker had lived like a "veritable beast of prey."

Alvin Karpis and Harry Campbell had just left the Barkers and were

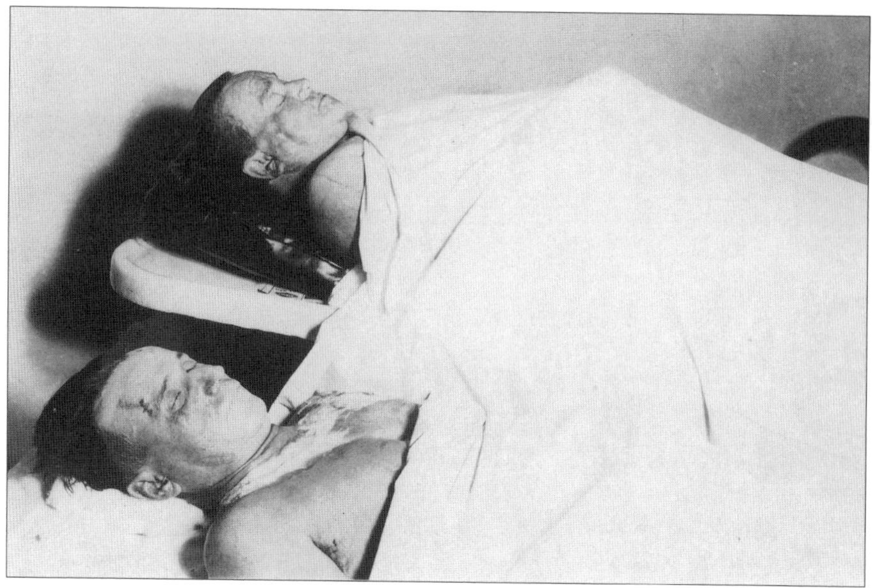

The bodies of Fred and Kate Barker went unclaimed for eight months.
(Author's Collection)

fishing in the Gulf Stream, Biscayne Bay, and Everglades City. Upon their return to Dolores and Harry Campbell's girlfriend, Wynona, they learned the fate of Fred and his mother. Telephone calls from their Cleveland connections streamed into Dolores' apartment. In a panic, the four headed for Joe Adams' place. They collected $1,000, which Adams had been holding for them. He directed them to their next stop, the Danmore Hotel in Atlantic City, New Jersey.

Dolores gritted her teeth and listened to her instructions. In a panicked daze she ran around her apartment as the list rang in her head: Pack the booties, the baby hats, and the tiny sweaters. These were the "baby things," as Dolores called her layette. She'd made everything herself. As Karpis and Campbell embarked by car, she stuffed her swollen feet into shoes and, accompanied by Wynona Burdette, climbed onto a train. She bumped along the eastern seaboard while Karpis enjoyed the comfort of an automobile.

On January 19, 1935, Earl Connelley received information regarding the whereabouts of Karpis. A nurse who had been caring for Dolores became panicked when she discovered that the woman had fled. She was upset at the sudden flight of Dolores, whom she said was due to give

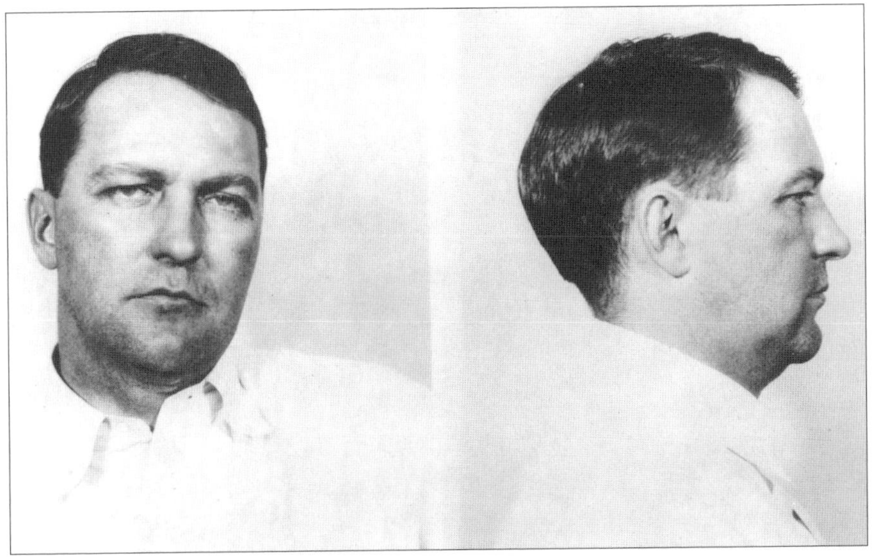

Harry Campbell accompanied Karpis on his flight from Atlantic City, leaving Wynona Burdette to face harboring charges. (National Archives)

birth between January 15 and 20. This nurse was rumored to have given the license number of Karpis' Buick to authorities. Florida police notified Atlantic City to watch for a 1935 Buick.

Atlantic City in the 1930s was a seedy resort situated on a murky New Jersey beach. At dawn on January 20, the four were sleeping in the Danmore Hotel, a stop enroute to New York, which they hoped to reach the next day. After Patrolman Elias Saab found the car near the boardwalk, police acted on a tip and stationed themselves in the front and rear doors, the lobby, and on the fourth floor. Detective Dan Wulhern knocked on the door and identified himself as a police officer.

In the shooting fray that followed, Dolores was hit in the thigh by a ricochet from either Karpis' or Campbell's gun. A detective was hit in the face by a splinter nicked off the wall by bullets. Karpis, who claimed to have tied Dolores' wound with a sheet and helped her into some clothes, left her in a stairwell as he climbed out a window. Campbell, dressed only in his underwear, joined the descent down the window, running off to steal a Pontiac sedan while Karpis exchanged shots with the officers. Karpis later claimed he'd gone back to the alley to find Dolores. When he went returned, both women were gone.

Dolores, shot in the leg, was taken to a hospital, her age listed as

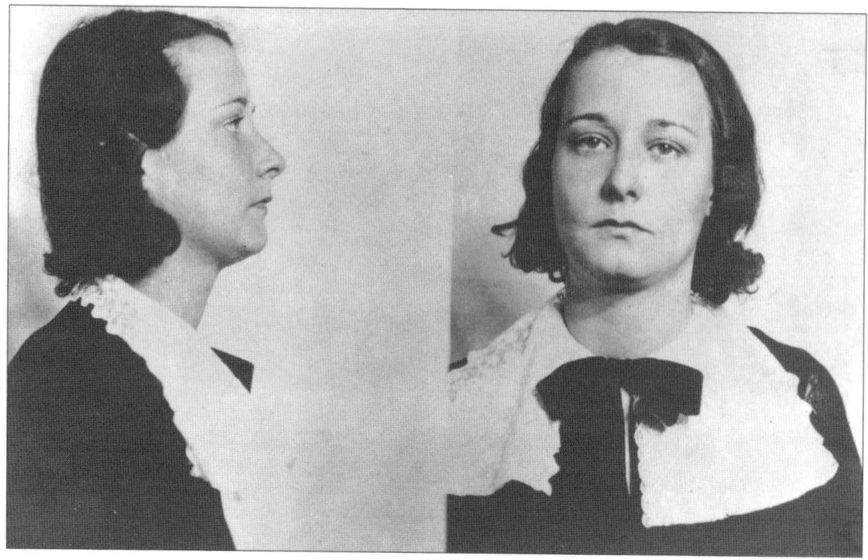

Wynona Burdette, captured in Atlantic City with Dolores Delaney, had once turned down a deal to turn Harry Campbell over to authorities. He showed his appreciation by leaving her stranded in a shootout. (National Archives)

twenty-one. Winona gave her age as twenty-two.

A few days later, after the two women were taken to Philadelphia, Dolores gave birth to a son. Karpis' parents traveled from Chicago to pick up the boy, named Raymond Alvin after his father. They were living at 2842 North Francisco Avenue, where they worked as custodians. Karpis' two sisters also lived in the apartment. His mother, who could not read English, depended upon his sisters to translate for her. Father and son would meet twenty-three years later, in the visiting room at Alcatraz.

Dolores Delaney and Wynona Burdette were treated as siamese twins from the moment of their arrests until their sentencing. On February 7, 1935, the Dade County Federal Court indicted Dolores Delaney in the harboring of Karpis in Miami. She was pinpointed to the Miami apartment on one specific day, January 15, 1935. Karpis was identified as a federal fugitive by virtue of an indictment filed the previous May 4, 1934, charging him with "conspiracy to violate the act of Congress approved June 22, 1932" in the Bremer affair. Dolores was charged not only with cohabiting with Karpis on January 15, but of doing so with the knowledge that he was indicted for Bremer.

On February 17, a scant two weeks after giving birth, Dolores was moved back to Miami with Wynona. From there she went to Jacksonville on March 5, where she was locked in a cell on the thirty-fifth floor to prevent escape. They had been brought in secret to Miami from Jacksonville, with the usual precautions taken out of fear that Karpis would return to free his woman. The women had by then agreed to plead guilty but refused to trade information for a light sentence recommendation.

On March 26, 1935, both women went before Judge Halsted L. Ritter of the U.S. District Court. They were not represented by counsel. They made no comment in their own defense, asking only what they were pleading to and answering "guilty" as W. Sanders Gramling, U.S. Assistant District Attorney, read the indictments.

A Department of Justice agent told of their association with Karpis and Campbell through Miami, and their flight to Atlantic City while Karpis and Campbell were sought for the kidnapping of Edward Bremer. Judge Ritter said,

"Kidnapping has taken the country and it is up to us to stop it. The girl companions of kidnappers must understand that it is not heroic to associate with them."

The prison sentence was divided by Judge Ritter into three parts:

I. three years each on indictments of a felony by failing to report Karpis' whereabouts to federal officers;

II. two years each on an indictment naming both of the women in a conspiracy to harbor and conceal Karpis. In addition, they were to be served concurrently with:

III. two years each on another conspiracy indictment and six months each on indictments charging them individually with harboring and concealing Karpis while knowing that a fugitive from justice warrant had been issued against him are to be served concurrently with the three-year term.

After the passing of sentence, Dolores asked that her "baby things," which she made and purchased, and her own jewelry and clothes be given back to her. Judge Ritter ordered the return of her property.

The district was a feeder for progressive cottages at Alderson, but

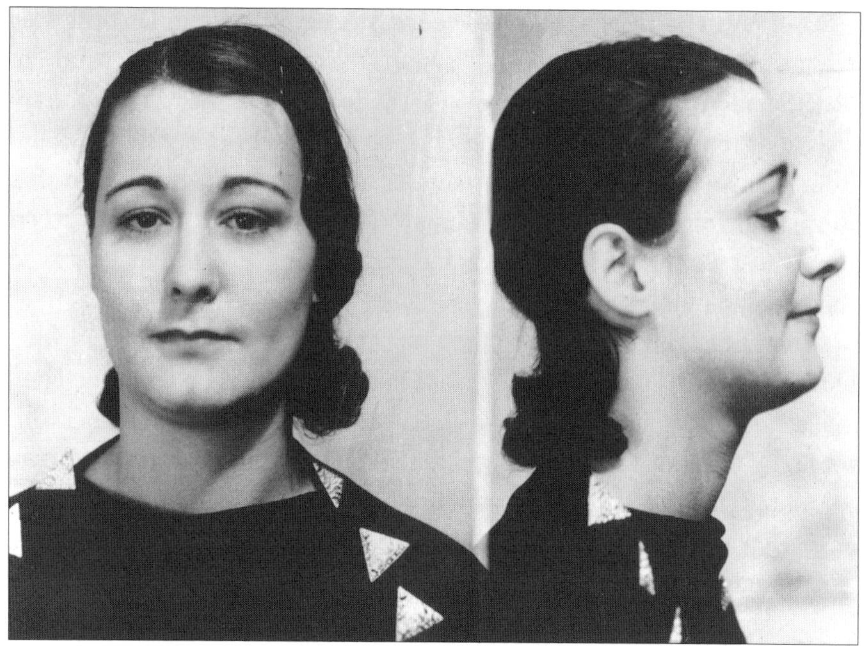

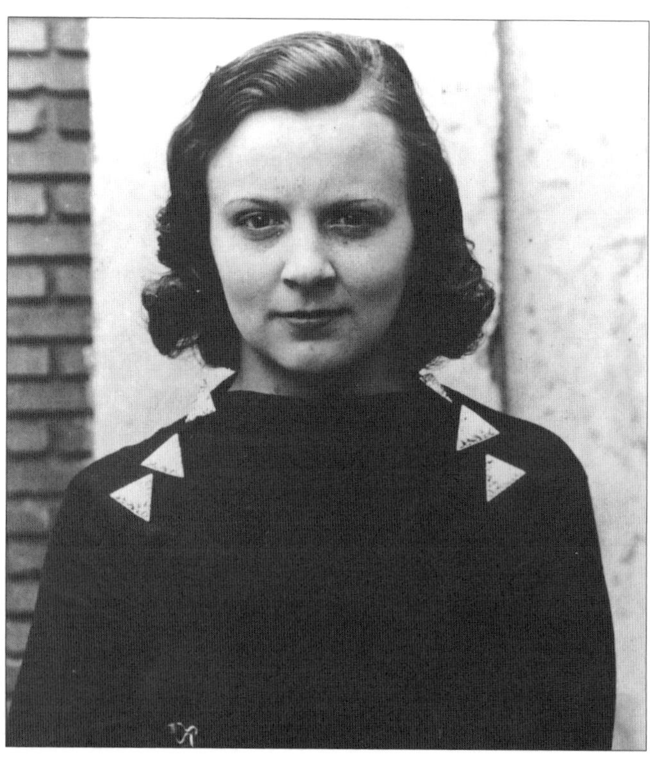

Wynona Burdette and Dolores Delaney, wearing identical dresses, were given equal treatment in court. (National Archives)

Dolores was not to be placed with her sister, Jean Delaney Crompton. Yet other relatives had been incarcerated together; Kathryn Kelly served out much of her life term with her mother, Ora Shannon. By virtue of her two-year commitment to Alvin Karpis, Dolores was placed into the "incorrigible" category. She'd serve her time in the steel cells of Milan with the other wives and girlfriends of public enemies who had steadfastly refused to testify.

Her time, all together, would amount to five years, more than any other woman of the era had gotten. While the harboring law only provided for a maximum of two years on each count, her sentences in two cases would run consecutively, with only the third case running concurrently. Winona Burdette was given the same sentencing arrangement, but her entry into Milan listed her anticipated stay as being six months. Both women were delivered to Milan on March 29, 1935.

One month after the birth of Dolores' child, federal prosecutors in Chicago requested the return of Helen Gillis. They placed a hold against her in Illinois. Now a ward of Sanford Bates, Director of the Federal Bureau of Prisons, Mrs. Gillis' removal to Chicago in March of 1935 sparked a controversy. The publication of the book, *Ten Thousand Public Enemies*, by Courtney Ryley Cooper, under the auspices of Hoover, had forced Bates to a confrontational question.

"If [Gillis] gives you any stories of a confidential nature about the jail are you going to sell them out to some novelist to write stories on?"

E.A. Tamm was astonished.

"Have you ever known us to do that?" he responded by letter.

"I certainly have, you have a book full of them just printed . . . '*Ten Thousand Public Enemies* . . . '" Bates continued. "It's just a little bit of a sarcastic inquiry as to whether we can do business with you. . . . "

On May 29, 1935, Helen Gillis was indicted by the grand jury in San Francisco along with the roster of people who had worked with Gillis there. "Fatso" Negri, Tobe Williams, John Paul Chase, Jack and Grace Perkins, among others, were featured in the indictment.

Fatso Negri pleaded guilty and became the government's chief witness in the trial of the other defendants. In a dramatic moment during the trial, he would tell a story of two gangsters very much at odds with each other. During the nights of planning the South Bend robbery, behind the schoolhouse outside of Chicago, Gillis had turned to Dillinger.

"You're worth $15,000. I'm only worth $5,000. But pretty soon I'll have as much reward offered for me as there is for you," Gillis had said.

Negri's six-month sentence would expire on June 25, 1935. He had pleaded guilty to violation of the Dyer Act, had been sentenced to two years, sentence suspended, and was placed on probation for five years. The roster continued.

- Thomas C. "Tobe" Williams, who gave his age as seventy-five, and who had an amputated leg with the other leg infected, was tried and convicted. His original sentence of eighteen months and a $5,000 fine, which he paid, was reduced to one year and one day.
- John Paul Chase was confined for life in Alcatraz. He was found guilty of the killings of Agents Cowley and Hollis.
- Frank Cochran, a Reno garage man who'd been acting secretely as a government informant, stood trial and was convicted, sentenced to one year and one day, and fined $2,000. His wife, Anna, resisted removal from Carson City, Nevada. The government later charged him with a double-cross.
- Jack Perkins pleaded guilty and was sentenced to two years and fined $1,000.
- Clarence Lieder, who arranged the ammunition buy on the day Gillis died, pleaded guilty, and was sentenced to one year and one day and fined $1,000.
- Anthony "Soap" Moreno, who provided Gillis with hideouts, stood trial, was found guilty and sentenced to six months in the county jail.
- Louis Tambini was acquitted. Arthur Pratt entered a nolle prosequi.
- Henry Hall was found guilty by a jury, sentenced to six months in the county jail, and fined $2,000.
- Eugene Mazet, a service station operator, was acquitted.
- Frankie Field and Vincent Markovich, bartenders at the Bank Buffet where Gillis' gang hung out, got a directed verdict of "not guilty."
- Grace Perkins was acquitted and danced on the steps of the

courthouse, in spite of the fact that her husband had received a two-year sentence.

- William Schivo and Ralph Rizzo got nolle prosequi.

Sally Backman, while not a defendant in *U.S. v. Chase et al.*, was held and, in June 1935, admitted to her activities with Chase until the time Gillis was killed.

She testified against John Paul Chase, and her interviews with agents and prosecuting attorneys left them with the impression that she had given a straightforward account of her activities.

She sat in the courtroom, her eyes screened beneath a veiled hat, as Marino, Tambini, Grace Perkins, and Vince Markovich watched her. She related how Tambini had driven her out to see Gillis and "Johnny" Chase, near Louis Parente's resort in El Verano. She implicated Vince Markovich, who brought a note from Chase and took her to another rendezvous. That was the juncture that brought the gang into Nevada, she explained. California had become "too hot," as Frank Cochran had been acting secretly as a government informant. Her testimony relayed the tough circumstances that Gillis and his wife had fallen into. They'd slept in the woods, rolled up in blankets. Higher-class accommodations would be a bed in a car already loaded down with machine guns.

"We traveled across the country. We always parked along some riverbank and camped and bought our food in some town and cooked it in camp. We went in some restaurants and ate and brought food out to Gillis. He never went into a restaurant."

"Who would bring out the food?

"Helen Gillis . . . and Mrs. Perkins and I would help her."

With the indictments of the other defendants, in April 1935, came a request by the Justice Department to hold Helen Gillis at the U.S. Detention Facility at Milan, "in order to insure her apprehension and ultimate removal to California." A change in attitude would occur, and by September 1935 she'd been in prison less than a year. With "good time" allowance, her impending release was scheduled for September 26. The U.S. Attorney's office in San Francisco had reconsidered prosecuting her. H.H. McPike cited several reasons why a jury would sympathize with the woman. First and foremost was the precedent-setting acquittal of Grace Perkins. The wife of Jack Perkins had been acquitted by a jury who believed that "she was a woman, therefore dominated and coerced into the life by her husband."

"Especially persuasive is this defense where Gillis is concerned," he penned. "It is widely recognized that Gillis was a mad outlaw, a killer with a lust for killing. Even his own gang didn't trust him, dreaded his murderous will and tendencies. Was Mrs. Gillis dominated and her actions controlled by her fear of him?"

Suddenly the harboring law, which was, at its zenith, the strongest weapon the government had, came up for inspection. "It is a misdemeanor only, and the maximum punishment is a fine of $1,000 and imprisonment for six months."

Although Purvis had always maintained that Helen Gillis had reloaded during the battle of Barrington, and had somehow escaped being sentenced to life along with Chase for the murders of Ed Hollis and Sam Cowley, the fact remained that she was not prosecuted. The facts regarding Joseph "Fatso" Negri, without whose testimony she could not be convicted, were such that he was a dubious witness. He was out on probation, and as a suspected member of the South Bend plot he was not considered credible. The San Francisco Federal Court also had its political reasons for not wanting to further prosecute Helen Gillis. It feared that an unfavorable conclusion would damage their reputation after the conclusion thus far had satisfied the people of San Francisco. In conclusion, H.H. McPike said,

"It is my judgment . . . that if Helen Gillis stands trial the jury will not, as matters now stand, convict her."

The Justice Department was not so willing to put Barrington behind them. The recently resigned Melvin Purvis had written a book which demanded that someone take another look at Helen Gillis' involvement in the gunfight that had killed Cowley. Hoover, who was putting distance between himself and Melvin Purvis, nevertheless demanded further prosecution.

"She accompanied her husband during the major portion of the period he was a fugitive," wrote Special Agent Jay Newman in response to McPike's suggestions. With the eleventh hour approaching and her release just hours away, the dispute had still not been resolved. Things became further scrambled when the government's witness against her, Fatso Negri, was injured in a car accident and installed in a hospital in

Sacramento. As she was arraigned at Milan prior to her release, she admitted to being Helen Gillis but denied being the Helen Gillis mentioned in the indictment. Regardless of his condition, Negri was scheduled as a witness for October 10.

Father Coughlin left Chicago on March 1, 1935. He was transferred to the Holy Family Parish in Canute, Oklahoma, under the supervision of Reverend L. Hugo. His sister, Mrs. Carney, directed FBI agents to that location, where they served him with a subpoena, with an affidavit of service.

He was brought out to San Francisco on March 21, 1935, to identify John Paul Chase. Claiming not to have known the true identity of Helen Gillis, he admitted that she brought her dying husband to him. In spite of some reports that had depicted the priest as having administered last rights, Father Coughlan might not have known at that point how close to death the gangster was. No mention is made in his testimony as to having administered the final prayers to the gangster.

"Mrs. Gillis begged me to take Gillis into the house," testified Coughlan.

"I refused to do so. I got into my car and told them to follow me down the road."

With Chase installed in Alcatraz for life imprisonment, the federal prosecutors allowed Helen Gillis to serve out her term.[2]

After the arrest of Dolores Delaney, Alvin Karpis went to Grace Goldstein's house in the early summer of 1935. Calling himself Ed King, Karpis lived with Fred Hunter, who lived with Connie Morris, an associate of Grace Goldstein. In Hot Springs, Arkansas, a wide-open town flourished. The Chief of Detectives, Herbert "Creeping Jesus" Akers, and Chief of Police Joe Wakelin presided over the operation of Grace Goldstein, who ran a brothel at 123 Palm Street. Under his guidance she moved her business to the Haterie Hotel at 233 Central Avenue. Karpis stayed there safely for several months. Karpis' hideout was eventually discovered. The officials who had comprised the police net sanctioning his presence were prosecuted. During the FBI presentation to the federal court in Little Rock, the defendants were Akers, Wakelin, Lieutenant Cecil Brock, and Goldstein.

All of the defendants were sentenced to serve two years each. Grace Goldstein alone took the stand. Like Dolores Delaney, she was sentenced harshly. In addition to the boiler plate two years, an additional five years for violation of the White Slave Traffic Act was added on. Investigations had revealed that she'd transported her niece, Margaret, from Blossom, Texas, to Hot Springs to engage in prostitution.

In contrast to the government's attitude toward Little Rock and Hot Springs, Arkansas, Hoover had made the determination one week after Dillinger's death that conditions in the East Chicago, Indiana, Police Department would never be pursued on a federal level:

"I do not see that it falls within our jurisdiction at all," he wrote the Acting Attorney General, "as to what the conditions are in Lake County insofar as they do not involve any violations of Federal Statutes . . . I do not see why this Divison should be drawn into the controversy."

Dillinger had lived with Mrs. Sage for five weeks, enough time for Sergeant Martin Zarkovich, a close friend of Sage, to have known about Dillinger's whereabouts without notifying anyone higher up. Because he had assisted in the apprehension, Zarkovich was exonerated by Sam Cowley. The Justice Department lauded East Chicago as a good example of cooperation between local police and federal officers.

At this news, Indiana State Police Captain Matt Leach balked. Three days after Dillinger's death, on July 27, Matt Leach had called Sam Cowley, who'd been promoted to inspector. A confidential informant had given Leach information that Anna Sage, Polly Hamilton, and Sergeant Martin Zarkovich "put Dillinger on the spot" in order that they might gain possession of Dillinger's wealth. He insisted that Zarkovich had known where Dillinger was for the last sixty days. In a far-fetched charge, he declared that Polly Hamilton and Anna Sage were responsible for the deaths of two East Chicago Police officers who were killed by Dillinger gangsters. Matt Leach requested that the division cooperate with him in investigating these charges.

Cowley retaliated. He challenged the police captain to conduct an investigation into the murder of the two East Chicago policemen, "particularly if it involved a dishonest Police Department." Leach had charged at the time of the murder of the two policemen, on May 25, that they were killed because they "knew too much." Leach had associated the death of the policemen with the Dillinger gang from the first minutes of the investigation. After Dillinger's death, the East Chicago police sent two containers of ammunition found in the bodies of Detectives O'Brien and Mulvihill to the Chicago office for comparison with the ammunition found in Lake Michigan after Dillinger's death.

Leach reacted to Sam Cowley's suggestion to investigate it on the state level.

"Dillinger is only one thing we have to investigate in Lake County . . . the killing last May of two East Chicago police, presumably on a hunt for Dillinger, will be among the incidents investigated," Leach stated.

Sam Cowley confided to Hoover that jealousy was the driving force behind Leach's accusations.

"Leach is the cause of a great deal of trouble," said Hoover.

The Chicago *Tribune*, which had taken an interest in Leach's statements, released long-suppressed rumors and innuendoes that never grounded themselves conclusively. There were "corrupt conditions," as the city editor phrased the East Chicago elements. Hoover detested the Washington correspondent of the *Tribune*, Mr. Duffield, whom he called a "colossal liar." He refused to speak to anyone or acknowledge the minefield that Matt Leach had opened with his accusations. Hoover believed that Leach had been true to his tendency toward exploiting and involving the press to achieve his end.

"The story," began Hoover, "is actuated solely by jealousy and envy because of the fact that the Chicago, Illinois police and the Indiana State Police, together with the *Chicago Tribune*, did not have an inside scoop on the killing of John Dillinger."

Anna Sage was saying that she knew Dillinger as Jimmy Lawrence. Dillinger paid protection to her from the proceeds of the South Bend robbery and was planning to go to Mexico when he couldn't pay any more. The city editor penned a memo that said,

" . . . the Indiana crowd decided it was about time to have him taken and, fearing he might talk, to arrange to have him taken in such a way that he would be killed instead of captured. No reflections cast on government men, but rumor is that Indiana men wanted Dillinger dead, not alive."

This sent ripples back to Crown Point, where Judge Murray felt the Zarkovich controversy emanating toward his county seat. The judge emphatically denied that Sage had ever gotten clemency because of her friendships with the local police.

By October 1935, the government was contacting its potential witnesses in the identification of Louis Piquett and the linking of him, physically, to John Dillinger. It was fairly intimated that there had been a bribe that had precipitated Dillinger's escape, yet it was not actively named due to lack of evidence. Called up from Crown Point, Indiana, however, were Sheriff Holley, Edwin Saager, Warden Lew Baker, and Ernest Blunk, who were subpoened based on Piquett's visits to Crown Point with Meyer Bogue. Anna Patzke, who'd seen Piquett together with Dillinger in the home of Jim Probasco, received a writ, as did Piquett's legal secretary and reputed mistress, Esther Anderson. A summons went to the police station in East Chicago, Indiana, addressed to P.O. Hobart Wilgus. He'd been the chief witness to the death of his friend, Officer O'Malley, the man Dillinger stood accused of killing. He'd traveled to the Crown Point county jail to identify Dillinger during the time the bandit was there.

Piquett was put on trial twice, first for his role in the harboring of Dillinger, and the second trial for protecting Van Meter. In both trials, his conduct during Evelyn Frechette's St. Paul trial would come under scrutiny. The U.S. Attorney requested transcripts. He wanted to pour over Piquett's remarks, especially about Dillinger, made to the jury in the opening phases of Evelyn's defense.

Piquett's trial was conducted in the face of diminished public interest. It was felt that Dillinger was now history. Alongside the continuing saga of the trial of Bruno Richard Hauptmann for the kidnapping of the Lindbergh baby, and the Third Ocean Crossing of Amelia Earhart, sat tired accounts of the Piquett's main defense: He'd been planning to turn in his gangster client.

Art O'Leary testified that Piquett had introduced Dillinger to James Probasco.

"Did Piquett introduce Probasco to Dillinger?"

"Yes."

"What did Piquett say?"

"He said, 'Jimmy, this is my famous client, John Dillinger.'"

Art O'Leary was joined by Dr. Loeser and Dr. Cassidy, who all testified for the government. Piquett insisted that their testimony was not to be believed. In a three-hour effort to clear himself, he painted a picture of himself as trying to bring about Dillinger's surrender. To his temporary satisfaction, he was found not guilty of harboring John Dillinger on

January 15.

His elation was tempered by the immediate announcement of U.S. Attorney Dwight D. Green that "we will proceed to the trial of Piquet on the charge of harboring and concealing Van Meter." On March 2, 1935, he attempted to file a pleading which declared that he'd been previously acquitted on January 14. This far-fetched attempt to free himself didn't go further than his typewriter. On June 25, 1935, a jury convicted him for harboring Homer Van Meter during the period of the gangster's plastic surgery.

Louis Piquett was received in Leavenworth on May 9, 1936, after his jury verdict of "guilty" for violation of Sec. 88 and 246 Title 18 U.S.C., and fined $1,000. Judge Sullivan sentenced him to two years and a fine of $1,000. He immediately appealed it. The Court of Appeals later affirmed the conviction. Evidence had been obtained during the Van Meter case that he had tried to bribe a deputy marshall so as to influence the jury. Because he was closely watched, he was unable to complete his plans. The government branded him "arrogant," a word that would prevent his early release and would follow him through a penal system that would describe him as "self-confident, brazen, contemptuous, evasive, antagonistic and bitter."

He came up for parole in 1936 but was denied on the grounds that he was to be considered a menace to society. In contrast to Piquett, who never recovered from the ravages of the Dillinger era, Anna Sage faced a deportation hearing with a surprising lack of bitterness. Held before the Department of Labor in 1935, the hearing was instrumental in insuring that the woman would leave the United States permanently. Melvin Purvis was by now a former agent, having left the Justice Department's Division of Investigation. In spite of his diminished standing, Purvis did what he could to help her. The ex-Special Agent in Charge testified that he had promised Mrs. Sage that he'd have the deportation order dismissed in return for her participation in Dillinger's capture.

A federal judge ruled that such a promise was not within the jurisdiction of an officer outside the Department of Labor. When she was deported in 1936, New York reporters asked if she felt she had been "double-crossed by the Government in the deportation proceedings."

"I have never felt that way," she replied.

Pat Cherrington came up for her first parole hearing on April 26,

1935. Her sister, Opal Long, had already been released and was caring for Pat's child. During the course of her interview, Cherrington refused to implicate Pat Reilly as the person who had driven her onto the property owned by Emil Wanatka called the Little Bohemia. Reilly was sentenced at Madison, Wisconsin, to fourteen months in the El Reno, Oklahoma, penitentiary.

"I don't want to appear stubborn or hateful about it, she explained. "I hate to see somebody else get into trouble over some foolishness of mine."

"As I said before, the only reason for interrogating you is in order to develop to the satisfaction of the Board, the facts as to your character . . . if you take your stand with the underworld or with society, if you prefer to stand with the underworld and protect them, it follows that you are not a good parole risk," stated a member of the Parole Board.

Upon hearing this, she agreed to name Pat Reilly.

"Oh, I see," the board responded. "Well, it didn't make a particle of difference whether you told us or not, who you left with, we have it right here in the record."

After establishing that Pat had employed Mrs. Betty Neatz to take care of her daughter, the parole board challenged her character as a mother.

"You tried to bring the girl up right?"

"I certainly have."

"Don't you realize you were setting a terrible example for that poor kid?"

"She never knew about what I did."

"Do you realize you marked her for life?"

"I do now. I always tried to keep her clean and gave her a good home and everything she needed."

The board was less than impressed.

"You put a stigma on her life she will never live down and may be the result of her ruin later; with a gangster's moll for a mother . . . "

Pat felt aggrieved. "I have taken care of the youngster ever since she was born," she cried. "I could have adopted her out, some of the best people wanted her, but I couldn't give her up."

The parole board concluded that "the applicant's attitude does not forecast reformation."

Ultimately, Pat Cherrington's maximum term expired on July 5, 1936. After serving nineteen months on the Wisconsin conviction, she was paroled in October 1935. As her release became imminent, a new order for a bench warrant was written to rearrest her for harboring Dillinger at the home of Hamilton's sister on April 19, 1934. It was issued on May 15, 1935. Four months after her maximum term expired, Pat Cherrington was again arrested and held on $5,000 bail. On February 28, 1936, Pat Cherrington officially pleaded guilty before Federal Judge Fred M. Raymond to another charge of conspiring to harbor and conceal Dillinger. She admitted in Grand Rapids Federal Court to charges of conspiring to harbor and conceal Dillinger along with Mrs. Anna Steve, John Hamilton's sister. Pat Cherrington was officially sentenced to serve five additional months at Milan.

Anna Steve had been hounded since the grand jury convened at Sault Ste. Marie, Michigan, on January 8, 1935, to study an indictment charging Anna Steve with being an accessory in the theft of the car. This stemmed from the charge that she accepted a car from Hamilton, which he had said was "too hot" for him to drive. According to the indictment, Hamilton had told her not to use the car until 1935. Her son was included in the indictment for allegedly parking the car in their garage. Her attorneys, Robert Hudson and Claude Coates, served a motion to quash the indictment. The motion was denied as the trial, originally set for January 8, 1935, was postponed in order to allow two witnesses, Special Agents R.D. Brown and Harold Reinecke, the opportunity to appear at the trial of Louis Piquett.

Unfortunate as Mrs. Steve's predicament was, she appears to have had more help than the indigent Pat Cherrington in stating her case. Her physicians and attorneys were standing by, trying to help her. By February 1935, her health was deteriorating, a matter that her attorneys tried to bring to the attention of the court. The physicians treating her were concerned about her weakened heart muscles, liver and kidney condition, which was causing her to experience dropsy. Her attorneys argued that she could not afford additional expense by having the venue moved from Sault Ste. Marie to Marquette. She was suffering from severe anxiety and protectiveness toward her five children, ranging in age from two to seventeen years. The attorneys feared the children would be summoned to testify the way Wallace Salt had been called at the St. Paul trial of his mother, Augusta Salt.

Indeed, the seventeen-year-old son of Anna Steve was arrested with her. On April 3, 1935, the two were brought in on a bench warrant, and held on $1,000 bail. The trial commenced in Grand Rapids, from June 3 to 7, 1935. Several lawmen testified, among them Special Agent A.E. Lockerman, who had been at the Biograph Theater. Joining him was Special Agents H.H. Reinecke, R.D. Brown, and J.H. Rice, along with Willard Welsh, the sheriff of Sault Ste. Marie. The roster was expanded with the testimony of Lillian Holley, Ernest Blunk, and Edwin Saager of Crown Point, who were called to identify Dillinger's likeness.

Mrs. Steve's son was acquitted on June 7, 1935, by a jury; she was found guilty after testimony by newspaper employee James Ripley. He arrived under a subpoena to bring with him "records of subscription of Mr. or Mrs. Anna Steve to the *Evening News* of Sault Ste. Marie . . . which contained any news items pertaining to the activities of John Dillinger and John Hamilton."

The ironies in the ordeal of John Hamilton's sister were many. Certainly the most tragic component was the fact that, throughout her four months served in the Grand Traverse Jail, she didn't know whether her brother was dead or alive.

To Louis Piquett, the irony was his lifelong disbarment. When Dillinger's attorney was released from Leavenworth in 1938, he attempted, unsuccessfully, to reinstate himself as a citizen and as an attorney in the state of Illinois. His attempts continued until March 1951, when Piquett wrote a letter of desperation to the Supreme Court. He would die before the end of the year:

" . . . Fifteen years of my life have been obliterated . . . My case became Cause Celebre at the time of my conviction because of the unfavorable publicity of my then client, which resulted in great misfortune to me. Any person who has known me can readily understand that I at no time desired to strengthen the elements of the criminal class of our society . . . I have laid open my heart to [the Justice Department] . . . and their only answer was that it was not because of me but because of the stigma of the name of Dillinger. . . ."

Through dead letters, strange remnants of emotion outlived the era. A poem once written by Pat Cherrington remains in her old prison file.[3]

"Love heals the wounds that sorrow leaves, love brightens darkest skies, love wipes away the burning tears, Love mends the broken heart & brings the smiles to lips again, love holds the magic something, that brings gladness [*sic*] out of peace.

Patricia Young."

*"I've never gotten anyone in trouble. "I've always refused to 'talk' and that's my policy for the future."*

*—Opal Long,*
*interviewed in the Minneapolis Workhouse*

# Postscript
# "Souls of the Just"

Out of the collective body of Dillinger's female associates, only Mary Kinder, Mary Longnaker, Polly Hamilton, and Pearl Elliott escaped prosecution.

Dillinger's funeral in the home of Emmett and Audrey Hancock was constantly interrupted by reporters bent on tabloid speculation. Reporters listed many former girlfriends of Dillinger appearing, such as Mary Longnaker and Pearl Elliot. Mary Kinder, who had to fight off reporters while hiding in the arms of Hubert Dillinger, did attend the funeral with her sister, Margaret Behrens.

At the time of Dillinger's wake, Pearl Elliott was in no condition to attend. She had returned to her mother's home. There she suffered from advanced cancer. When federal agents tried to interview her, they learned that she was numbed by morphine. Her abdomen was filled with spreading cancerous cells. She died on August 10, 1935, at the age of forty-seven. She was buried in Greenlawn Cemetery in Frankfort, Indiana.

Dewey Elliott survived Pearl. He lived in Indianapolis into the 1940s, when his mother, Anna, passed away. At the time of Anna's death, the family still resided at 1136 South Delphos Street, the house they had inhabited since the 1920s.

Mary Longnaker had married her boyfriend, Sherman Claude Constable on July 19, 1934, and lived in a Dayton basement apartment with him. Their hope, that her association with Dillinger might bring in some money, faded with Dillinger's death. She and Constable were divorced, and Constable soon remarried. Howard Longnaker, the man who Dillinger had so bitterly fought on Mary's behalf, would die tragically. After the divorce from Claude Constable, Mary married a third time, and was divorced again in 1953. Claude Constable died in October, 1976, in Fort Lauderdale, Florida. Mary's brother, James Jenkins, who'd been imprisoned with Dillinger in the June 10, 1928, murder of grocer Jack Burton, was buried in Nashville, Indiana. Mary died in 1991.

The brother of Mary Kinder and Margaret Behrens, Earl "The Kid" Northern, died in 1936 of tuberculosis on June 29, 1936, at thirty-five years of age, while incarcerated in the Indiana State Penitentiary at Michigan City. He was interned in the Harley J. Carlisle Funeral Home, Michigan City.

The least known of the Dillinger girlfriends, Elaine Dent, remained an enigma. The woman who accompanied John "Red" Hamilton through the fall of 1933 failed to appear in court on a felony charge of accessory to murder on September 19, 1934. Her bail of $2,000 was forfeited. Her name appeared once more through an article which alleged that Hamilton, Dillinger, Elaine, and Evelyn Frechette had attended the Roman Catholic Confirmation ceremony of Elaine's daughter in Galesburg, Illinois, in November 1933.

John Dillinger's father, John Wilson Dillinger, accepted an offer to appear at an Indianapolis Theatre. He wrote off the commercial prospects by paying for his son's funeral with the proceeds. Dillinger's sister Audrey, her husband, Emmett Hancock, and Hubert Dillinger appeared with him. The Lyric Theatre vaudeville act ran for five days, then it went on the road. In garnering sympathy for his son, the elder Dillinger became a symbol of survival. George Bazso, the bartender of the Little Bohemia Lodge where Mr. Dillinger appeared, got to know him.

"He was a nice, slow-moving, Indiana farmer," Bazso related in an interview.

In Mr. Dillinger's public affability, he garnered legal immunity for his family members and moral amnesty for his deceased son.

While John Dillinger found a posthumous vindication, the women he'd left behind suffered. Hoover continued to exercise power over the incarcerations of the Dillinger women. On November 11, 1935, he penned a letter to the Superintendent of the U.S. Detention Farm, Milan. In it he said that Warden Johnson, from Alcatraz, had called to his attention the fact that four women in Milan had husbands at Alcatraz: Kathryn Kelly, Patricia Cherrington, Evelyn Frechette, and Dolores Delaney, the sister of Jean Delaney Crompton. Cherrington and Spark were receiving letters every month from Milan. Evelyn Frechette had gotten on friendly footing with Welton Spark, from whom she still had not obtained a divorce.

Hoover wanted all the "cases treated alike": The wife may write to her husband only one letter every two months. She could receive one answer every two months, provided they had not forfeited their privileges. Correspondence must deal with matters of a legal or business nature, and not for the purpose of "institution gossip or comparison." Johnson was authorized to withhold any letter of "frivolous or improper character."

Welton Spark remained married to Evelyn throughout his incarceration. Evelyn Frechette didn't obtain her divorce from Welton Spark as quickly as she had hoped. They were still married as late as 1941, when Spark expressed hope to the Federal Bureau of Prisons that he might some day return to her. According to Alvin Karpis, Spark and Cherrington posed as members of the Dillinger gang while on The Rock. They remained blood brothers in Alcatraz, living in adjoining cells, numbers 199 and 200. On March 28, 1940, after serving his time in Alcatraz since his transfer there in September 1934, he was again returned to Leavenworth. At the time of his transfer, he reported that his wife, Evelyn Frechette, was "traveling with a road show and not in need of relief." He expressed the hope that he could become reunited with his wife, "if she could be located."

Spark became eligible for parole in September 1942. His freedom brought no changes of behavior or attitude. He continued on the path of petty infractions and imprisonments.

Arthur Cherrington was transferred to Alcatraz from Leavenworth on September 4, 1934, along with Welton Spark. His record as AS-199

Evelyn Frechette after the Dillinger Era.
(William J. Helmer)

was initially troubled. He lost one week yard privileges in 1935 for passing a magazine to Spark in his adjoining cell. In May of the same year, he helped Spark, AZ-200, beat up Blackwood, AZ 180, a stool pigeon. Both Spark and Cherrington went into solitary confinement on a "restricted diet," that is, bread and water. In 1936, Cherrington participated in strikes and refused to work. He was again placed in solitary on the dreaded "piss and punk," the vernacular term at Alcatraz for bread and water. When asked why he continued to place his impending parole in jeopardy, he said,

"I cannot be a heel. I have to go with the rest. I would not feel right if they gained something, and I was to get benefit of it, and not have a share in getting it."

He was thrown back into solitary in 1939 due to another work action. This one was based on his charges that he'd been fired from his job in the laundry ironing room due to discrimination. By 1939 his privileges were again restored. Cherrington began steering his rebellion and intelligence into legal research. That same year, in District of Northern California before Judge Sure, he filed a writ of habeas corpus based on his allegation that the original sentence, which imposed five years on count three, comprised double jeopardy and that his imprisonment after May 1939 was illegal. He was deemed eligible for parole in 1942. He died in September, 1970.

Evelyn Frechette traveled with the road show referred to by Welton Spark in his interview with the administration at Leavenworth. Along with Mary Kinder, she carved out a marginal existence on the coat tails of the Dillinger publicity until 1941, when she listed her address as being c/o *Billboard Magazine*, Cincinnati. She was freed from the Federal Facility at Milan on January 30, 1936, and immediately returned to her home on the Menominee Reservation in Neopit. She'd been issued a conditional release on a "pauper's oath" on January 30, 1936. The U.S.government later levied a tax against the Menominee Tribe for $1,000, the amount of her unpaid fine. It was repaid twenty-one years later. The U.S. government took the fine in annual deductions from the funds of the Menominee Indian tribe, based on the per capita share that would have gone to Evelyn Frechette as a member of the tribe.

In addition to her carnival "Crime Does Not Pay" show, Evelyn Frechette co-authored a morality pamphlet, a trendy genre popular in the late 1930s. This series tackled subjects as diverse as anti-communism and isolationism. Evelyn's "book," as she proudly called it, preached a stern message:

"It is my sincere wish that this publication be a warning and an object lesson to other young girls and boys," she wrote.

After her deportation in 1936 to Romania, Anna Sage lived in a quiet town in southwestern Romania, Timisoara. For the record and for infinity, Anna Sage never admitted having taken him in with knowledge that he was John Dillinger. He was known to her, she maintained, as Jimmy Lawrence, Chicago Board of Trade Clerk. This lie would contribute to the mythology of Dillinger having somehow escaped death, with Jimmy Lawrence being there in his place and stead.

By August 1935, a few radical factions were calling Dillinger's death an "assassination." The state's attorney's office, whose representative couldn't give his name, said, "Dillinger could have been taken peacefully

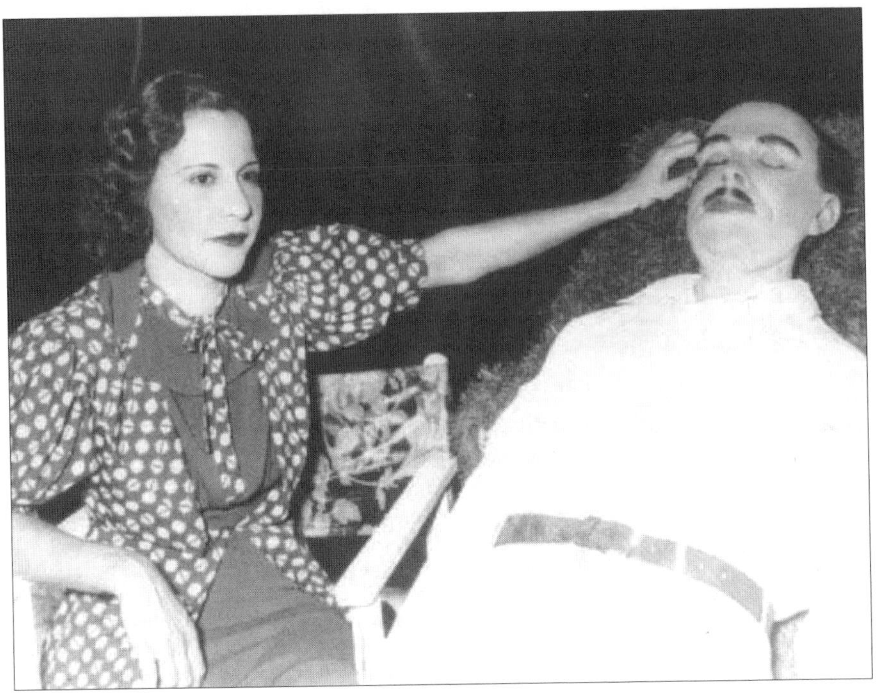

Evelyn Frechette, shown beside a wax figure of Dillinger. "Crime Does Not Pay" show, 1936. (Sandy Jones/The John Dillinger Historical Society)

. . . he could have been taken to headquarters for a seven cents fair on a street car."

The insinuations were:

- Dillinger used a real gun, not a wooden gun, in the Crown Point escape.
- His delivery was arranged by a group of men who received $3,500 in payment.
- These men protected him while he was a fugitive.
- These men wanted him killed for two reasons—his money ran out. If he were to remain alive, he would implicate them.
- Policemen Lloyd Mulvihill and Martin O'Brien of East Chicago were mysteriously murdered on May 24, 1934, because they had unwittingly interrupted a meeting of the conspirators, who feared they "saw too much."
- Dillinger had arranged to flee Chicago in a Chicagoan's car on July 23 and go to Mexico. The price was to be $10,000.

- Anna Sage had a triple motive: to get the reward; to remain in the country; and to help her friend, Martin Zarkovich.
- In 1936, an attack on Hoover and the FBI was launched when it became known that the U.S. Secret Service was secretly investigating the murder of Dillinger and Ed Green.

By the close of 1935, some of the women who had been incarcerated for harboring the "public enemies" were reclaiming their freedom.

Opal Long was visited by the Justice Department shortly after Dillinger's death in the Minneapolis Workhouse. "I've never gotten anyone in trouble," she told them angrily. "I've always refused to 'talk' and that's my policy for the future."

At that point she concluded the interview, leaving the agents frustrated and annoyed. She was released earlier than the other women. On November 29, 1934, Opal Long was released from the Minneapolis Workhouse and returned to her niece, J. Young (a pseudonym). The child remained in her care during the remaining years that Pat would stay in prison.

Patricia Cherrington went back to her life in Chicago after her troubles wound to a conclusion. She'd served two sentences in Milan for essentially the same crime. After her parole she was demonized by J. Edgar Hoover, who wrote scathing essays about her well into the late 1930s. She managed to obtain a divorce from Art Cherrington and made the news again in 1938 when an associate was arrested.

After the Dillinger era, she made her living as a waitress. The health problems that had plagued her undoubtedly shortened her life. Her obituaries mention that no family members stepped forward after she died in her sleep on May 3, 1949, at 1424 North Clark Street. Pat's death was reported by Opal Long, who visited the county morgue on the condition of anonymity. Before Pat's internment in an unmarked grave in Wunders Cemetery, her remains were tended by a funeral director at 716 North State Street. Opal Long died of heart failure at the age of 63 on July 31, 1969 in Chicago, where she'd married a former Pearl Elliott associate.

Anna Steve died on May 20, 1948, in Sault Ste. Marie. Her nephew, Bruce Hamilton, insists that John Hamilton survived.

Dolores Delaney moved around quite a bit before her "conditional release" from Milan was granted on November 30, 1938. She was released on writ to the U.S. Marshal in St. Paul, Minnesota, on January

3, 1936. She returned to Milan for a brief period and went to the Southern District of Florida on writ on May 17, 1937 to June 18, 1937. She was transferred to the Detroit House of Correction on November 15, 1937, and transferred back to Milan on January 17, 1938. She was tracked by a probation officer until 1940.

J. Edgar Hoover was instrumental in suggesting to the attorney general that Dolores receive three sentences for harboring, thus preventing her from contact with her infant son through the years of his early childhood. At the same time, he accused Alvin Karpis of cruelty toward the pregnant woman, for abandoning her in Atlantic City. Had Hoover been sincere, he would have tried to obtain an earlier parole for Dolores, out of consideration for her right to know her own child.

He compounded the hypocrisy by writing essays about the woman in the same year she would be released and, ostensibly, try to build a new life. In 1938, Hoover wrote a book in which he accused Dolores of being a "cheap, deluded, silly little moll."

Helen Gillis' commitment to Milan as Inmate Number F-43 and later F-44 was filled with transfers. She entered on December 7, 1934. On December 28, 1934, she was taken to the Cook County House of Correction. She was returned on January 5, 1935. She was released to the Chicago Division on March 9, 1935, and returned on March 13, 1935. She was released overnight on November 29, 1935 to the U.S. Marshal for the Eastern District of Michigan. She was turned over to the marshall for a further hearing on bail default for $10,000, which was heard on November 29, 1935. Her transfer to San Francisco took place on December 7, 1935. She died on July 3, 1987. She was buried as "Wife" next to her husband, Lester Gillis, in St. Joseph's Cemetery in Chicago.

Also laid to rest in the Gillis family plot, alongside of Lester and Helen Gillis, is Mary R. Gillis, Lester's mother. She died in October 1961.

Marie Comforti's release the following year should have signaled her return to normal life. Instead she took a giant step back to jail. She was released from Alderson on October 11, 1935, only to be rearrested for harboring Van Meter in another location. On October 12, 1936, the paroled woman became the subject of a bench warrant issued in Chicago. She was again arrested on December 7, 1936.

Ella Finerty had similarly been rearrested on June 19, 1936, but was brought to the District Court in Chicago and freed on her own recognizance of bail. Marie's natural mother, Eleanor Krause, died on June 17, 1943, in the sanitarium in Bremen Township, where she'd lived since 1920.

After teaching courses in the U.S. Federal Penitentiary at Leavenworth on "elementary and criminal law," Louis Piquett was officially released from prison on January 10, 1938, on an oath of poor convict. His wife remained loyal to him, having written dozens of letters to the prison administration asking for his release. He was never reinstated to the Illinois Bar. Louis Piquett died on December 12, 1951, in Chicago.

Viola Carroll, the notorious "Rattlesnake" who tried to get possession of Tommy Carroll's body after his death, also challenged Carroll's brother, Charles, for Carroll's meager estate.

After Dillinger, Anna Sage lived the life of a well-to-do citizen. She died on April 28, 1947, having lived through the Second World War without being deported out of Romania, and seeing the Communist takeover come throughout her country. She resumed her maiden name of Ana Cumpanas when she returned to Romania. Her age at her death of a liver ailment was fifty-eight years old. She claimed until her death that she'd been cheated out of her reward, which she told the people of Romania had been $70,000 rather than the $10,000 it had actually been. Her son served in the Marine Corps in World War II. She often expressed her nostalgia for the United States.

Some rumors about Anna Sage after her return to Romania, which was soon to undergo persecution by the Nazis and would become a war-ravaged country, say that she was victimized by the Romanian protection racket who demanded money, thinking her a rich American who had been highly paid by Uncle Sam. She was rumored to have gotten plastic surgery and then fled to Egypt. In Cairo she entered a sanitarium. She tried acting, and working as a hostess in a resort. She died of a liver ailment in 1947 in the little Romanian town of Timisoara.

Her friend, Polly Hamilton, returned to her hometown of Fargo, but didn't remain there long. She went back to Chicago, where she lived until her death, on February 19, 1969, as Edythe Black.

After Sam Cowley's death, Mrs. Cowley was given a job with the FBI. She stayed with the Justice Department until 1948, when she asked to resign in order to spend more time with her two sons.

Likewise, the widow of W. Carter Baum worked for the FBI until her

1944 resignation. The wife of Special Agent W. Carter Baum, killed by Gillis at twenty-nine years of age, was left in Washington, DC, with two children. J. Edgar Hoover, knowing her plight, offered her a job with the bureau. She accepted, and would go on to stay with the FBI for ten years. W. Carter Baum is buried at Rock Church Cemetery, Silver Spring, Maryland. Doris Lockerman, secretary to Melvin Purvis, wrote an article about her experiences in the FBI offices in the 1930s.

After Cowley's death, Earl J. Connelley, then SAC, Cincinnati, took charge of the Special Squad in Chicago. He helped run down the gang members in the Dillinger, Barker-Karpis, Kansis City Massacre and other major cases. He had entered the Justice Department in 1920, became an inspector in 1936, and then served as a field assistant director from 1940 until his retirement in 1954.

Jessie Levy died Jessie Levy Shusler in 1976.

A museum was opened by Emil Wanatka after Dillinger's death. It was at that time that Dillinger Sr. went up there to provide interviews.

"I took his father fishing once," said the late George Bazso. "Nice Indiana people. They will never argue. John Dillinger was just like that."

The Northern Lights resort is now gone. The Lodge at Little Bohemia and the neighborhing Voss' Birchwood Lodge are still thriving. In contrast to the publicity once sought by the Little Bohemia, the Voss Birchwood Lodge has sought to distance itself from the tragic events of years before.

Henry A. Voss, who coined the famous phrase, "the man you want most is up here," died with his wife, Ruth M. Voss, in a Florida automobile accident in 1958.

Father Coughlan was permitted to relocate as a parish priest in a remote part of the Archdiocese of Oklahoma City, Oklahoma. No record of his existence is found in the Archdiocese Directory. While the priest who sheltered Coughlan is listed, the gangster cleric's name has not been added to the roster. Father Coughlan did not make it into the index, entitled "Souls of the Just."

With everyone either dead or imprisoned, the brunt of the government's wrath was later visited upon the one remaining character who bore culpability in the South Bend robbery of the Merchants Bank.

Having been found guilty in the San Francisco harboring trials, on March 25, 1935, Jack Perkins was brought before four South Bend witnesses: Detective Henderson; P.G. Stahly, the bank vice president; Detective McCormick; and a teller. They identified him as having been one of the five who robbed the bank there with Dillinger, Gillis, and Homer Van Meter. Perkins would serve his two-year term for harboring Gillis and would be indicted by a grand jury on November 26, 1936, for his alleged role in South Bend. Charges that he'd killed P.O. Wagner would be dropped as late as February 1937 in a state court, with no federal prosecution to follow.

Russell Clark spent his life in prison. He first became eligible for parole in April 1954, but his application was denied. He spent at least fourteen years in solitary confinement at the Ohio State Prison in Columbus. He was released in 1968, at age seventy. Shortly after his release, on December 24, 1968, he died of cancer.

Jean Delaney Crompton was released from Alderson on March 31, 1935. She was officially released from supervision on June 12, 1935, and resumed her trade as a cashier. She walked into court with her mother and sister, Babe, to obtain a divorce from her husband, Edward, on December 20, 1935. She denied that any children had been born. Babe Delaney, as "Helen Reilly," appeared with Jean's mother to testify that Edward Crompton had abandoned Jean. Mrs. Delaney, who had resisted moving to the "wicked city," relented and moved to 6045 Kenmore Avenue in Chicago. Jean moved in with her mother after being paroled.

Beth Green was conditionally released on May 24, 1935. She was held a bit longer, and physically left the institution on August 22, 1935. She resumed a lawful life, working in the restaurant trades and remarrying. She knitted sweaters for her nieces and was a popular member of her family. Her great-niece, Myrna Otte, remembered her.

"In her later years, she worked in or managed restaurants, taverns, night spots or liquor stores. While still in her thirties, she remarried briefly and again divorced, remaining single, then, for the rest of her life. She maintained a good but somewhat risque or salty sense of humor. We loved Aunt Bess; she was the favorite aunt of all the children in the family. She quickly won a place as our children's favorite babysitter, too, when she cared for them once while we took a vacation. She certainly could adjust her behavior to the situation. It's amazing, given the level of her knowledge and involvement with the criminal element in the Twin Cities, what a closely guarded secret her experiences were."

Beth Green died on September 17, 1983, in Minnesota. Before her death, she'd returned to her former, given name of Bess. The federal agent who had been instrumental in obtaining her confession, Hugh H. Clegg, retired from service in 1954. He continued to work in the private sector of academia until his death on December 12, 1979.

The FBI agent who had led the ambush against Fred Barker and his mother, Earl J. Connolley, received a commendation from Vice President Richard Nixon for his work on the Alger Hiss investigation. He retired from active duty in 1954 and died on January 20, 1957.

Melvin Purvis retired from the Justice Department of Investigation in 1936 after a series of disputes with Director J. Edgar Hoover. He died on February 29, 1960, when a gun he was cleaning discharged and hit him.

Similarly, Matt Leach, the captain of the Indiana State Police, left his job under pressure in 1937. He was fired as a result of his refusal to withdraw his accusation that the Justice Department had overlooked the corruption in East Chicago, Indiana.

Kathryn Kelly served most of her time at Terminal Island, California, after her transfer on October 30, 1939, along with her mother, Ora L. Shannon. Kathryn served as an Editor for the *Terminal Island Gull*. In that capacity she wrote stirring articles. "The Government can never fashion from steel and stone a prison that will mean 'home' to any of its inhabitants," she wrote bitterly. She remained incarcerated until 1958, when she hired an attorney who reopened the case. Originally convicted to life imprisonment on the testimony of handwriting expert D.C. Patterson, who said that the Urshel ransom notes had been written in her handwriting, Kathryn was the victim of thinking that had attributed to her "feminine" intelligence (i.e., wiles).

The attorney filed an appeal in the U.S. District Court in Oklahoma City, which challenged the policy of keeping her on bread and water to "weaken her resolve." It also reputed the original trial judge's refusal to grant her the right to have the letters examined by another expert.

An FBI lab report dated September 23, 1933, long suppressed, was produced. It said that "detailed analysis indicated that Mrs. Kelly did not write these letters." She was conditionally released and entered into a barter arrangement with the State of Oklahoma. She was offered a job as a bookkeeper for the Oklahoma Country Home and Hospital, with the promise of a pension. One condition of her employment was her agreement not to discuss her case. She is buried in Oklahoma.

Mary Kinder lived in Martinsville, Indiana, for most of her life. She worked on an assembly line for P.R. Mallory & Co. Mary died on May 21, 1981. At the time, she was survived by three of her sisters, Margaret, Martha and Agnes. She was buried in the Floral Park Cemetery in Indianapolis.

Mary Kinder's sister, Margaret "Silent Sadie" Behrens, made the U.S. Army her career. "Marge" died in Florida on August 8, 1987.

Evelyn Frechette died on January 13, 1969, at the age of sixty-one, of a tumor that had occurred a few months before. She is buried in Woodlawn Cemetery in Shawano, Wisconsin.

Evelyn's life after Dillinger had been pocked with tragedies—her marriage to Wally Wilson, of the Menominee Reservation, was halted with his sudden death. She remained on friendly terms with Dillinger's niece, Mary.

Mary spoke of Evelyn Frechette in a letter dated October 15, 1988, to the author. She wrote:

"We enjoyed Evelyn's visits to us, as we liked her very much."

Evelyn stayed close to her home and at the age of fifty-eight married Art Tic, seventy-five, of Shawano, Wisconsin. The marriage license had been issued in Lake County, Illinois, on September 8, 1965. She knew happiness with Art Tic, who was protective of her, refusing to allow her to work outside of their home. Before his death, he shared his stories in a telephone interview with the author. He related that Evelyn liked to cook wild game and could speak some of the native language of the Menominee Tribe. She always dressed well, "never wearing slacks," he boasted. In a conversation before her death, she spoke her own eulogy to Art Tic.

"I've had one hell of a life," she said.

"I've had one hell of a life," Evelyn Frechette said in retrospect. (William J. Helmer)

# Chapter Notes

Abbreviations:

**National Archives and Records Administration (NARA):**

| | |
|---|---|
| NA — | National Archives, Washington, DC |
| NA-Region, city | NA-Region, City |
| RG — | Record Group Subtext within National Archives Citations |

**Agencies of the U.S. Federal Government:**

| | |
|---|---|
| BIA — | U.S. Department of the Interior, Bureau of Indian Affairs |
| FBOP — | U.S. Federal Bureau of Prisons |
| FBI — | U.S. Department of Justice, Federal Bureau of Investigation |
| Justice Dept. — | U.S. Department of Justice, Division of Investigation (as the FBI was known in the Dillinger era) |

**File Designations:**

| | |
|---|---|
| DF — | Dillinger File (Prefix 62-29777-) Unless otherwise noted, file designation is Reading Room, Federal Bureau of Investigation, Washington, DC |

Note:
The term "Director" refers to J. Edgar Hoover, Director, Federal Bureau of Investigation (known in 1933–1935 as the Bureau of Investigation of the Justice Department).

## Notes for Chapter 1

1. State of Illinois, Cook County, Marriage License of Evelyn Frechette to Walter Sparks, File No. 1348716, 3 August 1932; H.H. Clegg, St. Paul, to File, 4 May, 1934, DF-1665.
2. Admission Summary, Spark, Welton AZ-200, U.S. Penitentiary, General Records of the Bureau of Prisons, Records of the U.S. Penitentiary, Alcatraz, Record Group 129, Box 215, NARA, San Bruno, California: Admission Summary, Spark, Welton AZ-200, U.S. Penitentiary, General Records of the Bureau of Prisons, Records of the U.S. Penitentiary, Alcatraz, RG 129, Box 215, NA, San Bruno, CA.

   Spark was born in Milwaukee on July 22, 1907, and was raised in Sheboygan, Wisconsin, by his grandmother and widowed mother, Mamie, who worked as a cleaner and dyer. While Mamie Spark kept the family financially secure with a strong, personal work ethic, her fatherless boy ran loose. He served two years in the St. Charles School for Boys, 1922—1924 for car theft. He went on to one year in the Chicago House of Corrections. On January 22, 1926, he was sentenced to three to twenty years in Joliet for robbery. Welton Spark met Arthur Cherrington at Joliet. Welton Spark had been married in Wisconsin in approx. 1923 to Evelyn Morse. She divorced him during his imprisonment;

   Breakdown of sentence of July 20, 1932 for post office robbery: ten years on count 1, five years on count 2, five years on count 3, all to run concurrently.

   Further information on Spark: M.C. Spear, Kansas City, to Chicago, 8 March 1934; DF-118-NR5.

   Evelyn Frechette's activities in Chicago: Purvis to Michigan Division, March 18, 1934; DF-163, p. 2; Whitley, New Orleans to File, 18 March 1934; DF-161.

   Evelyn Frechette's activities prior to her marriage to Welton Sparks and the information relating to her cohabitation with her half-sister, Frances, at 3512 North Pinegrove: Metcalf to File, 23 March, 1934; -181, p.8.
3. Report on Writ of Habeas Corpus, Cherrington, Arthur AZ-199, U.S. Penitentiary, General Records of the Bureau of Prisons, Alcatraz; RG 129, Box 215, NA, San Bruno, CA: Cherrington's parents both died, his mother in childbirth. An orphan, he was sent to live with an uncle. Claiming his guardian was forcing him to study for the priesthood, he ran away to live on the streets. He was a repeat offender from 1915 to 1918, and served jail time for truancy and larceny during those years. In 1920, a more serious charge of auto theft stood with a twenty-seven-month prison sentence. In February 1925, he was arrested and sentenced to the Illinois State Penitentiary at Joliet for larceny.

4. U.S. Detention Farm Milan, Michigan, Board of Parole Hearing on Patricia Cherrington, April 26, 1935; D.E. Buehler, to Dr. Mary B. Harris, Superintendent, U.S. Industrial Institution for Women, Alderson, W.Virginia, August 16, 1934, Cherrington, Arthur AZ-199, General Records, FBOP, NA, San Bruno, CA.; "Case History of Patricia Young," U.S. Department of Justice, Federal Bureau of Prisons, Archive, FOI, 320 First St., N.W. Washington, DC 20523. She may have been born in 1904, although 1903 is generally found in the record.
5. Evelyn Frechette's nickname, Billie, is noted in a memo written by an agent of the Bureau of Investigation: J.J. Metcalf, Agent, to File, Chicago, March 23, 1934; DF-181, p. 7.
6. Birth date of Evelyn Frechette: State of Wisconsin, *Original Certificate of Death,* Evelyn Wilson (nee' Frechette), January 13, 1969, Registrar of Deeds, Shawano, WI 54166, V-39, p. 200; Art Tic, Interview, stated she was born on September 15, 1907 in Keshena, WI.
7. Menominee Chronology: (httip://www.menominee.ns/HistoryPeriods1600-1800Revised.ht)
8. Richard Polenberg, *War and Society*, New York: J.B. Lippincott Co. 1972, p. 75.
9. Frechette family birth and death: Register of Deeds, Shawano, WI. Reference to attendance at Tomah School: "Indian Girl Singer Here, Friend of Dillinger's Sweetheart, Tells How City Lured Gang Moll," *Wisconsin State Journal,* April 25, 1934; "What I Knew About John Dillinger, By His Sweetheart," *Chicago Herald & Examiner,* August 27, 1934, Pt.1, pp. 1—3; http://www.menominee.ns.../History; Telephone interview with Art Tic, by author 1988.
10. The documents relating to the population of Tomah, comprised of letters, reports, and memoranda, are Superintendent, Tomah Indian School, to Cato Sells, Commissioner of Indian Affairs, Washington, DC, June 13, 1916, Preliminary Inventories No. 163, Vol. II, p. 465, Education 800, BIA Central Classified, 1907—1939, Record Group 75, NARA, American West Division, Washington, DC.

    Gibbee, Inspector, to Commissioner, Vol. II, BIA 1907—1939, March 10,1916, RG 75, NA; Gibbee, Inspector, to Commissioner, Vol. II, BIA 1907—1939, April 19, 1916, RG 75, NA.
11. Cato Sells, Commissioner of Indian Affairs, Washington, DC, to Charles F. Peirce, Superintendent, March 10, 1922; Preliminary Inventories No. 163, Vol. II, p. 399, Flandreau, Box 820, BIA 1907—1939, RG 75, NA, American West Division;

    Byron J. Brophy, Superintendent, to Commissioner, October 2, 1935, Vol II, Flandreau, Box 820, BIA 1907—1930, NA; C.M. Knight, Inspector, to Commissioner, January 31, 1917, Vol II, Flandreau, Box 820, BIA 1907—1930, NA.

W.W. Coon, Assistant Supervisor of Schools, Flandreau School, to Commissioner, February 9, 1916; Box 810, BIA 1907—1939; Flandreau, RG 75, NA.

J.F. House, Supervisor, to Charles F. Pierce, Superintendent, March 11, 1922; Box 806, BIA 1907—1939; Flandreau, RG 75, NA; Edna Groves, Supervisor Home Economics, to Supervisors House and Stevens, November 8, 1922; Box 800, BIA 1907—1939; Flandreau, RG 75, NA; Edna Groves to House and Stevens, June 25, 1924; Box 800, BIA 1907—1939; Flandreau, RG 75, NA; Commissioner Indian Affairs to Congressman C.A. Christopherson, Sioux Falls, S.D., June 12, 1923, Vol II, Flandreau School, Box 810, BIA 1907-1939; RG 75, NA.

12. J.J. Waters, Chicago, to File, March 22, 1934, DF-173, p 8.

13. Employment records of the Menominee Lumber Mill contained information on the position and responsibilities of Charles Frechette: M.J. Wallrich, Chairman Citizens Committee, to Hon. E.B. Meritt, Assistant Commissioner of Indian Affairs, March 9, 1929; Menominee Indian Reservation, Neopit, Wisconsin, BIA 1907—1939; RG 75, NA; Charles J. Frechette Chairman, Advisory Board, Menominee, to J. Henry Scattergood, Assistant Commissioner, Washington, DC, January 9, 1933; Menominee, BIA 1907—1939; RG 75, NA; Scattergood to Charles Frechette, January 13, 1933; Menominee, BIA 1907—1939; RG 75, NA. Meeting of Employees, Menominee Indian Mills, by Mr. Smith, January 9, 1933; Menominee, BIA 1907—1939; RG 75, NA.

14 Secretary of the Interior to The Commissioner of Indian Affairs, Washington, DC, April 12, 1929; Menominee, BIA 1907—1939; RG 75, NA;

Charles H. Burke, Commissioner, copy to Secretary of the Interior, Washington, DC, to George C. Hammer, Manager, Menominee Mills, April 19, 1929; Menominee, BIA 1907—1939; RG 75, NA. Citizens' Committee report, Menominee Mills, Menominee logging operations, April 1929, BIA 1907—1939; RG 75, NA, maintained that venereal disease was their "greatest problem."

Dr. L. Culp, in one month alone during 1929, had already established a friendly relationship with the people. He'd worked on the reservation for ten years, laboring under the name "government eye doctor." Ironically, he had lost his eye while treating what he'd called a "mechanical accident" that occurred during the treatment of an unsuspected case of gonorrhea during his first year of practice. Understandably, he now harbored a fear and a hatred for this line of medicine. "These same conditions obtain apparently, in the vile holes just off the reservation, and are an added lure to the continuance of vicious thought and act. It is apparent the county itself does not realize the kind of seed they are sowing, for absolutely no honest effort has ever been made to curb these evils."

While Dr. Culp's analysis leaned heavily towards moral judgement that precluded an understanding of underlying causes, he did feel qualified to lend conclusions: "Unless law and order be firmly established and permanently maintained the venereal situation will remain the same for all time. The local disrespect for common laws and decency are openly and continuously violated. Self-respect or honest pride is conspicuous by absence. Illegitimacy is at a premium, and has been for years. What about it? Establish law and order as the very first and fundamental act, and do it very promptly. It must be done within the reservation just as certainly as without." L.L. Culp, Special Physician, to Commissioner of Indian Affairs, Washington, DC, Copy to Emil Krulish, Medical Director, Menominee Indian Mills, November 15, 1928; Menominee Files, BIA 1907—1939; RG 75, NA; Hon. E.B. Meritt, Assistant Commissioner, to Culp, February 6, 1929; Menominee, BIA 1907—1939; RG 75, NA; Culp to Commissioner, January 28, 1929; Menominee, BIA 1,1907—1939; RG 75, NA.

15. The flight to Milwaukee, and involvement with four men in Greshem, one of whom fathered Evelyn Frechette's child: Metcalfe, Chicago to File, 15 March, 1934, DF-170, p. 5; Evelyn's attempts to secure medical treatment at the Bryant Hospital, and later at the Salvation Army Hospital, in Chicago for her pregnancy: J.J. Waters, Chicago, to File, 22 March, 1934, DF-177, p. 15.

16. The Beulah Home was corroborated in a series of newspaper articles, discovered by Dillinger researcher Tom Smusyn: "Charges Baby Home Owner Sent Girls Out to Beg Food," *Chicago Times,* 27 January 1935; "Beulah Baby Home Bleak and Deserted," *Ibid.* 27 January 1935; Kay Hall, "Death Farm" *Ibid.* 27 January 1935; "Frechette Baby In Paper Coffin," 27 January, 1935, p.1; Interview with Proprietor of Beulah Home confirmed the statement of the Director, (67C) to Bureau that baby had "died at the age of 3 months of syphlis," in Metcalfe, Chicago to File, 15 March, 1934, DF-170, p. 5. This important FBI document confirms the validity of the letter published in the *Chicago Times* on 27 January, 1935, allegedly hand-written by Evelyn Frechette one week prior to May 22, 1934.

   In the aforementioned memo, with names blacked out under classified disclaimer 67C, Agent Metcalfe states: "(67C) furnished a specimen of the handwriting of Evelyn Frechette in the form of a letter addressed by her to (67C) which is signed 'From Evelyn.' This letter was written from (67C) on May 15, 1928. It pertained solely to the child that was born to her. This letter is being kept in the Chicago files as a specimen of her handwriting, and is to be returned to (67C) after it has served its purpose."

   In the article published by the *Chicago Times* on 27 January 1935, another letter from Evelyn Frechette, not directly confirmed by the memo of Agent Metcalfe of 15 March, 1934, was published.

## Notes for Chapter 2

1. Dillinger's intake admission, published in "Dillinger's Own Story of his Wooden Gun Escape," *New York Sunday Mirror*, 2 December, 1934; Display of Original Letter, John Dillinger Historical Museum, Nashville, Indiana, 1988, viewed during visit by author; actual date of offense was Sept. 6, 1934. The dates of John Dillinger's incarceration at Pendleton Reformatory, and his subsequent transfer to Michigan City: "John Dillinger Parole Under Fire of Jurors," *Chicago Daily Tribune,* 15 March 1934.
2. Telephone Interview with Delbert Hobson, 1988, by author.
3. Telephone Interview, February 1999, author to Mary.
4. Telephone Interview, Hobson.
5. Telephone Interview, Mary.
6. Date of birth, wedding, and divorce of Dillinger to Beryl Hovious provided by Tony Stewart, author, *Dillinger: The Hidden Truth.*
7. Author visit, Dillinger's home in Mooresville, 1988.
8. Dillinger's prison record of infractions: "Indiana Blamed for Dillinger's Career of Crime," *Chicago Tribune,* 1935.
9. Aspects of the personality of Homer Van Meter were taken from interviews with Beth Green, associate of Van Meter in St. Paul, after her arrest in April 1934: W.A. Rorer, St. Paul, to File, 9 April, 1934, DF-491; Cowley to Director, 11 April 1934, DF-514; Criminal record: I.D. Order No. 1222, April 1934, Homer Van Meter aliases Kenneth Jackson, DF-426-430.
10. The descriptions of Pierpont, Clark, Makely, Van Meter, and Hamilton were found in a series of charts once maintained in the Indiana State Prison and now available in a vertical file stored at the Indiana State Library in Indianapolis. Van Meter: T.P. Baughman to File, 6 April 1934, DF427 p. 1.

    The personality profiles of Pierpont, Clark, Makely, and Hamilton were compiled through their quotes and interviews that were conducted after their arrest in Tucson, Arizona. Much of this was obtained through the Tucson Historical Society, which holds a large vertical file of newspaper clippings, articles, and essays that were written about these men by reporters who were on the scene. These articles number in the hundreds and are too voluminous to list separately. However, these reporters took a strong interest in the men as individuals while dubbing them collectively as the "Terror Gang," after their sensational arrest in January 1934.
11. Russell Clark received no visit from Opal Long aka Bernice Clark while incarcerated in Michigan City before the escape, nor was he visited by anyone fitting her description who may have come in under an assumed name. Given the ferocious nature of her attempts to see and communicate with him after his Tucson arrest and conviction to life imprisonment, the author contends that Opal Long's relationship with Clark began after the Michigan City escape; Russell Clark's World War I Marines enlistment: "Enlistment

News," *Terre Haute Star,* 2 May 1919, p. 21 c. 4.; Descriptions: Wm. Larson, Detroit, to Director, 20 October 1933, DF-12, p. 5.

12. Larson, Chicago, to H.H. Clegg, St. Paul, 11 April 1934, DF-490, p. 1.
13. Indiana State Penitentiary at Michigan City, author tour and interview with Barry L. Nothstine, Sr., Administrative Assistant, State of Indiana, Dept. of Correction, 1989; "History of the Indiana State Prison," Pamphlet.

## Notes for Chapter 3

1. Author visit, Dillinger's home in Mooresville, 1988.
2. Elizabeth Fields Dillinger Obituary: *The Mooresville Times*, 25 May 1933.
3. Harry Pierpont's arrest and trial in New Harmony, Indiana: "Police Arrive with 2 Alleged Bandits," *Kokomo Dispatch*, 4 April 1925, "Police Deny Skeer Confessed Robbery," *Dispatch*, 5 April 1925, "Skeer Relates Robbery Story in Confession," *Dispatch*, 6 May 1924; While initially visiting the Elliotts alone, Dillinger and Copeland brought Frechette and Patricia Cherrington in fall 1933: E.J. Wynn, Indianapolis, to file, 28 December, 1934, DF-4996, p. 6.
4. Kokomo hideout: Klein to File, 12 April 1934, DF-530, p.3.
5. V.W. Peterson, to file, DF-1478 pp. 39, 49.
6. *Ibid.*; State of Indiana, County of Clinton, *Local Record of Death*, Pearl McDonald Elliott, Filed 12 August 1935, Bk D-10; P 70; Local No. 100.; Marital history: Kokomo-Howard Public Library; "Kokomo Woman Was Friend of John Dillinger," *Kokomo Tribune*, 9 September, 1962; alleged political connections: E.J. Wynn, Indianapolis, To File, 28 December 1934, DF-4996; E.J. Wynn, 28 December, 1934, DF 4996, p. 6; Dewey, William (Family of), 1920 Census, Soundex, Indiana, Vol. 38; Sheet 12; Line 37; Dewey Elliott's connection to the Nitti gang was told by Ed Shouse to Michigan City officials after his arrest: V.W. Peterson to file, Chicago, 17 May 1934, DF-1478; Pearl Elliott's other friends included Sylvia and Tillie Clevinger, and Pearl Hellman, also known as Pearl Applegate, 305 Harrison Street, Mishawaka, Indiana; Pearl Elliott's "Joint": E.J. Wynn, Indianapolis, to File, 28 December 1934, DF-4996; pp. 5,6.
7. Kokomo "business" letters went to Pierpont in Michigan City under a variety of names, one of which was Homer Parker: E.J. Connelley to Director, Cincinnati, 28 October 1933; DF-9; The guns smuggled into the prison in a box of thread was taken from interviews with Deputy Warden Schmuhl, who gleaned the information from Walter Detrich upon his return to the prison after being captured: Agent Mullen to File, Chicago, 18 March 1934, DF-163.
8. Muncie prostitutes Sarah Goodnight and Mickey Shea: V.W. Peterson, Chicago, to file, 23 May 1934; DF-1668; Mary Longnaker's divorce: State of Ohio, County of Montgomery, *Decree*, Mary R. Longnaker v. Howard E. Longnaker, No. 13633 D.R. 4 December 1933; John Dillinger's trip to the Chicago World's Fair and Michigan City with Mary Longnaker, along with

Dillinger in Dayton with Mary Longnaker: K.R. McIntire To File, Chicago; 13 April 1934; DF-526; Mary Longnaker's divorce attorney's meeting with Dillinger: N.B. Klein to File, Cincinnati, 10 April 1934, DF- 447, pp. 7,8; Researchers have long debated the rumor that James Jenkins was Dillinger's prison lover while in Michigan City—this writer found no primary evidence to support the theory.

9. Dillinger's activities with Sam Goldstine (misspelled Goldstein) and Clifford Mohler; Mullen, Agent, to File, Chicago, 8 March 1934; DF-115; Memo to file, Chicago, 18 June 1934, DF-173, p. 3. Homer Van Meter's date of parole: Homer Van Meter alias Kenneth Jackson, DF-426-430. Dillinger's meeting with Lester Gillis in East Chicago, Indiana in May 1933: Peterson to File, Chicago, 9 March 1935; File No. 62-29777-; College Park; RG129; 95-57-8; Sec. 8; National Archives 2, Washington, DC; Dillinger's rental of an apartment with Sam Goldstine under the alias Donovan: Receipt, Beverly Apartment Hotel, Gary, Indiana, Basil Gallagher Series.
10. Hilton Crouch's account of the robbery of the Massachusetts Avenue Bank in Indianapolis was found in an FBI account of an interview that the bank robber gave to Deputy Warden Schmuhl. Crouch was eager to talk, without implicating anyone who was not already known to the law, because he wanted to get an interesting work detail at Michigan City. The file contains Sam Goldstine's accounts to the FBI of the robberies that he committed with Dillinger:

    Mullen to File, Chicago, 18 March 1934, DF-163; Details of the robbery of the State Bank of Massachusetts Avenue in Indianapolis on September 6, 1933; the arrest in Dayton, the interaction between attorney Jack Egan and Judge Patterson, with jurisdiction resulting in Lima transfer:

    Andrews, Larry, "I was There When They Captured John Dillinger," *Dayton Daily News*, 29 July, 1984; Dillinger's Dayton arrest: *Dayton Daily News*, 22 September 1933.

    *Dayton Journal Herald*, 23—26 September 1933; Transfer of Dillinger's Essex Terraplane to Hubert Dillinger: E.J. Connelley to Director, Cincinnati, 28 October 1933; DF-9.

10. Mary Longnaker after Dillinger: N.B. Klein to File, Cincinnati, 10 April 1934, DF- 447, pp. 7, 9–10.

## Notes for Chapter 4

1. Andrews, Larry, "I was There," *Dayton Daily News*, 29 July 1984.
2. Ousted Deputy Warden H.G. Claudy related that in a conversation had between Dillinger and himself while the former was incarcerated at Tucson, that Dillinger admitted to having thrown three guns over the wall of the prison: "Blames McNutt 'Spoils System' in Prison Break, *Tribune*, 2 November 1934.

3. The physical layout of the Indiana State Prison at Michigan City arose from the following sources: Interview and tour of facility with Barry L. Nothstine, Sr., Administrative Assistant, Indiana State Prison. Mr. Nothstine corroborated, in an informal conversation, that the old practice of firing guards with a change of administration did indeed occur. "You could be Warden on New Years Eve," he said, "and on New Years Day you could be dog catcher."
4. Pierpont's associates in Michigan City: Connelley to Director, Cincinnati, 28 October 1933, DF-9; Danny McGeoghan's wife, Marie; Larry Streng and his relationship with Opal Long: V.W. Peterson, to File, 23 May 1934, DF-1668.
5. "His Own Story of How Felons Kidnaped Him," *Tribune*, 29 September 1933.
6. Harry Pierpont's letters to New Harmony jurors: E.J. Wynn, Indianapolis, to File, 28 December, 1934, DF- 4996; The death of Earl Northern: State of Indiana, County of LaPorte, *Certificate of Death*, Earl Northern, Filed 30 June, 1936.
7. Mary Kinder's personal memoirs: Mary Kinder, "Four Months With the Dillinger Gang," *Chicago Herald,* 30 July 1934: Mary said that she visited Pierpont in prison, not specifying whether these visits were at Pendleton or at Michigan City. While she said, "I used to take flowers and cake to him and I fell deeper and deeper in love with him each time I went to the prison," a check of Pierpont's visiting list at Michigan City does not reflect her name, nor does his mailing list. She most likely visited him under an assumed name, as her status as his co-defendant's sister may have forced her to disguise her identity. Some of the facts as stated in Mary's series were documented in a subsequent national series: Avery Hale, "The Inside Story of Dillinger," *True Detective*, January 1934; Mary Kinder's parents: State of Florida, County of Pasco, *Original Certificate of Death,* Margaret Ann Flory, (Margaret "Silent Sadie" Behrens) #87 083938, Filed 14 August, 1987;

   State of Indiana, County of Hendriks, *Certificate of Death,* Mary Ellen Grimsley (Mary Kinder).

   Mary's admission that she had attended Catholic elementary school, and the Emmerich Manual Training H.S.:

   "Had Wonderful Time As Moll," *Indianapolis Star*, 2 February 1934.
8. Robbery of the New Harmony Bank, with subsequent trial re: Earl Northern and Harry Pierpont: (Articles provided to Author by Dillinger researcher Tom Smusyn)

   "Officers on Trial of Bank Robbers," *Evansville Courier Journal,* 11 March 1925;

   "Make Away with Loot from S. Kokomo Bank," *Kokomo Dispatch,* 28 March 1925;

   "Part of Loot from Kokomo Bank Found," *Dispatch,* 3 April 1925;

   "Police Arrive with Two Alleged Bandits," *Dispatch,* 4 April 1925;

   "Police Deny Skeer Confessed Robbery," *Dispatch,* 5 April 1925;

"Man Arrested in Indianapolis is Put in Jail Here," *Dispatch,* 29 April 1925;
"Arraign Bandit Suspect Today," *Dispatch,* 30 April 1925;
"Pierpont Begins to Serve Prison Term," *Dispatch,* 7 May 1925;
"Skeer Tells of Intimidation in Northern Trial," *Dispatch,* 4 June 1925;
"Guilty of Robbing Local Bank However," *Dispatch,* 6 June 1925.

9. State of Indiana, County of Marion, *Application for Marriage License*, Dale R. Kinder to Mary E. Northern and Mary E. Northern to Dale R. Kinder, Filed 3 March 1931; "Four Months with the Dillinger Gang," *Chicago Herald,* 30 July 1934; Mary Kinder's 1932 arrest:
E.A. Tamm to Director, U.S. Dept. of Justice, Bureau of Investigation; 7 August 1934; NA, Dillinger; 95-57-8; Sec. 5; Call No. 3241.
10. "Deputy Warden Tells Own Story of Prison Break," *Tribune*, 27 September 1933; "10 Felons Flee Indiana Prison, Kidnap Sheriff,"*Chicago Daily Tribune*, 27 September 1933.

## Notes for Chapter 5

1. "Chicago Police Hunt Escaped Felons in City," *Tribune*, 27 September, 1933; Ralph Saffel's apartment; surveillance of Clark family in Hamilton, Ohio; Mary Longnaker after Dillinger's arrest: Klein to File, Cincinnati, 10 March 1934; DF-447; 12 April 1934; Klein to File, 12 April 1934, DF-530; R.D. Brown to File, Cincinnati, 26 February 1934; DF-81; Mary Kinder's status as gang member: Joe Pinkston, Author's interview, Nashville, Indiana, 1989; Viola Paterson's address: Peterson to file 7-19-34, DF-2782; The death of James Jenkins: Wm. Larson to File, Detroit, 4 November 1933; DF-24; N.B. Klein to File, Cincinnati, 12 April 1934.
2. Mary Kinder, "Four Months With the Dillinger Gang," *Chicago Herald,* 30 July 1934; State of Indiana, County of Marion, *Certificate of Death*, Fern M. Pierpont, Filed August 1919; Obituary (Newspaper unknown), "Pierpont, Fern M., Age 19 years." Documents furnished by Lori Hyde to author; Mr. and Mrs. Pierpont's arrest after New Harmony: DF-2775, p. 17.
3. Opal Long's recollections: Bernice Clark, "My Adventures With the Dillinger Gang," *Chicago Herald and Examiner,* 12 September 1934, Chapter III.
4. Lima: Prior published accounts of the encounter between Harry Pierpont and Sheriff Jesse Sarber have quoted Pierpont as producing a gun with an epitaph. This is a somewhat different version of the phrase, "Here's my credentials." Aftermath of Lima breakout, with investigation conducted on Pierpont farm: Wm. Larson to Director, Detroit, 20 October 1933, DF-12, 1-9; Newspaper articles: "Kill Sheriff; Take Robber from Ohio Jail," *Chicago Tribune*, 13 October 1933.
5. Peru raid: Larson, Detroit, to File, 4 November 1933, Df-24, p. 3.

6. The Steuben Club and Dewey Elliott's connection to the Nitti gang was told by Ed Shouse to Michigan City officials after his arrest: V.W. Peterson to file, Chicago, 17 May 1934, DF-1478; Background on Frank Nitti: Bill Davidson, "How The Mob Controls Chicago." In *The Chicago Crime Book*, ed. Albert Halper, Cleveland: The World Publishing Co., 1967, p. 507.

## Notes for Chapter 6

1. The Chicago hideouts, with Captain John Stege's involvement after Lima: M.H. Purvis to Director, 31 March 1934; DF-226; V.W. Peterson to File, Chicago, 1 February 1935, File No. 62-29777-; NA, College Park, MA., RG 129; Notorious Offenders; 95-57-8; Sec. 8., Call No. 3241.
2. "Case History of Patricia Young," U.S. Department of Justice, Federal Bureau of Prisons, Archive, FOI, 320 First St., N.W., Washington, DC 20523; S.L. Greely, Investigator, The Central Howard Assn. to Social Services Division, Leavenworth, Cherrington, Arthur AZ-199, General Records, FBOP, NA, San Bruno, CA.
3. Opal Long: General Register, 1933—1935 Workhouse commitments, Opal Long aka Clark, Bernice; Municipal Library, Minneapolis City Hall, Room 300M; V.W. Peterson to File, 17 May 1934, DF-1478 p. 63; the Marshall Hotel, was identified as "a hangout for hoodlums" by Opal Milligan in D.L. Nicholson, St. Paul, to File, 5 September 1934, DF- 3788; Description of Marshall Hotel: Personal visit by author, 1989; Patricia Cherrington and Harry Copeland hung out in the Olympia Lounge at 1101 North Clark Street, Chicago.
4. J.J. Waters, Chicago, to File, 22 March 1934, DF-173; The physical description of the Menominee Reservation at Neopit, Wisconsin, author's visit, 1989.
5. Larsen to File, Chicago, 20 March 1934; DF-210, p. 16; T.E. Billings to File, Chicago, 9 April 1934; DF- 452, p. 3; Patricia Cherrington's medical condition: Medical Records, Patricia Cherrington (nee' Patricia Young), BOP, Washington, DC, Federal Industrial Institution at Alderson, W. Virginia, Archive.
6. Pat Cherrington's daughter and the details surrounding her babysitter Betty Naetz Minor: Larsen to File, Chicago, 20 March 1934; DF-210; U.S. Detention Farm Milan, Michigan, Board of Parole Hearing on Patricia Cherrington, 26 April 1935; Cherrington, Arthur AZ-199; General Records, FBOP, NA, San Bruno, CA.
7. Mary Kinder, "Four Months With the Dillinger Gang," *Chicago Herald,* 30 July 1934; Evelyn's color preference based on inventory of her wardrobe in St. Paul: H.H. Clegg, St. Paul to Director, Washington, DC, 31 March 1934; FN -380; Harry Copeland's Chicago addresses: T.E. Billings to File, Chicago, 9 April 1934; DF- 452; John Hamilton's addresses: Devereaux to File; Chicago, 22 November 1933; DF-43.

8. Ed Shouse's information on the internal philosophy of the gang with regard to their split after Greencastle: Mullen to File, Chicago, 9 March 1934; DF-81; Ed Shouse's role in the fencing of the Greencastle Bonds: Peterson to File; 1 February 1935; File No. 62-29777-, NA, College Park, MA, RG129; 95-57-8; Sec. 8; NA2.
9. The information on Marty McGinnis and four other informants that were used by the Indiana and Illinois State Police: Agent Mullen to File, Chicago, 18 March 1934, DF-163;

   Newspaper coverage of the ambush of Dillinger and Evelyn Frechette in front of the office of Dr. Eye: "Dillinger and Woman Shoot Way Out of Trap in Chicago," *Indianapolis Star*, 16 November 1933, "Raid Apartment to Seize Outlaw Who Fled Trap," *Chicago Daily News,* 17 November 1933, "Trail Outlaw on North Side," *Chicago Times*, 2nd Ed., 16 November 1933, "Police Find Indiana Gang's Lair," *Chicago Daily News*, 16 November 1933, "Fight 16 Police; Elude Trap," *Tribune*,16 November 1933, p. 1.
10. Police memoranda that mistakenly attributed the activities of Evelyn Frechette to Pearl Elliott: M.H. Purvis to Director, Chicago, 31 March 1934; RR FBI

    The surveillance memo of Matt Leach of the Indiana State Police, which listed the descriptions of Pat Cherrington and Opal Long, Russell Clark and Mary Kinder, and which placed Pearl Elliott at the Parkside address, was found in a series of memoranda penned by Matt Leach in Indianapolis, November 1933: Exhibit, The Little Bohemia Restaurant, Silver Star Lake, Wisconsin; Author's note: the racist quotes attributed to Matt Leach have not been censored in order to depict the historical climate of the 1930s.

11 Racine associate Casey Jones was documented in: V.W. Peterson, Chicago, to File, 23 May 1934, DF-1668; Newspaper coverage: "Rob Racine Bank, Shoot 2, Kidnap, Free 2," *Tribune*, 20 November 1933, p. 1; "Racine Banker is Kidnapped," *Milwaukee Journal*, 20 November 1933, "Fire Shots on Street in Racine Robbery,"*Journal*, 20 November 1933, "Warrants for Dillinger Gang in Racine Raid," *Journal*, 21 November 1933, "There was Plenty of Shooting in Racine," *Journal*, 21 November 1933.

12. Harry Copeland's arrest: Purvis to Director, 31 March 1934, DF- 226; "Seize Indiana Outlaw, Pal of Dillinger," 20 November 1933, *Chicago Tribune*, "Copeland, Hoosier Desperado, Seized," 20 November 1933, *Muncie Morning Star.*
13. Pearl Elliott's illness, her activities upon leaving Kokomo with Elliott, and her hosting of Dillinger and Copeland in her boarding house: E.J. Wynn, Indianapolis, to File, 28 December 1934, DF-4996.

## Notes for Chapter 7

1. John Hamilton's whereabouts in the fall of 1933:Devereaux to File; Chicago,

22 November 1933; DF-43; Newspaper coverage:"Dragnet Out for Killer of Police Hero," *Chicago Times*, 15 December 1933; "Indiana Prison Break Leader Foils Capture," *Chicago Tribune,* 15 December 1933; "Widow and Four Children Mourn Slain Policeman," *Tribune,* 15 December 1933; "Dragnet Out For Killer of Police Hero," *Chicago Times,* December 15, 1933.

2. "Ten Squads Assigned to Capture Outlaws,"*Tribune*, 18 December 1933; "50 Police Led by Stege Hunt Convict Gang,"*Tribune*, 19 December 1933; "Police Storm Outlaws' Flat; Girl Arrested,"*Tribune*, 18 December 1933; The testimony of Arthur "Fish" Johnson regarding the Chicago activities of the Dillinger gang; telephone message point in the Sheridan Billiard House:

   V.W. Peterson to File, 1 February 1935; File No. 62-29777-576; NA, College Park, MA, RG 129; Notorious Offenders; 95-57-8; Sec. 8., Call No. 3241."Robbers Killed in Gun Battle," *Tribune*, 21 December 1933; 26 December 1933; "Bullet Intended for Gangster Hits State Policeman," *Indianapolis Star*, 21 December 1933; "Officer Slain in Gun Battle," *Tribune*, 21 December 1933; the arrest of Hilton Crouch: "Jail Ex-Convict," *Tribune*, 25 December 1933;

   "Third Convict in Dillinger Hunt Seized,"*Chicago Herald and Examiner*, 25 December 1933;

   "Dillinger Mob Holding Daily Gun Rehearsal," *Herald*, 26 December 1933; "Nab Dillinger Thug Without Firing Shot," *Chicago Times*, 24 December 1933; "Nab Convict as 'Outside Man' of Dillinger Gang," *Tribune*, 24 December 1933; Agent Mullen to File, Chicago, 18 March 1934, DF-163.

3. Russell Clark's purchase of the Ford V-8 in November 1933: T.E. Billings to File, Chicago, 9 April 1934; DF-453; Bernice Clark, "My Adventures With the Dillinger Gang," *Chicago Herald,* 12 September 1934, Chapter III; Evelyn Frechette's movements; gang activity at the Daytona Beach address at 901 South Atlantic Avenue; transfer of the Essex Terraplane to Evelyn Frechette: R.L. Shivers to File, Jacksonville, Florida, 9 April 1934; DF-424; H.H. Clegg, to Birmingham, Alabama, 14 April 1934, DF-518; M.M. Davis to Special Agent, Kansas City, Missouri, March 1934, DF-188NRS;

   Evelyn's revelations regarding her feelings toward the experience of driving the Essex Terraplane, told to an informant and reported to: J.J. Waters to File, Chicago, 4 April 1934; DF-314;Opal Long's refusal to cook while in Daytona: H.H. Clegg, St. Paul to Director, 15 April 1934, DF-567; Pat Cherrington's observations of John Dillinger in Daytona, will provoke controversy as Patricia has never been placed in Daytona with the gang. She confided that she was in Daytona, offering her opinion of Dillinger's behavior there, within interviews found in: *Inmate Patricia Young,* Archive, Federal Industrial Institution at Alderson, W. Virginia, BOP. It is probable that she traveled to Daytona from Kansas City, to which she had gone from Chicago shortly before Copeland's arrest.

The caretaker placed the entire group as having been gone from the Daytona house after Christmas, with one member of the gang returning on January 13 to pick up mail. The person, described as in his 40s, matches Makley, as does the Studebaker that belonged to Makley. Given the stretch in age and the unreliability of eye-witness reports, and assuming the gang member to pull up on January 13 was Dillinger, it would provide part of the alibi that he had been in Daytona at least two days before the killing of Officer William O'Malley in East Chicago, Indiana. He always maintained that he could not have traveled from Florida to East Chicago within the prescribed travel time of one or two days.

## Notes for Chapter 8

1. Milwaukee: J.J. Waters, Chicago, to File, 22 March 1934, DF-173, p 8; J.J. Waters, Chicago, to File, 22 March 1934, DF-177, p. 7.
2. Evelyn Frechette lived at 901 Addison sporadically between January and March 1934. The following document, which records the telegram exchange between Evelyn Frechette and Pat Cherrington as "Ann Jackson," place the rental at around January 13. The telegrams; the Milwaukee transfer of the Essex Terraplane was found in: J.J. Waters to File, Chicago, 22 March 1934; DF-177; Larsen to File, Chicago, 20 March 1934, DF-180.
3. The January 7, 1934, arrest of Jack Perkins:V.W. Peterson to File, 1 February 1935; DF- 576; NARA, CP MA, RG 129; Notorious Offenders; 95-57-8; Sec. 8., Call No. 3241; Walter Detrich arrest with shooting death of Jack Klutas: "Dillinger Ally and 2 Others are Captured," *Chicago Tribune,* 7 January 1934.
4. Frechette: J.J.Metcalf to File, Chicago, 23 March 1934; DF,-181; Descriptions of the scene at the bank robbery in East Chicago, Personal Visit by author, 1989. Wilgus' identification of Dillinger at East Chicago: "Dillinger Robs Bank, Kills Policeman," *Tribune*, 16 January 1934; "Thrilling Robbery Story Recounted," *Arizona Citizen*, 29 January 1934; "Wilgus Tells of O'Malley Death in Bank Robbery,"*Citizen*, 29 January 1934; Rebuttal based on statement of Jeff Scalf, Dillinger's great-nephew, with excerpts (used by permission) of his interview with Mary Kinder conducted in 1980.
5. Hamilton's convalescence after East Chicago and Pat Cherrington's role in his recovery was revealed by Jean Burke, girlfriend of Art "Fish" Johnson and is recorded in:V.W. Peterson, Chicago, to File, 25 August 1934, DF-3607.
6. Mr. and Mrs. Frank Sullivan's purchase of Hudson club sedan: J.O. Hichew to File, St. Louis, Missouri, 7 April 1934, DF-353; Leroy and Naomi H. had gone to Phoenix, Arizona in December 1933, returning to Hamilton, Ohio, with Arizona license plates. It is probable that this Arizona connection was known to the police via the many informants operating around the gang. This information, with the fact of Evelyn Frechette's prior visit to Arizona, was shown in these two documents: J..J.Metcalf to File, Chicago, 23 March 1934; DF-181; Larsen to File, Chicago, 20 March 1934; DF-180.

7. There are conflicting stories around the circumstances that brought about the Tucson arrests. This version has tried to incorporate the most credible elements, those that have been confirmed by various primary sources. The magazine articles that comprised much of this background are as follows: Chief C. A. Wollard, "Clark! Makley! Pierpont! Dillinger! Captured,"*True Detective*, June 1934; Basil Gallagher, *The Life Story of John Dillinger*," Indianapolis, Stephens Publishing Co., 1934; The women's version of Daytona and Tucson: Bernice Clark, "My Adventures," *Chicago Herald,* Part 5, 14 September 1934; Mary Kinder, "Four Months," *Chicago Herald*, 30 July 1934; "Chief Proud of His Police," *Arizona Star*, 27 January1934; "Who Gave Tip for Dillinger Arrests," *Star*, 3 February 1934; Previous accounts of the apprehension of Harry Pierpont have reported that he attempted to swallow a paper with Dillinger's Tucson address in order to prevent the police from finding it. This is disputed as not having occurred by the agent sent by the bureau to the Pima County Jail: C.J. Endres to File, 27 January 1934, DF-69.

## Notes for Chapter 9

A large newspaper archive molded the facts of the Tucson extradiction. Provided by the Arizona Historical Society in Tucson, they are: "Dillinger Gang is Held," *Tucson Citizen*, 26 January 1934; "Indiana Sends Police Detail," *Citizen*, 26 January, 1934; "I'll Kill You Yet...Pierpont," *Arizona Star*, 29 Jan 1934; "Outlaws Struggle to Return to Wisconsin," *Citizen*, 29 January, 1934; "Moeur Signs Requisition Papers," *Citizen*, 29 January, 1934; "Deputies Given Battle," *Star*, 30 January, 1934; "Three Dillinger Bandits and Woman," *Citizen*, 30 January, 1934; "Arizona Rules Indiana Gets Dillingers,"*Chicago Tribune*, 27 January 1934; "Dillinger Gang Facing Death as States Act," *Tribune*, 27 January 1934; "Dillinger Women Granted Clothing," *Star*, 28 January 1934; "Tucson Sighs As Gangsters Leave Arizona," *Star*, 31 January, 1934; "Dillinger Women Depart from City," *Star*, 1 February, 1934; "Pierpont's Moll is Given Freedom," *Star*, 15 February, 1934; "Mary Had Wonderful Time as Moll," *Star*, 2 Feb. 1934; "First Rewards Paid to Police," *Star*, 1 February 1934.

1. Bureau of Investigation's jurisdiction fell under the "possibility of the violation of the National Motor Vehicle Theft Act." The bureau had tried to enter the case after the murder of Sheriff Sarber, when it was learned that an automobile found abandoned by these subjects at Hamilton, Ohio, had been stolen from its owner in Chicago, Illinois. This stands in dispute with previous accounts of the FBI's entry, which place the date as occurring after Dillinger drove a stolen car over state lines as he left the Crown Point County Jail in March 1934; Mary Kinder's rebuttal given in an interview conducted by Jeff Scalf, great-nephew of John Dillinger, in 1980 (used with permission).

Before Crown Point, Hoover was required keep a low profile in his interest in Dillinger, as long as the gang members legitimately purchased the cars that they drove over state lines. Having no federal jurisdiction, he was powerless to act. It is interesting to note that, while no state charges stuck against Opal Long and Evelyn Frechette in Tucson, within a few short months both women would be wanted on serious, federal harboring charges that superseded individual state warrants. In the following correspondence, J. Edgar Hoover dates the bureau's involvement as occurring "shortly after the murder of Jesse Sarber:" Director to Attorney General, 31 January 1934; DF-70; Director to C.A. Wollard, Tucson, 7 March 1934; DF-684.

2. The destination of Opal Long and Evelyn Frechette upon leaving Tucson was discovered by Grover C. Lutter, Chief of Police, Racine, Wisconsin, and told to Chester Sherman, Tucson City Detective: C.J. Endres, Los Angeles, to File, 30 March 1934, DF-343.

## Notes for Chapter 10

The physical description of the Crown Point County Jail in Crown Point, Indiana: Author's visit, 1990. The record of Lillian Holley's tenure and of her nephew, Carroll Holley's, term as sheriff was found in the Lake County Courthouse, Crown Point, Indiana.

1. The accounts of Dillinger's arrival at Crown Point; photo session and biographical notes on Sheriff Lillian Holley: "Dillinger Is Jailed," *Chicago Tribune,* 31 January 1934, p. A1; "Slim Woman, Mother of Twins, Controlled Dillinger as Sheriff," *Tribune*, 4 March 1934, p. A2; "Sheriff Holley Says Her Men Were Yellow," *Tribune*, 6 March 1934, p. A2; "Maybe, Stege Wants to Be a Deputy," *Indianapolis Star,* AP Photo caption, 2 February, 1934; "Fear Dillinger Jail Delivery," *Tribune*, 5 February, 1934; James "Fur" Sammons' appointment to the Chicago Crime Commission's "Public Enemy" List: William J. Helmer and Rick Mattix. *Public Enemies: America's Criminal Past, 1919—1940,* New York: Facts on File, Inc., 1998, p. 298.
2. The intelligence that chronicled the activities of Evelyn Frechette during the period of Dillinger's incarceration at Crown Point County Jail: J.J. Metcalf, Agent, to File, Chicago, 23 March 1934; DF-181; Evelyn and Frances "Patsy" Frechette's September, 1933 visit to Neopit was discovered by requesting information from the Keshena Indian Agency in Keshena, Wisconsin, and documented in: J.J. Waters to File, Chicago, 22 March, 1934; DF-81; Melvin Purvis, Chicago, to Director, 10 April, 1934, DF-385.
3. The origins of the relationship between Arthur O'Leary, Louis Piquett, and John Dillinger: "Piquett Hid Dillinger," *Chicago Tribune*, 10 January 1935, p. 1;"Piquett Fights U.S. Version of Dillinger Plot," *Tribune*, 11 January 1935, p. 1.
4. Evelyn Frechette's conversation with Indianapolis-bound pilot Oscar

Hanole: J.J. Waters, Chicago, to File, 4 April 1934, 314; Welton Sparks' correspondence list and record of divorce from Evelyn Frechette: Agent Mullen to File, Chicago, 18 March 1934,DF-163.

5. The account of Hilton Crouch's interview with Deputy Warden Schmuhl, where he recounts the fact that Meyer Bogue had connections to Stege's informant Happy Miles: *Ibid.*; V.W. Peterson, Chicago, to File, 19 July, 1934, DF-2782; Evelyn Frechette's coded conversation with Dillinger at Crown Point: "Outlaw's Auto Found, But He Eludes Pursuit," *Chicago Tribune,* 6 March 1934, p. A1; Sheriff Holley's account of Evelyn Frechette's Crown Point visit: T.F. Mullen, Agent, to File, Chicago, 9 March 1934, DF-182; The Tochida party that Evelyn attended with Marge Edwards. J.J. Metcalf, Agent, to File, Chicago, 23 March 1934, DF-181; the aftermath of Dillinger's escape and the subsequent public interest generated in "Mrs. Dillinger," including the inaccurate reference to the visit having been made by Mary Kinder: "Quick Getaway Indicates Help From His Aides," *Chicago Tribune,* 4 March 1934.

6. The account of the Crown Point escape, as told in this chapter, was pieced together by this report, which attempted to straighten out the conflicting versions of the sequence of events: Agent Mullen to File, Chicago, 9 March 1934; DF-81; the official explanation of how the wrong license plate number was released, which gave Dillinger the time he needed to escape, was issued through the newspapers:

"An unidentified employee went to the Main Street garage, to pick up the next consecutive number from a second Auburn car. Because there had been a system in place to keep track of the cars by numbering them chromatically, the mathematical equation of deducting one number from the license, should have given them the correct digits of the stolen car. The unknown person sent to the car garage, performed the equation correctly. The problem was, he picked it up from the wrong Auburn car, which accounted for the incorrect number being broadcasted."

This writer was brought to the apartment building of Piquett's secretary, Esther Anderson, where Dillinger was reunited with Evelyn, by Dillinger researcher Tom Smusyn in 1989, when new information started to circulate among Dillinger scholars. FBI memoranda attributed Evelyn's address with Frances "Patsy" Frechette and Marge Edwards as being located on 3215 Halsted Street: J.J. Metcalf, Agent, to File, Chicago, 23 March 1934, DF-181. This information is confusing in light of the other address kept by the women at this time, which places the reunion between Dillinger and Evelyn after Crown Point at 516 Cornelia Street.

The newspaper articles that helped to frame out the events surrounding the escape are too numerous to mention. The *Chicago Tribune* leant comprehensive coverage: "Prison Warden Blames Sheriff and Officials," *Tribune*, 3 March 1934; "Slayer's Bold Escape Made with Toy Gun,"

*Tribune*, 4 March 1934; "Outlaw's Auto Found," *Tribune*, 5 March 1934; "Quick Getaway Indicates Help from his Aides," *Tribune*, 5 March 1934; "Sheriff Holley Says Her Men Were Yellow," *Tribune*, 6 March 1934, A2; "Dillinger Escape Perils Rule of Democrats in Crown Point", *Tribune*, 6 March 1934; "Indiana Moves for Ouster of Sheriff Holley," *Tribune*, 8 March 1934; "Judge Orders New Inquiry on Jailbreak," *Tribune*, 9 March 1934; "Dillinger Seen on South Side," *Tribune*, 9 March 1934; "New Dillinger Hunt On," *Tribune*, 9 March 1934; "State to Accuse Two Dillinger Guards of Plot," *Tribune*, 10 March 1934; "Two Lost Jurors Delay Inquiry of Dillinger Break," *Tribune*, 10 March 1934; "New Hitch Halts Dillinger Quiz for Third Time," *Tribune*, 14 March 1934; "Seize Two for Questioning," *Tribune*, 30 October 1934; the editors of the *Chicago Tribune* had knowledge of the bribe paid by Piquett to Lake County officials. They were unable to publish due to lack of solid evidence: Memo to file; City Editor, Ed., Tribune Copy; Dated July 1934, File No. 95-57; Sub. 8; 12-2-34 – 3-12-35; Section 6; NA, MD; Investigative articles about the relationship between Sergeant Zarkovich, Dillinger, and the organized crime syndicate as protected by the East Chicago Police Department: "Indiana's Police Launch Quiz on Dillinger Death,"*Tribune*, 29 July 1934; "Records Shed New Light on Dillinger Assassination," *Tribune*, 21 July 1935; William J. Helmer and Rick Mattix. *Public Enemies: America's Criminal Past, 1919–1940,* New York: Facts on File, Inc., 1998, p. 204, which lists amounts much higher ($11,000) in bribe money than was originally believed. The attempt to break the alleged coded conversation between Evelyn Frechette and Dillinger, made by Mr. George Howard of Indianapolis: Melvin H. Purvis, Special Agent, Chicago, to Cincinnati, 10 March 1934, DF-185.

## Notes for Chapter 11

1. The grand jury investigation into Mary Kinder's role in the Michigan City escape: "Ohio Will Get 5 of Dillinger Mob," *Indianapolis Star*, 9 February 1934; "Pierpont's Moll is Given Freedom," *Arizona Star*, 15 February 1934; Mary Kinder's feelings of isolation after her release and exoneration were recorded in: Kinder, "Four Months," *Chicago Herald*, 30 July 1934; The surveillance of Mary Kinder, the illegal wiretapping of Jessie Levy's office, and the surveillance of the Leipsic farm: E.J. Connolley, Dayton, to File, 9 April, 1934, DF-530; The transfer of Dale Kinder: "Kinder Among 50 in Prison Move," *Indianapolis Star*, 22 February 1934.
2. The harassment of Louis Piquett and Esther Anderson in Lima: DF-1804; The newspaper coverage of the Lima trials was complete and concise. Highlights from the collection of articles used to frame out the trials are as follows: "Pierpont Goes on Trial in Ohio," *Tucson Citizen*, 6 March 1934; "Pierpont Tough Guy Says Mark Robbins," *Star*, 7 March 1934; "Sarber's

Son Retells Death of his Father," *Star*, 8 March 1934; "Guards Circle Courthouse at Pierpont Trial," *Citizen*, 8 March 1934; "Captain Jay Smith Tells Jury in Ohio of Taking Gun Away,"*Citizen*, 9 March 1934; "Dillinger Cellmate Tells of Jail Delivery," *Citizen*, 9 March 1934; "Pierpont takes Witness Stand," *Star*, 10 March 1934; "How Dillinger Fled Revealed," *Star*, 11 March 1934; "Gunman Denies Killing Sarber," *Star*, 11 March 1934;"Defense Made Tight by Lima Jail Watchers," *Star*, 11 March 1934; "Makley State Witness Balks," *Star*, 15 March 1934; "Jury Declares Makley Guilty," *Star*, 17 March 1934; "Makley Sent to Death Row by Lima Jury," *Star*, 17 March 1934; "Clark to Face Murder Count at Lima Today; Arrest Attorney," *Star*, 18 March 1934; "Russell Clark Expects to Die," *Star*, 22 March 1934; "Mother Defends Russell Clark," *Star*, 23 March 1934.

The unsigned letter regarding Harry Pierpont, written in Lima and delivered to Dillinger, was found in the latter's raided Lexington Avenue apartment in St. Paul on March 30, and recorded as inventory: H.H. Clegg, St. Paul, to Director, 31 March 1934; DF-380.

The shooting death of Herbert Youngblood: "Dillinger Aide Dies in Fight with Deputies," *Star*, 16 March 1934; "Outlaw Flees from Police in Michigan," *Citizen*, 16 March 1934.

3. "Prison Gates Close on Dillinger's Pals," *Star*, 1 April 1934; Sioux Falls and Mason City bank robberies: "Raid Iowa Bank; Get $52,000 and Shoot Way Out," *Chicago Tribune*, 13 March 1934.
4. The reference to Evelyn Sparks was Pierpont's way of protecting her identity. The "B." is most likely Russell Clark, who was called "Boobie" by the gang: letter, author's collection.

## Notes for Chapter 12

1. The interview with Ed Shouse wherein he identified Evelyn Frechette: Agent Mullen to File, Chicago, 9 March 1934, DF-115; the clerical process that resulted in the circulation of the I.D. Order of Frechette: Agent Dunn, Los Angeles, to Director, 5 April 1934, DF-376; Frechette family funeral: J.J. Waters, Chicago, to File, 4 April 1934, DF-314; Frechette in Detroit: W. Larson, Detroit, to File, 28 March 1934, DF-210.
2. The background on the role played by Harry Sawyer and Pat Riley in the St. Paul underworld: S.P. Cowley, Chicago, to Director 8 April 1934, DF—468; Cowley to Director, 11 April 1934; DF-514; and Clegg to Director, 15 April 1934; -560; Sioux Falls and Mason City bank jobs: Synopsis: "Edward Green, with aliases," 23 July 1936; F.B.I. No. 62-29777, Record Group 65; File No. 95-57-8; NA, College Park, MD.
3. Dr. Mortensen's admission of administering medical attention to the bullet wounds of Dillinger and Hamilton: "Dillinger Dead? Federal Police Are Now Asking," *Arizona Star*,

3. April 1934; "Dillinger Shot Twice," *Star*, 27 April 1934;The theories of isolationism that characterized the national mood in the 1930s: Richard Polenberg, *War and Society*, New York: J.B. Lippincott Co., 1972.
4. The events taking place inside the home of Mrs. Mae Clark and Mr. Andy S. in Detroit , reported by two people named Wilson, living inside, recorded by: W. Larson, Detroit, to File, 28 March 1934, DF-210; Cernocky's place after Dillinger, Gillis and Van Meter left Minneapolis was reported to the bureau in a conversation with Bessie Green, who added that Cherrington and Opal Long had preceded Dillinger into St. Paul: H.H. Clegg, St. Paul, to Director, 15 April 1934, DF-560.

## Notes for Chapter 13

1. Many of the physical descriptions of the wives and girlfriends of St. Paul gangsters were taken from interviews with Bess Green after her arrest. The contents of these conversations: H.H. Clegg, St. Paul, to Director, 15 April 1934, DF-560. This document also contained details of the social interactions between the Greens and Dillingers, especially the banter surrounding the movies. The Greens' aversion to living around the corner from Dillinger in Minneapolis were reported in: Cowley to Director, 11 April 1934; DF-514;The background on Eugene Green: H.H. Clegg, St. Paul to File, 7 April 1934; DF-407; Bess Green's appearance and background: W.A. Rorer, St. Paul, to File, 9 April 1934; DF-491; Memo to Director, 3 April 1934, -370; H.H. Clegg, St. Paul, to Director, Washington, 15 April1934; DF-503; H.H. Clegg, St. Paul, to File, 7 April 1934, DF-407; and Earl Van Wagoner, Chicago, to File, 11 April 1934; DF-538.

   Biographical information was offered with permission by Myrna Otte, great-niece of Bess Green.

   The rental of the Girard Street apartment by the Dillingers; the Greens' daily habits as members of the "respectable" community; and Marie Conforti's confinement to St. Paul Samaritan Hospital were documented in: Synopsis: *Edward Green, with aliases;* 23 July 1936; Federal Bureau of Investigation No. 62-29777, Record Group 65; File No. 95-57-8;

   National Archives at College Park, MD. Eddie Green's impressions of Evelyn Frechette were taken from his bedside ramblings shortly before his death and recorded in: Sam Cowley to Director, 4 April 1934; FN. 62-29777 DF-325; Other dynamics between the two couples were taken from BessSkinner's interviews: H.H. Clegg, St. Paul, to File, St. Paul, 7 April 1934, DF-407.

   Evelyn continually wore the striped shirtwaist and suede jacket she'd been arrested in during her visit to Detroit, when informant Mrs. Wilson observed her in the Clark home at the end of February. This and Pat Cherrington's visit to Harry Copeland enroute from Detroit to Chicago, and the activities in Detroit surrounding herself, Evelyn Frechette, Opal Long, and J. Young (a pseudonym) were documented in: W. Larson, Detroit, to File, 28 March 1934; DF- 210;

Pat Cherrington's inappropriate correspondence with Welton Spark was noted in the following:

**Admission Summary**, Spark, Welton AZ-200; 9 April 1940, U.S. Penitentiary, BOP, Alcatraz, San Bruno, California. Within this document, the Associate Warden's Report advised, "[Sparks'] correspondence list . . . should be closely checked inasmuch as in the past he has made efforts to correspond with the wife of his co-defendant Cherrington." Frechette's telegram to Pat Cherrington : J.J. Waters, Chicago, to File, 4 April 1934, DF-314; Telegram of Agent Purvis, Chicago, to E.J. Connelly, Cincinnati, 1 April 1934, DF-320 NR16.

2. Evelyn Frechette's round-trip flight from Minneapolis to Chicago and Indianapolis, with trip back to Minneapolis accompanied by two women, was recorded in: J.J. Waters, Chicago, to File, 4 April 1934, DF-314; Telegram of Agent Purvis, Chicago, to E.J. Connelley, Cincinnati, 1 April 1934, DF-320 NR16, which also noted that Evelyn had ridden "the plane with a man named Mr. Macy, who was not registered at the Congress Hotel, which he claimed was his address."
3. Beth Green's further descriptions of Evelyn Frechette: H.H. Clegg, St. Paul to File, 7 April 1934; DF-407; Evelyn Frechette's story of viewing John Dillinger's father in a movie newsreel: Frechette, Evelyn, "What I Knew About John Dillinger," *Chicago Herald & Examiner,* 30 August 1934; The manager of the Lincoln Court Apartments, Mrs. Coffey, who made a report to the U.S. Postal Inspectors of suspicious persons in the Lexington Avenue apartment; and Rorer's admission of advising Coulter and Nalls to secure extra police assistance: W.A. Rorer, St. Paul to Director, Washington, DC, 1 April 1934; DF-387; The circumstances of the rental of the Lexington Avenue apartment were told to the bureau by Mrs. Meidlinger and recorded with the inventory taken at the Lexington Avenue apartment after it was vacated by Dillinger and Frechette: D.L.Nicholson, St. Paul, to File, 9 April 1934. DF-466.
4. The source of the photos that Evelyn brought back from Indianapolis, the family of John Dillinger, was reported by Bess Green: H.H. Clegg, St. Paul, to Director, 15 April 1934, FN -560; Telephone interview with Mary, niece of John Dillinger, by author, February 1, 1999; Apartment inventory: H.H. Clegg, St. Paul to Director, Washington, DC, 31 March 1934, DF-380; The surveillance on Opal Long noted her movements and activities during March 1934. This intelligence was augmented through the unintentional omissions of her friend, Larry Streng, to the bureau informant, and was recorded in the following: Melvin Purvis, Chicago, to Director, Washington, DC, 1 April 1934; DF-385; J.J. Waters, Chicago, to File, 4 April 1934, DF-314; H.H.

Clegg, St. Paul, to File, 29 March 1934, DF-211; Purvis, Chicago, to Director, Washington, DC, 2 April 1934, DF-260; Purvis, Chicago, to Director, 6 April 1934. DF-390; Matthew Leach's role in the surveillance of Opal Long: H.H. Clegg, St. Paul, to Director, Washington, DC, 21 March 1934, DF-200.

5. Bess Green's safe deposit box activities at the Midway National Bank and Liberty National Bank: L.J. Rauber, St. Paul, to Director, 9 April 1934, DF-409; Beth Green's assistance in the purchase of Dillinger's new Hudson Sedan: W.A. Rorer, St. Paul, to File, 9 April 1934; DF-491; Beth Green's account of social interactions between Dillinger, Frechette and the Greens: H.H. Clegg, St. Paul to File, 7 April 1934; DF-407.
6. A synopsis of Dillinger's strategies when cornered in St. Paul, including details of the escape down the back stairs, and the confrontation with the "soap salesman:" S.P. Cowley to Director, 11 April 1934, DF-514; The account of the Lexington Avenue shootout as depicted in this chapter was augmented by the account told to Bess by Evelyn Frechette, when she drove to the Greens' apartment immediately after the incident. The details were related by Skinner to the bureau in the various interviews captioned in these notes.

   Newspaper coverage was unreliable due to the confusion in the immediate aftermath of the shootout, with Van Meter not identified until days afterward. However, some details were provided by the following newspaper articles:

   "Dillinger Named as Gunman," *St. Paul Sunday Pioneer Press,* 1 April 1934, p. 1, Sec. 1;

   "Hamilton and Woman Escape After Battle," *Arizona Star*, 1 April 1934; Harry Sawyer's involvement with John Hamilton after the shoot-out on Lexington Avenue, and the facts of Hamilton's ammunition and bullet-proof vest found in the apartment: H.H. Clegg, St. Paul, to Director. 15 April 1934, DF-560; Inventory, including the unsigned letter from Lima: Clegg, St. Paul to Director, Washington, D.C., 31 March 1934, DF-380.

## Notes for Chapter 14

1. The medical treatment obtained for Dillinger after the Lexington Avenue shootout:

   T.F. Baughman, St. Paul, to Director, 6 April 1934, DF-427; H.H. Clegg, St. Paul, to Director, 15 April 1934, DF-560; Cowley, Chicago, to Director, 8 April 1934,DF-468; The immediate aftermath of the shootout, as told to Bess Green by both Evelyn Frechette and Homer Van Meter:

   Clegg to Director, 15 April 1934, DF-560; Skinner's conflicts with Van Meter: W.A. Rorer, St. Paul, to File, 9 April 1934, DF-491; Cowley to Director, 11 April 1934, DF-514; Hamilton's activities after the shootout, and the lifting of Hamilton's fingerprint and identification of same, with allegation of a print of Evelyn Frechette: Notesteen, St. Paul, to File, 12 April 1934, DF-539. The activities of Dr. Clayton E. May and Augusta Salt in the treating of Dillinger's leg wound are recorded in the following newspaper accounts of the court trial of the two:

"Threatened, Dr. May Says, in Statement," *St. Paul Pioneer Press,* 18 May 1934; ". Dr. May Describes Dillinger Meeting,"*Pioneer Press*, 19 May 1934.

2. Hoover's sardonic response to W.A. Rorer's request for police backup was recorded in: Transcript of telephone conversation between Mr. Hoover and W.A. Rorer, Memo of Apr. 1, 1934, DF-264. The events which brought Lucy and Leona Goodman and Opal Whyte to the apartment on Marshall Avenue: Clegg to Director, 31 March 1934; DF-380; Cowley, to Director, 3 April 1934, DF-293; Cowley, to Director, 8 April 1834, DF-468;Clegg, to Director, 15 April 1934, DF-560; Van Wagoner, Chicago, to File, 11 April 1934, DF-538. The bureau's version of the shooting of Eddie Green: Clegg, to Director, 4 April 1934, DF-467.
3. The conditions of Bess' incommunicado incarceration: Cowley to Director, 12 April 1934, DF-515; Automobile and safe deposit transactions: Cowley, to Director, 4 April 1934. DF-325; Green's behavior in the hospital after the shooting: Clegg, to Director, 4 April 1934, DF-467;T.E. Billings, Chicago, to File, 9 April 1934, DF-453; Tom Filbin's involvement in the sale of Dillinger's car to Bess Green: Director, Washington, to Cowley, 10 April 1934, DF-511.

Newspaper coverage of the shooting of Eddie Green, and the subsequent public information on "Beth Green" are as follows:

"Dillinger Pal is Wounded in Gun Fight," *Arizona Citizen*, 4 April 1934;"Beth Green Rejects Attorneys' Efforts to Obtain her Release," *St. Paul Pioneer Press*, 11 April 1934; "Beth Green Talks,"*Pioneer Press*, 12 April 1934.

Background information on Tom Filbin, Dillinger's automobile financier, is related in detail, along with other extensive information on the St. Paul crime scene, in the following work:

Maccabee, Paul, *John Dillinger Slept Here,* St. Paul: Minnesota Historical Society Press, 1995.

The further background on Bessie Skinner, including the tangled social connections to the St. Paul underworld, the details of the meeting with Dr. Clayton E. May; the details of the bureau agents' meeting with Leona Goodman and Lucy Jackson, were found in the following document:

Synopsis: *Edward Green, with aliases,* 23 July 1936, Federal Bureau of Investigation No. 62-29777, RG 65; File No. 95-57-8; NA, College Park, MD; Payment to the Anker Hospital for Green's treatment: Clegg, to Director, 14 April 1934, DF-541.

## Notes for Chapter 15

1. Opal Long's recollections of the Lexington Avenue shootout, and the immediate aftermath: "My Adventures with the Dillinger Gang," *Chicago Herald and Examiner*, 15 September 1934; The raid on the Green Lantern Inn: "Dynamite and Guns Seized in Dillinger Hunt," *St. Paul Pioneer Press*, 6 April 1934, p. 1.; Opal Long's complicity in St. Paul was established in: Purvis, Chicago, to Director, 8 April 1934, DF-393.
2. Dillinger's plan to release Pierpont, Clark, and Makley from the Ohio Penitentiary, and the letters to the three prisoners: Peter J. Nolan, Cincinnati, to File, 14 April 1934, DF-588; Lima escape plan: S.P. Cowley, Chicago, to File, 12 April 1934, DF-515; The letters to the prisoners in Lima from Mary Kinder and Opal Long, had been copied word-for-word by agents before being censured and/or withheld: Nolan, Cincinnati, to File, 16 April 1934, DF-588.

   The conversations within the prison visits between Pierpont, his family, and Mary Kinder, with her deceptive visitor status as his "wife:" Klein, Cincinnati, to File, 12 April 1934, DF-530.

   The raids on Mary Kinder's houses at Daly Street and Luett Street in Indianapolis, the retention of Mary Kinder in custody, and the questioning of the other women in the family: Connolley to File, 9 April 1934. DF-530; Connolley, Telegram to Director, 9 April 1934, DF-408; The telegram sent to Detroit, earmarked for Opal Long by Jessie Levy: N.B. Klein, Cincinnati, to File, 10 April 1934, DF-447; The decision to watch the activities of Jesse Levy: E.J. Connolley, Cincinnati, to File,11 April 1934, DF-530; The surveillance placed upon Jesse Levy recorded the writer and sender of the telegram to Opal Long as sent by "a woman between 40-45 years, plump build, graying hair and eyeglasses."

   Jessie Levy had reason to be cautious. E.J. Connolly, the agent in charge in Cincinnati, decided that Jesse Levy should be watched. This arrangement was made through the prosecuting attorney at Lima.
3. The interrogations of Evelyn Frechette's friends and family members, and their findings: Waters to File, 22 March 1934, DF-173; FBI Interview with Patsy Frechette and Marge Edwards: Purvis to Director, 10 April 1934, DF-385; J.J. Metcalfe, Chicago, to File, 23 March 1934, DF-181; Frechette with Dillinger in home of Augusta Salt was revealed in the subsequent trial testimony, and reported in: "Dillinger Kidnapped Him, Dr. May Asserts,"

   *Pioneer Press*, April 27, 1934, p. 1; The detainment of Mrs. Betty (Chico) Marx was recorded in:

   F.X. Fay, New York, to Director, 5 April 1934, DF-326; The series of articles ghost-written by John Dillinger, Sr., helped to piece the visit of Dillinger and Evelyn Frechette to Mooresville. They are: "Dillinger's Own Story of his Wooden Gun Escape," *New York Sunday Mirror*, 2 December 1934, magazine p. 10; "How the Hunted Bandit Chose His Own Grave,"*Mirror*, 16

December 1934, magazine p. 13; "Crimes Now Revealed by his Father," *Mirror*, 25 November 1934, magazine p. 11; The bureau's intelligence regarding the Mooresville Family Reunion, which included the fact that John and Hubert Dillinger had driven unrecognized past three agents: Connolley to File, 11 April 1934, DF-530.

4. Evelyn Frechette's further attempt to divorce Welton Sparks: Conroy, Kansas City, Telegram to H.H. Clegg, St. Paul, 5 April 1934, -392NR5; Larry Streng was the informant who notified the bureau that Dillinger would be at the 416 State Street location. Streng was inadvertently giving information over his wiretapped telephone, or speaking to someone else who was acting as an informant. This conclusion is based upon the fact that it was the FBI's unbending policy to black out the names of their informants in the documents revealed under the Freedom of Information Act, and made available in the Reading Room in Washington, DC. There is no attempt to conceal Streng's name in the scores of pages where it is mentioned. If Streng were an informant, his name would be available only if a clerk had overlooked it with the black censuring marker that disguised an informant's name; Larry Streng's admissions to the bureau informant, and the wiretap affixed to Streng's telephone: Director, to Chicago, 2 April 1934, DF-261; Purvis, Chicago, to Director, 6 April 1934, DF-390; Klein, Cincinnati, to File, 10 April 1934, DF-447; Opal Long's activities with Larry Streng just prior to Frechette's arrest: Purvis, Telegram to St. Paul Division, 5 April 1934; DF-546NR8; Streng later claimed he didn't know Evelyn Frechette was the "Billie" connected with Dillinger until as late as March 29, 1934. Streng's April 9 date with Evelyn at the State Street Tavern was confirmed in: Earl Van Wagoner, Chicago, to File, 11 April 1934, DF-538.
5. After Cowley told Purvis to tell the truth to the press about Evelyn's arrest, Hoover documented his veto to the decision by noting on a copy of Cowley's memo to file: "I told Purvis to not make any statement at this time. 4-11-34 J.E.H." The memo from Purvis to Cowley regarding the advisability of informing the press of Frechette's arrest, and Hoover's subsequent reaction: Sam Cowley, Chicago, to Director, 11 April 1934, DF-517; Director to Cowley, 11 April 1934, DF-524.
6. The formal charges against Frechette, with evidence: Notesteen, St. Paul, to File, 12 April 1934, DF-539; Identification of her coat: D.L. Nicholson, St. Paul, to File, 9 April 1934, DF-466; Warrant for removal to St. Paul, with bail: "Frechetti Woman to be Tried in St. Paul," *St. Paul Pioneer Press*, 13 April 1934; "Frechette Bond Set at $60,000 on Compromise," *Pioneer Press* 14 April 1934; Piquett's statement to the press regarding the proposed reduction of Frechette's bail: "Dillinger Just a Nice Boy," *Pioneer Press*, 22 April 1934. Agent H.H. Reinecke steadfastly denied having used physical force or psychological inducements to get Evelyn to discuss Dillinger with the Bureau: "Frechette Got No 3d Degree, U.S. Aid Avers," *Pioneer Press,* 17 May 1934.

Conclusion: Evelyn's rebuttal was told to family and friends by Frechette in later years. Individuals known to Evelyn Frechette related the story to the author in interviews. Their names are withheld.

## Notes for Chapter 16

1. The specifics of the Federal Harboring Law were cited in:
   Agent Gordon Dean, Washington, to Joseph Keenan, upon request of U.S. Attorney McPike, San Francisco, 25 September 1934;
   File No. 62-29777; National Archives 2, College Park, MA, Record Group 129; Notorious Offenders; 95-57- 8; Sec. 8., 5-16-35 — 12-3-35; The Court procedings of Beth Green: District of Minnesota, Third Division, *Complaint*, U.S. v. Beth Green and Edward Green, 10 April 1934;
   D. Minnesota, Third Div., *Transcript of Proceedings*, U.S. v. Beth Green and Edward Green, 10
   D. Minnesota, Third Div., *Final Mittimus*, U.S. v. Beth Green and Edward Green, 10 April 1934.
2. The tracking of Helen Gillis' activities around her husband's escape from the Statesville Prison at Joliet, Illinois, are taken from statements made to the Justice Department after her arrest at the Little Bohemia: L. Nicholson, St. Paul, to File, 14 May 1934; DF-1460. More comprehensive background on Lester Gillis, with his wife, Helen, including his earlier affiliations with Tommy Carroll and Homer Van Meter, and San Francisco and Reno, Nevada: U.S. v. Chase, Gillis, Negri, et al., No. 25287-; and Synopsis: "Lester Gillis, with aliases;" 28 November 1934; F.B.I., No. 62-29777, Record Group 65; File No. 95-57-8; Sec. 2, Pt. 2; 4-26-34 — 5- 18-34, National Archives at College Park, Maryland; The facts regarding the rental of Lester Gillis' cottage near the Indiana Dunes and Homer Van Meter's residency: Peterson to File, Chicago, 9 March 1935; File No. 62-29777-; NA, College Park, MD, RG129; 95-57-8; Sec. 8; also filed under V.W. Peterson, Chicago, to File, 9 March 1935, U.S. v. Chase, et al. No. 25287, RG 65, Pt. 2, 4-26-34 – 5-18-34, NA, College Park, MD;
   Facts on the genealogy of Helen Gillis were supplied by Dillinger researcher Steve Nichols: State of Indiana, County of Porter (Valparaiso) Marriage License, Lester Gillis to Helen Warwrzyniek, 30 October 1928; Steve Nichols supplied the dates of the births of Helen Gillis' children, Darlene and Ronald. Other sources: V.W. Peterson, Chicago to File, 19 July 1934, DF-2782; Leona (Mrs. William) McMahon's name and Bremerton, Washington address: I.D. #2941 and #3020; *Helen Gillis with Alias;* Helen Gillis' quote that she wanted to "die with Les," was obtained in an interview with Jean Delaney Crompton: E.A. Tamm to Director, 14 June 1934, DF-2006; The description of the Andromeda Cafe at 155 Columbus Avenue in San Francisco: Author's visit, 1998. Lester Gillis' presence: H.H. Clegg, St. Paul, to Director, 15 April 1934, DF-560.

3. Jean Delaney Crompton's dislike of Comforti: *Ibid.*; The activities surrounding Marie Comforti's trail to the Little Bohemia, and the origin of her relationship with Van Meter were found in her statements made to the bureau after her arrest: D.L. Nicholson, St. Paul, to File, 14 May 1934;

   DF-1460; Purvis to File; 2 May 1934. DF-1451; Peterson to File, 4 June 1934, DF-1775; "Comforti Girl Pleads Guilty," *Wisconsin State Journal*, 12 September 1934; Hoover to Attorney General, 26 December 1934, DF-4982: commented and embellished a *Chicago Tribune* article entitled, "Comforti Member of 42 Gang."Information about the Silver Slipper and the Forty-Two Gang was also published in: Alvin Karpis, and Bill Trent, *The Alvin Karpis Story,* New York: Coward, McCann & Geoghegan, Inc., 1971.

   Hoover to Attorney General, 26 Dec. 34 – 4982, which reported the publication of the article entitled, "Comforti Member of 42 Gang." This article also mentioned Marie's Boston bull puppy, a gift from Van Meter.

4. Crompton's statement that Comforti was the "most convenient thing available" to Van Meter: E.A. Tamm to Director, 14 June 1934, DF-2006; Van Meter (and Ed Green): "Edward Green with Aliases," 23 July 1936; File No. 62-29777-576; NA, College Park, MD, Record Group 129; Notorious Offenders; 95-57-8; Sec. 8., Call No. 3241; Jean Delaney Crompton's version of the April 19 dinner at Louis Cernocky's "Louie's Place" was revealed in a prison interview with Alderson Supervisor Hironimus: Lee F. Malone, Pittsburgh, to File, 11 July 1934, DF-2569; Other background information on Cernocky: F..W. Peterson, Chicago, to File, 19 July 1934, DF-2782; The destination of Van Meter and Dillinger after the April 13 police station raid: Tamm to Director, 4 June 1934, DF-1877; Federal District Court:Western District of Wisconsin, Report of Grand Jury in re: John Hamilton, et al., Filed 19 May 1934.

5. Dillinger's stay at Sault Ste. Marie on April 17, 1934, with John Hamilton and Pat Cherrington: *Ibid.*; *Hoover to Attorney General*, 26 April 1934; Federal Bureau of Investigation No. 62-29777, Record Group 65; File No. 95-57- 8; Sec. 2, Pt. 2; 4-26-34 – 5-18-34, NA, College Park, MD; and V.W. Petersen, Chicago, to File, 23 May 1934; FN62-29777-1668; Hoover to File, I.D. Order, 62-29777-2941, p. 12; Newspaper coverage: "Hamilton's Sister Held Under $1,000 Bond," *Wisconsin State Journal*, 24 April 1934; The opening of Pat Cherrington's Chicago safe deposit box, and the raid on the Warsaw police station, were reported in:

   "Frechette Bond Set at $60,000 on Compromise," *St. Paul Pioneer Press*, 14 April 1934, p. 1;

   The connection between Father Coughlan, Louis Cernocky, and Frank Traube with Lester Gillis: V.W. Peterson, Chicago, to File, 19 July 1934, DF-2782; Dillinger's hopes of getting in touch with Victor Fasano were reported by Traube to:V.W. Peterson, Chicago, to File, 23 May 1934, DF-1668; Pat Cherrington's role in the Little Bohemia incident, including her trip to St.

Paul to see Dr. Mortensen for medical care, were taken from her own testimony given at her parole board hearing: U.S. Detention Farm Milan, Michigan, *Board of Parole Hearing Pat Cherrington,* 26 April 1935; Cherrington, Arthur AZ-199, BOP, Alcatraz, RG 129, San Bruno, California;

Peterson to Chicago File, 4 June 1934, DF-1775; Hoover to Tamm, 12 June 1934, FN-1971.

Pat Cherrington's insights into the gang members were revealed when she was interviewed by Special Agent Madela shortly after her Chicago arrest: D.L. Nicholson, St. Paul, to File, 20 July 1934, DF-2767; Dillinger's feelings on Evelyn's imprisonment: V.W. Petersen, Chicago, to File, 17 May 1934, FN-1478.

6. Author's interviews with Audrey Voss, George Bazso, and Kal LaPorte were conducted during personal visits to the Little Bohemia Lodge in Manitowish Waters by the author in August 1989.

   The clothing worn by the gang was left behind in the melee, and was made available for viewing to the author at the Little Bohemia Lodge.

## Notes for Chapter 17

1. Details of the agents' drive to Manitowish Waters from Rhinelander were taken from Purvis' recollections in: Melvin Purvis, *American Agent,* New York: Garden City Press, 1938 (1 ed.), pp. 4—8; Details of the Voss' ride to Rhinlander provided by Audrey Voss, interview with author, 1989; Newspaper articles had placed as many as fifty agents at the Lodge. This number was exaggerated. Agent Clegg placed the number at twelve. "Tip Delayed on Dillinger," *St. Paul Pioneer Press,* 23 April 1934; "Outlaw Holds Resort 3 Days in Wisconsin," *Madison Capital Times,* 23 April 1934, p. 1.; Hoover's influence in resisting the help of local law enforcement in the raid: Turner, William W., *Hoover's F.B.I.*, New York: Thunder Mouth Press, 1993, pp 217—219. In contrast and in fairness, it should be stated that the official FBI explanation regarding local police intervention published in Whitehead, p. 96.
2. Frank Traube's and H.H. Clegg's eyewitness account of the shooting was found in the transcript of the depositions taken immediately following the shooting:

   Examination of: H.H. Clegg, J.M. Roberts, Dr. R. Oldfield, Trank Traube and Emil Wanatka; 23 April 1934, DF-1461; H.H. Clegg wrote a rebuttal disputing the transcription and adding his own changes to the testimony, in a letter to the Director on May 15. This testimony and rebuttal are filed in:Clegg, St. Paul, to Director, 15 May 1934, DF-1465; Werner Hanni's version of the raid is found in:W. Hanni to Director, 22 May 1934, DF-1753; Coroner's Inquest, 23 April 1934; DF-1462; Examination of Mr. Lang, 23 April 1934, DF-1461;H.H. Clegg's Rebuttal Letter to Director, 15 May 1934, DF-1465.

3. The visit by Pat Cherrington has been documented here as being solely for medical purposes, although there have been other, unsubstantiated yet published reports to the contrary. A tiny, 35-cent book was published in 1950 by Ken Krippene, who claimed to have been privy to further information as follows. In his book, Mr. Krippene alleged that Cherrington's purpose in visiting St. Paul while Dillinger resided at the Little Bohemia Lodge was to fence (in Minneapolis) a suitcase full of stolen securities. After the negotiations, the million dollars were sold for two hundred thousand dollars cash. All in small bills, it was packed in a suitcase and she returned to Wisconsin with it, returning safely on Sunday morning. She gave the suitcase to Dillinger and left for the west side of Chicago, and was gone by early Sunday afternoon. After escaping from the Little Bohemia, Dillinger buried this money "five hundred yards straight north."

   For purpose of comparison, this version has been entered to the record. The only fact that can substantiate this fantastic story is that Dillinger did run in a northerly direction to affect his escape from the Lodge. The story of Dillinger's alleged buried money is found in:

   "Dillinger's Buried Loot," Ken Krippene, *Buried Treasure*, New York: Garden City Publishing Co., 1950, pp. 64–68.

   The more credible evidence, which supports the claims for medical treatment, are found in Cherrington's parole testimony, and are also backed by her troublesome medical history as recorded in her file from the Alderson, W. Va. facility, as well as:

   U.S. Detention Farm Milan, Michigan, *Board of Parole Hearing Pat Cherrington,* 26 April 1935; Cherrington, Arthur AZ-199; U.S. Penitentiary, General Records of the Bureau of Prisons, Records of the U.S. Penitentiary; Alcatraz, Calif. Record Group 129; Box 215; National Archives at San Bruno, San Bruno, California.

   In addition, agents reported that a Packard sedan, which is the car that Reilly had been driving, had entered the roadway for a brief moment during the raid and had careened out of the roadway, disappearing.

4. Lester Gillis' shooting of Agents Newman and Baum, with Constable Christiansen, with his prior activities at Lang's and Koerner's lodge: D.L. Nicholsen, St. Paul, to File, "Summary Report on murder of Sp. Agent W. Carter Baum by Lester Gillis," 3 May 1934, DF- 1979; J. Hoover to Attorney General, 26 April 1934; Federal Bureau of Investigation No. 62-29777, Record Group 65; File No. 95-57-8; Sec. 2, Pt. 2; 4-26-34 — 5-18-34, NA at College Park, MD. Frank Traube's and H.H. Clegg's eyewitness account of the shooting was found in the transcript of the depositions taken immediately following the shooting:

   Examination of: H.H. Clegg, J.M. Roberts, Dr. R. Oldfield, Trank Traube and Emil Wanatka; 23 April 1934, DF-1461; H.H. Clegg wrote a rebuttal disputing the transcription and adding his own changes to the testimony, in a letter to the Director on May 15. This testimony and rebuttal are filed in:Clegg, St. Paul, to Director, 15 May 1934, DF-1465; Werner Hanni's version of the raid is found in:W. Hanni to Director, 22 May 1934, DF-1753; Coroner's Inquest, 23 April 1934; DF-1462; Examination of Mr. Lang, 23 April 1934, DF-1461;H.H. Clegg's Rebuttal Letter to Director, 15 May 1934, DF-1465; Robert Johnson's account of being kidnapped by Dillinger, Hamilton and Van Meter:

"Carpenter Tells of Driving Auto for Gangsters," *St. Paul Pioneer Press,* 24 April 1934, p. 2; "Dillinger Gives Aid to Resort Woman," *Pioneer Press*, 24 April 1934, p. 4.

Conclusion: The roles of George Baszo, Audrey Voss and Calvin La Porte were reported to the author in personal interviews during a visit to Manitowish Waters in the summer of 1989.

## Notes for Chapter 18

1. The earliest pleadings that indicted Comforti, Gillis, and Crompton were written under their assumed names:D. Wisconsin, Western D., *Temporary Mittimus,* U.S. v. Rose Ancker, Ann Southern and Marian Marr, 25 April 1934; Confirmation of the story of the reporters who instigated the petition to remove Purvis after the shootings: Federal Bureau of Investigation No. 62-29777, RG 65; File No. 95-57-8; Sec. 2, Pt. 2; 4-26-34 — 5-18-34, NA, College Park, MD.
2. "Dillinger Gang Girls In County Jail," *Madison Capital Times,* 24 April 1934, p. 1; "Molls' Under $150,000 Bail," *Capital Times*, 25 April 1934, p. 1; "Gang Girls Crack Under Grilling," *Wisconsin State Journal*, 26 April 1934, p. 1; "Three Girls Under Airtight Guard," *Wisconsin*, 24 April 1934.

   J. Edgar Hoover's statements regarding the women of the Dillinger gang were later embellished in the following three works:

   Cooper, Courtney Ryley, *Ten Thousand Public Enemies*, Boston: Little, Brown & Co., 1935;.

   Cooper, *Here's To Crime,* Boston: Little, Brown & Co.,1937; and Hoover, J. Edgar, *Persons in Hiding,* Boston: Little, Brown & Co., 1938.

   Marie Comforti's parentage: State of Illinois, County of Cook, Dept. of Commerce, *Certificate of Death*, Eleanor Krause, Filed 30 June 1943, File No. 480; The census listed the Costello Family as William and Sarah Costello, 224 South Winchester, who had one "unrelated child" in their home, named "Marie Sacarino," aged 4½, in addition to their own child, Charles Costello: State of Illinois, County of Cook, Dept. of Commerce, *1920 Population Census*;

   William Costello, d. 21 February 1933; Comforti biography as pieced together by the Justice Dept. : Peterson to File, Chicago, June 4, 1934, DF-1775; D.M. Ladd to Director, 9 July 1934, DF-2569; D.L. Nicholson, St. Paul, to File 14 May 1934, DF-1460; Hoover to Attorney General, 26 December 1934, DF- 4982, which reported the publication of the article entitled, "Comforti Member of 42 Gang." This article also mentioned Marie's Boston bull puppy, a gift from Van Meter; Comforti's allegations of desertion: Melvin Purvis, Chicago, to Clegg, St. Paul, 15 June 1934, DF-2002.

3. *Ibid.*: Jean Delaney Crompton told Agent Clegg that she had been pregnant at the Little Bohemia, that Carroll knew it, and that he had "come to her rescue," which would indicate that an abortion was performed shortly after she was released on probation; "Gang Girl's Sister to Visit Her in Cell," *Wisconsin*, 24 May 1934.

4. The Barker-Karpis Gang: *The Kidnapping of Edward George Bremer, St. Paul, Minnesota*, 19 November 1936, General Records of the Federal Bureau of Investigation, 95-57-8, Sec. 5, Call No. 3241, NA, College Park, MD:

After the death of Arthur Old Man Dunlap, the Barker gang scattered, having picked up William Weaver along the way. His association sprang from an incarceration in the Oklahoma State Penetentiary with Doc Barker, serving time with his boyhood friend Volney Davis for the 1921 murder of night watchman James J. Sherrill.

Now the Barker-Karpis household moved to Kansas City, Missouri. There, the organized crime protection avenues of Johnny Lazia and Judge Cas Welch spawned the prostitution houses and gambling dens of the Prohibition era. Kansas City operated on two distinct levels. Through this junction flowed cattlemen and salesmen to sell their wares in this bustling center of industry and commerce. Through the underground flowed a criminal empire seeking protection and finding it. Francis Keating and Thomas Holden, escaped prisoners from Leavenworth Federal Penitentiary, met the Barkers there. With Harvey Bailey, Larry DeVol, from Kansas City; and Bernard Phillips, an ex-policeman, they robbed a Fort Scott, Kansas bank on June 17, 1932. Along with the Barker-Karpis gang, they were then joined by Jess Doyle, who had been released from the Kansas State Penitentiary that same day.

5. Prime suspect Vern Miller was known as a quiet killer who'd learned his trade as a decorated World War I veteran. As a local hero returning from war, he'd ascended to post of sheriff in his home town in South Dakota, before being arrested and sentenced to jail for misappropriation of county funds. After his parole he got into bootlegging and joined forces with both Vi Matthias, who kept her daughter with her while living with Miller, and a Capone mob connection who recognized the gunman in Miller and took him on.

Clayton, Merle, *Union Station Massacre: The Shootout that Started the FBI's War on Crime*, Indianapolis, The Bobbs-Merrill Co., 1975: The author sets forth the theory that the law enforcers who died at the hands of Vern Miller, Adam Richette, and Arthur "Pretty Boy" Floyd in the transfer attempt of prisoner Frank "Jelly Nash" were the victims of the syndicate of Johnny Lazia, who had local cops on the payroll in Kansas City, MO.

Miller associate Earl Christman, wounded after the Fairbury bank robbery the previous April, had been brought to the home of Miller and Matthis. There, on a bloody cot, he died in the attic. In a chilling antidote, children who played with Vi Matthis' daughter were ordered away from the bolted door of the attic death room; Edna Murray's prison record of escapes Missouri State Prison, Register of Inmates, Edna Muray #28973, Missouri State Archives, D/R 1925, V. 25, P6HA. The Bremer tie-in with Jean Delaney Crompton, and the connection between the Slim of the Little Bohemia and the Slim who was a go-between in handling Bremer ransom money: V.W. Peterson, Chicago, to File, 17 May 1934, DF-1478, p. 9; "Bremer Cash Still Waiting,"*Wisconsin*, 27 January 1934; The biography of Doc Moran:

Cooper, *Here's To Crime*, Boston: Little, Brown & Co., 1937, p. 76.

6. Helen Gillis' refusal to cooperate with Justice Dept. : Melvin Purvis, Chicago, to Clegg, St. Paul,15 June 1934, DF-2002; The frustration of agents, who'd used "every method of attack," in getting Helen Gillis to break: D.L. Nicholson, St. Paul, to File 14 May 1934, DF-1460; "Hill to Defend Mrs. Nelson, Gangster Girl," *Wisconsin*, 4 May 1934; Ole Catfish: "Indians Track Fleeing Dillinger Aide," *Wisconsin State Journal,* 27 April 1934; Jimmy Murray's restaurant:

V.W. Peterson to File, Chicago, 23 August 1934, DF-3642; This cite also contained allegations by an unknown informant that Dillinger and Van Meter were in Fort Wayne, Indiana, on May 2, that they had plenty of cash, ammunition, and license plates with them.

7. "Dillinger Hideout Believed in St. Paul," *St. Paul Pioneer Press,* 24 April 1934, p. 1;"Bloody Car Found; Police Close in Pursuit," *Wisconsin,* 23 April 1934, p. 1; There is doubt that the corpse found in the Aurora gravel pit was not John Hamilton. FBI reports have included a description of the corpse's clothing. It is far-fetched that Hamilton's burial clothing allegedly survived intact while his fingers decomposed. FBI reports listed the corpse dressed in a "blue serge suit," and his hat: *Recovery and Identification of the Body of John Hamilton, 18 March, 1938,* General Records of the Federal Bureau of Investigation, 95-57-8, Sec. 5, Call No. 3241, NA, College Park, MD. The connection between Doc Moran and John Hamilton was suggested in: Cooper, *Here's To Crime,* Boston: Little, Brown & Co., 1937, pp. 83, 84.

The connection between Frankie Pope, soldier of Frank Nitti, and the Dillinger gang was confessed by Ed Shouse: V.W. Peterson to File, Chicago, 17 May 1934, DF-1478; Death of Pope, listed in Chicago Crime Commission directory, information provided by Rick Mattix; Order denying the petition of Anna Steve: *Pioneer Press*, April 24 1934; Purvis to U.S. Attorney Dwight H. Green, 26 December 1934, DF-4970; Assistant U.S. Attorney Thurman

B. Doyle to United States Attorney General, Washington, DC, 24 September 1934; General Records of the Federal Bureau of Investigation, 95-57-8, Sec. 5, Call No. 3241, National Archives at College Park, MD.

8. "Gang Girls Win Probation" *Wisconsin State Journal*, 25 May 1934; "Trio Ordered Held by U.S. Justice Chiefs," *Wisconsin State Journal*, 26 May 1934; *Madison Capital Times*, which provided, among others, the following articles:

"Dillinger Girl Sobs as Sister Comes to Aid," 11 May 1934;

"Nelson's Bride, Mother of Two Children," 15 May 1934;

"Leave City After Tour of Stores," 26 May 1934;

"Dillinger Girls Go Shopping, Drink Beer, Leave Our City, 27 May 1934.

Conclusion: Evelyn Frechette's experience in St. Paul: "Dillinger Cop Proof, Woman Pal Asserts," *Pioneer Press,* 26 April 1934, p. 1; Inside knowledge that Evelyn Frechette was brought in and out of solitary confinement in St. Paul was found in: H.H. Clegg, Inspector, to SAC, Detroit, 11 June 1934, DF-1970.

## Notes for Chapter 19

The chronological narrative was developed by comparing the newspaper reportage to a hand-written trial log that was found among the court transcripts. Unsigned, but most likely kept by Court Reporter L. Ayer, this journal provided an hourly account of the events as they unfurled in the courtroom. The newspaper articles that provided the backdrop to the courtroom pleadings are cited as follows:

"Doctor and Nurse Lack Bail," *St. Paul Pioneer Press*, 19 April 1934;

"Dillinger Cop Proof, Woman Pal Asserts," *Pioneer Press,* 26 April 1934, p. 1;

"Dillinger Just A Nice Boy," *St. Paul Pioneer Press*, 22 April 1934;

"Frechetti Woman to be Tried in St. Paul," *St. Paul Pioneer Press*, 13 April 1934; p. 1;

"Bail Cut for Dr. May," *St. Paul Dispatch*, 1 May 1934;

"Frechette Pleads Not Guilty," *Dispatch*, 2 May 1934;

Various Articles, *Dispatch,* 2—4 May 1934;

"Beth Green Guilty," *Dispatch*, 5 May 1934;

Various articles, *Dispatch*, 6—14 May 1934;

"Evelyn Frechette Nearly Escapes," *Pioneer Press,* 15 May 1934; p. 1;

"Frechette Placed at Shooting Scene," *Pioneer Press*, 16 April 1934, p. 1;

"3d Degree Denied in Frechette Quiz," *Pioneer Press*, 17 April 1934, p.1;

"Government Jails Witness," *Arizona Star*, 15 May 1934;

"Threatened, Dr. May Says," *Pioneer Press*, 18 May 1934, p. 1;

"Dr. May Describes Dillinger Meeting," *Pioneer Press*, 19 May 1934, p. 1;

"Jury Gets Case," *Pioneer Press*, 22 May 1934, p. 1;

"Frechette and Dr. May Get 2 Years," *Pioneer Press*, 23 May 1934; p. 1;

"Judge to Alter Prison Order for Frechette," *Pioneer Press*, 24 May 1934; p. 1;

"U.S. Helped by Beth Green," *Pioneer Press*, 29 May 1934, p. 1.

1. During his own trial for harboring that occurred after Dillinger's death, Louis Piquett relayed his educational background and political history. He revealed the telephone call from Dillinger that involved him in the defense of Evelyn Frechette, which occurred immediately following her arrest, and the $500 payment for Frechette's defense delivered to Arthur O'Leary, go-between for Piquett. The facts were reiterated during O'Leary's own trial testimony: "Piquett Hid Dillinger," *Chicago Tribune*, 10 January 1935, p. 1; ""Piquett Fights U.S. Version of Dillinger Ploy," *Tribune,* 11 January 1935, p. 1.

   Evelyn Frechette's enforced solitary confinement in St. Paul: H.H. Clegg, Inspector, to SAC, Detroit, 11 June 1934, DF-1970; Louis Piquett's criminal history was taken from:

   Purvis to Director, 6 September 1934, DF-3784;

2. Case of Beth Green:

   Green's admission that Dillinger had contributed to Tom Brown's political campaign: Director to Mr. Tamm, SAC Pittsburgh, 12 June 1934, DF-1971;

   U.S. District Court, Minnesota, Case No. 6037, Beth and Eugene Green, Dr. May and Nurse Salt; and Case Nos. 6388, 6375 and 6373:

   City of Chicago, Northern District of Illinois, Seventh Circuit, Eastern Division, *Complaint*, U.S. v. Mary Evelyn Frechette, 12 April 1934;

   City of Chicago, No. Dist. Illinois, Seventh Cir. Eastern Div., *Warrant to Apprehend,* 13 April 1934;

   City of Chicago, No. Dist. Illinois, Seventh Cir. Eastern Div., U.S. v. Mary Evelyn Frechette, alias etc., *Mittimus on Adjournment,* 13 April 1934;

   City of Chicago, No. Dist. Illinois, Seventh Cir. Eastern Div., U.S. v. Mary Evelyn Frechette, alias etc., *Warrant for Removal,* 18 April 1934;

   District of Minnesota, Third Division, U.S. v. Mary EvelynFrechette (with aliases), *Mittimus*, 25 April 1934;

   D. Minnesota, Third Div., *Complaint*, John Doe and Jane Doe, 14 April 1934;

   D. Minnesota, Third Div., *Warrant of Arrest*, U.S. v. John Doe and Jane Doe, 18 April 1934;

   D. Minnesota, Third Div., *Findings of Grand Jury*, April 1934;

   D. Minnesota, Third Div., *Mittimus*, U.S. v. Beth Green and Edward Green, 23 May 1934;

   D. Minnesota, Third Div., *Transcript of Proceedings*, U.S. v. Evelyn Frechette, with alias, Clayton E. May, Mrs. A. Salt with alias, Filed 26 May 1934;

D. Minnesota, Third Div., *Order Requiring Witness to Give Recognizance with Surities*, Dolores Smart, Filed 15 May 1934;

D. Minnesota, Third Division, *Writ and Commitment*, filed 23 May 1934;

Milan, Michigan, U.S. Detention Farm, *Return Writ*, Filed 3 June 1934;

D. Minnesota, Third Division, *Notice of Appeal*, Filed 6 August 1934;

D. Minnesota, Third Division, *Assignments of Error*, Filed 6 August 1934.

3. Correspondence regarding Frechette's alleged escape attempt: H.H. Clegg, St. Paul, Telegram to Hoover, 16 May 1934. DF-1447/1448.
4. Many local citizens were interviewed for the jury, and newspapers occasionally published some of the wrong names. To add to the confusion, the "*List of Jurors*" within the transcript was written out by hand, with names crossed out as prospective jurors were dismissed. Yet the jurors listed in this chapter were confirmed by checking several lists against each other and comparing those with written and published accounts.

   They were Louis Grunwaldt, a forty-two-year-old blacksmith; Herbert McGrath, a forty-year-old pole and timber salesman; Charles M. Gregory, a twenty-eight-year-old antique shop operator; Ambrose Keene, a twenty-two-year-old stock room employee; Edward W. Ensley, a thirty-four-year-old depot ticket seller; George Murdock; a thirty-two-year-old draftsman from Wabasha; Edward A. Effertz, a forty-eight-year-old shop foreman; Gust Schmidt, of Winona; George Carrier, a fifty-three-year-old oil station operator; Reinhold Engfer, a sixty-year-old farmer; and John J. Fredericks of Bald Eagle. After they were empaneled and sworn, the judge ordered that two alternate jurors be selected and sworn. Cushing F. Wright and Frank Stoppel stepped in to served as petit jurors, as alternates were formally called.
5. The age of Wallace Salt is questionable. Some accounts list Wallace Salt as being as young as eleven, others date him at thirteen years of age.

   The source of Dr. Clayton E. May's conduct with Dolores Smart on the night of Dillinger's injury is formed from an interview with Beth Green; his reputation as an abortionist stemmed from an indictment filed in Hennepin County District Court, Criminal Docket No. 29214, dated February 26, 1931: D.L. Nicholson, St. Paul., to File, 15 May 1934, DF-1440.

   Conclusion: Bess Green's letter to Hugh Clegg: H.H. Clegg, Inspector, St. Paul, to Director, 4 June 1934, DF-1800.

## Notes for Chapter 20

1. Justice Department memoranda regarding Beth Green in Chicago: Purvis, Chicago, to Director, June 1934, DF-1821; Underworld belief in St. Paul that Bess had talked: DF-2006; The intake procedure applied to Beth Green at Alderson: Inmate Beth Green, U.S. Industrial Institution for Women, Alderson, W.Virginia, General Records, FBOP, Archive, FOI, 320 First St., N.W. Washington, DC 20523.

The historical and operational background on the Federal Industrial Institution for Women at Alderson, West Virginia: U.S. Dept. of Justice, "Federal Offenders, 1931—32," "1932—33," "1933—1934," "1934—35," "1935—36," "1936—37," "Milan, 1938—40." U.S. Bureau of Prisons, "The Alderson Saga;" "Federal Industrial Institution for Women," "Federal Reformatory for Women," "Federal Correctional Institutional, Milan, Michigan." Archives, Federal Bureau of Prisons, Washington, DC.

Beth's letter to Green's mother: DF-3086.

2. The Federal Harboring Indictments against Pat Cherrington, Homer Van Meter, Tommy Carroll, Lester Gillis, et al: U.S. District Court, Northern District of Illinois, Eastern Division, Case No. 10923, June 1934; U.S. District Court, Western District of Wisconsin, Case No. 10922 and 10923 Criminal, July 1934; "Indict Dillinger Gang Here," Wisconsin State Journal, 19 May 1934; Federal Crime Bill Information: Whitehead, p. 102.
3. In the wake of the Little Bohemia Debacle, Cowley had been taken from Washington and installed as the head in Chicago of a division that would be called the Special Squad. This somewhat aggrandized quote was most likely a variation on Hoover's true charge to Sam Cowley. Cooper, *Persons In Hiding*; p. 98.
4. Fugitives often used houses of prostitution as hideouts. Gillis was never tracked to East St. Louis on any other occasion. He was a creature of habit who visited the same places with regularity. The relevance of this information bears scrutiny. While there is no proof that Lester Gillis was faithful to Helen at all times, they were together at every opportunity: Peterson, Chicago, to File, 23 May 1934, DF-1668.
5. The Justice Department memoranda regarding the surveillance of Helen Gillis, Jean Delaney Crompton, and Marie Comforti after their release on probation: M.H. Purvis, SAC, to Director, 1 June 1934 DF-1810; Cowley to Director, 11 June 1934, DF-1924; Father Coughlan's call to Cowley regarding movements of Baby Face Nelson, Marie Comforti surveillance lifted; Crompton & Carroll in New Lawrence Hotel; DF-2782. p. 54; Helen Gillis' attempt to get her car: H.H. Clegg, St. Paul, to George F. Sullivan, U.S. Attorney, St. Paul, 8 June 1934, DF-1889;

Wiretap placed on Fitzsimmins' phone: W.A. Smith to Director, 5 June 1934, DF-1798;

Agents lose track of Gillis' phone tap: Memo of Tamm to Director, June 4, 1934, DF-1877;

Relating to Gillis' request for car: Clegg to Carl Hill, Madison, June 8, 1934, DF-1889;

Director to Cowley, June 2, 1934, DF-1776; Nelson's visit to Fitzsimmons home on May 27; Background on Tom Filbin, financier of Helen's car: Peterson, Chicago, to File, 23 May 1934, DF-1668.

6. The arrest and court actions of Opal Long and Pat Cherrington:

"Police Seize 2 of Dillinger Gang Women," *Tribune*, 1 June 1934; "Opal Pleads Guilty to Harboring Outlaw Here in March," *St. Paul Dispatch*, 29 June 1934;"Patricia Flies Here to Deny Gang Charge," *Wisconsin State Journal*, 20 June 1934;Clark, Bernice, "My Adventures with the Dillinger Gang," *Chicago Herald and Examiner*, 15 September 1934.

The court proceedings in U.S. v. Opal Long: U.S. District Court, District of Minnesota,

Third Division, Case No. 6046-3, Opal Long a/k/a Bernice Clark, June 1934; NA, Great Lakes Region.

The court proceedings in U.S. v. Patricia Young: U.S. District Court, Northern District of Illinois, Eastern Division, Case No. 10923, June 1934; U.S. District

Court, Western District of Wisconsin, Case No. 10922 and 10923 Criminal, July 1934.

Justice Department memoranda relating to arrest of Cherrington and Long:

Information on Jean Burke, Opal Long's letters from prison, Cherrington's incarceration: V.W. Peterson, Chicago to File, 19 July 1934 DF-2782. Burke was somehow thought to be a friend of Dr. Alice Wynekoop. The aged physician had been recently convicted for the gruesome murder of her daughter-in-law, Rheta Wynekoop, in the basement of their mansion. Captain Stege connected Jean Burke to the Wynekoop story, announcing that the two were friends. This is a mystery; prior to her involvement with her daughter-in-law's murder, Wynekoop limited her associations to clubs and hospital philanthropies. Stege had gotten the confession from Wynekoop after a typical twenty-four-hour grilling. Neither he nor others would be totally satisfied with her confession, feeling that she'd tried to protect her son, the philandering husband of the unfortunate murder victim. The only connection that Jean Burke might have had to Dr. Alice Wynekoop must have been a shared space in the county jail.

Information on the payout of $100 to Copeland's mother in Muncie, Opal Long's letter to Clark's mother offering the car:-Wm. Larson, Detroit, to SAC Chicago, 8 June 1934, DF-1855 NRI;

Opal Long's correspondence with Mrs. Clark and Russell Clark, subject the retrieval of her car, clothes, and rings: H.B. Harris, Cincinnati, to File, 26 June 1934, DF-2237.

The manner in which Opal Long and Pat Cherrington were notified of John Hamilton's death was found in a letter she kited out to Bernice Norton in August 1934. The "Frank" referred to is an alias they used when referring to Dillinger. This letter is found in: Wm. Larson, Detroit, to SAC, Chicago, 3 August 1934, DF-3153.

Background on the story of Dr. Alice Wynecoop, Frank Nitti, and "Bugs" Moran was taken from:

Halper, Albert (Ed.,) *The Chicago Crime Book*, Cleveland: World Publishing, 1967.

Opal Long's proposed meeting with Dillinger at a place called Turkey Run State Park, in the vicinity of Clinton, Indiana, and the car crash in Chicago before Detroit: DF-1855 NRI; and DF-1688 (with deletions under the 67D exemption).

Pat Cherrington's activities immediately before, during, and after the incident at the Little Bohemia: Peterson to Chicago File, 4 June 1934, DF-1775; Hoover to Tamm, 12 June 1934, DF-1971;

Opal Long's fight for her possessions from Tucson: "Dillinger Lawyer Wins Legal Tilt," April 21, 1934, *Arizona Star*; Official Opinion that Opal Long had forged marriage papers in order to gain visitor's status at Ohio State Penitentiary: V.W. Peterson to File, Chicago, 17 May 1934, DF-1478. (Note: After her arrest, Opal Long wrote to Mrs. May Clark, addressing her as Mom. It was a source of frustration for the faithful Opal Long to be cast as a mere mistress, even if that is what she actually was. "They know that I am Russell's wife," she said, "but had a warrant for me in the name of Long."

Opal Long's basic statistics as recorded: Opal Long/Bernice Clark #3309, General Register, 1933–1935 Minneapolis Workhouse Commitments, Minneapolis City Hall, Municipal Library.

Opal's letter from the Minneapolis Workhouse was kited out to Bernice Norton, Clark's mother, in late July 1934, right after Dillinger's death. Norton left the letter lying around the house that had two active informants spying throughout the house. The letter was delivered to the bureau and filed under: Wm. Larson, Detroit, to SAC Chicago, 3 August 1934, -3153

Pat Cherrington's medical condition upon her intake to the Alderson Industrial Reformatory was found in: Inmate Patricia Young, Alderson, Archives, BOP, Washington, DC.

Pat Cherrington's personal account of her activities after the Little Bohemia was found in: Sparks and Cherrington, Archives, Federal Bureau of Prisons, Washington, DC.

D.A. Sullivan's payment to Mrs. Daisy Coffee to testify against Opal Long and Pat Cherrington was found in: D.L. Nicholson, St. Paul, to File, 13 June 1934; DF-3032.

## Notes for Chapter 21

1. Jean Delaney Crompton was not found to be with child one week later upon her arrest at Waterloo, Iowa. Hugh Clegg's opinion that Crompton had a miscarriage, and thoughts that she had offered the story as an excuse for her returning to Carroll: E.A. Tamm to Director, 14 June DF- 2006; Bugs

Moran/The Doll House Connection to Dillinger gang and Tommy Carroll: V.W. Peterson, Chicago to File, 19 July 1934, DF-2782;

Helen Gillis' admissions to the Bureau as to the activities at Lake Como: V.W. Peterson, Chicago, to File, 20 February 1935; 95-57-8, Section 8, 5-31-35 – 11-26-35; National Archives, College Park, MD; Jean Delaney Crompton's stay at the New Lawrence Hotel in Chicago, and her admissions to Beth Green: Lee F. Malone, Pittsburgh, to File, 11 July 1934, DF-2569; and timing at leaving Helen Gillis: Telegram from Ladd to Purvis; 8 June 1934, DF-1951NRII.;

The Delaney family members: V.W. Peterson, Chicago, to File, 19 July 1934, DF-2782, p. 21.; Viola Carroll's story: "I Married Tommy Carroll," *Actual Detective*, April and May 1935.

2. *Ibid.*; Jean Delaney Crompton's Divorce: State of Illinois, County of Cook, Complaint for Divorce, Jean Delaney Crompton v. Edward Crompton, Filed 19 December 1935, Superior Court of Cook County; Radio Sally Bennett: V.W. Peterson, Chicago to File, 19 July 1934 — 2782.

Interview with Charles H. Carroll, brother of Tommy Carroll, concerning both Viola Carroll and "Radio Sally" Bennett : H.H. Clegg, St. Paul, to Director, 13 June 1934, DF-1990; Director to Tamm, dated June 11 1934; S.P Cowley to SAC St. Paul, 18 June 934, DF-2002, which stated that Radio Sally Bennett was harboring Joseph Burns of the Michigan City escape; *Radio Sally Bennett*, V.W. Peterson, Chicago to File, 19 July 1934, DF-2782;.Newspaper articles re death of Tommy Carroll:

"Carroll's Moll Jailed," *Wisconsin State Journal*, 9 June 1934;

"Dillinger Gang Gunman Slain by Iowa Police," *Tribune*, 9 June 1934;

"Carroll Moll Faces Prison After Probation is Revoked," *Wisconsin*, 11 June 1934;

"Tommy Carroll, Aide of Dillinger, Is Slain," *Wisconsin*, 8 June 1934;

"Slain Carroll's Girl Ordered to Prison for Year," *Tribune*, 9 June 1934;

"Grief-Stricken Carroll Sweetheart Sobs Her Woe," *Wisconsin*, 10 June 1934.

Interviews conducted with eye-witnesses to the aftermath of Carroll's death:

Text from interview with Francis Veach, Journalist, and Dr. Wade Preece conducted in 1991 by telephone, wherein Veach told the story of his prevention of the cruel hoax about to be perpetrated on Miss Crompton. Text from interview with Wade Preece, M.D., conducted in 1991 by telephone with author.

This interview with Dr. Wade Preece disputes the earlier accounts of Tommy Carroll's death-bed speech, "Take care of the little girl . . . she doesn't know what it's all about." According to the physician, Carroll made two statements. "I'm hit, buddy," was one. The other was, "Don't think you're gonna steal my watch." Author also conducted a telephone interview in 2000 with Peg Nelson, who directed her toward her article, found in the Waterloo Library, entitled, "His 'Waterloo'," and suggested the author compile the facts in the shooting from the article.

The controversy surrounding the availability of reward money and it's potential for appropriation to Officers Walker and Steffen: 95-57-8, Section 3 5-22-34 – 6-16-34 National Archives, College Park, MD.

3. Pat Reilly's arrest:"Dillinger's Pal is Seized in Bed By Federal Men," *Chicago Sunday Tribune*, 27 June 1934; "Reilly, Accused Dillinger Aid, to Face Court, *Tribune*, 8, July 1934; Chicago Office to Hon. Joseph M. Donnelly, U.S. Attorney, 27 December 1934 – 4986).

   Pat Reilly's arrest: "Dillinger's Pal is Seized in Bed," *Chicago Tribune*, 27 June 1934.

   The investigation into Helen "Babe" Reilly: St. Paul Field Office to Director, 9 June 1934, DF-1956. The specific charges against Pat Reilly were that he escorted Dillinger and John Hamilton to the home of Dr. Neils Mortensen after Sioux Falls and Mason City. He was held on $50,000 bail.

   The correspondence between Jean Delaney Crompton and her family members from Alderson: J.J. Water, Chicago, to SAC Chicago, 2 August 1934, DF-3121; Crompton's placement in Beth Green's cottage at Alderson: Tamm to Director, 12 June 1934, DF-1988; and Clegg to Director, 13 June 1934, DF-1988; Jean Delaney Crompton's meeting of Beth Green at Alderson: V.W. Peterson, Chicago to File, 19 July 1934, DF- 2782;

## Notes for Chapter 22

1. The Probasco kitchen revelations were reported by Peggy Doyle in her interviews with the FBI, and recorded in: V.W. Peterson, Chicago, to File, 17 May 1934, DF-1478; Peggy Doyle's recollections of Dillinger as he lived in Probasco's home and other related events in the Crawford Avenue house are found in: V.W. Peterson to File, Chicago, 23 August 1934, DF-3642.

   The arrangements made between Louis Piquett and Art O'Leary with Probasco were found in *U.S. v. Piquett et al.* Federal District Court, Northern District of Illinois, Eastern Division; 95-57-8 Sec. 2, Pt. 2, 4-26-34 — 5-18-34, National Archives, College Park, MD.
2. The preliminary research that the Dillinger gang put into their bank robbery methodology was described by Pat Cherrington to federal agents after her arrest. If she knew about the Merchants National Bank at South Bend, she didn't reveal it. The description of the bank robbery preliminary get-away run was told by Pat Cherrington to the Bureau of Investigation at the County Jail in Madison, Wisconsin, before her incarceration in the Federal prison system. It is found in: A. Rosen to Mr. Tamm, 21 July 1934, DF-2839.
3. Much of the background information assembled for the South Bend narrative was gleaned from a vast, yet virtually unintelligible FBI file. It is cited as follows:

File No. 91-15, Subject: "John Dillinger; Homer Van Meter; Lester Joseph Gillis aka Baby Face Nelson; John Hamilton; Jack Perkins—Merchants National Bank, South Bend, Indiana." Some items:

South Bend witnesses' post-mortem identification of Dillinger: pp. 25746–9;

Van Meter and Comforti's activities after Dillinger's death: p. 25745;

Ted Bentz cleared: p. 25743;

Activities of Cassidy; O'Leary and Finery, with signed statement of Reinaldo "Fatso" Negri: p. 25512;

Trial of Jack Perkins; p.25506.

Ted Bentz cleared: p. 25743;

South Bend robbery vis a vis Negri and Chase's involvement:

V.W. Peterson, Chicago, to File, 9 March 1935, U.S. v. Chase, et al., File No. 95-57; Sub. 8; 12-2-34 – 3-12-35; Section 6; National Archives, College Park, MD.

South Bend newspaper articles:

"Bloody Dillinger Escape Machine Found in Indiana," *St. Paul Sunday Dispatch*, July 1, 1934, p. 1

"Dillinger Head of Fatal Bank Raid, Say Police," *Chicago Tribune*, 1 July 1934

"Dillinger Gang Kills Officer in Bank Robbery," *Tribune*, 1 July 1934

"Dillinger Pals Force Doctor's Help; Slug Him," *Tribune*, 2 July 1934.

4. Interview with Pat Cherrington re: South Bend: A. Rosen to Mr. Tamm, 21 July 1934, DF-2839; Interview with Kathryn Kelly, Milan, which revealed her thoughts that the identity of the large, 200-pound man who participated in the South Bend robbery was thought to be "Big Homer," who was already imprisoned, to twenty-eight years in the State Prison at Waupun, WS (Helmer, and Rick Mattix, p. 198) for the Racine bank robbery, staged with the Dillinger gang on November 20, 1933 holdup: W. Larson, Detroit, to SAC, Chicago, 23 July 1934, DF-2854.
5. The "consider the source" argument has been used to question the truthfulness of Helen Gillis' rebuttal. There isn't any evidence to suggest a reason as to why she would have lied. She continually denied Floyd's involvement at a time when she implicated everyone else surrounding Baby Face Nelson. There would have had to be a viable reason for Helen Gillis to protect the memory of the deceased Pretty Boy Floyd. Floyd, who weighed in at 200 pounds and was identified at the Kansas City Massacre as the "fat man," did fit the physical description.
6. Theodore Bentz complicity in South Bend, his admission of Hamilton's death, Marie Comfort's admissions of the whereabouts of Van Meter immediately before and after the South Bend affair, and evidence of Frank (Connolly) who hung around with Van Meter after South Bend, was found in: D.L. Nicholson, St. Paul, to File, 5 September 1934, -3788.

Ted Bentz' identification is discredited because as many people who identified him, also identified John Hamilton, unofficially dead. An investigator, F.G. Huntington, entered the case. By the time Bentz fell under an active investigation, he was serving life for a previous bank robbery in Michigan. On November 10, 1934, the Assistant U.S. Attorney said he didn't believe Ted Bent was implicated, and the indictment was dropped.

With Detective Henderson identifying Jack Perkins, he would be arraigned in the Bremer Case and was then lined up as a suspect in South Bend, on February 4, 1935. Jack Perkins and his wife, Grace, would be charged with Harboring Baby Face Nelson on February 5, 1935. The Federal Grand Jury in the case wanted to charge Jack Perkins with the murder of P.O. Wagner. On March 25, 1935, Det. Henderson; P.G. Stahly, the VP of the bank; Det. McCormick ; and a teller identified Jack Perkins. Perkins, a gambler who hung around the poolroom at 3939 Sheridan Road with Art "Fish" Johnson, would serve two years at Leavenworth for harboring Nelson. On November 26, 1936, the St. Joseph County Grand Jury in South Bend, returned an indictment charging Jack Perkins with auto banditry, bank robbery, murder in the first degree, murder in participation of a robbery and would be tried in State court in February 1937. The murder charges were eventually dropped and the futility of the case became apparent when it was decided that no federal prosecution would follow the State prosecution. On June 28, 1936, Melvin Purvis transferred the investigation to the Indianapolis office of the FBI. On October 7, 1936, the state finished its presentation into the Perkins case. On February 22, 1937, the state rested its case. The government finally admitted defeat in its attempts to identify the other two bank robbers at South Bend. They would, toward the end of their indictments, be forced to name as plaintiff, John Doe and Richard Roe.

Conclusion: Van Meter's fear of Dillinger's new girlfriend: Peterson, Chicago, to File, 17 May 1934, DF-1478; Peterson to File, Chicago, 23 August 1934, DF-3642.

## Notes for Chapter 23

1. Letter from Eddie Green's mother to Beth: Hoover to Tamm, July 30, 1934, DF-3086; Location of Green's grave: St. Peter's Cemetery in Mendota, MN: Maccabee, p. 235; Mary Kinder's letter about Evelyn Frechette's condition in Milan: E.J. Connelley, Cincinnati, to SAC Chicago, 27 August 1934, DF-3652. Edythe Hamilton: 1920 U.S. Census—N.D., Cass C., ED 19, Sheet 17.
2. Sam Goldstine and Clifford Mohlar's incarceration in Michigan City:

   "Open War on Gang Contacts Here," St. Paul Pioneer Press, 25 August 1934; Polly Hamilton's series of interviews after Dillinger's death: "Polly Hamilton, Dillinger Sweetheart, Found," Chicago Herald and Examiner, 24 October 1934; State of Indiana, County of Lake, Roy O. Keele v. Rita Keele,

Filed 13 February 1934; Probasco with Piquett: U.S. v. Louis Piquet, Wilhelm Looser, Harold Bernard Cassidy and Arthur W. O'Leary; District Court of the United States, Northern District of Illinois, Eastern Division; Chicago, Criminal Records, Criminal Case Files, Case No. 28,342; R. 21, Records of the District Courts of the United States, NA, Great Lakes Region.

3. Anna Sage's police record: Cowley to Director, 30 July 1934, DF-3013; Purvis to Hoover, 31 July 1934, DF-3077; Divorce records of both Zarkovich and Sage (Located by Researcher Tom Smusyn, who shared them with the author) State of Indiana, County of Lake, Petition of Divorce; Anna Chiolak v. Mike Chiolak, Filed 12 December 1923; State of Indiana, County of Lake, Lake Superior Court, Hammond, Petition of Divorce, Temporary Alimony & Attorney's Fees; Elizabeth Zarkovich v. Martin Zarkovich, Filed 17 March 1920.

   Investigative articles that explored relationships between Sergeant Zarkovich, Dillinger, the East Chicago Police Department, and Anna Sage:

   "Indiana's Police Launch Quiz on Dillinger Death," *Chicago Tribune*, 29 July 1934.

4. A list of most of the agents who were stationed at the Biograph, their positions and actions, found in Cowley to Director, 24 July 1934; -2895, is as follows:

   C.O. Hurt; H.E. Hollis; J. McCarthy; R.G. Gillespie; J.R. Welles; A.E. Lockerman; E.L. Richmond; C.G. Campbell; J.J. Metcalfe; Val C. Zimmer; T.J. Connor; M.F. Glynn; R.C. Suran; J.T. McLaughlin; W.C. Ryan; Woltz; D.P. Sullivan; Brown; Purvis; and Agent Winstead; Sam Cowley.

   Internet article: Rick Mattix, "The Lawmen Who Slew Dillinger."

   East Chicago, Indiana police were Sergeant Zarkovich; Captain Timothy O'Neill and Officers Arthur Sopsic and Stretch Conroy.

   Neither Agent Cowley nor Purvis fired at Biograph: Hoover to Tamm, 24 July, -2957.

   Agent Winstead fired the shots that hit Dillinger, the number being three. Agent Hollis fired one shot. There was the possibility that five shots were fired. Two went through Dillinger and hit two women. Winstead fired the fatal shots.

5. Sam Cowley's search for Polly Hamilton after Dillinger's death: Hoover to Tamm, 24 July 1934, DF-2964; Recovery of Dillinger's munitions at the Lincoln Park Gun Club:

   S.P. Cowley to Director, 1 August 1934; DF-3102; Direction of Anna Sage's case to Frances Perkins:

   Stanley to D.W. McCormick, Commissioner, Immigration and Naturalization Service, Dept. of Labor, Washington, DC; 13 August 1934 DF-3390; Holger Burglum claim of having been defrauded by Mrs. Sage: Purvis To Hoover, 31 July 1934, DF-3077;

Polly Hamilton's identification and Cowley's denial: Telegram Cowley to Director, 27 July 1934, DF-2971; August 3 location of Polly Hamilton, at South Haven, Michigan:

V.W. Peterson, Chicago, to File, 8 August 1934, DF-3607; Cowley's control over Sage after Dillinger's death: Hoover to File, 24 July 1934, DF-2882; Hoover to Tamm, 24 July 1934, DF-2956, DF -3086; Hoover to Tamm, 24 July 1934, DF-2957. This cite also contains information on the July 24 luncheon agreement made between Purvis, Tim O'Neill, Sergeant Zarkovich, and the Chief of Police of East Chicago.

The agents accompanying Dillinger's body to the Alexian Hospital and Cook County Morgue affirmed that no one had taken any of Dillinger's money or belongings. These are documented in: Memo to File, Agents C.O. Hurt, H.E. Hollis, R.G. Gillespie, J.V. Murphy, D.P. Sullivan, 3 August 1934, DF-3366. Revisionist theories have altered this view, and it is considered a given that one of the East Chicago police officers, most likely Sergeant Zarkovich, relieved Dillinger's corpse of its money.

Documents pertinent to the Dillinger reward money:

William Stanley, Asst. Attorney General, to Sergeant Martin Zarkovich, 4 October 1934;

File Memorandum, Dept. of Justice, Subject: Dillinger Reward:

File No. 95-57; Sub. 8; 12-2-34 – 3-12-35; Sec. 6; National Archives, College Park, MD.

Death of James Probasco: "Dillinger Face Surgeon Said to be an Ex-Convict," *Chicago Tribune*, July 1934; James Probasco's death: S.P. Cowley to Director, 27 July 1934, DF-2924; References to question about ropes and wires: -E.A. Tamm to Director, 26 July 1934, DF-2884.

Sage's pending deportation: Hoover to Tamm. 30 July 1934, DF-3031.

Newspaper coverage on Dillinger's death was national. The *Chicago Tribune* covered it extensively. It began:

"Dillinger Shot to Death by 15 U.S. Agents in Front of Movie Theater; *Tribune*, 22 July 1934;

Extending to the funeral: "Dillinger Given Church Burial as Downpour Soaks Curious," Tribune, 26 July 1934.

Matt Leach's contentions regarding East Chicago corruption, with regards to Crown Point County Jail and Dillinger's escape: Hoover, J. Edgar, "Memo for Acting Attorney General;

City Editor, Ed., Tribune Copy; "Records Shed New Light on Dillinger Assassination," *Tribune*, 21 July 1935.

Polly Hamilton's series of interviews after Dillinger's death:

"Polly Hamilton, Dillinger Sweetheart, Found," *Chicago Herald & Examiner*, 24 October 1934;

"Dillinger's Last Hours—With Me, by his Sweetheart," *Herald & Examiner*, 25—28 October 1934.

## Notes for Chapter 24

1. Comforti's remarks on shadow team: Hoover to Attorney General, 26 Dec. 34 — 4982; Frank Kirwin's admissions:

   U.S. v. Thomas Gannon et al., District Court of the United States, D. Minnesota, 5th Division, No. 5213; R. 21; Subgroup UDC Minnesota, 5th Div. Criminal Case Files 1907-1955; File No. 5213; National Archives, Central Plains Region.

   Thomas Gannon in St. Paul: D.L. Nicholson to File, St. Paul, 5 September 1934, DF-3788;

   The events surrounding Van Meter and Comforti's stay in Calumet City:

   U.S. v. William Finerty, Ella Finerty and Marie Comforti alias Mrs. Hank Adams, U.S. District Court, Northern District of Illinois, Eastern Division; Chicago, Criminal Records, Criminal Case Files, Case No. 28344; RG 21, Records of the District Courts of the United States, National Archives, Great Lakes Region.

   U.S. v. Finerty et al.; U.S. v. Kirwin et al., File No. 95-57; Sub. 8; 12-2-34 – 3-12-35; Section 6; NA, College Park, MD.

   William Finerty's admissions regarding Van Meter and identification of Dr. Cassidy as the physician who treated his head wound after South Bend: Telegram to Director from Purvis dated 27 August 1934, DF-3653.

   Marie Comforti surveillance lifted, DF-2782 — p. 54; Van Meter's facial evidence of plastic surgery: E.A. Tamm to Director, 24 August 1934, DF-3628.

   Opal Milligan's revocation of parole and memoranda disputing her role in the death of Van Meter: D.L. Nicholson, St. Paul, to File, 5 September 1934, DF-3788; E.A. Tamm to Director, August 24, 1934, DF-3623; The underworld's deal with Tom Brown to finger Van Meter: D.L. Nicholson to File, St. Paul, 5 September 1934, DF-3788; Van Meter's death: S.P. Cowley Memo, Chicago, to File, DF-3787.

   Van Meter's death was covered nationally. The articles are voluminous, starting with August 24, 1934. A sampling is as follows: "Dillinger Ace Shot Down in St. Paul," *Madison Capital Times*, 24 August 1934; "St. Paul Police Kill Desperado in Street Trap," *Chicago* Tribun*e*, 24 August 1934; *"Tom Brown Describes Van Meter Battle*," St. Paul Pioneer Press, 24 August 1934."

   Marie Comforti's arrest: 26 August, 1934, E.A. Tamm to Director, DF-3636.

2. "Victim's Kin Glad Dillinger is Out of Way," *Chicago Herald & Examiner*, 24 July 1934. Evidence to support the trail of Van Meter before his death, located in trial transcripts:

   U.S. v. Thomas Gannon et al.; District Court of the United States, D. Minnesota, 5th Division, No. 5213; R. 21; Subgroup UDC Minnesota, 5th Div. Criminal Case Files 1907—1955; File No. 5213; National Archives, Central Plains Region.

U.S. v. William Finerty, Ella Finerty and Marie Comforti alias Mrs. Hank Adams; District Court of the United States, Northern District of Illinois, Eastern Division; Chicago, Criminal Records, Criminal Case Files, Case No. 28344; RG 21, Records of the District Courts of the United States, NA, Great Lakes Region;

U.S. v. Finerty et al.; U.S. v. Kirwin et al.,

Arrests and Indictments of plastic surgery team:

U.S. v. Louis Piquet, Wilhelm Loeser, Harold Bernard Cassidy and Arthur W. O'Leary;

District Court of the United States, Northern District of Illinois, Eastern Division;

Chicago, Criminal Records, Criminal Case Files, Case No. 28,342; R. 21, Records of the District Courts of the United States, National Archives, Great Lakes Region.

3. The activities of the Nelsons and John Paul Chase from end of May 1934 to the Battle of Barrington in November 1934:

   V.W. Peterson, Chicago, to File, 20 February 1935; 95-57-8, Section 8, 5-31-35 – 11-26-35; National Archives, College Park, MD.

   July 30 and 31, Gillis in El Verano. From -3596, E.P. Guinane, San Francisco, to File August 18, 1934, DF-3596.

   Details of the Battle of Barrington and the death of Baby Face Nelson:

   V.W. Peterson, Chicago, to File, 9 March 1935, U.S. v. Chase, et al., File No. 95-57; Sub. 8; 12-2-34 – 3-12-35; Section 6; NA, College Park, MD.

   Agent Connelly to Director, 30 November 1934; -4983:

   Nelson's two children were being kept in Chicago with Juliette Fitzsimmons, causing bureau confusion as to identity of Perkins child: E.A. Tamm to Director, 23 August 1934, DF-3621;

   E.A. Tamm to Director, 28 December 1934, DF-5007.

   Newspaper articles regarding the death of Baby Face Nelson are voluminous. A sampling from the period of November 27 through December 6 are as follows: "Baby Face Nelson Dead after Killing 2 Agents," *Madison Capital Times,* 27 November 1934.

4. The details of the aftermath of Nelson's death, with the address of 1605 Walnut Street listed as the location of Gillis' death, and the investigation into the activities of Nelson through testimony of Helen Gillis: U.S. v. Chase, et al., File No. 95-57; Sub. 8; 12-2-34 — 3-12-35, Section 6, National Archives, College Park, MD; 1627 Walnut Street: Helmer with Mattix, p.224.

5. "Shoot Widow of Nelson, Is Agents' Order, *Wisconsin State Journal,* 28 November 1934; "Judge Scolds, Sends Mrs. Gillis to Cell," *Times*, 7 December 1934; "Judge Will Invoke 18 Month Term," *Times*, 7 December 1934; "Widow of Baby Face Sentenced," *Times*, 6 December 1934.

## Notes for Chapter 25

1. The reaction of J. Edgar Hoover to Marie Comforti's interview regarding Sam Cowley: Hoover to Attorney General, 26 December 1934, DF-4982; Hoover's letter to the Acting Attorney General, 31 July 1934, 95-5708 Sec. 5, National Archives, College Park, MD.;

   Hoover to Assistant Attorney General Mahon, 18 May 1936; 95-57-8 Sec. 2, Pt., 4-26-34 — 5-18-34., NA, College Park, MD.;

   "7 in Dillinger Net are Cited," *Indianapolis Star*, 7 September 1934;

   "Comforti Girl Pleads Guilty," *Wisconsin State Journal*, 12 September 1934;

   Transcripts, U.S. v. William Finerty, Ella Finerty and Marie Comforti alias Mrs. Hank Adams; District Court of the United States, Northern District of Illinois, Eastern Division; Chicago, Criminal Records, Criminal Case Files, Case No. 28344;RG 21, Records of the District Courts of the United States, NA, Great Lakes Region.
2. V.W. Peterson, Chicago, to File, 9 March 1935, U.S. v. Chase, et al., File No. 95-57; Sub. 8; 12-2-34 – 3-12-35; Section 6; NA, College Park, MD.; U.S. v. Chase, et al., File No. 95-57; Sub. 8; 12-2-34 — 3-12-35, Section 6, National Archives, College Park, MD;

   Newspaper articles regarding the roundup of the Nelson harborers were voluminous:

   "U.S. Opens Drive against Men Who Aided Baby Face," 1 January 1935; *San Francisco Examiner*; "Chase Confession;" "Chase Charges to Be Pressed," 5 January, *Examiner*;"U.S. Seizes 4 More in Hiding of Baby Face," 14 January 1935; *Examiner*.

   Mary Kinder's remarks regarding her mother's reaction to her involvement with Dillinger gang: Radio Interview, July 29, 1934, Transcript: Author's collection; Mary Kinder's letter about Evelyn Frechette's condition in Milan: E.J. Connelley, Cincinnati, to SAC Chicago, 27 August 1934; DF-3652. Frechette's unrequited wish to attend her mother's funeral: Frechette, Evelyn, "The Story of Evelyn Frechette, "March of Crime." Mary Kinder's final letter to Pierpont: E.J. Connelley, Cincinnati, to SAC Chicago, 27 August 1934, DF-3652; Lena Pierpont's admissions re Mary Kinder's activities: DF-1818, Telegram to Director, 7 June 1923. Mary LaBelle Frechette's death: *Wisconsin Evening Star,* p2, c5, 6 July, 1934 (Lori Hyde).

   Barker shooting: Ocala Evening Star, Star Banner; Hoover, Persons In Hiding; Author visit; Interview: Warren E. McGahagin.

   The trail through Cuba and Florida of Karpis and Delaney are found in:

   U.S. District Court:Southern District of Florida, U.S. v. Joseph H. Adams, et al., National Archives, S.E. Region, East Point, Georgia.

   Karpis' ambush in Atlantic City, Dolores' trail to Philadelphia and back to Florida are found in:

"Karpis Associates Get 5 Year Terms," *Miami Herald*, 26 March 1935;

"Federal Agents Here Check Movements of Karpis,"

"Police Believe They Have Karpis Penned Up in Atlantic City," *Ocala Evening Star*, 21 January 1935;

"Karpis Fled from Miami," *Ocala Evening Star*, January 22, 1934;

"Karpis Trailed to Canada Line,"

"Karpis Companion Same Girl Who was Here with Barkers," *Evening Star*,;

"Where Karpis Escaped Trap," (Danmor) *Ocala Evening Star*;

"Kidnapping of Doctor Gives U.S. New Clues," *Ocala Evening Star*, 22 January;

Karpis' ambush in Atlantic City, Dolores' trail to Philadelphia and back to Florida are found in:

"Karpis Associates Get 5 Year Terms," *Miami Herald*, 26 March 1935;

"Federal Agents Here Check Movements of Karpis,"

"Police Believe They Have Karpis Penned Up in Atlantic City," *Ocala Evening Star*, 21 January 1935;

"Karpis Fled from Miami," *Ocala Evening Star*, January 22;

"Karpis Trailed to Canada Line,"

"Karpis Companion Same Girl Who was Here with Barkers," *Ocala Evening Star*,;

"Where Karpis Escaped Trap," (Danmor) *Ocala Evening Star*;

"Kidnapping of Doctor Gives U.s. New Clues," *Ocala Evening Star*, 22 January;

Other papers who carried Karpis stories during this time were the *Chicago Tribune* and the *San Francisco Examiner*.

The trail through Cuba and Florida of Karpis and Delaney are found in:

U.S. District Court:Southern District of Florida, U.S. v. Joseph H. Adams, et al., National Archives, S.E. Region, East Point, Georgia.

The dispositions of the defendants accused of harboring Karpis are as follows:

U.S. District Court:Southern District of Florida, U.S. v. Dolores Delaney, with alias; U.S. v. Wynona Burdette, National Archives, S.E. Region, East Point, Georgia.

Newspaper articles regarding the round-up of Baby Face Nelson's network were voluminous, beginning with:

"U.S. Opens Drive against Men Who Aided Baby Face," *San Francisco Examiner*, 1 January 1935

"Chase Confession"; "Chase Charges to Be Pressed," *San Francisco Examiner*, 5 January 1935.

"U.S. Seizes 4 More in Hiding of Baby Face," *San Francisco Examiner*, 14 January 1935;

"Action taken after Nelson Widow 'Talks,'" *San Francisco Examiner*, 16

January 1935; and with daily coverage of the arrests, investigations and trials, ending with:

"Missing Reno Banker Victim of Baby Face," *San Francisco Examiner*, 29 March 1935;

"Sally Backman Bares Life With Nelson Gang," *San Francisco Examiner*, 29 March 1935;

"Frisch Death Clues Found," "Moreno in Terror of Life," *San Francisco Examiner*, 4 April 1935;

"Baby Face's Jealousy of Dillinger Told," *San Francisco Examiner*, 27 March 1935;

"Two Set Free," *San Francisco Examiner*, 2 April 1935;

"Bay Doctor Aid to Karpis Gang Bared," *San Francisco Examiner*, 7 April 1935;

"Jury Expected to Get Nelson Case Today," *San Francisco Examiner*, 5 April 1935;

A detailed analysis of the movements of Baby Face Nelson, Chase and Helen from the Lake Como period immediately prior to Waterloo, up to and including Dillinger's death and until the Battle of Barrington and the aftermath, with Father Coughlan's transfer to Holy Family Parish in Canute, Oklahoma, are found in:

V.W. Peterson, Chicago, to File, 9 March 1935, U.S. v. Chase, et al., File No. 95-57; Sub. 8; 12-2-34 – 3-12-35; Section 6; National Archives, College Park, MD.

Further confirmation of Father Coughlan's transfer to a quiet Oklahoma parish is found in:

"Priest Points Out Chase as Nelson's Pal," San Francisco Examiner, 21 March 1935.

Helen Gillis' trail after her arrest continues with:

A detailed analysis of the movements of Baby Face Nelson, Chase and Helen from the Lake Como period immediately prior to Waterloo, up to and including Dillinger's death and until the Battle of Barrington and the aftermath, with Father Coughlan's transfer to Holy Family Parish in Canute, Oklahoma (this fact is in a subsequent chapter) are found in:

V.W. Peterson, Chicago, to File, 9 March 1935, U.S. v. Chase, et al., File No. 95-57; Sub. 8; 12-2-34 – 3-12-35; Section 6; National Archives, College Park, MD.

Further confirmation of Father Coughlan's transfer to a quiet Oklahoma parish is found in:

"Priest Points Out Chase as Nelson's Pal," *San Francisco Examiner*, 21 March 1935.

3. Justice Department investigation over the police protection of Grace Goldstein's brothel in the harboring of Alvin Karpis; an account of the prosecution of the Hot Springs defendants after the arrest of Alvin Karpis and

Fred Hunter: Collins, pp. 195—201; Cowley's denial of East Chicago murders as being under Federal jurisdiction: Telegram from S.P. Cowley to Director, 27 July 1934, DF-2938; Cowley challenged Matt Leach to conduct an investigation into the murder of the two East Chicago policemen, "particularly if it involved a dishonest Police Department:"

Cowley to Director, 27 July 1934, DF-2978; Hoover's remarks that "Leach is the cause of a great deal of trouble:"Hoover to Tamm, 27 July 1934, DF-2966; Matt Leach's outrage after Dillinger's death: Turner, pp. 219—220; Matt Leach's statements after Dillinger's death:

Hoover, J. Edgar, "Memo for Acting Attorney General;City Editor, Ed., Tribune Copy;

Records Shed New Light on Dillinger Assassination," *Tribune*, 21 July 1935;

Anna Steve: Purvis to U.S. Attorney Dwight H. Green, 26 December 1934, DF-4970;

The trial of Patricia Cherrington and Anna Steve:

The prognosis on Anna Steve's case: Hoover to File, I.D. Order May 1934 DF-2941;

Purvis to U.S. Attorney Dwight H. Green, 26 December 1934, DF-4970;

Memo, Chicago to Hon. Joseph M. Donnelly, U.S. Attorney, 27 December 1934, DF-4986;

Director to Tamm, 8 June 1934, DF-1877; .

U.S. v. Anna Steve, et al., U.S. District Court, Western District of Michigan,

Southern Division, Grand Rapids, Criminal Records, Criminal Case Files, Case 4235; NA, Great Lakes Region, RG 21, Records of the District Courts of the United States.

Pat Cherrington's Parole Hearing, Transcript: Director to Superintendent, U.S. Detention Farm, Milan, Michigan, 11 November 1935; Report on Writ of Habeas Corpus, Cherrington, Arthur AZ-199, U.S. Penetentiary, BOP, Alcatraz, California. RG 129, Box 215; NA, San Bruno, California; Pat Reilly's conviction: "Reilly Pleads Guilty to Madison Charges," *Wisconsin State Journal*, 21 September 1934;

Trials of Louis Piquett and Arthur O'Leary:

"Piquett Accused as "Master Mind," *Journal,* 2 September 1934

"Dillinger Lawyer is Held Victim of Double Cross," *Wisconsin State Journal*, 4 September 1934;

"7 in Dillinger Net are Cited," *Indianapolis Star*, 7 September 1934;

"Dillinger, Weary, Planned to Give Up," *Wisconsin State Journal*, 4 September 1934;

"Jury Completed to Try Piquett," *Chicago Tribune*, 9 January 1934;

"Lawyer's Part in Face Lifting is Told to Jury," *Tribune*; 9 January 1934;

"Piquett "Hush" Payment Told," *Tribune*, 10 Jaunary 1934;

"Piquett Fights U.S. Version of Dillinger Plot," *Tribune*, ll January 1934;

"Jury Expected to Get Piquett's Case Today, *Tribune*, 14 January 1934;

"Lawyer Found Not Guilty of Dillinger Plot," *Tribune*, 15 January 1934;

Evaluations made on Louis Piquett after his incarceration:

Louis Piquett, #48972-L, Declassified file; Leavenworth, Kansas; U.S. Department of Justice, Federal Bureau of Prisons, Washington, DC; North Central Regional Office, Kansas City, Kansas.

Letter penned by Louis Piquett:

Piquett, L. to Honorable Jesse Simpson, Chief Justice of the Supreme Court, State of Illinois, Springfield, Illinois; 3 March 1951; Author's collection.

Pat Cherrington's undated Poem: Inmate Patricia Young, Alderson, Archives, BOP, Washington, DC.

## Notes for Postscript

Mary Longnaker's marriage to boyfriend Claude Constable:

Agent Klein to File, Cincinnati, 25 July 1934, DF-2865; Lawrence Royer and Lori Hyde provided other documentation.

Pearl Elliott's death:

State of Indiana, County of Clinton, *Local Record of Death*, Pearl McDonald Elliott, Filed 12 August 1935; Clinton City Dept. of Health, Bk D-10; P 70; Local No. 100.

Evelyn Frechette:

"Dillinger's Moll Pays Debt to Society, *Indianapolis News*, 9 February 1955.

Tic, Arthur and Mrs. Evelyn M. Wilson, License for Marriage, 8 September 1965. Filed Lake County, Illinois;

Arthur Tic, Interview with author by telephone, 1988.

Frechette, *The March of Crime,*

Arthur Cherrington and Welton Spark:

Report on Writ of Habeas Corpus, Cherrington, Arthur AZ-199, Spark, Welton AZ-200, U.S. Penetentiary, General Records of the Bureau of Prisons, Records of the U.S. Penitentiary; Alcatraz, California. RG 129, Box 215; NARA, San Bruno, California; Blackwood — AZ180, status as stool pigeon: Alvin Karpis with Robert Livesey.

Anna Sage & Polly Hamilton:

"Women You Can't Forget," *Indianapolis News*, 11 January 1958; "Woman In Red Dies," 28 April 1947. Information on Polly Hamilton's death provided by Dillinger Historian Sandy Jones.

Elaine Dent:

"When John Dillinger Came to Galesburg," *Galesburg Times*, Litvin, Martin; 8 June 1989.

John Hamilton:

"Recovery and Identification of the Body of John Hamilton," 18 March 1938, "General Records of the FBI," 95-57-8, Sec. 5, Call No. 3241, NARA, CP, MD; Anna Steve death date: Bruce Hamilton, who shared his John Hamilton survival theory with author by telephone, May 2002.

Louis Piquett:

Louis Piquett, #48972-L, Declassified file; Leavenworth, Kansas; U.S. Department of Justice, Federal Bureau of Prisons, Washington, DC; North Central Regional Office, Kansas City, Kansas.

Mrs. Cowley and Mrs. Baum: Whitehead.

Father Coughlin:

"Souls of the Just," Archdiocese of Oklahoma City, lists Reverend L. Hugo as having practiced in Oklahoma. The priest assigned to him there, Father Coughlan, is not listed.

Jean Delaney Crompton's divorce:

State of Illinois, County of Cook, *Complaint for Divorce,* Jean Delaney Crompton v. Edward Crompton, Filed 19 December 1935, Superior Court of Cook County.

Opal Long's interview at the Minneapolis Workhouse:

E.A. Tamm to File, 30 August 1934; RR FBI -3751

Opal Long's November 29, 1934 date of release from the Minneapolis Workhouse:

General Register, 1933—1935 Workhouse commitments, Opal Long aka Clark, Bernice; Municipal Library, Minneapolis City Hall, Room 300M

Opal Long, death of: Cook Cty. #722708, courtesy Robert Bates.

Viola Carroll's challenge to Charles Carroll for Tommy Carroll's estate:

Letter from Paul Maccabee to author, December 27, 1993.

Russell Clark:

"Last of the Dillingers," *National Detective*, 1950.

Earl Northern, Mary Kinder and Margaret "Silent Margaret" Behrens:

State of Indiana, County of LaPorte, Local No. 138, Indiana State Board of Health, *Certificate of Death*, Earl Northern, Filed 30 June 1936.

State of Florida, County of Pasco, *Original Certificate of Death,* Margaret Ann Flory, (Margaret "Silent Sadie" Behrens) #87 083938, Filed 14 August 1987; New Port Richey, Florida

State of Indiana, County of Hendriks, *Certificate of Death,* Mary Ellen Grimsley, (Mary Kinder) Filed 28 August 1989;

John Wilson Dillinger:

Interview with Frank Basco, Bartender at the Little Bohemia Lodge, co-worker to elder Dillinger when the latter ran the John Dillinger Museum at the location.

Russell Clark's release from Ohio State Penitentiary at Columbus:

Reception Diagnostic Center, 737 Moon Road, Plainfield, IN.

Russell Clark: Incarceration at the Indiana State Penitentiary at Michigan City; State of Indiana, Parole Dept., Memo to File, 12 February 1934.

Patricia Cherrington, Death of:

State of Illinois, County of Cook, Original Certificate of Death, Pat Cherrington, Filed 13 May 1949, #13650; Obituaries.

Kathryn Kelly:

U.S., Appellant, v. Kathryn Thorne Kelly, and Ora L. Shannon, Appeal from the United States District Court for the Western District of Oklahoma, Criminal Records, Criminal Case Files, File No. 109-61, NARA, CP, MA., Records of the District Courts of the United States;William F. Turner. *Hoover's F.B.I.,* New York: Thunder's Mouth Press, 1993, pp. 21–22.

Evelyn Frechette: State of Wisconsin, *Original Certificate of Death,* Evelyn Wilson (nee' Frechette), 13 January 1969, Registrar of Deeds, Shawano, WI 54166, V-39, p. 200.; Arthur Tic, Interview with Author by telephone, 1988.

## Books

Barnes, Bruce. *Machine Gun Kelly: To Right a Wrong*. Perris, California: Tipper Publications, 1991.

Callahan, Clyde C. and Byron B. Jones. *Heritage of An Outlaw, The Story of Frank Nash*. Hobart, Oklahoma: Schoonmaker, 1979.

Clayton, Merle. *Union Station Massacre: The Shootout that Started the FBI's War on Crime*. Indianapolis: The Bobbs-Merrill Co., 1975.

Collins, Frederick L. *The FBI in Peace and War*. Foreword by J. Edgar Hoover. New York: G.P. Putnam's Sons, 1943.

Cook, Fred J. *The FBI Nobody Knows*. New York: The Macmillan Co., 1964.

Cooper, Courtney Ryley. *Ten Thousand Public Enemies*. Foreword by J. Edgar Hoover. Boston: Little, Brown & Co., 1935.

__________. *Here's To Crime*. Boston: Little, Brown & Co., 1937.

Cromie, Robert and Joseph Pinkston. *Dillinger: A Short and Violent Life*. New York: McGraw Hill, 1962.

Davidson, Bill, "How The Mob Controls Chicago." In *The Chicago Crime Book*, ed. Albert Halper. Cleveland, Ohio: The World Publishing Co., 1967.

DeNevi, Don and Philip Bergen. *Alcatraz '46: The Anatomy of a Classic Prison Tragedy.* San Rafael, California: Leswing Press, 1974.

Edge, L.L., *Run The Cat Roads: A True Story of Bank Robbers in the 30's*. New York: Dembner Books, 1981.

Girardin, G. Russell with William J. Helmer. *Dillinger: The Untold Story*. Bloomington: Indiana University Press, 1994.

Helmer, William J. and Rick Mattix. *Public Enemies: America's Criminal Past, 1919–1940.* New York: Facts on File, Inc., 1998.

Hinton, Ted with Larry Grove. *The Real Story of Bonnie and Clyde*. Fredericksburg, Texas: Shoal Creek Publishers, Inc., 1979.

Hoover, J. Edgar. *Persons in Hiding*. Foreword by Courtney Ryley Cooper. Boston: Little, Brown and Co., 1938.

Jenkins, John H. and H. Gordon Frost. *I'm Frank Hamer*. Austin, Texas: State House Press, 1993.

Karpis, Alvin with Bill Trent. *The Alvin Karpis Story*. New York: Coward, McCann & Geoghegan, Inc., 1971.

__________. with Robert Livesey. *On The Rock: Twenty-Five Years in Alcatraz.* Mississauga, Ontario, Canada: L.B.S. Inc. Publications, 1988.

Krippene, Ken. *Buried Treasure*. New York: Garden City Publishing Co., 1950.

Leuchtenburg, William E. *Franklin D. Roosevelt and the New Deal, 1932–1940.* New York: Harper & Row, 1963.

Louderback, Lew. *The Bad Ones: Gangsters of the '30s and Their Molls*. Grenwich, Connecticut: Fawcett, 1968.

Maccabee, Paul. *John Dillinger Slept Here: A Crooks' Tour of Crime and Corruption in St. Paul, 1920–1936*. St. Paul: Minnesota Historical Society Press, 1995.

Nash, Jay Robert and Ron Offen. *Dillinger: Dead or Alive?* Chicago: Henry Regnery Co., 1970.

Ness, Eliot with Oscar Fraley. *The Untouchables*. New York: Julian Messner, Inc., 1957.

Polenberg, Richard *War and Society*, New York: J.B. Lippincott Co., 1972.

Purvis, Melvin. *American Agent*. New York: Garden City Publishing Co., 1938.

Quimby, Myron J. *The Devil's Emissaries*. New Jersey: A.S. Barnes & Co., 1969.

Schott, Joseph L. *No Left Turns: The FBI in Peace & War*. New York: Praeger Publishers, 1975.

Sitkoff, Harvard. *A New Deal for Blacks: The Emergence of Civil Rights as a National Issue.* New York: Oxford University Press, 1978.

Sullivan, William C. with Bill Brown. *The Bureau: My Thirty Years in Hoover's FBI.* New York: W.W. Norton & Co., 1979.

Toland, John. *The Dillinger Days*. New York: Random House, 1963.

Touhy, Roger with Ray Brennan. *The Stolen Years*. Cleveland, Ohio: Pennington Press, Inc., 1959.

Treherne, John. *The Strange History of Bonnie and Clyde*. New York: Stein and Day, 1984.

Tully, Andrew. *The FBI's Most Famous Cases*. Introduction by J. Edgar Hoover. New York: William Morrow & Co., 1965.

____________. *Inside the FBI*. New York: McGraw-Hill Book Co., 1980.

Turner, William F. *Hoover's F.B.I.* New York: Thunder's Mouth Press, 1993.

Wallis, Michael. *Pretty Boy: The Life and Times of Charles Arthur Floyd*. New York: St. Martin's Press, 1992.

Welch, Neil J. & David W. Marston, *Inside Hoover's FBI: The Top Field Chief Reports.* New York: Doubleday & Co., 1984.

Whitehead, Don, *The FBI Story: A Report to the People.* Foreword by J. Edgar Hoover. New York: Random House, 1954.

## Articles and Pamphlets

Frechette, Evelyn, "What I Knew About John Dillinger: By His Sweetheart," *Chicago Herald & Examiner,* 27 August 1934, Pt. 1, pp. 1-3.

"History of the Indiana State Prison," Pamphlet, Provided by Barry L. Nothstine, Sr. Administrative Assistant, Indiana State Prison

Andrews, Larry, "I was There When They Captured John Dillinger," *Dayton Daily News*, 29 July 1984

Kinder, Mary, "Four Months With the Dillinger Gang," *Chicago Herald,* 30 July 1934.

Hale, Avery Hale, "The Inside Story of Dillinger," *True Detective*, January 1934.

Clark, Bernice "My Adventures With the Dillinger Gang," *Chicago Herald & Examiner,* 12 September 1934.

Wollard, Chief C. A., "Clark! Makley! Pierpont! Dillinger! Captured" *True Detective*, June 1934.

Gallagher, Basil "The Life Story of John Dillinger," Indianapolis: Stephens Publishing Co., 1934.

Frechette, Evelyn, "The Story of Evelyn Frechette," *The March of Crime: Public Enemies*, Chicago: Stein Publishing House, 1939.

U.S. Bureau of Prisons, Archives, Washington, D.C.,

"The Alderson Saga"

"Federal Industrial Institution for Women,"

"Federal Reformatory for Women,"

"Federal Correctional Institutional, Milan, Michigan." (Provided by Anne Diestel, BOP)

Adult Corrections Facility, Hennepin County, Dept. of Community Corrections, 1145 Shenandoah Lane, Plymouth, MN 55447: "History of the Workhouse: Part I, 2000 Annual Report, p. 34 (Re: Minneapolis Workhouse, Provided by Kathy Wellersheim, Assistant Business Services Officer)

Viola Carroll, "I Married Tommy Carroll," *Actual Detective*, April and May 1935.

# Acknowledgments

America in the 1930s, under the vicious crime waves launched in the Midwest, was in the grips of an unexplainable evil. The police officers and federal agents empowered to stop the 1930s "Public Enemies" were the heroes of their day. They fought a home-grown, desperate terrorist. The campaign was no less dangerous than anything we face in today's world. I wish to thank the police officers; federal agents; and one particularly vulnerable, female sheriff named Lillian Holley; for their heroism.

When I started the research for this study, there was no Internet. My initial interaction with a published writer in the Dillinger field, Joe Pinkston, now deceased, sounds as antiquated as the pony express. I had read the dust jacket of a then out-of-print edition of his published classic, *Dillinger, A Short and Violent Life*. The biographical information stated that Joe worked for Motorola at the time of the publication in 1962. It was 1988 and a longshot—I wrote to Motorola. A few weeks later I was surprised to find in my mailbox a letter from Joe Pinkston. In his well-mannered, gallant manner, he asked how he could help.

The Curator of the John Dillinger Historical Museum in Nashville, Joe served as a one-man clearinghouse for all the information disseminated around the nation on the outlaw. To him I extend gratitude—especially for the ride in the 1934 Ford V-8 in which we careened, Bonnie and Clyde-style, through the woods of Indiana.

Through my association with Joe Pinkston, I met William "Bill" Helmer, the co-author of *Dillinger: The Untold Story* and *Public Enemies: America's Criminal Past*.

Bill's parties at the Biograph Theater, an offshoot of his efforts to immortalize the location, helped 1930s crime researchers find each other. In addition to coining the title of this book, Bill has helped its development through advice, praise, humor, and the sharing of his technical expertise.

I wish to thank Tom Smusyn, genius of research, who showed me around Chicago and sent me to "Little Bo" equipped with his personalized map. Tom uncovered certain valuable documents that support the text, including the divorce pleadings of Martin Zarkovich, Mary Longnaker, Jean Delaney Crompton, and Polly Hamilton Keele. It was he who found the New Harmony Bank robbery articles, the "Baby Billie" scandal, and other untold aspects of the Dillinger story. He read between the lines, questioned everything, and made the tiny details important.

I'd like to extend my appreciation to Paul Maccabee, the author of *John Dillinger Slept Here: A Crook's Tour of St. Paul.* Paul kindly referred me to Myrna Otte, the great-aunt of Bess Green, who generously shared her recollections with me.

I wish to express my deep appreciation to other researchers who shared their friendship, and help, with this book. Among them, a special thanks to Lori Hyde, who went out of her way to help with photographs and fact-checking; Sandy Jones, who helped me differentiate the automobiles, and Tony Brucia, co-founders of the Partners In Crime internet group. (Tony wishes to extend an invitation to 1930's crime buffs to visit the PIC site by writing him at Aibrucia@aol.com.)

Thanks also to Rick Mattix, co-author *Public Enemies: America's Criminal Past*; Steve Nickel, author of *Baby Face Nelson: Portrait of a Public Enemy*; Robert Bates; Todd Moore; Kathi Harrell; Tony Stewart, author, *Dillinger, The Hidden Truth*; Jim McKnight, the author of a forthcoming book on Bonnie and Clyde; Jeff Scalf, great-nephew of Dillinger; Jack Kelly; Brad Smith, author of *From Lawman to Outlaw: Verne Miller and the Kansas City Massacre,* and Jonathan Davis.

A warm expression of gratitude also goes to Patterson Smith, antiquarian bookseller. Pat provided many of the books that served as secondary sources. He also leant editorial assistance in crafting the bibliography. I wish to thank Susan Sheehan of the Arizona Historical Society, and Don Bowdon of Wide World, for their help in locating photos.

I want to thank survivors, eye-witnesses and descendants, among them Red Underhill, the cousin of Wilbur Underhill; Myrna Otte, niece of Bess Green; the late Frank Bazso, the bartender at the Little Bohemia Lodge; Audrey Voss Dickerson; Calvin La Porte; and Fred Theosen, who took me on a tour of "Little Bo," and Bruce Hamilton. A posthumous debt of appreciation goes to Art Tic, Mary Gallagher, and Delbert Hobson, who shared their memories of Dillinger and Evelyn Frechette with me. I wish to thank Warren E. McGahagin, who remembers the Barkers when they lived in Ocala, Florida, and was a witness to the shootout that resulted in their deaths; Dr. Wade Preece, Reporter Frances Veach, and Peg Nelson, eye-witnesses to the death of Tommy Carroll at Waterloo, Iowa, and the subsequent arrest of Jean Delaney Crompton.

Among my professional mentors in the Borough of Queens in New York City, I wish to thank the staff of the English Department at Queens College-CUNY for their guidance. I send a loving thanks to Professor Joe Cuomo, Director, Queens College Evening Reading Series. Joe Cuomo read the early drafts during vacations from his hectic schedule, making the suggestions that bound notes into a "spine." Queens Public Librarian Rudolph Bold tirelessly applied for newspaper-on-microfilm and made his microfilm machine available whenever I needed it. The library staff at the Rosenthal Library at Queens College were also helpful in obtaining microfilm through interlibrary loans. Professor Warren, History Department, Queens College, with whom I studied the 1930s and The New Deal, brought the social and political conditions of the 1930s alive in his classroom. My appreciation also goes to the staff at Northwestern University, in Evanston, Illinois, for making the *Chicago Tribune* on microfilm readily available. Thanks to Max Misch, my Web site designer; and

Shane Cappuccio, for his photo shop and Web site enhancement skills. Thanks to Betty Cooney, Editor at *The Queens Chronicle*, for giving me the range to explore; Ro London, with whom I shared the writers' workshop; and Richard Cappuccio, who shared my early enthusiasm and the road.

Most helpful were the genealogists who helped to compile the family backgrounds. I wish to thank Marge Topps, Don McGuire, Virginia Martin, and Carol J. Graf, Genealogy Assistant in the Kokomo-Howard Public Library. Other librarians who assisted with the book are Deborah Bischoff, Central Florida Regional Library; Nancy Sherrill, Genealogy Librarian at the Vigo County Public Library; John R. Gonzales, California State Library; Noraleen Young, Indiana State Library; and Lori Davisson, Research Historian, Arizona Historical Society, Tucson.

The research assistants at the National Archives who provided me with court records, and to whom I extend my appreciation, are Charles Reeves, Southeast Region; Rosemary Kennedy, San Bruno, California; Fred Romanski, College Park, Maryland; Kenneth Shanks, Great Lakes Region; Richard Fusick and Ken Hawkins of the American West Division, Washington, D.C.; and Glen Longnaker, Chicago Office.

Prison officials who helped are Barry L. Nothstine, Sr., Administrative Assistant at the Indiana State Prison, who took me on a tour of the facility at Michigan City. Ray S. Hooker, Executive Assistant, U.S. Federal Penitentiary at Milan, Michigan, uncovered the old index cards kept on the prisoners who served their time between 1934 and 1936.

I wish to thank Anne Diestel, Archivist, Office of Communications & Archives, U.S. Federal Bureau of Prisons; Donna Daun, U.S. District Court Records Clerk, Minnesota; F.B.I. Reading Room Staff members Toni Yassin, Janet Hawkins, Judy Janet, and Mike, who was very helpful to me. Also, Kathy Wellersheim, of the Hennepin County Department of Corrections, obtained print material on the Minneapolis Workhouse.

Thanks to Marc Taylor, New York-based author of *A Touch of Classic Soul*, for steering me in the right publishing direction.

A long-lasting thanks to Andrew Prunella, my husband. You offered your unwavering support and encouragement. Special thanks to Alma Ortiz and Alice MacLarty, my proofreaders.

To my children, Eva, Keith, Shane, Catherine and Andrea, I say, "Thanks for understanding that delineating history does not require taking sides, that researching a criminal era does not mean you've glorified crime."

A special thanks to my book designer, Liz Tufte, without whom this book could not have been written.

In conclusion, I wish to thank, in advance, the next generation of researchers. You are the jury to whom this charge is being directed—the peers who will decide if these stories bear further research. To you I pass the torch.

# Index

## Banks

- New Carlisle National Bank, June 10, 1933. $10,600.
- First National Bank of Montpelier, August 4th, with a third man. $10,110.
- Commercial Bank of Daleville, July 17, $3,500.
- The Citizens National Bank of Bluffton, Ohio. August 14, 1934. $2,100.
- Massachusetts Avenue State Bank, Indianapolis, with Hilton O. Crouch and another man, between $21,000 and $24,000.
- First National Bank at St. Mary, Ohio, with members of Terror Gang, $11,000, October 3, 1933.
- Central National Bank of Greencastle, Indiana, October 23rd, Pierpont, Dillinger, and Makley. $18,000 in cash; over $56,000 in stocks and bonds. Ed Shouse drove the getaway car. Fight over the split would result in Shouse's eviction from the gang.
- American Bank and Trust Company in downtown Racine, Wisconsin. The gang had planned the job in the Triangle Bar in Milwaukee, under the protection of Casey Jones, an ex-con from Leavenworth. There they hung out with a Pearl Elliott connection named Heck Trimby. With Pierpont, Dillinger, Leslie Homer, Makley and Clark. This job always referred to informally as "Racine." The take amounted to over $50,000.
- First National Bank in East Chicago, Indiana, planned with John Hamilton and Fort Wayne associate Victor Fasano. Officer William O'Malley was shot and killed. Dillinger was going to be charged with his murder while awaiting formal charges in the Crown Point County Jail, Indiana, from which he escaped. January 15, 1934, $20,376.00.
- Securities National Bank at Sioux Falls, South Dakota, on Tuesday, March 6, 1934. Dillinger, Lester Gillis, John Hamilton, Homer Van Meter, Eddie Green and Tommy Carroll. The take, $49,500.00.
- First National Bank at Mason City, Iowa, on March 13, 1934 (exactly one week after Sioux Falls and with the same people). Dillinger, Lester Gillis, John Hamilton, Homer Van Meter, Eddie Green and Tommy Carroll. March 13, 1934. Cash estimated at $52,000.
- Merchants National Bank at South Bend, Indiana, June 30, 1934; Dillinger, with Homer Van Meter, Lester Gillis, Jack Perkins, and an unidentified 200 pound man, $28,323.29.

## Addresses

| | |
|---|---|
| 324 West First Avenue in Dayton, Ohio | Mary Longnaker's boardinghouse |
| 714¼ North Washington, Kokomo, Indiana | Pearl Elliott's rooming house 1925–1934 |
| 606 N. Market Street, Kokomo, Indiana | Pearl Elliott lived here as Pearl Mullendore, c. 1920's |
| 2029 South Elwood Street, Elwood, Indiana | Ruby Ickes lived with "Uncle" George Boonham, Mayor of Elwood, Indiana, 1933–1934. |
| 604 Third Street, Fort Wayne, Indiana | Visited by Dillinger in July, 1934 |
| 1052 South 2nd Street, Hamilton, Ohio | Hideout after Michigan City break |
| 54th and Keystone Avenue, Indianapolis | Pierpont family home in 1920's |
| 343 McCleed Avenue, Indianapolis | Ralph Saffel's apartment |
| 316 North Luett Street, Indianapolis | Home of Mary Kinder, Silent Margaret Behrens and Viola Paterson in 1933–1934. |
| 1244 North Dearborn Street | Pat Cherrington's address in 1932 |
| Hotel Wil-Mar, 11 West Division Street | Pat Cherrington's address in 1932 |
| Marshall Hotel, 1232 N. LaSalle, Chicago | Opal Long's home 1930–1933 |
| 1832 Belmont Avenue, Chicago | Home of Art Cherrington's brother, Ira, and his wife, Vera |
| 4310 Clarendon Avenue, Chicago | Rented by Pierpont, Mary Kinder, Dillinger and Evelyn Frechette |
| 115 N.Parkside, 150-54 N. Parkside, Chicago | Rented by Dillinger Gang, October, 1933 |
| Nut House, 1022 North Clark, Chicago | Mary Kinder's hangout, October, 1933 |
| 1742 Humboldt Boulevard, Chicago | Home of Jean Burke and Arthur "Fish" Johnson |

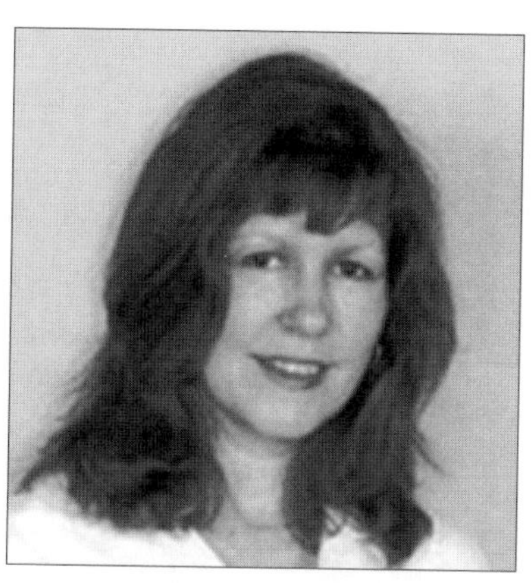

Ellen Poulsen was born in New York City in 1953. She holds a B.A. in Literature from Queens College-CUNY, and has received the Sandra Schor and Helen Viljoen Awards for Non-Fiction. She's worked as a newspaper staff writer and columnist. *Don't Call Us Molls*, reflecting fifteen years of research, is the result of lifelong interest in John Dillinger.

# Notes

# Notes

# Notes

nna Sage, the Woman in Red, is kissed by
ergeant Martin Zarkovich as she is deported
Romania. (AP/Wide World Photos)

# What They Are Saying

"Until Ellen Poulsen stepped forward with this meticulously researched book, the story of the 1930's Public Enemies-era focused exclusively on gangland's men, from Dillinger to Creepy Karpis – a tale of male bravado, bullets, bank vaults and banditry. The extraordinary accomplishment of *Don't Call Us Molls* is Poulsen's revealing, for the first time, the hidden lives of the women who loved these nefarious outlaws. It is an untold story of desperate romance, astonishing escapes, unspeakable brutality, covert abortions and intra-gang rivalries for the affection of men, both in and out of prison. Alternately funny and horrifying, *Don't Call Us Molls* brings back to life a band of strangely compelling women – many of whom said farewell to their men as they witnessed their boyfriends' arrest or death in a shoot-out." —Paul Maccabee, author, *John Dillinger Slept Here: A Crooks' Tour of Crime and Corruption in St. Paul*

"Ellen Poulsen has spent many years painstakingly researching, and has miraculously revealed the truth behind these women labeled as gun molls. A very riveting book." —Lori Hyde, John Dillinger Historian

"Poulsen's book fills a serious void in true crime annals by telling the real stories, mostly sad, of the girlfriends and wives of John Dillinger and his accomplices." —Anthony Brucia, co-founder, Partners In Crime (PIC)

"Poulsen brings an era to life. She strips away the façade of legend to give us the gritty reality of the Depression-era outlaws, the sound and smells and pure desperation. Her emphasis on the women of the gang opens a refreshing new perspective. The meticulous research and gripping story here will appeal to all those who continue to be intrigued by this fascinating time." —Jack Kelly, author, *Mad Dog* and *Mobtown*

"In *Don't Call Us Molls*, Ellen Poulsen has produced an indispensible addition to the library of any '30's crime afficionado. The result of careful research and crammed with enough new information and insights to satisfy the most rabid gangster buff, Poulsen retells the Dillinger gang story by a unique slant — from the amazing case histories of the gang's women. Forget the cardboard stereotypes of the past: the "cigar-smoking gun moll" image projected by Bonnie Parker and the "disease-ridden harlot" fantasized by J. Edgar Hoover. Evelyn Frechette, Mary Kinder, Helen Gillis, Pat and Opal and all the rest emerge as real women and products of their era and environments." —Rick Mattix, co-author of *Public Enemies: America's Criminal Past, 1919-1940*; and *Thompson, the American Legend: The First Submachine Gun*

# Order Form

**Don't Call Us Molls: Women of the John Dillinger Gang**

**Fax orders: (718) 357-4993**

**On-line orders: www.dillingerswomen.com**

**Postal Orders: Clinton Cook Publishing Corp.**

**P.O. Box 640356**

**Oakland Gardens, New York 11364-0356**

**Telephone: (718) 357-4991**

**Name ______________________________________________**

**Address ____________________________________________**

**City ________________________ State _____ Zip _________**

**Telephone ( ___ ) ____________________________________**

**e-mail ___________________________________________**

| | |
|---|---|
| **Price:** | **19.95 each** |
| **Postage & Handling** | **3.00** |
| **Total:** | **22.95** |

**(N.Y. Residents add 8¼% sales tax @$1.65=total $24.60)**

**Make check or money order out to**

**Clinton Cook Publishing Corp.**